SECURING H. IN THE AGE OF RISK: NEW CHALLENGES FOR TRAVEL, MIGRATION, AND BORDERS

By Susan Ginsburg

April 2010

Migration Policy Institute
Washington, DC

Library of Congress Cataloging-in-Publication Data

Ginsburg, Susan, 1953-
Securing human mobility in the age of risk : new challenges for travel, migration, and borders / by Susan Ginsburg.
       p. cm.
Includes bibliographical references.
ISBN 978-0-9742819-6-4 (pbk.)
1. Migration, Internal. 2. Emigration and immigration. 3. Travel.
4. Terrorism. I. Title.
   HB1952.G57 2010
   363.325'991--dc22
                                            2010005791

Cover photo: Daniel Clayton Greer
Cover design: April Siruno
Interior typesetting: James Decker

Printed in the United States of America.

TABLE OF CONTENTS

PREFACE

The core contention of this volume is that our overall approach to immigration and border security is off-kilter; it is not keeping pace with changes in the scale and scope of people's movement around the world and our expectations for and attitudes toward freedom of movement. I elaborate here on this premise and suggest some practical steps for realigning our approach to human mobility, one key aspect of globalization and an arena for homeland security. The undertaking has been animated by three sources.

First, the book is a successor publication to a 2006 report published by the Migration Policy Institute (MPI) titled *Countering Terrorist Mobility: Shaping an Operational Strategy*.[1] That 2006 report argued that immigration for economic or family reasons and movement in connection with global terrorism raise largely distinct sets of policy concerns that have to be clearly separated in order to address each most effectively. Aimed at the government policymakers, managers, and frontline practitioners concerned with ensuring that terrorists do not cross US borders undetected, the report proposed specific steps to detect, disrupt, and exploit terrorist mobility. The publication expanded on a recommendation in the 9/11 Commission report that terrorist and criminal travel, even more than terrorist finance and money laundering, should become a prominent vehicle for counterterrorism and crime control. The perspective and recommendations in *Countering Terrorist Mobility* have gained some currency but have not been fully absorbed. So this book takes another crack at explaining why and how countering terrorist mobility is an important aspect of homeland security and counterterrorism.

Second, shortly after the publication of *Countering Terrorist Mobility*, two government officials, one a political appointee at the Department of State and the other a former federal agent serving in a senior intelligence position at the Department of Homeland Security, separately made the same comment to me: An effort must be made to determine how the United States should interact with global partners to establish an international framework — legal, strategic, and operational — for dealing with terrorist mobility and border security. This book takes up that challenge. Many of us have been confused about how domestic policy on immigration, border management, and travel should join up with foreign policy and security strategy relating to terrorism and crime control. This book attempts to sort that out.

Third, many voices in civil-society organizations; in the military, intelligence, and law-enforcement communities; in academia; and in public policy circles have insisted that the US government has too closely linked immigration policy and security strategy surrounding the movement of people.[2] I share the view that the United States has boxed itself in to a position where an oversimplified version of border security and immigration enforcement, which results in the detention of thousands of people, is equated with counterterrorism. The United States also seems to be trapped in a system in which we act as if it is inevitable that errant tourists and students are occasionally shackled and detained as if they were terrorists or dangerous criminals. Yet these actions disrupt the lives, offend the sensibilities, and undermine the rights of law-abiding persons. They also impose unnecessary costs on families, institutions, and US public diplomacy.

I believe that sloganeering politics has prevented acknowledgement of the importance of expanding the rule of law in global mobility channels, and denied attention to the full range of what needs to be done to improve security relating to the movement of people. So, I have tried with this book to sketch a broader spectrum of mobility policy, from taking action against terrorists and human traffickers to sustaining the integrity and resilience of mobility channels, and preventing illegal and uncontrolled movement that is dangerous to migrants, populations, and states.

My book contains four different elements — some description of the movement, both positive and negative, that is occurring; a proposed strategic framework for understanding the new mission of securing human movement in the context of homeland or civil security; an account of some of the policy arenas that are rising in importance because of this mission; and proposals that address these issues. By highlighting the new contours of illicit mobility and measures to preclude harms and bolster resilience, I aim to build consensus around moving away from the type of narrow approach that concentrates resources on border security and illegal immigration enforcement. Much more discussion, research, and reporting are needed to build that consensus and develop appropriate strategies; my hope is that this book contributes to this effort by proving a solid framework for debate and elaboration.

One criticism of *Countering Terrorist Mobility* was that it was insufficiently denunciatory of government policy at the time and too optimistic about what could be achieved going forward. It runs against my grain to attack individuals who are dedicating themselves to the public's well-being and who have a great deal more public exposure and accountability than I do, even if I disagree with their beliefs. Writing here as a policy analyst, I aim to discover productive, responsive, feasible policy innovation, and to develop ideas drawn from discussions with current practitioners, scholars, and thinkers within a theoretical frame that suits current conditions. Realistic, sometimes tough assessments are a necessary condition of successful policymaking, and uphill battles and profound disagreements about direction are inevitable. But in spite of such conflict, there are usually good options to be seized, options that not only are true to what people most want for themselves and from government but which will be undertaken by government officials under the right circumstances. This book endeavors to be explicit about my basic principles relating to these issues and specific about how current policy and practice should be further developed, modified, or abandoned.

There are fundamental theoretical questions that underlie any discussion relating to security, terror, crime, and mobility that I do not address comprehensively. For example, while I provide some views on such basic issues as the meaning of "security" and the degree to which terrorism constitutes war or crime, I do not try to resolve them. Instead I settle on what seem to me to be defensible usages and hybrid terms and positions from which to adopt practical approaches to recognized problems. I try to give an account of homeland security, proposing that we rename it civil security. I also do not try to resolve the question of what scale of immigration is right for the United States, or how it should be apportioned between employment needs and family reunification. I assume that it is important that our country remain a preeminent state for drawing in a diverse group of temporary and long-term migrants and immigrants, whether for demographic, economic, or humanitarian reasons. I also anticipate that Americans will continue to grow into global citizens, through study, travel, commerce, international service, and other forms of engagement. I believe the United States should take a leadership role in securing human movement by promoting collective arrangements.

I have been fortunate to serve as senior counsel and team leader on the staff of the National Commission on Terrorist Attacks Upon the United States (9/11 Commission), where I was responsible for research and policy recommendations concerning the entry of the 9/11 hijackers, terrorist travel, and border controls. I also serve on the Homeland Security Advisory Committee's Quadrennial Review Advisory Committee, which has allowed me to understand the issues with which homeland security officials are currently grappling. The book is principally aimed at policymakers, government officials, policy analysts, and scholars who shape US policy and operations concerning mobility security, and who are working to understand what it means in the context of the homeland security enterprise. In addition, this book is aimed at all the groups that have a major stake in US strategy relating to the movement of people, and in promoting changes in today's border security and immigration enforcement approaches.

I hope this mix of theory, policy analysis, commentary, and suggestion will shed light on how to expand freedom of movement and build a secure and well-ordered immigration, travel, and border system — one that acknowledges the world of markets, evolving state alliances, and core human rights commitments while providing security measures against those who would attack, disrupt, or exploit such a system.

Susan Ginsburg
Migration Policy Institute, April 2010

Introduction: The Limits of Border Security

Travelers have always needed to protect themselves from exploitation by criminals and others, and sovereign states have long sought to maintain the integrity of their border and immigration systems. However, in the twenty-first century, which has witnessed major enhancements in the ease of travel, unprecedented complexity of migratory movements, and devastating terrorist attacks on airliners and other modes of public transportation, security issues surrounding the movement of people have taken on new urgency in the policymaking, intelligence, law-enforcement, and travel industry communities. Mobility security strategy and law are about upholding the right to legal travel, ensuring that crossing borders is a source of vulnerability for terrorists and criminals, and preventing the large-scale illegal movement and hazardous displacement of populations. It is an aspect of homeland (civil) security, comparable to cybersecurity or financial system security. This book seeks to move beyond the conventional focus on *border security* and *immigration enforcement*, proposing a new migration-related security paradigm referred to here as *securing human mobility*. This new framework points the way toward security measures that are more proactive, systematic, and far-reaching in protecting legitimate travelers, limiting travel by terrorists, human traffickers, and other criminals, and precluding uncontrolled, high-volume migration.

As with global communications and international financial flows, the opportunities that global mobility affords the United States and its citizens are overwhelmingly positive, and central to US character and identity. US citizens seek to maximize their ability to go wherever and receive whomever they wish. As much as these opportunities — and the principles they represent — are celebrated, and as much as they benefit the United States, we must act to safeguard them while we minimize the new types of risks in this era and their potentially catastrophic consequences.

As such, the new approach to securing human mobility articulated in this volume proposes the following policy recommendations:

- New mobility security agreements with Canada and the European Union (EU)
- Improved programs to prevent violations of visa terms and conditions
- A redress system for temporary visa denials
- An international organization to promote global mobility security
- An interagency, extraterritorial criminal network strike force
- A program to thwart transnational gang migration
- A second deputy secretary at the Department of Homeland Security (DHS) to oversee the civil security arena

*   *   *   *   *

The potential for significant devastation and a breakdown of public order — whether caused by terrorists or state agents using weapons of mass destruction (WMDs), by natural disasters, or by system failures — injects into daily life risks of a significance previously associated chiefly with conventional war. The September 11, 2001, terrorist attacks accomplished what an earlier era of airline hijackings did not; they forcefully woke citizens up to the fact that ordinary travel channels are vectors and sites for some of these risks.

To deal with the threats inherent in terrorist and criminal travel and with two other major problems associated with the movement of people — high levels of illegal immigration and pressures and emergencies arising from mass displacements of people — the United States has relied on the traditional combination of border security and immigration enforcement.[3] This two-part concept, coexisting with the goal of facilitating the lawful movement of people, currently defines the US approach to managing the movement of people. Improved border and immigration security is widely credited with being an operational deterrent to terrorist travel to the United States.[4]

Still, this strategic approach should be reexamined. Mobility is a primary instrument for terrorists, and it is a given that terrorists continuously innovate in response to security measures and expectations. Hence, new solutions have to be continually sought as well. While some terrorists will get through — the odds favor the individual who slips into the stream of the hundreds of thousands who enter or depart daily — new security methods can make travel and migration riskier for people who are threats and can reduce the pressures of illegal migration.

The border security–immigration enforcement paradigm may be inadequate to the challenge, particularly as the strategic environment is changing. The current paradigm focuses on the vulnerabilities associated with immigration more than on the contributions and the opportunities that mobility offers. Under the framework articulated in this volume, the United States would safeguard the opportunities presented by global mobility while minimizing the evolving risks and consequences of this new era.

Gaps and New Directions

The view of mobility as a source of vulnerability has led to distortions in US policy. These include too many detained people; too much emphasis on incarceration and deportation; damage to the United States' image abroad; oppressive policies in border communities; and undue costs to the scientific, education, and business communities. Some of these problems are being addressed and mitigated, but they will not be solved simply by doing a better job at what we are already doing; assumptions, programs, roles, and organization must be rethought.

Adherence to the border security–immigration enforcement paradigm has led to an unduly narrow and sometimes misguided approach, with three primary weaknesses that could be remedied. First, the United States could be much more proactive in curbing terrorist and criminal travel. This means identifying terrorists and their methods of movement; hobbling their ability to travel; disrupting human-trafficking organizations (HTOs) and human-smuggling organizations (HSOs), especially where there may be a link with terrorists; and countering the corruption that facilitates illicit travel. Transnational gang migration — the travel of gang members, particularly between the United States and Central America — cannot be a given. The US focus on interdicting, arresting, prosecuting, detaining, or deporting unauthorized immigrants absorbs almost all investigative resources dedicated to the illicit movement of people.

Second, we could focus more resolutely on building security into day-to-day operations of US border and immigration programs. Making the watchlists function well, strengthening the security of birth certificates and travel documents, finding a way to deter visa overstays — these types of improvements require a broad commitment over many years.

Third, enlarging our vision beyond border security and immigration enforcement would enable us to more effectively engage partners and allies such as Canada and the European Union in accomplishing what is most essential to us as US citizens — instituting the rule of law in global mobility channels. Only collective endeavors will provide the security, reassurance, and resilience needed to protect the United States and its interests and allies, reduce the dangers and harms of mass migration, and expand the ability of individuals to move freely throughout the world in an era of risk.

Because the paradigm of border security and immigration management does not spark these kinds of efforts, it is reaching the limit of its usefulness as the framework for responding to the new risks associated with the movement of people in the twenty-first century. Rather than trying to fit goals and objectives that are either newly important or altogether new into a strategic construct designed for a prior era, it makes more sense to adjust the framework. This will allow room for fresh initiatives and enlarged goals, and provide support for innovations for which the programmatic, budget, and organizational frameworks lag.

Securing Human Mobility

This book proposes making the transition from seeing through the double lens of *border security* and *immigration enforcement* to a new paradigm based on *securing human movement*. (It uses the terms *movement* and *mobility* interchangeably.) The goal of securing human mobility is to minimize risks associated with the movement of people that can turn into catastrophes. This goal does not substitute for border enforcement, immigration security, or facilitating lawful travel. Rather, *securing human mobility* incorporates *border security* and *immigration enforcement* and situates it in a more encompassing framework. This is not a radical change, but it is one that will make a significant difference. It permits a wider range of threats and risks to be addressed, new practical approaches to security to emerge, and strategic outcomes to be clarified and enlarged. This new framework includes:

- Building international institutions to establish and maintain the integrity of global mobility channels

- Providing incentives and training so that developing countries can strengthen their border capacities and mobility policies
- Upholding the right of freedom of movement and other rights that come into force when people travel, migrate, and seek protection and refuge
- Putting in place security strategies suitable to the different categories of people on the move, including those that aim to preclude terrorist travel, criminal mobility networks, and the risk of mass movements of people
- Ensuring the responsiveness, integrity, and resilience of the US mobility infrastructure (including border and immigration systems) with effective regulation, incentives, sanctions, and technology
- Forming bilateral and regional mobility security relationships that reduce risk and lower barriers to lawful movement
- Denying access to the global mobility system to terrorists, criminals, corrupt officials, and human rights violators

These types of policies are necessary to *securing human mobility* as a dimension of successful homeland security strategy. They may at first sound like good government bromides that are either uselessly general or can be taken for granted as an integral part of homeland security, defense, and international relations. Not so. As it stands, the public and Congress are concerned mainly with bolstering traditional border security and immigration enforcement. In relation to the list above, for example:

1. No standing strike force has been funded to target human smugglers who have a potential terrorist nexus.
2. Many aspects of the mobility infrastructure have fallen below the radar and are undersupported, including critical aspects of identity management.
3. The concept of mobility security agreements barely exists, even with a close ally such as Canada.
4. No international institution has been established to support efforts against terrorist travel, criminal movement, and the integrity of mobility channels the way the Financial Action Task Force (FATF) assists states in countering terrorist finance, money laundering, and financial system integrity.
5. DHS and the Department of State (DOS) do not have a program dedicated to security assistance that would build developing states' abilities to manage their borders and immigration systems.
6. Law schools, advocacy groups, and government agencies have not devoted sufficient attention to defining the scope and contours of the right to move.

7. The concept of governing global mobility channels as a public good, free of corruption and violence, is inherent in the imposition of global travel bans but remains unarticulated.

Achieving the mission of securing human mobility would be helped by changes within the US government, especially at DHS, and around the world. Such changes would (1) sharpen the focus on mobility, as distinct from other homeland security missions associated with the nation's infrastructure; (2) distinguish mobility security from immigration policy; and (3) advance international mobility security efforts.

Terminology

The term *mobility* refers herein to how people travel, use transportation, immigrate, or migrate. *Terrorist travel* is used here synonymously with terrorist mobility, although in some quarters the former is a narrower term that excludes reference to modes and means of transportation. In the migration policy context, *mobility* refers to a person's ability to move to another jurisdiction and reside or work there, as in *labor mobility*.

Travel typically refers to short-term movement or the process of getting from one place to another, regardless of how long one will stay at the destination. *Terrorist mobility* and *terrorist travel* are accepted terms. *Travel regulation*, as used here, is a form of mobility regulation covering the rules that apply to all travel, including for US citizens.

People usually think of immigration as being permanent, although because the Immigration and Naturalization Act prescribes rules for all conditions and lengths of stay in the United States, the term *immigration* is often used to describe the rules for temporary visits as well as permanent residence. The term *access regulation* is also used to encompass rules governing foreign citizens' visits and immigration.

The term *mobility*, when used as an adjective (i.e., *mobility facilitators* and *mobility crimes*), refers to the spectrum of people and functions associated with illegal or legal global mobility. These include travel agents, transportation companies and officials, consular officers, intermediaries and illicit facilitators, port-of-entry inspectors, border patrol, immigration adjudicators, passport producers and examiners, US Customs and Border Protection (CBP) and DHS officials or their counterparts in foreign countries or international organizations, as well as intelligence or military officers focused on terrorist travel and illicit pathways or criminals (such as human smugglers and traffickers) associated with the flow of people.

Mobility security is a goal that the United States must reach through government programs and common efforts to preclude potentially catastrophic risks associated with the movement of people.

The Current Paradigm

Since 9/11 in particular, the federal government has focused on building border security and immigration enforcement. The key building blocks have been:

- Tightening of terrorism laws and expansion of investigative authorities to reduce risk in the immigrant and nonimmigrant admissions process
- Toughening of the visa, admission, and travel-screening procedures at consulates, refugee facilities, airports, and ports of entry
- Reinforcement of border security through expansion of the Border Patrol especially at the southern border with Mexico, and by the Coast Guard in maritime channels
- Substantial technology infrastructure innovation and investment in biometrics and databases like watchlists, surveillance systems, and physical border barriers
- Expanded domestic and international information and intelligence collection, sharing, and analysis, including automated analysis relating to mobility

Notwithstanding the retention of the legacy paradigm, the evolution to securing human mobility is being driven by three developments: the new and devastating risks to the United States associated with mobility in this century, the scale and scope of global movement, and the significance of mobility to both US citizens and their economy.

The New Negatives

The existing paradigm predates today's era of potentially catastrophic terrorism. While there were meaningful precursor events and responses that foreshadowed current realities, the 9/11 attacks caused a reassessment. The greatest threat associated with mobility today is not illegal immigration but rather travel by terrorists with chemical, biological, radiological, nuclear, or high yield explosive (CBRNE) WMDs. These attacks could cause death and destruction on a scale not seen in past eras. Mobility-related terrorist attacks, human trafficking and smuggling, and cross-border criminal violence are not new, but terrorism and transnational crime pose risks today that significantly strain traditional enforcement doctrine. At the same time, the right to movement has significantly grown in importance to US citizens, other free peoples, and global market participants everywhere.

Terrorists and Weapons of Mass Destruction

The emergence of al Qaeda combined with the trafficking of CBRNE weapons and technology, as exemplified by the accused nuclear proliferator A.Q. Khan of Pakistan, initiated an era of significant new dangers posed by a small numbers of terrorists and corrupt individuals. The risks that these weapons pose in the hands of terrorists or subversive foreign agents are real and ever present. The difference between contemporary and earlier acts of terrorism is the potential access to WMDs through traffickers and bribable or complicit officials. Violent extremists who may acquire such weapons pose the greatest danger of violence to populations not at risk from conventional or nuclear war. Terrorists and CBRNE traffickers can launch an attack to kill people in mobility channels, disrupt service, or exploit these channels to commit crimes elsewhere.

The threat of terrorism crosses borders in both directions. US citizens can exploit global mobility channels by traveling for terrorist training and other activities. For example, Terry Nichols, one of the 1994 Oklahoma City bombers and an associate of a US pro-gun extremist group, learned his bomb tradecraft when he traveled to the Philippines and met with a bomb maker from the Abu Sayyaf Brigade. In 2009 it was revealed that US-based known and suspected terrorists traveled to Pakistan and Afghanistan for al Qaeda training and planning and then returned to the United States, or traveled to and from Canada. And US citizens of Somali descent have traveled to take part in internecine Somali warfare, including on the side of an extremist faction associated with al Qaeda.

Human Trafficking and Smuggling Organizations

Human trafficking represents a second and virulent dimension of global migration. This scourge arises from criminal exploitation of mobility channels and leveraging of market inequalities, wage and standards gaps, and demand. Human trafficking, which first became a prominent focus for US law enforcement in the mid-1990s, has grown with the increase in the number and size of market economies throughout the world. The total number of human-trafficking victims identified in 71 countries rose by more than 27 percent between 2003 and 2006 — from 11,706 victims in 2003 to 14,909 in 2006.[5] HTOs do not generally profit from the movement of people, which is a cost to them, but raise revenue by forcing trafficking victims into prostitution (79 percent of victims) and forced labor (18 percent).[6]

HSOs, which profit from the movement of people, also pose a major problem. They range in importance from those with a nexus to terrorism or HTOs, to those that are less coercive and are without links to other criminal enterprises. Even then, HSOs are a corrupting influence, undermining good governance and the rule of law.

Organized Crime and Diaspora Community Vulnerabilities

Transnational movements of members of other types of crime organizations, including the circular movement of criminals to and from particular communities in the United States and other countries, represent another dark side of enhanced global mobility. International criminal organizations originating elsewhere are active in the United States. For example, Mexican drug-trafficking organizations (DTOs) have a presence in 195 cities, and Salvadoran and Chinese violent gangs are a problem in many cities throughout the country.[7] In the United States, most ethnic violence is directed at fellow members of the community, not at other ethnic groups. Terrorists, transnational criminals, and violent gangs all exploit mobility channels and migrants. Ethnic or national immigrant communities can fall prey to terrorist recruiters, to crime patterns associated with their communities of origin, and to vulnerabilities associated with being new arrivals in monolingual communities.

Mass-Scale Movement of People

The border security–immigration enforcement paradigm also fails to sufficiently address concerns over the large-scale uncontrolled movement of people. This movement can take the form of mass displacement due to a natural disaster or political upheaval, or a large-scale, steady movement of economic migrants in search of better labor markets.

Illegal Migration to the United States

Much illegal migration can be attributed to this gap between the mobility engendered by economic globalization and national laws that regulate legal admissions based on labor-market needs. In the US context, the risk to human life associated with illegal migration and the nonmonetary cost to families and communities is especially troubling. Large numbers of migrants have died during border crossings. Border-crossing deaths along the US-Mexico border almost doubled during the six-year period from 1999 to 2005, jumping from 241 to 472, before dropping to 390 in fiscal year 2008.[8] The majority of these deaths occurred in the Border Patrol's Tucson sector, which covers the Arizona desert.[9] The phenomenon isn't unique to the rugged US-Mexico border. According to unofficial estimates, 1,861 migrants died trying to reach Europe from Africa across the Atlantic Ocean and Mediterranean Sea in 2007.[10]

The separation of families is another disturbing cost of unregulated and illegal labor migration, with spillover social problems for communities. The problem is at both ends. Communities in sending countries that benefit from remittances also suffer from family separation, as well as from vulnerability to economic swings. The separation is voluntary in a very attenuated meaning of the word. People choose to leave, but they make the decision because they lack economic opportunities afforded in their own countries, and as in some areas of Mexico, suffer other forms of insecurity due to crime, corruption, and weak governance. The case that migration is positive or negative for purposes of development has not been determined, but the stripping of human resources in communities and family separation and uncertainty are strong negative forces.[11]

Beyond apprehensions at the US-Mexico border, which accounted for 91 percent of the 723,840 apprehensions made by the Border Patrol in FY2008,[12] US Immigration and Customs Enforcement (ICE) has increased the number of unauthorized immigrants it has detained and removed from the United States. ICE removed 50,924 noncitizens in FY1995; that number increased to 358,886 in FY2008.

Illegal immigration to the United States continues to be substantial. Although the unauthorized immigrant population decreased from an estimated 12.4 million in 2007 to 11.9 million in 2008, largely as a result of the recession, the number still remains large.[13] An estimated 4.2 million unauthorized immigrants entered in 2000 or since,[14] and unauthorized immigrants made up 4 percent of the total US population and 5.4 percent of the US workforce (or 8.3 million individuals) in 2008[15] — an increase from the 4.3 percent share in 2003.[16]

Most migrants entering illegally do so outside the ports of entry. Between 6 and 7 million unauthorized immigrants living in the United States in 2006 had evaded immigration inspection by crossing between the ports of entry.[17] The fact of large-scale uncontrolled movement proves borders can be breached and invites territorial violation by people who represent more serious threats.

Migrants who cross borders unlawfully or who overstay visas to seek a better life do not present a threat of terrorist violence or, as a rule, of criminal violence. Describing this group as a security threat or treating it as such is, in this sense, excessive and disproportionate. However, large-scale illegal migration corrodes democracy. When Congress and the president adopt a set of immigration laws, it is reasonable to expect them to be respected and enforced. Wholesale disrespect for the law undermines democratic consent. Ultimately, a loss of control over demographic choices can undermine a state's ability to exercise its strategic power.

Large-Scale Illegal Movement as a Security Issue

Insecurity and lack of democratic governance have been factors in illegal and life-threatening migration from south to north and south to south for a long time.[18] In this context, the movement can be dangerous, precipitous, disorderly, and illegal in ways not fully addressed by international refugee law and institutions. The Office of the United Nations High Commissioner for Refugees (UNHCR) estimates that there were 42 million forcibly displaced people worldwide at the end of 2008, including 15.2 million refugees, 827,000 asylum seekers, and 26 million internally displaced persons.[19] Millions of others who are not counted as refugees nonetheless are forced to leave their countries due to weak or failed governments, political violence, oppression, or intense poverty. These include the 500,000 to 3 million Zimbabwean migrants in South Africa.[20] Military conflicts, such as along the Armenian-Azerbaijani, Uzbek-Kyrgyz, and Uzbek-Tajik borders also cause humanitarian flows. The United States has seen such flows from Cuba during the Mariel boatlift in 1980, from Haiti most recently in the 1990s, and currently from Mexico, with individuals fleeing to US border communities to escape DTOs.

Large-scale, unregulated migration is problematic not only due to the crime with which it may be associated — human trafficking, human smuggling, or complicity and corruption among government officials — but also because of the threat to the migrants themselves. In addition, refugee flows may overwhelm or destabilize underdeveloped or weak states. States subjected to such demands may be drawn into war. Uncontrolled flows may result from genocide, war crimes, ethnic cleansing, or human rights violations. They may result from a lack of rights and from economic insecurity.

This troubling, sometimes interlaced, set of problems cannot be addressed without strong leadership from the United States and its partners. Humanitarian and development assistance, such as in recent years to Pakistan and to South Asia after the tsunami, are becoming an increasingly important element of foreign policy for a combination of reasons, not least of which is their role in forestalling the mass displacement of people.

The Scale and Scope of Cross-Border Movement

The phrase border security implies territorial defense, the repelling of armed invaders, and the general exclusion of foreigners. But the ability of citizens to travel safely and the admission of people who support market and social goals are also primary objectives. Today's volume of humans on the move and their geographic scope — including global travel for tourism, study, and work, as well as for migration — render the traditional vision of border security and immigration enforcement anachronistic.

Travel and temporary stays. Cross-border travel volume is enormous. Half a million people cross borders somewhere in the world every hour.[21] In 1950 there were 25 million international arrivals, according to the United Nations World Tourism Organization (UNWTO); by 2004 that number had reached 763 million, with an average annual growth rate of 6.5 percent. With 925 million international tourist arrivals recorded worldwide in 2008,[22] we will soon see 1 billion arrivals a year.[23] International student travel to industrialized countries increased 50 percent between 2000 and 2005, growing to approximately 2 million students in 2005.[24]

All told, CBP processed 409 million[25] pedestrian and passenger entries into the United States in FY2008 — a number that exceeds the population of the United States by over a 100 million.[26] Although the number of temporary (nonimmigrant) admissions to the United States has generally declined since 1997, particularly of Canadians and Mexicans,[27] there were still 175.4 million nonimmigrant admissions of foreign nationals to the United States in 2008.[28]

Americans have themselves become world travelers on a significant scale. Approximately 28 percent of Americans have a passport, with 85.5 million US passports in circulation as of February 2008.[29] Between 2004 and 2007, the number of US passports issued annually more than doubled, reaching nearly 18.5 million.[30] Sixty-four million US residents (21.2 percent of the population) traveled abroad in 2007 — 400,000 more than in 2006.[31] US citizens traveled mostly to Europe (31.1 percent), the Caribbean (14.1 percent), and Asia (13.7 percent).[32] Travel to Mexico and Canada comprised 14.6 percent and 8.9 percent of all US citizen air traffic overseas.[33]

Globalization is also drawing US citizens away from home for longer periods, whether for work or to live with family members. At least 5 million Americans live outside the United States, excluding Americans on military bases.[34] This diaspora is not well documented, but it comes vividly to the public's attention during crises when US citizens are victims of terrorist attacks or natural disasters, such as the devastating January 2010 earthquake in Haiti, which killed more than 100 Americans and left others wounded.

Permanent migration. Permanent migration, unlike short-term travel, has been comparably high at previous points in history, but it is substantial today. In addition, citizens in virtually all countries now travel outside their borders — a new phenomenon that gives more countries a stake in global mobility. Political changes, economic globalization, and structural inequality among the world's economies have led to the upsurge in international migration.

Overall, there is net emigration from poorer regions of the world and net immigration into more developed regions.[35] However, migrants from developing countries move to other countries in the developing region of the world, south-south, in greater numbers than they move to countries with advanced economies, south-north.

All told, more than 200 million people live outside their countries of origin, a total of 3 percent of the world's population and more than 2.5 times the number of migrants 50 years ago.[36] The relative size of foreign-born populations as a share of total national population can be significant. Twenty-five percent of the total population in Australia in 2007 was foreign born;[37] 39.6 percent in Luxembourg in 2006;[38] 12.6 percent in the United States in 2007;[39] and 80.5 percent in Qatar and 25.5 percent in Oman in 2005.[40] Canada in 2006 had approximately 6.2 million foreign born — 19.8 percent of its total population and the highest proportion since 1931. Over the past 75 years, Canada's foreign-born population has almost tripled.[41]

Immigration has been integral to the history, culture, and society of the United States. While the share of the foreign born in the United States is below the levels recorded between the 1860s and 1920s (the historic high of 14.8 percent was in the 1890s), the United States still has the largest foreign-born population in the world: 38 million individuals were foreign born, comprising 12.5 percent of the total US population in 2008.[42] The annual number of new lawful permanent residents (LPRs) has quadrupled since the 1950s, from an annual flow of 250,000 in 1950 to an annual average of roughly 1 million from 2000 to 2008.[43] The nearly 10 million individuals granted permanent residence in the United States over the past decade exceed the total populations of many countries, including Austria, Denmark, El Salvador, Israel, Sweden, and Switzerland.[44] Figure A, below, shows the US foreign-born population in absolute numbers and as a percentage of the total population.

Figure A. Foreign-Born Population in the United States as a Percentage and Share of Total Population, 1850–2007

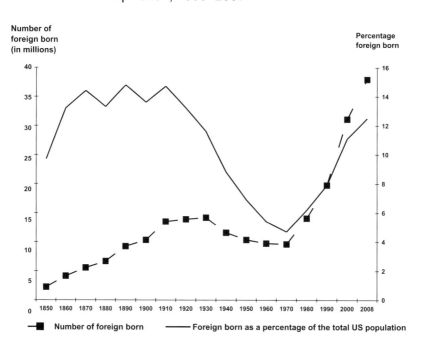

Source: The 2008 data are from the 2008 American Community Survey; the 2000 data are from Census 2000. All other data are from Campbell Gibson and Emily Lennon, "Historical Census Statistics on the Foreign-Born Population of the United States: 1850 to 1990," Working Paper No. 29, US Census Bureau, US Government Printing Office, Washington, DC, 1999.

War or terrorism could disrupt patterns of mobility, but for now continued increases in temporary and long-term flows of people seem likely over the next several decades, including for the United States.[45] The causes of these flows are not likely to ebb. These include the development and labor-market gap, historical ties, family ties, market opportunity, and economic insecurity. Under current conditions, annual net migration from the developing countries to the developed regions of the world is expected to average 2.3 million persons annually from 2010 to 2050.[46] The total future flow of migrants annually would still be 40 percent higher than the 1.6 million annual average migration flow to developed countries between 1960 and 2005.[47]

The Significance of Mobility Today

Beyond the sheer scale of human movement around the globe, the importance of human mobility in globalizing economies and in individual lives is a second reason why a new strategic vision for security associated with the movement of people is necessary. It is not simply that people are choosing to move; it is that their decisions have such significant consequences.

Increasing numbers of people respond to the opportunities of the global market economy by temporarily studying, working, and living in another country. In 2006 the Organization for Economic Cooperation and Development (OECD) countries[48] experienced 2.5 million entries of temporary labor migrants, approximately triple the number of entries of permanent labor migrants.[49]

Migration increasingly delivers an economic edge to advanced and advancing nations. The competition for foreign talent has intensified in recent years. Many advanced industrialized economies are not producing enough native talent to satisfy the demands of employers, driving them to seek foreign employees. Relatively small differences in talent can have huge impacts on innovation and hence on economic outcomes. Global labor mobility of the highly skilled, particularly for transnational corporations, is viewed as critical to overcoming inefficiencies in domestic labor markets.[50] With rapidly growing economies such as India and China both producing and searching for talent, the competition for labor will increase, not only among developed economies but also among emerging and middle-income economies.[51]

Globalization has transformed immigration from a largely ignored reality or unknown phenomenon into a prominent strategic interest, which governments now actively try to manage for their benefit. At least 158 countries, according to the United Nations (UN), have policies that seek to raise, lower, or maintain immigration levels, depending on specific national needs.[52]

Advanced economies actively seek to manage immigration levels. Access to scientific talent has become a political issue in the United States. Some 114 countries — among them the United Kingdom, Australia, Canada, New Zealand, Singapore, and the Czech Republic — have policies to manage highly skilled immigration through selection systems that facilitate the entry of and, in some instances, make the countries more attractive to immigrants possessing a variety of skills and talents.[53] Both temporary and permanent migration policies will play an increasingly large role in countries' competitiveness. In addition, migration is often seen as an important means to spur development, whether through remittances, direct investment, or diaspora engagement.

Tourism also has become an intensely competitive sector. Travel and tourism account for an estimated one-tenth of the global gross domestic product (GDP), nearly 11 percent of world exports, and more than 9 percent of world investment.[54] International tourism generated $944 billion in 2008.[55] All regions of the world share in the receipts of inbound tourism, including Europe (51 percent), Asia and the Pacific (22 percent), the Americas (20 percent), the Middle East (4 percent), and Africa (3 percent).[56]

Visitors to the United States in 2007 spent more than $122 billion.[57] Figure B depicts annual entries between 1999 and 2008 from the five countries associated with the highest number of temporary admissions to the United States in 2008.[58]

Figure B. Nonimmigrant Admissions, 1999–2008, from the Five Countries Sending the Highest Number of Nonimmigrants to the United States in 2008

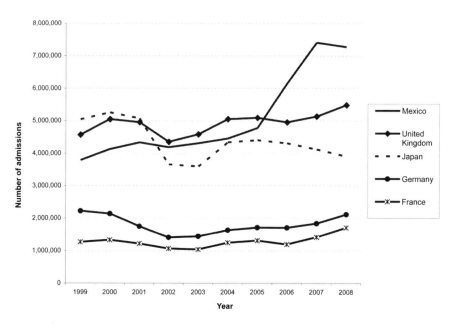

Source: DHS, Yearbook of Immigration Statistics, 2008.
Notes: United Kingdom includes the United Kingdom, Anguilla, Bermuda, British Virgin Islands, Cayman Islands, Falkland Islands, Gibraltar, Guernsey, Isle of Man, Jersey, Montserrat, Pitcairn Island, St. Helena, and Turks and Caicos Islands; France includes France, French Guiana, French Polynesia, French Southern and Antarctic Lands, Guadeloupe, Martinique, New Caledonia, Reunion, St. Pierre and Miquelon, and Wallis and Futuna.

We live in an "age of mobility."[59] One political theorist proposes that regulating mobility now constitutes the core role of the state, central to how government affects people's lives. By regulating mobility, the state determines people's access to security, markets, social benefits, and opportunity.[60] Nations are distinguished by their mobility regimes, citizens by their different degrees of freedom and access. Our strategic vision for security should reflect the ways in which human mobility is critical to Americans and to US strategic interests.

Deficiencies of the Current Paradigm

The prevailing policy language of *border security–immigration enforcement* suggests that borders and enforcement can stop anyone or anything. Yet perfect security cannot be achieved by any set of methods, and terrorist incidents may occur even when real progress is being made in enhancing security through prevention and mitigation, often based on lessons learned from calamitous incidents.

Border security–immigration enforcement also suggests that problems are best addressed at the border and in the interior. But mobile bad actors either originate or return from travel outside the United States, and their use of global mobility channels must be addressed at least in part elsewhere. A recognition of this imperative has, to some extent, been built into homeland security thinking through the concept of *layered defense*, with visa officers considered a first layer. Unlike for cargo, however, which is treated as flowing though a global supply chain to be secured through all its links, the United States has developed few cooperative agreements with homeland security allies to stem illegal immigration or control organized crime associated with mobility. Traditional immigration enforcement also will not work to eliminate the transnational movement of violent gang members active in immigrant communities and sending countries.

Another deficiency of the border security–immigration enforcement paradigm is that the risk assessment that results from it almost inevitably treats everyone on the move as a potential malefactor. We have remained transfixed by the problem that everyone is a potential terrorist but in fact the likelihood is miniscule. Concentrating attention on all individual unauthorized immigrants crowds out the development of more targeted tools necessary to identify potential malefactors and respond to or prevent new actual threats and greater risks. With the emphasis on border security and immigration enforcement, these complex problems are neglected.

Reducing illegal immigration and bringing migration under regulatory controls remains an essential dimension of securing global mobility, but looking for a solution for this problem primarily in border security and immigration enforcement has not worked. Hundreds of thousands of people enter the United States illegally or overstay their visas every year.

For all three problems — terrorist travel in and out of the United States, criminal mobility organizations, and high-volume illegal immigration — centering attention on the border and the interior distracts policymakers from focusing on where illegal movement begins and what can be done to change migration push factors, whether from Mexico and Central America, Canada, or overseas.

Furthermore, at the tactical level the border security–immigration enforcement paradigm results in distortions to US policy that are reflected in large-scale detention, an overemphasis on incarceration and deportation, and oppressive policies in border communities.

In sum, the scale and the significance of human mobility are now too substantial for border security and immigration enforcement to be an adequate paradigm. The traditional framework has these major deficiencies:

- It does not reflect the homeland security mission of providing sufficient security so that citizens can take the full advantage of the opportunities afforded by mobility.
- It leads to treating everyone on the move as a potential terrorist.
- It monopolizes resources and promotes, rather than quells, public fears.
- It does not lead to risk assessment strategies that consider other sites for homeland security, e.g., cyberspace, financial flows, cargo.
- It prevents the development of new tools and results in distortions, human costs, and the sacrifice of core principles.
- It suggests that the problems of mobility today can be diminished to a manageable size and shaped through tightening traditional civil and criminal processes.
- It confuses immigration policy with the homeland or civil-security mission, and therefore precludes the kind of policy analysis needed to protect this vital strategic asset.

The Persistence of the Legacy Paradigm

The border security–immigration enforcement paradigm is stubbornly persistent. From today's vantage point, without a longer-term perspective, it appears that the public policy debate about mobility and security in the twenty-first century remains largely confined to the terms of the immigration debate of the twentieth century. Viewpoints and policy prescriptions associated with the period following the 9/11 attacks seem stuck in place.

The exploitation of the lawful mobility system that led to the 9/11 attacks caused Americans to look at the nation's immigration system, national borders, and global transportation and travel differently. Suddenly the public had legitimate concerns about mobility security. At the time, other factors compounded a sense of threat, particularly the high level of illegal immigration. Border violence associated with Mexico-US DTOs also reinforced this perspective.

Two distinct issues — terrorist travel and uncontrolled illegal immigration — immediately became fused. One member of Congress explained that the attacks still raised questions about how immigration authorities allowed terrorists to enter the United States and highlighted the importance of improving US immigration enforcement.[61] Like nearly everyone else, Congress members saw immigration regulation as the one-stop way to accomplish two goals: reduce illegal immigration and preclude terrorist travel to the United States. It has been almost impossible to see the problem any differently.

Immigration enforcement has remained fixed as a significant concern in the public discourse for two reasons. It assumed policy prominence beginning in the mid-1990s, when the increased trade promoted by the North American Free Trade Agreement (NAFTA) began exposing American workers to greater competition. As many have pointed out, policymakers effectively permitted employers to skirt the law prohibiting the hiring of unauthorized workers. Because of this generally accepted neglect and corruption of the rule of law, considered more or less benign at the time, policymakers ultimately became vulnerable to attack. This gave the political upper hand to those who wanted to restrict or even end legal migration.

A second cause of the durability of the emphasis on immigration enforcement is that the United States has tended for some time in the direction of the criminalization of illegal migration in the name of security. The trend began with the passage of laws in the 1990s that expanded the class of "aggravated felons" who can be deported without consideration of their individual equities and who are subject to mandatory detention. It continued through the fight over the criminalization of "illegal presence" that took place during the comprehensive immigration reform legislative debate in 2005. The criminalization approach treats law enforcement as the solution to all security issues relating to immigrants. Emphasis on criminal immigration law enforcement as a primary tool against immigrant terrorists fits naturally within this mindset and has been frequently employed.[62]

Immediately after 9/11, the government toolkit for enlisting border and law-enforcement agencies in preventing terrorist travel was in fact very limited.[63] Cargo security was the focus of creative policy thinking, but there was no corresponding attention to security relating to human mobility.[64] A bolstered terrorist watchlist was more or less the only tool the intelligence and security community initially had to offer. The US intelligence community prior to 9/11 did not have a strategic operational function called "countering terrorist travel" that was analogous to the multiagency "countering terrorist finance" with its range of preventive and protective intelligence and regulatory programs. Border security and immigration enforcement then became the accepted substitute.

Moreover, the development of new tools was not encouraged in the overall strategy toward violent extremism. To a very large degree, leaders took a military approach and made the Iraq war the central front on terrorism, emphasizing "fighting them over there in order not to fight them over here." This gave less scope for high-level attention to developing nonmilitary tools and figuring out how mobility issues fit into homeland security and counterterrorism. A terrorist travel strategy was developed, but its lack of explicit benchmarks effectively left the priority of addressing illegal immigration intact.

The dramatic failure of the immigration reform legislation in Congress in 2007 solidified the enforcement and border security approach. It has remained an assumption that until the American public can be confident that immigration laws are being enforced effectively and the US border secured sufficiently — or until the stakeholders feel sufficient pressure to compromise — there will be no resolution of the status of immigrants already here or reform of underlying legal immigration laws.

The establishment of DHS in 2004, which absorbed the functions of the US Immigration and Naturalization Service (INS) along with those of 21 other agencies, formally conflated *immigration policy* and *border security* with *homeland security*. Its authorizing legislation made protection against terrorism the overriding mission of DHS, but also made DHS carry over existing immigration mandates. All of these factors reinforced the sense that suppression of illegal immigration through border security and immigration enforcement represented the best method of managing security risks associated with the movement of people.

A Transition to Mobility Security

Authorities have made thousands of changes since 9/11 to reduce risk in travel, border-crossing, transportation, and immigration channels. Because the deficiencies of the border security–immigration enforcement paradigm have been largely recognized, the transition to mobility security can be accomplished in an evolutionary, rather than revolutionary, fashion.

From the first homeland security strategy, there has been real and growing recognition of and attention to the facilitation of travel for economic benefit, the civil liberties at stake in travel, and the human rights implicated in the mass displacement of people. *Facilitation*, long a priority for customs and immigration officials, and *redress*, a new concern that has arisen in response to problems travelers encounter in the new, stricter screening regime, are frequently invoked in homeland security circles.

To some extent, also, the meanings of *border security* and *immigration enforcement* are evolving in response to the new imperatives. For example, border security, it is now emphasized, involves "pushing out" the borders to deepen the layered defense of the United States in a way that coincides with the military concept of layered defense. Measures described as *border security* no longer just involve controlling US air, land, and sea borders or even reinforcing virtual borders by screening at consulates, but rather mitigating risks in shared travel channels through international agreements. For example, CBP posts inspectors in foreign airports such as Amsterdam and London and reciprocally accepts their foreign counterparts in major US hubs such as the John F. Kennedy International Airport in New York and the Miami airport. In these settings, there is joint responsibility for managing the risks of unlawful travel.

Immigration enforcement is notably more focused than previously on measures beyond US borders in the interior of the country, through worksite enforcement and other means. Moving toward mandating an electronic system for employers to verify the eligibility of their employees to work acknowledges the reality that illegal labor migration cannot be stopped with border security alone but also requires a sound immigration compliance policy.[65] Agents from ICE and the State Department Diplomatic Security (DS) division are critical members of the Federal Bureau of Investigation (FBI) Joint Terrorism Task Forces (JTTFs), which act to preempt plots and not only to enforce laws after they are violated.

In addition, all along there have been programs that do not fit obviously within the border security–immigration enforcement paradigm. In the 1990s, for example, US officials laid the groundwork for international agreements to fight against human trafficking and smuggling.[66] Since 9/11 terrorist travel has emerged as an entire new focus for intelligence analysis, and increasingly DHS has expanded its vision of border security and immigration enforcement to encompass safeguarding lawful travel and disrupting illicit pathways.

Because the border security–immigration enforcement paradigm is not as rigid as public rhetoric sometimes suggests, its evolution into a new framework is within reach. The outline for a new "mobility security" framework can be found in risk assessment methodologies and tools, in strategies against terrorist travel and criminal mobility, and in a variety of mobility access and security agreements with Mexico, Canada, the European Union, the Asia-Pacific Economic Cooperation (APEC) countries, and in visa-free travel agreements. It can also be found in the international regulation regime for passports and merchant mariner identification, airline reservation systems, airlines, and the commercial maritime domain.

Article 13 of the Universal Declaration of Human Rights recognizes the right to freedom of movement. However, the law and practice relating to the security of human movement would benefit from more attention. The global systems for the movement of goods are far more developed than the systems that sustain the movement of people. Just as trade is the subject of ongoing discussions about lowering barriers and harmonizing customs rules, with global trade rules overseen by the World Trade Organization (WTO), the security of human movement should receive far more systemic and international attention.

Securing human mobility is a critical homeland security mission. This book articulates some of the tasks that could advance it.

Section I describes the goals of mobility security, how they fit into the homeland security enterprise, how mobility security relates to immigration policy, and how government can be better organized to accomplish this mission. Beyond the macro perspective, the section places terrorist travel and key methods of criminal movement in a conceptual framework.

Section II proposes a list of the most important threats from people that are relevant to the mobility security mission, and programs that address several of them.

Section III discusses select aspects of ensuring the integrity and resilience of mobility infrastructure, from compliance and sanctions to fairness and privacy.

Section IV highlights the evolving task of preventing dangerous, illegal, and uncontrolled large-scale human movement, and some of the emerging tools and institutions with which the United States is engaging to carry out this task.

Notes

1. The report was part of a series of studies conducted for the Independent Task Force on Immigration and America's Future, which was convened by the Migration Policy Institute and cochaired by former Sen. Spencer Abraham (R-MI) and former Rep. Lee Hamilton (D-IN).

2. See, for example, Stephen Yale-Loehr, Demetrios G. Papademetriou, Betsy Cooper, *Secure Borders, Open Doors: Visa Procedures in the Post-September 11 Era* (Washington, DC: Migration Policy Institute, MPI, 2005), www.migrationpolicy.org/pubs/Secure_Borders_Report0905.pdf; Doris Meissner, Deborah W. Meyers, Demetrios G. Papademetriou, and Michael Fix, *Immigration and America's Future: A New Chapter* (Washington, DC: MPI, 2006), www.migrationpolicy.org/ITFIAF/finalreport.pdf; Doris Meissner and Donald Kerwin, *DHS and Immigration: Taking Stock and Correcting Course* (Washington, DC: MPI, 2009), www.migrationpolicy.org/pubs/DHS_Feb09.pdf; Edward Alden, *The Closing of the American Border: Terrorism, Immigration, and Security Since 9/11* (New York: Harper Perennial, September 2009).

3. The issue of cross-border threats to health and epidemiological risks will not be covered in this volume and awaits subsequent attention.

4. Marc Sageman, *Leaderless Jihad: Terror Networks in the Twenty-First Century* (Philadelphia: Univ. of Pennsylvania Press, 2008), 151.

5. UNODC (United Nations Office on Drugs and Crime), *Global Report on Trafficking in Persons* (Vienna, Austria: UNODC, 2009), www.unodc.org/documents/human-trafficking/Global_Report_on_TIP.pdf. On a country-by-country level, many of these 71 states reported a decline in the number of human-trafficking victims they identified during this period.

6. Ibid.

7. DOJ (US Department of Justice), National Drug Intelligence Center, *Situation Report: Cities in Which Mexican DTOs Operate within the United States* (Washington, DC: DOJ, 2008), www.usdoj.gov/ndic/pubs27/27986/appendb.htm#start.

8. Congressional Research Service, *Border Security: The Role of the U.S. Border Patrol* (Washington, DC: Congressional Research Service, 2008), www.fas.org/sgp/crs/homesec/RL32562.pdf. According to a report by the American Civil Liberties Union of San Diego and Imperial Counties and Mexico's National Commission of Human Rights, the estimated number of deaths along the US-Mexico border between 1994 and 2008 ranged from 3,557 to 5,607.

9. GAO (US Government Accountability Office), *Illegal Immigration: Border-Crossing Deaths Have Doubled since 1995: Border Patrol's Efforts to Prevent Deaths Have Not Been Fully Evaluated*, GAO-06-770 (Washington, DC: GAO, 2006), www.gao.gov/new.items/d06770.pdf.

10. Frontex, "Frontex and Fortress Europe," May 29, 2008, http://frontex.info.pl/content/frontex_and_fortress_europe.

11. Kathleen Newland, Dovelyn Rannveig Agunias, and Aaron Terrazas, *Learning by Doing: Experiences of Circular Migration* (Washington, DC: MPI, 2008), www.migrationpolicy.org/pubs/Insight-IGC-Sept08.pdf; Dilip Ratha, *Leveraging Remittances for Development* (Washington, DC: MPI, 2007), www.migrationpolicy.org/pubs/MigDevPB_062507.pdf; Dovelyn Ranneveig Agunias, ed., *Closing the Distance: How Governments Strengthen Ties with Their Diasporas* (Washington, DC: MPI, 2009).

12. DHS (Department of Homeland Security), Office of Immigration Statistics, *Immigration Enforcement Actions: 2008* (Washington, DC: DHS, Office of Immigration Statistics, 2009), www.dhs.gov/xlibrary/assets/statistics/publications/enforcement_ar_08.pdf.

13. Jeffrey S. Passel and D'Vera Cohen, *Trends in Unauthorized Immigration: Undocumented Inflow Now Trails Legal Inflow* (Washington, DC: Pew Hispanic Center, 2008), http://pewhispanic.org/files/reports/94.pdf.

14. Ibid.

15. Jeffrey S. Passel and D'Vera Cohn, *A Portrait of Unauthorized Immigrants in the United States* (Washington, DC: Pew Hispanic Center, 2009), http://pewhispanic.org/reports/report.php?ReportID=107.

16. Ibid.
17. Pew Hispanic Center, *Modes of Entry for the Unauthorized Migrant Population* (Washington, DC: Pew Hispanic Center, 2006), http://pewhispanic.org/files/factsheets/19.pdf.
18. Rey Koslowski, "International Migration and Human Mobility as a Security Issue," International Studies Meeting, New York, February 15–18, 2009.
19. The size and proportion of humanitarian flows relative to overall permanent migration vary from country to country. In 2006, humanitarian flows accounted for 0 percent of all permanent migration flows to Japan and Portugal and 28 percent and 24 percent of all permanent migration flows to Sweden and the Netherlands. Another 51 million people in the world were internally displaced. See UNHCR (United Nations High Commissioner for Refugees), *2008 Global Trends: Refugees, Asylum-seekers, Returnees, Internally Displaced and Stateless Persons* (Geneva, Switzerland: UNHCR, 2009), www.unhcr.org/4a375c426.html.
20. Jonathan Crush, "South Africa: Policy in the Face of Xenophobia," *Migration Information Source*, July 2008, www.migrationinformation.org/Profiles/display.cfm?ID=689.
21. Joseph Atick, personal conversation with the author.
22. UNWTO (United Nations World Tourism Organization), "Testing Times for International Tourism," News Release, June 2009, www.unwto.org/media/news/en/press_det.php?id=4421&idioma=E.
23. Jennifer Blanke and Thea Chiesa, *The Travel & Tourism Competitiveness Report 2009: Managing in a Time of Turbulence* (Geneva, Switzerland: World Economic Forum, 2009), www.weforum.org/pdf/ttcr09/ttcr09_fullreport.pdf.
24. OECD (Organisation for Economic Co-operation and Development), *International Migration Outlook Annual Report 2008 Edition* (Paris: OECD, 2008).
25. DHS, Customs and Border Protection (CBP), *Performance and Accountability Report Fiscal Year 2008* (Washington, DC: DHS, 2008), www.cbp.gov/linkhandler/cgov/newsroom/publications/admin/par_fy08_pub.ctt/par_fy08.pdf.
26. According to the US Census Bureau, the US population was 307.9 million on November 10, 2009.
27. This number includes those who were issued an I-94 and those who were admitted temporarily without an I-94 from Mexico and Canada. See DHS, Office of Immigration Statistics, *Yearbook of Immigration Statistics: Table 25, Nonimmigrant Admissions: Fiscal Years 1997 to 2006* (Washington, DC: DHS, 2006), www.dhs.gov/xlibrary/assets/statistics/yearbook/2006/table25.xls.
28. DHS, Office of Immigration Statistics, *Yearbook of Immigration Statistics: Table 25, Nonimmigrant Admissions by Class of Admission: Fiscal Years 1999 to 2008* (Washington, DC: DHS, 2008), www.dhs.gov/xlibrary/assets/statistics/yearbook/2008/table25d.xls.
29. GAO, *Comprehensive Strategy Needed to Improve Passport Operations*, GAO-08-891 (Washington, DC: GAO, 2008), www.gao.gov/new.items/d08891.pdf.
30. Ibid.
31. DOC (US Department of Commerce), International Trade Administration, Office of Travel & Tourism Industries, "US Sets New Records for Travel Abroad in 2007," Press Release, June 30, 2008, http://tinet.ita.doc.gov/outreachpages/download_data_table/2007_Outbound_Analysis.doc.
32. DOC, International Trade Administration, Office of Travel & Tourism Industries, *US Citizen Air Traffic to Overseas Regions, Canada & Mexico 2008* (Washington, DC: DOC, 2009), http://tinet.ita.doc.gov/view/m-2008-O-001/index.html.
33. These numbers reflect only nonstop air traffic from a US port to a foreign port. See DOC, US Citizen Air Traffic to Overseas Regions, Canada & Mexico 2008.
34. AARO (Association of Americans Resident Overseas), "5.25 Million Americans Abroad Map," (map), http://aaro.org/.
35. UN (United Nations), Department of Economic and Social Affairs (DESA), Population Division, *International Migration 2006* (New York: UN, 2006), www.un.org/esa/population/publications/2006Migration_Chart/Migration2006.pdf; UN, DESA, Population Division, International Migra-

tion from Countries with Economies in Transition: 1980–1999 (New York: UN, 2002), http://.
un.org/esa/population/publications/ewmigration/E-W_Migrationreport.pdf.

36. UN, Department of Economic and Social Affairs, Population Division, *Trends in International Migrant Stock: The 2008 Revision*, UN database, POP/DB/MIG/Stock/Rev.2008 (New York: United Nations, 2009), http://esa.un.org/migration/index.asp?panel=1.

37. ABS (Australian Bureau of Statistics), *Migration 2006–07* (Belconnen, Australia: ABS, 2008), www.ausstats.abs.gov.au/ausstats/subscriber.nsf/0/F15E154C9434F250CA2574170011B45B/$File/34120_2006-07.pdf.

38. Serge Kollwelter, "Immigration in Luxembourg: New Challenges for an Old Country," *Migration Information Source*, March 2007, www.migrationinformation.org/Profiles/display.cfm?id=587.

39. US Census Bureau, *American Community Survey: Citizenship Status in the United States — Universe: Total Population in the United States* (Washington, DC: US Census Bureau, 2008), http://factfinder. census.gov/servlet/DTTable?_bm=y&-geo_id=01000US&-ds_name=ACS_2008_1YR_G00_&-SubjectID=17632063&-_lang=en&-mt_name=ACS_2008_1YR_G2000_B05001&-format=&-CONTEXT=dt.

40. In some countries, the foreign born may only comprise a small portion of the total population. In 2005 the foreign born comprised 2.6 percent of the total population in South Africa, 1.6 percent in Japan, 0.4 percent in Brazil, 1.2 percent in South Korea, 0.5 percent in India, and far less than 1 percent in China. See UN, *Trends in International Migrant Stock*, http://esa.un.org/migration/index. asp?panel=1.

41. Statistics Canada, *Immigration in Canada: A Portrait of the Foreign-Born Population, 2006 Census: Immigration: Driver of Population Growth* (Ottawa, Canada: Statistics Canada, 2009), www12. statcan.ca/census-recensement/2006/as-sa/97-557/p2-eng.cfm.

42. MPI (Migration Policy Institute), *Foreign-Born Population and Foreign Born as a Percentage of the Total US Population, 1850 to 2008* (Washington, DC: MPI, 2008), www.migrationinformation. org/DataHub/charts/final.fb.shtml.

43. These flows include both status adjusters (those already residing in the country under temporary status) and new arrivals. See DHS, Office of Immigration Statistics, *Yearbook of Immigration Statistics: Table 1, Persons Obtaining Legal Permanent Resident Status: Fiscal Years 1820 to 2008* (Washington, DC: DHS, 2008), www.dhs.gov/xlibrary/assets/statistics/yearbook/2008/table01.xls.

44. UN, DESA, Population Division, *Statistics and Indicators on Women and Men* (New York: UN, 2009), http://unstats.un.org/unsd/demographic/products/indwm/tab1a.htm.

45. Demetrios. G. Papademetriou, Will Somerville, and Hiroyuki Tanaka, "Talent in the 21st Century," in *Talent, Competitiveness and Migration*, ed. Bertelsmann Stiftung and Migration Policy Institute (Gütersloh, Germany: Bertelsmann Stiftung, 2009).

46. International Organization for Migration, *World Migration Report 2008: Managing Labour Mobility in the Evolving Global Economy* (Geneva, Switzerland: International Organization for Migration, 2008), www.iom.ch/jahia/webdav/site/myjahiasite/shared/shared/mainsite/published_docs/studies_and_reports/WMR2008/Ch1_WMR08.pdf.

47. Ibid., 36.

48. OECD members include: Australia, Austria, Belgium, Canada, the Czech Republic, Denmark, Finland, France, Germany, Greece, Hungary, Iceland, Ireland, Italy, Japan, Korea, Luxembourg, Mexico, the Netherlands, New Zealand, Norway, Poland, Portugal, Slovak Republic, Spain, Sweden, Switzerland, Turkey, the United Kingdom, and the United States.

49. OECD, *International Migration Outlook*, SOPEMI 2008.

50. Jane Millar and John Salt, "In Whose Interests? IT Migration in an Interconnected World Economy," *Population, Space and Place* 13 (2007): 41–58; Jane Millar and John Salt, "Portfolios of Mobility: The Movement of Expertise in Transnational Corporations in Two Sectors — Aerospace and Extractive Industries," Global Networks 8, no. 1 (2008): 25–50; Jonathan V. Beaverstock and James T. Boardwell, "Negotiating Globalization, Transnational Corporations and Global City Financial Centres in Transient Migration Studies," in *Competing for Global Talent*, ed.

Christiane Kuptsch and Pang Eng Fong (Geneva, Switzerland, International Institute for Labour Studies, International Labor Office, Singapore Management Univ., 2006).

51. Papademetriou, Somerville, and Tanaka, "Talent in the 21st Century."

52. UN, *International Migration 2006*.

53. Ibid.

54. Blanke and Chiesa, *The Travel & Tourism Competitiveness Report 2009*.

55. UNWTO, "Testing Times for International Tourism."

56. Ibid.

57. DOC's International Trade Administration totals include passenger fares and travel payments. See DOC, International Trade Administration, Office of Travel & Tourism Industries, "2007 Sets All Time International Tourism Record for US," Press Release, March 10, 2008, www.commerce.gov/NewsRoom/PressReleases_FactSheets/PROD01_005355.

58. CIA (Central Intelligence Agency), *The World Factbook: Rank Order — GDP (Purchasing Power Parity)* (Washington, DC: CIA, 2008), https://www.cia.gov/library/publications/the-world-factbook/rankorder/2001rank.html.

59. Demetrios G. Papademetriou, *The Age of Mobility: How to Get More out of Migration in the 21st Century* (Washington, DC: MPI, 2007), www.migrationinformation.org/transatlantic/age_mobility_032307.pdf.

60. John Torpey, *The Invention of the Passport: Surveillance, Citizenship, and the State* (Cambridge: Cambridge Univ. Press, 1999); Kamal Sadiq, *Paper Citizens: How Illegal Immigrants Acquire Citizenship in Developing Countries* (Oxford: Oxford Univ. Press, 2009).

61. Comments by Rep. Ellen Tauscher (D-CA) at the Transatlantic Satellite Debate, *What Lessons in the War against Terror Can the EU and US Exchange?* (Washington, DC: Friends of Europe, 2005), www.friendsofeurope.org/Portals/6/Documents/Reports/Atlantic%20Rendez-Vous%20-%2025%20April%202005.pdf.

62. Richard H. Friman, "Migration and Security: Crime, Terror, and the Politics of Order," in *Immigration, Integration, and Security: America and Europe, Comparative Perspective*, ed. Ariane Chebel d'Appollonia and Simon Reich (Pittsburgh: Univ. of Pittsburgh Press, 2008), 130–44.

63. National Research Council of the National Academies, *Making the Nation Safer: The Role of Science and Technology in Countering Terrorism* (Washington, DC: National Academies Press, 2002); Paul R. Pillar, Terrorism and US Foreign Policy (Washington, DC: The Brookings Institution Press, 2003).

64. Stephen E. Flynn, *America the Vulnerable: How Our Government Is Failing to Protect Us from Terrorism* (New York: Harper Collins, 2004).

65. It remains to be seen whether such a system can be deployed prior to comprehensive immigration reform that responds to the business community's perception of its labor needs. See Doris Meissner and Marc R. Rosenblum, *The Next Generation of E-Verify Getting Employment* (Washington, DC: MPI, 2009), www.migrationpolicy.org/pubs/Verification_paper-071709.pdf.

66. The White House, *International Crime Control Strategy* (Washington, DC: The White House, 1998).

Section I: Mobility Security Facts and Principles

Introduction

Good policies integrate facts with the basic principles and interests at stake. In any given arena, one has to look both at macrolevel policies and at the often unpredictable microlevel events and facts relevant to the challenges at hand. At the macro level, border security and immigration enforcement have been held up as the key means of providing protection from the movement of dangerous people. This perspective derives from a conflation of immigration and national security based on a specific set of assumptions and historical factors. In recent years, security needs have radically changed due to the risk of terrorism with weapons of mass destruction (WMDs). At the same time, the ability of individuals to cross borders has become central to economic vitality and the exercise of freedom. In the absence of sufficient legal mobility channels, the United States has experienced high levels of illegal movement, endangering the lives of migrants and undermining the rule of law.

Border security–immigration enforcement is no longer an adequate paradigm because there is more at stake than stopping illegal immigration. Even if illegal labor and family migration to the United States ceased, there would still be exploitation of mobility channels by US citizens, foreign terrorists, and members of organized criminal networks. There would still be migratory surges resulting from sudden destabilizations in migrant source countries.

The combination of new security imperatives and evolving human rights norms argues for the adoption of a new framework for mobility security. This new paradigm seeks to go beyond the missions of border security and immigration enforcement.

Specific and comprehensive information about illicit travel is necessary to design and implement any strategy for securing human mobility. Without a clear picture of the operations of illicit travel and immigration, options for protective measures will be limited and possibly misguided. With an operational picture that details (1) the organization of the illicit travel market, (2) the methods that comprise illegal movement, and (3) prevalent patterns of movement, policymakers would have a more solid basis for deciding how best to accomplish the mission of securing human mobility and the public would have a greater ability to assess the chosen policies.

A fourth dimension of analysis is the convergence of transnational threats, including human smuggling and trafficking, money laundering, corruption, arms trafficking, and trafficking in other commodities. Ultimately, policymakers must focus on the nodes where threats converge and on the greatest vulnerabilities. This book highlights the criminality associated with mobility as one element of this larger picture that has not received systematic attention.

While illicit markets will always be hard to measure and pinpoint, success in doing so can provide information that allows governments to allocate enforcement resources, find terrorists and criminals, disrupt and dismantle criminal organizations, use regulatory authorities more effectively, seek new laws, undertake diplomatic initiatives, and educate the public.

Chapter 1 addresses a puzzle that has flummoxed the policy community since the concept of homeland security first gained currency after September 11, 2001: the interconnections among immigration policy, immigration enforcement, border security, homeland security, national security, and counterterrorism. It describes the transformation of the mission that occurred when the Immigration and Naturalization Service (INS) was dismantled and its pieces rearranged within the Department of Homeland Security (DHS). It describes the elements of a proposed new mission of securing human mobility. Chapter 2 provides an overview of the types of professional criminals and other actors who drive the illicit market in mobility. Chapter 3 takes a closer look at their tools and methods as well as the key geographic and legal pathways that facilitate illegal mobility. These chapters lay the groundwork for the policy-oriented chapters that follow.

CHAPTER 1: SECURING HUMAN MOBILITY AS A HOMELAND SECURITY MISSION

Securing human mobility requires that new concepts and objectives be defined, new roles assigned, and existing organizations reoriented and restructured. The pieces of the security puzzle include: mobility security, immigration enforcement, counterterrorism, immigration policy, travel regulation, homeland security, border security, national security, and homeland defense. The key challenge is to determine how these pieces fit together. While these relationships may not be fully clarified for years, this chapter makes an effort to start sorting out mobility-related security roles and responsibilities, particularly in federal agencies.

Mobility Security as Homeland Security

Securing the movement of people implicates many of the core activities of the government, including defense, diplomacy, intelligence, crime control, and market regulation. Each lever of power reinforces mobility security. Law-enforcement and immigration agencies, for example, secure mobility by engaging in *immigration enforcement* and *trafficking investigations*. *Enemy troop movement* and *control of the air, land,* and *maritime domains* are classic concerns in intelligence and military science. In the counterterrorism context, major mobility-related subjects include *infiltration* and *exfiltration, terrorist targeting,* and *special operations at borders*. Diplomacy has shaped international agreements on *civil aviation* and *human trafficking* and *smuggling*.

Securing human mobility is not associated with any of these traditional contexts. Nor is it the same as "facilitating the lawful flow of people." The phrase takes on a clear and straightforward meaning only in the framework of homeland security, which is itself a relatively new concept that speaks to the need to preclude harm to citizens, our way of life, and our strategic interests arising from potentially catastrophic risks. Americans require and expect access to safe and lawful mobility channels, but mobility channels can be sites and vectors of attack, exploitation, and systemic collapse.[67] This makes securing human mobility a major mission of homeland security, comparable to securing cyberspace, financial flows, and the energy supply.

The Department of Homeland Security (DHS) is principally in charge of determining how US mobility-related risks are to be managed and addressed. The United States, in turn, works through bilateral agreements, regional organizations, the United Nations, and other multilateral fora to safeguard mobility channels worldwide.

Why Homeland Security?

Why should a homeland security formulation dislodge border security–immigration enforcement as the strategic framework for protecting travel, borders, and immigration? The short answer is that homeland security aims to protect citizens and others from threats and risks that are different or more significant than those posed by the traditional criminal and immigration threats. This section examines homeland security as a strategic concept, as distinct from the traditional understanding of national defense. It suggests how the goals of homeland security differ from, but relate to, the goals of immigration policy.

The precipitating threat that spurred the development of the homeland security paradigm, with its strategic reliance on risk management, was terrorist violence against US citizens — not illegal immigration or mass displacement of people. Travel and migration facilitate, but do not cause, terrorism. Networked terrorism associated with weapons of mass destruction (WMDs) is instead a phenomenon arising from changes in the strategic environment.[68]

The possession of overwhelming military power by certain governments, especially by the United States, led to the emergence of asymmetric forms of attack by adversaries. Whatever their views, violent extremists engage in terrorism to delegitimize and weaken governments and to coerce them toward a political or social end. Other factors critical to the emergence of the new homeland security concept include:

- The global marketplace, which — supported by communications, information technology, and transportation — has made WMDs available to outlier states and to nonstate extremist groups
- The vulnerability to attack and disruption of societies that rely on technological networks and the globalized market
- The world's deepening belief in human freedom and dignity, expressed in the law of human rights

Security must protect human life and freedom of movement. Democratic states, in particular, demand a high degree of civil protection.[69] The relationship between state sovereignty and individual rights is being tested by the emergence of transnational threats, and the United States' constitutional commitment to civil liberties and human rights informs its response to such threats.

Homeland security seeks to mitigate or prevent the destruction and constitutional collapse precipitated by hazards such as terrorist violence, natural disaster, and the breakdown of critical infrastructure and resources.[70] The September 11, 2001, attacks exemplified the death, destruction, economic cost, and psychological impact that terrorist groups seek to achieve. The aftermath of Hurricane Katrina illustrated the civil disorder and delegitimizing of government authority that can follow a catastrophic natural disaster. Fortunately, we have not experienced a catastrophic collapse of cybersystems or other critical infrastructure in a context outside natural disaster.

In the same way that traditional military defense protects the United States against aggressors using conventional armed forces, strategic nuclear forces, or unconventional warfare, homeland security protects the country from catastrophic consequences arising from: (1) terrorist attacks, especially using chemical, biological, radiological, nuclear, or high yield explosive (CBRNE) WMDs; (2) pandemics and natural and environmental disasters; and (3) the collapse of technological systems or key resources. Whereas the goal of conventional war is to defend against the use or threat of military force, the goal of homeland security is to preclude catastrophes that could emerge from a broad spectrum of risks.

Homeland Security Is Civil Security

Other terminology may help to clarify the meaning of homeland security. *Civil security* is a term used in Europe, where references to *homeland* and *motherland* are too closely associated with discredited ideologies.[71] More so than *homeland security, civil security* conveys the root concerns with the control of civil unrest, service disruption, and other challenges that can result from major, natural, people- or technology-induced catastrophes and lead to serious breakdowns in the constitutional order.[72] The phrase also evokes the legacy of *civil defense*.[73]

The phrases *civil security* and *civil protection* are more intuitively meaningful than *homeland security* for other reasons. First, they omit any reference to *land* or *territory*. Terrorists are not defined principally by a nationalist or territorial goal. Border security is an important element of homeland security, but terrorists target the constitutional order of the state, not its territory.[74]

The term *homeland security* also could suggest, erroneously, that no concern is owed the millions of citizens and the substantial US interests abroad, which cannot be true. Being able to issue passports to US citizens overseas and to issue warnings are, for example, critical aspects of mobility security. *Civil security* and *civil protection* evoke the harms that are sought to be precluded — the breakdown of law, violations of rights, and human and material destruction.

Although the terms *national defense* and *national security* also carry the connotation of security for US citizens and interests beyond American soil, they have a different meaning and cannot substitute for *civil security*. *Defense* traditionally connotes actions to detect, deter, and defeat aggression from external adversaries. Civil security, on the other hand, seeks to preclude breakdowns due to threats to the interior such as terrorist attacks, natural disasters, and technological vulnerabilities. *National security* is understood to encompass homeland security: the National Security Council (NSC), for example, carries out homeland security functions. These functions are, however, distinct from other national security functions, so that the two terms are not interchangeable.

Homeland security as a descriptive term has another limitation. It is usually taken to mean something other than war. This tends to suggest that military and intelligence activities are illegitimate in the context of homeland security, and reside legitimately within the sole preserve of traditional *national defense*. The Department of Defense (DOD) makes a sharp distinction, very important to current strategic thinking, between *homeland defense* and a function set apart from traditional defense: *defense support to civilian authorities* (DSCA). One form of DSCA was apparent in the immediate aftermath of 9/11 when DOD assigned the National Guard to airports. DSCA is being further developed and now notably encompasses a standing, specialized unit to respond to nuclear incidents.

Although *civil security* is a preferable term, *homeland security* is the term most frequently used in the United States. Hereafter the two terms are used interchangeably. The core goal of *homeland* or *civil security* is to preclude catastrophic events and to minimize their consequences when they occur. The military has a role in meeting this goal, but the purposes and methods of counterterrorism differ from those demanded by war. Wars against predatory and violent nonstate organizations defend the citizen in order to defend the state, as Christopher Coker wrote in *War in an Age of Risk*. The military's role against such human adversaries is still being determined.

The proper role for the military at land, air, and sea borders is also unsettled. Border concerns may implicate illegal immigration, organized crime, or violence. At times, military or military-style assets have been deployed.[75] DOD has a legitimate role in achieving homeland security, although not necessarily as it is traditionally configured. Similarly, law-enforcement and intelligence agencies are contributing to homeland security, although they are not necessarily being used in the same way as in the past.

DHS asserts that homeland security cannot be achieved by a narrowly defined group, but rather requires the involvement of a wide range of organizations and institutions in society, including international, federal, state, and local authorities and individuals. DHS refers to this joint endeavor as the *homeland security enterprise* and sees one critical task as achieving unity of effort among all participants. How to the draw the lines of the entire homeland security enterprise and assign roles to the full array of players is not the focus here. Instead, this chapter seeks to explain enough about homeland security to be able to discuss how securing human mobility contributes to it.[76]

The Functions of Homeland Security

Like criminal justice and military action, civil security has its own functions, tools, and methods. It is important to have a sense of these functions in order to see how they apply in the context of mobility security. DHS has argued that *homeland security* reflects the evolution and increasing coordination — in response to new threats and hazards — of traditional government responsibilities for *civil defense, emergency response, customs, border control, law enforcement,* and *immigration.*[77]

For the first seven years after 9/11, government officials articulated homeland security in terms of four main contributing elements: *prevention, protection, response, and recovery.*[78] More recently, DHS has begun to modify this understanding by identifying three pillars of homeland security:[79]

- *Security*: protecting the United States and its people, vital interests, and

way of life; relying on shared efforts to prevent and deter attacks; protecting the nation's critical infrastructure and key resources
- *Resilience:* fostering individual, community, and system robustness; ensuring the capacity for rapid recovery through information, training, and material and psychological preparedness
- *Customs and exchange:* expediting and enforcing lawful trade, travel, and immigration in such a way as to promote a strong and competitive US economy, protect civil liberties and the rule of law, and expand cooperation with international partners

Building on these pillars, homeland security can be achieved through:

1. Assessing risks realistically so as to inform priorities
2. Being aware of current threats and risks
3. Fostering unity against shared risks in society, government, and the international community
4. Precluding attacks, disruptions, and failures through short- and medium-term methods
5. Building security features into people's ways of life, critical infrastructure, and key resources
6. Preparing for attacks, system collapses, and natural disasters by fostering resilience in people, systems, and the environment
7. Responding effectively to incidents
8. Recovering rapidly and fully from incidents; minimizing trauma, disruption, and damage; and strengthening systems and structures in response
9. Diminishing the risk of future attacks, disruptions, and failures through long-term efforts
10. Making new laws and adapting existing legal regimes to the new realities of risk while upholding fundamental commitments and rights

Integrated strategically, these elements serve to preclude high-consequence events that disturb society and its constitutional governance. Successful preclusion can be achieved by (1) proactively preventing the event as it begins to unfold; (2) thwarting it by hardening the target; (3) vitiating its impact through robust resilience; and (4) seeking political, cultural, scientific, or other changes that will diminish the risk of potentially disastrous events.

Key Homeland Security Tools for Securing Human Mobility

While most homeland security tools associated with mobility security are sufficiently self-evident for the purposes of this discussion, a few points are worth emphasizing both because of their importance and their somewhat unsettled terminology.

Risk Assessment

Risk assessment is implicit in any protective approach. Leaders have always assessed where threats come from, and therefore where risks are. But in the homeland security context risk assessment, not *threat* assessment is primary. Risk assessment involves a different methodology than traditional military strategic planning or cost-benefit analysis.

Risk is such an important concept that DHS has produced a *Risk Lexicon* that defines key terms associated with this core task. "Risk," according to DHS, is the "potential for an unwanted outcome resulting from an incident, event, or occurrence, as determined by its likelihood and the associated consequences." It is "the potential for an adverse outcome assessed as a function of threats, vulnerabilities, and consequences associated with an incident, event, or occurrence."[80]

Risk assessment in the context of civil security is important because the environment is one where significant hazards are unpredictable, even unknowable; vulnerabilities are extensive; and consequences may be massive. Risk, DHS notes, "may manifest at the strategic, operational, and tactical levels."[81] Choosing to focus on the right risk, in the right way, with the right level of resources is an extremely difficult challenge. Risk assessment has relevance to securing human mobility because there are so many vulnerabilities. New methods and technology will have to be developed and applied to risk assessments that have not been used in traditional immigration enforcement or border security.

Prevention and Security

The proactive element in homeland security is often signified by the terms *security* and *prevention*. It can involve such action as law enforcement, intelligence, military forces, deradicalization, vaccination, and quarantine.

Resilience and Protection

Homeland security also influences how we build infrastructure, design business processes, and conduct our lives. It enables us to go about our daily lives without undue deviation while feeling as protected as possible from the risks around us. In other words, it gives us a sense of *resilience, protection, security*.[82] Legal, virtual, and physical infrastructure are arenas for resilience. Sensors in the ocean to record seismologic measurements and detect and trigger warnings of disturbances contribute to resilience. So does a well-functioning travel, border, and immigration screening system.

Short-Term vs. Long-Term Prevention

In addition to short-term proactive efforts that may preempt unfolding incidents, we may undertake long-term measures to preclude or mitigate catastrophes, including those associated with the movement of people — from development assistance to diplomacy and institution building.

Securing Human Mobility as a Homeland Security Mission

A definition of mobility security follows from this overall framework. As a dimension of civil security, securing human mobility means to preclude the disabling of mobility channels from performing their normal and legitimate functions. It means preventing the risks and threats that materialize from standing in the way of people's lawful choices to travel, visit, and immigrate. Mobility security represents one element of civil security, comparable to securing the flow of goods and other critical infrastructure and resources.

Traditional methods frequently fail to fully address new needs. Homeland security seeks to preclude the crimes that pose the gravest risks, rather than to address them through traditional administrative and criminal remedies. Securing human movement as a mission of civil security encompasses three broad goals:

1. Blocking and degrading the travel channels of terrorists, serious criminals, and conspirators

2. Ensuring the integrity and resilience of mobility infrastructure, including immigration, border, and refugee programs

3. Preventing life-threatening, uncontrolled, and illegal migration through medium- to long-term structural change

While most objectives and functions of mobility security fall squarely within the civil security mission, some relate as much or more to criminal justice or national defense, or fall outside the security arena. Table 1.1 lists some of the objectives — and federal agencies — that serve these three goals.

Proactive Efforts against Terrorists, Criminals, and Conspirators

The first purpose of securing human movement is to act against terrorists, criminals, and other conspirators who threaten or exploit mobility channels.[83] The goal, of course, ought to be to deter or prevent these evils altogether. A long-term effort to persuade individuals to repudiate violence is at the heart of counterinsurgency strategy, counterradicalization, and community or constabulary policing. Success in preventing terrorism may be possible without recourse to war, martial law, or other extreme measures. The Irish Republican Army (IRA) has, for the most part, ceased its armed attacks. The Italian mafia in the United States is reduced in size and activity. It has been demonstrated that youth gang violence can be precluded through innovative forms of deterrence. But as long as globally networked terrorists pose a threat, any program of human security must include actions against terrorists and serious criminals on behalf of vulnerable populations.

There are three focal points for policy and practice that specifically involve securing mobility as a means of protecting people from imminent or anticipated violence:

- Terrorist travel and radicalization
- Criminal mobility organizations and facilitators
- Other transnational criminal networks

Terrorist Travel and Radicalization
Although human mobility does not cause terrorism, it is one of the preconditions for networked terrorism and transnational crime. As a result, mobility channels are an important venue for offensive and defensive counterterrorism. Programs to prevent or address radicalization should be a part of securing human mobility against violence.

Table 1.1 Securing Human Movement as a Homeland Security Mission

Goals	Acting Against Terrorists, Criminals, and Conspiracies			Ensuring Mobility Infrastructure Integrity	
Policy Focus	Terrorist Travel	Criminal Mobility Facilitators	Diaspora, Immigrant, and Other Trans-border Criminals andNetworks	Right to Movement	Refugees and Asylum Seekers
Key Purpose	Disrupting terrorist travel	Countering HTOs and HSOs	Countering trans-national crime other than mobility crimes	Balancing mobility rights and responsibili-ties	Meeting humanitarian commitments
Example of Programs or Objectives	Terrorist watchlists and informa-tion-sharing agreements	Extraterrito-rial Criminal Travel Network Program	Ending circular violent gang migration	Upholding citizens' right to return	Refugee resettlement
Primary Federal	DHS NCTC State DOJ DOD	DHS NCTC State DOJ DOD	DHS DOJ State DOD	DHS DOJ State DOD	DHS State HHS DOD

Source: Migration Policy Institute.

Table 1.1 (cont.)

Ensuring Mobility Infrastructure Integrity			Preventing Life-threatening, Illegal, and Uncontrolled Movements		
Upholding Civil and Criminal Immigration Laws	Security of Lawful Travel and Entry	Boundary Control (between ports of entry)	Life-threatening, Illegal, and Uncontrolled Migration	Travel Bans and Rule of Law	Mobility Security Capacity Building
Immigration law compliance and enforcement	Screening, compliance, and international agreements	Border policing, defense, and management	Advancing human and state security and managing risk	Isolating corrupt officials and human rights violators	Strengthening borders and weak links in global mobility channels
Status adjudication	Secure passport issuance and identity verification	US-Canada joint maritime patrols	US-Cuba migration negotiations	Banning travel by corrupt passport officials	Assistance for border control in South Asia
DHS State DOJ DOL DOD	DHS State DOJ DOL	DHS DOJ DOD	DHS State HHS DOD	DHS State DOJ DOD	DHS State DOD

Criminal Mobility Organizations and Facilitators

The two types of criminal mobility organizations are human-smuggling organizations (HSOs) and human-trafficking organizations (HTOs). Third-party facilitators are the private and government officials who provide assistance to HTOs and HSOs, which must corrupt public officials in order to function. Terrorists in collaboration or independently can exploit the mobility channels that these groups and their facilitators establish. Such groups typically do not attack or disrupt mobility channels; their goal is to exploit these channels for profit. HTOs cannot leverage different labor markets or exploit women and children without using illegal mobility channels. HSOs exploit travel, immigration, border, and transportation agencies. They violate the law and have been associated with terrorist travel.

Other Transnational Criminal Networks

Finally, violent drug-trafficking organizations (DTOs) and other transnational criminal networks — some of which are linked to terrorist organizations — require priority attention.

Tackling crime in global travel channels or in immigrant communities may fall short of being a top homeland security priority, as compared, for example, with getting watchlists right. But even so, instituting homeland or civil security does not mean abandoning criminal investigations or policing; it means *adding* a new dimension of security. International organized crime cannot be ignored.

Moreover, at the community level, crime control often *is* homeland security. Gang violence overwhelms certain communities. In addition, serious criminals such as fugitives, international child abductors, or human traffickers may exploit global mobility channels. Criminal mobility activities such as visa and passport fraud and non-mobility-related organized crime such as smuggling and trafficking are forms of corruption that undermine the rule of law in mobility channels. Finally, as police executives have repeatedly pointed out, effective policing in immigrant communities engenders trust that leads to more effective counterterrorism.[84]

Ensuring Mobility Infrastructure Integrity and Resilience

Human mobility requires legal, institutional, operational, and technological infrastructure. One of the three fundamental goals of securing human mobility is to ensure that all the dimensions of this infrastructure maintain their integrity and resilience. Usually the phrase *infrastructure protection* is used to refer to this goal and function. *Protection* is an accurate term because all security is about protecting people. But there are different forms of protection, and a more precise term would be helpful in the context of homeland security. Mobility infrastructure is like cyber or financial infrastructure. *It has to maintain its integrity and resilience, that is, it has to be able to perform its positive missions well and reliably, and not be destabilized by catastrophic events.* If it does not, society cannot function and people cannot go about their normal routines.

The United States first has to reinforce its own mobility infrastructure, but in order to protect its markets and the rule of law in mobility channels, it has to foster collective action among partners and allies. In particular, it must work with other countries to secure the integrity and resilience of North American, transatlantic, and transpacific travel channels. Not only are they vectors for risk, but US citizens and their business associates and families outside the United States depend on them.

Reinforcing mobility channels with new layers of security reduces the risk of attack, disruption, exploitation, or failure. It also increases the ability to respond and to recover from incidents and to mitigate their impact. These security mechanisms, which are built into infrastructure and processes, operate during what DHS officials sometimes refer to as "steady state" or normal daily functions. They go on without reference to any specific proactive effort by law-enforcement or intelligence units to pursue a known or suspected terrorist, corrupt travel agency, HSO, or transnational criminal organization. Designing, improving, and maintaining this steady state implicates the core activities of homeland security. Security must become axiomatic, a standard part of the system. This will contribute to people's resilience. They need to have confidence in the integrity and resilience of mobility infrastructure to use it in the ways that the law provides. Conversely, they must comply with the law for this infrastructure to function efficiently, responsively, and as openly as possible.

These are five aspects of mobility infrastructure that are important to a normative steady state:

- Defining and ensuring the individual's right to movement
- Meeting obligations to refugees and asylum seekers
- Upholding civil and criminal immigration law and processes
- Securing lawful travel and entry channels
- Maintaining control of the border between ports of entry

Right to movement has not been a focus for major jurisprudence or civil liberties and human rights litigation since the Cold War period when there were efforts to deny passports based on ideological views. But if a mission of homeland security is to defend the ability of citizens to move in global channels, it becomes important to understand the legal foundation on which that ability rests. What are we to make of this right in the twenty-first century?

As most recognize, the right to movement is limited by prevailing ideas about sovereignty. No one questions seriously the US government's authority to limit who enters the United States, consistent with its international humanitarian obligations. The sovereign determines the citizens' right to enter, and the sovereignty of states remains the foundation of the international order embodied in the UN Charter.[85]

Individuals nevertheless have a natural expectation of movement, a kind of inalienable right. The right to free movement is enshrined, for example, in Mexico's Constitution. Such a right is also embodied in the human rights charters to which the United States is a party. Although considered somehow secondary, and usually narrowly interpreted, this right encompasses a citizen's ability to move within, depart from, and return to her nation.[86] The free world has articulated this right in defense of citizens trapped by totalitarian regimes.

Given the threat of devastating terrorist attacks and the new strategic context that has emerged in the twenty-first century, the prevailing understanding of a right to movement may be questioned in a number of respects. One set of issues concerns the role of the state in guaranteeing and limiting this right. Does this right have the same meaning among free societies? Can one free and democratic society allow its people to enter another free and democratic society illegally and in large numbers when global mobility channels are pathways for terrorists who pose major threats to public safety and civil order? What about when citizens die in foreseeable numbers while intending to violate the destination state's sovereignty such as in illegal migration to the United States or European Union? Do we have to reconsider a sending state's obligation to ensure a safe, lawful, and orderly departure — perhaps consider it part of its responsibility to protect? These are questions facing us going forward.[87]

A second set of issues concerns the individual's rights. The mission of securing human mobility arises because the ability to move to see one's family, pursue economic opportunity, or find security, has become a crucial dimension of life for hundreds of millions of people. As government increases its regulation of movement in the interests of security, this right must be carefully guarded. On what basis and through what process should governments be able to impose travel bans? Should travelers be able to appeal rejections of their visa applications? On what grounds should US citizens be denied passports? Answering these pressing questions will become an important dimension in ensuring the integrity of human mobility. To the extent possible, democratic societies ought to vest most decisions about lawful free movement in the individual, thus protecting him from abuse by the state.

Obligations to refugees and asylum seekers need no elaboration here; they are much discussed elsewhere.[88]

Immigration law and practice constitute the third pillar of mobility infrastructure. The homeland security mission includes responsibility for ensuring that this infrastructure can function as expected by citizens and as most benefits the United States, in spite of risks. In particular, the immigration system must support the economy as directed by Congress and ensure that particular immigration and visitor policies do not present unacceptable risk. It means ensuring sound adjudications, compliance with the law, and meaningful enforcement. It encompasses the design of the security dimensions of laws. It includes the processes for status adjudication, detention, removal, and earned legalization. Integration programs are also an ongoing function of immigration policy into which some security features may be built.

Lawful travel and entry policy and practice together compose the fourth pillar of human mobility infrastructure. Citizens born in the United States, temporary visitors, and immigrants all use the lawful travel system. Travel and entry policy and practice have two security functions: screening to preempt entry by dangerous people and compliance programs. Information sharing and redress systems (for those incorrectly identified as a risk) are new elements intended to reinforce the integrity and resilience of travel and entry practice. The challenge is building effective security into this system in such a way as to reinforce the willingness and ability of people to cross borders despite the risk of terrorism.

Control of the boundaries of the United States between ports of entry, and in the maritime and air domains is the fifth pillar of mobility infrastructure. Ensuring integrity and resilience in this context means to counter terrorism and minimize illegal immigration consistent with US law, the interests of communities, and the health of the environment along the border. One goal should be to prevent circumstances that could give rise to the need for military defense at the border.[89]

Preventing Dangerous, Illegal, and Uncontrolled Movement

The third goal of securing human mobility concerns upstream factors — precluding dangerous, illegal, and uncontrolled movement. Preclusion has rapidly emerged as a core function of securing human mobility.

Prevention or preclusion as an element of securing human mobility refers to long-term prevention of flows of people who either represent a danger to migrants, refugees, and others, or of flows that are illegal, precipitous, or uncontrolled. In FY2008, the Border Patrol apprehended 723,840 people.[90] The US goal should be to preclude the movement of people who believe that they must migrate in order to survive, reduce the number of people who endanger themselves in doing so, and reduce the number of people who migrate illegally.

Prevention has become an important arena for policymaking in the migration and broader mobility arena and is destined to become more important, for a variety of reasons. One reason is the threat of terrorism. Terrorists can come and go virtually anywhere. It is an axiom of homeland security theory that security layers and offensive counterterrorism will not deter or preempt all attacks. Preventing the emergence of illegal streams in which terrorists may hide is one method of mitigating risk.

Another reason for emphasizing prevention is the cost to those on the move — in risk to life and in destabilized and reduced communities. Helping a country's

government and civil society establish the rule of law, democratic accountability, and conditions for economic productivity advance human security and
reduce the need to migrate.

Yet another reason is that the number of people who want to flee their countries exceeds the capacity of the world's legal immigration and refugee systems. Expansion of these legal migration systems is unlikely in the short term.
Instead, the best approach to illegal or uncontrolled movement is to dismantle
the conditions that impel it, to convince source nations to fulfill their responsibility to protect their own citizens, and to assist them in developing their own
nations.

Finally, prevention is important because current strategies to combat illegal immigration have not been effective in substantially reducing illegal immigration
and have had high costs to individuals and communities.

Deciding that prevention is central to securing human mobility represents a
policy shift. It is not an absolute shift, because preventive efforts have taken
place already. But there is now a consensus that the level of illegal flows to the
United States is unacceptable, which moves prevention higher up the homeland security agenda. There are different views on appropriate migration levels
and enforcement measures. If real results are to be achieved, prevention will
command real resources.

The tools of long-term prevention in this context are easily stated because they
coincide with other areas of development. They include:

- Working with sending countries to improve conditions so that people are
  able to develop their capabilities at home
- Assisting other countries in improving their mobility management and
  control capacities, including their travel, border, and immigration programs, so as to make it possible for them to exercise some control over
  immigration and emigration
- Anticorruption efforts
- Making new laws concerning human movement, including imposing travel
  bans on leaders whose corrupt and oppressive practices contribute to the
  creation of conditions that drive emigration
- Building international institutions that support the rule of law in sending
  countries and in global mobility channels

"Homeland Security" and the Responsibilities of DHS

Shifting from the perspective of border security–immigration enforcement to mobility security can be accomplished without major changes. Before making a few suggestions about possible adjustments, however, it is necessary to explain the role of DHS in furthering homeland security, as distinct from carrying out its traditional immigration policies and programs.

DHS's role in relation to homeland security is not as straightforward, for example, as DOD's role in national defense in two ways. First, the human resources for achieving homeland security — the troops, as it were — are not all contained within DHS. On the contrary, one of the hallmarks of civil security is that it depends on participation by a wide range of people and institutions, everyone from the military to ordinary citizens. This larger collective effort and its shared responsibility have been coined the *homeland security enterprise*. DHS is thus, on its own, much smaller than the homeland security enterprise.

The second difference runs in the opposite direction. DHS has responsibilities over and beyond homeland security. Unlike DOD, which is exclusively concerned with defense, DHS has many legacy responsibilities inherited from the 22 agencies it assumed. For example, it carries over the missions of the former US Customs Service in enforcing intellectual property law and in collecting duties. Some legacy roles are more compatible with homeland security than others, such as the Secret Service's protection of the president and other key government leaders, and some are irretrievably outside the frame, such as the Coast Guard's inspections for vessel seaworthiness.

DHS has two legacy sets of responsibilities relating to the movement of people that go well beyond the authority it exercises in any other arena. First, DHS and the Department of State (DOS) are nearly completely responsible for *carrying out the day-to-day steady state operating functions of the US laws and systems supporting human mobility*. As discussed above, DHS runs the immigration system, manages airline travel security, patrols the borders and coasts, and staffs the ports of entry. Second, DHS is deeply involved in creating immigration-, travel-, and customs-related trade policy in the sense of deciding how to use its substantial resources and prioritize programs within the broad parameters of the positive policy goals established by Congress.

DHS does not exercise comparable operational and policy responsibilities in other sectors. For example, it does not have the same type of policy leadership or hands-on responsibilities for cyberspace, financial flows, energy, public health, food supply, the chemical industry, and all other critical sectors and infrastructure, which are vital to homeland security. DHS does not regulate banks or the energy supply, or set food policy. Nor is it responsible for law enforcement in any of these sectors.

In these and other arenas, DHS has a distinctly more limited policy role. DHS has exercised authority over response to pandemics, for example, but the Department of Health and Human Services (HHS) manages public health policy. DHS has responsibility for the security of water infrastructure, but the Department of the Interior oversees water policy more generally. When it comes to the movement of goods and cargo, other major entities such as the US Trade Representative, the Departments of Treasury and Commerce, the World Trade Organization (WTO), even the World Customs Organization and the private market have more important policy roles and influence than DHS. Even with respect to terrorism, a core DHS focus, DHS is part of a larger structure of authority, including elements of the intelligence community such as the National Counterterrorism Center (NCTC) and the Directorate of National Intelligence (DNI), as well as the Federal Bureau of Investigation (FBI) and Department of Justice (DOJ), and DOD.[91]

By contrast, DHS and DOS oversee visa policy, supply travel documents, manage travel and border crossings, build border infrastructure, run the immigration system, negotiate with foreign governments on migration matters, and establish policy and programmatic priorities within the parameters of the Immigration and Nationality Act. Immigration responsibilities outside the realm of homeland security are not small or insignificant. Just to take two issues currently being debated in policy circles, DHS must decide whether to develop civil detention standards relating to immigration violators and it must decide how to shape the role of its Office of Citizenship. These examples raise full-blown policy issues in the absence of terrorist or other contemporary risks.

The distinction between homeland security and its other more traditional immigration functions is reflected in Congress's articulation of the DHS mission:

- Prevent terrorist attacks within the United States.
- Reduce the vulnerability of the United States to terrorism.

- Minimize the damage and assist in the recovery from terrorist attacks.
- Carry out all the functions of the entities that it assumed, including acting as a focal point regarding natural and manmade crises and emergency planning.
- *Ensure that the nonsecurity functions of the entities it inherited are not diminished* (emphasis added).
- Ensure that the nation's homeland security activities do not threaten or undermine economic security.
- Coordinate efforts to sever connections between drug-trafficking organizations and terrorism, and otherwise contribute to anti-drug-trafficking efforts.[92]

This statutory list comprises an initial definition of homeland security, one that Congress intends to be incorporated and elaborated in the first Quadrennial Homeland Security Review. By referring separately to legacy responsibilities, the statute acknowledges that while immigration policy and practice have to take security and resilience into account, these are not the only purposes of US immigration policy.

Immigration policy primarily derives from demographic and labor-market needs, family reunification imperatives, refugee and other legal and moral obligations, considerations relating to national groups, and beliefs about human freedom. These needs and considerations do not fit under the homeland security rubric. But they are of as profound strategic interest to the United States as a sound financial system and a reliable supply of natural resources.

Government Organization

DHS should be organized to: (1) support its exercise of authority over aspects of homeland security within its direct purview; (2) provide the strongest possible foundation for its exercise of authority in the areas in which it has primary operational and policy authority (mostly in mobility matters); and (3) enable its special legacy roles and responsibilities to be managed in the strategic interest of the United States. The legacy role of primary concern is immigration policy because no other department has a significant say in it.

At present, these organizational needs are not fully realized. The main problem is double-sided: on one hand, mobility functions so dominate DHS in terms of personnel and budget that it easily can appear as if border security and immigration enforcement compose most of homeland security, rather than being important elements of a much larger enterprise. On the other, mobility functions are not consolidated in such a way as to give them the kind of attention they merit, as a distinct form of critical infrastructure with strategically important legacy purposes.

DHS's organizational structure should reflect that homeland security entails a risk management strategy that accounts for all catastrophic risks (not just those that are mobility related) in the same way that national defense is directed against any source or form of aggression. Mobility infrastructure is simply one sector that requires security and resilience among many other "top-tier" sectors or activities. Some of DHS's legacy immigration and other non-mobility-related functions are no less important or central to homeland security.

The best way to carry out DHS's responsibilities for the security of mobility channels and for other top-tier sectors would be to install two deputy secretaries (as has been done at the DOS and the DOJ). One deputy secretary would have the portfolio for movement security covering the movement of goods and people   S2(M). The other would have the portfolio for all the other infrastructure and resource sectors and aspects of civil security — S2(C).

S2(M) would oversee: the Transportation Security Agency (TSA); US Coast Guard (USCG); CBP; US Citizenship and Immigration Services (USCIS); the Federal Law Enforcement Training Center (which trains the personnel for most of these agencies); and possibly the United States Secret Service, which protects the president, visiting foreign heads of state, and designated sites and events in the United States, and also safeguards the nation's financial infrastructure and payment systems (because of its strong link to CBP).

S2(M) could be supported by a senior assistant to coordinate all aspects of immigration policy implementation and coordination.[93] It may be that Congress would want more substantial attention paid to immigration policy, due to its increasing strategic importance to the United States. Already, Congress is concerned that trade issues do not receive sufficient policy attention within the homeland security framework. Canada, for example, has a separate migration ministry.

The offices that support both deputy secretaries — Intelligence and Analysis, the Privacy Office, Legislative Affairs, General Counsel — could also continue to support all functions of the department, but similarly divide their units into two basic divisions. The United States Visitor and Immigrant Status Indicator Technology Program (US-VISIT), formally known as the US Visitor Information and Status Technology, could be designated as being under S2(M) or S2(C) or otherwise.

As was proposed by former homeland security secretary Michael Chertoff, there should also be an under secretary for policy, rather than just an assistant secretary as currently exists.[94] DHS is simply too large and complex to meet its policy responsibilities effectively without this level of attention. The under secretary for policy should have a range of assistant secretaries. With reference to the movement of people and goods, there should be an assistant secretary for mobility security policy overall or, possibly, assistant secretaries for different subject areas such as mobility crimes, mobility infrastructure, and international information sharing and foreign assistance.

To give legacy responsibilities the special attention they need would also require an assistant secretary for immigration policy and an assistant secretary for travel and trade policy. The under secretary would report to the secretary through one of the two deputy secretaries. The assistant secretary for immigration policy would work in partnership with the proposed Standing Commission on Labor Markets, Competitiveness, and Immigration (discussed below) in the same way that elements of the Department of the Treasury complement or work in tandem with elements of the Federal Reserve, which has a major research unit. The assistant secretary for travel and trade would work in tandem with counterparts at the Department of Commerce (DOC) and the Office of the Special Trade Representative. As long as these legacy responsibilities remain in DHS, they must be fully reflected in the agency's policy architecture.

Another way to strengthen immigration policymaking would be to provide a focal point for immigration policy analysis outside of DHS. The Migration Policy Institute (MPI) has suggested that such a focal point be established in the form of a Standing Commission on Labor Markets, Competitiveness, and Immigration, which would conduct research and inform Congress on an ongoing basis about the immigration policy interests of the United States.[95] As stated above, travel policy already has focal points in government outside of DHS, in the Department of Commerce and DOS.

Other Organizational Issues

In addition to ensuring the integrity and resilience of mobility operations, securing human mobility requires proactive programs and long-term preclusive programs. For both of these, DHS and other entities have to collaborate closely.

Proactive efforts against terrorists. Violence related to mobility is partly a homeland security function and partly a matter of crime prevention and control. Either way, security from mobility-related violence is mainly a DHS responsibility because DHS possesses almost all the relevant expertise and personnel. Other critical assets are DOS consular affairs officers, who issue passports and adjudicate visas, and DOS diplomatic security agents, who investigate passport and visa fraud.

NCTC has authority over "strategic operational planning" concerning terrorist travel.[96] DHS has the lead in countering HSOs and HTOs. Human-trafficking policy and practice extend to other departments, but tackling the criminal infrastructure is a DHS mission. Attacking transnational criminal networks at the federal level is a responsibility DHS shares with State Department consular officers and DS agents, as well as the FBI; Bureau of Alcohol, Tobacco, Firearms, and Explosives (ATF); Drug Enforcement Administration (DEA); and prosecutors. But *all* the expertise on visas, passports, border crossing, transportation, and immigrant communities and integration resides in DHS and the two State Department operational agencies, and in their intelligence community partners. Therefore, it is primarily a DHS responsibility to take the lead in figuring out how to use mobility needs to attack or prevent transnational crime and to provide the personnel to do so.

The FBI, ATF, and DEA lead the effort to control and end transnational crime. DHS and the DOS agencies can contribute to this effort by developing tactics that relate to criminal mobility and smuggling.

Chapter 4 proposes to strengthen the Human Smuggling and Trafficking Center as a way to bring greater strategic coherence to securing human mobility.

Prevention in the mobility context. There is no one-size-fits-all approach to prevention, making organizational streamlining difficult. Where good governance is the goal, efforts to support the rule of law and anticorruption programs are critical. To upgrade border control requires capacity building related to customs collection, border control, travel documents, and physical infrastructure. Military assistance and training may be required to solidify border defense in certain circumstances.

All the challenges inherent in delivering aid effectively, assisting other countries in raising their prospects, and gaining cooperation from other countries, come into play in prevention efforts. Inevitably, the process must involve negotiation among immigrant-sending and -receiving countries to stabilize migration and provide for security. Political cooperation over travel sanctions will also present a challenge, just as it has for financial sanctions.

The variety of purposes and methods that make up preventive efforts requires that a number of departments, agencies, and international organizations be involved. DHS, DOS, and DOJ — with DOD support — must establish a vehicle for priority setting, coordination, and calibration of efforts. Like other complex coordination problems that arise in the security context, this one raises the question of whether White House direction is needed. At a minimum, the entire effort needs to be discussed in the context of the US strategic approach to foreign assistance and military intervention.

Chapter 2: Terrorists, Criminal Mobility Enterprises, and Third-Party Illicit Travel Facilitators

Illicit travel — including travel by terrorists, human smugglers, and traffickers — is facilitated by three sets of actors. *Insider mobility facilitators* act within insurgent, terrorist, and other illicit networks. *Criminal mobility facilitators*, whether cottage-industry operators or members of major transnational criminal organizations, include human smugglers and traffickers and specialists in counterfeit documents. *Third-party mobility facilitators* are the unwitting, negligent, complicit, or corrupt officials who work in transportation agencies, travel agencies, airports, and government offices. They include employer and immigration-related intermediaries; police officers; foreign embassy officials; and passport, visa, and immigration adjudicators. Poorly designed regulatory systems and ineffective government agencies also facilitate illegal travel and residence.

Each of these actors has a lawful counterpart, whether the savvy traveler organizing a family vacation or the law-abiding professional working in travel, immigration, or transportation.

The three types of illicit mobility facilitators raise strategic concerns related to: (1) precluding terrorism and serious transnational crime by denying freedom of movement to dangerous individuals, (2) preserving the legal and physical integrity of mobility channels, and (3) providing the opportunity for law-abiding travelers to move securely and safely within a framework of laws.

It is important to become familiar with the myriad roles that facilitate the illicit movement of people in order to understand who sustains it, how this work is organized, what motivates them, and what can be done to limit their activities.

Within *terrorist* or *organized* criminal networks (other than human-smuggling organizations [HSOs] and human-trafficking organizations [HTOs]), there may be individuals who specialize in supporting travel, either as part of a portfolio of logistical responsibilities or as a niche skill or function. Their roles range from that of logistics director and travel document counterfeiter to courier (with the ability to deliver airline tickets, money, or information at relatively low risk) or harbor of people on the move. Some insiders coach others in how to respond to questions at a port of entry. Illicit travel facilitators may also serve as recruiters.

HSOs and their networks are motivated by profit. They range from family and social networks to sophisticated global criminal enterprises. The illicit mobility market has local, regional, and increasingly global dimensions. Its main customers are economic migrants, persons seeking to join family members, and (sometimes) refugees escaping violence or persecution. Terrorist organizations, too, have used the services of human-smuggling networks.[97] HTOs, meanwhile, may either smuggle victims themselves or outsource this activity to HSOs. The traffickers' financial gain derives from the transfer or exploitation of trafficked victims, not from the movement itself, which represents a cost.

Public- and *private-sector officials, intermediaries,* and *employees* of immigration, border, travel, and transportation organizations intentionally or unintentionally collaborate with terrorists and criminal mobility facilitators. Those in the know supply their services for a range of ideological, familial, financial, and other reasons. Whether intentional or not, such third-party mobility facilitators play a key role in all illicit travel networks. Regulatory and law-enforcement policies must distinguish among third-party facilitators — from family members and officials to immigration sponsors to organized criminals.

These three sets of actors — insider, criminal, and third-party mobility facilitators — often overlap with one another. Some terrorist and criminal travel facilitators have connections with corrupt passport officers or travel agents. Human smugglers may also serve terrorist networks and criminal enterprises other than HTOs, including violent gangs, arms- and drug-trafficking organizations, traffickers in gray-market or counterfeit products, and money-laundering operations.

Terrorist Organizations

In-House Terrorist Travel Facilitators
Today's global and transnational terrorist groups have thrived in areas where illicit economies support trafficking in humans, drugs, arms, and commodities from baby formula to cigarettes. Terrorist groups raise funds in diaspora communities in the United States and elsewhere. Recently, American citizens have been linked to Somali-based terrorist activity and to al Qaeda in Pakistan and Afghanistan. For the purposes of mobility security, a terrorist's jumping-off point is not as important as his movement. The goal for homeland security agencies, then, is to be able to detect, track, and disrupt such movement.

The primary terrorist threats to the United States are groups, many of a fundamentalist Islamist persuasion, concentrated in Pakistan and Afghanistan, the Middle East and the Maghreb, East and West Africa, the Balkan and Caucasus regions, and (to a lesser extent) the triborder area of Latin America (the intersection of Brazil, Argentina, and Paraguay). Some European Union (EU) and Caribbean countries are also venues. The United States has designated 44 foreign terrorist organizations operating globally.[98] Active global terrorist networks, by definition, engage in mobility fraud by deceiving officials as to their travel intentions.

Al Qaeda and its Affiliates

Al Qaeda today consists of Osama bin Laden's original network — which was responsible for the September 11, 2001, attacks and operates along the Pakistan-Afghanistan border — and closely affiliated groups in Iraq, the Maghreb, and the Arabian Peninsula. Other organizations with ties to al Qaeda include Jemaah Islamiyah (which killed hundreds in a 2002 Bali car bombing), the Abu Sayyaf Brigade in the Philippines, Lashkar-e-Taiba in Pakistan, groups in the horn of Africa, and less organized groups that have also received terrorist training. Some of these groups are actively focused on attacking US civilians and US interests within and outside the United States. Such conspiracies include the Christmas Day 2009 attempted attack on a US jetliner by a Nigerian allegedly affiliated with al Qaeda in the Arabian Peninsula; the 2008 Lashkar-e-Taiba attack on a Mumbai hotel hosting Americans and other Westerners; and the July 7, 2005, bombings in London. The ongoing threat of attack, whether involving US- or foreign-based terrorists, makes al Qaeda's international travel activities of deep concern to US counterterrorism officials.

A key question is the extent to which al Qaeda and its affiliates manage travel for their operatives internally or outsource it to human-smuggling networks. At the time of the 9/11 attacks and immediately thereafter, al Qaeda managed much of its travel in-house, consistent with its need to maintain operational secrecy. Abu Zubaydah, who managed al Qaeda's travel as part of his oversight of a network of training camps, was able to provide al Qaeda operatives with genuine passports that he had secured from foreign fighters, corrupt and sympathetic officials, and others. Terrorist operatives used these passports, the least likely kind to draw official scrutiny, to transit through countries such as Yemen and Iran. During its peak years, al Qaeda developed elaborate travel tactics, such as supporting false biographies with real and forged entry stamps.

Following Abu Zubaydah's apprehension in 2002, al Qaeda leaders surely sought to replace him with new travel managers. However, the disruption of al Qaeda during the first phase of the anti-Taliban Afghan war and other operations against al Qaeda facilitators, including the arrest of Hambali in Thailand, appear to have diminished its ability to organize travel with its previous level of sophistication.

On the one hand, al Qaeda's alliances are ongoing and promise ample access to new documents and to travel facilitator networks. On the other hand, due to increased post-9/11 efforts to intercept terrorist communications and financial transfers, al Qaeda has been forced to increase its reliance on couriers, which increases the network's vulnerability to travel-related detection.

Terrorist Travel and Human-Smuggling Organizations

Many al Qaeda adherents are capable of moving around the globe without assistance. Those who require assistance can either tap al Qaeda's internal resources or turn to outsiders to move them incognito. Al Qaeda uses local smugglers to cross back and forth along the Afghanistan-Pakistan border. Baluchi smugglers cover well-worn routes to Iran. Similarly, local travel facilitators move recruits from Saudi Arabia, Morocco, and other Maghreb countries into Iraq. In the absence of internal capacity, al Qaeda relies almost entirely on human-smuggling networks. For this reason, HSOs that operate across borders in war zones are of particular importance to mobility security. Smuggling enterprises may be linked to terrorist organizations through ideological, familial, or other personal associations or they may not be involved with terrorism in any way.

Systematic cooperation with purely profit-driven groups is not, however, in al Qaeda's interest. Terrorists prefer to deal with their own kind, rather than with criminals who might betray them. That said, far too little is known about the nexus between terrorist groups and criminal travel facilitators. Human smuggling and trafficking is a high-profit, low-risk business; most criminals want to avoid the attention that moving terrorists and major international criminals would bring to their business. Still, notwithstanding the increased risks, terrorists and HSOs do cooperate with each other. Co-nationals are more likely to cooperate, but there is also evidence of smugglers assisting terrorist groups with whom they have no ethnic or ideological links. In general, terrorist organizations tend to use smugglers in South Asia and the Middle East, but are more cautious in Western countries. That said, there is active cooperation between terrorists and human-smuggling networks throughout

Europe and in North Africa, making EU passports easy for terrorists to obtain. Hubs for false documents, such as in Thailand, may be found around the world.

Terrorists can exploit human-smuggling networks that have little knowledge or concern about the background of the people they are moving. Unless an individual stands out and is likely to attract unwanted attention, a smuggling organization has little incentive to find out more than whether a customer has the ability to pay. Still, it seems likely that some smugglers are in the know. Although handling a terrorist raises the risk of law-enforcement attention, it may also reap greater profit. In addition, some smugglers may help terrorists because of personal or ideological associations.

There are no published cases of HSOs transporting al Qaeda terrorists to the United States from Canada or Mexico. (There have been cases of HSO figures in Mexico and elsewhere in the western hemisphere with tangential associations with terrorist organizations.) But a case involving an HSO in Latin America demonstrates the potential for this to occur. In 2006 eight Colombians, one Venezuelan, and one Palestinian national were charged in US federal court with arranging travel to the United States for individuals they believed to be members of the Revolutionary Armed Forces of Colombia (FARC). In reality, their client was an informant working for US law enforcement.

The group provided fraudulent identity documents from Colombia, genuine Colombian passports issued in the name of dead people, Spanish identity documents, and trade association cards. It also arranged to procure Spanish passports, most with substituted photographs, which would have enabled the supposed FARC members to enter the United States without visas. The informant used a Spanish passport to board a plane from Panama City. Charging more than $20,000 for its services, the group included a Colombian immigration service detective and an immigration inspector, who arranged undetected passage through immigration controls at the international airports in Bogota and Panama City through which clients were to travel to Miami.[99]

Even without the participation of human smugglers, experienced terrorists can and do use smugglers' illicit travel infrastructure: that is, they exploit the regulatory vulnerabilities, routes, corrupt officials and police, and other third-party facilitators that provide passports and other assistance in crossing borders. Extremists are often told to seek out local contacts who have travel connections.

The line between human-smuggling networks and such individual actors is blurred at best.

Al Qaeda in Iraq relies on a network of sympathetic facilitators and profit-seeking human smugglers to move operatives into Iraq from Syria. These operatives come to Damascus from elsewhere in the Middle East, and from North Africa and Europe. The attraction of the Syrian route includes loose transit visa regulations, the long Syrian-Iraqi border, and a Syrian regime that is at best ambivalent toward the United States.

Al Qaeda associates are believed to be concentrating on recruiting operatives who look nonthreatening, who have no known association with terrorism, and who are able to obtain passports of countries from which travel to the United States does not require visas. Such operatives are what the Department of Homeland Security (DHS) has referred to as "clean skins," a term originally used for drug traffickers without prior records. A more precise and less dehumanizing term is "unknown clandestine operatives" (UCOs), which will be used hereafter. After US passports, the most valued are those from Canada and the 35 countries participating in the US Visa Waiver Program (VWP). The new US Electronic System of Travel Authorization (ESTA), however, makes it more difficult to exploit the VWP. (ESTA is discussed in chapter 10.)

These passports may be genuine. A frequent tactic is to use fraudulent identity documents acquired in South Asian countries — for example, residency cards, driver's licenses, identification cards, and voter-registration cards — to acquire passports from European countries participating in the VWP. The higher the rank of the terrorist traveler, the less likely he or she is to rely on smuggling organizations. Dhiren Barot, a British al Qaeda conspirator sentenced to life in prison based on evidence of plots to blow up UK railroad stations and a London tube train, had nine British passports — seven in his true name and issued to him by the British passport authority, the other two for false identities. He obtained new passports by reporting previously issued passports as lost or stolen.

Al Qaeda has had access to false document providers in Europe — most of them known sympathizers — since before 9/11. In Italy, for example, al Qaeda associates sold passports outside of mosques. In 2008 British investigative journalists uncovered a Bangladeshi operation peddling Bulgarian passports at two mosques, mostly for labor migrants but also for purported Islamic extremists.[100] Document facilitators who provide genuine, altered, and counterfeit passports to al Qaeda are particularly active throughout the Maghreb, especially in Libya, Algeria, and Morocco, and they are connected to mosques throughout Europe, from the United Kingdom to the Balkans.[101] European authorities make periodic arrests of passport forgers, for example, in February 2009 Spanish police arrested 15 people suspected of forging passports for use by al Qaeda members. The group allegedly stole passports in Spain and forwarded them to Thailand for alteration. Portugal is another country where al Qaeda members have been involved in the production of false documents.[102]

Whatever the status of their passports, when al Qaeda operatives fly commercial carriers, they must obtain tickets through the existing reservations systems and must pass through airline and government screening systems. They have an incentive to use third-party facilitators to avoid the regulated travel system.

Al Qaeda also uses vulnerabilities in visa-screening processes to move their operatives around the world. In the United Kingdom, security officials have noted that because the UK Border Agency does not sufficiently screen all visa applicants from countries such as Pakistan, Somalia, and Yemen, a number of individuals with UK visas (predominantly student visas) may be current members of sleeper cells, ready to attack at any moment.[103] Between October 2008 and April 2009, the UK Border Agency may have allowed up to 13,000 visa applicants from Pakistan to enter the United Kingdom without conducting checks on their supporting documentation.[104]

Al Qaeda has used outside human-smuggling networks to facilitate its operatives' movements, including across land and sea borders outside of established ports of entry.[105] For example, al Qaeda operatives have hidden in the backs of trucks and bribed truck drivers and border guards.[106] The smugglers involved in these operations may or may not have been aware of the full identity of their clients, although al Qaeda operational security practices make it unlikely that they were informed. Operatives who are not distinguishable by appearance or behavior are the ones most likely to be moved by nonterrorist smuggling organizations.

The United States introduced the systematic use of biometrics — the use of intrinsic physical traits to identify individuals — in 2004 with the establishment of US-VISIT, a program to take fingerprints from arriving passengers with visas. As the use of biometrics becomes more prevalent worldwide, it will be riskier for al Qaeda to use legal entry channels. The dominant assumption since

2001 — that al Qaeda and associated organizations would seek to use legal systems — may no longer be valid. Even sophisticated and experienced terrorists may find it necessary to take advantage of illegal mobility channels. As of yet, however, the US government has not reported that any terrorist operatives connected to al Qaeda or its affiliates have crossed into Mexico.[107]

Hezbollah's Global Smuggling Network

Hezbollah is a global, terrorist network of significant concern to the United States. To date, its targets have mainly been in Lebanon and Israel, although it has also mounted attacks in Latin America, where (as perhaps in Mexico) it has been involved in the drug and arms trade.[108] Hezbollah raises funds from donors and from its criminal operations in the United States. Because of its backing from Iran, it can maintain the most sophisticated travel operation of any major terrorist organization, including a global network of complicit government officials. In Latin America, Venezuela has provided passports at Iran's urging to a number of Hezbollah members to facilitate their travel to Mexico and to European countries that do not require visas for travel from Venezuela.[109] Other terrorists, not connected to Hezbollah, have used fraudulent Venezuelan passports.[110]

Scores of HSOs operate in Mexico, including those based in nations with a significant anti-US terrorist presence. That said, Hezbollah has the only known terrorist nexus to an HSO in Mexico. Mexico's substantial Lebanese community makes it an attractive staging area for Lebanese citizens interested in entering the United States. Prior to his arrest in 2002, a Lebanese citizen who owns a restaurant in Tijuana helped at least 80 Lebanese citizens cross the US-Mexico border into California. There is no indication that this facilitator himself had any terrorist connections, but some of his clients had ties to Hezbollah.[111]

Generally, further linkages between terrorist groups and HSOs moving people to the United States from Mexico have not been identified. However, Hezbollah appears to be an intermediary organization used by Mexican DTOs to sell drugs to Europe and the Middle East. In addition, arms providers in the Middle East, Latin America, and Bulgaria sell arms through Hezbollah to the DTOs.[112] The significant increase in the capabilities of DTOs seems to be aimed primarily at Mexican military forces and other cartel opponents. But it also has ramifications for those communities in the United States, whether at the border or beyond, where the organizations sell drugs and carry out turf battles.

Terrorist Relations to Human-Smuggler Organizations

The potential exists for terrorist organizations to use human smuggling and human trafficking as means of raising funds. From what is known about al Qaeda and Hezbollah, however, formal links with human traffickers appear to be fewer and weaker than with arms and drug traffickers. While terrorist networks may occasionally smuggle people or a smuggling group may engage in terrorist tactics, the two appear to be for the most part separate enterprises.[113] At the same time, connections do exist and intelligence on deeper integration may be weak since human smuggling and trafficking are usually handled in law enforcement rather than in intelligence channels. The Liberation Tigers of Tamil Eelam (LTTE), recently defeated by the Sri Lankan military, took tribute from HSOs, for example. A Thai document forger arrested in 2008 had a history as a human and arms smuggler, including for LTTE.[114] As this example suggests, to the extent that human smugglers engage in a variety of criminal activities, they may be more attractive to terrorists.[115]

Human-Smuggling Organizations

US officials believe that most people crossing illegally into the United States receive assistance from HSOs.[116] The European Police Office (Europol) estimates that most illegal immigrants into the European Union use a facilitator, usually an organized criminal group.[117] The ten nationalities with the highest level of illegal border crossings into the European Union in 2008 were Albanian, Afghan, Moroccan, Somali, Iraqi, Tunisian, Nigerian, Eritrean, Palestinian, and Algerian. Turkey is a major hub for organized criminal organizations that smuggle people from the Middle East, Asia, and Africa into the European Union.[118]

The United States has been battling the Mafia and other organized-crime groups for nearly a century, and law-enforcement organizations are authoritatively knowledgeable about their structure, finances, and culture. In contrast, law enforcement is only beginning to have a deeper understanding of HSOs and HTOs, which are also evolving rapidly.

The Structure of HSOs

The architecture of HSOs is very different from the hierarchy historically associated with the Mafia and other transnational organized crime. HSOs are generally not centralized monoliths and do not take the form of corporate franchises. Instead they are decentralized, usually consisting of networks formed in concentric circles around a small core group. The ringleaders draw on smaller enterprises and individuals linked, in turn, with other service providers. Complementary service providers do business at nexus points along pathways where there is demand for illegal travel.

Because of the unique profiles and needs of travelers, HSOs are often defined along national or ethnic lines. In addition, they have only limited reach and are competitive with one another in their geographic and social space.

Figure 2.1 The Enterprise Structure of Human-Smuggling Organizations

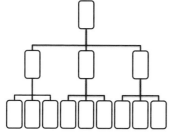

Human Smuggling Organizations (HSOs) Enterprise Structure

Traditional Organized Crime Hierarchy

- Key individuals define activities, command allegiance, and determine alliances
- Such groups may not consider themselves organized criminal entities, e.g. neighborhood gangs

New Core Criminal Groups

- Includes a core group that consists of a limited number of individuals forming a relatively tight, horizontal structure
- Core group is surrounded by a loose network of associates, among whom are a small group helping to maintain internal discipline
- Activities based on opportunities for profit
- Group comprised of several nationalities, reflecting the countries in which they operate

Source: Migration Policy Institute.

Small HSOs with personal, community, cultural, or ethnic ties to customers are typical for the first stage of a journey. Iraqi migrants fleeing violence and chaos being smuggled out of Jordan to Europe, for example, prefer smugglers who have previously helped their relatives or friends, or people with whom they share religious ties or have a direct relationship. The requirement that the traveler provide a significant percentage of the $4,000 to $6,000 smuggling fee up front makes such trust particularly important.[119]

While HSOs may be stand-alone organizations only involved in human smuggling, some have core groups that smuggle people as an adjunct to other criminal activities. Within Europe, for example, Russian- and Albanian-based organized crime appears to be the main source of human smuggling from Eastern Europe to Spain, the Netherlands, and Belgium. For such groups, drug trafficking, document fraud, and firearms trafficking often go together.

Smuggling networks in Mexico are primarily comprised of Mexican nationals and run the gamut in size and organization structure. On one end of the spectrum are family businesses that act as independent operators exploiting well-placed family-owned land. At the other end are organized criminal groups often linked to or paying Mexican DTOs. These HSOs typically charge a higher price for non-Mexicans who blend in less easily, are more likely to draw attention, and are therefore more risky to move. These criminal groups also include current and former Mexican military and police officers who have received US counternarcotics training. Some have sophisticated equipment, including body armor, fully automatic weapons, and encrypted radios.[120]

Most smugglers on the US side of the border are US citizens or lawful permanent residents (LPRs), many of them women.[121] Transporting people can be a gateway to other criminal activities for human smugglers. Migrants who regularly cross the border may start out by being pressured by relatives or friends to help someone cross. If successful with this task, they may feel confident to take people another time, then a few more people, until it becomes a business. Once established in the human-smuggling business, they may branch out to drug trafficking, which is more profitable.

Recently, criminal gangs have become intermediaries at the final stage of crossing into the United States. Drug traffickers and gangs have seen how lucrative human smuggling can be and now use it as a source of revenue along with other illegal activities. Different gangs control particular territories and are linked to the Mexican DTOs. They include both ethnic Mexican gangs and the Mara Salvatrucha (or MS-13), with roots in El Salvador and Salvadoran communities in the United States.[122]

The current routes into Texas, for example, appear to be controlled by two sets of gangs. On the Mexican side of the border, Los Zetas, who emerged from the Gulf drug cartel, act as enforcers, collecting intelligence, managing logistics, and conducting operations, including transshipment and recruitment. Comprised of former members of the Mexican special forces, corrupt law-enforcement officials, and civilians, Los Zetas have also brought MS-13 gang members into the organization as expert, violent smugglers. MS-13 members also manage some operations on the US side of the border, receiving and distributing migrants and sometimes kidnapping them from other HSOs in order to extort extra money. Deported gang members of Salvadoran origin also operate coyote services in Central America. Los Negros members act as enforcers, intelligence collectors, operators, and logistics managers. They are involved in transshipment and recruiting on the Mexican side of the border, and partner with the Latin Kings on the US side of the border.

Chinese Snakeheads and Other Global HSOs

There are two at least partial exceptions to the prevailing model of decentralized HSOs defined by national or ethnic identity. Chinese HSOs, led by so-called snakeheads, provide point-of-origin to point-of-destination mobility. Snakehead recruiters draw on an extensive network of family members and business ties that provide information to potential clients and their families in China. (Human smuggling is an accepted social activity in China.) But snakeheads also use local HSOs and facilitators in Latin America, as well as Chinese who have settled in Latin America and have no known family connections. Criminals who profit from smuggling or trafficking systematically corrupt government and private officials. Chinese smugglers enjoy access to government intelligence and are among the first to take advantage of changes in laws and regulation. They also have a reputation of being ruthless, and may order that debtors or family members be killed if they do not pay. It is estimated that snakeheads earn up to $7 billion per year from their human-smuggling activities.[123]

Second, a few HSOs have recently evolved into multinational networks run by a single core group that liaises with service providers globally. By spending a significant amount of time and money reinvesting in business connections and partnering with other HSOs and corrupt authorities, an HSO network can effectively go global and reap greater profits. Under this model, the network head typically operates in a country other than where the bulk of operations occur. This marked trend toward global networking and increased sophistication represents a major new challenge for government policymakers and law-enforcement authorities. However, at present, only a handful of HSOs have known multinational reach.

The first significant case of a global HSO was one operated by a Ghanian naturalized citizen of Mexico, Mohammed Kamel Ibrahim, known as Hakim, who originally operated a smuggling organization based in Mexico that transported people to the United States. His East African clients were supplied by a smuggler in Belize, who obtained the crucial Mexican visas from a corrupt Mexican employee in that country's embassy in Belize. Hakim gradually expanded his reach by flying to Africa to enlist new network providers, including recruiters and transporters in Africa, smugglers in South and Central America, and guides and money collectors in Mexico. At various times his network's smuggling routes included Eritrea, Ethiopia, the United Arab Emirates, Sudan, Kenya, and South Africa in Africa; Italy in Europe; and Brazil, Bolivia, Cuba, Panama, Nicaragua, Honduras, Guatemala, and Mexico in the Western Hemisphere. Hakim personally flew to various countries to identify and bribe corrupt officials, and used money services, express mail, and e-mail to conduct business. The HSO had access to fake and real South African, Belizean, Bolivian, Chilean, Peruvian, and Mexican visas.[124]

The emergence of global HSO networks is not surprising. Increasing levels of border security are expanding the opportunities for larger, more sophisticated organized-crime groups that can more efficiently smuggle people across borders. Smaller HSOs, absent sufficient capital, are becoming less able to produce newer travel documents that contain greater security features. Violence is also a factor driving the emergence of large networks. The human-smuggling and human-trafficking trades are becoming more violent throughout the world. While there is no sign that the number of smuggling organizations dropped in the past ten years, prices for smuggled individuals increased when demand was robust. Stepped-up enforcement efforts contributed to escalating prices. Smaller organizations need financial backing to acquire expertise in using the police or military-grade equipment needed for securing passage across better-defended national boundaries, and to pay higher bribes where enforcement or intelligence operations are increasing risks.[125]

Third-Party Facilitators of Human Smuggling

HSOs depend on the full spectrum people who run the immigration, border, and global travel system. These third-party facilitators include corrupt, complicit, and unwitting[126] immigration and border officials and intermediary organizations that recruit migrants for foreign institutions; travel and transportation workers; and senior government officials, police, and contractors from the full range of passport, customs, visa, and border-guarding organizations, as well as those from agencies producing the birth certificates, driver's licenses, and other breeder documents necessary to acquire passports and ultimately visas.

Third-Party Facilitators in the Private Sector

Human smugglers regularly use sham business facades to facilitate their trade. They also exploit otherwise legitimate businesses and corrupt private- and public-sector officials to support smuggling and trafficking enterprises.

Travel agencies. Travel agencies may be complicit or not in human smuggling. In cases where travel agencies are not complicit, the traveler with ulterior motives may use a tour as cover, leaving it when it reaches his destination. In some instances, travel agencies are front companies.[127] Travel agencies advertise travel packages geared toward would-be migrants, including visa services. They also instruct migrants on how to behave in encounters with consulate staff, border guards, or other immigration authorities. Migrants are reluctant to testify or give any information about such arrangements because they and their families face possible retribution from the security officers of these companies.

Within the European Union, convenience-store-style travel enterprises offer migrants everything from untraceable phone numbers to airline tickets.[128] Such agencies operate much like a normal tourist agency would, giving advice and selling products to consumers, but offer an outlet for document counterfeiters and human smugglers to market their products, creating a useful link in the smuggling process.[129]

For example, migrants fleeing the violence and turmoil in Iraq for Jordan can use local travel agencies there that specialize in smuggling foreign domestic workers into Europe and the United States. Ultimately they may seek refugee or asylee status. Visas obtained in Jordan are occasionally counterfeit; in the majority of cases, however, they are legitimate, though obtained with illegitimate documents provided through fraudulent means, for example, letters of invitation from ghost companies in Europe.

Schools and employers. Within the European Union, smuggling organizations have established sham schools that offer "admission" as a way to exploit the availability of student visas. This type of fraud is difficult to track. For example, Denmark issued residence permits for 1,800 agricultural trainees from the Ukraine in 2006, but Ukraine sent only 400 trainees. This means that 1,400 people somehow obtained trainee documentation permitting them to stay in

Denmark.[130] Similar scams have been discovered in the United States and the United Kingdom.

Another frequent sham occurs when a broker sets up a front company that does not conduct any real business, charges people to file a work petition, and pockets the profit.[131]

Religious institutions. HSOs often work through religious institutions. Since at least the 1990s, mosques in Europe have frequently been used to provide information on how to migrate, how to distribute financial resources from abroad, and how to arrange for travel to the United States and Europe. This is consistent with the common role of mosques as community centers, and as is typical in migrant communities, friends and family who have already migrated relay information back to would-be migrants; sometimes this advice encompasses illegal methods. Smuggling organizations have also apparently submitted religious worker petitions on behalf of putative religious institutions. As a result, US Citizenship and Immigration Services (USCIS) has now tightened the rules for religious worker visas.[132]

Shipping and transport. Shipping companies have been used to smuggle Chinese migrants into North America in 10-by-40-foot containers. This method was common in the 1990s but appears to have declined. More recently, nonexistent shipping companies have submitted letters of guarantee, confirming that they hired an individual to work on a ship in the United States; such fraudulent papers are then used to illicitly obtain C1 transit visas.

Many airlines have been involved to some degree or another in human smuggling, most often unwittingly. Of those who knowingly helped, Bulgaria's Jes Airlines was so heavily involved in human smuggling that it was denied landing rights in the United States and ultimately went out of business.[133] Turkmenistan Airlines moved Tamils from Sri Lanka without proper travel or visa authorization to the Netherlands in 1997.[134] Airlines in Central American have also been implicated in smuggling, as have airline charter companies. Airport employees and security personnel have been caught helping to move people through airport check points, through guarded doors, and off planes without inspection.

Land transport companies are potentially powerful enablers of human smuggling. Some companies have falsified work documents or have transported undocumented workers, for example, from the southwest border of the United States to other major US cities. US authorities have prosecuted at least one bus company for transporting thousands of undocumented workers from the Mexican-US border to cities on the West Coast. Golden State Transportation of Los Angeles moved approximately 50 to 300 unauthorized migrants every day.[135] Bus lines, such as Golden State Transportation, and taxis, some of which have special compartments to smuggle people, appear to be the main commercial modes of smuggling.

Third-Party Facilitators in the Public Sector: Official Corruption

In many parts of the developing world, corruption among immigration, border, and transportation officials is endemic. Not only is corruption tolerated by the public, but there are few government constraints to prevent or to stop it. Economic motivations and political and cultural factors contribute to high levels of corruption. Democratically established tax systems are underdeveloped, remuneration for civil servants and police is low, and it is expected that government employees will supplement their salaries by accepting additional payments from citizens seeking services.

In some countries, racketeering officials extort fees for the full range of travel-related services: to supply the breeder documents needed to apply for passports and visas, to verify eligibility, to speed the passport application process, and to distribute passports. Where government corruption is prevalent, it is exploited to facilitate human-smuggling operations, terrorist travel, and all forms of transnational criminal movement. There is a strong correlation between Transparency International's corruption index and migrant-transit countries: corruption is often the determining factor in route selection.

The platform for illicit travel created by across-the-board government corruption is reinforced by several factors. Even where there are laws and policies in place to prevent corruption, they are uneven and subject to misuse. Progress toward mitigating corruption is slow, as the same officials that benefit from corrupt practices are the ones who have to implement changes. In addition, legitimate applicants may be less likely to try to obtain travel documents through legal means if they know that they can obtain documents more cheaply, easily, and predictably in the illicit market. The World Bank has documented the existence and impact of two policies in migrant-sending countries that drive migrants into the illicit market: high passport costs and restrictions on legal emigration.[136] Increased demand for illicit documents typically increases the supply of those documents.

In addition, officials who extort funds from legitimate travelers are often willing — for a larger "fee" — to help applicants seeking to travel under a false identity. Most often such travel is for the trafficking of contraband. Officials may not know or care why the individual wants to travel clandestinely. Routine graft, however, can evolve into broader and deeper criminal arrangements, where levels of payment are higher and risks are greater.

Participants in such clandestine activities — from Chinese snakeheads and coyotes at the Mexican-US border to the many supporting officials in sending and transit countries — are not typically viewed as criminals in their homelands or diaspora communities. In fact, they are often seen as heroes.

The problem of corruption in the global mobility system is pervasive. Passport offices in parts of the Middle East, Africa, and South and East Asia appear to be the most rife with corruption. Embezzled funds from the Indonesian Embassy and Consulate in Malaysia have amounted to 36 billion rupiahs (about US$3.8 million).[137] Russia's Federal Migration Service (FMS) has similar levels of corruption. The raids it conducts in connection with corruption cases frequently incriminate high-level management within the FMS and net several hundred thousand dollars.[138] The intelligence service in Papua New Guinea uncovered a visa racket in which facilitators collected $5,000 from would-be immigrants for payment to senior Papua New Guinean immigration officials.[139]

The one known instance of a nexus between passport office corruption and terrorist travel occurred in South Africa. The South African passport is difficult to counterfeit, but wide-scale corruption within the nation's Department of Home Affairs has resulted in the illicit sale of thousands of government-issued travel documents.[140] UK authorities have arrested members of al Qaeda for illegal possession of legitimate South African passports allegedly obtained from sources in the Department of Home Affairs, and in March 2009 the United Kingdom suspended visa-free travel from South Africa.[141] Corrupt South African sources have also fed travel documents to economic migrants, smugglers, asylum seekers, and terrorist suspects. Five years ago, a criminal group inside Home Affairs sold documents for as little as $77.[142] The same group also took part in a larger illicit scheme to sell South African passports to unauthorized Indian migrants being smuggled into England, who paid around £8,000 for their new, apparently legal, travel documents.[143]

In South and Central America and the Caribbean, a lack of resources and corruption within immigration, customs, and law-enforcement agencies, as well as the judicial branch, contribute to the ease of illicit travel. Directors of immigration services, supreme court justices, cabinet officials, a national security adviser, and one president (Panama) have been implicated in corruption relating to the movement of people. Paraguay's triborder region is a prime example of an area with ineffective immigration and customs controls due to corruption.[144] Corrupt officials in Venezuela have provided passports to terrorists, specifically to members of Hezbollah.[145]

With large emerging markets, newly industrialized countries such as Brazil, China, and India are attractive places for foreign investment and trade. This has led to pressure to reduce travel restrictions on these countries, and even the complete waiver of all visa requirements, at least among regional groupings of states. (The Association of Southeast Asian Nations, or ASEAN, and Asia-Pacific Economic Cooperation, or APEC, are two regional organizations that are facilitating travel among their member states.) States unable to regulate and control the distribution of their breeder documents and consequently their travel documents form a weak link in global travel security.

While the illicit sale of passports and visas in developing countries is common, such documents are of somewhat limited use, since the United States and EU Member States require extensive visa applications for passport holders from these countries. Travel documents from developing countries are used more as a supplement to a traveler's primary passport, allowing terrorists to travel to countries such as Afghanistan or Pakistan without "dirtying" their primary passports with stamps that would alert Western authorities to their possible identities and intentions.

Corruption in US Consular, Border, and Immigration Agencies

In contrast to developing or newly industrialized countries, most developed countries have relatively minor problems with corruption in the public sector, but significant risks do exist and they appear to be growing.

There is little evidence that government sources consistently supply individuals with highly desired valid visas and passports from the United States and the EU Member States.[146] Disgruntled visa applicants, whose applications have been turned down, frequently lodge accusations of corruption against locally hired employees at embassies, but these complaints are rarely justified. Nevertheless, significant instances of corruption occur with some consistency, albeit fewer involving US-citizen officers.

A single foreign service or immigration officer can provide a large number of documents over time and facilitate the movement of a large number of people. As with other corrupt individuals, these officers do not necessarily focus on the identity of their buyers — identities that in any event may be difficult to confirm with routine visa screening. For example, in April 2008, authorities arrested a US citizen and former US Embassy employee in Mexico City for selling 180 US visas out of the embassy and taking at least $345,000 in bribes.[147] This is far more than the number of visas used by the al Qaeda operatives responsible for the 9/11 attacks. In 2003 the State Department had to shut down the visa section of the US consulate in Nuevo Laredo due to a major episode of corruption among a number of Mexican employees.[148]

Cases of bribery, extortion, and document fraud have occurred in US Customs and Border Protection (CBP), USCIS, and US Immigration and Customs Enforcement (ICE). In the United States, there were 200 open corruption cases against DHS law-enforcement employees as of May 2008, and corruption investigations doubled between 2003 and 2007.[149] Rapid hiring and training of large numbers of new agents have perhaps contributed to the increase in corruption.

Those found guilty of corruption typically took money or were persuaded by sexual favors to allow unauthorized immigrants, firearms, and illicit drugs into the United States, as well as to release smugglers and unauthorized immigrants who authorities had detained.[150] Although official corruption accounts for few of the total unauthorized entries into the United States, the trend is problematic. Medium to large sums of money seem to be the usual motivating factor for officers, and the sums of money involved are growing. One CBP agent caught accepting bribes from drug smugglers for four years was sentenced to 20 years in prison and ordered to give up $5 million.[151] An even more troubling development is that CBP is uncovering an increasing number of efforts by DTOs to place agents in US law-enforcement agencies to facilitate smuggling operations.[152]

The lack of consistent, predictable access to US or EU visas or to European residence permits makes it difficult for organized criminal or terrorist enterprises to plan travel with valid documents. Unreliable and limited access can mean extended wait times, so that spontaneous criminal activity or terrorist activity is unlikely. However, al Qaeda has shown notable patience; signs of long-term planning; a preference for entry by legal channels; and an ability to adjust mobility tactics to enforcement, circumstances, and opportunities.

Conclusion

How terrorist and criminal networks are engaging in illicit mobility today is complex and evolving. The security community is in a position to provide significantly improved estimates and analysis about HSOs derived from investigative and intelligence sources — with necessary interagency and international cooperation. Going forward, it will be particularly important to understand the role of travel facilitators in diaspora communities; the linkages between HSOs and other organized crime groups; and the scale and type of complicity and corruption among officials in passport, border, immigration, and other mobility services and commercial companies.

In addition to better HSO estimates and analysis — derived from investigative and intelligence sources, with interagency and international cooperation — Congress and the public need to know more about how HSOs intersect with terrorist and other criminal actors. This is important to obtain necessary funding for deterrence and protection and to provide citizens a better understanding of what DHS and other agencies should be, and are doing, to counter the threats.

CHAPTER 3: METHODS OF ILLICIT MOVEMENT

Understanding the specific methods that human-smuggling, human-trafficking, and terrorist organizations use to move their loads and operatives allows regulators and law enforcement to focus on the most important problems and develop tailored countermeasures. Strategically the best approach to diminishing illegal human movement would be to address the forces that prompt it and align US visa policies with the nation's economic and labor-market needs. But even this would not stop illicit movement associated with terrorism and crime. With the understanding that such movement is likely to continue, the ability to disrupt it is becoming increasingly important. This chapter covers key issues that are generally known to varying degrees and are or should be the subject of analysis and response by officials involved in securing human mobility.

Illegal movement methods can be as simple as walking over a mountain pass or across a desert, hiding in the trunk of a car, or attempting to use a phony visa or an obviously counterfeit travel document. The means used for illicit travel are fast becoming more sophisticated.

Terrorists travel selectively; most trips are short and not to the same location. Often terrorists and criminals depend on others to obtain travel and supporting documents, to acquire an alias, and to make travel arrangements. They dispense large sums of money to maintain secrecy. The more experienced or professional the terrorist or criminal, the more he can jeopardize the integrity of the international mobility regime. They also tap into human-smuggling networks and exploit the same corrupt individuals that smugglers do, using established routes or even embedding people in smuggled groups. But their most secure operational strategy is to minimize the use of outsiders.

The business of illicit human transport is characterized by agility. Successful human-smuggling organizations (HSOs) change routes to gain efficiency and avoid scrutiny, and adapt tactics to changing immigration, transportation, and border laws and processes. They are able to match visa requirements to passports, to decide the most profitable routes for the passports they have in hand, and to secure streams of genuine visas from corrupt officials. Smugglers also choose airports based on the effectiveness of entry and exit checks.[153]

Table 3.1 Human-Smuggling Organizations: Roles and Functions

Network head	Oversees all smuggling activity; acts more as a broker than as a facilitator; typically makes all pertinent decisions (money, priority of people, routes); spends his/her time developing network infrastructure. Normally of the same nationality as that of the people being smuggled or with some other cultural or religious tie to them. Usually based outside the destination country; for example, the US network head may be based in the Western Hemisphere but outside the United States. May have started out as a transit facilitator/smuggler and moved into the dominant position.
Local facilitator/ smuggler	Oversees large-scale human smuggling; located in country of origin; facilitates acquisition of legitimate and fraudulent travel and identity documents; employs guides, drivers, money collectors, and recruiters; arranges for staging of aliens and smuggling via land/air/sea; normally of nationality of source or transit country.
Recruiter	Recruits people to be smuggled by local facilitator; located in the country of origin; normally of the same nationality as the people being smuggled. In the case of a global HSO, there may be different recruiters for the different nationalities being smuggled.
Money broker (foreign)	Lends, holds, and transfers money; receives all or initial payment of smuggling fees; located in country of origin; normally of the same nationality as the people being smuggled.
Guide, transporter, or stager	Meets people being smuggled and takes them to a load house or other staging area; may operate in the source, transit, or destination country.
Corrupt local law enforcement	Provides protection to organization's operations located in country of origin or transit; is of the nationality of the staging or transit country.
Document provider	Provides fraudulent travel documents to local and transit facilitators/smugglers; for travel to the United States, usually located in the Western Hemisphere; typically of the nationality of the source or transit country.

Table 3.1 (cont.)

Corrupt travel-industry employee	Facilitates travel via commercial means (agents, airlines, trucking, shipping, bus companies, lodging, and car rentals); located in staging or transit countries; typically of the nationality of those countries.
Corrupt immigration officer	Facilitates entry/exit of smuggled people; located in staging or transit countries; of the nationality of those countries.
Transit facilitator/ smuggler	Acts as intermediary along the route, ensuring that smuggling fees are collected, corrupt officials are bribed, and the like; located in staging or transit countries; usually of the nationality of the people being smuggled.
Domestic facilitator	Receives smuggled people upon their arrival; arranges temporary staging; retrieves travel documents; has guides lead groups across the border; contacts respondents to make payment arrangements; maintains contact with drivers and loadhouse operators; located in transit or destination country; typically works along the border; often of the same nationality as the people being smuggled.
Harborer/security person	Maintains smuggled people at a harboring site; detains smuggled people pending receipt of smuggling fees; detains them pending coordination of travel; houses, feeds, and maintains control of the smuggled people until the transporters are ready to move them; works with money collectors to coordinate payment; maintains loadhouses along the border and interior cities; located in destination country; often of the same nationality as the people being smuggled.
Respondent	Makes final payment for release of smuggled individual; is usually a family member or friend of the individual being smuggled; located in the destination country.
Money broker (US)	Lends, holds, and transfers money and coordinates receipt of fees paid by relatives and friends of smuggled people (using Western Union, Money Gram, Popular Cash, etc.); located in the destination country; usually of the nationality as the people being smuggled.
Transporter/driver	Transports smuggled people between the staging area and the destination; transports smuggled persons to airport hubs for distribution throughout the destination country; located in the destination country; normally of the same nationality as the people being smuggled.

Source: Migration Policy Institute.

Terrorists and human traffickers are both likely to tap into human-smuggling networks, which range from family operations to violent global organizations engaged in drug and arms trafficking. This section describes HSOs and their methods; methods which, of course, are also used by individuals not involved in human smuggling.

Human-Smuggling Methods

HSO members carry out a standard set of functions, listed in table 3.1. Most HSOs are decentralized networks directed by a core group of four or five key people. These tend to be of the same nationality but often live in different locations, even different countries. Each brings unique assets to the organization — primarily connections to the right people. The HSOs employ local (point-of-origin) facilitators who in turn connect with a range of service providers, including document providers, harborers, transporters, enforcers, and money brokers. Transporters move the clients, helped by corrupt or unaware immigration and transportation officials.

A single smuggling ring typically cannot provide the requisite support on the ground for the entire journey.[154] Rather, a group of people will be moved from country to country and region to region by a succession of organizations. The last transporter associated with one core group may deposit the clients in a location and leave them entirely to their own devices, or tell the clients where they can find the next HSO, or provide them with a telephone number. The next HSO — which may or may not be under contract with the previous one — is usually made up of citizens of the transit country, with better local ties.

Figure 3.1 HSO Roles in HSO Global Networks

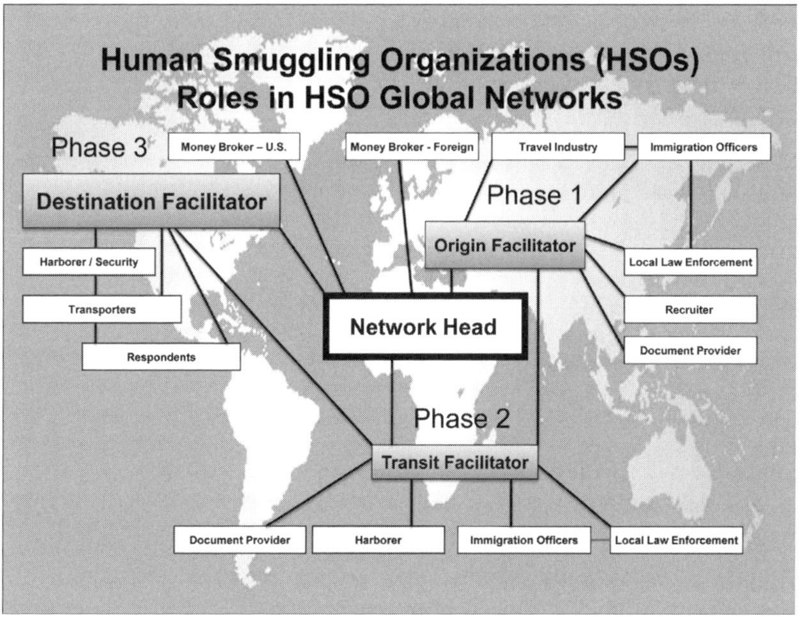

Source: Migration Policy Institute.

Long-distance smuggling routes are rarely direct and are likely to shift in re-sponse to changing circumstances, whether natural conditions, the location of corrupt government officials, the availability of fake documents, or intensified enforcement efforts. Such routes often involve transit through multiple coun-tries. Thus, an HSO in Syria may move clients in transit to the United States through Russia, Greece, Italy, the Netherlands, France, and Spain, dealing with different core groups in each of these transit countries. HSOs in those countries move migrants in various combinations to the Americas, often arriving first in Sao Paolo, Brazil. From Sao Paolo, different HSOs may take Syrian migrants to Ecuador, Cuba, El Salvador, or Guatemala before traveling to Mexico. A Syrian-born Mexican citizen may then work for a Mexican-based HSO that organizes travel to the United States.

HSOs should be distinguished from human-trafficking organizations (HTOs).[155] Since human traffickers profit from the long-term activities of victims after they have been moved, there is little incentive for HTOs to incur the costs of smuggling. Traffickers may occasionally engage in smuggling but only when they can save money by doing so. By keeping transportation in-house, the trafficker increases operational security, has better control of victims, and decreases the vulnerability to infiltration by law enforcement or interference by other criminal groups. However, more often than not, traffickers tend not to be smugglers. Instead, they use smugglers.

While human smuggling and terrorist travel are linked, there is almost no known nexus between human trafficking and terrorist travel. Unlike other criminal activity, there are no reported cases of trafficking proceeds being used to finance terrorist organizations, either directly or indirectly.

Illicit movement is highly organized. Smugglers guiding people through ports of entry on foot usually walk six to ten people ahead in order to act as lookouts and bolster confidence in those behind them. At most ports of entry into the United States, crossing is done by vehicle because typically the US Customs and Border Protection (CBP) inspector only touches one document, that of the driver. Vehicle smugglers may not see the people they are transporting, in an attempt to preserve some deniability in case the load is spotted. Smuggled passengers in vehicles, if not concealed, may make a false claim to citizenship. They may carry passports, many of which have been lost or stolen. Spotters — who report information about CBP inspector shift changes, inspection routines, and tolerance levels — typically outnumber CBP inspectors. Spotters relay information back to handlers.

Document providers are key figures in HSOs. These may have links to corrupt officials or one or more small-scale counterfeiters. A group arrested in March 2009 in Kuala Lumpur is typical. Three Indonesian nationals falsified about six or seven passports and supported them with 17 Malaysian immigration stamps used in various Malaysian ports of entry.[156]

HSOs use cell phones and commercial-shipping services to send and receive travel documents; the Internet to advertise; and e-mail to negotiate and communicate regarding fees, to coordinate delivery of travel documents, and to plan activity. In Tijuana smuggler services are offered at hotels through concierge services. Document vendors stroll the sidewalks in front of hotels. Part of the art is matching people with the right passport and visa. Iraqis smuggled into Peru for passage to Los Angeles were stopped by an airlines official when it was noted that, although they carried Dutch passports, they could not speak Dutch.

HSOs may incorporate fraudulent tactics to move through otherwise legal channels. Smuggled people may be brought to a border and advised to turn themselves in and apply for asylum, receiving coaching in the asylum process. Ramzi Yousef, the key figure in the first World Trade Center bombing, in 1993, famously used a fake Iraqi passport (he is thought to be Pakistani) and asked for asylum when he entered the United States in 1992. And in 2008, US Immigration and Customs Enforcement (ICE) uncovered a Russian-born immigrant ring that made millions of dollars by coaching would-be asylum seekers on how to lie to immigration officials. However, very few of its hundreds of clients prevailed in their claims.[157]

Payment varies according to the client and service. A local client will pay less than someone from a more distant location. At the Mexican border, women pay about $100 more than men. Jobholders and family men pay more than young male gang members. A passport's price varies according to its date of issue, whether it has been altered, or whether it is an e-passport. Clients usually provide at least some initial payment to a point-of-origin money broker, usually half the fee with the other half to be collected by a money broker at the final destination. However, some organizations accept full payment upon delivery to the destination. The local facilitator may ensure passage to any point along the travel path, usually to the next transit country. High-end Chinese smuggling organizations, which move Chinese nationals in groups of 10 to 300 all over the world, are often linked to underground banks. Prices for smuggling persons range from $60,000 to $80,000 on the high end to not less than $25,000 for transport and $35,000 for transport and a job. Smugglers may demand advance money at high interest rates, extort work from migrants, and kill those who do not make the payments demanded.

Fraudulent Use of Travel Documents

The document provider is a key member of HSO networks since travel documents — passports and visas — are essential tools of clandestine travel. Terrorists and criminals frequently possess multiple travel documents, often from different countries and under different names.

Passports and visas are also critical tools for counterterrorism experts, criminal investigators, and border and immigration management. All known terrorists who have entered the United States presented travel documents, many of which had a detectable indicator of fraud.[158] While asylum seekers may destroy the passports they used to exit a country, most people who enter illegally carry travel documents. It is therefore important to understand something about travel document fraud.

A passport is a document that allows a citizen to travel abroad and reenter his or her country. A visa is a document issued by a country of transit or destination that enables the traveler to apply for admission at that country's port of entry, where border officials adjudicate eligibility for entry. Travel document fraud is a broad term that refers to the deceptive acquisition and use of a passport or visa, whether under one's own name or that of a false alias. There are numerous methods of travel document fraud involving the passport- and visa-issuance process; the creation of fraudulent documents, whether through counterfeit or tampering; and the use of fraudulent supporting documentation.

Use of Two Legitimate Passports

Individuals with dual nationality may legitimately possess two passports, with or without legal variations in their name. Under the current standards for passport design and issuance, a government's border service has no immediate way of knowing whether a citizen is a dual national with a second passport. Individuals may use their second passport for legitimate reasons — where states do not recognize dual citizenship — or to hide travel to places that will elicit attention from visa or port-of-entry officials. Some British-Pakistani travelers fly from London to Dubai on a UK passport, then go to Pakistan on a Pakistani passport and return using the same method. The same screening problem arises in the United States for dual citizens of countries with a terrorist presence, as in the case of Somali-Americans.

Acquisition of Multiple Passports in One's Own Identity

New passports may be obtained as part of a scheme to alter and/or sell them for use by terrorists, criminals, or economic migrants or as part of an effort to hide previous travel history. New passports enable terrorists or criminals to hide a record of previous travel that might suggest involvement in criminal or terrorist activity. Knowing that a new passport may be a cover for previous suspicious travel activities, visa officials are wary of applicants with new passports. Meanwhile, economic migrants may use counterfeit stamps in otherwise blank new passports to build a falsified travel history that supposedly adds credibility to their visa applications (see discussion of counterfeit passport stamps further in this chapter).

Deception as to Identity

The most basic and ubiquitous form of fraud, and a frequent terrorist tactic, is the acquisition of a legitimate passport or visa through the use of fraudulent applications; that is, applications that omit information or include false information. The fraud may consist of applying for a passport in a false identity, but using genuine evidence of nationality and/or a stolen or improperly obtained identity. Typically such deceptive applications are accompanied by counterfeit breeder and other documents. These documents pose a one-time risk to users at the time of application, as compared to the continual risk posed by the use of counterfeit passports. Depending on the circumstances, fraudulently obtained documents can be easier to obtain than can counterfeit passports or visas. For example, a common practice of experienced criminals is to acquire passports in the name of dead people.

Use of False "Breeder" Documents to Obtain Passports

The most fundamental problem underlying passport fraud is the lack of security in "breeder" documents. Breeder documents are those documents used to obtain other critical documents like social security cards, driver's licenses, and passports. Eligibility for a passport is based on evidence of citizenship and identity. In the United States, evidence of citizenship is usually a previous US passport, a certified copy of a birth certificate, a certificate of citizenship (for derivative citizenship), or a certificate of naturalization (for naturalized citizens). Identity can be proven by presenting a driver's license or other official ID issued by a competent government authority.

Some countries require an electoral roll certification, a good-behavior certificate from police authorities, or other documents. If the underlying document used to establish identity and citizenship does not tie a person to a fixed identity, the validity of the passport cannot be relied upon because passport issuers establish identity based on breeder documents. Any of these breeder documents can be counterfeited, made on stolen blanks, stolen from rightful owners, or obtained through fraud or corruption. The insecurity of the primary documentation used to obtain passports is a pervasive problem. To some extent, there is also a lack of rigorous scrutiny in the issuance process, whether due to under-staffing, corruption, or a lack of consistent standards by which officials verify identification. Extremists frequently use false breeder documents.

Passport Employee Malfeasance

Graft is typically used to persuade passport employees to issue false passports. Terrorists and sophisticated criminals often have the resources to pay more for breeder and travel documents than government officials earn in their weekly or monthly salaries.

Impersonation and Imposter Passports

Impersonation is the use of a legitimate passport by someone posing as the person to whom the passport rightfully belongs, by relying principally on a similar physical appearance. Photographs may also be altered; in fact, this is likely the most frequent form of passport fraud at present. Passports used by imposters may have been acquired legally — or not. Travel document specialists in HSOs obtain passports by buying or stealing them from tourists and diaspora citizens.

Both HSOs and terrorist organizations also lend their members' passports to others in the network or obtain new passports under the identities of family members or associates. This method is common in Yemen, Turkey, and other nations in the Middle East where photo identification can easily be obtained in someone else's name due to easily corrupted, abused, or very informal local government systems. Because of their authenticity, the illegal use of these passports is hard to detect.

Developing countries, which may lack the ability to check databases or to use or verify biometric data encoded on the passport, are more susceptible to imposter passport fraud. In the developed world, passports acquired by theft are of limited value for long-term use, because many countries enter key information about stolen passports into a database against which passports are checked at entry, alerting border authorities to the fraud. Interpol maintains a central repository for lost and stolen passport information that border officials may be able to access. There are, however, variations in the timing of entry of the data on lost and stolen passports into the Interpol database, which clandestine travelers can exploit. Nearly all use of such passports within a couple of weeks of theft is safe for the bearer. The greater the passage of time since the loss and the more advanced the receiving country, the greater the risk to the bearer.

Absent the biometric identifiers and related technology, impersonation is the most difficult form of passport fraud to detect and the most commonly used method of travel document fraud. To optimize the impersonation, the services that provide fraudulent passports also provide disguises and makeup close to the point of embarkation. Smugglers often collect imposter passports at the destination point, returning them to their country of origin for reuse.[159]

Acquisition of Used Passports for Imposter Use or Alteration. Legitimate passports can be acquired for use by look-alikes, also known as imposters, from a variety of sources, as can passports with replaced photographs or biodata. They may be stolen by individuals acting on their own or as part of a theft ring working for illicit document providers. Document providers also may acquire passports from their original owners, usually tourists willing to sell them for cash. Members of terrorist and criminal organizations may share passports, replacing the photograph where impersonation is not an option. Despite advances in passport security, photo-substituted passports are still used, especially in older but still valid passports. These passports often contain valid visa foils (the name of the visa is taken from the material used to make it).[160]

Economic migrants sometimes carry forged passport stamps and visas that show regular returns to their home countries. Illegal acquisition of passports from visa-waiver partners can be prohibitively expensive. Meanwhile, criminals and terrorists usually use multiple passports and, often, identities to keep their activities hidden from authorities. They often travel to a mix of developed, developing, and failed states, and must show visas as required.

Counterfeit Passports

Counterfeit passports are created through a fraudulent production process. They contain all elements of a legitimate passport, including a photograph and biodata page, and sometimes also fictitious entry and exit stamps and visas to establish the travel history of a false identity. A high-value counterfeit passport includes forged or simulated security features, including holograms or vignettes, which are images where the borders are undefined and fade away until they blend into the background. Nevertheless, this most expensive form of fraudulent travel document retains a major element of risk because the counterfeit elements can be detected by trained and technologically supported border inspectors.

Security features are shared only to a limited degree by passport authorities. No country will share all of its security features, which is why collaboration in real-time passport verification is critical. Coordination should go beyond passport authorities to include other sectors of society. For example, even if US and EU border officials would know to recognize counterfeit US and EU passports, such documents are often used as a form of identification for other than travel purposes, for example, as identification presented to a prospective employer or to open a bank account and for travel to third countries where its security features will not be able to be verified. The use of counterfeit passports is declining at present due in part to a new generation of security features.[161]

Replacement of the Computer Chip

There are no reported cases of illicit replacement of the computer chip, which contains biometric and other data, in the new electronic US passports. Replacement is unlikely in a properly deployed system, because the encryption and matching keys thus far appear to preclude the ability to make a change without being detected. More realistic problems include the possibility of disabling the chip and the failure of border authorities to use the chip to its maximum capability; that is, to provide a live-capture image against the image contained in the chip. In order to tell if the data have been altered, officials examining a passport have to check a digital signature. To do so, the issuing country must share its cryptographic key with the international agency that sets travel document standards, the International Civil Aviation Organization (ICAO). About 70 countries have electronic passports (with several more in line to make the change), but only 15 of those have shared their key through ICAO, primarily due to cost, although some are sharing it manually. Fewer yet are actually using this elaborate data security system.

Replacement of the Biodata Page

Replacement of the biodata page, a widespread technique, allows any individual to hold what appears to be a valid passport regardless of the physical appearance of the original holder. Forgers typically replace only certain elements of the biodata page, especially the physical description and the decade of birth, in order to match the description of the new illegitimate passport holder. This is more difficult to do than simply replacing the photograph, but this method increases the range of potential users — and thus potential passport customers for the travel document provider.

Replacement or Alteration of the Photograph

In this technique, the photograph of an authentic passport is subtly altered to confuse facial-recognition systems while all other data and passport pages are left intact and unaltered. The physical descriptions on the biodata page of the passport must closely match the new passport holder. US border officials can easily spot or feel with their fingers photo-substituted US passports, but photo substitution remains a viable technique in countries that have not yet adopted digitized photos.

Theft and Use of Stolen Blank Passports

Corrupt officials sometimes provide blank passports to illicit brokers. In addition, theft rings in Europe and Asia have been able to steal large batches of blank passports from government offices and passport-manufacturing facilities. Blank passports without inventory control numbers on them can be virtually undetectable. In London in 2008, authorities uncovered an organization that counterfeited passports of an older design, using stolen blanks. The 1,800 passports seized were worth over £1 million.[162] The effects of insecure passport-issuance systems can be far-reaching. For example, until 2003, Belgium distributed passports on a local level through town halls and other local authorities. Repeated burglaries of blank Belgian passports have made older versions of the passport prevalent on the illicit passport market and highly valued by smugglers.[163]

Counterfeit Passport Stamps

Fraudulent or forged entry and exit stamps, supplied by corrupt officials or counterfeiters, are used to make new passports appear less suspicious. For terrorists, fraudulent stamps are used to cover other stamps that indicate travel to locations that would draw attention. Fraudulent applicants and *mala fide* travelers, meanwhile, use fraudulent stamps to indicate previous travel and add credibility to their applications. For example, it is unlikely someone from Thailand would go to Belgium as his first travel destination. However, if the traveler appears to have traveled frequently and widely, Belgium might not seem such an odd destination. Counterfeit stamps are more easily produced than visas and harder to detect.

Use of False Documents to Obtain Visas

False documentation pervades the travel and immigration arenas. A visa often requires an interview and documentary evidence of the visa status for which the individual is applying, as well as evidence of sufficient ties to the home country. Fraudulent visa applications, whether supported by legitimate or illegitimate passports, use a variety of falsified papers — bank statements, job-related documentation, real estate papers — that either buttress the individual's false identity or present false qualifications for the class of visa the applicant is seeking.

Forged Visas

Forged visas provide benefits similar to false passport stamps. Some visas, often from developing countries, are nothing more than ink stamps with handwritten notations and are thus easy to alter or counterfeit. Visa foils, issued by more technically advanced authorities such as those in the United States and the European Union's Schengen region (where internal travel among countries does not require showing a passport), contain multiple overt and covert security features. They are more difficult to counterfeit and thus are more risky to use, but they can also substantiate a traveler's apparent legitimacy.[164] Visas are usually required to visit the Schengen countries and the United States. A visa from one of these countries in an applicant's passport would make the passport look more "used" (and therefore less suspicious), and would make the applicant appear less likely to overstay a visa. Forged visas are useful for terrorists, criminals, and economic migrants. Patterns and practices differ depending on the country. Third-rate documents are sufficient in transit countries that are developing nations. It is more difficult to use fraudulent documents in developed countries.

Violations of the Visa and Terms-of-Entry System

With or without a false passport, and short of actually forging a visa, the US visa and admissions system can be violated in two areas: the visa-application system and the terms of entry. For the United States and many other countries, consular officers grant visas that provide permission to come to a country's border. Customs and immigration officials then decide upon the terms of entry. Restrictions on terms of entry are sometimes part of the visa and entered in the passport by the immigration authority at the border, who usually determines the period of stay. In some countries, immigration officials issue visas at the port of entry to certain designated nationalities.

In FY2008, the US Department of State (DOS) issued 6.6 million temporary nonimmigrant visas for reasons such as tourism, business travel, and medical care.[165] The denial rate varied across applicant nationalities and averaged around 22 percent overall.[166] In some US consulates, however, the view is that up to 90 percent of applications for US visas are fraudulent. DOS has begun to tally denials specifically associated with fraud detection. Local document providers and travel facilitators often set up businesses near US consulates and study the practices of US consular officers. Among other methods, they interview applicants and use informants within the consulate to obtain sample questions and information about officers. Travel facilitators are known to have prepared complete guides with descriptions of each officer in a consulate, alongside information on his or her denial rates and interview style.

Abuse of the entry system, either by staying longer than the time granted or lying to consular or border officials about the reason for travel, poses a significant challenge. Exact figures for people staying longer than their terms of entry and visas permit have only recently begun to be estimated, as have those for Mexican border-crossing card violators. The Department of Homeland Security (DHS) reports varying numbers from alternate data sources. Migrants overstaying their visas contribute anywhere between 39 and 50 percent of the annual flow of the 700,000 to 850,000 unauthorized migrants who remain and stay in the United States every year.[167] Although they represent a large portion of unauthorized migrants, those overstaying their visas constitute a very small percentage of nonimmigrant visa holders.[168]

Visa applicants must have a legitimate reason to visit the United States, show significant ties to their home country, and be vetted against the terrorist watchlist and other records. But fraudulent visa applicants can lie and produce counterfeit documents to show fictional financial means, business activity, and intentions with regard to their stay in the United States. Fraudulent visa applicants include economic migrants, criminals, and terrorists. Immigration and border-control authorities allowed all 19 of the September 11, 2001, hijackers into the country on nonimmigrant (temporary) visas (though five conspirators were denied visas) and denied entry to only one would-be conspirator on a tourist visa.[169] Most experts think that terrorists are most likely to seek visas based on true identities that show no history of travel to nations with a terrorist presence; otherwise, they are likely to be holding passports for travel between visa-waiver partners. Four of the July 2005 London train bombers did not have problematic histories, nor did Richard Reid, the would-be 2004 British shoe bomber. .

Types of Visa Fraud

Visa fraud occurs in all visa programs; no category, whether nonimmigrant or immigrant, is immune. In the United States, certain categories have received special attention or have been analyzed with new rigor. There has been sustained focus in recent years on misuse of the religious worker visa for migrants from countries where terrorist organizations are active. The diversity lottery visa system, which selects visas by lottery, has long been rife with fraud. Despite efforts to automate it and to require electronic filing, the lottery continues to be subject to fraudulent schemes. Fiancé and marriage fraud are also among the more common forms of visa fraud.

Fraudulent applications for student visas are increasingly an issue of concern for immigration officials. Counterfeit university degrees and university documents such as transcripts and recommendations are used to obtain genuine US visas. The documents come from both legitimate and fake universities and have become increasingly popular in the United States and abroad, with one company producing more than 10,000 diplomas for customers in 131 countries.[170] The use of Internet advertising that can reach both domestic and foreign audiences has enabled this type of document fraud to become increasingly prevalent.

Business-related visas, such as L (intracompany transferee) and H (guest workers) visas have also been targeted by visa-fraud facilitators. Eurasian organized-crime members have used L visas to enter the United States. Their schemes often involve seemingly legitimate front companies used for other criminal activities such as financial fraud, contraband smuggling, and money laundering.

The UK refugee system appears to be highly vulnerable to fraud. Pilot DNA tests in two refugee sites in Kenya in 2008 were able to validate only 13 percent of the family relationships claimed by applicants.[171] For the same reason, the United Kingdom has initiated a policy to check the DNA of asylum seekers from Africa.[172]

The line between fraud with criminal intent and fraud spurred by desperation is often hard to draw. Most Somalis apply to enter without a visa, since there is no US Embassy in Somalia that would make lawful visas available. Individuals from Iran and Sudan, for example, often first acquire tourist or other visas (B1, B2, F1, F2, K1) to enter the United States, then file an asylum application, casting doubt on the veracity of statements made in the initial visa application.

DHS and DOS would have a better understanding of visa fraud if the US Citizenship and Immigration Services (USCIS), CBP, and State's Bureau of Consular Affairs (CA) worked together to study adjudicated visa fraud by category and showed the distribution of fraud.

Exploitation of Legal Regimes

Terrorists and HSOs study legal mobility regimes and systematically take advantage of regulatory weakness.

Passports of Convenience

"Passports of convenience" are sold by governments to persons who agree to invest a required amount in the issuing country. Such passports can be used to overcome travel restrictions. They can allow their owners to avoid any stigma or extra regulations that might otherwise arise after their primary passport has been legally taken by their country of birth. They can also be used to hide the true identity of the purchaser, as countries that sell citizenship and investor passports rarely conduct due-diligence background checks on the buyers.

Primary users are business moguls seeking tax advantages. "Luxury" passports of convenience from Switzerland, Monaco, and Liechtenstein cost more than $1 million per head of household. Designed for high-profile celebrities and investors, they are not well suited for terrorists and serious criminals. Less expensive passports of convenience, which still contribute significantly to the overall gross domestic product (GDP) of the smaller nations that offer them, are well within the budgets of terrorist and criminal organizations. Today, the countries that offer such passports include Tonga, Samoa, the Marshall Islands, Vanuatu, and Nauru. Pacific Island countries charge between $4,000 and $50,000 for each passport/citizenship, with reduced costs for the family members of purchasers. Samoan officials have advertised passports and citizenship in Hong Kong newspapers for amounts ranging between $30,000 and $50,000.[173] Between 1998 and 2002, Nauru made 8 percent of its GDP from the sale of passports of convenience.[174] Other countries have requirements like obligating buyers to invest a certain amount of money ($250,000 in the case of the Marshall Islands) or restrictive conditions such as prohibiting them from owning land in the issuing country's territories.[175]

Passports of convenience can and have been exploited by terrorists and organized criminals in the past. In 2000 officials in the Philippines arrested a Russian, holding a passport from Nauru, who was suspected of involvement in an international terrorist network. Among those caught with Nauru passports are a terrorist from Azerbaijan and members of the Turkestan Liberation Organization and al Qaeda.[176] In 2007 Samoa admitted that it could not account for 712 passports, which is not unusual. In most countries that supply passports of convenience, such documents come both from legitimate government sources and corrupt officials, and the entire system is poorly regulated.

Visas are required for holders of passports of convenience traveling to developed countries, and their holders receive additional scrutiny from visa officials. But the system can be exploited by criminals and terrorists who may use their passports of convenience for travel in the developing world, where there is often less scrutiny given to travel documents.

Such passports are too costly for most labor migrants, but the concept is attractive. Chinese migrants are known to have purchased passports from a Caribbean country in an attempt to travel to the United States and Canada. The Kaweah Indian Nation in Kansas attempted to sell tribal memberships to migrants, promising that membership would confer US citizenship. It sold $1.2 million worth of memberships to more than 13,000 people before being stopped by authorities.[177]

Registered-Traveler Systems and Visa-Free Travel

A country's decision to lift its visa requirements or to dilute them substantially can prompt an overnight change in HSO routing. Ecuador lifted all visa requirements in 2008, an action that immediately opened up a preferred route through Ecuador for illegal Chinese immigrants to the United States. Intense diplomatic activity initiated by the United States resulted in an adjustment of Chinese and Ecuadorean practice that has mitigated the impact of this particular channel. The Ecuador experience followed a similar episode in which Mexico dropped transit-visa requirements for Brazilians, resulting in a wave of Brazilians being apprehended at the US-Mexico border. When Mexico reinstated transit visa requirements for Brazilians, Border Patrol apprehensions fell dramatically.

The US Visa Waiver Program (VWP) is a source of particular concern for counterterrorism officials because of terrorists' interest in it. Business-facilitation programs in consulates and registered-traveler programs run by border agencies are also thought to have been used by terrorists.

Hot Spots and Channels of Illicit Mobility

The scale and complexity of global migration, while measures of human freedom and opportunity, pose a daunting challenge for policymakers focused on terrorist travel and organized crime. Such factors provide serious malefactors with ample opportunity to shift routes and transportation methods. At any given moment, US policymakers and other governments have to decide where to focus attention and resources based on the location of targeted groups, HSO and HTO hubs, illegal travel document source sites, pressure points for travel, and vulnerabilities.

Transit Zone Case Studies: Canada, Mexico, and the Caribbean

Illegal movement across the borders of the United States is inevitably a major concern. People with reported or suspected associations with terrorist entities, including a number of US citizens, move in both directions across the US borders with Canada and Mexico. Sri Lankan extremists associated with the now-defeated Tamil Tigers and US gun traffickers enter Canada from the United States. Mexican HSOs and drug-trafficking organizations (DTOs) have US resident and citizen operatives who smuggle guns and money into Mexico, then take delivery of migrants and receive their final payments. Sometimes these groups kidnap migrants and extort ransom from their families. Although not preferred, al Qaeda and other terrorist organizations consider illegal entry into the United States via legal travel through Mexico or Canada an option.

Mexico. Because of the overall volume of illegal labor migration into the United States from Mexico —more than half of the estimated 11.5 million unauthorized immigrants living in the United States in 2006 were Mexican —[178] and the violence of Mexican DTOs, there is greater border agency attention toward Mexico than Canada.

Mexico itself does not have a large extremist population, although it does have some indigenous guerillas and extremists. There have been no published reports of actual known al Qaeda terrorists entering the United States from Mexico, through ports of entry or in between. But there is Mexican territory that is effectively ungoverned by the federal government. Massive corruption, DTO subversion of government, and weak border controls are endemic. The US security community faces the possibility that Iraqi, Somali, or other al Qaeda–affiliated terrorists will use Mexican pathways. Overall, less than 1 percent of the people apprehended at the southwest border by the Border Patrol are from countries with a significant terrorist presence (known as special-interest aliens). Iraqi nationals requesting political asylum, virtually all of them identifying themselves as Chaldean Christians, constituted 40 percent of all non-Mexicans entering at the southwest border in 2008 from countries with a significant terrorist presence.[179] Most of the East Africans apprehended by the Border Patrol cross the Rio Grande at the southwest border, while the Marfa and Del Rio sectors in Texas are the most frequent crossing locations for migrants from the Middle East.[180]

Mexico itself has a major problem with illegal movement from Central America. In 2004 12.5 percent of all land-border entries along Mexico's southern border were unauthorized.[181] More than 300,000 migrants from other countries — mainly from Central America — illegally entered Mexico with the aim of migrating to the United States.[182] Among them 240,000 were returned to their countries of origin by Mexican immigration authorities.[183] The remaining migrants may be assumed to have traveled to the United States. Guides help their clients to evade border checkpoints at the Guatemalan border. After gathering in Mexico City, they travel by bus to Monterrey and on to Nuevo Laredo or Reynosa. From there, they enter the United States. In addition to maritime passages, there are four major routes through Mexico to the United States: the California corridor, the Arizona corridor, the west Texas–New Mexico corridor, and the south Texas corridor. The Mexican DTOs are fighting for control of these entry channels and for the revenues at stake from drugs and (increasingly) from human smuggling.

Migrants also travel by air. For example, Iraqi migrants may travel legally to Turkey using Iraqi passports and then use smugglers to enter Greece by boat, truck, or on foot. From Greece, they contact other travel facilitators who arrange additional travel. With Greece shifting to new e-passports, travel facilitators are providing Iraqi travelers with forged or other types of fraudulent European passports, often from Cyprus, Poland, or Bulgaria. Transiting through Madrid and Paris, Iraqis then take direct flights to Guatemala City, Cancun, Monterrey, and, less frequently, Mexico City. Afterwards, smugglers usually take back the fraudulent passports for reuse.

The Caribbean. Border-security efforts in the Caribbean are uneven.
Because some Caribbean countries' border-security agencies are understaffed, underresourced, undertrained, and underpaid, they are vulnerable to corruption. Cubans increasingly are transiting Mexico to claim asylum at US borders, which is granted by law once they step onto US soil under the "wet foot, dry foot" policy. More than 11,500 Cubans transited Mexico in 2007, compared with more than 7,800 Cuban migrants who came through the turbulent Florida straits. The most notable channel for illegal movement through the Caribbean

is via the Bahamas and St. Martin. Migrants then move by small vessels to Puerto Rico, and from the British Virgin Islands to the US Virgin Islands.

Canada. According to Canadian intelligence, 40 terrorist groups operate in Canada. Some are not a current threat to the United States. The presence of these groups in well-established diaspora communities in Canada makes terrorist entry from Canada to the United States a significant concern. Individuals applying for visas from US consulates in Canada regularly show up on terrorist watchlists. (For more discussion of Canada, see chapter 12.)

In 2009 roughly 14,000 suspected unauthorized immigrants were detained in Canada.[184] Many of those who are smuggled into Canada are Chinese and Vietnamese nationals who have transited through Thailand, acquiring forged travel documents to use in entering Canada.[185] Recently, there has been an upswing of illegal Indian migrants using forged travel documents. And between May 2006 and May 2008, immigration officials were notified of at least 31 foreign nationals who were likely human-trafficking victims.[186]

Canada has a more extensive list of visa-free travel partners than does the United States. There is a notable risk that people holding visa-free passports for entry into Canada may actually intend to reach the United States. Soon after Canada gave visa-waiver status to the Czech Republic and Hungary, large numbers of Roma, holding Czech and Hungarian passports, arrived at Canadian airports and made claims for asylum. Mexico faced a similar situation when it extended visa-free travel status to all EU Member States.[187]

South Korean and Chinese nationals use South Korean passports to enter Canada under visa-waiver arrangements and are then smuggled to the United States; numerous female Korean trafficking victims entered the United States through Canada or Mexico.[188] As of 2008 South Koreans may also travel visa-free to the United States.

Global HSO Routes

Global HSO routes constantly change; the following descriptions offer a snapshot of one period of activity in 2008.

Routes through and from Africa. South Africa and countries in East and West Africa are commonly used as transit countries, particularly by Chinese migrants, because of their high degree of official corruption. East Africans —

Somalis, Eritreans, Ethiopians — seeking to get to the United States typically depend on Latin-America-based HSOs and East African associates. Smugglers use established facilitator networks of corrupt officials and document forgers in Africa and in Latin America. The HSOs choose routes based on their ability to bribe officials at key points and use those connections to improve their access to fraudulently obtained travel documents. Smuggled individuals may transit through Kenya, Angola, the Congo, or Tanzania, but most pass through Johannesburg before flying to Sao Paolo. Alternative routes include Abu Dhabi, Dubai, or Rome to Bolivia, Venezuela, Cuba, or Mexico. There is intelligence on African smuggling routes, but the routes are not fixed and levels of traffic and specific locations frequently change.

Routes to Europe. The majority of illegal migration and terrorist travel to the European Union is via a North African or West African Atlantic Coast route, navigating the Straits of Gibraltar or the Mediterranean with target destinations of Rome, Malta, and Madrid. Additional routes include the Eastern Mediterranean using Iran, Turkey, and other Middle Eastern nations as transit countries to Athens. Due to its location, Turkey is the main transit point for people from the Middle East being smuggled into the European Union. A Balkan route goes through the West Balkans and ultimately to Greece, Italy, Slovenia, Austria, Bulgaria, Romania, and Hungary. Smuggling may begin in Asia and take a route through Kazakhstan, Kyrgyzstan, Uzbekistan, Tajikistan, and Turkmenistan to Russia and from there to Ukraine, Slovakia, and the Czech Republic.

These Central and Eastern European routes, which are of growing importance, also use the countries of the former Soviet Union to enter Poland, Hungary, Bulgaria, and Romania.[189] Entries to Poland from the Ukraine number 30,000 a year. Once in the EU Schengen zone, unauthorized migrants can travel virtually unimpeded to most EU countries.

Routes to the United States. Typical routes from the Middle East to the United States are through Rome or by air to Johannesburg, then by air to South and Central America for land routing through Guatemala. Chinese nationals are often smuggled into the United States on Japanese or South Korean passports through transit countries such as Chile or Peru.[190] Routes through Canada are associated with fewer illegal entries but more terrorism-related incidents, albeit only a few in total.

Routes to Australia. Migrants from the Middle East or South Asia aim for Christmas Island or other points on Australia's west coast, which are a short haul from the Indonesian archipelago.[191] Entering Malaysia, people are moved south by ferry to Batam, onward to Jakarta, and from there to the Indonesian islands of Bali, Flores, or Lombok, for the final leg to Australia.[192]

HSO Hubs

Markets, geography, corruption, and infrastructure, including the presence of organized- crime networks, come together at nexus points or criminal hubs for HSOs. The hubs act as routers for criminal activity including drugs and trafficked people and products. While geographic routes change, nexus points for the most part remain fixed.

Greece. Its location as a gateway to Europe, its heavy Russian and Albanian organized crime presence, and the demand for movement into the European Union are all factors making Greece an important HSO hub for entry to Europe from the east.

Asia and Europe. With the increase in the number of airlines and the historical decrease in the overall cost of tickets, unauthorized migrants are increasingly coming by air.[193] Because Belgium, Switzerland, and Japan are convenient transportation hubs within their respective regions, these countries have become the major transit countries for human smuggling. Thailand is a hub because it has the preeminent industry for illicit travel documents.

Pakistan. Pakistan's porous borders, corruption, and sympathetic government officials have made it a safe haven for al Qaeda and a major facilitator of terrorist travel.[194]

Africa. Johannesburg, which is host to African, South Asian, Chinese, Russian, and Albanian organized crime and corruption, is the key hub for human smuggling that originates in and transits through Africa. Since the introduction of direct flights between Angola (a former Portuguese colony) and Brazil, Angola is used often for transit to Rio and Sao Paolo.

Sao Paolo. Sao Paolo is the major air entry point for HSOs into the Western Hemisphere.

Triborder area/Ciudad del Este, Paraguay. Latin American hot spots for terrorist financing include Venezuela, Trinidad and Tobago, and the Iquique area of Chile, the triborder area where Argentina, Paraguay, and Brazil come together and where Paraguay has established the free trade zone of Ciudad del Este. The latter is also a major center for organized crime — Middle Eastern, Mexican, Colombian, Japanese, Chinese, and Russian. Hezbollah, Hamas, and other terrorist groups have a presence here, although the extent of their activities is unclear.[195] The area's criminal infrastructure and central location make it an HSO hub.

Diaspora communities. Europol highlights what it terms "seclusion criminal hubs" that are made up of non-EU-origin ethnic communities within the European Union, which in essence create their own regions and are vulnerable to exploitation by organized-crime groups. Diaspora communities, in other words, frequently serve as criminal hubs and terrorist transit points as well as HSO operational centers.

Travel Document Fraud Centers

It is generally accepted that terrorists prefer to acquire official documents and to appear to travel legally. Passport fraud of all kinds, for travel and for economic migration purposes, is pervasive and is a primary vulnerability of the global mobility system. Therefore, travel documents and their modes of acquisition are a major concern. While all HSO hubs have document acquisition capabilities, some locations are notorious for their document fraud.

Bangkok. Thailand is the current counterfeit capital of the world and is the primary global source for imposter, altered, and counterfeit travel documents. Most passports sold on Thai streets are legitimate and make up a significant, but unknown, proportion of the 10 million lost or stolen passports on the illicit world market. Thai passport rings are sizable. An investigation of one ring led to the May 2008 arrest of 12 people and the seizure of 20,000 passports from countries as diverse as Brunei, Burma, Canada, France, Germany, Malaysia, Russia, Sweden, and the United States.

Thai-sourced passports can sell for $200 to $10,000 depending on the type of passport and associated visas.[196] The majority of Thai-produced passports are mediocre counterfeits, sold for a retail price between $25 and $50. While not good enough to fool immigration officials, they are useful for individuals and criminal organizations to open up bank accounts or gain residency. There have been a number of cases where expatriate European document couriers were apprehended while carrying hundreds of counterfeit blank EU passports from Thailand to Europe. Travel-document providers in Thailand are also thought to have the best nonstate forgery technology in the world. Counterfeit or altered passports for travel purposes, particularly those with visas to the United States or United Kingdom, are worth $2,400 to $2,900 on the illegal market.[197] Real or counterfeit Japanese and South Korean passports are also highly valued, because of these countries' visa-waiver agreements with various Western countries.

Manila. Manila is a major source for fraudulent documents and is known for widespread corruption in the border services as well as extremist groups.

African countries. Ghana is known for its document forgeries and Nigeria for counterfeit passport production. North African countries also have significant levels of document fraud production. Document producers in Ghana serve both Europe and groups using the Sahara as a logistics base, including the border regions of Algeria, Mauritania, and Mali. South African passports are still favored by Eritreans, Somalis, and others coming illegally to the United States. Although South Africa redesigned its passport in 2007, adding new and improved security features, corruption in passport and civil document issuance is common, and inventory control on passports and on breeder documents is still insufficient. The older passport series, which will be valid until 2017, remains an area of vulnerability. As a result, the United Kingdom has suspended visa-waiver travel from South Africa.

Europe. Several European cities are prime locations for counterfeit passport production, marketplaces for North-African-produced travel documents, and venues for stolen passports. The Netherlands is a long-time center for the production of altered and counterfeited passports and visas. London has a large-scale false-travel-document industry. The United Kingdom has an organized crime and terrorist group presence, making it a persistent problem as a point of origin for visa-free travel to the United States. The UK passport is one of the most secure travel documents, making it among the most sought-after passports for illicit movement. One-third of those who had committed terrorist attacks in the United Kingdom as of 2009 had been involved in identity fraud and improperly obtained passports, and officials estimate that authorities detect only one in ten forged immigration documents in the United Kingdom.[198]

Counterfeiters usually produce a variety of passports. In a July 2007 raid on a Bulgarian organized-crime group in London, for example, police found 1,800 completed passports for a dozen countries, including 200 UK passports and others for Albania, Belgium, Denmark, Finland, France, Greece, Italy, Korea, Latvia, Portugal, and Slovenia. The Bulgarian group was also producing immigration stamps and driver's licenses. Criminal organizations in England have increasingly provided falsified documents to support the creation of front businesses that offer fake jobs to back up visa and work-permit applications and falsified documentation for student visas.[199] Documents include fake bank account statements and university acceptance letters. During investigation of a foiled terrorist plot to blow up shopping centers in Manchester, police discovered that the man in charge had helped other alleged members of his terrorist cell enter the United Kingdom under student visas.[200] A police official noted that the United Kingdom does not have much incentive to thoroughly inspect student visas as international students generate millions of pounds for the country every year.[201]

Latin America. In Latin America, false travel documentation is so ubiquitous that it extends beyond low-wage economic migration to professions where foreign countries tightly limit visas. Sports are an example. Professional Argentine soccer players have acquired fraudulent Italian passports to overcome EU restrictions on foreign players.[202] Somalis and other East Africans have access to counterfeit and genuine Bolivian, Peruvian, Chilean, Belizean, and Mexican, as well as South African, visas.

Tijuana. Mexican cities near the US border have a thriving illegal-document market where travel documents needed to enter the United States can be purchased or rented. These documents range from state driver's licenses to passports from visa-waiver countries; US passports and border-crossing cards are prevalent. These documents previously were only available to citizens of Mexico and Central American countries, but an increase in visitors from abroad to Mexico and growing demand have meant that this is no longer the case.[203]

The United States. The United States has a strong illicit market for counterfeit documents, including driver's licenses, social security cards, green cards, and other identification documents. Gangs within the United States, such as the Latin Kings, have been involved in the production of fake ID cards. During an investigation of several Latin King members in 1999, authorities discovered 31,000 manufactured IDs and travel documents.[204] Gangs, organized crime syndicates, and even otherwise legitimate businesses are involved in the industry, which primarily caters to unauthorized workers, although customers are diverse and include US citizens.

Some Pressure Points for Illicit Mobility to the United States

US consulates and US border authorities are an intelligence target for terrorist organizations, HSOs, and traffickers of all kinds. For every form of visa there are applicants seeking to subvert the process. Often, efforts to acquire and disseminate information about the policies and practices of consulates are quite elaborate. Intelligence can include detailed written reports describing individual consular officers by appearance, interview approach, and decision-making pattern. The Internet has facilitated the dissemination of this information.

At ports of entry along the Mexican border, the intelligence operations of the HSOs and DTOs place more people on-site than there are CBP officers on duty. These operatives use encrypted communications to relay information regarding who is on duty, what type of screening is occurring, what the time frames are, and in what lanes.

The government of Venezuela has issued thousands of fraudulent passports to launder the identities of Colombian members of the Revolutionary Armed Forces of Colombia (FARC) and individuals of Middle Eastern origin, including a network of people raising funds for Hezbollah in Venezuela.[205] Over the years, thousands of blank unissued Venezuelan passports have been reported missing or stolen from the passport-issuing agency and embassies. A former US intelligence official notes that US authorities know of cases in which terrorists have used fraudulent Venezuelan passports.[206]

Iraqis, Somalis, and others from war-torn countries in which there is a significant al Qaeda presence have been delivered by HSOs to Mexico and advised to turn themselves over to Mexican authorities. After presenting themselves as asylum seekers and being detained by the Mexican immigration service for ten days, they are generally released with an order to depart. They then may use other HSOs to enter the United States or present themselves to US border officials and claim asylum. If these individuals travel without passports and other forms of identification, screening is a particular challenge for US officials.

Systemic Weaknesses

Breeder documents. The production of false breeder documents throughout the world constitutes a significant weakness for the international mobility regime. In the United States and elsewhere, a frequent technique is to apply for passports in the name of dead people. In some countries, for example, in India, Malaysia, South Africa, and Pakistan, millions of unauthorized migrants from neighboring countries acquire citizenship through the use of false breeder documents. Their true names may or may not be used, but the claimed nationality is false. Once these migrants acquire citizenship, they may also acquire genuine travel documents. The US visa-issuance system, as well of those of all other countries, rests on a flimsy foundation when adjudicating applications from countries where breeder documents are notoriously insecure and where "paper citizenship" is a widespread reality.[207]

Blank passport theft. Stolen blank passports remain a problem in some countries in Europe. Today fully centralized passport issuance exists in Belgium, the Baltic countries, the Czech Republic, Germany, Luxembourg, the Netherlands, and Sweden. Decentralized issuance — which makes securing passports more difficult and theft in transport a possibility — continues in Italy and Spain. Many thefts in France precipitated a push to centralization, which is not complete. Ireland maintains two passport issuance sites.

Dual passport possession. Use of two passports to hide suspect travel has been a problem for the UK government in addressing risks from UK citizens who retain dual Pakistani citizenship and travel to Pakistan or Afghanistan, using their Pakistani passports, for terrorism-related training. Now it is becoming a problem for travel to Somalia by US- and UK-based Somalis. The complete breakdown of the Somali state has driven many refugees — now with dual nationalities — to London (which has the largest Somali community in Europe), Sweden, the United States, and elsewhere. (Al Shabaab, al Qaeda's Somali affiliate, has been fighting to take control of the Somali state.)

Border agency corruption and incompetence. Border agency corruption defeats even the most advanced passport security measures. In many developing countries, border agencies are underfunded and underresourced. They also suffer from inadequately trained personnel and inadequate technology and equipment. Often at the lower end of their country's law-enforcement hierarchy, border security personnel are often underpaid, making them especially vulnerable to bribery.

Priority Vulnerabilities

Terrorist access to false travel documents. The topmost concern for US counterterrorism officials with regard to terrorist mobility is the movement of unknown clandestine operatives, who are not detectable by officials. Unknown clandestine operatives, such as the would-be shoe bomber Richard Reid, use their own identity, present authentic travel documents, and have no record that would draw the undue attention of immigration officials. Despite the validity of the concern, however, the major al Qaeda events in Europe since 9/11, including the March 2003 Madrid bombings and the July 7, 2005, London bombings, have involved the use of false travel documents. Thai authorities in August 2005 arrested a Syrian-born British national with ties to the July 7, 2007 bombers, with 186 fake French and Spanish passports. Extremists have difficulty obtaining documents legitimately even through deception, but prefer official documents that present the appearance of traveling legally.

Homegrown terrorism in Canada and entry from Canada. Canada is confronting the potential for violence among young second- and third-generation immigrants, who come from a secular background but are drawn to extremism linked to Islam. In spring 2008 the Royal Canadian Mounted Police investigated seven suspected terrorist plots and nearly 850 national-security cases. And a terrorist group known as the Toronto 18 was disrupted in 2006 during the planning of a plot to blow up parliament, kill the prime minister, and bomb the Toronto Stock Exchange. (Canada is discussed further in chapter 12.)

Conclusion

This chapter is illustrative of the type of analysis that DHS and other US agencies should be conducting on a systematic basis. While practices and routes are constantly changing, HSOs and HTOs are motivated by profit to find the least-expensive, most-trouble-free means of illicit travel. To counter terrorist travel, DHS and its partner agencies need to create a picture of the illicit market's operations and travel patterns that is as accurate and current as possible. Such a picture requires the use of intelligence methods, international information sharing, investigations, and computer-assisted analysis performed on a regular basis. The analysis must then focus on the organizations, hubs, methods, regulatory processes, and operating environments that support the illicit-travel market. One of the most difficult problems is to establish priorities. The workings of this market are global in scope and cannot be addressed by US law enforcement alone. The solutions will come not only from law enforcement but from raising regulatory standards, strengthening legal frameworks, and finding new solutions to difficult problems such as how to identify bad-faith actors. Only an all-out effort to bring the rule of law to global mobility channels will enable democratically ordered societies to secure human mobility. Understanding the current state of affairs is a necessary starting point.

NOTES

67. Fiona B. Adamson, "Crossing Borders: International Migration and National Security," *International Security* 31, no.1 (2006): 165–99.

68. Philip Bobbitt, *Terror and Consent: The Wars for the Twenty-First Century* (New York: Knopf, 2008). The discussion that follows is based on my reading of this book.

69. Gary Hart and Warren Rudman (cochairs) and Stephen Flynn (project director), *America – Still Unprepared, Still In Danger* (New York: Council on Foreign Relations, 2002), www.cfr.org/publication/americastill_unprepared_still_in_danger.html_.

70. *Homeland Security Act of 2002*, Public Law 107-296, 107th Cong., 2nd sess., November 25, 2002, www.dhs.gov/xlibrary/assets/hr_5005_enr.pdf.

71. David McIntyre, "Borders, Technology and Security: Strategic Responses to New Challenges," New Mexico State Univ.–US Army Strategic Studies Institute Colloquium, Los Cruces, New Mexico, March 31, 2008.

72. European Commission, Security Budget, 2007–13 "EU Funded Research Will Tackle Themes Linked to Civil Security (Anti-Terrorism And Crisis Management)," http://ec.europa.eu/research/fp7/index_en.cfm?pg=security.

73. Conversation with Philip Bobbitt; Matthew Dalleck, "Civic Security," *Democracy* 7 (2008), www.democracyjournal.org/article.php?id=6567; James Fallows, "Civilize Homeland Security," *The Atlantic*, July/August 2009, www.theatlantic.com/doc/200907/ideas-homeland-security.

74. The phrase *societal security* is currently used as the name for the international standard, ISO 223, for what is understood in the United States to be emergency preparedness and resilience. That ordinary members of society have an essential role in civil security is well captured by this terminology, but it does not evoke the fact that the ultimate harm to be precluded is the breakdown of civil order.

75. Border management in Afghanistan today, for example, involves counterinsurgency, counterterrorism, controlling cross-border crimes, and enforcing customs and immigration rules.

76. The term *enterprise* refers to the collective efforts and shared responsibilities of federal, state, local, tribal, territorial, nongovernmental, and private sector partners, as well as individuals, families, and communities. David Heyman and James Jay Carafano, *Homeland Security 3.0: Building a National Enterprise to Keep America Free, Safe, and Prosperous* (Washington, DC: Heritage Foundation and the Center for Strategic and International Studies, 2008), www.csis.org/files/media/csis/pubs/080918_homeland_sec_3dot0.pdf.

77. DHS (US Department of Homeland Security), *Quadrennial Homeland Security Review* (QHSR) (Washington, DC: DHS, February 2010), viii, www.dhs.gov/xabout/gc_1208534155450.shtm.

78. DHS, National Preparedness Guidelines (Washington, DC: DHS, September 2007), iii, www.fema.gov/pdf/government/npg.pdf; The White House, Homeland Security Council, *National Strategy for Homeland Security* (Washington, DC: The White House, October 2007), www.dhs.gov/xlibrary/assets/nat_strat_homelandsecurity_2007.pdf.

79. DHS, QHSR, ix; DHS, "Remarks by Secretary Napolitano at the Council on Foreign Relations," Press Release, July 29, 2009, www.dhs.gov/ynews/speeches/sp_1248891649195.shtm.

80. DHS, Risk Steering Committee, *DHS Risk Lexicon* (Washington, DC: DHS, 2008), www.dhs.gov/xlibrary/assets/dhs_risk_lexicon.pdf.

81. Ibid.

82. Stephen Flynn, *The Edge of Disaster* (New York: Random House, 2007).

83. James Lebovic, *Deterrence and Homeland Security: A Defensive-Denial Strategy Against Terrorists* (Baltimore, MD: John Hopkins Univ. National Center for the Study of Preparedness and Catastrophic Event Response [PACER 2006]), www.pacercenter.org/pages/publications_briefs.aspx.

84. Anita Khashu, *The Role of Local Police: Striking a Balance between Immigration Enforcement and Civil Liberties* (Washington, DC: Police Foundation, 2009), www.policefoundation.org/pdf/strikinga-balance/Narrative.pdf.

85. Colin Harvey and Robert P. Barnidge, Jr,, *The Right to Leave One's Country Under International Law*, (Geneva, Switzerland: Global Commission on International Migration, 2005), www.gcim.org/att-

tachments/TP8.pdf.

86. Jeffery D. Kahn, "International Travel and the Constitution," *American Bar Association National Security Committee Law Report* 30, no. 4 (November/December 2008): 13–15.

87. Similar questions are illuminated in Robert Bach, "Global Mobility, Inequality and Security," *Journal of Human Development and Capabilities* 4, no. 2 (2003): 227–45.

88. Susan F. Martin, Patricia Weiss Fagen, Andrew Schoenholtz, *The Uprooted: Improving Humanitarian Responses to Forced Migration* (Lanham, MD: Lexington Books, 2005).

89 Timothy J. Dunn, *The Militarization of the U.S.-Mexico Border 1978-1992: Low-Intensity Conflict Comes Home* (Austin, TX: CMAS Books, 1996).

90. The number of people that the Border Patrol apprehends on an annual basis has dropped sharply from 1,676,438 in FY2000. See DHS, Office of Immigration Statistics, *Yearbook of Immigration Statistics: Table 35, Deportable Aliens Located by Program and Border Patrol Sector and Investigations Special Agent in Charge (SAC) Jurisdiction: Fiscal Years 1999 to 2008* (Washington, DC: DHS, 2008), www.dhs.gov/xlibrary/assets/statistics/yearbook/2008/table35.xls.

91. The inadequate coherence of the postwar national security structure for new security requirements is widely recognized. See Project on National Security Reform, *Forging a New Shield* (Arlington, VA: Project on National Security Reform and the Center for the Study of the Presidency, 2008).

92. *Homeland Security Act*, Sections 101(b)(1)(A)-(G) cited and discussed in Doris Meissner and Donald Kerwin, *DHS and Immigration: Taking Stock and Correcting Course* (Washington, DC: MPI, February 2009), www.migrationpolicy.org/pubs/DHS_Feb09.pdf.

93. Meissner and Kerwin, *DHS and Immigration*, 94–95.

94. DHS, "Secretary Michael Chertoff, US Department of Homeland Security Second Stage Remarks," Press Release, July 13, 2005, www.dhs.gov/xnews/speeches/speech_0255.shtm; DHS, "Homeland Security Secretary Michael Chertoff Announces Six-Point Agenda for Department of Homeland Security," Press release, July 13, 2005, www.dhs.gov/xnews/releases/press_release_0703.shtm.

95. Demetrios G. Papademetriou, Doris Meissner, Marc R. Rosenblum, and Madeleine Sumption, *Harnessing the Advantages of Immigration for a 21st Century Economy: A Standing Commission on Labor Markets, Economic Competitiveness, and Immigration* (Washington, DC: MPI, 2009), www.migrationpolicy.org/pubs/StandingCommission_May09.pdf.

96. *The Intelligence Reform and Terrorism Prevention Act of 2004*, Public Law 108-458, 108th Cong., 2nd sess., December 17, 2004, www.nctc.gov/docs/pl108_458.pdf.

97. John Rollins, Liana Sun Wyler, and Seth Rosen, *International Terrorism and Transnational Crime: Security Threats, U.S. Policy, and Considerations for Congress*, R41004 (Washington, DC: Congressional Research Service, 2010), http://assets.opencrs.com/rpts/R41004_20100105.pdf.

98. DOS (Department of State), Office of the Coordinator for Counterterrorism, www.state.gov/s/ct/rls/other/des/123085.htm.

99. "US Attorney Reports Palestinian National and Former Colombian Detective Guilty of Conspiring to Support FARC and Alien Smuggling," *LawFuel.com*, November 15, 2007, www.lawfuel.com/show-release.asp?ID=16112; Eric Green, "US-Colombian Cooperation Nets Arrests of Alien Smugglers: Panama Also Helps in Solving Smuggling Case," *America.gov*, January 27, 2006, www.america.gov/st/washfile-english/2006/January/20060127170932AEneerG0.6159937.html.

100. Mazher Mahnrood, "Passport to Evil: We Smash Ring that Could Help Terrorists Slip Net," *News of the World*, August 24, 2008, www.newsoftheworld.co.uk/news/article16763.ece.

101. Statement for the record of Lorenzo Vidino, deputy director, The Investigative Project, "Islamic Extremism in Europe," before the House Committee on International Relations Subcommittee on Europe and Emerging Threats, 109th Cong., 1st sess., April 27, 2005, www.investigativeproject.org/documents/testimony/303.pdf.

102. "Arrests after Spain 'Forgery' Raids," *Aljazeera*, February 3, 2009, http://english.aljazeera.net/news/europe/2009/02/200923105422941176.html.

103. Author's communication with US government officials. Senior UK foreign service official, private communication with the author's research assistant on June 19, 2009.

104. Duncan Gardham, "Hidden Threat from Al-Qaeda Sleeper Cells: Al Qaeda Terrorists are Exploiting Loose Visa and Immigration Rules to Enter Britain, the Security Services Fear," *The Telegraph*, November 27, 2009, www.telegraph.co.uk/news/6672806/Hidden-threat-from-al-Qaeda-sleeper-cells.html.

105. "Al Qaida South of the Border: Rumsfeld — Human Smuggling Rings Tied to Bin Laden's Terrorist Network," *WorldNetDaily*, February 16, 2004, www.wnd.com/news/article.asp?ARTICLE_ID=37133.

106. Brooke Loren, "Mexican Border Vulnerable to Al Qaeda," *Associated Content*, February 19, 2009, www.associatedcontent.com/article/1470457/mexican_border_vulnerable_to_al_qaeda.html?cat=75; "Report: Mexico is Al-Qaida Route to U.S.: Plans to Use Migrant Smuggling Paths to Set Up Operatives," *WorldNetDaily*, September 17, 2004, www.wnd.com/index.php?fa=PAGE.view&pageId=26596.

107. Individuals have entered the United States legally from Canada who were later found to be al Qaeda associates.

108. Sara A. Carter, "EXCLUSIVE: Hezbollah Uses Mexican Drug Routes into US," *The Washington Times*, March 27, 2009, www.washingtontimes.com/news/2009/mar/27/hezbollah-uses-mexican-drug-routes-into-us/print/.

109. Robert Morgenthau, "The Link between Iran and Venezuela: A Crisis in the Making?" *The American Interest Online*, September 9, 2009, http://blogs.the-american-interest.com/contd/2009/09/09/the-link-between-iran-and-venezuela-a-crisis-in-the-making/.

110. "Passport Investigation Suggests Security Hole," *NBC News*, December 28, 2007, www.msnbc.msn.com/id/22419963/page/4/.

111. Siobhan O'Neil, *Terrorist Precursor Crimes: Issues and Options for Congress*, RL34014 (Washington, DC: Congressional Research Service, 2007), www.fas.org/sgp/crs/terror/RL34014.pdf.

112. J. Jesús Esquivel, "U.S. Government: Hamas, Hezbollah Collaborating with Mexican Drug Cartels," *Proceso*, July 16, 2008, www.blacklistednews.com/?news_id=550.

113. Russell D. Howard and Colleen M. Traughber, "Summary of Conclusions: Combating Terrorism Working Group (CTWG)," *Connections* 6, no.1 (2007): 104–05.

114. Zachary Abuza, "Second Thai Counterfeit Passport Ring Broken Up This Month: Nearly 22,000 Passports Seized," *Counterterrorism Blog*, May 10, 2008, http://counterterrorismblog.org/2008/05/second_thai_counterfeit_passpo.php.

115. Thomas Davidson, "Terrorism and Human Smuggling Rings in South and Central America," *Terrorism Monitor* 3, no. 22 (2005), www.jamestown.org/programs/gta/single/?tx_ttnews[tt_news]=611&tx_ttnews[backPid]=180&no_cache=1.

116. US government officials, interviews with the author.

117. Europol (European Police Office), *Facilitated Illegal Immigration into the European Union* (The Hague, The Netherlands: Europol, 2008), www.europol.europa.eu/publications/Serious_Crime_Overviews/Facilitated_illegal_immigration_2008.pdf; Europol, *Facilitated Illegal Immigration into the European Union*, 2009 Fact Sheet (The Hague, The Netherlands: Europol, 2009), www.europol.europa.eu/publications/Serious_Crime_Overviews/Illegal_Immigration_Fact_Sheet_2009.PDF.

118. Ibid.

119. Géraldine Chatelard, *Iraqi Forced Migrants in Jordan: Conditions, Religious Networks, and the Smuggling Process* (Helsinki, Finland: UN Univ. Institute for Development Economics Research, 2003), www.wider.unu.edu/publications/working-papers/discussion-papers/2003/en_GB/dp2003-34/_files/78091728636347261/default/dp2003-34.pdf.

120. Blas Nuñez-Neto, Alison Siskin, and Stephen Viña, *Border Security: Apprehensions of "Other Than Mexicans" Aliens* (Washington, DC: Congressional Research Service, 2005), 21, www.au.af.mil/au/awc/awcgate/crs/rl33097.pdf.

121. An increasing number of women are involved in the business of human smuggling to obtain power, money, and drugs. The sentence for female smugglers who are caught is shorter than those given to men because they are mothers or daughters. See Claudia Nuñez, "Women Are The New Coyotes,"

La Opinión, December 23, 2007, http://news.ncmonline.com/news/view_article.html?article_id=170 fbf6eecdd019ad7e93f66eda8d6b8.

122. Celinda Franco, *The MS-13 and 18th Street Gangs: Emerging Transnational Gang Threats?* (Washington, DC: Congressional Research Service, 2008), 16, www.fas.org/sgp/crs/row/RL34233.pdf.

123. Mary Lagdameo, "Human Smuggling from Fujian to New York," Master Thesis, Univ. of Southern California, 2008, http://digitallibrary.usc.edu/assetserver/controller/item/etd-Lagdameo-2050.pdf; Patrick Radden Keefe, *The Snake Head: An Epic Tale of the Chinatown Underworld and the American Dream* (New York: Doubleday, 2009), 107.

124. DOJ (US Department of Justice), "Foreign National Pleads Guilty to Conspiracy and Alien Smuggling Charges," Press Release, September 22, 2008, www.justice.gov/opa/pr/2008/September/08-crm-844.html.

125. Europol, *EU Organized Crime Threat Assessment 2007* (The Hague, The Netherlands: Europol, 2007), 20–36, www.europol.europa.eu/publications/European_Organised_Crime_Threat_Assessment_%28OCTA%29/OCTA2007.pdf.

126. The distinction between corrupt, complicit, and unwitting help was noted by the author Kamal Sadiq in a book discussion on the "Illicit Market for Citizenship in the Developing World," MPI, Washington, DC, October 1, 2009; see Kamal Sadiq, "Networks of Complicity," in *Paper Citizens: How Illegal Immigrants Acquire Citizenship in Developing Countries* (New York: Oxford Univ. Press, 2009), 57–69.

127. FBI (Federal Bureau of Investigation), Human Smuggling and Trafficking Center (HSTC), *Front Companies: An Invaluable Source for Alien Smuggling Organizations* (Washington, DC: FBI, 2004).

128. Europol, *Facilitated Illegal Immigration into the European Union*, 2009.

129. Rey Koslowski, "The Mobility Money Can Buy: Human Smuggling and Border Control in the European Union," in *The Wall Around the West: State Borders and Immigration Controls in North America and Europe*, ed. Peter Andreas and Timothy Snyder (New York: Rowman & Littlefield, 2000), 212.

130. Danish report says 1,400 Ukrainians are in Denmark on false pretenses. See Undocumented Worker Transitions, *Denmark Country Report: Work Package 2* (Roskilde, Denmark: Undocumented Worker Transitions, 2007), www.undocumentedmigrants.eu/londonmet/library/s15990_3.pdf.

131. DHS (US Department of Homeland Security), US Immigration and Customs Enforcement (ICE), "Los Angeles Man Arrested for Filing Nearly 1,000 Fraudulent Work Visa Petitions: Defendant Made Nearly $5 Million Charging Aliens for Fraudulent Filings," Press Release, July 31, 2008, www.ice.gov/pi/nr/0807/080731losangeles.htm.

132. FBI, *Front Companies*.

133. US Government officials, interview with the author.

134. "Once More Group of Tamils Landed," *De Telegraaf*, March 4, 1997, www.lankaweb.com/news/items00/0503-1.html.

135. James Sterngold, "Bus Company is Accused of Traffic in Illegal Aliens," *The New York Times*, December 11, 2001, www.nytimes.com/2001/12/11/us/bus-company-is-accused-of-traffic-in-illegal-aliens.html.

136. David J. McKenzie, "Paper Walls are Easier to Tear Down: Passport Costs and Legal Barriers to Emigration," Policy Research Working Paper 3783, World Bank, Washington, DC, December 2005.

137. Muninggar Sri Saraswati, "Government to Make Immigration Office More Independent," *The Jakarta Post*, December 31, 2005.

137. "Russian Federal Migration Service Offices Raided in Corruption Probe," *ITAR-TASS News Agency*, April 26, 2007.

138. Steve Marshall, "PNG Immigration Officials Face Bribery Allegations," *ABC News*, October 8, 2008, www.abc.net.au/news/stories/2008/10/08/2384898.htm.

140. DOS, *Country Reports on Terrorism 2007* (Washington, DC: DOS, 2008), www.state.gov/documents/organization/105904.pdf.

141. Other reasons why the United Kingdom suspended visa-free travel for South Africans to its country include the issuance of genuine South African passports by corrupt South African officials to illegal immigrants, refugees, and criminals. See Adriana Stuijt, "UK Cracks Down on South African Passport Holders from March," *Digital Journal*, February 10, 2009, www.digitaljournal. com/article/266934; "UK: Some Won't Need Visa Yet," *News 24*, February 9, 2009, www.news24. com/Content/SouthAfrica/News/1059/c3c88c0980a04b16916f5eaa6d678f0a/09-02-2009-11-01/ UK_Some_wont_need_visa_yet; Senior UK Border Agency official, conversation with the author's research assistant on January 16, 2009, in London, United Kingdom. See Home Office, UK Border Agency, "New Countries Face Tough Visa Rules," Press Release, February 9, 2009, www.bia. homeoffice.gov.uk/sitecontent/newsarticles/newcountriesfacetoughvisarules.

142. "Terrorists obtain S. Africa Passports," *The Associated Press*, July 28, 2004, www.chinadaily.com. cn/english/doc/2004-07/28/content_352358.htm.

143. Stone Martin, "The People Smuggling Gang Who 'Imported' Thousands to Britain," *Financial Times*, January 22, 2008.

144. DOS, *Country Reports on Terrorism 2007*.

145. See Robert Morgenthau, "The Link between Iran and Venezuela: A Crisis in the Making?" *The American Interest Online*; NBC News, "Passport Investigation Suggests Security Hole."

146. Peter Mascini, "Can the Violent Jihad Do Without Sympathizers," *Studies in Conflict and Terrorism* 29, no. 4 (2006): 343–57.

147. Jay Weaver, "Kendall Woman Sold Phony Visas, Feds Say," *Herald.com*, April 7, 2004, www.amren. com/news/news04/04/08/visafraud.html.

148. T. A. Badger, "Probe Closes Visa Section of U.S. Consulate," *The Associated Press*, January 30, 2003.

149. Randal C. Archibold and Andrew Becker, "Border Agents, Lured by the Other Side," *The New York Times*, May 27, 2008, www.nytimes.com/2008/05/27/us/27border.html.

150. Ibid.

151. Ibid.

152. US government officials, interview with the author.

153. Mahesh Buddi, "'Immigration' Check Required," *The Times of India*, May 27, 2008, http://timesofin-dia.indiatimes.com/articleshow/msid-3075082,prtpage-1.cms.

154. Europol (European Police Office), *Facilitated Illegal Immigration into the European Union* (The Hague, The Netherlands: Europol, 2008), www.europol.europa.eu/publications/Serious_Crime_Overviews/ Facilitated_illegal_immigration_2008.pdf.

155. According to the Department of State's (DOS's) annual *Trafficking in Persons Report 2009*, the International Labor Organization (ILO) estimates there are 12.3 million individuals trafficked for purposes of supplying forced, bonded, and commercial sex labor with an estimated 1.39 million of these tied to sex trafficking. See DOS, *Special Reports: Trafficking in Persons Report 2009* (Washington, DC: DOS, 2009), www.state.gov/documents/organization/123357.pdf.

156. "Malaysia Unravels Indonesian Passport Forgery Syndicate," *Antara News*, March 3, 2009.

157. Maryclaire Dale, "Feds: Russian Ring Made $3 Million on Asylum Fraud," *The Associated Press*, July 30, 2008, www.cis.org/node/707.

158. National Commission on Terrorist Attacks upon the United States, "Entry of the 9/11 Hijackers into the United States: Staff Statement No.1," (Washington, DC: National Commission on Terrorist Attacks upon the United States, 2004), http://news.findlaw.com/hdocs/docs/terrorism/911comm-ss1.pdf; interviews with multiple US government officials.

159. Geraldine Chatelard, *Iraqi Forced Migrants in Jordan: Conditions, Religious Networks, and the Smuggling Process* (Florence, Italy: European Univ. Institute, 2002), www.aina.org/articles/chatelard.pdf.

160. A visa foil is the sticker placed on the visa pages of a foreign passport for nonimmigrant or immigrant travel to the United States. It contains the full name of the applicant, the visa type and class, the location of the visa-issuing office, the passport number, sex, date of birth, nationality, the number of applications for admission or the letter "M" for multiple entries, date of issuance, date of expiration, and visa control number. Currently there are two types of visa foils for the United

States: the Teslin and the Lincoln. It is manufactured by a contractor under the supervision of the Government Printing Office and DOS.

161. Remarks by an Immigration and Customs Enforcement (ICE) Forensic Document Lab senior official on September 30, 2009, at MPI in Washington, DC.

162. "Officers Seize 'Fake' Passports," *British Broadcasting Company News*, July 4, 2007, http://news.bbc.co.uk/1/hi/england/london/6269210.stm; "£1m Haul of Fake Passports as Police Smash Counterfeit Ring," *Daily Mail*, July 4, 2007, www.dailymail.co.uk/news/article-466192/1m-haul-fake-passports-police-smash-counterfeit-ring.html.

162. Thomas Fuller, "EU Passports: An Easy-to-Steal Tool for Terrorists," *The New York Times*, January 8, 2002, www.nytimes.com/2002/01/08/news/08iht-passport_ed3_.html?pagewanted=1; Interpol (International Criminal Police Organization), *Trends in Illegal Immigration and Travel Document Fraud* (The Hague, The Netherlands: Interpol, 2007), 17.

164. Visa foils may soon be superseded by virtual electronic visas.

165. DOS, *Report of the Visa Office 2008: Table I, Immigrant and Nonimmigrant Visas Issued at Foreign Service Posts Fiscal Years 2004–2008* (Washington, DC: DOS, 2008), www.travel.state.gov/pdf/FY08-AR-TableI.pdf.

166. DOS publishes the number of B visas it denies every year on its web site. The statistics for FY2009 can be found at DOS, *Adjusted Refusal Rate — B Visas Only by Nationality Fiscal Year 2009* (Washington, DC: DOS, 2009), www.travel.state.gov/pdf/FY09.pdf.

167. Pew Hispanic Center, *Modes of Entry for the Unauthorized Migrant Population* (Washington, DC: Pew Hispanic Center, 2006), http://pewhispanic.org/files/factsheets/19.pdf.

168. Ibid.

169. National Commission on Terrorist Attacks upon the United States, *9/11 and Terrorist Travel* (Franklin, TN: Hillsboro Press, 2004), 11.

170. Diana Jean Schemo, "Diploma Mill Concerns Extend Beyond Fraud," *The New York Times*, June 29, 2008.

171. "DNA Test for UK Asylum Seekers Triggers Protests," *The Times of India,* November 6, 2009, http://timesofindia.indiatimes.com/world/uk/DNA-test-for-UK-asylum-seekers-triggers-protests/articleshow/5201462.cms.

172. Ibid.

173. Anthony van Fossen, "Citizenship for Sale: Passports of Convenience from Pacific Island Tax-Havens," *Commonwealth & Comparative Politics* 45, no. 2 (2007): 138–63.

174. Ibid.

175. Ibid.

176. Van Fossen, "Citizenship for Sale," 138–63.

177. Roxana Hegeman, "Kan. Tribal 'Secretary of State' Gets Prison Term," *The Associated Press*, October 10, 2008, www3.signonsandiego.com/news/2008/oct/10/immigration-indian-tribe-10-10-08/.

178. DHS (US Department of Homeland Security), Office of Immigration Statistics, *2007 Yearbook of Immigration Statistics, Table 3: Persons Obtaining Legal Permanent Resident Status by Region and Country of Birth: Fiscal Years 1998 to 2007* (Washington, DC: DHS, 2007), http://.dhs.gov/xlibrary/assets/statistics/yearbook/2007/ois_2007_yearbook.pdf.

179. DHS officials, interview with the author.

180. DHS officials, interview with the author.

181. Ernesto Rodriguez, Martín Iñiguez, Jesús Gijón, and Roselí Venegas, *Flujos de entradas de extanjeros por la frontera sur terrestre de México registradas por el Instituto Nacional de Migración* (Mexico City, Mexico: Secretaría de Gobernación, Instituto de Migración, Centro de Estudios Migratorios, 2005), http://.inami.gob.mx/estudios/foros/documentos%20basicos/1%20dossier%20flujo%20de%20entradas%20de%20extranjeros%20por%20la%20frontera%20sur%20terrestre%20de%20mexico%20registradas%20por%20el%20instituto%20nacional%20de%20migracion.pdf.

182. Alma Arámbula Reyes and Gabriel Mario Santos Villarreal, *El flujo migratorio centroamericano*

hacia México (Mexico City, Mexico: Servicios de investigación y análisis, Subdirección de Política Exterior, 2007), http://.diputados.gob.mx/cedia/sia/spe/SPE-ISS-19-07.pdf.

183. Ibid.

184. Kathleen Harris, "Report: 14,000 Suspected Illegal Immigrants Detained Last Year," *Toronto Sun*, January 11, 2010, www.torontosun.com/news/canada/2010/01/11/12425881-qmi.html.

185. Interpol, *Trends in Illegal Immigration and Travel Document Fraud*, 20.

186. The Univ. of British Columbia, "UBC Legal Expert Releases Canada's First Stats on Foreign Human Trafficking Victims," Press Release, October 28, 2008, www.publicaffairs.ubc.ca/media/releases/2008/mr-08-143.html.

187. Official in the National Institute of Migration, personal communication with an official.

188. DOS, *Special Reports: Trafficking in Persons Report 2009*, www.state.gov/g/tip/rls/tiprpt/2009/123136.htm.

189. Europol, *Facilitated Illegal Immigration into the European Union*.

190. Interpol, *Trends in Illegal Immigration and Travel Document Fraud*, 13–30.

191. Ibid.

192. Interpol, *People Smuggling* (The Hague, The Netherlands: Interpol, 2009), www.interpol.int/public/THB/PeopleSmuggling/Default.asp.

193. Europol, *EU Organized Crime Threat Assessment 2007* (The Hague, The Netherlands: Europol, 2008), 20–36.

194. Delcan Walsh, Jason Burke, and Giles Tremlett, "Al-Qaida Connection: Foreign Passports Linked to Attacks on West Recovered," *The Guardian*, October 29, 2009, www.guardian.co.uk/world/2009/oct/29/al-qaida-pakistan-taliban-link.

195. Benedetta Berti, "Reassessing the Transnational Terrorism-Criminal Link in South America's Tri-border Area," *Terrorism Monitor* 6, no. 18 (2002), www.jamestown.org/programs/gta/single/?tx_ttnews[tt_news]=611&tx_ttnews[backPid]=180&no_cache=1.

196. Interpol, *Trends in Illegal Immigration and Travel Document Fraud*, 7.

197. Alisa Tang, "Thailand Now Fake Passport Capital for Criminal Underworld, Terrorists," *The Associated Press*, September 8, 2005, www.irrawaddy.org/article.php?art_id=4963.

198. Martin Rudner, "Misuse of Passports: Identity Fraud, the Propensity to Travel, and International Terrorism," *Studies in Conflict and Terrorism* 31, no. 2 (2008): 95–110.

199. Europol, *Facilitated Illegal Immigration into the European Union*.

200. Sandra Laville, Richard Norton-Taylor, and Vikram Dodd, "Student Visa Link to Terror Raids as Gordon Brown Points Finger at Pakistan," *The Guardian*, April 10, 2009, www.guardian.co.uk/uk/2009/apr/10/student-visa-terror-arrests-link.

201. The percentage of student visa applications made in Pakistan rejected by the UK Home Office increased from 64 percent in 2008 to 74 percent in 2009. See Duncan Gardham, "Hidden Threat from Al-Qaeda Sleeper Cells: Al Qaeda Terrorists are Exploiting Loose Visa and Immigration Rules to Enter Britain, the Security Services Fear," *The Guardian*, November 27, 2009, www.telegraph.co.uk/news/6672806/Hidden-threat-from-al-Qaeda-sleeper-cells.html.

202. Daniel Schweimler, "Passport Scandal Hits Argentina," *British Broadcasting Company News*, July 13, 2008, http://news.bbc.co.uk/go/pr/fr-/2/hi/americas/7503844.stm.

203. Statement for the record of Brian Zimmer, Senior Associate, Kelly, Anderson & Associates Inc., "Interrupting Terrorist Travel: Strengthening the Security of International Travel Documents," before the US Senate Committee on the Judiciary, Subcommittee on Terrorism, Technology and Homeland Security, 110th Cong., 1st sess., May 2, 2007, http://judiciary.senate.gov/hearings/testimony.cfm?id=2733&wit_id=6437.

204. Andrew W. Papachristos, "Gang World," *Foreign Policy* March/April (2005): 53.

205. William F, Jasper, "Communism's Resurgence," *The New American*, January 24, 2005.

206. "Passport Investigation Suggests Security Hole," NBC News, December 28, 2007.

207. Kamal Sadiq, *Paper Citizens: How Illegal Immigrants Acquire Citizenship in Developing Countries* (New York: Oxford Univ. Press, 2008).

SECTION II: ACTING AGAINST TERRORISTS, CRIMINALS, AND CONSPIRATORS

INTRODUCTION

A primary goal of securing human mobility is to act against terrorists, members of organized crime networks, and other criminals. In the context of human mobility, enforcement policy seeks to uphold immigration laws at a nation's border and in its interior. In recent years, enforcement policy has focused on how best to prioritize the use of resources against the estimated 12 million unauthorized US residents and the hundreds of thousands entering annually through illegal channels.

This focus needs to be reexamined. The homeland security mission cannot be met by assuming that its intelligence and investigative resources should primarily be used against unauthorized people, even those who are criminals. Instead, the United States must begin with a "zero-based" assessment of the threats to citizens, long-term residents, and others in global travel channels.

Like zero-based budgeting, a zero-based risk assessment of human mobility channels has to begin with identifying the most important missions. This introduction to section II outlines the key threats that the United States and US citizens and residents face with respect to mobility. The three chapters that follow discuss approaches to addressing selected threats.

The key zero-based risk assessment question is: *what are the greatest threats and risks that the global and US mobility infrastructure should address, either because it must be safeguarded from them or because it can respond to them?* Both aspects of the question are important, because US and global mobility channels both comprise critical infrastructure and serve as conduits for terrorists, criminals, and the life-threatening or disruptive movement of people in the form of illegal, precipitous, or uncontrolled large scale migration that places migrants, transit or receiving communities, or states at risk.[1]

The Department of Defense (DOD) and Department of Homeland Security (DHS) have both identified the most important threats from the perspective of defense of the United States and its citizens. Threat lists are the right starting point for defining mobility-related security missions.

Table II.1 Priority Threats and Security Challenges Associated With Human Mobility

Key security challenges identified by DOD Violent extremist movements Spread of weapons of mass destruction (WMDs) Rising powers with sophisticated weapons Failed or failing states Increasing encroachment across the global commons
Major threats identified by DHS High-consequence WMDs Al Qaeda and affiliated terrorist movements Cyber attacks, exploitation and intrusions, and disruptions Natural hazards, pandemics, and infectious diseases Illicit trafficking and transnational crime Smaller-scale terrorism
Combined DOD and DHS security priorities associated with human mobility Trafficking in high-consequence WMDs Major terrorist movements focused on the United States Human trafficking and transnational crime Smaller-scale terrorist and extremist attacks Failed or failing states Increasing encroachment across the global commons

Table II.1 (cont.)

Proposed list of mobility-related security priorities   Terrorist attacks, exploitation, and disruptions of mobility infrastructure   Human smuggling associated with terrorists or serious organized crime   Human traffickers and other high-concern gangs and transnational criminals   Insecure borders that enable safe havens, insurgency, banditry, and uncontrolled illegal flows   Corrupt regimes and human rights violators that contribute to the dangerous movement of people

Source: DOD, "2010 QDR Terms of Reference Fact Sheet," Press Release, April 27, 2009; Homeland Security Council, National Strategy for Homeland Security (Washington, DC: The White House, 2007); DHS, Quadrennial Homeland Security Review (Washington, DC: DHS, 2010).

Both departments' strategists roughly agree that one of the most important threats to national security at present is that posed by terrorists, in particular those who emerge from violent extremist movements and who have potential access to chemical, biological, radiological, nuclear, or high yield explosive (CBRNE) weapons or, in different terms, to weapons of mass destruction (WMDs).[2]

Terrorist attacks are also the most important threats in relation to global mobility infrastructure. Similar to the cybersystem, terrorists may directly attack, disrupt, or exploit human mobility infrastructure. Airline hijackings represent the prime example of terrorist attacks involving human mobility infrastructure. Examples of disruption to critical mobility infrastructure include the systematic corruption of a visa, passport, or border office; sabotage of the international reservations system; or a border- or visa-related terrorist incident leading to curtailing of these channels. Terrorist and criminal exploitation of mobility systems may take the form of exploiting entry channels and mechanisms to gain legal status.

Other than asymmetric terrorism and increased access to WMDs, DOD and DHS do not designate any common security priorities relating to mobility.

DHS highlights two additional mobility-related priorities: illicit trafficking and transnational crime and smaller-scale terrorist and extremist attacks. DOD highlights two others: failed states and encroachment on the global commons (the natural assets outside national jurisdictions, such as outer space or Antarctica). Each of these four is crucially linked to mobility security. Transnational crime and terrorism are on a continuum because terrorist organizations may obtain funding and resources from criminal activity. Transnational crime and failed states come together when large-scale gangs effectively control large swaths of state territory. In both these senses, transnational criminal organizations represent a potential strategic threat.

In the context of illicit trafficking and crime, the most important threats relating to human mobility are human smuggling and human trafficking. Human smuggling is especially important when it may be linked to terrorism, human trafficking, organized crime, or life-threatening illegal migration. Other transnational crimes relating to mobility include abducting children across international borders and traveling to commit sexual abuse.

Transnational crime is also committed by members of groups residing in the United States and traveling back and forth to other countries. US-based transnational criminals include members of MS-13, the Bloods and the Crips, Mexican-US drug-trafficking organizations (DTOs), and groups that prey on new arrivals. Many of these gangs terrorize neighborhoods and block residents from full participation in society.

DOD's list highlights failed or failing states and increasing encroachment across the global commons. Since global travel channels are situated in the global commons, and the global commons are the location of movements of concealed nuclear and radiological materials, DOD's list clearly covers mobility security issues.

Failed or failing states pose a mobility-dimension risk in three ways. First, failed and failing states are characterized by corruption that poses a major problem in preventing terrorist and criminal travel. Terrorists, human-smuggling organizations (HSOs), human-trafficking organizations (HTOs), and other serious organized crime organizations that take part in the illicit market in travel depend on third-party facilitators, from document suppliers to transportation officials. The most important third-party facilitators, as discussed earlier, are corrupt government officials, whether passport officials, visa officers, port officials, or immigration authorities. Finding ways to eliminate the corruption associated with failing states is critical to mobility security.

Second, failed or failing states often have weak border controls. Insecure borders enable terrorist safe havens, insurgency, banditry, and uncontrolled movement of people generally.

Third, states with poor governance, human-rights-violating regimes, and high levels of corruption are potential sources of precipitous, uncontrolled migration. These flows represent a danger to law-abiding people on the move and they may violate other countries' border procedures and immigration laws. Most refugees and labor migrants do not pose threats of terrorism, violence, or criminality. Large uncontrolled movements, however, undermine the rule of law and may pose challenges to the absorptive capacities of societies; screening is no less important for these groups.[3]

DHS and DOD threats lists can be drawn upon to create a consolidated list of the areas of attention that are most important for securing human mobility:

- Terrorist-caused attacks, disruption, and exploitation of mobility infrastructure
- HSOs associated with terrorists, serious organized crime, and corruption
- HTOs and other high-concern transnational criminals
- Insecure borders that enable safe havens, insurgency, banditry, trafficking, and uncontrolled illegal flows
- Corrupt regimes and human rights violators that contribute to life-threatening, illegal, and uncontrolled movement of people

In the future, considerations relating to migration caused by global warming and other environmental and resource-related changes may need to be added to this list since they could overwhelm even the most well-managed and governed mobility channels.

The three chapters in this section focus on some of the key groups responsible for the negative side of international mobility: terrorists; corrupt regimes; human smugglers associated with terrorism, human trafficking, and serious organized crime; and transnational criminal gangs preying on residents of US and Central American cities. The chapters highlight new methods of countering these groups and preventing their attacks and crimes.

Chapter 4 highlights the need to prioritize terrorist travel and to modernize law-enforcement and administrative processes to deal with globally networked terrorist organizations and HSOs. Chapter 5 proposes that prevention of violent crime become the hallmark of US Immigration and Customs Enforcement's (ICE's) approach to eliminating gang crime in immigrant communities. Chapter 6 highlights travel bans, a relatively recent tool for marshalling global resolve against terrorists and major human rights violators.

Chapter 4: Terrorist Travel and Human-Smuggling Organizations: Information, Analysis, Action

Policy Preview: *Terrorist and criminal travel should be an area of systematic focus by domestic and international law-enforcement and intelligence organizations. In particular:*

- *The National Terrorist Travel Strategy produced by the National Counterterrorism Center (NCTC) should be updated*
- *Mobility-related agencies should establish dedicated strategic operational analysis units and coordinate this work*
- *The Human Smuggling and Trafficking Center (HSTC), a fusion center operated by the departments of Homeland Security, Justice, and State (DHS, DOJ, and DOS), should be strengthened and charged with producing an annual report on illegal movement and its market*
- *US Immigration and Customs Enforcement's (ICE's) Extra-Territorial Criminal Travel Strike Force (ECT) should be funded and expanded to include other agencies*
- *Intelligence from ICE should be used to initiate more criminal investigations and prosecutions, as well as more civil penalties*
- *The number of Bureau of Diplomatic Security's (DS's) Resident Security Officer-Investigator (RSO-I) positions should be increased*
- *Congress should legislate increased penalties for human-smuggling crimes that have a nexus with terrorism or transnational organized crime, especially by groups operating in conflict zones*

Based on a zero-based assessment, and relying on current DOD and DHS strategic assessments, the foremost threats to the United States in the context of securing human mobility are:
- Terrorist attacks, disruption, and exploitation of mobility infrastructure
- Human smuggling associated with terrorists, human traffickers, and organized criminal enterprises
- Human trafficking and other transnational criminal activity
- Insurgency, banditry, trafficking, and uncontrolled illegal flows created by insecure borders
- Life-threatening, illegal, and uncontrolled movement of people

The United States targets terrorists unilaterally, regionally, and through multilateral efforts at the United Nations (UN) and elsewhere. Its multidimensional approach should be brought to bear more effectively on transnational organized crime, including human trafficking and smuggling, consistent with relevant UN agreements (discussed in chapter 11). To take a leading role in strengthening multilateral capacity against transnational organized crime, the United States needs a strong foundation in its own strategy and use of domestic resources. This chapter concerns domestic agencies with the key resources to counter human-smuggling organizations (HSOs) and human-trafficking organizations (HTOs) and the illicit market in movement.

Because of the way ICE, DS, and other law-enforcement agencies count and report investigations, the level of activity on these priorities is hard to discern. Despite some effective investigative strategies, however, it appears that sufficient attention is not afforded to them.

Terrorist attacks with weapons of mass destruction (WMDs), enabled by terrorist travel and facilitated by human-smuggling networks, are the top threat against which mobility-related investigative resources must be directed. DHS is giving top priority to supporting the government of Mexico's efforts against drug-trafficking organizations (DTOs). With congressional backing, ICE has focused on the southwest US border including working with federal prosecutors to create zero-tolerance zones for immigration violations, however minor. Overall, investigations, deportations, detentions, and removals involving criminal aliens and other immigration law violators consume most ICE resources.

Seeking out and dismantling terrorist cells and the illicit travel pathways they use is a critical dimension of counterterrorism. Yet ICE has devoted more resources to its cross-border drug, gun, and money criminal cases than it has to investigations of human smugglers who may have a terrorist nexus. Similarly, DS, which has jurisdiction over visa and passport fraud, tends to focus more on single-offender malfeasance at consulates or passport offices than on dismantling the market in illicit travel documents, which intersects with terrorist travel, human trafficking, and other serious criminality. To some extent, existing priorities are mandated by Congress. The number of national-security-related investigations relative to available leads and opportunities is unclear.

But with the asymmetric potential of chemical, biological, radiological, nuclear, and high yield explosive (CBRNE) WMDs, a serious debate needs to occur at DHS, DOJ, DOS, and the National Security Council (NSC) about how to allocate resources within and across federal agencies against the different streams of illicit movement. This chapter seeks to make some specific suggestions that might help shape the debate.

National Strategy to Secure Human Mobility against Terrorism

There is a consensus in the counterterrorism community that since September 11, 2001, security throughout the US travel-and-entry system and in global travel networks generally has lowered the risk of clandestine entry by terrorists, raised obstacles and costs, and had a deterrent effect by denying easy access. But the problem of attacks, disruptions, and exploitation of travel channels by terrorists and serious criminals persists. In addition, the methods used by such networks continually change. Thus, efforts to thwart terrorist entry must continue to adapt and to improve.

What is the current strategy to counter illicit movement? There are many useful programs, especially new ones in which ICE's immigration and customs financial crimes tactics are brought to bear against HSOs and HTOs. In addition, DS is using more sophisticated tactics against illicit travel document networks. Nonetheless, a coherent interagency strategy to act against terrorists and criminals who exploit mobility channels must still be developed. A sense of goals and benchmarks would be helpful, especially in the context of long-term nuclear and other chemical, radiological, and biological threats, and the war against Mexican DTOs. This challenge will be significant, however, given the multiple departments and agencies and types of authorities that exist at the federal level alone, as shown in Box 4.1.

Box 4.1 Federal Departments and Agencies with Roles in Securing Human Mobility

White House
National Security Council (NSC)

Homeland Security Council

Department of Homeland Security (DHS)
DHS senior leadership

Offices of Intelligence and Analysis, Policy, United States Visitor and Immigrant Status Indicator Technology Program (US-VISIT), Risk Assessment, and other support offices

US Customs and Border Protection (CBP)**

US Immigration and Customs Enforcement (ICE)*

US Citizenship and Immigration Services (USCIS)**

US Coast Guard (USCG)

Transportation Security Administration (TSA)**

Department of State (DOS)
Bureau of Consular Affairs (CA)**

Bureau of Diplomatic Security (DS)*

Coordinator for Counterterrorism

International Narcotics and Law Enforcement (INL)

Population, Refugees, and Migration

Office to Monitor and Combat Trafficking in Persons

Intelligence and Research (INR)

US Agency for International Development (USAID)

Economic Bureau

Regional bureaus

Department of Justice (DOJ)
Criminal Division

National Security Division

Civil Rights Division

US Attorneys/Executive Office

Federal Bureau of Investigation (FBI)/ Counterterrorism

FBI's Terrorist Screening Center (TSC)

Intelligence community (outside listed departments)

Directorate of National Intelligence (DNI)

National Counterterrorism Center (NCTC)

Central Intelligence Agency (CIA)

National Security Agency (NSA)

Department of Defense (DOD)
Joint chiefs of staff and strategic components

DOD components relating to trafficking

DOD components involved in border operations and training

DOD combatant commanders

Defense Intelligence Agency (DIA)

* Investigative agency **Referral agency

In 2006 NCTC produced the National Strategy to Combat Terrorist Travel (NSCTT).[4] While NSCTT highlighted some key operational approaches, it was little more than a compendium of different agency programs and lacked goals and benchmarks. The NSCTT needs to be reconceived with the full participation of the Homeland Security Secretary and coordination by NSC and DNI. Almost a decade after 9/11, a broader strategy that covers terrorist travel, mobility crimes, and the other threats and risks is achievable — and long overdue. A team for this purpose could be built at the Human Smuggling and Trafficking Center (HSTC), which is a DHS-Justice-State fusion center statutorily linked to the NCTC.

The initial NSCTT stated that its goal was "to fight terrorist travel globally."[5] A second edition of the strategy would be on firmer footing if it were retitled the National Strategy to Secure Human Mobility (NSSHM) and if it set specific goals with respect to terrorist travel and other purposes.

The NSCTT had two pillars and six strategic objectives:

1. Enhance US and foreign-partner capabilities to constrain terrorist mobility overseas
- Suppress terrorists' ability to cross international borders
- Help partner nations build capacity to limit terrorist travel
- Deny terrorists access to resources that facilitate terrorist travel

2. Deny terrorists the ability to enter, exit, and travel within the United States
- Inhibit terrorists from crossing US borders
- Enhance US government capabilities to detect and constrain terrorist travel within the United States
- Strengthen US identity-verification systems[6]

The problem of clandestine and uncontrolled travel rests, in part, on the immense variety of pathways available for travel and the complex forces that drive movement. Global movement of people involves a dynamic network of travelers, travel agents, transportation companies, private and public legitimate intermediaries and complicit facilitators, and mobility officials of all kinds — passport, consular, territorial and marine border, port of entry, and immigration/customs — dispersed across various countries. The challenge is to judge where the most powerful and pernicious nodes and weakest links are, and to dismantle and strengthen those, respectively, with the right short- and long-term approaches. Only proactive strategies can create the resilient and secure mobility channels that our era of mobility and risk demands.

First, the concept of risk management should drive the strategy so that appropriate priorities can be set and challenges defined. Risk management takes into account threats, vulnerabilities, and consequences, enabling resources to be directed toward those activities where risk is highest. Second, the divide between US activity domestically (inhibiting terrorists from crossing US borders) and outside the United States (suppressing terrorists' ability to cross international borders) should be eliminated, since HSOs are transnational organizations. This would be consistent with the 9/11 Commission's conclusion that the United States failed in large measure to detect the plot because of a domestic/foreign divide that existed among intelligence and law-enforcement agencies.

The NSSHM should take as its terrorist-travel-related goal preclusion of terrorist attacks, and disruption of terrorist activity in global travel channels directed at the United States and at US persons and interests. The reduction in risk could be measured against a risk assessment prepared by HSTC, discussed below. Third, the full range of methods should be considered, as discussed in box 4.2.

Box 4.2 Methods of Mobility Security in the Context of Homeland Security

The concepts of border security and immigration enforcement convey a limited sense of the potential operational strategies against terrorists, criminal organizations, and illegal migration. The following protective approaches apply to securing human mobility in the context of homeland security.

Preclusion: the strategic goal of making impossible the events sought to be avoided. *Example:* as long as there are no entries by foreign terrorists, the sum total of protective approaches may be deemed successful.

Preemption: proactive measures to stop an occurrence before it can take place. *Example:* to dismantle a terrorist travel cell before it can insert its operatives into the United States.

Disruption: to interfere with or set up obstacles to a terrorist event or a long-term threat. *Example:* intelligence operations in terrorist travel channels.

Interdiction: to physically block movement. *Example:* arrest of a migrant crossing a border illegally or in transit to a border with the intent to cross illegally.

Box 4.2 (cont.)

Prevention: strategies, including law enforcement, that end or reduce the occurrence of unwanted events.
Example: fingerprinting fixes identities of visa applicants, preventing identity switches between visa acquisition and presentation at a port of entry.

Deterrence: strategies to change people's motivations and actions such that they do not engage in the unwanted activity.
Example: combined enforcement tactics, community moral suasion, and provision of opportunities to deter youth gangs from violence and drug dealing.

Dissuasion: tactics that persuade people not to engage in the unwanted conduct.
Example: programs that persuade young women that human smugglers may turn out to be human traffickers.

Source: Author's compilation.

The NSCTT presents many of the fundamental concepts and unclassified methods with which to move forward. These include a focus on travel documents, screening, and action against HSOs. In a revised strategy, more thought should be given on how to:

- Make the rule of law in global mobility channels a norm
- Build the travel-ban program
- Identify and close weak links in the lawful system of travel
- Enhance US and multilateral coordination in action against terrorist travel networks, HTOs, and larger HSOs
- Establish accepted minimum standards for port-of-entry and border management and a systematic means of working toward their implementation
- Further upgrade the travel-document regime and work toward globally interoperable screening functions
- Bring successful anticorruption norms and practices into global movement channels
- Enhance strategic operational analysis of terrorist and other illicit-travel methods
- Unify across agencies and improve accuracy and fairness in border screening
- Coordinate foreign assistance for mobility management

Strategies can be more trouble than they are worth and there has been a proliferation of them in recent years. In the case of securing human movement, there is a need to concentrate attention on the most consequential risks, to employ the highest value methods, and to make optimal use of investigative, intelligence, prosecutorial, and other resources. Such strategies can help shape the implementation of goals and objectives that are set forth in the first Quadrennial Homeland Security Review (QHSR) and subsequent reviews.

Strategic Operational Analysis Units

Policy discussion on terrorist and criminal access to the United States virtually always omits reference to a body of empirical findings and to specific goals. Instead it refers to limited descriptions of illegal movement and typically invokes the general merits of border security, interior enforcement, or various types of investigations. In the immediate period following 9/11, it was understandable that action to prevent dangerous individuals from traveling to and entering the United States would be taken as swiftly as possible, based on the information at hand.

But illicit movement (in general) and terrorist travel (in particular) present major challenges for preclusive strategy. Unlike human trafficking, for example, where the organizational head of the HTO maintains long-term relationships with HSOs, terrorist travel is for the most part episodic and hard to spot. This makes finding terrorists through their travel practices difficult.

The single most important next step would be for the several agencies involved in securing human movement — DS, CBP, ICE, USCIS, CA, USCG, the United States Visitor and Immigrant Status Indicator Technology Program (US-VISIT), and TSC, among other operational agencies — to form separate or joint strategic operational analysis units that support their own agencies, and support the DHS Office of Intelligence and Analysis, DHS Office of Policy, HSTC, and NCTC. Of course, this type of analysis should also be a priority for NCTC, which exercises strategic operational authority over efforts to counter terrorist travel. The goal is to move from tactical to strategic operational analysis and to share this analysis extensively through HSTC.

The emphasis of all of these agencies since 9/11 has not been on strategic operational analysis. It has been on "connecting the dots"; that is, on ensuring that each agency's investigations do not miss crucial information by improving collection, building an information-sharing environment, and providing operational and tactical support in the form of analysis to frontline investigators and field agents. A second area of emphasis has been on developing more effective screening processes, including biometrics, to support passport, visa, and immigration-benefit decisions.

Actionable Regulatory and Strategic Operational Information

Notwithstanding these critical and ongoing agendas, mobility-related investigative, screening, and adjudicatory units must make better use of the information they generate, separately and jointly. Law-enforcement and adjudicatory agencies have absorbed the concept of developing actionable or tactical intelligence and analysis; now they must invest in the idea of actionable regulatory and strategic operational information. That means organizing the information that is in the possession of DHS and other agencies with mobility-related responsibilities so that it can be used for purposes beyond the immediate function of referring cases; analyzing travel documents; and making visa, entry, and immigration-benefit decisions. Actionable regulatory information is a description of a pattern or practice gleaned from analysis of the facts on the ground, enabling policymakers and managers to propose new regulations, laws, diplomatic initiatives, and programs. Actionable strategic operational information is a description of a pattern or practice gleaned from analysis of the facts, enabling policymakers and managers to adjust frontline resources, investigations, or processes.

There are five reasons why strategic operational analysis is important for securing human movement. First, it would help with very difficult problems of resource allocation. The various screening methods and intelligence programs now in place — including US-VISIT, the Student and Exchange Visitor Information System (SEVIS) run by ICE; other programs run by USCIS, CBP, and TSC; as well as passport and visa officers — generate thousands upon thousands of leads or hits against various databases. By setting up a strategic operational analysis unit that routinely assesses the number of true hits relative to the number of referrals and that looks at the types of cases that emerge from them, the homeland security, crime control, and immigration compliance communities can set priorities and devise solutions based on the specific patterns they are actually seeing. New models can be tested and algorithms adjusted.

Second, strategic operational analysis enables law-enforcement agencies to shift from after-the-fact response to prevention, from a reactive to a proactive or preventive posture. For example, CBP's National Targeting Center (NTC) uses machine-aided information analysis, while ICE uses leads generated by SEVIS; but these are screening procedures, not operational analysis. Third, in the context of terrorism and serious crime, it is very important to know what information an agency possesses and its implications — as well as for that information to be shared across relevant agencies. As the 9/11 attacks demonstrated, "not knowing what you know" can lead to catastrophic consequences. Fourth, basic knowledge about the methods and patterns of movement of people that governments perceive to be dangerous, that pose risks, or that undermine lawful order is a necessary foundation for policy and strategy about how best to prevent such movement. Fifth, making a reasonable amount of information about the market in illegal travel available to the public will also build congressional support, public awareness, confidence, participation in mobility security, and resilience after an incident occurs.[7]

What Information Matters?

Law enforcement in the context of movement typically analyzes the number of agents needed; hours per full-time employee; and how many arrests, prosecutions, and convictions occur in a year. Strategic operational questions inform enforcement, regulatory, intelligence, and foreign policy. The following information should be developed in order to inform policymaking:

- Major channels of terrorist travel
- Major channels of organized-crime travel
- Major HTOs and HSOs and routes identified and disrupted, by nationality
- Travel documents of choice for terrorists and criminals
- Country-by-country travel-document security assessments
- Visa and passport policies that draw HSOs to transit particular countries
- Annual figures on the number of watchlisted individuals, broken down by those identified by consular offices, at ports of entry, and within the U.S.
- The number of intercepted watchlisted individuals by visa category they obtained or sought
- Criminal laws that provide insufficient deterrence to HTOs and HSOs
- The number of lost and stolen passports by country and year
- The number of fraudulent passports by type, nation of origin, and the government officials or agencies that detected them
- The number of incidents referred for criminal investigation by visa category
- Country-by-country corruption assessments (document, immigration, border)
- Assessments of corruption within transportation organizations

Individual government officials, especially agents, inspectors, and analysts possess considerable information about these subjects based on their field experience. But this knowledge has not been systematically captured and analyzed in order to inform policymaking. For these reasons, the baseline of common knowledge with respect to how terrorists, criminal networks, or individuals move around the globe is considerably lower than the level of understanding about the people and practices underpinning the illicit movement of terrorist finance, arms, and drugs, although these arenas overlap considerably.[8]

Strategic operational policy questions provide actionable regulatory and strategic operational information. For example, strategies to counter terrorist travel might be based on information related to terrorist reliance on insiders, in particular human smugglers and corrupt officials. Passport design issues might be driven by information on the reliance by illegal entrants on multiple passports or fraudulent documents. Strategies to address corruption might be based on assessments of the level and location of travel-and-immigration-system-related corruption. And regulatory structures and enforcement strategies could be revisited based on the prevalence of fraud by visa category.

Strategic operational units in the relevant agencies could also coordinate in establishing metrics and benchmarks.[9] The point of this discussion, however, is to emphasize their ability to improve investigative and preclusive outcomes. Policymakers, managers, and law-enforcement analysts and investigators would have a direct interest in the success of such units.

The Human Smuggling and Trafficking Center

Congress established the HSTC in the Intelligence Reform and Terrorism Prevention Act of 2004. It is a fusion center and distribution point for intelligence and information about terrorist travel, human trafficking, and human smuggling. The secretary of state, homeland security secretary, attorney general, and members of the intelligence community oversee it, though its day-to-day operations are managed by ICE. Its five responsibilities are to:

- Facilitate the broad dissemination of all-source information
- Prepare strategic assessments
- Identify issues for interagency action
- Coordinate select initiatives when requested by operational agencies
- Work and exchange information with allied foreign governments and organizations

HSTC is important because of the complexity of the illicit market in movement and available pathways for clandestine travel. There have and will always be simple smuggling schemes that involve hiding someone in the trunk of a car, walking many miles across the Arizona desert, swimming across a river, or trying to use an obviously counterfeit travel document. But these schemes are not the major concern related to terrorist travel. Today's human smuggler is sophisticated enough to match the visa requirements to the passports and determine the most affordable routes for his loads. Or even more effective, the HSO head may invest in relationships with corrupt officials to obtain a genuine visa. Only a fusion center without the blinders of a particular agency can bring all the necessary players together to make assessments and decide what can be done to address sophisticated threats of this kind.

The idea for HSTC originated about a decade ago but the center still has not fully hit its stride. Fusion centers at the federal level, like those at the state level, are still an organizational novelty and an interagency puzzle to be solved. A basic problem for HSTC is a breakdown in its relationship with NCTC, and the lack of participation by the FBI since the inception of HSTC. In particular, it is unclear how HSTC can fulfill its statutory mandate to serve as a fusion center for all-source information or even to prepare its annual report on terrorist travel, The Threat from Terrorist Travel and How Illicit Facilitators Try to Defeat US and Foreign Security Systems. (This report is classified and provided to Congress and customers in the executive branch.) The HSTC report should provide the factual foundation for a future National Strategy to Secure Human Mobility.

HSTC should be revitalized and its relationship with NCTC clarified and put on a sound footing. One possibility is instead of ICE running HSTC exclusively, which it does now as part of its National Security Investigations Division, there should also be a reporting line to the DHS Office of Intelligence and Analysis (I&A), with part of the HSTC budget falling under the DHS intelligence budget. HSTC, to that extent, would act within the current National Implementation Plan for the War on Terror[10] (and its successors) and submit collection priorities through I&A as a participant in the intelligence community. There could also be rotating directors from the three founding departments or alternately from DS, ICE or I&A, DOJ, and NCTC. However it is done, there needs to be a means of bringing NCTC back to the center (enabling HSTC to perform its function of supporting NCTC in its efforts to counter terrorist mobility) and of integrating the FBI into the organization.

In reconsidering the HSTC structure, one goal should be to vest enough authority in the organization such that it can take over the operational targeting role of the NSC. If everyone can be brought to the table at HSTC, it seems unnecessary to locate these decisions in the White House, although the NSC could still oversee the function.

HSTC has played an important role in communicating with foreign governments over sensitive questions of visa policy, where it has identified significant weak links exploited by HSOs and HTOs. This initiative should expand. HSTC could also take a coordinating role in US agency training and assistance for foreign partners. Finally, it could play a role in supporting the development and implementation of travel bans, serving as a clearinghouse for bans imposed by the UN Security Council (UNSC), the European Union, and individual countries, as well as those imposed by the United States. (Travel bans are discussed in chapter 6.) However, if it is to perform leadership functions and effectively serve its constituent departments, HSTC must be led by senior-level officials.

Extra-Territorial Criminal Travel Strike Force (ECT)

The ECT is a joint DOJ-ICE initiative that targets global smuggling organizations that have or potentially have a nexus to terrorism, whether or not the smugglers are aware of the linkage. It aims at disrupting smuggling pipelines and criminal travel networks that terrorists could use to enter the United States. It is a proactive initiative that relies on intelligence, investigation, prosecution, and often also ancillary diplomatic activity.

Like HSTC, ECT needs attention and support, but recommendations to improve its effectiveness are simpler. First, ECT should become an interagency strike force run by ICE, much as the Joint Terrorism Task Forces (JTTFs) are run by the FBI. Second, it should be responsive to an interagency, NSC-approved list of targets for prosecution. Third, it should be adequately resourced.

The ECT concept has predecessors in the Alien Smuggling Task Force (ASTF) formed pursuant to a presidential directive issued by President Clinton. This task force disrupted dozens of criminal-smuggling networks, many with nodes in the Middle East.

The NSC Migrant Smuggling and Trafficking Interagency Working Group (IWG) identifies the most dangerous HSOs for coordinated interagency action.[11] The NSC working group has provided targeting information to investigators, prosecutors, analysts, diplomatic, regulatory personnel, and others who assemble on an ad hoc basis. Scores of cases have been prosecuted, with ICE in the lead on most of them.

As originally designed, ECT is strictly an ICE unit that therefore cannot be designated as the interagency group responsive to the IWG list of HSOs with a potential nexus to terrorism. Instead, a case is given ECT status by determination of a board of ICE and DOJ senior staff, which meets periodically to review the human smuggling and trafficking investigative and intelligence file. The ICE list, in contrast to the IWG list, remains at ICE rather than being assigned to an interagency group. Rather than being supported exclusively by ICE, ECT should essentially become the global jump team for the IWG. The strike force should be expanded to include agents and analysts from other agencies, which have supported the IWG. DS is especially important to include, because it has expertise in illicit travel documents and production cells and networks touching consulates around the world. ECT should also reach out to the noninvestigative agencies that participate in IWG.

A presidential directive or congressional action ought to be able to create a targeting group based at HSTC. Investigations taken on by ECT would resemble the following ICE cases:

- *United States v. Jalal Sadat Moheisen,* in which several defendants were prosecuted and convicted for smuggling to Miami four confidential informants who identified themselves as the Revolutionary Armed Forces of Columbian (FARC) guerillas.[12]

- *United States v. Maher Jared,* in which an Ecuadorean-based, Palestinian national was prosecuted and convicted for smuggling US-bound Middle Eastern aliens.[13]

- United States v. Mohammad Hussein Assadi, in which a well-known Latin-American-based Iranian national was prosecuted and convicted for smuggling aliens to the United States.[14]

- *United States v. Ashraf Abdallah,* in which a Guatemalan-based Egyptian national was prosecuted and convicted for smuggling aliens from Egypt and other Middle Eastern countries to the United States.[15]

- *United States v. Neeran Zaia,* in which a Canada-based Jordanian national was prosecuted and convicted of operating front businesses in Canada and Jordan, as well as recruiting and smuggling Middle Eastern aliens to the United States.[16]

The ECT-IWG should target what could be called "super HSOs," which operate across continents and individual human-smuggling groups as well as HSOs with a possible nexus to terrorism. The ECT-IWG might also consider injecting another element into the case-selection process: sowing distrust in travel networks for clandestine travelers. What clandestine travelers seek is complicit travel networks. The need for trust runs two ways: clandestine travelers want trustworthy travel facilitators, and HSOs and their travel facilitators want to know that their clients are trustworthy. Using undercover agents to imitate travelers could help catch and prosecute illicit travel facilitators and make the others who hear about such operations less willing to deal with new customers. Using undercover agents to imitate illicit travel facilitators — setting up "sting" fake-ID shops, for example — can catch unknown clandestine travelers and make others less willing to seek out illicit-travel facilitators. Such operations could be done by placing an informant in an existing HSO or other travel node or by constructing a new operation on either side of the transaction. Sowing distrust has a deterrent effect, over and above the incapacitation of specific terrorist groups or service providers.[17] That same penetration could also find possible links to terrorist organizations. This makes cases important for what they preclude even more than for the level or number of travel facilitators prosecuted.

Because of the complexity of these cases, the need to work with foreign counterparts, and the mix of tactics involved, the program should be assessed not on numbers of prosecutions of individuals but on the value of subjects being investigated and their role in the illicit mobility market. What ECT is trying to do is preclude access to mobility by threats to the United States. As one DOJ official said, "ECT is in the business of not knowing when you stop something bad from happening, with the added bonus of absolutely knowing that you don't."[18]

To address the globalization of HSOs, ICE has made real progress in helping to establish vetted units in foreign law-enforcement agencies with which it can partner in ECT investigations. Almost a dozen units are active in about nine locations in Mexico, Latin America, and the Caribbean. These efforts are forming a solid foundation for US leadership in UN and other multilateral efforts against human trafficking and smuggling organizations.[19] The new

Mutual Legal Assistance Treaty (MLAT) signed with the European Union and taking effect February 1, 2010, will create new transatlantic investigative opportunities by facilitating information sharing and providing for integrated investigations.[20] This treaty may serve as a model for future relations with other partners, for example, Canada. (International information-sharing agreements are discussed in chapter 9.)

ECT is an unfunded program; that is, it has so far been funded by scraping the bottom of the barrel for monies in other ICE accounts. That is not to say that human-smuggling investigations are unfunded. ICE commits resources to investigating human smuggling, human trafficking, HSOs, and HTOs, although the resource allocation slipped in 2008. ICE dedicated 986,600 hours to human-smuggling and human-trafficking casework, which corresponds to approximately 583 full-time agents. In fiscal year 2008, ICE conducted 432 human trafficking investigations, of which 262 were of commercial sexual exploitation and 170 of forced labor. These investigations led ICE and prosecutors to make 189 criminal and 483 administrative arrests, and secure 126 indictments, 126 convictions,[21] and $2,368,435 in seized assets. ICE also led over 2,300 human-smuggling investigations that year leading to 2,138 arrests, 1,353 indictments, 1,468 convictions,[22] and $16,660,574 in seized assets.

In FY2008, ICE dedicated 789,463 hours to the same type of casework, corresponding to approximately 465 full-time agents and $11,848,763 in asset seizures.[23]

Notwithstanding the ongoing casework, ECT targets the highest-priority threats and has had some very promising accomplishments. It deserves dedicated funding for agents, analysts, and prosecutors; strong interagency participation; appropriate targeting authority; and support from Congress.

Diplomatic Security Resident Security Officer Investigators

DS, DHS's law-enforcement arm, is best known for its resident security officers (RSOs) whose mission is to protect US embassies and consulates. In the same way that the US Secret Service protects the president and other officials, and also has jurisdiction over counterfeit currency, financial, and identity crimes, DS also has a legal mandate to protect the integrity of the US passport and visa. Its Criminal Investigation Division has a Passport Fraud Branch and a

Visa Fraud Branch, responsible for investigating the issuance, acquisition, and use of fraudulent passports and visas.

DS visa investigations have historically given priority to malfeasance in consulates.[24] Since 9/11, at the direction of Congress, DS's investigative strategy has expanded to incorporate a focus on travel-document production cells and networks. DS has 75 RSO-Is on board, posted throughout Asia, the Middle East, Russia and former Soviet states, Canada, Central and South America, and the Caribbean, with 48 additional positions recently approved.[25] This coverage is beginning to give DS the ability to systematically monitor and probe visa applications that pose a potential security risk, as well as to develop a global picture of the market in illicit travel documents and associated HSOs and HTOs and the methods by which illicit-travel facilitators target US consulates. Already present in US embassies and trained in the language, DS investigators routinely work with foreign law-enforcement agencies. DS has close ties to CA but more limited dealings with ICE, which has few agents involved with immigration cases overseas — an additional reason for establishing the ECT.[26]

One of the unexpected decisions in the aftermath of 9/11 was to establish DHS/ICE Visa Security Officers in consulates to investigate suspicious visa applications with the authority to veto visa issuance. DS agents have skills relevant to the position, including language training, well-established liaison relationships, clearances, familiarity with the visa process, knowledge of counterintelligence, and experience of foreign postings. ICE requires none of this training and has none of this experience; its singular asset is its databases. Rather than assigning less-prepared DHS Visa Security Officers to this task, consideration should be given to DS agents. In particular, DS agents should be given access to DHS databases. If DHS does not want to give up the program and Congress wants to preserve it, DHS should reimburse DS for supplying its agents to fill at least some of these positions, especially where they have the language skills, clearances, and local or regional experience.

Regardless, DS by the summer of 2010 should have in place full-time investigators in all visa-issuing posts or regionally to cover small posts. Building on the experience of an interagency ECT, ICE should also place investigators overseas dedicated to conducting HSO and HTO investigations and illicit travel investigations generally, including in partnership with DS. DS and ICE should be building a strong global partnership to dismantle HSOs and HTOs and the document networks linked to them. Sooner or later the thorny, unresolved matter of how to organize an expanded law-enforcement presence in general, and mobility-related and other DHS investigators in foreign countries in particular, has to be resolved.

Resources for Parallel Construction of Intelligence-Driven Cases

The collection of evidence usable at trial, when the subject was initially identified using intelligence information, is known as parallel construction. As it stands, ICE devotes insufficient resources to parallel construction. This may be the reason why intelligence officials estimated in 2008 that as many as 50 percent of potential cases failed to be fully developed. Where no further investigation is conducted, ICE may instead deport the individual.

Action against al Qaeda and associated terrorist organizations takes place in military, intelligence, law-enforcement, and mobility-related arenas, which include administrative processes and civil and criminal enforcement methods. Border and immigration agencies usually encounter terrorists who have already been identified and placed on a classified terrorist identities list. However, they may also encounter terrorists in the first instance, on the visa line, at ports of entry, or outside ports of entry.

Counterterror successes against al Qaeda and similarly networked groups almost always have a link to intelligence collection. Terrorist groups strive to maintain secrecy so as not to be discovered. Intelligence and counterterrorism programs are secret to protect classified sources and methods and to prevent the release of information that would be useful to adversaries.

One of the problems that arise from dependence on classified information is that the information it provides about potential terrorists may not always be pursued effectively. Some form of judicial process should be the default position. In the absence of special courts and procedures dedicated to terrorist cases, it is a laborious and legally challenging process to figure out ways to re-create intelligence that may legally and effectively substitute in a judicial proceeding for information obtained through classified means. This has been a problem for US law-enforcement agencies dealing with mobility-related intelligence. Investigators and analysts should be assigned in sufficient numbers and provided sufficient training to perform this critical role. The perfecting of criminal cases can lead to the development of more evidence and intelligence. Even if all the possible cases were being developed and referred to prosecutors, there would still be instances where DHS would choose to repatriate an individual rather than seek to develop the case further. In some cases it is not possible to re-create intelligence as evidence. Some suspected terrorists are let go for this reason. While this is a problem that extends well beyond terrorist-travel cases, these investigations comprise a pool of cases or operations that can be monitored and examined as a basis for considering whether the current rules of evidence are sufficient to support terrorism prosecutions or actions in civil immigration proceedings.

A second problem with the need to rely on classified intelligence is that efforts against terrorists are largely secret from the public. Without knowing about DHS successes, the public cannot gain sufficient confidence that DHS is doing its job. Some middle course of public reporting between total secrecy and tipping off criminals and terrorists or revealing intelligence sources and methods needs be found. Some annual public reporting, perhaps through the HSTC, would provide the public with the ongoing reassurance that contributes to public confidence in DHS's management of the border and immigration systems, and therefore to the long-term resilience of the US population.

Corruption Associated with Human Smuggling and Trafficking

Human smuggling and human trafficking may facilitate a range of criminal and terrorist activities. Corruption and trafficking in conflict zones are among the collateral crimes that should receive priority in the human-smuggling and human-trafficking context. Like the Mexican-US DTOs, HSOs and HTOs corrupt government and private-sector officials, and in doing so, undermine and weaken fragile states, destroy good governance, and fuel violent conflict.

The fight against corruption in the context of securing human mobility must be waged against the human smugglers and traffickers who bribe officials; against US agents and inspectors who take bribes; and against foreign public- and private-sector officials who take bribes, initiate corrupt activities, and run criminal enterprises.

Corrupt officials can be prosecuted for allowing unauthorized persons to cross borders at ports of entry or in between, or for operating as members of human-trafficking or smuggling rings, or for distributing visas and passports out of legal channels.

In general, corruption of the travel and immigration sector has received almost no attention. The World Bank, Transparency International, US Treasury, and other institutions committed to opposing corruption have not focused on this set of problems. The United States has paid some attention to these crimes overseas, but at the level of individual cases and not in terms of a broad policy approach. In 1999, for example, the United States revoked the visa of the Panamanian chief of intelligence. US Embassy officials in Panama declared the revocation was due to her suspected involvement in the visa ring that used Panama as the entry point for Chinese aliens headed clandestinely by land to the United States. (Travel bans are discussed in chapter 6.)

Domestic corruption cases are increasing along with the size of the Border Patrol. By the end of 2009, the US Border Patrol was expected to reach 20,000.[27] In May 2008, there were 200 cases pending against law-enforcement employees working at the border.[28] Between October 1, 2004, and June 11, 2008, 61 current or former CBP employees had been arrested, indicted, or placed under prosecutorial review for suspected corruption.

In addition to the FBI, which is the leading anticorruption investigating agency for the United States, a number of multiagency task forces are working to combat corruption along the border. DHS has three internal affairs units that are involved in investigating corruption: the CBP Office of Internal Affairs, the ICE Office of Professional Responsibility, and the DHS's Office of Inspector General (IG). Agencies are not always willing to share information with one another and, depending on the case, there may be disputes about which team should take the lead on an investigation; however, these investigations have been productive.[29]

The CBP Office of Internal Affairs has the responsibility "to promote the integrity and security of the CBP workforce."[30] It takes an innovative, multipronged approach of preventing, detecting, and investigating threats to integrity within the agency. It uses preventive methods before hiring, monitors during employment, invests in research partnerships with academic institutions to develop better responses to corruption in US agencies, and provides its investigators to FBI-led anticorruption investigative teams.

This integrated approach makes sense because it enables Internal Affairs to transform what it learns about patterns and practices of corruption into new screening methods and development of investigative targets. Thus it enables Internal Affairs investigators and its FBI partners to move beyond initiating cases based on tips and instead take a proactive approach built on evidence and expertise. In contrast the DHS IG's office is more limited to traditional means of learning of malfeasance. From the perspective of DHS, having both the Office of Internal Affairs and IG engaged in pursuing corruption cases makes sense, especially because the pace of hiring at Internal Affairs is not abreast with CBP hiring of border personnel. However, at the end of the day, without violating the autonomy of IG, DHS and Congress should insist on annual integrated statistics about cases and sharing at a minimum of closed case files to permit an integrated analysis of trends and patterns. (Integrated reports of DS and State Department IG investigations, and closed cases of corruption at consulates and passport offices should also be required.)

As of June 2008, 9 percent of CBP employees were deemed unsuitable for their jobs. Those with less than five years of work experience at CBP and arrested for corruption primarily worked in Puerto Rico and states such as Texas, New Mexico, Arizona, California, Illinois, and New Jersey. As of June 2008, CBP's Office of Internal Affairs had 495 open investigations involving CBP employees, ICE's Office of Professional Responsibility had 307 open investigations, and DHS's IG had 488.[31] CBP should continue to increase its Internal Affairs investigative capacity in tandem with the increase in border personnel.

Agents who allow human and drug smugglers to pass through ports of entry without inspection are also putting their country in danger of admitting terrorists, weapons, and other national security threats. DHS, along with the departments of State and Treasury, should put together an anticorruption campaign aimed at US and foreign corrupt officials and human traffickers and smugglers who endanger security, undermine the rule of law, and weaken institutions. The campaign should prioritize dismantling HSOs with extensive corruption practices, sentencing enhancements for using corruption to aid human smuggling and trafficking, and reallocation of agents' time to focus greater attention on cases known or suspected to involve corruption.[32] Building anticorruption elements into training and assistance programs, as CBP's Office of Internal Affairs is already doing, should also be an element of the program.

Conclusion

Counterterrorism and mobility crime control are essential dimensions of civil security and continue to be spheres of experiment and innovation. Some of the newest ideas have significant potential and should be given more attention and support, especially HSTC, ECT, DS's RSO-I program, and efforts against corrupt officials in the United States and overseas, and against their HSO links. The most important next step is to establish strategic operational analysis units among agencies involved in securing human movement. These units will allow agencies to "know what they know" and, as a result, to improve their allocation of resources and tactical methods. These types of activities should be at the core of a new strategy to secure human movement as a homeland security mission.

CHAPTER 5: VIOLENT TRANSNATIONAL GANG MIGRATION: FOCUSED DETERRENCE

Policy Preview: *The Department of Homeland Security (DHS) should begin taking a more strategic, preventive approach to gang crime in ethnic and immigrant communities, aiming not only to punish and deport, but to preclude the violence. To break the cycle of transnational migration of violent gang members among the United States and El Salvador, Honduras, Guatemala, and Mexico, as well as between these other nations, US Immigration and Customs Enforcement (ICE) should join other federal, state, and local law-enforcement agencies and community organizations in applying focused deterrence, also called "pulling levers," a decade-old preventive enforcement strategy that takes a zero-tolerance approach to gangs for select offenses. Through the Merida program with Mexico, the United States should also explore the possibility of supporting preventive approaches like focused deterrence in the Central American states afflicted by regional gang violence.*

One vision of the world foresees growing disorder fomented by nonstate actors including terrorist organizations; insurgents; transnational organized crime groups; and ethnic, youth, and other types of gangs and groups. Even today's level of violence is too much; taking action to preclude violence and other forms of criminality by nonstate actors is central to securing human mobility. *Preclusion* may take the form of *preemption*, which in this context means taking action to stop processes or events that are already in motion, whether outside or inside the United States. The focus may be transnational criminals in the United States, immigrants committing crimes against members of their own community, or conspirators working with terrorist groups outside the country. Deradicalization of known terrorists is preemptive in this sense.

Preclusion may also take the form of *proactive prevention*. Whereas the goal of preemption is to stop acute, known threats in progress, the goal of proactive prevention is to prevent risks from developing into threats. Proactive prevention ranges from methods meant to be efficacious in the short to medium term, to those that are less immediate and more indirect forms of risk reduction. Those focused on long-term risk reduction are discussed in section IV.

The highest mobility-related priority should be to detect, dissuade, and disrupt immigrants to the United States who may have become radicalized here and who may seek to assist extremist groups, whether by sending funds to terrorists, harboring extremists, or traveling themselves for training or planning in terrorist camps. ICE's internal investigative programs and the Federal Bureau of Investigation's (FBI's) Joint Terrorism Task Force (JTTF), in which ICE participates, as well as border-screening programs, address aspects of radicalization among immigrants; however, an integrated strategy for counterradicalization is needed.[33] One vehicle for outreach to immigrant communities is hometown associations (HTAs), which are immigrant organizations whose members — who come from the same hometown— come together for social, cultural, political empowerment, and economic development goals. One proposal emphasizes the potential for strengthening immigrant integration and development in migrant-sending communities through partnerships between the government(s) of the sending country, nongovernmental organizations (NGOs), and HTAs.[34]

A second priority in securing human movement is to preempt and proactively prevent serious transnational mobility crimes, particularly human trafficking and human smuggling that is associated with terrorism and violence. (Methods against human-trafficking organizations, HTOs, and human-smuggling organizations, HSOs, are discussed in chapter 4.)

Another priority is to act against transnational criminals of all kinds. The term gangs usually refers to organizations that are distinct from, but may interact with, global HSOs and HTOs. Most street gangs focus on controlling their own neighborhoods and compelling respect for individual members.[35] Other types of gangs, including ethnic gangs, become managers of overt drug markets. Street gangs and those associated with illegal commerce are associated with high levels of violence. Many US gangs have a transnational element; for example, US members may maintain connections to members now in Central America since deportation from the United States. Assisting Central American governments in reducing gang violence should be a policy priority, as should consideration of US policies to deport gang members who have lived nearly their entire lives in the United States.

A range of federal, state, and local agencies — especially ICE and the Bureau of Diplomatic Security (DS) at the federal level, the Drug Enforcement Administration (DEA), the Bureau of Alcohol, Tobacco, Firearms, and Explosives (ATF), and the FBI share authority for dealing with the immigration and lawbreaking associated with violent and otherwise criminal gangs. Ultimately, officials seek to use their authority to preserve security, civil order, and community well-being. This means dismantling these groups, persuading gang members to desist from violence, or causing them to dissolve without new ones being formed. Crime control in US ethnic communities has implications for counterterrorism and transnational crime control. Investigations and policing can either exacerbate or help to resolve racial and ethnic tensions, extremism, violence, and disorder. When a community is willing to cooperate with the police, crime is likely to diminish.

This chapter argues that violence in immigrant communities and in the countries of origin of gang members would decrease if ICE were to move from its current preemptive and punitive strategy to a proactive preventive approach. The preclusive methods described here can also provide lessons for counter-radicalization techniques in communities.

Crime among Noncitizens

The number of foreign-born criminals in US federal prisons grew between 2001 and 2004 from 42,000 to 49,000.[36] As of December 2009, approximately 55,500, or 26.7 percent, of all inmates in federal prisons were non-US citizens.[37] Mexicans alone accounted for 17.9 percent of the total federal inmate population.[38] Contrary to the fears of some, the incarceration rate of people born in the United States (3.5 percent) was four times the rate of the foreign born (0.9 percent) in 2000.[39]

Despite the relatively small size of the foreign-born incarcerated population, violent gangs and drug dealing involving foreign-born residents are a serious problem in many cities and increasingly also in smaller communities throughout the country. The National Network for Safe Communities, a group of police chiefs, prosecutors, community leaders, service providers, mayors, and others, has identified 75 jurisdictions that could benefit from cooperating on reducing crime in the areas of gang violence and drug markets.[40] A number of these have sizeable immigrant populations and gang problems associated with them, for example, Los Angeles; Chicago; Providence, RI; and Stockton, CA.[41]

Central and South American and Asian immigrant communities predominate in these jurisdictions.[42] Mexican drug-trafficking organizations (DTOs) are present in 235 cities in 48 states and the District of Columbia (see map).[43]

Figure 5.1 Cities Reporting the Presence of Mexican DTOs

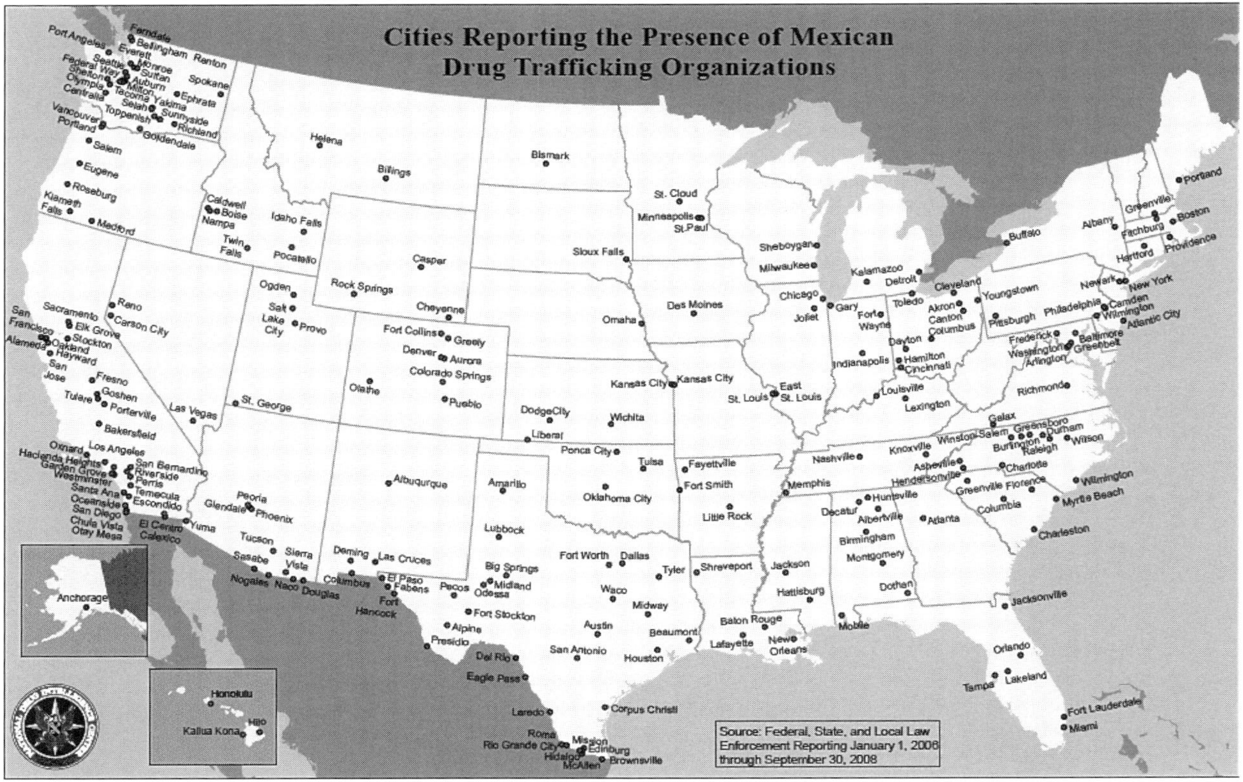

Cities Reporting the Presence of Mexican
Drug Trafficking Organizations

Source: Federal, State, and Local Law
Enforcement Reporting January 1, 2008
through September 30, 2008

Source: DOJ (US Department of Justice), National Drug Intelligence Center, National Drug Threat Assessment 2009,
www.usdoj.gov/ndic/pubs31/31379/appenda.htm#Map5.

Types of Gangs

Public reports often refer to gang-related problems without distinguishing among particular gangs and the level of violence associated with each. Knowing the specific gang can dictate tailored strategies and approaches. Max Manwaring of the Army War College divides gangs into three types:[44] The first is the traditional street gang whose members primarily defend turf and demand respect. The second type pursues illegal commerce. Its leadership tends to be more centralized and concentrated on trafficking and market protection. To protect markets, such gangs use violence selectively internally or in recruitment, against competitor gangs, and against police and other local and national security organizations. This type of gang often has links to transnational criminal organizations and insurgents. The gangs providing border-crossing services to Mexican DTOs are an example.

The third type of gang expands on the initial set of illegal activities, adding others — human smuggling and trafficking, trafficking in cars and weapons, money laundering, kidnapping, robbery, and other crimes. It may take over territory and reach deeper into governments. The gang leader functions like a warlord, drug kingpin, or insurgent leader, and the gang may participate in mercenary activities and have explicit political objectives.[45] The Mara Salvatrucha in El Salvador, and the Mexican and Colombian DTOs are of this kind.

Ethnic and Immigrant Gang Violence

Ethnic gangs are of all three types. The Mexican Mafia has become a real organized-crime group, working with the Mexican drug cartels and taxing other gangs across the southwest. The Latin Kings operate across the United States, and like the Mexican Mafia are active in US prisons. Russian and other East European gangs are profit-seeking groups but operate differently than the foregoing. Traditionally African American gangs such as the Bloods and Crips have some national elements. MS-13 seems to be something of a hybrid, encompassing local street gangs, acting as the arm of Mexican DTOs along the US border, and engaging in a wide range of criminality and corruption in Central American countries.

Although ethnic organized crime is widespread, most visible gangs that include recent migrants fall into the category of street gangs. In gangs of this type, violence is typically concentrated among small groups of active offenders. Such groups drive most homicide and gun violence in their communities, including most of the homicides in US cities and virtually all public drug-related activity.[46] Most of these gang activities are local, personal, and impulsive. They tend to arise in poor urban neighborhoods where there is also drug dealing. Offenders and victims of gang violence tend to be young, have criminal records, and be known to the law-enforcement community. Many are on parole or on probation. Relations with the police are often characterized by toxic racial and ethnic tension and conflict; community respect for the rule of law is undermined by high levels of police harassment.[47]

Violent gangs victimize communities; gang intimidation leads to restrictions in daily life and prevents business development. Criminal histories damage individuals for life, and the prevalence of such histories in a community helps create a street culture that works against successful immigrant integration. Dropping out of school, never taking a legitimate job, and imprisonment become the norm. By raising hurdles to integration and choking off human potential, gangs deprive families and communities of crucial human resources. There is often despair among residents and law enforcement that communities are broken and nothing can be done to turn them around. State and federal taxpayers foot the bill for consequences in medical care and law enforcement, and lose the benefits that otherwise productive members of society would contribute.

As with Black gangs that fight mostly other Black gangs, Hispanic gangs mostly fight other Hispanic gangs and Asian gangs other Asian gangs. The Mara Salvatrucha gangs, known as MS-13 and MS-18, were formed after refugees fleeing civil wars in Nicaragua, El Salvador, Honduras, and Guatemala coalesced in Los Angeles among other locations of immigrant communities. Young Central American immigrants encountered gangs in their neighborhoods and in a perversion of immigrant integration became involved with and imitated them. Today, Mexicans are also members of MS-13; in fact, most MS-13 members are foreign born. The FBI tends to see MS-13 as highly organized and therefore amenable to a Racketeer Influenced and Corrupt Organizations Act-type enforcement strategy; other observers tend to believe that MS-13 is violent but not particularly directed from outside.[48] MS-13's largest rival is known as the Mara 18 or 18th Street Gang.[49]

In the mid-1990s, after peace agreements ended civil wars in Central America, some of these violent young men returned home voluntarily. Others were deported from the United States as part of the precursor to what is now DHS's

Secure Communities program, a program by the then–Immigration and Naturalization Service (INS) to deport convicted felons. In El Salvador, Honduras, and Guatemala, these deported youths formed gangs in the mode of MS-13. Some then returned to the United States illegally, sometimes with gang members who had joined in their countries of origin.[50]

US Policy and the Maras in Central America

In crafting strategy for dealing with the Maras and other immigrant or ethnic gangs in the United States, it is important to recognize how different the US situation is from that in Mexico, El Salvador, Honduras, and Guatemala. Only in some cases are the Maras involved in drug trafficking and human smuggling.[51] As the government of Mexico puts pressure on the Mexican DTOs, traffickers are shifting southward, solidifying an already developed set of connections between the Maras and the Mexican DTOs. Honduras has as many as 40,000 Maras among their youth, and the gang problem is given highest priority among national security issues. The specter of the DTOs enlisting Maras in a more formal way than they do at present is a major concern.

The Merida foreign assistance package to support the government of Mexico's armed suppression of DTOs provides a small amount of funds for assistance to Central American governments. Just as the United States has accepted coresponsibility with Mexico for the cross-border traffickers who supply American consumers with drugs and Mexican DTOs with guns and cash, the United States should explicitly acknowledge shared responsibility for the problem of the Maras, in which the United States is similarly implicated. It should provide substantial assistance for addressing this problem in Central America and help develop innovative approaches.

ICE Enforcement Policy and Practice

The United States has relied heavily on the criminal justice system for dealing with violent gangs. ICE's overall strategy for enforcing laws relating to human mobility is the same as the rest of US law enforcement — arrest, prosecution, and incarceration — with one additional tool: deportation. ICE seeks to deport as many criminal aliens residing illegally in the United States as possible. The arrest and prosecution strategies have led to about a fivefold increase in the rates of incarceration since the 1970s (from about 140 per 100,000 to about 700 per 100,000 in 2008).[52] In addition, there has been an increase in the number of immigrants detained on a daily basis. Between 1994 and 2007, the number of immigrants detained daily grew nearly fivefold, from 6,785 to 30,295.[53]

The level of removals is also at a peak. ICE has removed increasing numbers of noncitizens over the past decade: 50,924 in FY1995, 189,026 in FY2001, and 358,886 in FY2008,[54] about 97,133 of whom had criminal records.[55] Over the past 15 years, criminal prosecutions for immigration-related offenses have sharply increased: from 8.6 percent of all federal criminal referrals in FY1987, to 9.9 percent in 1997, and 27.2 percent in 2007.[56] In June 2009 ICE and DEA signed a new interagency agreement to enhance cooperation in dealing with drug traffickers by increasing the number of agents, improving information and intelligence sharing through the Organized Crime Drug Enforcement Task Force (OCDETF), and coordinating more effectively and efficiently between the two agencies.[57] Under this initiative, ICE will select agents who will also work for DEA in the United States and overseas to investigate violations of the Controlled Substances Act, 21 USC. §§ 801, et seq., commonly known as "Title 21," and target drug smugglers.

ICE is also making a fresh effort to target unauthorized immigrants based on criminal violations beyond their violation of US immigration laws and to direct enforcement activity by level of criminality. Under ICE's Secure Communities program, the agency attempts to identify noncitizens who have been arrested and place serious criminals in removal proceedings. The program has established three levels of crime corresponding to the risk to public safety. Level 1 includes those convicted of major drug offenses and violent offenses (murder, manslaughter, rape, robbery, and kidnapping); level 2 comprises those convicted of minor drug offenses and property offenses (burglary, larceny, fraud, and money laundering); and level 3 involves those convicted of other crimes. Secure Communities began as a pilot program in October 2008 in 48 counties, and is expected to operate at almost all local jails by the end of 2012.[58]

The estimated cost to remove convicted criminal foreigners each year is roughly $2 to $3 billion.[59] This is nearly on par with federal prison expenditures for incarcerating criminal foreigners, which totaled approximately $5.8 billion between 2001 and 2004.[60] Most of ICE's resources will remain focused on deportation. The intensified focus on deportation of foreign-born criminals necessitates a parallel increase in the number of prosecutors, immigration judges, detention beds, and other resources.

ICE's Operation Community Shield

ICE's approach to gang violence and criminality in immigrant communities is similar to its approach to illegal migration: it seeks to identify and deport noncitizen gang members.

Figure 5.2 Operation Community Shield, ICE Surge 2008; Total Arrests by City

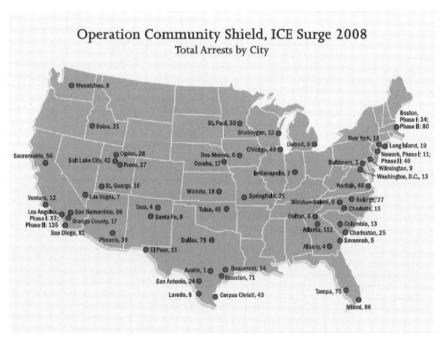

Source: DHS, Immigration and Customs Enforcement, www.ice.gov/doclib/pi/investigations/comshield/operation_surge_map.pdf.

ICE initiated Operation Community Shield in 2005 to target violent transnational street gangs.[61] Originally intended to target MS-13, ICE subsequently expanded the program to encompass all transnational criminal street and prison gangs.[62] Since the program's inception, ICE has arrested 11,106 individuals whom it identifies as street gang members and associates.[63] Of those arrests, 145 were reputedly gang leaders, 2,018 were identified as MS-13 members or associates, and 4,331 had violent criminal histories. ICE also seized 388 firearms through Operation Community Shield between February 2005 and September

2008.[64] Between 2005 and 2007, 59 percent of those arrested were Mexicans, 17 percent Salvadoran, 5 percent Honduran, and 3 percent Guatemalan.[65] Nine percent of those arrested were US citizens. Of the gang members that ICE arrested, more than one-third (36.0 percent) have been charged with criminal offenses, while the others have been deported on immigration grounds.[66]

Transnational Gang Migration

Deportation of gang members is to some extent only a stop-gap measure. Gang members — almost all are young men — frequently try to return to the United States. DHS has increased its focus in recent years on border enforcement to reduce unauthorized immigration from Mexico, but it has not eliminated recidivism. There is no formal count as to how many gang members return, but some do.[67]

The United States quadrupled its border enforcement spending between FY1993 and FY2006, and tripled the size of the Border Patrol from 5,876 in FY1996 to 17,819 in FY2008.[68] The Secure Fence Act of 2006 mandates 670 miles of new fencing along the US-Mexico border, 643.3 miles of which were completed as of January 15, 2010.[69] DHS also has worked with federal prosecutors to increase immigration-related prosecutions, with some border-state district US attorneys' offices adopting a "zero-tolerance" approach and criminally prosecuting (prior to deporting) everybody caught for crossing the border illegally.

DHS in 2009 reported a decline in numbers of people it apprehended at the US-Mexico border, which it attributed in part to its increased enforcement efforts and their deterrent impact.[70] But the decline may also be explained by other factors, particularly the economic recession and associated unemployment. In addition, increased border enforcement may have a deterrent effect on migrants living illegally in the United States, causing them to remain in the country rather than return to Mexico.

Stepped-up border enforcement measures have not discouraged deported migrants from attempting to the cross the border illegally again, and they appear to be able to do so quite successfully. Of migrants from Jalisco in 2005 and 2007, more than 92 percent were able to enter the United States after having been apprehended, according to a survey by the Mexican Migration Field Research and Training Program of the University of California, San Diego

(UCSD).[71] Unauthorized migrants from Yucatan and Oaxaca reentered at even higher rates.[72] The increase in border enforcement since 1994 has had no significant impact on the ability of individuals to cross the border illegally.[73] While approximately 45 percent of migrants are apprehended at least once while attempting to cross, about 97 percent eventually make it through to the United States, and this has been the case since 1995.[74] Since 1977, the average number of apprehensions per unauthorized immigrant fluctuated between 0.3 and 1.3.[75]

Illegal migration persists despite migrants' knowledge of the significant dangers it entails. Of the 1,031 UCSD survey respondents, 64 percent stated that evading Border Patrol agents when crossing the border was very difficult, 21 percent said it was somewhat difficult, and the great majority believed that crossing the border without papers was very dangerous. The migrants' views are consistent with the evidence: migrant deaths have increased as the United States has stepped up its border enforcement efforts. A total of 5,046 deaths were recorded between January 1995 and March 2009.

Violence, Capabilities, and Migration

The precise rate of return of deported migrants needs to be known in order to assess the effectiveness of ICE's strategy to address gang violence. Migrant deaths are a high price to pay for enforcement and for source governments' permitting the unregulated departure of their nationals. The impact on the societies to which gang members return is another problem. Countries in Central America have significant problems with transnational organized crime and gangs, problems that are raising the level of violence and corroding the rule of law in these countries. El Salvador is one of the five most violent countries in the world, with an average of nine murders and several carjackings reported daily.[76] The homicide rates for every 100,000 people in El Salvador, Guatemala, Nicaragua, Honduras, and Mexico were 57.5, 36.4, 17.4, 32.2, and 11.3 respectively in 2004, in comparison with 6 per 100,000 in the United States.[77] Violence in Central America is worsening as the Mexican government puts pressure on DTOs. While illegal migration flows from Mexico to the United States have fallen sharply in recent years, Mexican drug violence has led to significant numbers of political asylum claims by Mexican nationals and may ultimately create the conditions that lead to large-scale migration.

Is it possible to get out of the cycle of deportation and return of violent offenders? The United States has the right and the responsibility to safeguard its communities from violence by removing unauthorized immigrants who commit crimes. Yet transnational violent gang migration is clearly part of the etiology of a serious crime problem on both ends. The reactive approach does nothing to prevent or deter these gang members from committing gang-related crimes, whether in the United States or in their countries of origin. Rather it makes it likely that the crimes will continue at both ends, feeding the illegal migration-deportation cycle, and seriously undermining US efforts to foster the rule of law and deter corruption in Central America. While DHS continues to expand operational resources at the border, HSOs make it possible to reenter and to defeat the Border Patrol's announced "deterrence through prevention" strategy. What alternative approach could the US government adopt to deter and prevent gang activities from recurring? The experience of an innovative law-enforcement strategy known as focused deterrence or "pulling levers," demonstrates that violence can be reduced. In fact, it is possible to all but eliminate and prevent violence in some locations.

From Enforcement to Preclusion

Proactive prevention when core law-enforcement authorities are used results in *deterrence*. When something is deterred, it is prevented. This is why the Border Patrol refers to its southern border strategy as *prevention through deterrence*. But in non-law-enforcement "prevention" circles that deal with street crime, "prevention" has come to mean "not about authority."[78] Law enforcement dealing with street gangs typically does not think about prevention at all.

As discussed in chapter 4, *preclusion* through a range of methods is the core goal of counterterrorism and other efforts against as-yet-unknown threats and risks not yet materialized. The goal — whether considered a war aim or simply the strategic purpose — is to preclude events with catastrophic consequences, whether precipitated by terrorists, states, criminals, natural hazards, or technological vulnerabilities. Preclusion or prevention does not mean that there is no offensive or assertive action. On the contrary, it requires the proactive use of all levers of national power.

Preclusion is not only a core concept of counterterrorism. Proactive preventive strategies have become rooted in some arenas of federal and local law enforcement. For example, ATF's primary focus until 1997 was on arresting felons in possession of firearms; that it now conducts targeted investigations of firearms traffickers incorporates systematic prevention tactics into what was a predominantly reactive strategy.[79] The expanded targets range from corrupt gun dealers to straw purchasers and now, with ICE, to smugglers into Mexico. The goal of proactive prevention of gun trafficking is to prevent access to guns and in turn to prevent gun violence or to make it more costly. Disruption of small arms trafficking to Mexico as one tool to curb the escalation of violence is integral to the US effort to support Mexico's war on DTOs.[80]

Local police are also adopting prevention as a strategic hallmark. The precinct accountability policy for the New York Police Department (NYPD) enables the command staff to surge new resources when they see evidence of a spike in crime in a particular neighborhood, preventing escalation of the problem and often substantially reducing it. In 2008 the police force in High Point, North Carolina, building on ten years of experience,[81] made prevention its core operational strategy, combining key operational and intelligence functions into a new Major Crime Deterrence and Prevention division. Following the interventions in High Point, drug markets have closed and the city has witnessed large reductions in violent and drug-related crime, with no displacement. Overall, the High Point model, which has been adopted by other cities, is producing 40 to 50 percent reductions in violent and drug-related crime.[82]

Using Focused Deterrence to Prevent Gang Violence

Focused deterrence is a form of proactive preventive law enforcement aimed at suppressing gang violence and other criminal activity.[83] It concentrates enforcement resources to deter particular types of criminal activity among particular groups rather than to deter individuals generally or specifically. Focused deterrence is also known as "pulling levers" because it uses the full range of existing legal tools on a variety of offending fronts to deter a selected offense: for example, street drug enforcement becomes one of the penalties imposed on an entire gang for a homicide committed by one gang member.

As one type of community policing, focused deterrence is an effective way to prevent gang violence that has emerged from community and problem-oriented policing.[84] Although there are important parallels in gang activity across cities, the character of gangs and the violence with which they are associated varies widely both within and across cities.[85] Not all gangs are violent, and gangs and violence associated with them take many forms.[86] The problem-oriented policing approach promotes analysis of the precise nature of local gangs and associated gang violence so that responses can be logically linked to specific problems.[87]

DOJ's Office of Juvenile Justice and Delinquency Prevention suggests that gang violence prevention programs that hold promise generally take a blended approach that includes suppression, social intervention, opportunity provision, and community organization.[88] A number of jurisdictions seeking to prevent gang violence have been experimenting with problem-oriented frameworks. These focused deterrence strategies are typically centered on enforcement activities and include a collectively embraced, centrally devised, and commonly implemented program that incorporates all four elements of the blended approach.

Because it deploys the full range of resources, pulling levers as a method to reduce crime in communities is analogous to the 9/11 Commission's suggestion that all means of national power be used to address terrorism. Counterinsurgency theory also turns on engaging a comprehensive range of resources to change the dynamic in communities. It is inspiring veterans of the Iraq and Afghanistan wars, who are teaching or studying in the United States at institutions such as the Naval Postgraduate School, to experiment with and offer advice to public officials on countergang interventions based on their counterinsurgency experience.[89]

To convey the meaning of focused deterrence as a law-enforcement strategy, this section examines instances of its use and their impact. The cases offer lessons for how policymakers could address immigrant-related gang violence in the United States.

Two distinct but closely related strategies have been developed to deal with these core crime problems. The Ceasefire approach to violent groups was developed in Boston more than ten years ago and aimed at Boston's gangs. It assumes that a small number of criminals commit a disproportionately high number of serious, violent crimes. Once such offenders are identified, police require them to attend a meeting where they are told that they and fellow gang members will suffer swift and severe punishment. In return for better behavior, the city, in partnership with social workers and academics provide life coaching and job-counseling services.[90] The program cut youth homicide by two-thirds and homicide citywide by one-half, and became known as the "Boston Miracle."[91] Based on the success of Ceasefire, the DOJ National Institute for Justice supported the program's adoption in other US cities with gang violence problems. The strategy has since been implemented in Minneapolis, Indianapolis, Los Angeles, Cincinnati, Chicago, and other jurisdictions. The more recently developed High Point approach, which follows the Ceasefire strategy,[92] resulted in the virtual elimination of drug markets in that North Carolina city and won a 2007 Kennedy School of Government Innovations in Government Award.

Rather than applying a law-enforcement strategy of arresting and prosecuting gang members after they commit violent crimes, the police use a strategy of focused deterrence, which employs law-enforcement authorities to pull six levers. The strategy:

1. Establishes an interagency task force comprised of representatives from local and federal law-enforcement agencies, community leaders, and social-service providers who can provide alternative support such as job training
2. Conducts background research and analysis on gangs and their activities in the area, mapping gang territory and rivalries, and allowing the task force to know about tensions with each other before they escalate
3. Provides a special social-service program to help gang members with education, work, and other lawful needs
4. Organizes community members, often family members, who are willing to say to gang members that their own community rejects their violent and criminal behavior
5. Creates an integrated federal, state, and local law-enforcement strategy that can respond to gang member violence and can enforce all available laws (exercised by each of the federal, state, and local agencies) for any crimes committed by any gang members
6. Involves direct and repeated communication to all gangs, often in face-to-face meetings with an array of law-enforcement representatives, that help is available, that their own communities want them to behave, and that all gang members will be sanctioned if any are violent

Despite some general similarities, gangs and their reasons for and modes of violence differ in important ways. Thus, the focused deterrence strategy requires a tailored approach based on strategic problem analysis in customizing pulling levers to local conditions.

Each of the six steps is critical to a comprehensive gang-prevention strategy.

The wide array of agencies and groups represented in the interagency task forces is essential to the program's success. The participation of all the partners allows a broad "no violence" and "no dealing" message to be delivered. The participation of the full spectrum of agencies permits the task force to be able to state credibly that all available laws (among other levers) will be used against all members of a group if a single member of that group engages in violence.

As these rather complex strategies have been implemented in jurisdictions around the country, dramatic reductions in violence and the elimination of drug markets have resulted. The success of the programs has depended on the willingness of the participating agencies to "pull their lever" by using the sanctions available to their agency that most delivers the community message in response to breaches of the requirements imposed on gangs. ICE appears to be the only major federal law-enforcement agency that does not participate, yet the sanction that ICE uniquely could impose — deportation of gang members — is potent. The following is a brief description of select programs.

Hispanic Gangs in Stockton, California

Under Operation Peacekeeper, in 1997 police in Stockton, California, led an intervention aimed to reduce gang violence between the Hispanic Norteño and Sureño gangs. The strategy in Stockton focused directly on identified gangs. The interagency task force held forums on a regular basis to communicate to gangs that their violence would not be tolerated, to offer social services, and to communicate strong community norms against violence. When violence occurred and a gang was sanctioned, the police and others involved in the interagency task force also informed other gangs why they were taking certain actions and responding in the way they were. Between September 1997 and December 2002, the interagency task force held 44 such forums. Gang-related homicides fell from 18 in 1997 to 1 in 1998 and stayed down for the next several years.[93] The formal evaluation found a 42 percent reduction in gun homicide.[94]

Asian Gangs in Lowell, Massachusetts

Project Safe Neighborhoods (PSN) in Lowell, Massachusetts, addressed violence by Asian street-gang members of all ages by enforcing gambling laws against older gang members, who were told explicitly that the raids on their gambling parlors were being triggered by shootings. The task force's approach corresponded with 100 gambling-related arrests between October 2002 and June 2003.[95]

Other Locations

There is also a large and growing number of cities and other jurisdictions in which the strategy has been implemented with apparent impact. A focused deterrence strategy in Indianapolis reduced homicides by slightly more than one-third, with larger impacts among the neighborhoods and groups most affected by violence.[96] In Chicago, a focused deterrence program in several extremely violent neighborhoods adopted a quasi-experimental design using other neighborhoods as controls; the pulling levers group achieved a 37 percent reduction in homicide.[97] Minneapolis removed a street gang called the Bogus Boyz in the first week of June 1997 and began face-to-face meetings with gang members. In the summer of 1996 there were 42 homicides in Minneapolis; in the summer of 1997, there were 8.[98]

Conclusion

These results demonstrate that focused deterrence is a promising strategy relevant for ICE in its mission is to reduce cross-national gang activity, including drug smuggling involving migrants and immigrants. Certainly, the focused deterrence strategy provides an additional tool for ICE.[99] Instead of limiting ICE's enforcement policy to arresting and deporting violent immigrant gang members — a process that actually fuels transnational gang dynamics — ICE should seek to engage in targeted initiatives such as those described above with the goal of preventing gang violence. As long as there is a market-focused deterrence, task forces will not end the illegal-market activities of commercially focused gangs. But the strategy can work to dramatically reduce and in some circumstances preclude the gang violence and patterns of drug dealing that are tearing apart immigrant families and communities in the United States.

ICE agents should be represented in the interagency task forces that are leading focused deterrence strategies in cities around the country where there are immigrant populations and gang violence problems. This would allow the team to communicate to gangs that there will be deportation consequences if they engage in gun violence and other violent gang activities. Such an approach would increase the effectiveness of the strategy, and supplement ICE's existing

Community Shield program, also aimed at targeting violent gang members who are a threat to public safety and national security.

As in the classic structure of focused deterrence described above, the possibility should be considered of enlisting widespread community support — especially from family members of violent gang members — by making it clear that indiscriminate deportations will not be pursued, because ICE's mission is "to target the people, money, and materials that support terrorist and criminal networks."[100] Rather, deportations will be focused on violent gang members. ICE agents would then have an opening to work with the affected communities to reset norms and standards with gang members, and to prevent violence from occurring over the long term.

DOJ has required that each of the 93 US Attorney's offices develop a local effort to reduce gun crimes and gang violence, incorporating PSN principles.[101] Another 43 cities have joined a public-private partnership called the National Network for Safe Cities. At least 24 have an ICE Office of Investigation field office either in or within close proximity.[102] Ensuring that ICE participates in focused deterrence task forces should be a priority. At the same time, DOJ and DHS should explore transmitting what has been learned in the focused deterrence program to Central American states dealing with high levels of gang violence.

CHAPTER 6: TERRORISTS AND HUMAN RIGHTS VIOLATORS: TRAVEL BANS

Policy Preview: Travel bans imposed by the US government against terrorists and corrupt officials from foreign governments rally other countries to the cause of upholding the rule of law in global travel channels. Further developing the US travel-ban program is an important way in which the Department of Homeland Security (DHS) and the Department of State (DOS) can move beyond border security and immigration enforcement to promote a global alliance to secure human movement against terrorist and criminal travel. There is precedent for such an alliance, notably US leadership in the international effort to secure global flows against terrorist finance and money laundering. Depriving individuals of freedom of movement cannot be undertaken lightly, however, and there should be more transparency to the travel-ban programs operated by the United States and the United Nations (UN).

Travel bans have operational utility and strategic significance for mobility security. On the practical level, travel bans target three of the groups that matter most for mobility security: regime leaders whose corrupt and failed governance contributes to the prospect of dangerous and illegal migration, corrupt officials who directly facilitate illegal travel, and terrorists. The bans also potentially target human traffickers and other major criminals. Strategically, travel bans embody a collective determination to uphold democratic and human rights norms in global mobility channels. For these and other practical and strategic reasons, travel bans should be an important focus — both for the DHS, as it develops programs to secure human mobility, and for the DOS, in its work in foreign policy and global counterterrorism.

A travel ban is an executive order that extinguishes an individual's right to movement: i.e., to enter, to transit through, or to find safe haven in a particular country or in *any* country or region. The United States, the European Union (EU), and the United Nations Security Council (UNSC) are now using travel bans to varying degrees as a means to pressure leaders who pose a threat to peace and security, to fight corruption, and to counter terrorists. Travel bans are a relatively new international instrument. US and EU travel bans represent largely unilateral decisions of the executive branch. US travel bans are secret and rely on classified information, while EU travel bans are public. UNSC travel bans differ from national watchlists in that they are mandatory for all countries and ban all international movement.

Travel bans have evolved from two roots. One is the international sanctions movement, the other sovereign terrorist watchlists. DOS, which is responsible for sanctions policy and which originated the terrorist watchlist, oversees US travel-ban policy. However, travel-ban policy is also a DHS responsibility because safeguarding the legal, operational, and market infrastructure of mobility is a paramount homeland security mission. Travel bans represent an important innovation in securing human mobility for several reasons.

First, a travel ban uses their desire to travel to pressure leaders and officials to alter their conduct. This adds physical reality to political isolation, making the impact of the travel ban both practical and symbolic. Travel bans are one of the "smart sanctions" that offer a new method, short of military action, of opposing kleptocratic regimes and those failing in their protection responsibility. Because illegal movements that threaten human security and undermine the rule of law frequently result from corrupt governance, travel bans are an important policy tool for DHS and DOS.

Second, in countering terrorism, travel bans have the dual benefit of being offensive in nature and of operating through international law. They are preventive rather than reactive — disrupting terrorists and other malefactors from moving freely and, thus, from pursuing their aims. Travel bans are neither immigration-law-enforcement nor criminal investigative actions, although they may operate through these laws at the sovereign level; they are a new kind of collective action in counterterrorism.

Third, the use of international bans is an implicit acknowledgement that governments cannot rely solely on their own border-control measures against asymmetric threats. The challenge of stopping particular individuals among the mass of legitimate travelers is too great to be met by one government through its own border-security regime. Governments must cooperate in preventing and disrupting the movement of terrorists and other banned individuals. Travel bans constitute an important form of collective effort, and should be a centerpiece of DHS mobility security policy.

Fourth, travel bans commit governments to prevent the entry and the departure of people who represent a threat to others. The latter responsibility has significant implications for governments' roles in preventing illegal migration. Fifth, travel bans raise questions about the law of human mobility: in exercising legal authority to ban an individual's movement, travel bans put the spotlight on the relatively undeveloped right to movement, its legal foundation, and how this right may be denied and forfeited.

There has been little or no analysis of the logic, efficacy, or policy implications of US, EU, or UNSC travel bans. Many questions arise about their operation and fairness. Given the world's myriad travel channels — and the many weak links in the global travel system — travel bans may be circumvented. But they potentially offer a powerful incentive to change conduct while constraining the movement of dangerous individuals. This chapter describes their history and operations and makes recommendations for their continued development.

US Travel Bans

The mechanism for US travel bans is the suspension of access to visitor or temporary visas, referred to as nonimmigrant visas, and sometimes also the suspension of access to immigrant (i.e., permanent) visas. Section 212(f) of the *Immigration and Naturalization Act* provides for suspension of entry or imposition of restrictions on foreign officials by the President of the United States. It states that:

> Whenever the President finds that the entry of any aliens or any class of aliens into the United States would be detrimental to the interests of the United States, he may by proclamation, and for such period as he shall deem necessary, suspend the entry of all aliens or any class of aliens as immigrants or nonimmigrants, or impose on the entry of aliens any restrictions he may deem to be appropriate.[103]

US travel bans are imposed and administered by DOS under delegated authority from the president. They have evolved in their purposes with the shift in US foreign policy and security strategy from Cold War concerns to human rights, democracy building, and counterterrorism.

Proclamation 7750, Corruption, and Mobility Security
By far the most significant travel ban for mobility security policy is Proclamation 7750 (January 12, 2004).[104] This ban suspended the entry of individuals engaged in or benefiting from corruption. The purpose of this ban was to provide a tool against corruption and, thus, to promote security and to strengthen democratic institutions and free market systems. The "No Safe

Haven" policy, endorsed by G-8 leaders in their Evian Declaration in 2003, was a foundation for the proclamation.

Corruption is a major factor in the illegal movement of people, in two ways: direct and indirect. First, corruption of authorities involved with mobility directly facilitates illicit travel, including by terrorists. Human-smuggling organizations (HSOs), human-trafficking organizations (HTOs), and sometimes terrorists rely on such third-party facilitators to function in the illegal travel market. Corruption may take the form of bribes or graft. It may also involve complicity; for example, a public or private official may assist relatives, friends, or associates outside of formal channels, not necessarily for money, but perhaps for political, among other, reasons.[105] Second, high levels of corruption are a key aspect of poor governance in developing countries. Poor governance is a major contributing factor to refugee flows and to the dangerous and uncontrolled flows of other migrants, many of whom perish as they attempt to cross borders illegally.

DHS has to be concerned with travel bans on corrupt officials, even those whose activities are not directly facilitating illegal migration. One key aspect of securing human mobility is to uphold the rule of law in global travel channels. Policies and processes that prevent the provision of safe haven for corrupt officials help preserve the integrity of global mobility channels.

Proclamation 7750 represents the most comprehensive extension of US government power to restrict the mobility of foreign officials. It is unprecedented in that it did not specifically target any single person, group of persons, country, or situation. Instead, it expands the State Department's authority to deny a visa if there is any reason to believe that any foreign official is corrupt to the detriment of the US national interest. The official need not have been convicted in his or her home country, nor done anything illegal in the United States. The proclamation covers public officials who take bribes, people who bribe public officials, and public officials who appropriate public funds or interfere with judicial, electoral, or other processes. It also covers any spouses, children, and dependent household members who are beneficiaries of any articles of monetary value or other benefits obtained by such officials.[106]

Proclamation 7750 defines US national interests to include the international economic activity of US businesses, US foreign assistance goals, the security of the United States against transnational crime and terrorism, and the stability

of democratic nations and institutions. The security, integrity, and function-
ality of global human mobility channels are implicated in all of these areas.
In August 2006, President George W. Bush issued the National Strategy to
Internationalize Efforts against Kleptocracy to confront high-level, large-scale
corruption among public officials and to target their proceeds.[107] The strategy
included a provision to deny safe haven to corrupt officials, to deny or revoke
their visas, and to suspend information sharing with them.[108] Congress, by
passing in 2007 the Department of State, Foreign Operations, and Related
Programs Appropriations Act of 2008, directed the Secretary of State to "compile and maintain a list of officials of foreign governments and their immediate
family members who the Secretary determines there is credible evidence to
believe have been involved in corruption relating to the extraction of natural
resources of their countries."[109] The United States vowed to deny entry to
those on the list.[110]

Implementation of Proclamation 7750

Because of the secrecy surrounding individual travel bans, it is difficult to
assess the effect of Proclamation 7750, particularly with respect to securing
human mobility. The Secretary of State has extremely broad discretion with
regard to this program.[111] At present, travel bans that counter corruption are
not strategically directed at complicity and corruption in mobility channels,
such as corruption by passport agency directors, immigration service heads,
border guard directors, port operators, etc., or by major human traffickers or
other types of serious criminals who drive or capitalize on illicit movement.
DHS policy involvement in the selection could help bring these considerations to the fore.

The selection process at present is somewhat unclear. Generally speaking,
personnel in US embassies and civil-society organizations are among those who
bring information about possible travel-ban candidates to the attention of the
DOS Office of International Narcotics and Law Enforcement (INL). Consular
officials must investigate corruption allegations before denying or revoking a
foreign official's visa. INL then produces a detailed memorandum justifying the
denial. The memorandum is reviewed in an interbureau and interagency process
and is ultimately signed by the Under Secretary of State for Political Affairs.[112]

The proclamation provides the Secretary of State specific legal authority to
establish and maintain a list of persons who could be denied entry. DOS does
not, however, administer a list of individuals who could fall within the scope of

Proclamation 7750. Rather, officials make decisions on denying entry or revoking visas on a case-by-case and an as-needed basis. The statute does not require the Secretary of State to make the names of banned individuals public or accessible to external entities. According to DOS, it keeps the issuance and refusal of visas confidential on the grounds that release of the information could obstruct US law enforcement and create foreign-policy complications. DOS will confirm whether an individual was denied entry under the proclamation if a request is made. However, the list of people subject to bans under proclamation 7750 is otherwise classified. These two rules are inexplicably contradictory and should be reviewed with an eye toward bringing transparency to this important program. The department has not even made public the number of travel bans it has imposed pursuant to Proclamation 7750.

Some subjects of travel bans come to light, usually by their own complaints to the media or by statements by civil-society organizations. The degree to which travel bans are linked to terrorism is not clear, but a Honduran interior minister was denied a visa in 2006 for reasons relating to alleged terrorist activities. Some cases are tied to corporate corruption, others to drug trafficking. One Panamanian president alleged that his US visa had been cancelled because he refused to allow the United States to set up an anti-drug-trafficking intelligence center in his country.[113] Corruption directly tied to mobility has been a factor in at least a few cases.[114]

Other cases make it clear that civil-society activists have had a significant role in providing derogatory information to DOS about individuals who are subsequently banned from travel to the United States.[115] Global Witness, an international NGO combating the corrupt exploitation of natural resources and international trade systems, welcomed the news that the United States endorsed travel sanctions against corrupt Cambodian government and military officials.[116] On other occasions, however, civil-society groups have opposed US sanctions against government officials.

These known cases suggest that the DOS view of corruption is a broad one, and US sanctions usually target political cases and high-level officials, and behavior that implicates democracy and rule-of-law issues. The secrecy that blankets the program makes it difficult to fully assess the merits of the decisions that have come to light, and even to have a clear understanding of the types of corruption being addressed. This makes it hard to determine how well the program is navigating the line between politics and anticorruption, and reduces the potential impact of the travel bans. It also prevents the integration of the program into a strategy to secure human movement.

EU Travel Bans

The European Union also imposes travel bans. EU Member States are asked to take all necessary measures to prevent the entry into, or transit through, their territories of listed persons.[117] The European Union sees travel bans — which may include visa restrictions on individuals, groups, or entities — as one tool in a broader array of sanctions or restrictive measures that may be imposed for reasons that range from strengthening security to promoting democracy and the rule of law.[118] As of January 2010, EU travel bans applied to persons from Belarus, Bosnia and Herzegovina, Burma, the Democratic Republic of Congo, Côte d'Ivoire, Croatia, the Republic of Guinea, Iran, Lebanon, Liberia, Moldova, Montenegro, North Korea, Serbia, Sierra Leone, Somalia, Sudan, Syria, and Zimbabwe, as well as to Osama bin Laden and al Qaeda and Taliban operatives.

UNSC Travel Bans

Chapter VII of the UN Charter requires states to carry out measures to combat threats to peace and security. Such measures include preventing terrorist travel by controlling movement across borders and access to safe havens. Like the US and EU travel bans, UNSC travel sanctions do not depend on prior criminal convictions under national law. UNSC travel bans are similar to DHS firearms trafficking and nuclear materials movement policy initiatives in that the bans require border authorities to prevent the departure and entry of the named individuals. UN travel bans have roots in counterterrorism and in the sanctions movement.

The Counterterrorism Context for Travel Bans
In response to the al Qaeda bombings of US embassies in Africa in 1998, the Security Council passed Resolution 1267 (1999) and simultaneously established the al Qaeda and Taliban Sanctions Committee (the 1267 Committee) to implement the resolution.[119] The initial objective of Resolution 1267 was to push Taliban leaders to hand over al Qaeda leader Osama bin Laden through an asset freeze and arms embargo. The resolution did not include a travel ban on al Qaeda.

Following the September 11, 2001, attacks by al Qaeda, the Security Council, as part of its overall deliberations concerning terrorism, considered the movement of people in terrorist operations. On September 28, 2001, the Security Council passed Resolution 1373, which mandates that UN Member States treat terrorism as a crime and:

- Deny safe haven to terrorists and their supporters
- Prevent terrorists and their supporters from using their respective territories for terrorist purposes against other states or their citizens
- Prevent the movement of terrorists or terrorist groups through effective control of borders and controls on the issuance of identity papers and travel documents, and through measures aimed at preventing counterfeiting, forgery, or fraudulent use of identity papers and travel documents[120]

The Security Council widened the Resolution 1267 mandate in a series of seven resolutions from 2000 to 2008.[121] Prior to 2001, travel bans had already served as a form of targeted or "smart" sanctions against regimes. By adopting Resolution 1390 (January 2002), the Security Council applied this tool for the first time to nonstate actors, both groups and individuals. It committed states to preventing "the entry into or the transit through their territories" of named individuals.[122]

As of May 12, 2009, 142 individuals associated with the Taliban and 255 associated with al Qaeda appeared on the 1267 Sanctions Committee's consolidated list, which is comprised of all of the individuals and entities on whom the Security Council has imposed sanctions.[123] The 1267 Sanctions Committee attempts to update the list on a real-time basis. Between the second quarter and end of 2008, the committee added 31 individuals and one entity to the list (compared with eight people in 2007), and it made changes to 289 existing entries on the list, including removing deceased people from the list.[124]

The State Sanctions Context for UNSC Travel Bans
Under Chapter VII of the UN Charter, the Security Council may impose sanctions instead of using armed forces to affect the behavior of regimes that its members agree are undermining international peace and security.[125]

The Security Council imposes a range of sanctions, from those targeted against individuals and groups, to comprehensive economic and trade sanctions that apply to entire populations. But during the mid-1990s, the United Nations moved from adopting comprehensive sanctions that could affect entire popula-tions to targeted sanctions, in response to the ethical or human-rights consid-eration that the United Nations should not hurt or negatively impact innocent civilians through its sanctions.[126] It began to design more targeted sanctions that would motivate political elites but have minimal negative humanitar-ian impact on innocent civilians. Travel bans are one element of a trio of new "smart" sanctions, with bans on arms shipments and on financing. UN travel-related sanctions may require states to restrict the landing of aircraft in particular countries; deny shelter, asylum, or safe havens to certain groups and named individuals; or prevent entry into or transit through their territory by such persons.

Implementation and Oversight of UNSC Travel Bans

At present, 11 UNSC resolutions authorize sanctions committees to manage and maintain lists of individuals and groups on whom the Security Council has imposed targeted sanctions, including travel bans.[127] As of mid-2009, ten sanctions committees maintained travel bans against individuals and enti-ties. Seven of these administered travel bans against members of particular regimes, and their lists contained anywhere between three and 47 individuals. The three counterterrorism committees are made up of all 15 Security Council members. Chairs of these three committees have reported at least biannu-ally to the Security Council since 2005: the al Qaeda and Taliban Sanctions Committee (1267 Committee) and the Counterterrorism Committee (CTC, established by Resolution 1373), both of which deal with travel bans and the steps taken to effectuate them; and the Committee on Weapons of Mass Destruction and Terrorism (1540 Committee, not discussed here).[128] With listings of almost 400 individuals associated with either the Taliban or al Qa-eda, the 1267 Sanctions Committee oversees most of the travel ban listings.[129] The chair of the 1267 Committee briefs the Security Council once every four months and the UN Member States once every six months regarding updates to the consolidated list. The committees and their experts work closely with one another.[130]

The 1267 al Qaeda and Taliban Committee is responsible for monitoring and facilitating governments' implementation of the travel bans and other sanc-tions.[131] To carry out its duties, the committee has a Secretariat and Analytical Support and Sanctions Monitoring Team. Appointed by the UN Secretary General, these experts, together with political affairs officers from the UN Department of Political Affairs, assist the 1267 Committee in evaluating implementation of the sanctions. In 2008, the 1267 monitoring team visited 26 countries and conducted sanctions workshops in five Member States.[132]

Exemptions

One debate about travel bans has concerned whether visas should be denied to family members of targeted individuals. The prevailing view is that restrictions on the movement of family members, although sometimes affecting innocent civilians (such as students), can effectively exert pressure on the principal targets to change their actions.[133]

To avoid collateral harm, the Security Council may include provisions for exemptions in the text of its resolutions.[134] Air carriers and personnel from humanitarian or relief organizations may be permitted, for example, to deliver medical treatment to an individual or a state on the travel ban list, and individuals may likewise seek exemptions for medical, religious, or other humanitarian purposes. Resolution 1822 (2008) exempts states applying terrorist travel bans from denying entry into or requiring the departure from its territories of its own nationals, where entry or transit is necessary for the fulfillment of a judicial process, or where the Sanctions Committee determines that entry or transit is justified. The al Qaeda travel sanction is the only one that allows states (but does not require them) to deny entry to or require the departure of their own citizens. The Sanctions Committee can also grant individuals exceptions for medical treatment abroad and for the performance of religious obligations.

Short- and Long-Term Problems

The travel ban program is in an early stage of development and there are many issues and problems to be worked out, including appeal rights, identification and various listing issues, the scope of the right to movement, and lack of capacity in border and immigration systems.

Fairness in listing individuals. All UN Member States have a right to recommend that an individual be added to the 1267 Committee's single consolidated list. Governments must submit supporting evidence and the reason why they wish to include someone on the list. If none of the 15 Security Council members object to the proposal within five days, travel and other designated sanctions are imposed on that individual or group.[135] If an individual is in a country when the sanction is passed, the government of that country may choose to prevent that individual from leaving the country or to repatriate him to the

country of origin, unless the sanctions resolution specifies otherwise.
The processes for placing individuals on and removing them from the 1267 Committee's list are opaque.[136] Usually, national governments prepare a list of names based on their intelligence and law-enforcement information and submit that to the appropriate Security Council sanctions committee. Standards for proposing individuals for the list vary across countries. The United States is perceived to have high standards, even in comparison with the European Union, and its proposals are generally rapidly accepted by other members of the Security Council.[137]

It can be difficult to find out why an individual had been listed. There is no rule or enforcement mechanism covering the provision of information.[138] The Security Council has amended its process to require explanations. States must include identifying and background information when proposing new names to include on the 1267 Committee's list (Resolution 1526, 2004). States must include a "statement of case" that describes the basis of the proposal (Resolution 1617, 2005). They must also submit a standard form when proposing names to the 1267 Sanctions Committee, specify the nature of the information used in developing a case against the individual, and provide supporting documents, if available (Resolution 1735, 2006).

The sanctions committees have also expanded their requirements for notice to individuals and transparency to governments and publics. States must identify parts of the statement of case that can be made public to notify the proposed designee (Resolution 1735, 2006). The 1267 Committee is required to notify the designated individual of his or her addition to the list and the effect of that designation. It must also provide the publicly available statement of the case supporting the listing, notify the permanent mission of the country where the individual is believed to be and notify the individual's country of citizenship about the addition of his or her name to the list, and publish a summary of why the individual (or group) was put on its consolidated list (Resolution 1822, 2008; Resolution 1904, 2009).

Resolution 1526 (2004) established the Analytical Support and Sanctions Monitoring Team to offer independent reports and recommendations on implementing Resolution 1267 and its successors. The 1267 Committee now publishes, on its Web site, the reasons that individuals and groups are listed or delisted.[139] When the consolidated list is updated, the 1267 Committee issues a press release, transmits a diplomatic note, and sends e-mail notices to contact points in permanent missions in New York and national capitals.[140] It sends a hard-copy update quarterly.

Review and appeal procedures and rights. Individuals may wish to have their names taken off the consolidated list for a variety of reasons, including genuine mistakes, changes in the listed individuals' behavior, or the desire to seek an exemption based on judicial process. The standards for exemptions are not clear. The 1267 Committee posts some details on its Web site.[141]

Individuals who believe they are wrongly listed or those seeking an exemption may have their government or, in rare cases, a UN office or agency apply on their behalf by writing to the 1267 Committee's chairman.[142] The Security Council established an office, the Focal Point for De-listing, within the Security Council Subsidiary Organs Branch in March 2007[143] to receive requests from Member State governments for delisting names and granting humanitarian exceptions.[144]

These shifts toward greater transparency, review, and appeals came about because of lawsuits and the concerns voiced by human rights organizations — in particular European organizations and governments. It is unclear whether EU courts will find the limited right of appeal to be sufficient.

Identification and other listing issues. The consolidated list exists only in English, although it includes Arabic-script versions of most of the individual names and a few entities relating to al Qaeda and the Taliban. The process of writing all non-English names in their native scripts is ongoing. The 1267 Committee also maintains a delisting section on its Web site.

Continuing accuracy of the list is a problem, since individuals may die or their circumstances may change. In addition, all terrorist lists that governments develop are plagued by identification and information-sharing problems. To some extent, governments have erred on the side of inclusion, to the detriment of those who are undeservedly placed on terrorist lists. But even accurately identified terrorists can be elusive and some identification problems are unavoidable. The 1267 monitoring team has reported that the entries for many individuals on the 1267 Committee's consolidated list lack detail or adequate identifiers.[145]

Based on guidelines adopted in December 2008, the 1267 Committee will review all names on its list by June 30, 2010, and initiate reviews of small groups every quarter by circulating them to the designating state and the state of residence and/or nationality.

Countries are beginning to integrate the 1267 Committee's consolidated list into their national databases and watchlists, although some countries still require administrative orders or other legal procedures to allow them to enter the updates into their systems. The 1267 Committee teamed up with Interpol in 2005 to distribute its list more effectively to states without the ability to maintain an updated watchlist, but there are still many implementation problems.

The right to movement. Travel-ban programs raise a potential tension for democratic states. One purpose of democratic government is to protect the security of the state and its members. The other is to protect people's rights, which include freedom of movement as well as the due process of law.[146] The tension between security and freedom of movement is rooted in international law and is unavoidable, but it needs to be addressed.

Article 13 of the Universal Declaration of Human Rights (1948)[147] guarantees that "everyone has the right to freedom of movement and residence within the borders of each state," and "the right to leave any country, including his own, and to return to his country." Article 12 of the International Covenant on Civil and Political Rights (ICCPR) confirms this right.[148] It states:

- "Everyone lawfully within the territory of a state shall, within that territory, have the right to liberty of movement and freedom to choose his residence."
- "Everyone shall be free to leave any country, including his own."
- "The above-mentioned rights shall not be subject to any restrictions except those which are provided by law, are necessary to protect national security, public order (*ordre public*), public health or morals or the rights and freedoms of others, and are consistent with the other rights recognized in the present Covenant."
- "No one shall be arbitrarily deprived of the right to enter his own country."

The Security Council restricts movement through various means — blocking air travel to and from a targeted country, preventing travel of an individual seeking to leave a country, and barring travel by an individual seeking to enter a country. The initial travel bans aimed at terrorism were against state sponsors of terrorism who provided safe haven to terrorists. Resolution 1267 decreed that all states shall:

> deny permission for any aircraft to take off from or land in their territory if it is owned, leased, or operated by or on behalf of the Taliban [. . .] unless the particular flight has been approved in advance by the Committee on the grounds of humanitarian need, including religious obligation such as the performance of the Hajj.[149]

This generalized targeted sanction attempts to cut off the state sponsor of terrorism from access to global movement. It is not a stretch in principle to deny the right of movement to a state sponsor of terrorism. For example, the Taliban harbored al Qaeda, a global terrorist group that had by the time of the resolution's adoption launched a series of devastating attacks on civilians outside of Afghanistan.[150]

Resolution 1373 requires states to prevent the entry and exit of terrorists as a general rule. Travel bans are also, in principle, consistent with the UN Charter and successor articulations of the right to movement. The Security Council sanctions individuals and imposes travel bans on them pursuant to its mandate to ensure peace and security. Terrorists are placed on the list when they and their organizations intend to take the lives of individuals. In doing so, terrorists seek to substitute their will for people's lawful exercise of their fundamental human rights. The same is true for members of regimes that grossly violate human rights and threaten world order with nuclear or other aggression. Thus, travel bans both protect the security of states threatened by terrorist groups and the security of individuals.

UNSC travel bans tend to focus on restricting entry. Article 13 and other statements of the right to freedom of movement, as interpreted by courts, do not offer citizens of one country a blanket right to enter another country. A right to enter by anyone would override a state's ability to set and enforce immigration laws. Given that sovereign nations have the legal authority to decide who they admit in the first place, the act of restricting the admission of terrorists or human rights violators does not raise legal concerns in principle.

The scope of the right to international movement is not well understood or settled. There are two areas requiring further development: the right to depart and the right to reenter one's own country.

The incorporation of the freedom to depart and return to one's country as the chief element of the right to movement in post–World War II human rights charters was a response to the specter of totalitarian government, specifically to laws that restricted citizens' freedom to travel internationally. In fact, democratic governments may and do place limited restrictions on exit, for example, by individuals wanted for a crime, military service, or payment of taxes. (Other limitations are discussed in chapter 7.) Assuming that the grounds for a listing are accurate and fairly imposed, there is a basis for blocking departure. There is a long line of cases in US jurisprudence defining the scope of the right to depart, for example, in connection with the intersection of the right to travel with the exercise of free speech.[151]

With respect to an individual's right to reenter his or her own country, at least two governments, Canada and the United States, have considered the question of preventing the return of citizens on grounds of terrorism, and in Canada's case, of a dual citizen listed by the 1267 Sanctions Committee.[152] In August 2006, the United States denied two naturalized US citizens of Pakistani descent permission to reenter the United States from Pakistan unless they agreed to be interrogated by the FBI. The US government denied both men entry because they were relatives of a man convicted earlier that year for providing material support to terrorists. After their lawyer filed a complaint to the DHS in August 2006, the two were allowed return to the United States.[153] DHS conveyed to the lawyer that unspecified records had been modified "to address any delay or denial of boarding."[154] In such cases, the right to movement conflicts with the government's attempt to provide security against known terrorist risks.

Lack of mobility capabilities in developing countries. While international law authorizes the Security Council to decide upon the adoption of travel bans and to mandate an infrastructure to effectuate them, it is up to individual states to carry out these mandates.

Some nations are reluctant to implement travel bans for political reasons. In other instances, governments lack confidence in or object to the designation of specific individuals. Officials from a number of countries believe that travel bans or other sanctions by the Security Council reflect an exclusively Western-centric or "powerful-country" agenda and ignore the views of nations elsewhere around the world.

A fundamental challenge is gaining acceptance of the concept of travel bans as a legitimate counterterrorism and state sanction. Controls at borders seem at odds with the drive toward free trade, freedom of movement for people, and respect for the integrity of borderland communities and environments. Moreover, many states do not have sufficiently policed borders to make travel bans workable. Practically speaking, options for clandestine movement are robust.

By far the most important obstacle to more effective implementation is that many of the UN Member States amenable to fulfilling their obligations to ban travel and strengthen control at their borders lack the capacity and resources to do so. We need only consider the billions of dollars the United States continues to spend on modernizing its own border controls to grasp the magnitude of the task facing other governments. A UN implementation survey from June 2008 found, not surprisingly, that many countries were failing to implement border controls and to detect fraudulent documents.[155] As of October 2007, only one of the 13 countries in East Africa, a critical area for terrorists and smugglers, had fully implemented measures to screen travelers and nine had done so partially.[156] Of the 23 West and Central African countries, also critical areas for illegal transit and the backyard for al Qaeda in the Maghreb, none had fully implemented measures to prevent the illegal cross-border movement of persons.[157] This is not a resource gap that the United Nations can fill.

The Efficacy of UNSC Travel Bans

A critical question is whether travel bans can achieve the ends sought by the international community in imposing them. It is obvious how a financial ban can be effective — once a source of funds is located, it can be blocked using agreed-upon international mechanisms. The actual implementation of a travel ban is more complicated. In addition, travel bans have a mixed record of success in affecting regimes and countering terrorism. The Security Council Counter-Terrorism Executive Directorate (CTED) is unaware of any government having stopped any listed individual from crossing its borders, and several listed individuals are known to have traveled successfully. But it is not unreasonable to think that public bans constrain some terrorists and stigmatize listed individuals.

The UN Chapter 7 mandate increases the chances that a listed individual will be spotted by border or police authorities. In addition, travel sanctions can act as a deterrent to travel by listed terrorists. For example, radical cleric Abu Qatada, an al Qaeda associate living in the United Kingdom who is on the 1267 Committee's consolidated list, sought to — but did not take — a planned trip to Lebanon. But the vulnerabilities of the global travel system are an obstacle to full realization of terrorist travel bans. Senior members of al Qaeda, Hezbollah, and Hamas, whose identities and physical appearance are either known or captured by a biometric, are undoubtedly hindered by being on the UN list. Assuming the list is distributed effectively, border guards will be alerted. A travel ban may also deter terrorists from traveling simply by revealing that governments know who they are. With respect to lesser-known terrorists, particularly those whose photograph or other biometric identifier may not be available, the practical impact of a travel ban is questionable.

Conclusion

Despite the limitations of travel bans, they provide important benefits that go beyond their current operational efficacy. In the long run, travel bans increase the cost of travel — if not constrain it outright. A travel ban politically stigmatizes individuals and rallies governments and citizens against them. If there is a list of individuals of such significant concern that the Security Council attempts to block their finances and deny them weapons, it also makes sense that their movement be constrained.

To strengthen the US travel-ban program, DHS and DOS should take a number of steps to build on programs instituted by the European Union and Security Council:

- Travel bans should be incorporated more decisively and systematically into overall mobility security policy. Proclamation 7750, which focuses on corruption, should be reviewed, revised as needed, and reaffirmed. The scope of the US travel-ban program pursuant to Proclamation 7750 should be made public. There should be an annual Human Smuggling and Trafficking Center (HSTC) report that describes the number of travel bans imposed, the persons against whom they have been aimed, and the goals sought and benefits achieved. The degree of secrecy blanketing the US program and its list of names should be reexamined. The review should consider the purpose of the sanctions and the degree to which "naming and shaming" supports that effort. Other areas meriting review: issues of intelligence classification, the public's interest in knowing about a significant government program, privacy rights, and interest by DHS and DOS in promoting public resilience by providing reassurance of effective preclusive actions. Legal standards should be clear enough to withstand charges of political bias.

- DHS should contribute names to the Proclamation 7750 list of third-party government and private-sector facilitators who are responsible for corruption in mobility channels, especially those with a terrorist nexus or who participate in HSO networks linked to terrorist groups and HTOs.

- DHS and DOS should coordinate US and EU travel bans, perhaps using HSTC as a clearinghouse for travel-ban information internationally. Otherwise people banned from coming to the United States may travel to Europe, and vice versa. While there are many weak links in the global travel system, a consolidated effort by the European Union and the United States would remove a significant area of vulnerability. DHS should consider incorporating the issue of joint travel bans into negotiations concerning the mobility security agreements discussed in chapter 10.

- With respect to the Security Council sanctions, Congress should clarify the basis in US law for designating individuals for travel bans. It should also examine the question of whether and under what specific circumstances individuals on whom US travel bans are imposed should be recommended for Security Council travel bans.

- US officials should educate the public on the existence of the UN travel-ban list, the reasons for it, and the legal basis for abrogating the right to travel.

- Regular attention needs to be paid to keeping the Security Council Resolution 1267 consolidated list and other lists as updated and as accurate as possible. Consideration should be given to increasing the authority of the UN nonpolitical monitoring team to nominate individuals for addition and removal from the list.[158]

NOTES

1. Dangers range from life-threatening risks to migrants in desert or ocean crossings or at the hands of human traffickers to challenges for societies in absorbing large numbers of migrants or arising from migration precipitated by climate change. See Michael V. Hayden, "Transcript of Remarks," Landon Lecture Series, Kansas State Univ., April 30, 2008, www.cia.gov/news-information/speeches-testimony-archive-2008/landon-lecture-series.html.

2. DOD (US Department of Defense), *National Defense Strategy* (Washington, DC: DOD, 2008), www.defense.gov/news/2008%20National%20Defense%20Strategy.pdf; DHS (US Department of Homeland Security), "U.S. Department of Homeland Security Announces 6.8 Percent Increase in Fiscal Year 2009 Budget Request," Press Release, February 4, 2008, www.dhs.gov/xnews/releases/pr_1202151112290.shtm; DHS, *Quadrennial Homeland Security Review* (Washington, DC: DHS, 2010).

3. See, for example, Demetrios G. Papademetriou and Gregory Maniatis, lead writers, *Gaining from Migration: Towards a New Mobility System* (Washington, DC: MPI, 2007); Jonathan Laurence, *Integrating Islam: A New Chapter in Church-State Relations* (Washington, DC: MPI/Bertelsmann Stiftung, 2007).

4. NCTC (National Counterterrorism Center), *National Strategy to Combat Terrorist Travel* (Washington, DC: NCTC, 2006), www.nctc.gov/docs/u_terrorist_travel_book_may2_2006.pdf.

5. Ibid.

6. Ibid., 2–3.

7. The importance of analysis is widely recognized in the counterterrorism community, although the need for better specific analysis regarding clandestine travel channels, outside of tactical operations, has not been highlighted. See Rob Johnston, *Analytic Culture in the US Intelligence Community: An Ethnographic Study* (Washington, DC: Central Intelligence Agency, 2005); Richard A. Clarke, *Your Government Failed You: Breaking the Cycle of National Security Disasters* (New York: Harper Collins, 2008), 119–41.

8. See also Susan Ginsburg, *Countering Terrorist Mobility: Shaping an Operational Strategy* (Washington, DC: Migration Policy Institute, MPI, 2006), www.migrationpolicy.org/pubs/MPI_TaskForce_Ginsburg.pdf.

9. DHS (Department of Homeland Security), The Secure Borders and Open Doors Advisory Committee, *Preserving Our Welcome to the World in an Age of Terrorism* (Washington, DC: DHS, 2008), www.dhs.gov/xlibrary/assets/SBODAC_011608-Accessible.pdf.

10. The National Implementation Plan for the War on Terror, a classified document written by the NCTC, was first approved by the President in June 2006 and again in September 2008. It is the US government's comprehensive strategic plan that defines the objectives for over 500 discrete counterterrorism tasks for which different agencies are responsible.

11. GAO (US Government Accountability Office), *Combating Alien Smuggling: Opportunities Exist to Improve the Federal Response*, GAO-05-305 (Washington, DC: GAO, 2005), 58, www.gao.gov/new.items/d05305.pdf.

12. William Ho-González, "Combating International Criminal Travel Networks," *The United States Attorneys' Bulletin* 56, no. 6 (2008): 20–24, www.justice.gov/usao/eousa/foia_reading_room/usab5606.pdf.

13. Statement for the record of James W. Ziglar, Distinguished Visiting Professor of Law at The George Washington Univ. Law School, "Borders, Transportation, and Managing Risk," before the National Commission on Terrorist Attacks upon the United States, January 26, 2004, http://govinfo.library.unt.edu/911/hearings/hearing7/witness_ziglar.htm.

14. Michael Surgalla and Arthur Norton, "International Aspects of Criminal Immigration Enforcement," *The United States Attorneys' Bulletin* 51, no. 5 (2003): 14–20, www.justice.gov/usao/eousa/foia_reading_room/usab5105.pdf.

15. Ho-González, "Combating International Criminal Travel Networks."

16. Ibid.

17. Mark Kleiman, professor of public policy at the University of California, Los Angeles; personal communication with the author.

18. Ibid.

19. An excellent analysis and set of recommendations are provided in the International Peace Institute, *Transnational Organized Crime: Task Forces on Strengthening Multilateral Security Capacity* (New York: International Peace Institute, 2009), www.ipacademy.org/media/pdf/publications/toc_final.pdf.

20. Official Journal of the European Union, *Agreement on Mutual Legal Assistance between the European Union and the United States of America* (Brussels, Belgium: Official Journal of the European Union, 2003).

21. DHS, Immigration and Customs Enforcement (ICE), *ICE Fiscal Year 2008 Annual Report: Protecting National Security and Upholding Public Safety* (Washington, DC: DHS, 2009), www.ice.gov/doclib/pi/reports/ice_annual_report/pdf/ice08ar_final.pdf.

22. Ibid.

23. DHS, ICE, information obtained by the author.

24. DOS (US Department of State), *Investigations* (Washington, DC: DOS, 2009), www.state.gov/m/ds/investigat/index.htm.

25. DOS, Diplomatic Security (DS), information obtained by author. See also: Statement for the record of Joe D. Morton, Principal Deputy Assistant Secretary and Director, Diplomatic Security Service, DOS, "Pushing the Border Out on Alien Smuggling: New Tools and Intelligence Initiatives," before the House Judiciary Committee, Subcommittee on Immigration, Border Security and Claims, 108th Cong., 2nd sess., May 18, 2004, http://commdocs.house.gov/committees/judiciary/hju93716.000/hju93716_0f.htm.

26. Ibid.

27. Randal C. Archibold and Andrew Becker, "Border Agents, Lured by the Other Side," *New York Times*, May 27, 2008, www.nytimes.com/2008/05/27/us/27border.html.

28. Ibid.

29. Ibid.

30. DHS, Customs and Border Protection (CBP), *Office of Internal Affairs: Assistant Commissioner, James F. Tomsheck* (Washington, DC: DHS, 2009), www.cbp.gov/xp/cgov/about/organization/assist_comm_off/internal_affairs.xml.

31. James Tomsheck, Assistant Commissioner, Office of Internal Affairs, DHS, personal communication with the author.

32. Thanks to Jonathan Caulkins for the idea of sentence enhancements. See Jonathan P. Caulkins and Peter Reuter, "Towards a Harm-Reduction Approach to Enforcement," *Safer Communities* 8, no. 1 (2009): 9–23, www.ukdpc.org.uk/resources/Safer_Communities_Jan09_Special_Issue.pdf.

33. Task Force on Confronting the Ideology of Radical Extremism, *Rewriting the Narrative: An Integrated Strategy for Counterradicalization* (Washington, DC: The Washington Institute for Near East Policy, 2009), www.washingtoninstitute.org/pubPDFs/PTF2-Counterradicalization.pdf.

34. Will Somerville, Jamie Durana, and Aaron Matteo Terrazas, *Hometown Associations: An Untapped Resource for Immigrant Integration?* (Washington, DC: Migration Policy Institute, MPI, 2008), www.migrationpolicy.org/pubs/Insight-HTAs-July08.pdf. Foreign governments may seek to use nongovernmental organizations (NGOs) to pursue their own interests in connection with diaspora populations. See "Russia: Protecting Citizens Living Abroad," *Stratfor*, December 2, 2009, www.stratfor.com/memberships/149835/analysis/20091202_russia_protecting_citizens_living_abroad; Moscow is considering the establishment of a foundation for assistance and rights protection for compatriots living abroad, which would use NGOs to counter what Moscow perceives as mistreatment of Russian minorities in neighboring states.

35. The importance of respect has been described in several detailed accounts of ethnic gangs. See, for example, Ko-Lin Chin, *Chinatown Gangs: Extortion, Enterprise, and Ethnicity* (New York: Oxford Univ. Press, 1996); Ruth Horowitz, *Honor and the American Dream: Culture and Identity in a Chicano Community* (New Brunswick, NJ: Rutgers Univ. Press, 1983).

36. GAO (US Government Accountability Office), *Information on Criminal Aliens Incarcerated in Federal and State Prisons and Local Jails*, GAO-05-337R, Briefing for Congressional Requesters (Washington, DC: GAO, March 29, 2005), www.gao.gov/new.items/d05337r.pdf. The reliability of crime statistics relating to the foreign born and noncitizens has been questioned. See Steven A. Camarota and Jessica M. Vaughan, *Immigration and Crime, Assessing a Conflicted Issue* (Washington, DC: Center for Immigration Studies [CIS], 2009), www.cis.org/articles/2009/crime.pdf.

37. This number includes 10,877 individuals who are either not US citizens or whose citizenship is unknown. DOJ (US Department of Justice), Federal Bureau of Prisons, "Quick Facts about the Bureau of Prisons," Press Release, December 25, 2009, www.bop.gov/news/quick.jsp#1.

38. Ibid.

39. Rubén G. Rumbaut, Roberto G. Gonzales, Golnaz Komaie, and Charlie V. Morgan, "Debunking the Myth of Immigrant Criminality: Imprisonment among First- and Second-Generation Young Men," *Migration Information Source*, June 1, 2006, www.migrationinformation.org/Feature/print.cfm?ID=403.

40. National Network for Safe Communities, "Home," www.nnscommunities.org.

41. Los Angeles-Long Beach-Santa Ana, CA, at 34.9 percent; Stockton, CA, at 24.3 percent; Chicago-Naperville-Joliet, IL-IN-WI, at 17.6 percent; Sacramento-Arden Arcade-Roseville, CA, at 17.3 percent; Boston-Cambridge-Quincy, MA-NH, at 15.9 percent; Providence-New Bedford-Fall River, RI-MA, at 12.7 percent. Author's calculations based on US Census Bureau, *American Community Survey*, 2007 (Washington, DC: US Census Bureau, 2008).

42 . In the Los Angeles-Long Beach-Santa Ana, CA corridor, 57.4 percent of the foreign born were born in Central or South America and 33.6 percent in Asia. In the Chicago-Naperville-Joliet region, IL-IN-WI, 47.7 percent were born in Central or South America. In the Providence-New Bedford-Fall River, RI-MA region, 19.7 percent were born in Central or South America; in Boston-Cambridge-Quincy, MA, 29.6 percent of the foreign born were born in Asia, 22.4 percent in Europe, and 20 percent from Central or South America. Author's calculations based on US Census Bureau, *American Community Survey*, 2007.

43. For a comprehensive list of cities with a Mexican drug-trafficking presence, see DOJ, National Drug Intelligence Center, *National Drug Threat Assessment 2009* (Washington, DC: DOJ, 2009), www.usdoj.gov/ndic/pubs31/31379/dlinks.htm#Map5.

44. Max Manwaring, *A Contemporary Challenge to State Sovereignty: Gangs and Other Illicit Transnational Criminal Organizations in Central America*, El Salvador, Mexico, Jamaica, and Brazil (Carlisle, PA: Strategic Studies Institute, US Army War College, 2007), 4.

45. Ibid., 4–7. According to Manwaring these three types of gangs develop in a generational sequence, with one form evolving into the next. However, there is no evidence of such evolution.

46. Anthony Braga, "Analyzing Homicide Problems: Practical Approaches to Developing a Policy-Relevant Description of Serious Urban Violence," *Security Journal* 18, no. 4 (2005): 17–32; Anthony Braga, "Serious Youth Gun Offenders and the Epidemic of Youth Violence in Boston," *Journal of Quantitative Criminology* 19, no. 1 (2003): 33–54; Anthony A. Braga, David M. Kennedy, and George Tita, "New Approaches to the Strategic Prevention of Gang and Group-Involved Violence," in *Gangs in America*, 3rd ed., ed. Ronald C. Huff (Thousand Oaks, CA: Sage Publications, 2002); David M. Kennedy, *Deterrence and Crime Prevention: Reconsidering the Prospect of Sanction* (New York: Routledge, 2008); David M. Kennedy, conversation with the author.

47. Kennedy, *Deterrence and Crime Prevention*, 63–68, 142–43.

48. David M. Kennedy, personal communication with the author.

49. Ruben Castaneda, "Gang Members Describe Life Inside MS-13," *The Washington Post*, October 18, 2006.

50. Matthew Quirk, "How to Grow a Gang," *The Atlantic*, May 2008, www.theatlantic.com/doc/print/200805/world-in-numbers.

51. Ibid.

52. Mark Kleiman, *When Brute Force Fails: How to Have Less Crime and Less Punishment* (Princeton, NJ:

Princeton Univ. Press, 2009), 14.

53. Tom Barry, "Mass Incarcerations of Immigrants," *Border Lines*, May 24, 2009, http://borderlinesblog.blogspot.com/2009/05/mass-incarceration-of-immigrants.html.

54. DHS (US Department of Homeland Security), Office of Immigration Statistics, *Yearbook of Immigration Statistics: Table 36: Aliens Removed or Returned: Fiscal Years 1892 to 2008* (Washington, DC: DHS, 2008), www.dhs.gov/xlibrary/assets/statistics/yearbook/2008/table36.xls.

55. DHS, *Yearbook of Immigration Statistics: Table 37: Aliens Removed by Criminal Status and Region and Country of Nationality: Fiscal Years 1999 to 2008*, www.dhs.gov/xlibrary/assets/statistics/yearbook/2008/table37d.xls.

56. Doris Meissner and Donald Kerwin, *DHS and Immigration: Taking Stock and Correcting Course* (Washington, DC: MPI, February 2009), www.migrationpolicy.org/pubs/DHS_Feb09.pdf.

57. The Memorandum of Understanding between the US Immigration and Customs Enforcement (ICE) and Drug Enforcement Administration (DEA) will be reviewed after one year and every two years following that initial review. GAO, *Better Coordination with the Department of Homeland Security and an Updated Accountability Framework Can Further Enhance DEA's Efforts to Meet Post-9/11 Responsibilities*, GAO-09-63 (Washington, DC: GAO, 2009), www.gao.gov/highlights/d0963high.pdf; DHS, US Immigration and Customs Enforcement, "ICE and DEA Strengthen Partnership to Fight Drug Trafficking," News Release, June 18, 2009, www.ice.gov/pi/nr/0906/090618washington.htm.

58. Spencer S. Hsu, "US to Check Immigration Status of People in Local Jails," *The Washington Post*, May 19, 2009, www.washingtonpost.com/wp-dyn/content/article/2009/05/18/AR2009051803172.html.

59. DHS, ICE, "ICE Unveils Sweeping New Plan to Target Criminal Aliens in Jails Nationwide: Initiative Aims to Identify and Remove Criminal Aliens from All US Jails and Prisons," News Release, March 28, 2008, www.ice.gov/pi/news/newsreleases/articles/080414washington.htm.

60. GAO, *Information on Criminal Aliens Incarcerated in Federal and State Prisons and Local Jails*.

61. ICE, *Operation Community Shield: Targeting Violent Transnational Street Gangs* (Washington, DC: DHS, 2009), www.ice.gov/pi/investigations/comshield/.

62. Those arrested under Operation Community Shield have been members of the MS-13, Sureños, 18th Street Gang, Latin Kings, Vatos Locos, Bloods, and Varrio Northside, among others gangs.

63. ICE, *Operation Community Shield: Targeting Violent Transnational Street Gangs* (Washington, DC: US Homeland Security, 2008), www.ice.gov/pi/news/factsheets/opshieldfactsheet.htm.

64. Ibid.

65. Jessica M. Vaughan and Jon D. Feere, *Taking Back the Streets: ICE and Local Law Enforcement Target Immigrant Gangs* (Washington, DC: Center for Immigration Studies [CIS], 2008), www.cis.org/ImmigrantGangsAnnounce.

66. "Out of the underworld — Criminal gangs in the Americas," *The Economist*, January 6, 2006.

67. Author's interview with CBP officials. Mary Helen Johnson, "National Policies and the Rise of Transnational Gangs," *Migration Information Source*, April 1, 2006, www.migrationinformation.org/Feature/print.cfm?ID=394; Andrew V. Papachristos, "Gang World," Foreign Policy, March 1, 2005, www.foreignpolicy.com/articles/2005/03/01/gang_world; Celinda Franco, *The MS-13 and 18th Street Gangs: Emerging Transnational Gang Threats?* (Washington, DC: Congressional Research Service, 2008), www.fas.org/sgp/crs/row/RL34233.pdf.

68. Wayne Cornelius, *Evaluating US Immigration Control Policy: What Mexican Migrants Can Tell Us* (San Diego, CA: Center for Comparative Immigration Studies, 2009).

69. The 643.3 miles of fencing is comprised of 344.8 miles of primary pedestrian fencing and 298.5 miles of vehicle fencing. See DHS, Customs and Border Protection (CBP), "Southwest Border Fence Construction Progress," Press Release, January 15, 2010, www.cbp.gov/xp/cgov/border_security/ti/ti_news/sbi_fence/.

70. Statement for the record of Janet Napolitano, Secretary of the DHS, "Oversight of the Department of Homeland Security," before the US Senate Committee on the Judiciary 111th Cong., 1st sess., December 9, 2009, www.aila.org/content/default.aspx?bc=1019|6712|12178|30785; Cam

Simpson, "Border Arrests Decline Again," *The Wall Street Journal*, November 11, 2009, http://on-line.wsj.com/article/SB125781594948540097.html; Spencer S. Hsu, "Border Deaths Are Increasing," *The Washington Post*, September 30, 2009, www.washingtonpost.com/wp-dyn/content/article/2009/09/29/AR2009092903212.html.

71. Cornelius, *Evaluating U.S. Immigration Control Policy*.

72. Ibid.

73. Wayne A. Cornelius and Jessa M. Lewis, *Impacts of Border Enforcement on Mexican Migration: The View from Sending Communities* (Boulder: Lynne Rienner and UCSD Center for Comparative Immigration Studies, 2007); Wayne A. Cornelius and Idean Salehyan, "Does Border Enforcement Deter Unauthorized Immigration? The Case of Mexican Migration to the United States of America," *Regulation and Governance* 1, no. 2 (2007): 139–53.

74. Meissner and Kerwin, *DHS and Immigration*.

75. Wayne A. Cornelius, "Reforming the Management of Migration Flows from Latin America to the United States," Brookings Partnership for the Americas Commission Background Document BD-01, (Washington, DC: Brookings Institution, 2008), www.brookings.edu/~/media/Files/rc/reports/2008/1124_latin_america_partnership/migration_flows_cornelius.pdf.

76. Overseas Security Advisory Council, *El Salvador 2009 Crime & Safety Report* (Washington, DC: DOS, 2009), www.osac.gov/Reports/report.cfm?contentID=97810.

77. These rates are high-end estimates. UNODC (United Nations Office on Drugs and Crime), *International Homicide Statistics (IHS): Intentional Homicide, Rate per 100,000 Population, 2004, unless Otherwise Specified* (Vienna, Austria: UNODC, 2009), www.unodc.org/documents/data-and-analysis/IHS-rates-05012009.pdf.

78. David M. Kennedy, "A Tale of One City," in *Securing Our Children's Future: New Approaches to Juvenile Justice and Youth Violence*, ed. Gary S. Katzman (Washington, DC: Brookings Institution Press, 2002), 148.

79. Anthony A. Braga, *Problem-Oriented Policing and Crime Prevention* (Monsey: Criminal Justice Press, 2002), 78–81.

80. Alternatives to incarceration developed during the past two decades are discussed in Kleiman, *When Brute Force Fails*.

81. David M. Kennedy, *Drugs, Race and Common Ground: Reflections on the High Point Intervention* (Washington, DC: DOJ, 2009), www.ojp.usdoj.gov/nij/journals/262/high-point-intervention.htm.

82. DOJ, Office of Justice Programs, National Institute of Justice, "Editor's Note: Evaluating the High Point Intervention," Press Release, March 24, 2009, www.ojp.usdoj.gov/nij/journals/262/evaluating-high-point-intervention.htm; Kennedy, *Drugs, Race and Common Ground*.

83. Kennedy, *Deterrence and Crime Prevention*.

84. Scott H. Decker, "A Decade of Gang Research: Findings of the National Institute of Justice Gang Portfolio," in *Responding to Gangs: Evaluation and Research*, ed. Winifred L. Reed and Scott H. Decker (Washington, DC: DOJ, 2002); Ronald C. Huff, "Gangs and Public Policy: Prevention, Intervention, and Suppression," in *Gangs in America*, 3rd ed., ed. C. Ronald Huff (Thousand Oaks, CA: Sage Publications, 2002), 287–94.

85. G. David Curry, Richard A. Ball, and Robert J. Fox, *Gang Crime and Law Enforcement Recordkeeping* (Washington, DC: DOJ, 1994), www.ncjrs.gov/txtfiles/gcrime.txt.

86. See, for example, Richard H. Friman, "Drug Markets and the Selective Use of Violence," *Crime, Law and Social Change* 52, no. 3 (2009): 285–95.

87. A number of analysts have suggested that one of the crucial factors in responding to gangs is how the problem is understood. See, for example, Scott H. Decker "Gangs, Youth Violence, and Policing: Where Do We Stand, Where Do We Go From Here?" in *Policing Gangs and Youth Violence*, ed. Scott H. Decker (Belmont, CA: Wadsworth, 2003), 287–93.

88. Irving A. Spergel and G. David Curry, "Strategies and Perceived Agency Effectiveness in Dealing with the Youth Gang Problem," in *Gangs in America*, ed. Ronald C. Huff (Newbury Park, CA: Sage Publications, 1990), 288–309.

89. Karl Vick, "Iraq's Lessons, on the Home Front," *The Washington Post*, November 15, 2009, www.washingtonpost.com/wp-dyn/content/article/2009/11/14/AR2009111400915.html; John Brennan, "A New Approach to Safeguarding Americans," Remarks at the Center for Strategic and International Studies, Washington, DC, August 6, 2009.

90. John Seabrooke, "Don't Shoot," *The New Yorker*, June 22, 2009, www.newyorker.com/reporting/2009/06/22/090622fa_fact_seabrook.

91. David M. Kennedy, Anthony A. Braga, Anne M. Piehl, and Elin J. *Waring, Reducing Gun Violence: The Boston Gun Project's Operation Ceasefire* (Washington, DC: DOJ, September 2001), www.ncjrs.gov/pdffiles1/nij/188741.pdf; Anthony A. Braga, David M. Kennedy, Elin J. Waring, and Anne M. Piehl, "Problem-Oriented Policing, Deterrence, and Youth Violence: An Evaluation of Boston's Operation Ceasefire," *Journal of Research in Crime and Delinquency* 38, no. 3 (2001): 195–225.

92. For more details on the High Point approach, see Kennedy, *Drugs, Race and Common Ground*.

93. Stewart Wakeling, *Ending Gang Homicide: Deterrence Can Work* (Sacramento, CA: California Attorney General's Office, 2003), www.popcenter.org/problems/drive_by_shooting/PDFs/Wakeling_2003.pdf.

94. Anthony A. Braga, "Pulling Levers Focused Deterrence Strategies and the Prevention of Gun Homicide," *Journal of Criminal Justice* 36, no. 4 (2008): 332–43.

95. Anthony A. Braga, Glenn L. Pierce, Jack McDevitt, Brenda J. Bond, and Shea Cronin, "The Strategic Prevention of Gun Violence among Gang-Involved Offenders," *Justice Quarterly* 25, no. 1 (2008): 132–62.

96. Edmund F. McGarrell, Steven Chermak, Jeremy M. Wilson, and Nicholas Corsaro, "Reducing Homicide through a Lever-Pulling Strategy," *Justice Quarterly* 23, no. 2 (2006): 214–31.

97. Andrew Papachristos, Tracey Meares, and Jeffrey Fagan "Attention Felons: Evaluating Project Safe Neighborhood in Chicago," Working Paper, Columbia Univ., Institute for Social and Economic Policy and Research, September 2006, http://iserp.columbia.edu/files/iserp/2006_06.pdf.

98. David M. Kennedy and Anthony A. Braga "Homicide in Minneapolis: Research for Problem Solving," *Homicide Studies* 2, no. 3 (1998): 263–90.

99. Statement for the record of David M. Kennedy, Director, Center for Crime Prevention and Control, and Professor of Anthropology, John Jay College of Criminal Justice in New York City, "Making Communities Safer: Youth Violence and Gang Interventions That Work," before the House Committee on the Judiciary, Subcommittee on Crime, Terrorism, and Homeland Security, 110th Cong., 1st sess., February 15, 2007, http://judiciary.house.gov/hearings/February2007/021507kennedy.pdf?ID=736.

100. DHS, ICE, *ICE Fiscal Year 2007 Annual Report: Protecting National Security and Upholding Public Safety* (Washington, DC: DHS, 2007), www.ice.gov/doclib/about/ice07ar_final.pdf.

101. DOJ, "Project Safe Neighborhoods," www.psn.gov/about/index.html.

102. ICE Office of Investigations and its field offices are responsible for Operation Community Shield.

103. *Immigration and Nationality Act* (INA), 8 USC §1182 (2002).

104. Presidential Proclamation, "To Suspend Entry as Immigrants or Nonimmigrants of Persons Engaged in or Benefiting from Corruption Proclamation 7750," *Federal Register* 69, no. 9 (January 2004): 2287–88, http://edocket.access.gpo.gov/2004/pdf/04-957.pdf.

105. Kamal Sadiq, personal communication with the author.

106. Ibid.

107. The White House, "Fact Sheet: National Strategy to Internationalize Efforts against Kleptocracy," Press Release, August 10, 2006, http://georgewbush-whitehouse.archives.gov/news/releases/2006/08/20060810-1.html.

108. David M. Luna, "Strategies to Fight Kleptocracy," Press Release, US Department of State (DOS), September 28, 2007, www.scoop.co.nz/stories/WO0709/S00763.htm.

109. *Department of State, Foreign Operations, and Related Programs Appropriations Act, 2008*, 110 Cong., 1st sess., January 4, 2007, http://frwebgate.access.gpo.gov/cgi-bin/getdoc.cgi?dbname=110_cong_bills&docid=f:h2764enr.txt.pdf.

110. The measure, for instance, affects corrupt Cambodian officials. See Global Witness, "US Move to Ban Top Cambodian Officials Exposes Failure of Europe, Australia and Japan to Get Tough on Corruption," Press Release, January 22, 2008, www.globalwitness.org/media_library_get.php/569/ US_move_to_ban_top_cambodian_officials_exposes_failure_of_europe_australia_and_japan_to_ get_tough_on_corruption.doc.

111. President Proclamation, "To Suspend Entry as Immigrants or Nonimmigrants of Persons Engaged in or Benefiting from Corruption Proclamation 7750."

112. DOS (US Department of State), Bureau of International Narcotics and Law Enforcement Affairs, "US Strategy to Internationalize Efforts against Kleptocracy: Combating High-Level Public Corruption, Denying Safe Haven, and Recovering Assets," Fact Sheet, August 10, 2006, http://armenia. usembassy.gov/root/pdfs/kleptocracy.pdf.

113. Pablo Bachelet, "US Uses Visas to Combat Corruption," *Miami Herald*, February 19, 2006.

114. Cathy Majtenyi, "Prominent Kenyans Banned from Entering US," *Voice of America*, May 24, 2006, www.tingroom.com/voastandard/2006/5/33040.html.

115. Susan Jones, "US Denies Visa to Hindu Leader At Muslims' Urging," *Cybercast News Service*, March 18, 2005.

116. Global Witness, "US Move to Ban Top Cambodian Officials Exposes Failure of Europe, Australia and Japan to Get Tough on Corruption."

117. European Commission, External Relations, *Sanctions or Restrictive Measures* (Brussels, Belgium: European Commission, 2009), http://ec.europa.eu/external_relations/cfsp/sanctions/docs/index_ en.pdf#4.

118. Ibid.

119. UNSC (United Nations Security Council), "Security Council Committee Established Pursuant to Resolution 1267 (1999) Concerning Al-Qaida and the Taliban and Associated Individuals and Entities," www.un.org/sc/committees/1267/index.shtml.

120. UNSC, "Resolution 1373," S/RES/1373, September 28, 2001, http://daccess-dds-ny.un.org/doc/UN-DOC/GEN/N01/557/43/PDF/N0155743.pdf?OpenElement.

121. The seven resolutions are: 1333 (2000); 1390 (2002); 1455 (2003); 1526 (2004); 1617 (2005); 1735 (2006); and 1822 (2008).

122. UNSC, "Resolution 1390," S/RES/1390, January 28, 2002, http://daccess-dds-ny.un.org/doc/UN-DOC/GEN/N02/216/02/PDF/N0221602.pdf?OpenElement.

123. UNSC, "Report of the Analytical Support and Sanctions Monitoring Team Pursuant to Resolution 1735 (2006) Concerning Al-Qaida and the Taliban and Associated Individuals and Entities," May 14, 2008, and updated following an interview with UN staff, http://daccessdds.un.org/doc/UNDOC/ GEN/N08/341/88/PDF/N0834188.pdf?OpenElement.

124. UNSC, "Letter Dated 31 December 2008 from the Chairman of the Security Council Committee Established Pursuant to Resolution 1267 (1999) Concerning Al-Qaida and the Taliban and Associated Individuals and Entities Addressed to the President of the Security Council," December 31, 2008, http://daccessdds.un.org/doc/UNDOC/GEN/N09/206/16/PDF/N0920616.pdf?OpenElement.

125. These crimes constitute violations of a state's obligation to protect its civilian population. UNHCR (United Nations High Commissioner for Refugees), *Implementing the Responsibility to Protect: Report of the Secretary-General* (New York: UN General Assembly, 2009), www.unhcr.org/refworld/categor y,REFERENCE,UNGA,,,4989924d2,0.html

126. Aaron Halegua, "The Targeting of United Nations Sanctions: Political, Economic and Ethical Explanations of Normative Change," Paper presented at the Annual Meeting of the International Studies Association, Le Centre Sheraton Hotel, Montreal, Quebec, Canada, March 17, 2004, www. allacademic.com//meta/p_mla_apa_research_citation/0/7/3/1/8/pages73180/p73180-1.php.

127. The 11th UN Security Council Sanctions Committees are authorized respectively by Resolution 751 (1992) concerning Somalia; Resolution 1132 (1997) concerning Sierra Leone; Resolution 1267 (1999) concerning Al Qaida and the Taliban; Resolution 1518 (2003) concerning Iraq; Resolution 1521 (2003) concerning Liberia; Resolution 1533 (2004) concerning the Democratic Republic of

the Congo; Resolution 1572 (2004) concerning Côte d'Ivoire; Resolution 1591 (2005) concerning Sudan/Darfur; Resolution 1636 (2005) concerning Lebanon; Resolution 1718 (2006) concerning the Democratic People's Republic of Korea; and Resolution 1737 (2006) concerning Iran.

128. Security Council Report, "May 2008: Counter-Terrorism — Briefings to the Council," May 2008, www.securitycouncilreport.org/site/c.glKWLeMTIsG/b.4065781/k.C305/May_2008_brCounterTerrorism_Briefings_to_the_Council.htm.

129. UNSC, "Report of the Analytical Support and Sanctions Monitoring Team Pursuant to Resolution 1735 (2006) Concerning Al-Qaida and the Taliban and Associated Individuals and Entities," and updated after interview with UN staff.

130. For a comparison of what each committee is responsible for, see UNSC, "Comparative Table Regarding the United Nations Security Council Committees Established Pursuant to Resolutions 1267 (1999), 1373 (2001) and 1540 (2004)," www.un.org/sc/committees/1267/pdf/Revised%20comparative%20table_ENGLISH%20_7-11-2008_.pdf.

131. UNSC, "Security Council Committee Established Pursuant to Resolution 1267 (1999) Concerning Al-Qaida and the Taliban and Associated Individuals and Entities." The asset freezes require governments to "freeze without delay the funds and other financial assets or economic resources of designated individuals and entities." Arms embargo require governments to "prevent the direct or indirect supply, sale and transfer from their territories or by their nationals outside their territories, or using their flag vessels or aircraft, of arms and related material of all types, spare parts, and technical advice, assistance, or training related to military activities, to designated individuals and entities."

132. UNSC, "Letter dated 31 December 2008 from the Chairman of the Security Council Committee Established Pursuant to Resolution 1267 (1999)."

133. Michael Brzoska, ed., *Design and Implementation of Arms Embargoes and Travel and Aviation Related Sanctions: Results of the 'Bonn-Berlin Process'* (Bonn, Germany: Bonn International Center for Conversion, 2001), www.watsoninstitute.org/tfs/CD/booklet_sanctions.pdf.

134. Alistair Millar, Jason Ipe, David Cortright, George A. Lope, Anne Marbarger, and Kathryn Lawall, *Report on Standards and Best Practices for Improving States' Implementation of UN Security Council Counter-Terrorism Mandates* (Washington, DC: Center on Global Counter-Terrorism Cooperation, 2006).

135. UNSC, "Fact Sheet on Listing," www.un.org/sc/committees/1267/fact_sheet_listing.shtml; UNSC, "Guidelines of the Committee for the Conduct of Work," December 9, 2008, www.un.org/sc/committees/1267/pdf/1267_guidelines.pdf.

136. Eric Rosand, Alistair Millar, and Jason Ipe, *The UN Security Council's Counterterrorism Program: What Lies Ahead?* (New York: International Peace Academy, 2007).

137. Joshua Black (United Nations), in discussion with the author, 2009.

138. DOJ (US Department of Justice), Office of the Inspector General Audit Division, *The Federal Bureau of Investigation's Terrorist Watchlist Nomination Practices*, Audit Report 09-25 (Washington, DC: DOJ, 2009), www.usdoj.gov/oig/reports/FBI/a0925/final.pdf.

139. UNSC, "Resolution 1822 (2008)," S/RES/1822, June 30, 2008, http://daccess-dds-ny.un.org/doc/UNDOC/GEN/N08/404/90/PDF/N0840490.pdf?OpenElement.

140. UNSC, "Letter dated 31 December 2008 from the Chairman of the Security Council Committee established pursuant to resolution 1267 (1999)."

141. UNSC, "Fact Sheet on the Travel Bans and its Exemptions," www.un.org/sc/committees/1267/fact_sheet_travel_ban.shtml.

142. Ibid.

143. UNSC, "Letter dated 29 March 2007 from the Secretary-General Addressed to the President of the Security Council," March 30, 2007, http://daccessdds.un.org/doc/UNDOC/GEN/N07/291/00/PDF/N0729100.pdf?OpenElement.

144. UNSC, "Focal Point for De-listing Established Pursuant to Security Council Resolution 1730 (2006)," www.un.org/sc/committees/dfp.shtml.

145. UNSC, "Letter Dated 13 May 2008 from the Chairman of the Security Council Committee Established Pursuant to Resolution 1267 (1999) Concerning Al-Qaida and the Taliban and Associated Individuals and Entities Addressed to the President of the Security Council," May 14, 2008, http://daccessdds.un.org/doc/UNDOC/GEN/N08/341/88/PDF/N0834188.pdf?OpenElement.

146. Article 13 of the Universal Declaration of Human Rights; Article 12 of the International Covenant on Civil and Political Rights (ICCPR); Article 8 of the International Convention on the Protection of Rights of All Migrant Workers and Members of their Families (ICPMW); Article 5 of the International Convention on the Elimination of All Forms of Racial Discrimination; Article 10 of the Convention on the Rights of the Child; Article 5 of the General Assembly's Declaration on the Human Rights of Individuals Who Are Not Nationals of the Country in Which They Live.

147. United Nations, *The Universal Declaration of Human Rights* (New York: United Nations, 1948), www.un.org/Overview/rights.html.

148. International Covenant on Civil and Political Rights (ICCPR), adopted and opened for signature, ratification, and accession by GA Res. 2200A (XXI) of December 16, 1966, entered into force March 23, 1976, in accordance with Article 49, article 12, www2.ohchr.org/english/law/ccpr.htm. The United States ratified this instrument on September 8, 1992.

149. UNSC, "Resolution 1267," S/RES/1267, October 15, 1999, http://daccess-dds-ny.un.org/doc/UNDOC/GEN/N99/300/44/PDF/N9930044.pdf?OpenElement.

150. Marc Bossuyt, *The Adverse Consequences of Economic Sanctions on the Enjoyment of Human Rights: Review of Further in Fields With Which the Subcommission Has Been or May Be Concerned* (New York: United Nations, Economic and Social Council, 2000), www.unhchr.ch/Huridocda/Huridoca.nsf/e06a5300f90fa0238025668700518ca4/c56876817262a5b2c125695e0050656e/$FILE/G0014092.pdf.

151. Jeffrey Kahn, "International Travel and the Constitution," *UCLA Law Review* 56, no. 271 (2008): 271–350.

152. Paul Koring and Campbell Clark, "Pressure Mounts to Repatriate Canadian Citizen," *The Globe and Mail*, May 3, 2008.

153. Randal C. Archibold, "US Blocks Men's Return to California from Pakistan," *The New York Times*, August 29, 2006, www.nytimes.com/2006/08/29/us/29hayat.html?ex=1314504000&en=dcda49ed0eeae90b&ei=5090&partner=rssuserland&emc=rss; Randal C. Archibold, "Wait Ends for Father and Son Exiled by F.B.I. Terror Inquiry," *The New York Times*, October 2, 2006, http://query.nytimes.com/gst/fullpage.html?res=9505E7DE1430F931A35753C1A9609C8B63.

154. Ibid.

155. UNSC, "Letter dated 10 June 2008 from the Chairman of the Security Council Committee Established Pursuant to Resolution 1373 (2001) Concerning Counter-Terrorism Addressed to the President of the Security Council," http://daccessdds.un.org/doc/UNDOC/GEN/N08/375/56/PDF/N0837556.pdf?OpenElement.

156. Ibid.

157. Ibid.

158. Matthew Levitt and Michael Jacobson, *The Money Trail: Finding, Following, and Freezing Terrorist Finances* (Washington, DC: The Washington Institute for Near East Policy, 2008), www.washingtoninstitute.org/templateC04.php?CID=302.

Section III: Ensuring Mobility Infrastructure Integrity And Resilience

Introduction

The second of three missions of *securing human movement* is to ensure the integrity of the mobility infrastructure — encompassing laws, technology, and operations — so that it can achieve its purposes.

Most of the policy debate surrounding immigration and borders since September 11, 2001 has focused on the nation's mobility infrastructure: the immigration, border, and travel systems; the humanitarian obligations of refugee and asylum laws; and the constitutional law governing the right to movement.

One persistent theme since the September 11, 2001, terrorist attacks has been a perceived contradiction between security and openness. To some extent that tension is inescapable. But the metaphor of balancing two contradictory principles does not precisely describe the dilemma.

A government's provision of security is one of its core functions, and it responds to a fundamental right. Unless the risk is existential, however, security is something of a relative concept. People have to be and *to feel* sufficiently safe to act and they must be able to respond to and recover from incidents. Increased security measures both reduce the likelihood of attack and provide this kind of reassurance.

At the same time, the entire purpose of homeland security or civil protection is defense of the citizen and the civil order.[1] For the United States, civil liberties, human rights, openness, freedom, and thriving free markets are the foundation of that order. If the methods of protection undermine that order, then the protective measures will have failed in their strategic purpose and failed the American people.

To manage risks is to make judgments about where that line of failure is and how to stay on the right side of it. Because risk is to some extent subjective, views will differ markedly about that, but the debate has to take place. The debate is marred today with strident politics and mixes immigration policy apples with security consideration oranges.

This section looks at three arenas critical to human mobility, in which ensuring the integrity of mobility infrastructure will require the Department of Homeland Security (DHS) to shape its security mandate so as to maintain fundamental constitutional principles.

Chapter 7 discusses travel documents and personal identification, a US challenge as yet unresolved. Chapter 8 spotlights the temporary visa program, and the exercise of US sovereignty in adjudications of individual applications to travel to the United States. Chapter 9 addresses international mobility-related information sharing and privacy and data security protections necessary to prevent government and private abuse of personal information.

Chapter 7: Travel Documents and Identification

Policy Preview: *Identity management for international travel requires more systematic and priority attention, including long-term planning based on clearly articulated principles of security, access to lawful mobility, and privacy/data-security protections. Among other steps that should be taken immediately:*

- *Congress should follow through on its mandate to improve the integrity of birth certificate records, which are the foundational documents for obtaining passports and driver's licenses*
- *US passport adjudications should include electronic access to birth and death records.*
- *The Department of Homeland Security (DHS), Federal Bureau of Investigation (FBI), and other law-enforcement agencies should expand travel-document-related criminal investigations*
- *DHS should give new authority to its Screening Coordination Office to set standards for the issuance of travel documents and supporting documents and for consistent vetting of US passport applicants, foreign and US travelers, and immigrants*
- *The United States should proactively support improvement of passports, travel documents, and supporting national identity-management and civil registries worldwide, with the explicit goals of strengthening security and expanding and protecting access to global mobility channels for all legitimate travelers.*

Secure documents issued by government authorities are essential to establishing personal identification and protecting identity. Reliable personal identification is required to obtain passports, which are essential for freedom of movement. For terrorists, travel documents are "as important as weapons."[2] Authorities can potentially track, disrupt, and preempt a terrorist using travel documents and travel information developed in the context of a larger counterterrorism effort. In addition, screening of visa applicants and travelers comprises a key component of securing human mobility. The screening process occurs at each stage in the network from passport issuance to applications for visa or pretravel authorization through travel and up to naturalization, then for travel as a US citizen.

As air travel became more prevalent, nations cooperated to set standards for passport production in order to streamline passenger entry at airports.[3] The

United States and partner governments formed the International Civil Aviation Organization (ICAO) on the basis of the Convention on International Civil Aviation, better known as the Chicago Convention, which authorized the establishment of such standards.[4] Passports and supporting documents authenticate biographical information about individuals and provide access to benefits. Some are pressing for improved security of identification documents. The 9/11 Commission, for example, called for strengthening birth certificates and driver's licenses, and Congress imposed mandates to this effect in the Intelligence Reform and Terrorism Prevention Act of 2004 (IRTPA) and subsequent legislation.[5] The 9/11 Commission report also called for standards for screening checkpoints.[6]

After September 11, 2001, the United States and many other governments separately and jointly improved the security of passports and issuance procedures. DHS and the Department of State (DOS) recognize the central role of passports in enhancing travel-document security and identity management.[7] Since 9/11, DOS has redesigned the US visa and passport to make them more tamperproof and has bolstered its visa-issuance process. In addition, DHS has instituted ten fingerprint checks for foreign travelers through the United States Visitor and Immigrant Status Indicator Technology Program (US-VISIT), and created an interoperable fingerprint database with the FBI. Both agencies have opened access to databases to other agencies responsible for mobility security. But the United States is making only slow progress in improving personal identification, despite increasing problems with identity theft and the need to improve mobility security in the face of terrorism.

Civil-liberties concerns, cost, federalism conflicts, and fragmentation of the civil-security effort in the years since 9/11 are all factors in the failure to follow the recommendations of the 9/11 Commission and to meet congressional mandates to strengthen birth certificates and driver's licenses. The US passport has received even less attention than driver's licenses.

A fresh effort must be made to grapple with civil liberties, quality-control, and other issues surrounding US birth certificates and passports, and on standards for screening. This chapter focuses on important next steps for improving US travel-document security, for elevating and standardizing screening standards, and for fostering global cooperation in travel-document security.

The Role of Breeder Documents

There are four basic mobility security goals with respect to travel documents and the collection of supporting documents and biometrics associated with the acquisition and use of travel documents:

- preventing their exploitation by terrorists and criminals
- improving the ability to identify individuals and therefore to detect malefactors based on their travel documents
- promoting routine compliance with immigration regulation
- ensuring that citizens, residents, and refugees can acquire travel documents in emergency situations

To manage identity for these purposes, authorities issuing passports and civil registry documents such as birth and death certificates must establish identity, confirm citizenship, and determine entitlement to the documents. Identity is determined in three ways:

- Testing the applicant's knowledge in application forms, interviews, and increasingly through checking the "social footprint" — that is, how the person's claimed identity is actually being used in the community
- Collection and comparison of biometric information
- Review of the documents presented in support of the application for a travel document

Documents that provide the fundamental physical evidence accepted by national authorities to establish a prima facie claim to identity are known as *breeder documents* among mobility officials.[8] These include civil registration and identity documents authorized under national laws — birth certificates, driver's licenses, national identity cards, voter cards, and social security cards, among others.

US Travel-Document Security Priorities — Domestic

US legislative activity to strengthen domestic travel documents has largely focused on the role of driver's licenses in permitting the 9/11 hijackers to board airplanes, blend in, and carry out terrorist operations in the United States. All but one of the 9/11 hijackers acquired some form of US identification document and 18 hijackers fraudulently obtained 17 driver's licenses and 13 state-issued forms of identification.[9] An effort to establish national standards for driver's licenses predated the 9/11 attacks, and Congress quickly introduced legislation to this effect after the terrorist attacks.

At US borders, dependable travel documents remain the key screening tool for US and foreign travelers. The US passport is the gold standard for clandestine international travel outside the United States. Maintaining its integrity is critical to constraining terrorist and criminal travel across borders. The birth certificate is the key document to establish personal identity underlying the passport. Without reliable birth certificates, it is much more difficult to maintain the integrity of passports and driver's licenses. Thus, for the United States, the highest priority with respect to US-issued travel documents should be to prevent the exploitation of the US passport by strengthening its physical design, issuance process, and investigative protections, and to ensure the integrity of US birth certificates. The latter priority will also significantly improve the security of driver's licenses.

US Travel-Document Security Priorities — International

While the United States works to ensure the integrity of its birth certificates and passports, it must also work to secure travel documents globally. In short, the United States must prioritize passport security and national identity management. If passport security cannot be adequately assured, new forms of global travel identification may need to be considered.

The United States and partners in other developed countries have successfully promoted and supported enhanced passport-security measures globally. Digital facial and fingerprint and/or iris images contained in the passport are beginning to allow automation of biometric comparisons at points of visa issuance, border clearance, and immigration proceedings. The introduction of machine-readable e-passports using biometrics in a growing number of countries has been a major milestone.[10]

Over time, the change to e-passports with biometrics is expected to impede the most common form of passport fraud: imposter or look-alike fraud. Movement from decentralized to a more controlled and centralized issuance, and improved staff training have also made a significant difference. Recognizing the passport's critical role, Interpol and the US governments have undertaken systematic efforts to collect information about lost and stolen passports. (Interpol will be discussed further in chapter 11.) These improvements are resulting in a shift from document fraud to identity fraud. Rather than falsifying the passport itself, illegal travelers are presenting false identities with greater frequency.[11]

Breeder documents are national documents, but the civil registries that store and generate them can be state or local. Mobility authorities have a growing interest in these collections of personal information to authenticate credentials and verify identities of travelers and immigrants. The United States and other governments are confronting the need to improve their practice of national identity management involving the many types of documents used to acquire passports. With the transition from paper documentation to electronic databases, the registries and other databases used to verify the paper documents are critical security resources. They must achieve a certain level of quality and reliability; be secure from corruption, exploitation, and attack; and, in due course, become accessible in real time to cooperating mobility security authorities under a common set of rules.[12]

Four factors complicate the development of identity-management law and practice. First, support for a long-term commitment to strengthen identity management as a cornerstone of passport security has been overshadowed by the debates over driver's-license reform and whether the United States should adopt a national identification card.

Second, DHS's institution of biometric screening of foreign travelers in the US-VISIT program, and the EU decision to include fingerprints in EU passports, raises the question of whether US citizens will accept new biometrics in passports or driver's licenses.[13] This may have a polarizing political impact, similar to the issue of a national identification card, which is strongly opposed by civil liberties and privacy organizations.

Third, the United States and other developed countries are transitioning to digital records from paper documents. This transition raises significant issues related to privacy, data security, redress of errors, the enhanced impact of exclusion from vital records systems of minority and other vulnerable groups, and database interoperability.

Finally, two organizational issues slow the transition. DHS has authority over traveler and immigration-related identification requirements, but its Screening Coordination Office has not sought to set standards for screening across the spectrum of mobility agencies such as US Citizenship and Immigration Services (USCIS), Bureau of Consular Affairs (CA), and US Customs and Border Protection (CBP). DOS has authority over US passports, and no government agency has general authority over identity documents and management.

All four factors are reasons for DHS to take a broader and more assertive view of its role in identity-management and traveler-screening standards.

The Integrity of US Birth Certificates

Approximately 16,000 different entities issue birth certificates in the United States,[14] and there are over 14,000 different kinds of birth certificates in circulation.[15] There is no minimum federal standard for their issuance; state vital records offices and other local issuing entities have discretion over the security features and formats of the paper used for certified copies of birth certificates. In addition, every state has its own process for obtaining a certified copy of a birth certificate. Because of the number of agencies issuing certified copies of birth certificates there is no consistency in issuance requirements. Without fingerprints, photos, or other unique identifiers, there is no reliable way to confirm identification of the individual requesting a certificate. Vital records jurisdictions rely on the applicant having knowledge of the facts on the birth certificate and sometimes presenting a driver's license to establish identity and a right to the record.

As paper documents, birth certificates are highly susceptible to forgery, and are easier to produce than passports and visas. Ahmed Ressam, the Algerian known as the millennium bomber for his alleged intention to bomb Los Angeles International Airport on the eve of the millennium, forged a baptismal certificate for his own use and also admitted to forging birth certificates for fellow al Qaeda operatives.[16]

Birth-certificate fraud takes two forms: using another's identity or falsifying/altering a birth certificate. An estimated 85 to 90 percent of birth-certificate fraud seen by the US Immigration and Naturalization Service (INS, whose functions were later absorbed by the new DHS) and DOS Passport Services consisted of imposters submitting genuine birth certificates and identifying themselves with fake names — the most difficult type of fraud to catch.[17]

Delayed birth certificates or claimed births outside of hospitals raise other questions. School records, church records, even Bibles can be submitted to obtain a birth certificate.

Delayed Birth-Certificate Standards

The 9/11 Commission recommended that the federal government set standards for the issuance of paper birth certificates.[18] The IRTPA enacted to implement some of the recommendations of the 9/11 Commission, contained provisions requiring the Secretary of Health and Human Services to set minimum standards for paper birth certificates used for official purposes by federal agencies.[19] Yet more than five years after the law's passage, the regulations have yet to take effect.

According to IRTPA, the standards "at a minimum . . . shall require the use of safety paper or an alternative, equally secure medium, the seal of the issuing custodian of record, and other features designed to prevent tampering, counterfeiting, or otherwise duplicating the birth certificate for fraudulent purposes."[20] In addition, the issuing agencies would be required to verify identity before issuing a birth certificate, with additional security measures for issuing a certificate to an individual other than the applicant.[21] The federal government may not require a single national design of birth certificates to which the states must comply, and Department of Health and Human Services (HHS) has to accommodate differences among states in birth-certificate storage and production requirements.

The 2004 law required the Secretary of HHS to consult with the Homeland Security Secretary, the Commissioner of the Social Security Administration (SSA), other appropriate federal agencies, and state vital records offices in developing the standards. It authorized funding that would allow HHS to make grants to states to meet compliance standards, with each individual state slated to receive at least 0.5 percent of the grant funds.[22]

Federal agency and state registrar representatives met in the spring of 2005 to discuss steps for drafting and implementing the birth certificate regulations. They established five working groups to consider: (1) minimum paper and format standards, (2) standards for physical plant security, (3) standards for issuance of certificates, (4) minimum processing standards for issuance of the certificates, and (5) systems standards for states to qualify for grants to support computerization of vital registration systems.[23] The National Center for Health

Statistics (NCHS), in charge of the process for HHS, drafted the regulations.[24] While HHS reviewed the regulations, they have never been released to the Office of Management and Budget (OMB) for final approval.

The reasons for the delay run the gamut from the cost of implementation to general antipathy for issuing regulations, to the low priority HHS places on measures that arguably fall outside its primary activities and to the controversy that the regulations may generate.

The Costs of New Standards for Birth Certificates

States generally support IRPTA, although the legislation could ultimately result in significant costs and otherwise impinge on state practices. The National Association for Public Health Statistics and Information Systems (NAPHSIS), a nonprofit association formed by state vital records registration executives, actively supports establishing national standards.

Minimum standards for paper and format, for example, would likely involve some costs related to the use or upgrading of safety paper with security features such as watermarks. Additional costs likely would result from the requirement that the certificate be printed in the United States and from the need for secure transportation to vital records offices. Logs and numerical sequencing will be needed to detect and deter thefts, processes that implicate training if not additional work time. Most states already have some type of safety paper, and NAPHSIS has issued voluntary standards concerning paper that many states follow. Other states would have to impose statewide changes.

Standards for physical plants could have a significant impact and be contentious. Old courthouses and other recordkeeping sites often offer scant physical security, making safety paper vulnerable to theft. Sometimes local registrars work out of their homes. Although the statute prescribes some accommodation, a basic level of security would disrupt current practices.

Standards for recording delayed or out-of-hospital births would provide consistency among the vital records jurisdictions. There has been a spate of filings of delayed birth certificates by people seeking passports. The filings are based on claims to have been born at home, in the presence of a midwife (who may or may not have been licensed) or someone else. Objections will likely be raised to rulemaking in this area.

Setting national standards for processing requests for copies of certificates and determining who has the right to obtain a birth certificate also would have a significant impact, since the processes vary among jurisdictions. Most requests for a birth certificate come through the mail or the Internet so the identity of the person requesting the record is harder to confirm. Some states request to see a driver's license if the request for a birth certificate is made in person; others may request a copy of the driver's license if the request is made through the mail. Several states — including Maine, Massachusetts, Kentucky, Ohio, Vermont, and Washington — have completely open records, allowing anyone to walk in and obtain a birth certificate by filling out a form.

Standards could also reasonably require some kind of nationally accessible fraud alert system to prevent someone who is denied a birth certificate on the grounds of fraud in one state from obtaining a passport in another state. Although the American Association of Motor Vehicle Administrators (AAM-VA) has a system for sharing information about revoked or denied driver's licenses among about a dozen states, it is rarely used. NAPHSIS is pilot testing the AAMVA system in eight states for vital records use.

A congressional report raised concerns that the security measures might impede genealogical and historical research involving access to birth records.[25] If so, the concern would be limited to records for the past 100 years, since most states follow a model law which provides that birth records be open after 100 years.

Making birth certificates more difficult to produce and acquire could pose obstacles to the exercise of voting rights, issuance of social security cards and, therefore, identification for employment purposes. The hurdle could be the cost of obtaining a certified birth record. Similarly, these reforms might also impede the provision of social services, such as Medicare and Medicaid, which in some states require proof of citizenship. State officials criticized a 2006 federal rule requiring proof of citizenship to gain access to Medicaid, saying it excluded citizens who could not find birth certificates. For these reasons, it is essential to develop regulations that provide for more secure birth certificates, minimize costs, and assess the implications of access to birth certificates for voting, employment, and public benefits.

The largest cost of the regulations would likely be the digitization of legacy records and the electronic linkage of birth and death certificates to prevent fraud.

Electronic Verification of Vital Events (EEVE)

An electronic system that would allow authorities being presented with paper birth certificates to verify them would make birth certificates more secure. Electronic verification is particularly essential for the passport process, because it makes timely checks possible on a large scale, potentially enabling all applications to be checked in real time.

NAPHSIS had begun developing an online system for birth and death verification and certification before 9/11. The NAPHSIS system, called the Electronic Verification of Vital Events (EVVE), provides federal agencies a single interface for securely validating birth and death information, potentially for any jurisdiction in the country. It supports two forms of authentication: (1) *verification*, when an applicant presents a birth certificate and an agency needs to verify that it is valid, and (2) what NAPHSIS calls *certification*, which is when an applicant is seeking to rely on a birth certificate that he or she does not present to the agency. The EEVE system verifies and certifies by confirming or denying a match at a vital records office to the information being presented; it does not provide any personal information about individuals to the querying agency.

SSA funded EVVE's pilot program, which was initiated in eight states (California, Colorado, Hawaii, Iowa, Minnesota, Mississippi, Missouri, and Oklahoma) in the summer of 2002.[26] Previously, SSA verified certificates manually, usually by calling the state or local vital records offices, which receives fees for issuing certificates. As with the passport service, SSA's interest in EVVE was to save time and money.

After the EVVE pilot succeeded, SSA and NAPHSIS could not agree on a fee for service and SSA abandoned further participation in December 2003. DOS participated in the pilot, but did not invest further in the system. The Department of Transportation (DOT) stepped forward to fund EVVE through AAMVA, and three state departments of motor vehicles (DMVs) across the country enabled NAPHSIS to test EVVE further.

As of December 2009, EVVE is up and running or in the process of being implemented in 23 states.[27] DHS has provided NAPHSIS with a $3.8 million grant for fiscal year 2009 to finish EVVE installation in all vital records jurisdictions by 2011. Following a Government Accountability Office (GAO) report that starkly exposed passport fraud using birth certificates, DOS sought and obtained NAPHSIS's commitment to get seven high-population states on line in 2009 — California, Massachusetts, Michigan, New Jersey, New York, Ohio, and Pennsylvania.

A GAO undercover investigation revealed how the passport-issuance process was undermined by the failure to enhance the security features of birth certificates and challenges related to birth-certificate verification.[28] In March 2009, a GAO undercover investigator submitted four applications based on counterfeit documents, including birth certificates, driver's licenses, and real social security numbers for fictitious and deceased individuals. The investigator applied for a passport at three US Postal Service locations and the State Department's Washington, DC, passport-issuing office, and succeeded in obtaining four genuine passports — using one of them to board a plane from a major US airport.

The Cost of Transition to Online Birth Records

Funding the basic installation of EVVE is no longer a problem, but there are several financial barriers to its full implementation. First, while most (85 percent) of the birth certificates dating back to 1935 have been converted into a digital format, certificates prior to 1935 need to be converted.[29] Second, some of the entered information and the historical information is inaccurate and needs to be reentered. Clean files would raise the projected EVVE match rate to at least 95 percent.

Third, the system needs to be able to determine when an individual is using the birth certificate of someone who has died. To do that, states must have electronic death records, and all death records need to be linked with birth records. The link enables a query to be answered with a "deceased" notification that confirms fraud. While most jurisdictions have linked infant deaths, and some have linked deaths to people under 45, the remaining information is largely unavailable electronically. An estimated 15 percent of death records dating back to 1935 are not available in electronic form.[30]

It would cost more than $100 million for all states to input the old birth records, clean them, and link birth and death records.[31] Pending driver's-license-reform legislation known as PASS ID would replace an earlier law contested by many states, the 2005 REAL ID (an acronym for Rearing and Empowering America for Longevity against Acts of International Destruction.) PASS ID recommends that applicants present birth certificates and that states verify them before granting a license. But unlike REAL ID, the substitute PASS ID legislation would not include a list of acceptable identification documents and would not require their verification with the issuing agency wherever possible.[32] The PASS ID legislation, however, does authorize additional funding which at least makes it possible for HHS and DHS to establish EEVE as a standard for states.

Annual operating costs and birth-certificate jurisdiction fees associated with EVVE, which are paid to NAPHSIS, could be an issue. The fee is graduated based upon volume: once the projected number of transactions occur the fee is 95 cents when there is a match and eight cents when there is no match. DMVs do not want to pay these costs, which are fairly modest. It would cost about $15 million to verify birth data on the 245 million driver's licenses issued annually[33] — hardly a large sum given the need. Complicating matters, some vital records agencies are willing not to charge their DMV agencies.

Selected DOS passport officials now use EEVE, but only when a passport adjudicator suspects fraud. DOS relies on a 2004 memorandum that allows it access to SSA's main database, but the information it receives and uses from SSA is often outdated and cannot be obtained in real time. Privacy issues, coupled with the fact that passport adjudicators are not law-enforcement officials, often bar adjudicators from access to personal information such as death records.[34] EVVE solves these accuracy and privacy problems. DOS should use EVVE, in all the states where it is available, for passport applications.

Corruption in vital records offices is also a concern. There should be sufficient penalties for official corruption and for fraudulent use of birth certificates, including criminal prosecutions.

In sum, birth certificates are the critical input for obtaining passports and driver's licenses. There is fraud in the system, although it is not clear how much. Between July 2005 and August 2008, Diplomatic Security (DS) and the FBI identified 112 individuals who had fraudulently obtained US passports by using the birth certificates of deceased Americans.[35] The challenges to upgrading and safeguarding birth certificates are perhaps greater than for driver's licenses, which are issued by state and not local offices. For birth certificates, the standards for the document itself and its issuance are weak and there is no federal standard. In addition, the ability to verify birth certificates and to match them with death records remains a problem.

Ultimately, US citizen birth and death records are expected to become wholly electronic. But it is not clear whether this will happen in a decade, two decades, or some other period of time. In the interim, it is important to raise the standards for paper birth certificates.

Advancing National Identity Management Internationally

The United States has given primary attention internationally to upgrading passports, and secondarily, to international discussion relating to biometrics. As is true for the United States domestically, more attention needs to be given to breeder documents. Without reliable breeder documents, passport and visa issuance remain difficult and unduly subject to fraud.

The time is propitious for an international dialogue on how to strengthen breeder documents because so many countries are moving to improve their systems. India, for example, is embarking on a program to provide identification to all citizens.[36] Fraud relating to breeder documents is widespread, particularly in Asia. Often it is associated with government corruption or complicity. While abuse can affect the integrity of travel document issuance, tightening up can have enormous implications for people's ability to travel and for the exercise of other rights and benefits. In Malaysia, for example, almost one million illegal immigrants from Indonesia and the Philippines have acquired Malaysian identity cards.[37] They have obtained what author Kamal Sadiq calls "documentary citizenship," using illegally obtained but genuine credentials that enable them to function as full-fledged, voting Malaysians. If tightening up means depriving millions of such people the right to travel, it will be resisted.

Use of the information contained in paper or electronic civil registries or other national databases can implicate a wide range of civil and human rights. When working to tighten issuance standards, one cannot forget the millions of effectively stateless persons, many from minority groups, who lack identification cards because of systematic exclusion by governments.[38] Nor can one ignore the potential for other types of abuse. Warring Hutus and Tutsis, for example, used identification cards in Rwanda that included photos and listed tribal affiliation to identify one another.

The US biometric database in Iraq — which includes fingerprints, iris scans, and other information on more than 2.5 million Iraqis — has led to the identification of more than 400 "high-value" individuals. Turning the database over to the Iraqi military raises questions as to whether it could ultimately be used to identify persons for persecution.[39] The mixture of good and bad uses of breeder documents makes achieving a high level of integrity a complex human rights challenge.

Digitized registries will be amenable to rapid, automated search, potentially allowing for real-time verification. While national records have historically been off-limits to foreign immigration officials, these barriers should be reconsidered. For example, a consular officer may want to verify an applicant's driver's license or birth certificate, or a port-of-entry officer may want to check the issuance record of a passport reported lost and stolen. Consular and DS officers may have informal liaison relationships that permit records to be queried by counterparts who supply answers in due course. This is a time-consuming and inefficient process on both sides. However, there is no international law or standardized practice for providing mutual access to information contained in civil registries to verify travel-document information.

The United States, Australia, and New Zealand have launched a new system to provide real-time access to one another's passport databases for the simple, restricted purposes of a yes/no determination as to whether a particular passport was issued to the individual claiming it. (This system will be discussed in chapter 9.) In addition to greatly enhancing security by permitting multiple record checks, real-time verification would be a great boon to travelers, as it would further reduce the transaction time at consulates and ports of entry. But in developing minimal security norms for civil-status documents and databases, significant greater attention must be given to privacy and data security issues. Passport standards are set at ICAO. (ICAO and its activities are described in chapter 11.)

Technical issues associated with establishing trusted electronic communication should be reviewed in consultation with the National Institute for Standards and Technology (NIST). DOS and DHS will have to develop a program to provide foreign assistance relating to breeder document improvement, and consider with what other mobility initiatives participation in a documentary regime might be linked. (Foreign assistance is discussed further in chapter 11.) DHS' Policy, Privacy, and Screening Coordination offices all need to be involved in developing the US position on global breeder-document practice. Although such coordination will help the US government rationally improve its electronic communication standards, it should not come at the cost of the nimble pace that ICAO has demonstrated since 9/11 in advancing travel-document security.

The Integrity of US Passports

Congress and the DOS's CA bureau, which includes the Passport Services office, have considerably strengthened the design of US passports since 9/11. Because passports have to be read by border officials worldwide, the United States and partner countries develop passport standards through ICAO. In 2006 ICAO issued new specifications for the inclusion of internationally interoperable biometrics and an integrated circuit chip in the new generation of machine-readable passports.

An ICAO-sponsored "public-key infrastructure" and digital signature technology is intended to secure data from unauthorized access.[40] Public-key infrastructure (PKI) and digital signatures are two first-generation authentication or verification technologies. Based on public-key cryptography, PKI allows two communicating parties to exchange keys — comprising a mathematical formula — for encrypting and decoding messages. DOS also uses public-key cryptography and digital signatures in the e-passports introduced in 2006. The e-passport chip is encoded with the same information that is on the passport biodata page. This mechanism allows border officials to verify that the passport belongs to the person to whom it was issued.

The chip design makes counterfeiting new US passports prohibitively difficult at present. Passport designers have historically planned on about a five-year cycle of new design to reduce vulnerability to counterfeiting, although a forensic passport specialist recently reported that counterfeit techniques improve by an order of magnitude every six months. However, chip-protected passports have only been issued since 2006, so most of the passports in circulation are more easily altered and counterfeited. Even with the chip architecture, there are still some seemingly intractable problems associated with the design and usage of passports. The name on the passport may belong to the person, but not be spelled in the same way as on a watchlist or relevant criminal record. This can give rise to false negatives and false positives. One option would be for ICAO to mandate that all names be written in the script of their original language, and to provide for their universal transliteration into roman script.[41] For US citizens and foreigners, some process for obtaining more inviolable personal identifiers is the only way to mitigate this problem.

Problems also arise because individuals are lawfully entitled to possess more than one passport. There is no international system for enabling authorities to know when individuals use passports from multiple countries. Often this is a benign practice, allowing travelers to enter shorter lines or, in some circumstances, to use one passport rather than another for personal safety. More often people acquire more than one passport because they feel ties to more than one country. However, multiple passports may also be used to deceive authorities about travel. UK authorities worry, for example, about the possibility of traveling from the United Kingdom to Iran on Pakistani passport, continuing on to Pakistan, then returning to the United Kingdom using a UK passport. US authorities have similar concerns and should address this problem either through ICAO or through the Five Country Conference (a forum for collaboration among the United States, Canada, the United Kingdom, Australia, and New Zealand).

If the problem arising from people's entitlement to dual (or multiple) citizenship cannot be solved within the current framework, then the passport will not serve one of its core purposes: facilitating security screening in a significant way. If this comes to pass, consideration should be given to an international passcard with an integrated chip that records an individual's travel. This information would be stored in the most developed form of database security, accessible to national authorities based on a set of international rules.[42]

Protection against Passport Fraud

There are four primary ways a passport is obtained fraudulently from a country's passport services: (1) by using an assumed identity that is supported by genuine but fraudulently obtained identification documents; (2) by using the identity of a deceased person; (3) by submitting false claims of lost, stolen, or mutilated passports; or (4) by using counterfeit citizenship documents. DS has reported that approximately two-thirds of passport-fraud cases involve imposters using assumed identities supported by genuine but fraudulently obtained breeder documents.[43] The other one-third involve false claims of lost, stolen, or mutilated passports; child substitution; counterfeit citizenship documents; and acquiring of replacement passports by using expired passports of individuals with a close resemblance.

In theory, people who apply for legitimate passports with fraudulent documents put themselves at risk. Officials can scrutinize passport applications and refer applications to appropriate experts and authorities without the same time pressure to move lines of applicants for visas at consulates or for admission at ports of entry. But the risk is not as great as it should be. There are 8,000 passport-acceptance facilities in the United States. Places where individuals can apply for a US passport from agents trained by DOS include US Postal Service locations and courthouses. The agents must verify that the ID matches the applicant and send each applicant's proof of citizenship and passport application to DOS. Passport issuance in the United States is conducted at one of 17 facilities. To issue passports in a timely manner and to detect fraud, adjudicators need adequate information, training, support from document-fraud and other specialists, and reviews that are based on clear rules and well-crafted metrics.

In the aftermath of the GAO report, CA took a variety of steps to tighten the issuance process. CA had previously required passport adjudicators to meet numerical targets in issuing passports. After the GAO report, CA suspended its production targets and committed to rewriting performance standards for passport specialists to address quality-control issues. The suspension apparently only applied for 2009. It is not obvious why there should be only a temporary suspension of numerical targets. Rather than restoring production guidelines in the same manner, CA should establish a set of metrics that would track both false negatives and false positives based on regular, statistically valid reviews. Analysis of this aggregate information would enable CA to tailor improvements to locations and to remedy problems that arise repeatedly.

CA also committed to installing facial-recognition screening for all passport applicants, a program already in place for visa applications. Previously, CA required people to provide digital photographs of their faces, but did not test the photos in a "one-to-many" screening, which would reveal whether the applicant had previously applied under a different name or was on the DOS facial biometric database. To make this system work as well as it does for visas, photos would be required to have the same quality standards as visas.

US-VISIT has been sufficiently established to allow for an analysis of best practices related to facial, iris, and other forms of biometric identification. Such an analysis would look at the degree to which different forms of biometric identifiers lead to false negatives and positives, as well as to violations of civil liberties, privacy, and data-security rights. With US-VISIT now linked to FBI and soon with Department of Defense (DOD) databases, the biometrics used in the US passport should be reexamined.

Passport adjudicators need more access to information that enables them to verify the statements on applications. Not all states have electronic and linked birth and death records systems. Birth and death records cannot be matched to passport applications on any systematic basis without EEVE. As long as DOS is unable to verify in real time their authenticity, birth certificates will "present an exceptional challenge to fraud detection efforts, as there are currently thousands of different acceptable formats for birth certificates."[44] As stated above, passport adjudicators have limited access to the SSA database. They have access to vital records from only 17 states, available only to fraud-prevention officials. Driver's license information from 48 states through the National Law Enforcement Telecommunications System (NLETS) is also limited to select officials, not frontline passport adjudicators.

After the GAO report came out, CA provided senior passport-issuing officials with access to a commercial database that supplies personal information. The latter is proving as useful to passport adjudicators as it did to visa adjudicators. It is doubtful that commercial databases intrude less on privacy than do DMV or other state and federal records that adjudicators may not access. (Privacy law is discussed in chapter 9.) Whether the data is obtained directly from local, state, and federal government agencies or from commercial databases, it ought to be made available to frontline passport adjudicators immediately, supported by privacy protocols.

CA has also provided adjudicators access to fraud-prevention reference material, which comes in the form of e-mail fraud alerts based on findings in the field and at CA's central fraud offices. The information is good, but trying to keep track and remember all of it is impossible. Recall that there are thousands of different birth certificates in circulation, and even regional passport offices must deal with multiple state and local documents. CA should maintain a central electronic library of fraudulent exemplars (in cooperation with the US Immigration and Customs Enforcement [ICE] Fraudulent Document Lab) and initiate an information technology (IT) program that automatically cross-checks against applicant data.

CA is also committed to improving training for passport adjudicators. While that is a positive development, there should also be career specialists in fraudulent documents available in all facilities on all shifts to perform spot-checks and reviews, and to respond to queries. Specialists ought also to be available at consulates and ports of entry, especially where there are international flights.

At present, career travel-document specialists work in ICE's Forensic Document Lab and CBP's Fraudulent Analysis Unit.

Criminal Investigations of Passport Fraud

The prosecution of passport-fraud cases is a final element of passport adjudication that requires attention. These cases need to be pursued more systematically. In the wake of the GAO report, CA required a 100 percent review by supervisors, which is unsustainable. However, a rigorous review process, supported by metrics and baselines, is a necessity.

Cases are referred to DS whenever the adjudicator thinks there are sufficient indicators present to warrant that action. In FY2008, CA referred more than 4,400 passport-application cases for investigation, and DS made more than 940 domestic passport-fraud-related arrests.[45] It may be that there are only a tiny percentage of fraudulent passport applications among the millions being submitted annually. Policymakers could significantly benefit from a more reliable estimate of the level of fraud. Going forward, DS and CA should cooperate in a periodic study that reviews applications based on a statistical selection to determine the percentage of passports that warrant referral and prosecution.

To support better fraud detection and appropriate referrals, passport adjudication and issuance should be standardized based on best practices. Adjudicators currently are guided by a list of fraud indicators; beyond that, adjudicators are on their own. A set of general rules or guidelines is insufficient. Absent hard and fast rules and standards for recognizing fraud, and centralized review, practices deviate widely and can create significant vulnerabilities. A group of experienced adjudicators should be convened to guide the development of automated screening and to develop best practices for adjudication, review, and referral.

Enhanced Driver's Licenses and Passcards, REAL ID/PASS ID, and National ID

The driver's license debate implicates counterterror, immigration enforcement, and cross-border travel issues. Concerns about terrorist access to driver's licenses led to a standard-setting provision in IRTPA. Once that occurred, the focus turned to preventing illegal residents from obtaining driver's licenses, as a way of deterring them from coming to or staying in the United States. IRTPA's provision was replaced by the REAL ID Act, which placed more emphasis on lawful presence. REAL ID may, in turn, be replaced by the pending PASS ID legislation.

The Western Hemisphere Travel Initiative (WHTI), which was created by IRTPA, extended border-crossing identification requirements to travelers and commuters entering the United States from Canada, Mexico, and the Caribbean, including American citizens who had not previously been required to present identification. In borderland states, WHTI prompted an effort to expand the use of driver's licenses to include presentation at border crossings across the contiguous border with Canada, so as to maintain something close to the convenience in border crossing that local residents had enjoyed. At the same time, CA designed and issued a passcard for WHTI border crossing, to provide border-state residents with a more portable document than the normal passport book.

REAL ID, PASS ID, the enhanced driver's license (EDL), and the Passport Card (Pass Card) have different purposes. REAL ID and PASS ID seek to deny terrorists (who are unauthorized) with identity documents, access to government buildings and airplanes, and, thus, operational freedom. EDL and Pass Card seek to expedite and secure travel through the use of biometric and radio frequency identification (RFID) technologies under WHTI.

Each state must enter into an agreement with DHS to develop an acceptable EDL. DHS publishes accepted EDLs in the Federal Register.[46] EDLs must denote an individual's citizenship and identity; include technologies, such as a RFID chip and a machine readable zone (MRZ), that facilitate processing at ports of entry; and have built-in security features that protect it from tampering. DHS has worked to align EDL requirements, mandated under the WHTI, with REAL ID requirements.[47]

While both the REAL ID and EDL programs share the same objective of enhancing identification security, REAL ID requires proof of legal status in the United States, but state-issued EDLs require cardholders to be US citizens. In addition, REAL ID seeks to establish minimum standards for state-issued driver's licenses and identification cards for official purposes, but it does not require RFID technology.[48]

Driver's Licenses and Counterterrorism

Driver's licenses have not previously been considered a national security tool, but are important in four distinct security-related arenas:

- *Counterterrorism.* The primary impetus for license upgrades stems from the use of driver's licenses by the 9/11 hijackers to access airplanes and for general mobility. The hijackers were non-US citizens who obtained driver's licenses through legal and criminal channels, after having entered the United States illegally through legal entry channels.
- *Immigration law compliance.* Congress in repealing the driver's license provisions of IRTPA and replacing them with REAL ID intended to emphasize the need to ascertain immigration status; PASS ID does not have the same emphasis.
- *Crime control and underage drinking.* Inadequate identification and self-misrepresentation are significant problems for local law-enforcement agencies. Improved identification would assist local law enforcement in identifying recidivists and improving crime control for *low-severity crimes*, possibly preventing some individuals from spiraling downward into *more severe crimes*. While underage drinking is considered more of a social problem than a crime or security problem, underage drinkers are major users of false driver's licenses, so changes in license issuance and penalty practices could result in a major impact in this arena.
- *Dangerous driving.* The degree to which *false licenses* or *licenses issued erroneously* may be a significant factor in undermining public safety and health on the roads is not discussed herein.

To what extent the basic security goal of REAL ID — *preventing people from obtaining driver's licenses under false identities* — is met, and terrorism-related security is enhanced, requires understanding of how terrorists exploit driver's licenses and whether upgraded driver's licenses will make these uses more difficult.

Terrorists *exploit* or *use* driver's licenses in several circumstances. They use motor vehicles for operational transportation, as platforms for attack, and as deliverers of explosives. Lack of access to a license may complicate, increase the costs and risks, or disrupt any of these uses. The use of motor vehicles in terrorist attacks is illustrated by the DC metropolitan area sniper case, the first World Trade Center terrorist attacks, the Oklahoma City bombing, and the plotting of a homegrown cell in Toronto.

The process of obtaining a driver's license exposes a terrorist to scrutiny by governmental authorities and therefore at least potentially to the risk of being detected, tracked, and disrupted. Airlines use driver's licenses to confirm the identity of individual ticket holders, and as the basis for terrorist watchlist screening. Other forms of mass transport may use licenses in a similar way. Showing a driver's license to gain access to a particular location — a government facility or private building — may result in further scrutiny by government or other security specialists. Presenting a driver's license to state or local law-enforcement authorities during a traffic or other incident may result in a federal, state, or local law-enforcement official conducting a check through the FBI's National Crime Information Center (NCIC) or otherwise with the Terrorist Screening Center (TSC), which in turn may engage intelligence authorities or create a record for later use.

Neither prior nor current driver's license legislation fully addresses these circumstances. The 9/11 hijackers acquired state-issued driver's licenses and IDs through legal and illegal channels, including by providing fraudulently certified in-state addresses; they obtained and used false social security numbers (to open bank accounts); and they showed their identification in the process of boarding the airplanes. However, the terrorist threat most closely associated with driver's licenses is using motor vehicles as a mode of attack   by driving cars and trucks armed with explosives. This is the security threat that should be the principal benchmark by which changes to the driver's license system are assessed.

Although the purpose of driver's license reform legislation has been cast in terms of national and immigration-related security, its specific goals are not closely related to stopping terrorists from using motor vehicles as weapons. Issuance of a driver's license in an individual's true name will greatly assist local police and other law enforcement in identifying individuals and checking them against watchlists. But applying for a driver's license cannot by itself result in the individual's identification as a foreign visitor or home-based terrorist. To go from establishing a true name or problematic immigration status to determining a terrorist identity requires screening that name for terrorism purposes.

So far, congressional efforts at driver's license reform do not transform the driver's-license-issuance process into a means to deny terrorist access. There is no provision for driver's license applicants to be screened against terrorist-related databases such as the TSC watchlist accessible through NCIC. Even if a state DMV were to deny an applicant a license based on the new standards, the effective REAL ID Act policy is to deny a license but allow the individual to remain at liberty to circulate in the United States. That individual may have recourse to the illegal market in counterfeit documents, drive illegally, and gain access to facilities and services. In the absence of terrorist screening, the driver's license system does not deliver the most basic tool of counterterrorism.

Whether the cost of adding a layer of watchlist screening at DMVs is a worthwhile mobility security measure depends on a risk assessment based in part on what is known about the approximately 19,000 individuals who were a positive match to a watchlist of known and suspected terrorists in FY2009.[49]

The Importance of Birth Certificates

PASS ID legislation aims to improve the integrity of name-based identification and to impose obstacles to illegitimate license acquisition through setting higher standards for the primary identity documentation to be presented to DMVs. It also raises the level of DMVs' authentication of that documentation, encouraging DMVs to verify the named individual's identity through ascertaining date of birth, principal residence, and social security status.

The potential security enhancement to driver's licenses vary among three applicant groups: (1) US citizens who may present a state-level-generated birth record, a DOS-issued birth record, or an unexpired passport; (2) naturalized US citizens who lack state or DOS-issued birth documents, and who can present only an unexpired passport because DHS-issued certificates of naturalization are deemed unacceptable; and (3) noncitizens who may present a DHS-issued lawful permanent resident (LPR) card, an employment authorization document, or a foreign passport with a DOS-affixed US visa.

Most driver's license applicants will seek to acquire state or equivalent-level birth certificates as their primary identification document. Whether driver's licenses become more reliable as a source of identification depends in large measure on whether the birth record presented by the applicant conveys the applicant's true identity, along with documentation covering any subsequent name changes. The tightly linked implications of changes to birth certificates and the security of driver's licenses argue these changes should be closely coordinated. That way, the benefits of birth-certificate reform will be fully realized in the implementation of the driver's license legislation.

In contrast to driver's licenses as they would be reformed by Congress, EDLs and DOS passcards are issued only after the applicants undergo the same checks that are required for passports. As a result, these passport substitutes are more secure from the perspectives of counterterrorism and crime control. Given the limitations of PASS ID as a security measure, DHS should consider what appropriate counterterrorism processes should be built into the driver's-license-issuance process, including investigative follow-up on at least some denied applicants. At a minimum Congress, DHS officials, and AAMVA leadership should clarify that the primary function of driver's license reform legislation is to improve the security of driver's licenses and support immigration compliance, rather than counterterrorism.

Conclusion

Maintaining the integrity of travel documents is critical to securing human movement. In order to do so, more attention must be paid to the breeder documents that support US passport-issuance decisions. Citizens have many interests in sound identification, including access to voting, health care, and education. However, less than one-third of the US population has passports. Given current identification practices, securing birth certificates is of paramount importance in protecting travel and for other purposes as well. A concerted effort should be made to upgrade birth-certificate standards; record all birth and death certificate information digitally; and make this and other critical information, such as social security numbers, available in real time to passport examiners. Passport issuance should be based on hard and fast rules for fraud determination, complemented by a set of metrics for false positives and negatives that supply baselines against which improvements may be made.

DHS's Screening Coordination Office has developed a credentialing framework to guide DHS in setting consistent screening standards across all travel and immigration-related checkpoints, establishing standards for biometric use, and developing metrics for evaluating and improving these processes.

DHS should make this framework the basis for further discussion of identity management in an interagency council, which should include the departments and agencies with a stake in identity management and electronic communications, including NIST.[50] This effort should be linked to the public-private efforts of the American National Standards Institute (ANSI), which seeks to develop guidelines on identity verification with a view toward the adoption of an American national standard.[51]

The role of the Screening Coordination Office should encompass not only the standardization of identification but the screening standards envisioned by the 9/11 Commission. Thus, for example, there should be standards for the circumstances under which databases should be checked, the application forms that should be used, and the steps to be followed in communications with supervisors and interagency consultations.

There should also be a rule about checking the visa status of individuals whose names are provided to the National Counterterrorism Center (NCTC) for terrorism vetting. Enough time has passed since 9/11 to make it possible for an interagency committee to develop such procedures based on the different agencies' best practices. A consistent, reliable baseline for vetting is critical to quality control.

A process of standardization led by DHS must overcome stiff resistance due to agency cultures, practices, policies, and budgets. Practical experience with efforts to secure the social security number system, institute an employee immigration status verification system (E-Verify), and upgrade driver's licenses — none of which has been achieved — demonstrates that the United States is far from ready for a national identification card. Improving identity-management practice and using that improvement to leverage data to enhance vetting procedures is too pressing a need to be given short shrift. The incremental improvements being made in passport design and issuance are themselves a major challenge, but once instituted, will provide significant benefit.

Internationally, the United States should begin the dialogue about improvement and sharing of national civil registry information, consistent with national and international privacy and data-security rules. The challenges posed by moving toward better practices are considerable, especially with respect to developing countries. Improvements will depend in large part on overcoming related challenges of development, not only effecting civil registry infrastructure improvements but reducing corruption and crime that weaken the ability to maintain the integrity of the passport and other document systems. Reforms must be developed with full attention to human rights.

Countries have an incentive to develop interoperable systems that afford their citizens and economies the full benefits of globalization; but achieving consensus is not simple or easy. Outreach to developing countries will require technical and other foreign assistance, and perhaps other incentives. These next steps will stretch the capability and authority of existing multilateral institutions (such as ICAO) that have provided the vehicle for travel-document security collaboration. New institutions and arrangements may be needed as this effort unfolds.

Securing passports and civil registries is crucially important. However, most terrorist travel does not occur with US passports. In addition, even the best screening systems will not pinpoint unknown clandestine operatives who use deception to obtain travel documents and hide in plain sight. These limitations suggest some additional points to keep in mind in the approach to travel documents and identification.

First, more important than the technical means of identifying and screening individuals are: (1) strong relationships with other governments that address information sharing about known and suspected terrorists, transnational criminals, individuals using fraud in seeking access or traveling, and fraudulent travel practices; (2) strong analytic capabilities and fusion centers to make sense of intelligence, combined with information obtained during vetting; (3) incentives and rules that lead to a high level of compliance with immigration and travel laws; and (4) cultivating a strong civil security ethos among Americans, including good community-police relations.

Second, while travel documents are important for detecting malefactors, emphasis on individual screening should not be based on a determination by border officials that individuals are *desirable*. Rather, the issues should be whether they meet the terms of their visa or immigration status and are not violating or suspected of violating a prohibition. If they cease to meet the terms of their visas, their access to the United States should be revoked.

Third, improving travel documents and personal identification will be a long-term, incremental process. There needs to be clarity and transparency about what new systems are meant to accomplish with respect to security. That has been missing in the driver's license debate.

CHAPTER 8: THE TEMPORARY VISA PROGRAM

Policy Preview: *Maintaining the integrity and resilience of global mobility channels will allow people to travel reliably and efficiently, and with confidence that their movement will be safe and secure. The following measures would strengthen mobility security, fortify the right to movement, and help sustain US competitiveness:*

- *Professionalizing the Consular Service by making it a distinct service within the Department of State (DOS)*
- *Creating a DOS Office of Mobility and Security under a newly established under secretary for mobility and security. The office would merge the Bureau of Consular Affairs (CA); the Bureau of Diplomatic Security (DS); the Bureau of Population, Refugees, and Migration; the Office to Monitor and Combat Trafficking in Persons; and the Bureau of International Narcotics and Law Enforcement (INL)*
- *Clarifying visa practice to ensure that prudential revocations are issued when individuals are nominated to the terrorist watchlist through the Visa Viper system.*
- *Developing and standardizing procedures within and across relevant agencies regarding mandatory database checks in cases of suspected terrorists*
- *Giving visa officers access to all relevant databases currently withheld from them on grounds they are "non-law-enforcement" personnel*
- *Requiring the under secretary for mobility and security to report regularly, along with Department of Homeland Security (DHS) counterparts, on overstay rates of nationals and particular groups, and to report on the annual numbers of foreign citizens issued visas who are subsequently found to be ineligible*
- *Granting new authority to DHS and DOS to penalize visa overstayers*
- *Ending the doctrine of "consular nonreviewability" and mandating adequate supervision and review of junior officer decisions*
- *Providing certain groups of foreign citizens who are denied visas a meaningful opportunity for review*

The US immigration system does not yet fully meet the imperatives of securing human mobility. Ensuring the integrity and resilience of US mobility channels requires providing effective security from terrorism, achieving meaningful levels of compliance with immigration laws, preserving fairness through transparent rules and processes, and supporting US competitiveness through efficiency and responsiveness to market demands. Meeting these goals will require adjustment to many systems; this chapter focuses on the temporary visa program administered by the CA.

The United States issues about 6 million nonimmigrant visas and almost 500,000 immigrant visas annually, accepting about 22 percent of applications.[52] The temporary visa system, in particular, is the face of the United States in global mobility channels. An overly restrictive regime would harm individuals, families, and US competitiveness. An overly lax regime would permit terrorist travel to the United States and continued high rates of overstays.[53] The integrity of the visa system is thus a crucial element of mobility security and civil security. This chapter will examine how well this system promotes US competitiveness, security, and the needs of lawful travelers.

The Structure of Short-Term Visas

Foreign citizens may travel to the United States with or without a visa, depending on their country of origin and other factors (discussed in chapter 10). There are two types of visas issued under US law, nonimmigrant (temporary) and immigrant (permanent) visas. CA issues temporary visas, as well as immigrant visas. US Citizenship and Immigration Services (USCIS), a DHS agency, is tasked with adjusting the status of certain nonimmigrants to lawful permanent residence and considering lawful permanent residents (LPRs) for citizenship. As a precondition to awarding certain employment-related visas to noncitizens, the Department of Labor (DOL) determines whether there are US workers available to fill the positions in question.[54] USCIS adjudicates petitions for nonimmigrant workers in various categories, determining whether the position offered meets the statutory requirements and whether the prospective employee meets the qualifications for the visa category and the position offered.[55]

DOS consular officers determine whether the individual visa applicant qualifies for the visa requested and whether the applicant is admissible to the United States. Temporary visas are available to short-term visitors, such as tourists, and to longer-term residents, such as students who may stay ten years or more.[56] Visa policy, which DHS formulates in consultation with DOS, is an immigration and foreign policy tool.[57]

Visas permit individuals to travel to a port of entry, but they do not guarantee admission to the country. Consular officers issue visas outside the United States that authorize foreign citizens to travel to a US port of entry; the visa holder may be able to use that authority multiple times over a specified period of years. Port-of-entry officials (from US Customs and Border Protection, or CBP) determine how long a foreign citizen may stay for each visit, which they mark on the admission stamp placed in the passport and log into a central database. CBP can deny entry based on a determination that the foreign citizen is not admissible. In contrast to the United States, many other governments issue single-entry visas, and then require the traveler to register with locally based immigration authorities to obtain a reentry or residence permit that will often allow multiple visits.

US Competitiveness

There is a missing middle in US visa issuance. While the United States issues only temporary and immigration-related visas, many other countries provide the option for flexible, long-term, nonpermanent visas.[58] These are useful, of course, for people whose obligations and interests in a country are longer term, and who may or may not permanently stay. An independent task force convened by the Migration Policy Institute (MPI) has recommended that the United States adopt a "transitional" or "provisional" visa for certain categories of temporary visa holders.[59] Such visas would create a presumption of ability to stay in the United States for the same or related purpose for which the visa was originally granted. Provisional visas would better respond to labor market needs and equip individuals with a solid foundation for possible citizenship and integration into the US economy and society.

The Visitor Visa Process

Vital security determinations have improved since the September 11, 2001, terrorist attacks. CA and its enforcement partner DS examined 49,000 criminal arrest records in FY2009 and on average scrutinize 10,000 watchlist hits a month.[60] The mistakes in handling the multiple-entry visa of the alleged Christmas Day 2009 bomber, Umar Farouk Abdulmutallab, highlight the need for additional improvements.

At the same time, more elaborate and intrusive screening methods have interfered with legitimate travel by students, members of particular ethnic groups, scientists, business people, and family members of US citizens and residents.[61] Professionals, multinational employees, artists, and athletes have also been affected. The resulting harm to individuals, families, the economy, and US diplomatic interests undermines the integrity of the temporary visa program. Applications for US visas will far exceed the opportunities to travel here for the foreseeable future.

Visa adjudication must become more nimble and flexible. In addition, CA must be able both to respond instantaneously to threats and risks, and work to reduce negative perceptions of the visa-adjudication process by important stakeholders in the United States and outside of it.

The United States issues visas based on four types of criteria: nationality, purpose of travel, applicability of prohibitions, and individual adjudication. For example, all Russians need passports and visas to come to the United States. All mathematicians, including those from Russia, may be approved for specific visas to work in the US software development industry. All Russian mathematicians are subject to the standard prohibitions based on national security. Russian mathematician visa applicants are subject to an individualized background check to confirm their identities, their bona fides as mathematicians, their purpose in traveling, their criminal history status, and their compliance with security standards.[62]

Countries whose citizens travel visa free to the United States do so by bilateral agreement with the United States. DHS may look not only at current citizenship, but also nationality, place of birth, and ties to determine how to treat an individual. Under the post-9/11 National Security Entry-Exit Registration System (NSEERS), for example, Canadian citizens who maintained citizenship in, were born in, or had ties to one of the 25 special-registration countries were subjected to registration requirements as if they were citizens of one of those countries.[63]

As visa officers are able to acquire better information about individuals through real-time access to national civil registries (as discussed in chapter 7), it may be possible to shift from a two-tiered system — visa and visa-waiver jurisdictions — to a three-tiered system consisting of: (1) countries where all citizens must acquire visas, (2) countries whose citizens are entitled to visa-free travel using the Electronic System for Travel Authorization (ESTA), and (3) a new tier of countries with which the United States does not have visa-free travel agreements but from which select travelers would be permitted to travel visa free under a registered traveler program.

Counterterrorism and Consular Affairs

As of this writing, there has not been a full public rendering of the reporting through the Visa Viper process to the National Counterterrorism Center (NCTC) in the case of Umar Farouk Abdulmutallab, the suspected al Qaeda follower who allegedly attempted to detonate an explosive aboard an Amsterdam-to-Detroit flight. The Visa Viper Terrorist Reporting Program enables agencies in the field — consular and others — to report potential terrorists' names to NCTC and so to nominate them for inclusion on the watchlist used at border points.[64] DOS has testified that embassy officials sent a cable through proper channels, and also sought to check whether Abdulmutallab had a visa. However, they misspelled his name, although entering it correctly into the Consular Lookout and Support System (CLASS) database. In addition, the name-recognition program used in the visa-application process was not available at the embassy for checking records.[65] Absent knowledge of a visa, there could not be a request for a visa-revocation review of Abdulmutallab's multiple-entry visa from CA's Visa Office (VO) in Washington, as would have been the advisable course of action. The deputy assistant secretary over the VO has the authority to issue a "prudential revocation" of a still-valid visa, which permits revocation without declaring the individual definitively ineligible.[66] Under consular regulations, a visa may be reinstated if concerns prove invalid. In the Abdulmutallab instance, CA placed a quasi-revocation in the system, denoting that the individual was presumed to be ineligible for a visa in the future. A prudential revocation is a middle course between the step that CA took in this instance — flagging the name in the event of a future application — and a revocation. Going forward, however, if an individual is of sufficient concern to nominate him to the Terrorist Identities Datamart Environment (TIDE) list, then it would seem clear that the individual is also of sufficient concern to issue a prudential revocation.

The Abdulmutallab near disaster serves as a pressing reminder to take stock of the role, organization, and procedures of CA. CA has strenuously sought to improve its security, particularly through the use of technology backstopping. However, this change has been driven from Washington, and the culture in the field is apparently not as focused as it could be on security precautions.

Consequently, additional measures must be considered. Most importantly, DOS should no longer permit Foreign Service officers to serve in consular positions if they do not intend to become permanent consular officers. Foreign

Service officers often look down upon consular service, and wish to move on to more prestigious career paths within DOS. Such attitudes must be rooted out. Instead, the consular service should be professionalized, established as a desirable career path, and accorded a degree of law-enforcement status. As in Canada, this service should at least for now remain in DOS, into which it is deeply integrated. A few consular officers could cross into Foreign Service officer positions such as ambassadorships; most would not.

It would not make sense to move the consular service function to DHS, where there is no backbone of necessary language and other training. Such a move also would sever CA from its counterpart criminal investigative service focused on passports and visas. DS performs these functions with unmatched expertise. While greater efforts should be made to integrate US Immigration and Customs Enforcement (ICE) and DS in joint international investigations aimed at human-smuggling organizations (HSOs) with a potential terrorist nexus (as discussed in chapter 4), DS should remain within DOS, where it performs a range of other vital functions.

Instead, the DOS mobility functions should be consolidated under a new under secretary for mobility and security. Establishing an independent mobility and security office with its own professional cadre should elevate counterterrorism concerns within DOS. And consolidation of all mobility services and law-enforcement policy units under a new under secretary would focus DOS on meeting legitimate mobility needs while maintaining laser-like attention on security. The following departments would report to the under secretary for mobility and security: DS (which now reports to the under secretary for management); the Bureau of Population, Refugees, and Migration, and the Office to Monitor and Combat Trafficking in Persons (which now report to the under secretary for democracy and global affairs); and the INL (which reports to the under secretary for political affairs).

Beyond this longer-term institutional adjustment, there are three changes that should be adopted immediately. First, CA should promulgate a set of rules to be followed in the wake of every Viper case, regarding particular database checks, determination of visa status, and consideration of a prudential revocation. Second, Congress should ensure that CA officers have access to all relevant law-enforcement databases. At present, CA officers are denied access to certain databases due to the fact that technically they are not "law enforcement" under the terms of the US government personnel system. Third, the culture of impunity at CA fostered by the doctrine of consular nonreviewability should be ended immediately. There should be thorough supervisory and legal review of the work of junior officers, with the unambiguous authority by supervisors to reverse their decisions.

Improving Compliance with Duration-of-Stay Requirements

Illegal immigration remains a concern for the US public and for security officials who despair of detecting the terrorist amid the illegal flow of people. To have confidence in the integrity of the temporary visa system, the US public must be assured that visa holders are complying with the rules, and the rules themselves must be clear. Neither of these conditions exists today. Between 33 and 48 percent of the US unauthorized immigrant population in 2006 had entered the country legally, but subsequently overstayed the time allotted to them.[67]

Congress in 2007 delegated authority to DHS to establish a cutoff point after which the number of overstays from a country would disqualify that country from participating in the US Visa Waiver Program (VWP). There is no rational basis for specifying an acceptable overstay rate — whether the 2.5 percent rate set in the 2000 visa-waiver statute or the 10 percent rate established in 2007 legislation — without having a specific understanding of the details of overstay practice and their relation to security concerns. Unfortunately, this level of tactical analysis is as yet unavailable.

Exit Checkpoints and Data on Departures

DHS collects exit data from airlines but does not yet have a comprehensive method to calculate overstays and therefore does not have a good basis for pinpointing problems or adopting reasonable overstay rate benchmarks. A comprehensive exit system would provide a basis for systematically determining the number of overstays, their countries of origin, the types of visas on which they entered, and other characteristics. No administration has yet fully embraced the idea of a government-controlled exit system. Congress passed legislation that requires an electronic entry-and-exit system, but it has not forced the issue and indeed has in the past delayed implementation.[68] By way of contrast, under the United States Visitor and Immigrant Status Indicator Technology (US-VISIT) program, *entry* procedures are now in place at 116 airports, 15 seaports, and 154 land ports of entry.[69]

There would be significant benefits to an exit system for both individual travelers and government authorities. Such a system would be more likely to identify, penalize, and deter infractions, and thus likely would lead to a greater willingness by authorities to expand visa-free travel. As a result, more people would be able to travel more conveniently within regulated channels. The ability for authorities to know specifically who is going as well as who is coming would enable more targeted information sharing, enabling a global mobility security alliance to raise its level of cooperation against common security threats.

The cost-benefit value of an exit system has been considered primarily in terms of civil security — what it adds to real-time tactical and medium-term operational intelligence that allows officials to disrupt threats.

There are other reasons for collecting detailed, reliable data on departures. In Australia, for example, where there are government-administered exit checkpoints, departure information is used to analyze labor migration trends and make policy recommendations based on evidence.[70] As the transnational movements of temporary workers become more important for sending and receiving countries, such detailed measurements will likewise become more important. It is impossible to understand the full impact of labor mobility without knowing who is coming in and who is leaving. Anyone wanting to measure flows of trade or investment would demand minutely detailed statistics. Collecting entry but not exit data on people is akin to collecting statistics on imports but not exports.[71]

Overstay Estimates

Visa overstays are nonimmigrants who remain in the United States beyond their period of authorized stay and who, thus, join the illegally resident immigrant population.[72] As it stands, DHS can match some but not all outgoing air passengers' records against their entry records, to see whether they overstayed.[73]

In 2008 DHS estimated that only 0.6 percent of people traveling to the United States with and without visas had overstayed their period of permitted stay.[74] That same year, there were 17,645,381 admissions under VWP (excluding the Guam visa-waiver program).[75] If 0.6 percent of visa-waiver entrants overstayed in 2008, then 105,872 would have overstayed. This would translate to roughly 1.9 to 2.6 percent of the estimated 4 million to 5.5 million persons who overstay their nonimmigrant visas each year.[76]

Most visa overstays ultimately leave the country.[77] Many depart within days of their visa expiring and most depart within a year.[78] Thus visa overstays are not contributing anywhere near 4 million–5.5 million persons to the long-term unauthorized population each year. In fact, the number of VWP entrants who overstay their visas and become long-term unauthorized residents would be a small fraction of the roughly 105,000 persons who overstay their visas each year.

Obtaining Accurate Overstay Information

CBP and ICE cannot significantly improve the level of overstay compliance without first getting an accurate read on the number and identity of overstays. There continue to be problems with the quality of DHS overstay statistics. The Government Accountability Office (GAO) has for some years pressed DHS (and the US Immigration and Naturalization Service [INS] before it) to collect departure information and to make new estimates of overstays by air.[79]

GAO has criticized DHS for being unable to provide overall or country-specific overstay rates.[80] *The Secure Travel and Counterterrorism Partnership Act* of 2007 authorized DHS to consider expanding visa-free travel to countries to whom the United States refuses only a small percentage of short-term business and tourist visas (between 3 and 10 percent in the prior fiscal year).[81]

Importantly, in addition to identifying countries with visa-refusal rates between 3 and 10 percent, DHS must also certify that it can verify the departure of at least 97 percent of foreign nationals who exit from US airports and ensure that it has a fully operational ESTA. However, to calculate the departure rate of nationals from any country, DHS uses *departure* records as the starting point and "matches" these records to those of *prior* arrivals, departures, or change of status. The purpose of this undertaking is to identify foreign citizens who remain here illegally. But to use departure information as a starting point provides a poor basis for measurement. Rather, DHS must be able to identify overstays by using foreign citizens' *arrival* data as a starting point and by matching these data against *subsequent* departure records. This way DHS would learn who has departed by air and who has potentially overstayed.[82] Because of their inherent flaws, DHS overstay statistics have generated criticism from at least one Senate overseer.[83]

The inadequacy of the statistical method has not stopped enforcement efforts. DHS reports that the US-VISIT office, using the Arrival Departure Information System (ADIS), provides an average of more than 300 credible leads on overstays each week.[84] In 2008 ICE made 715 arrests for overstays based on such data, and more than 2,500 people were prevented from returning to the United States because they were confirmed overstays.[85] DHS's Office of Immigration Statistics through a cross-agency team should ensure that DHS is able to establish as accurately as possible the number of overstayers, where they come from, and their visa categories, travel patterns, and personal identities.[86] With this information, DHS can create a more effective compliance and enforcement program.

The Need to Achieve Better Compliance

Transparency about which countries have high overstay rates, combined with a clearer understanding of the reasons and circumstances for overstays, would contribute to the development of a more rational compliance policy. Just as CA posts visa-refusal rates, DHS should post overstay rates by country.[87]

Based on what it can learn through its matching program, DHS could explore new ways of creating incentives for full compliance. To begin with, adopting proposals for provisional long-term visas would likely cut down on the number of tourists and other short-term visa holders who illegally end up staying to work.[88]

It is important to set up a predictable and effective system for addressing visa overstays for several reasons. First, certain persons who overstay visas may present exceptional risks. Second, travelers need to understand the rules so that they can comply with them. The current system can be confusing to visitors because it provides a visa that is valid for a particular period and an I-94, which provides another time period for duration of stay in the United States. Third, the US public strongly supports compliance with the law. The goal need not be to punish every single overstaying visitor as a lawbreaker: law-enforcement officials should always exercise reasonable discretion within guidelines. Rather, the goal should be to maintain a level of integrity in the system and to provide a form of reassurance to citizens that the law will be obeyed. A high level of confidence in security measures makes for a more resilient system in response to inevitable harmful incidents.

Current options for dealing with overstays, including those from VWP countries, are not optimal. A high overstay rate creates a dilemma. If the country with a high national overstay rate is a European Union (EU) Member State with a high volume of travel to the United States, suspending the country from the program is not a good option. In addition to increasing costs for individuals and making Americans vulnerable to reciprocal requirements, suspension would harm US competitiveness by making tourist and business travel more difficult. It would also create diplomatic difficulties with the sanctioned country and with the European Union. Moreover, DOS lacks the capacity to adjudicate all the visas that would be requested from major VWP nations without this program, and reestablishing that capacity would be prohibitively expensive. Finally, VWP is grounded in mobility security agreements that provide for critical information sharing about terrorists and other serious risks. So, while suspending the program would mitigate an overstay problem, it could undermine counterterrorism and crime control if the partner country responded by suspending cooperation provided for under the VWP agreement.

Encouraging Compliance with Terms of Admission

There are different ways to promote compliance with visa requirements. At present, the consequences for overstaying vary. The main sanction is a bar to future admission. If the holder of a nonimmigrant visa overstays by 180 days and then leaves voluntarily, there is a three-year ban on returning to the United States. If he or she overstays one year or more and then leaves voluntarily, there is a 10-year bar. DHS may also initiate removal proceedings against persons who are unlawfully present.[89] For anyone wishing to travel to the United States, these penalties serve as a deterrent. However, they could operate as a greater deterrent if they were more prominently publicized, for example, on wall posters in consulates or when travelers enter at land, air, and sea ports.

Figure 8.1 Penalties for Overstaying in the United States, 2009

Days of overstay	Current legal penalty(ies)	Applicable provision of the Immigration and Nationality Act (INA) of 1952, as amended	Applicability of and exceptions to current legal penalty(ies)
1 or more	Deportation	§ 237(a)(1)(C)(i)	Applies only to nonimmigrant overstays
1 or more	Visa becomes void; alien is ineligible to be readmitted as a nonimmigrant without a new visa obtained at a consulate in his or her home country	§ 222(g)	Applies only to nonimmigrant overstays
181 to 364	Inadmissible for 3 years following departure or removal	§ 212(a)(9)(B)(i)(I)	Applies to all aliens who are unlawfully present in the United States on or after April 1, 1997
365 or more	Inadmissible for 10 years following departure or removal	§ 212(a)(9)(B)(i)(II)	Applies to all aliens who are unlawfully present in the United States on or after April 1, 1997

Source: INA (1952), Public Law No. 82-414, compiled by MPI.

The penalties provide a very limited a set of tools to DHS. An additional system of fines would be worth exploring as a possible deterrent and revenue source. If fines were used, bars to admission could be used as an alternative or in egregious cases. A fine-at-departure system, like those employed in Japan and India, would create swift and certain consequences for noncompliance. In Japan, for instance, if the police discover a visa overstay, that individual will be arrested and subject to a potential fine of up to 3 million yen (approximately $33,000) and then deported.[90] India imposes $30 fines on individuals who overstay their visas.[91] A downside of such a program is that overstayers attempting to leave could become stuck in the United States and subject to detention. This happens to US travelers overseas, who are then forced to delay their return and wire home for funds. A better option might be to impose fines when the would-be immigrant next applies for admission. Consideration should be given to undertaking a cost-benefit study of an exit system that operates in conjunction with a system of fines.

DHS could also consider requiring that foreign citizens who overstay their lawful periods of admission be interviewed by a DHS officer prior to departure. Such interviews would be aimed at determining why the foreign citizens overstayed, making a record of the overstay for future use, determining the identity of all foreign citizens who overstay, and determining whether it would be appropriate to question or to detain these overstays for security reasons. Distinctions would need to be made between foreign citizens who overstay because of medical emergencies, accidents, and similar situations, and those who willfully overstay and violate the terms of their admission, such as by working without authorization. An interview requirement would need to be structured and publicized so that it did not operate as a disincentive to depart from the country.

GAO in 2004 published a report on weaknesses in DHS' overstay tracking system, and the impact of these weaknesses and of high levels of overstaying on domestic security.[92] The report pointed out that "of the six hijackers who actually flew the planes on September 11 or were apparent leaders, three were out of status on or before September 11 — two because of prior short-term overstaying."[93] GAO also documented that some overstayers had obtained jobs in sensitive areas at US airports.

Over time, DHS should be able to determine which countries and what groups overstay at high rates. Based on a specific understanding of the nationalities and types of overstays, it should be able to develop more focused deterrent measures. The strengthened Human Smuggling and Trafficking Center (HSTC) proposed in chapter 4 should analyze the mobility tactics of overstays found to have a terrorist or criminal nexus.

Even with improvements in measurement and compliance, people may stay in the United States and never leave or may leave surreptitiously between ports of entry. Without the type of residential registration system imposed in some EU Member States — which the US public is not likely to embrace — overstayers will be difficult to find. Nonetheless, it is vitally important to maintain an accurate and updated overstay list that can be effectively accessed by law enforcement.

Appeals of Visa Decisions

As security standards tighten, more mistaken determinations will occur with severe consequences for individuals, the US economy, and US credibility as a fair arbiter of legitimate global movement. Consular officers, unlike government actors in most other contexts, make decisions about visa applications that are nearly inviolate in their finality. An applicant for a nonimmigrant visa has no means to seek review of an application denial. An internal review system, in which supervisors assess the decisions made by consular officers, is the sole formal method of review, supplemented by informal processes such as inquiry by a would-be traveler's attorney.

The exceptional power held by consular officers has come to be known as the doctrine of consular nonreviewability or consular absolutism. The culture of absolutism at CA is so unusual that it bears further comment. In bygone days, it made sense to grant plenary authority to consular officers, who often operated in far-off posts with which communication was difficult. This is far from the case today. E-mail and centralized databases put not only case-by-case review but aggregate analysis well within reach. Consular officials may issue more than 1,000 visas per day in busy posts, making errors inevitable. These decisions — often by relatively inexperienced employees — receive scant supervisory review. This upside-down structure has spawned a culture of arrogance and lack of accountability, with reports of junior officers contacting the department's inspector general when one of their decisions is questioned or failing to respond to inquiries by superiors who are seeking to resolve instances where CA and USCIS outcomes differ.

Consular nonreviewability has important policy ramifications in an era when the United States faces stiff competition for the benefits that legitimate visitors bring. Other countries have recognized that the nonimmigrant visa-application process represents a critical initial interaction between potential visitors and the host country, and are working to improve that experience.

The introduction of pretravel authorization for visa-free travel with ESTA may exacerbate this problem. ESTA applications from visa overstayers are denied. Thus, the inability of the United States to correct database errors may lead people erroneously listed as visa overstayers to give up attempts to travel to the United States. A year into ESTA's existence, all ESTA denials should be analyzed and systemic problems should be addressed in order to reduce the number of erroneous denials.

US consular officials recognize the deepening pressures to be more responsive to persons wrongfully denied visas. However, they raise three arguments in support of the status quo.

First, they play down their inability to alter decisions by junior officers they are ostensibly supervising by suggesting they can use informal methods to affect decisions. However, these methods remain obscure, undocumented, and unreliable. As such, they offer no reassurance to visa applicants. Moreover, there has been a perennial shortage of midlevel supervisors at consulates to provide even this informal level of review.

Second, consular officers argue that the fact that an applicant may reapply after being rejected is a reason why a more robust review and/or appeals process is unnecessary. In practice, however, consulates do not let visa applicants apply multiple times. Many have imposed local rules permitting reapplications only after 6 or 12 months. More importantly, a later application is not a "de novo" review, particularly for tourist and other visas. Instead, intent to remain permanently in the United States is presumed unless the applicant affirmatively proves he meets the required standards.[94] In such cases, there is a strong presumption against issuing a visa after an earlier denial, and the initial decision will only be overturned if the applicant can show "changed circumstances." Because the reapplication is not considered de novo, it tends to be held to a higher evidentiary standard.

Third, consular officers often fall back on the argument that they would be swamped and the resources required would be prohibitive if visa appeals were permitted, because so many people are willing to go to all possible lengths to come to the United States. Certainly these challenges would exist, and administrative and budget adjustments would be necessary. But other developed nations that are also highly attractive to migrants are finding ways of expanding the redress available to certain groups of prospective visitors. In short, this is a problem that can and should be solved. The lessons from the cautious steps taken by other governments facing similar pressures are discussed below. At a minimum, though, CA supervisors, like supervisors everywhere else in government, should be authorized to exercise controlling review over their juniors.

Visa Appeals Systems in Other Countries

Several developed countries have instituted a visa appeals process. The Common Consular Instructions for the Schengen countries (the 25 countries that have eliminated borders for purposes of intra-European travel) "set out the nuts and bolts of EU visa practice regarding third-country nationals who seek a short-stay visa to come to the EU."[95] However, they leave it up to each country to determine whether to provide for an appeal and how much information to provide on the grounds for an application's denial.[96] As a result, these nations have adopted a wide range of visa practices. For example, Belgium allows for appeals in some visa categories and requires that the grounds of denial be provided in writing to the applicant. If the visa is denied, the applicant can lodge an appeal with the Conseil d'Etat, the highest administrative court. Requests for an appeal must be sent by registered mail within 30 days of receiving the notice of refusal. The Council of State can annul the decision, but does not have the power to order that a visa be issued. Instead, the original authority must reconsider its original decision in light of the court's determination.

Visa appeals practice is a sensitive issue with consular officers. The cost of an appeals process must also be considered. The United Kingdom is considering a reconfiguration of some visa categories and appeal rights.[97] The French Senate recently commissioned a special rapporteur to investigate what it called the "headache" of visa processing, generating a list of recommendations that includes better use of its visa appeals commission.[98] Because countries like the United Kingdom, France, and Australia increasingly compete with the United States for nonimmigrant visitors, it behooves the United States to assess its system against the practices of these nations.

The UK System

The UK Border Agency is the agency in charge of visa operations in the United Kingdom.[99] As of April 2009, all border, immigration, customs, and visa services functions in the United Kingdom were united within the UK Border Agency.[100] In 2007–08, the UK government received 2.4 million visa applications and issued visas to 81 percent of applicants,[101] a slightly lower percentage than the US approval rate.

Internal Review. The UK Border Agency Web site does not mention the internal review process, but the Entry Clearance Guidance (ECG) describes this process.[102] All denials of family-based visitor visa applications, as well as other applications with limited rights of appeal, must be reviewed by an entry clearance manager (ECM) within 24 hours to ensure that the decision is reasonable, that it comports with the immigration rules, and that the refusal notice is properly worded. The ECG states that "[t]his review is in addition to the review undertaken following receipt of an appeal."[103]

Who Can Appeal. The following categories of visa applicants have the right to appeal a visa denial:[104]

- Visitors whose purpose is to visit close family members
- Children and dependent relatives who seek to settle in the United Kingdom
- Wives, husbands, or fiance/es who seek to settle in the United Kingdom
- Students who plan to study for more than six months
- Persons looking to take part in working holidays
- Au pairs who plan to live and work with a family
- Work-permit holders who wish to work full time
- Ministers who wish to work full time in a religious capacity

Many of these categories parallel US immigrant visa categories.

How the Appeals Process Works. Entry clearance officers (ECOs) make the initial decisions on visa applications in UK posts abroad. The ECO notifies applicants of denials, informs them whether they have a right of appeal, and provides them with the following forms: a written notice of refusal, which explains why the notice was refused; a notice of appeal form AIT2, which the applicant must complete, explaining why the refusal was incorrect; and a brochure describing how to fill out the notice of appeal form.

Applicants can lodge an appeal in one of two ways. First, they can appeal directly to the Asylum and Immigration Tribunal (AIT).[105] The tribunal hears appeals from decisions made by the home secretary and subordinates on asylum, nationality, and immigration matters. Appeals result primarily from refusals of asylum applications, refusals of entry into or leave to remain in the United Kingdom for permanent settlement, deportations, and refusals of entry into the United Kingdom for a family visit.[106] Applicants also can appeal to the overseas visa section where the visa was refused; the overseas post then forwards the appeal to the tribunal. There is no charge for filing an appeal. Applicants must file a notice of appeal within 28 days of receiving the notice of refusal.

Once the tribunal registers the appeal, it sends a notice of receipt to the overseas mission where the original visa application was filed, together with the supporting documents filed by those lodging an appeal. At that point, an ECM at the post reviews the visa application again, taking into account any additional materials in the notice of appeal. The ECM can then overturn the original decision. If the ECM does not overturn the original denial, an ECO writes an explanation of the reasons that the application was refused, which is sent with all the other appeal papers to the tribunal. The visa section overseas has 20 business days from the arrival of the notice of receipt to prepare and send the appeal papers to AIT if the appeal concerns a nonsettlement or family-visit case, and 60 business days for settlement cases.

Appellants have access to the case file, including the ECO's written statement, and can choose to have legal representation in the appeals process. They may also qualify financially for representation by the Legal Services Commission's Community Legal Service. In addition, another organization, the Immigration Advisory Service (IAS), which is independent of the government, can provide advice about the appeals process and representation in an appeal hearing. Cases can either be decided after an oral hearing or review of the case file.

An immigration judge hears the appeal. The judge makes a decision based on the facts of the case and on the governing immigration rules, taking into consideration evidence submitted by the applicant's representative and by the Home Office. A decision must be reported to the tribunal within 10 days of the hearing. The tribunal then notifies the parties. If the appeal is successful, the decision must be delivered to the overseas post within six weeks.

Judicial Review. As in the US system, applicants may apply again if a visa application is rejected. Visa applicants can also contest the ECO's decision through judicial review. In the United Kingdom, the exercise of power by public authorities is always open to challenge in the courts.[107] However, such a challenge is only available to determine the lawfulness of the decision. The standard for measuring lawfulness is low: i.e., whether a decision was "so outrageous in its defiance of logic or of accepted moral standards that no sensible person who had applied his mind to the question to be decided could have arrived at it."[108] Between October 2006 and March 2007, 13 appeals by applicants with limited rights of appeal were lodged with the courts: five of those were conceded by the government, four were contested, and four cases were still pending when these statistics were reported.[109]

The Independent Monitor. In addition to the appeals system, Section 23 of the Immigration and Asylum Act 1999 created the position of independent monitor for entry clearance refusals without the right of appeal (IM).[110] The IM, who has a full-time appointment, is independent of the government. The

IM must prepare two reports per year for the secretary of state. In these reports, the IM examines the information available to applicants with limited appeal rights; examines the handling of complaints made by the applicants; and assesses samples of files throughout the world.[111] The IM, who cannot change individual visa decisions, spends at least three months per year at overseas posts conducting monitoring activities.

The IM has authority over two main categories of visa applicants: nonfamily visitors (such as tourists or short-term business travelers) and some students.[112] Slightly more than one-half of all visa applications are made by nonfamily visitors. The IM also monitors applications from students who have been accepted for a course of study that will not last more than six months, as well as those who intend to study but who have not been accepted for a course of study. The IM's remit will expand once the Points Based System is fully implemented, as applications adjudicated under that new system will no longer have full rights of appeal.[113]

Proposed Changes. The right to appeal denials in family-visit visa cases was established relatively recently, in October 2000.[114] The Visitors Consultation Paper — which resulted from a process led by the UK Border Agency between December 2007 and March 2008 to assess the need for changes in UK visitor visa categories — argues that the issue of appeals for family-visit visa applicants should be revisited:

> [While the right of appeal] provides a safeguard for the Asylum and Immigration Tribunal to identify genuine applications, the appeal is often not heard until many months later, by which time the reason for the visit, such as a wedding, may have long since passed. With improvements in process and introduction of the sponsorship system, there may be a case for looking at whether the right of appeal is necessary. Options could include replacing the current arrangements with a form of administrative review, or, on the principle that those who wish to appeal should pay for at least part of the costs incurred, the full right of appeal could be retained, but some costs recovered through a stand-alone charge or though inclusion in the original application fee.[115]

UK Program Status. The full tribunal appeals process costs an estimated 30 million to 40 million pounds per year.[116] The UK Immigration Minister has conceded that the idea of ending appeals for family visit cases is unlikely to be welcomed.[117] The Visitors Consultation Paper, which resulted from a process led by the UK Border Agency in 2007 and 2008 to assess the need for changes in UK visitor visa categories, does not propose that appeal rights for family visitors be dispensed with altogether.[118] Yet policymakers must take into account that even a limited abridgment of family visitors' appeal rights is likely to be roundly criticized. If family-visit appeals were revoked, this could lead to an increase in cases brought under Article 8 of the European Convention on Human Rights, which protects the right to private and family life.

The Australian System

In the Australian system, certain decisions about visa applications are subject to the authority of the Migration Review Tribunal (MRT).[119] MRT was established under the authority of the Migration Act 1958 (Migration Act), and came into existence on June 1, 1999. It is a companion to the Refugee Review Tribunal (RRT), which reviews decisions related to protection visas.

The Migration Act and the Migration Regulations 1994 (Migration Regulations) govern which decisions MRT can review, who may seek review of a decision, and procedural issues such as how the application must be made, time limits for lodging a review request, and application fees.[120] Review of decisions to refuse or to cancel a visa based on lack of good character is conducted through a separate process, under the jurisdiction of the Administrative Appeals Tribunal.

The mandate for MRT is to provide "a mechanism of review that is fair, just, economical, informal, and quick."[121] The tribunal conducts merits reviews, administratively reconsidering the case in order to ensure that "the correct and preferable decision" is reached.[122] This standard allows MRT to reconsider each case in light of the facts, law, and government policy. MRT can obtain information from additional sources and can conduct its own investigations. In this sense the Australian visa-review process is arguably broader than in other systems, and reflects the policy priority of "improv[ing] the general quality and consistency of decision-making, and enhance[ing] openness and accountability."[123]

Who Can Appeal. Rights to review are limited to certain kinds of visas, and also to certain individuals with an interest in the application. When a visa is refused, the decision letter from the Department of Immigration and Citizenship (DIAC) explains whether the decision can be reviewed and who can apply for review. For visas applied for outside Australia, the reviewable categories include:

- A decision to refuse a visa for which the applicant must be sponsored or nominated by an Australian citizen, or by a company or partnership operating in Australia, or by the holder of a permanent visa, or by a New Zealand citizen who holds a special category visa
- A decision to refuse a visitor visa to visit an Australian citizen or permanent resident parent, spouse, child, brother, or sister

In the first set of instances, only the sponsor can apply for review. In the second, only the Australian citizen or permanent resident relative can apply.[124]

The DIAC decision letter must contain information about the time limits for lodging a review request, which vary depending upon the type of case. MRT cannot waive these time limits.[125]

MRT's principal member has overall responsibility for the operation of the tribunal and the RRT. The principal member is supported by three senior members, who provide support and advice to group members. The group itself is comprised of eight full-time and 82 part-time members. More than 50 percent of MRT members have legal training. The others have extensive senior-level experience in the public or private sectors, including having served on other tribunals. Two registries — one in Sydney and one in Melbourne — support MRT and RRT.

How the Appeals Process Works. MRT reviews each case on its merits, considering the case "in light of all the relevant facts, the law and government policy..."[126] The tribunal can affirm a primary decision, vary it, set aside a primary decision and substitute a new decision, or return the case with directions for reconsideration. It takes MRT, on average, 40 weeks from the time an application is filed to issue a decision.[127] This estimate includes all types of cases reviewable by MRT; family-visitor-visa review requests are only one part of this total.

The individual seeking review (the applicant)[128] is entitled to appoint a representative to assist with the preparation and management of the application for review. In most instances, the representative must be a registered migration agent.[129] The applicant is entitled to have access to the material before MRT in relation to the case, with certain limited exceptions. The minister and DIAC are not represented before the tribunal; they provide the documents relating to the case and in some instances can make written submissions.[130]

The applicant can make written submissions or provide documentary evidence at any stage in the review process. MRT must inform the applicant of "certain information that might lead to an adverse decision" and give the applicant the opportunity to comment on that information.[131] MRT may also issue an invitation for the applicant to provide further information or comment on particular information, which the applicant must do or risk losing the opportunity to appear before MRT. In some cases, a decision can be made based only on the case filings. These cases are generally reviewed by just one tribunal member. In general, though, MRT must invite the applicant to appear for a hearing at which she can give oral evidence and present arguments. Applicants are also allowed to bring witnesses and MRT provides translators if necessary. It is possible to conduct the hearing or take some of the evidence by telephone or video conference. During the hearing, the applicant can be assisted and accompanied by the designated representative or by a friend.[132] The MRT member deciding the case takes an active role in asking questions during the hearing, but the hearing is not adversarial.

Once a decision is made, MRT must provide to the applicant a written record, including an explanation of the reasons supporting the decision. Cases of "particular interest"[133] must be published and made available on the MRT Web site. Cases relating to individuals who applied for a protection visa are published in a way that does not reveal their identities. A total of 8,229 MRT cases were decided in 2008–09. [134] Overall, MRT and the RRT seek to publish 40 percent of their decisions.

Judicial review. MRT decisions are subject to final review by the courts. Cases can be appealed to either the Federal Magistrates Court or to the High Court. Visa applicants and the minister for immigration and multicultural affairs can seek judicial review. In 2008–09, 248 judicial appeals were made from MRT decisions, constituting 4 percent of all MRT decisions.[135]

France

In 2000 France instituted a visa appeals commission.[136] The commission, located in the Ministry of Foreign Affairs, is charged with hearing appeals of visa-application denials made by diplomatic or consular officials. Filing an appeal with the commission is a prerequisite to pursuing a case in court.[137]

The commission is comprised of a president (who must have served as head of a diplomatic or consular post); a member of the local administrative jurisdiction;

and representatives of the Ministry of Foreign Affairs, Migration and Population Ministry, and Ministry of the Interior. These members are named to a three-year term by the prime minister.[138]

Applicants who are refused a visa are not entitled to an explanation of the refusal, except in a limited number of cases. These categories include: spouses of French nationals, children of French nationals who are younger than 21 or still dependent, parents of French nationals, minor children who have been adopted, beneficiaries of an approval for family reunion, and certain persons with work authorization. Anyone whose visa application is refused can either reapply or submit an appeal.

Issues and problems. France's visa-processing system has traditionally been viewed as one of the least-transparent in Europe.[139] In 2007 the Senate Finance Committee commissioned a special rapporteur to compile a report assessing the system.[140] In 2006 a total of 300,000 visas were refused and of that number, only 4,198 appeals were initiated. The report attributes this low number to lack of information provided to applicants on how to appeal.[141]

Program status. The special rapporteur also concluded that erroneous visa denials were an important policy concern because of their significant negative impact not only on the individual but on the nation. Among other problems, erroneous denials were thought to result in a loss of economic power for France due to decreased tourism and business travel, to impede family well-being, and to create a negative image of France.[142] The rapporteur stressed the economic costs involved in errors that are not discovered until the traveler reaches a port of entry. The average cost of processing a visa application is 35, while on average the cost of a visa appeal is 100 per case. The report argued that an effective visa policy should be viewed as a budgetary goal.[143]

The French Senate commission report recommended that greater justification be provided for refusals as a way to improve the overall quality of visa decision making and to promote legitimate tourism, business travel, international student enrollment, and family visits. The report signaled France's commitment to reshaping its visa policy.

The US System

The idea of a foreign traveler having an opportunity to seek review and redress for mistakes made in connection with mobility is not unprecedented in the United States. DHS put in place its Traveler Redress Inquiry Program (TRIP) (discussed in greater detail in chapter 9) in response to complaints from passengers and governments about legitimate travelers being repeatedly delayed or detained as a consequence of watchlist errors.

The TRIP system is still being developed and has limitations. For example, the Primary Lookout Over-Ride (PLOR), which is used to correct border lookout errors, has not had the full capacity to override primary lookout errors. As it stands, if an individual is forced to undergo secondary inspection more than once, he can request CBP to enter a PLOR record in the database. The CBP officer, in turn, can create a PLOR record if the passenger is determined not to be a match to a lookout or watchlist record. The PLOR record will automatically suppress — but not delete — the hit the next time the individual is encountered, unless new derogatory information has become available.

Despite its limitations, TRIP reflects a recognition by the US government that redress is an important component of immigration management and mobility security policies. As former homeland security secretary Michael Chertoff noted, "[I]f you're going to incapacitate somebody for a period of time, you have to have a higher confidence level that you're being accurate."[144] Lack of review may not incapacitate all prospective travelers in the sense that incorrect placement on a watchlist or detention would. However, it can negatively affect the lives of visa applicants and the way they perceive the United States.

Consular Nonreviewability

In 1952 the McCarren-Walter Act put in place the statutory framework governing consular decisions. Within that framework, consular officers were granted the power to decide visa applications, and the Secretary of State was prevented from changing those decisions. Despite President Truman's objection to such unfettered power by government officials, the law was passed, and the same statutory framework remains in place today.[145] The umbrella authority giving consular officers nearly absolute control over visa issuance or denial is found in the Immigration and Nationality Act (INA). INA Section 104(a), provides that the Secretary of State "shall be charged with the administration and the enforcement of the provisions of this chapter and all other immigration and nationality laws relating to: (1) the powers, duties, and functions of diplomatic and consular officers of the United States, except those powers, duties, and functions conferred upon the consular officers relating to the granting or refusal of visas. . ." (8 USC §1104[a]). President Truman has not been the only critic of consular officers' power. An extensive roster of legislators, blue-ribbon commissions, academics, and legal practitioners have echoed and amplified his concerns.

A 2007 court decision addressing review of consular decisions provides a succinct summary of the doctrine of consular nonreviewability and its tenuous underpinnings:

> It is well-settled that the decision of a consular official to grant or deny a visa is nonreviewable by courts, absent a constitutional challenge by a United States citizen. This principle, now firmly rooted in our jurisprudence, has come to be known as the 'doctrine of consular nonreviewability.' The doctrine of consular nonreviewability provides that when a consular officer decides to negatively exercise the visa authority granted to the executive by Congress, a court has no jurisdiction to review the exercise of that authority. In other words, the decision of a consular official to deny a visa is final and is not reviewable. It is not entirely clear why this is so — but it is. It has been frequently challenged in the legislature and in the courts, but all judicial and legislative proposals to limit the doctrine have been soundly rejected.[146]

The court also noted that "[d]espite the fact that the doctrine took hold in the judiciary, no textual constitutional basis for the doctrine had been clearly identified."[147]

Formal administrative review of visa denials is not available either. Applicants for immigrant visas at consulates, the only place they are issued, have no access to a review process. Consular decisions, therefore, occupy a distinct space in the geography of administrative law. In other administrative law matters, recipients of negative decisions have avenues for formal review. Petitioners for US employment-based immigrant visas have access to a formal review process within USCIS, conducted by the Administrative Appeals Office (AAO), while the Board of Immigration Appeals (BIA) reviews denials of family-based immigrant petitions.[148] These petitions form the basis for the adjustment-of-status application or the immigrant-visa application. AAO reviews denials of nonimmigrant worker petitions. Applicants for adjustment of status in the United

States do not have a direct review process but can file a motion to reconsider or can renew their application for adjustment of status in removal proceedings. Thus, applicants denied nonimmigrant visas by consular officers uniquely lack redress within the US system. The DOS Visa Office can issue an advisory opinion on a particular case, but these opinions apply only to questions of law, not of fact.

A US court of appeals has recently issued a decision that departs from the extreme deference that the federal courts have shown to consular decisions. The court found that the district court had failed to exercise jurisdiction to consider a visa applicant's claim, notwithstanding the doctrine of consular nonreviewability.[149] Although the decision is significant, it likely has limited practical applicability to most visa applicants, because the case involved core First Amendment rights; i.e., the right of US citizens to hear the views of others from around the world, even those the State Department has banned from receiving a visa because of suspected terrorism ties.

In recent years, the distinction between review of adjudications made inside and outside US territory has been eroded by the increasing information and support being provided to consular officers from the United States. With the shift to Web-based visa applications this trend will continue.

Internal Review Policy and Practice

In addition to the INA, consular authority is also addressed in companion laws to the INA, such as the Enhanced Border Security and Visa Entry Reform Act of 2002, and in the federal regulations, rules, and guidance issued by DOS. In June 2006 a new rule was published in the Federal Register making a significant change to the DOS internal review process. Before that point, a section chief or designee within each consular post was required to review all visa refusals. Since the change, review of refusals has been reduced, with the stated objective of allowing "a greater emphasis to be placed by consular supervisors on the review of issuances."[150] As the instructions to consular employees detail, the revised policy seeks to enhance security: "While the review of refusals is essential to maintaining appropriate adjudication standards, it does little to promote border security. In order to enhance US border security, equal emphasis must be placed on reviewing issuances to ensure visas are indeed issued in compliance with law and procedures."[151]

Absent adequate reporting, it is hard to gauge the frequency or utility of internal reviews to correct errors in rejecting or approving applications. CA posts statistics relating to visa applications, approvals, denials, and numbers of denials overcome by fiscal year on its Web site. Since statistics have been posted only through 2005, it is not possible to assess the effect of the 2006 change in policy.[152]

Reassessing Consular Nonreviewability

Consular nonreviewability is a vestige of a different era. Both the Immigration Act of 1924 and the McCarran-Walter Act reflected a desire to preserve American racial and ethnic homogeneity, a goal that no longer exists. From a pragmatic standpoint, the finality of a consular officer's decision made some sense in an era when the physical isolation of consular posts and the lack of quick and reliable communication meant that any outside review would be unworkable. That concern has little meaning in the contemporary era of global connectivity.

The United States is not the only country that does not allow any appeal from the denial of a nonimmigrant visa application. The same is true of Canada and other developed countries. But US economic, social, and foreign policy interests arguably suffer to a greater degree based on the pervasively negative image of US visa policy.

Conclusion

Securing human mobility requires a more nimble temporary visa system, which responds instantaneously and reliably to information concerning terrorist risks and which meets the needs of the full range of people in mobility channels.

Consolidating the mobility and security functions at DOS under a new under secretary for mobility and security could greatly enhance security. This reform would professionalize mobility adjudications and remove Foreign Service officers who lack the necessary dedication and training from the process.

A revitalized and more effective overstay compliance system should be based on a system of fines and detailed reporting that uses CA validation studies and DHS exit data.

The quality of consular decision making is undermined by the culture of impunity that stems from doctrine of consular nonreviewability. This notion of the near infallibility of junior officers must be ended by Congress as soon as possible.

Applicants need to know why their applications have been denied in order to be able to pursue renewed applications or, potentially, to appeal. While CA rules require that grounds of refusal be provided in writing, applicants frequently report that the written notice consists of a box checked with the statutory reference.[153] A statutory citation is meaningless to most applicants. Attorneys report that family-based immigrant visa applications are routinely denied under the statutory provision barring admission for lack of a labor petition, although this provision is irrelevant to family petitions.

It undermines the quality of decision making to bar appeals of visa decisions. DOS should lay the groundwork for instituting an appeals system by standardizing its current adjudication process into three tiers. Tier 1 applications could be granted immediately. If there is a possibility of denial, the case should go to Tier 2, where adjudications would involve a more detailed interview. Although there would still be a significant number of issuances, there would be notes in the file about any issues that needed to be resolved. Cases contemplated for denial would be referred to Tier 3, which would primarily issue denials and document those denials for internal review and appeal purposes. All tiers would be subject to a rigorous internal review process by midlevel officers.

A three-tiered system would be rational and transparent. It would also help to organize data for the purpose of developing machine-assisted analysis. Such analysis would be useful for Congress in considering legislation to establish a visa appeals process.[154] In the interim, Congress and the courts should dismantle the doctrine of consular nonreviewability and empower CA supervisors to review, alter, or reverse decisions by junior officers.

Chapter 9: International Information Sharing and Privacy

Policy Preview: *The Department of Homeland Security (DHS) recognizes international information sharing as essential to civil security, including mobility security. Further progress with allies in shared surveillance as well as in the use and transfer of information will only come with a mutually agreed upon strengthening of privacy and data-security protections. DHS and the State Department should make it a priority to complete the binding transatlantic framework agreement on privacy for which they have laid a foundation through the DHS-European Union High Level Contact Group (HLCG). They should also develop a long-term plan for a broader mobility-related information-sharing program, seek to update US privacy law to cover non-US persons, and work with other departments to establish a uniform US framework and coordination point for bilateral and multilateral information-sharing negotiations supporting civil security. Overcoming transatlantic privacy and data-security disputes and deficiencies of law, including with Canada, is one way to build a broader and deeper civil security alliance.*

The new importance of information sharing marks the transition from seeing developed-country borders primarily as avenues for legal or illegal labor movement to seeing them also as vectors of risk and locations for civil security.[155] While information sharing became a pivotal element of securing mobility channels because of terrorism, three other trends made it inevitable: new preventive law-enforcement strategies aided by information technology (IT), the increased volume of mobility, and the market's push for seamless international travel.

Just as there is a new domestic focus on information sharing, a new transatlantic mobility diplomacy has emerged to formalize and expand intelligence and information-sharing relationships, including relating to mobility. The information must be shared by governments with other governments, by airlines with governments based on information submitted by their customers, and by travelers with governments pursuant to travel and immigration laws.

Information-sharing discussions have mostly focused on sharing the identities of known and suspected terrorists and other dangerous travelers. They have also focused on sharing information on lost and stolen passports. Other mobility-related information that may need to be shared systematically involves:

- Terrorist travel histories
- Known and suspected criminals
- Abducted and missing persons
- Human-trafficking organizations (HTOs) and human-smuggling organizations (HSOs)
- Biometric information concerning refugee and asylee claims
- Identities of overflying passengers
- Identities of particular groups traveling to terrorist safe havens or war zones
- Biographic and biometric information on visa applicants to a particular country[156]

Transatlantic Mobility Information-Sharing Agreements

Transatlantic information sharing has advanced significantly as a result of assertive US leadership and a common US-EU interest in countering terrorist groups and in ensuring orderly and efficient travel channels. Information-sharing agreements can be unilateral, bilateral, regional, multilateral, and international. The United States' deepest information-sharing relationships are with the Five Country Conference (5CC, the United States, Canada, the United Kingdom, Australia, and New Zealand), certain EU Member States, and a few other countries. The most significant technical advances in information sharing involve lost and stolen passports and have been made among English-speaking nations. Box 9.1 lists transatlantic agreements that authorize the transfer of information relating to the movement of terrorists, criminals, or passengers.

Box 9.1 Major Mobility-Related Information-Sharing Agreements

Information about terrorists and criminals
- US bilateral agreements with 16 countries to share terrorist and criminal identity information, negotiated pursuant to Homeland Security Presidential Directive 6 (2003–present)
- Agreement on Data Exchange on suspected terrorists and criminals (2008), with Germany and 12 other EU countries, comparable to the Prüm Treaty among Belgium, Germany, Spain, France, Luxembourg, the Netherlands, and Austria (2005)

Box 9.1 (cont.)

Criminal investigative and relevant administrative information
*   US-Europol (2001 and 2002) and US-Eurojust (2006) agreements among law-enforcement and criminal-justice agencies governing data exchange
*   US-EU agreement governing mutual legal assistance (2003), pending EU-wide ratification, establishing a legal basis for joint investigations as well as the sharing of traveler and other mobility information for criminal investigative purposes

Information about lost and stolen passports
*   Interpol General Secretariat (IPSG)–National Central Bureau (NCB) agreements that allow national law-enforcement officers to check travel documents against Interpol's Stolen and Lost Travel Document (SLTD) database
*   The Regional Mobility Alert System (RMAS) among Australia, the United States, and New Zealand and open to other countries, on lost and stolen passports. US participation in RMAS is formalized by a memorandum of understanding.

Information about refugee and asylum applicants
*   The High Value Data Sharing Protocol within the 5CC to share biometric fingerprint information of foreign criminals and asylum seekers as a means of preventing fraud.[157]

Information about all travelers
*   US Visa Waiver Program (VWP) agreements with 34 countries (1986–present);
*   EU-US agreement on the processing and transfer of Passenger Name Record (PNR) data by air carriers to the DHS (2007) and the agreement between the European Community (EC) and Canada (2005) on the processing of Advance Passenger Information (API) and PNR data.

Information about registered travelers
*   The Fast Low Risk Universal Crossing (FLUX) alliance between the United States and the Netherlands (2008), an agreement between the United States and the United Kingdom (2008) initiating an international expedited-traveler program based on mutual access to registered travel information. This program is expected to incorporate other existing bilateral programs, i.e. Sentri and Nexus.

Source: DHS; Interpol; Asia-Pacific Economic Cooperation (APEC) Business Mobility Group.

Several of these agreements are relevant to other aspects of counterterrorism and crime control. However, almost all of them were negotiated with the needs of mobility-related agencies taken into consideration.

US conflict with Canada and the European Union over privacy and data-protection standards has proven an obstacle to progress on information sharing. While it is not clear how much the European and US publics understand or care about privacy and data security, in fact, these issues are critical to people's confidence that mobility-security strategies honor democratic and human rights norms. Ultimately all information-sharing arenas have to be based on laws that protect privacy and provide appropriate ways to vindicate rights.

This chapter discusses the state of negotiations in three arenas: terrorist and criminal identities lists (watchlists), passport information, and passenger information.

Terrorist and Criminal Identities Information (Watchlists)

The highest-priority initiative for formal international agreements relating to terrorist mobility is the program to share biographic and biometric information about known and suspected terrorist identities. Since 2003 the United States has concluded 16 agreements with foreign governments to share terrorist-identity information.[158] The Department of State (DOS) leads these negotiations, with a team that includes representatives from the intelligence community, and the Departments of Justice (DOJ) and DHS.

Lost and Stolen Passports: Interpol and APEC Regional Movement Alert System

Terrorists and criminals use lost and stolen passports to hide their identities and travel histories. The United States participates in information sharing about lost and stolen passports bilaterally, through Interpol, and through a pilot information-sharing program sponsored by the APEC group called RMAS.

Interpol created the SLTD database in 2002. The Interpol partnership regularly produces five or more cases of fraud per month that would not have been identified without the system.[159] The European Union obligates all of its Member States to submit information on lost and stolen passports to Interpol in addition to their respective national databases and to the EU Schengen Information System.

The Regional Movement Alert System (RMAS)

While APEC has endorsed the Interpol program,[160] it has experimented with a different system, RMAS. The system was first piloted in 2005 by the United States and Australia and was joined by New Zealand in 2006.

RMAS allows participating countries to query each other's databases, thereby exchanging information in real time without storing data in a shared central database. Instead, a RMAS broker acts as a switchboard for directing information requests and their responses to and from the relevant officials at the border.

APEC's goal is to standardize the process of requesting information on travel documents across the region. RMAS is memorialized in a bilateral memorandum of understanding with individual states. In principle, either a bilateral or multilateral approach is acceptable, but in practice bilateral arrangements have proven more achievable than multilateral arrangements because it is less complicated to work out issues with one partner rather than multiple partners.

DOJ, DHS, DOS, and Congress should continue to promote, support, and use the Interpol program. Not only is the program accessible to a wide range of countries, but there is an infrastructure for its dissemination, and its international governance structure attracts political support, including from the United Nations (UN). The RMAS approach should be considered as a possible solution for the exchange of lost and stolen passport information in the transatlantic region.

Information about Travelers

Because terrorist movement draws on a network made up of links among travelers, travel-document agencies, reservation systems, travel agents and transportation companies, and border inspectors, the United States has an active set of programs to obtain biographical and biometric information about travelers as a means of attempting to detect threats. Other governments are beginning to follow suit, including Japan, the European Union, Mexico, and Canada.[161] There are multiple purposes for collecting information from travelers: identity verification, terrorist and criminal checks, mobility-law compliance, investigations, individual risk analysis, dynamic system improvements, and deterrence. Given the adaptability of terrorists, it is of paramount importance to use preventive intelligence to make systemic security improvements.

After September 11, 2001, the United States expanded the information it required airline companies to submit to it as a condition for entering US airspace. There are two primary airline data sets and systems: Advance Passenger Information (API) and Passenger Name Record (PNR). The Enhanced Border Security and Visa Entry Reform Act of 2002 required airlines to submit API data prior to their departure from a foreign country or arrival in the United States.[162] The reason for the change was to enable authorities to make a "no-fly" decision about individual passengers. API contains information that is encoded in the machine-readable zone of passports, including the number and type of travel document, nationality, full name, and date of birth.

PNR data were first collected by airline companies in the late 1950s to process international travel requests and reservations via a central computer reservation system. After 9/11, the United States passed the US Aviation and Transportation Security Act that made the US Customs and Border Protection (CBP) responsible for collecting, transferring, and retaining PNRs "for the purposes of preventing and combating terrorism and other serious criminal offenses that are transnational in nature"[163] and in order to facilitate bona fide travel. CBP collects information from airlines on all passengers traveling to, from, or through the United States, including US citizens. PNR data contains all the passenger information that booking agents and airlines need to process reservations. It is stored in interlinked global airline reservations systems (also known as global distribution systems) including Sabre, Amadeus, Galileo, and Worldspan.

According to internationally set standards, PNR fields, at a minimum, must include: the name of the passenger(s), itinerary or routing, the name of the individual making the reservation, a phone contact, and ticketing information such as a ticket number or the date by which the ticket must be issued.[164] Airlines may add supplemental information to the PNR in the special service request (SSR), other service information (OSI), or other remarks categories. Supplementary data may include a passenger's special dietary requirements, information on unaccompanied travel of minors, frequent flyer information, as well as requests for assistance at airports and on aircrafts.[165]

Impact of the Conflict over Privacy/Data Security Standards

The failure to agree upon a viable transatlantic privacy standard has significantly impeded information-sharing negotiations, with the following ramifications. First, privacy standards are the key hurdle to forging new agreements on sharing terrorism-related information. Second, agreeing on privacy standards is a key hurdle to renegotiating visa-waiver travel partnerships with European countries that are already in the VWP but are slated for review and renewal. Third, privacy standards can sometimes be a barrier to DHS being able to share investigative and intelligence information with EU Member States when a third country is involved. Fourth, lack of agreement over privacy standards is an obstacle to expanding the categories of mobility-related information that the United States and EU Member States exchange systematically. Fifth, CBP is encountering difficulties in collaborating with other countries to expand the nascent registered-traveler system, FLUX. In order to "certify" a registered traveler to another country's border authorities, there has to be some access to underlying data for verification (registered-traveler systems are discussed further in chapter 10). Sixth, lack of agreement over privacy rights is a factor in the failure of the United States and Canada to complete an innovative preclearance agreement that would make border crossing more efficient for both countries. Preclearance agreements elsewhere will not be possible absent an agreement over privacy rights (US-Canada preclearance is discussed in chapter 12). Seventh, the lack of a privacy agreement has led to a hodge-podge of information-sharing agreements, including a US-EU agreement, a US-Canada agreement, and a Canada-EU PNR agreement. Eighth, the dispute over privacy and data-security issues relating to information sharing is crowding out diplomatic exchange on broader mobility policy issues where transatlantic interests are at stake, for example, problem solving concerning exit controls, select visa categories, immigrant integration, refugees and asylum seekers, and mobility-security-related development assistance. Ninth, the transatlantic privacy standard stalemate is placing international institutions like Interpol and the International Civil Aviation Organization (ICAO) at the center of transatlantic controversy. Tenth, the PNR agreement itself may be reopened under the new governance arrangements adopted by the European Union in the Lisbon accords. The United States and the European Union have signed three PNR agreements — an initial agreement in May 2004, an interim agreement in October 2006, and the current one, valid until 2014, in July 2007. Disputes about how to protect individual privacy have sparked these successive agreements.[166]

Key Issues in the Transatlantic Dispute over Mobility-Related Data Protections

While the United States pursues terrorist-related information bilaterally, EU Member States are bound by EU law. Therefore, it ultimately makes sense for the United States to form an umbrella privacy agreement of some kind with the European Union as a whole. An agreement could also cover other nations with which the United States has close, expanding arrangements for sharing unclassified information about travelers, refugees, asylum seekers, and visa applicants. In June 2008, the EU-US HLCG on information sharing and privacy and personal data protection agreed on a set of 12 common principles concerning mobility-related privacy protections. One subject is outstanding: the scope and institutionalization of the right of individuals to obtain redress for flaws and failures in the collection and use of information about them. In November 2009 the United States and European Union agreed on data-sharing principles in the area of justice, freedom, and security (a key EU policy area), supposedly having worked out the outstanding issues that HLCG laid out in 2008.

While the European Union claims that all individuals have a right to redress regardless of nationality, the United States asserts that its constitution permits differential treatment of nationals versus nonnationals.[167] DHS has agreed that as a matter of policy it will provide certain redress mechanisms for watchlist misidentification issues as well as for problems encountered during screening and boarding procedures at ports of entry for non-US persons. This policy affords foreigners access to records and amendment rights, but not the four causes of civil action available to US persons, which include monetary damages.[168]

Also, the European Union asserts that adequate redress is not possible absent an independent data supervisor with authority to probe into commercial and government settings to determine compliance and to advocate on behalf of individuals. The United States does not have or recognize the need for a wholly independent privacy supervisory authority. However, US agencies have their own redress procedures, such as the DHS Traveler Redress Inquiry Program (TRIP), under which all individuals, including non-US citizens, can seek limited redress.[169] Among other sources of consternation in Europe is the period of retention of personal information under US policy, especially of people not suspected of anything. The EU standard is 24 hours. Under the PNR agreement, the United States can retain information that would be stored for 15 years in active and dormant files.

One key to resolving these differences is to acknowledge the complexity and dynamism of privacy and data-protection law on both sides of the Atlantic. EU data-protection standards are constitutional in nature and interpreted by EU judicial process. Privacy is recognized as a human right in the 1950 European Convention for the Protection of Human Rights and the EU Charter of Fundamental Rights (2000). Data-protection laws applicable to public and commercial information about these subjects include the EC Directive 95/46 on the protection of personal data (1995) (known as the Privacy Directive); the E-privacy Directive (2002); and the Council of Europe Convention for the Protection of Individuals with regard to Automatic Processing of Personal Data (1981).

EU privacy standards did not apply to criminal justice matters, including mobility security issues, until December 2008 when the European Union adopted the Council Framework Decision on the protection of personal data processed in the framework of police and judicial cooperation in criminal matters (Data Protection Framework Decision or DPFD). This agreement is intended to be implemented by EU Member States by 2010.

In the absence of DPFD, privacy and data-protection provisions have had to be negotiated separately. Under both sets of EU privacy standards, every EU Member State also has its own laws and methods of implementation and enforcement. The European Union has an independent European data protection supervisor that reports to the European Parliament. Each Member State also appoints a national data-protection authority (DPA). These entities, usually known as supervisory authorities, have some ability to intervene on behalf of aggrieved citizens by investigating claims. Most importantly, citizens from outside the European Union have the same privacy rights and redress opportunities as do EU citizens, including access to judicial review.

The US constitution does not explicitly recognize a right of privacy. Although the First and Fifth Amendments, and especially the Fourth Amendment right against unreasonable search and seizure, provide some protection, privacy is understood primarily as a common law and statutory right, not a human right. The linchpin statute is the Privacy Act of 1974, aimed at protecting Americans against the type of abuses perpetrated during Watergate. Other statutes apply under particular circumstances, for example, the Electronic Communications Privacy Act, the E-Government Act, and the Freedom of Information Act. States also have their own privacy laws.

The United States has a variety of privacy and data-security monitors within the executive branch. Authorities include the director of the Office of Management and Budget, chief privacy officers within federal agencies especially within DHS, and a civil liberties protection officer in the Directorate of National Intelligence (DNI).

Non-US persons have a right of action under the Freedom of Information Act (limited by that act's exemption for law-enforcement and national security information), but do not have a right of action under the nation's primary privacy law, the 1974 Privacy Act.[170]

The main form of redress that DHS is publicizing is its TRIP program. TRIP is administered by DHS's Transportation Security Administration (TSA). "Redress" in the TRIP context means that travelers may submit an inquiry for the purpose of ensuring that government records are accurate and are shared among all DHS screening programs in accordance with the law and DHS regulations. The Terrorist Screening Center (TSC) is a key reviewer of TRIP applications where the terrorist watchlist is involved. While the minimal available data suggest that the TRIP and Primary Lookout Override (PLOR) redress systems are having some positive impact, their success is not yet assured. Even some federal air marshals have not been able to get false positives overridden.[171] According to CBP frontline officers, TRIP remains a work in progress.[172] However well TRIP works as a single point of inquiry for travelers, its value is limited because it does not permit judicial remedies for non-US persons.[173] According to the DHS Office of Inspector General, TRIP fails to affect the travel experiences of individuals seeking redress, does not allow independent review of petitions, and does not share information on redress case results.[174] TRIP represents a good beginning, but it is not the necessary legislatively established comprehensive redress mechanism. The challenge is how to design a process that satisfies individual rights without tipping off terrorists. TSC, through TRIP, receives hundreds of queries from terrorists who are checking to see if they appear on the watchlist and can be removed from it.[175]

Channels for Advancing a Transatlantic Mobility-Related Privacy Framework

In addition to US bilateral discussions with Canada, there are several core channels through which transatlantic information sharing relating to mobility are being discussed: DOS-led bilateral, terrorism-related information-sharing negotiations; DHS-led bilateral, visa-waiver reviews and negotiations; the US-EU HLCG, led in the United States by DHS and US-EU negotiations over the new Mutual Legal Assistance and Extradition Treaties (MLAT), led in the United States by DOJ; the Committee of the Council of Europe and the largely European International Conference of Data Protection and Privacy Commissioners (ICDPPC), in which the United States participates only as an observer; and the multilateral Organization for Economic Cooperation and Development (OECD), in which the United States and 29 other countries with advanced economies participate.

Terrorist Identity-Sharing Negotiations and the Role of the State Department The DOS Consular Affairs (CA) Bureau has the lead in negotiating Homeland Security Presidential Directive 6 (HSPD-6) agreements on behalf of the US government, backed by DOJ and DHS, and the intelligence agencies. Congress should establish legislative authority for the DOS to continue negotiating new terrorist-identities-sharing agreements, in consultation with the DOJ, DHS, and the DNI, Central Intelligence Agency (CIA), and National Counterterrorism Center (NCTC).

Global negotiations by DOS over terrorist identity information sharing have to be coordinated with the DHS-State negotiation of visa-free travel agreements in order to fulfill Congress's mandate in the Secure Travel and Counterterrorism Partnership Act of 2007. The implementing recommendations of the 9/11 Commission Act of 2007 (H.R.1) required that terrorist identity information sharing be considered in renewal of VWP participation.

More thought needs to be given to how information-sharing negotiations are handled. Congress should establish a senior policy position within DOS with authority over global information sharing and privacy protection within the department. Congress should also address the question of how to achieve a coordinated and strategically directed US approach to all information-sharing agreements, encompassing law enforcement, terrorist financing, container security, commercial transactions, and public health. The compartmentalized approach to negotiations means that the different agencies that conduct such negotiations have ended up with quite different results.[176] The European Union, on the other hand, has the advantage of a consolidated position. To meet the urgent need to achieve and implement a common US position concerning transatlantic information sharing, the United States needs a central authority for privacy policy.

The US-EU High Level Contact Group

The mission of HLCG, which began its work in 2006, was to develop a set of common principles on the protection of privacy and personal data in the context of mobility-related information sharing that the European Union and the United States could agree upon despite differing legal regimes and historical contexts. HLCG has been a crucial forum that potentially serves either as the core or predecessor group for negotiations to establish the necessary legal framework for all information sharing across the US government with the European Union, and potentially with other state and regional entities.[177] The homeland security secretary represents the United States.

The DOJ-EU Mutual Legal Assistance Agreement Negotiations

The European Union and DOJ in 2003 successfully negotiated what might accurately be characterized as a revolutionary new US-EU MLAT in criminal matters.[178] In October 2009, the United States and European Union exchanged instruments on the treaty,[179] which will likely take effect in 2010.

Two aspects of the US-EU MLAT are particularly notable and have significant direct implications for mobility security. First, signatory states may establish joint investigative teams. This fuses US investigators and their counterparts in EU Member States into a single, integrated task force operating under one state's criminal law. The linkage is absolute; if an individual is prosecuted overseas, he will be protected by the double jeopardy clause of the US Constitution from prosecution in the United States. Such investigative teams are critical for effectively suppressing global HSOs and HTOs. Second, the agreement extends to "national administrative authorities." This means that regulatory and administrative agencies with the authority to make criminal referrals to law-enforcement agencies will be able to use the MLAT to gather information in connection with their investigations. Such agencies include the CA, CBP, and US Citizenship and Immigration Services (USCIS), as well as the various transportation agencies.[180] This treaty will become central to the US-EU mobility security relationship for years to come.

The Council of Europe's Section 108 Consultative Committee

(pursuant to Chapter V of the 1981 Convention for the Protection of Individuals with regard to Automatic Processing of Personal Data) and the International Conference of Data Protection and Privacy Commissioners (ICDPPC) EU privacy policy is guided by two bodies. The Council of Europe's Consultative Committee concerning data protection is composed of representatives and deputy representatives of parties to the convention, and observers admitted by decision of the Committee of Ministers, following consultation with the Parliamentary Assembly. It makes proposals to facilitate, improve, or amend the application of the 1981 Convention for the Protection of Individuals with regard to automatic processing of personal data and to offer opinions on its application.

The ICDPPC is an influential policy-developing body in the arena of privacy and data security that convenes government and private-sector privacy officials to advance dialogue and propose new standards. ICDPPC began as an all-European organization in 1978. However, it has since evolved to include non-EU Member States, Slovenia, Burkina Faso, and Argentina. Observer status has been granted to Mexico and Japan, as well as in the United States to DHS and the Federal Trade Commission (FTC). These observer nations have not been formally admitted due to their democracies' failure to establish a data supervisory authority with sufficient independence from the executive branch to meet ICDPPC charter requirements.[181]

Because ICDPPC convenes data and privacy officials from throughout the world and is a leading forum on privacy and data security, it is important for US views to be represented and considered in the discussions. US data-security experts should be included as participants in light of the practical impact of US views.[182]

Without full membership, the United States will not be able to participate formally in the series of meetings that follow up on ICDPPC's Strasbourg Resolution calling on the United Nations to create a binding international convention on data-protection standards. DHS and DOS should ensure that the United States participates fully in the UN-related processes, and press for admission of the United States into ICDPPC.

The Organization for Economic Cooperation and Development

OECD, the first international organization to develop and issue privacy guidelines, is opening up its influential 1980 Principles for renewed dialogue.[183] The

United States ought to take the OECD discussions seriously and fully partici-pate in them, with a government wide set of positions approved by the White House Office of Management and Budget (OMB).

Recommendations for Next Steps to Resolve the Transatlantic Privacy Dispute

Several points are relevant to keeping the US-EU dialogue productive. First, it should be acknowledged that privacy law has not kept abreast of changes in IT, business practice, or criminal threats. Current privacy law and policy are widely regarded as inadequate by experts, many with substantial government experience.[184]

US advisory groups' critiques are extensive, deep, and significant. With respect to government use of information, they make recommendations concerning such fundamental issues as the need to strengthen oversight and redress mecha-nisms, the need to regulate transfers to third parties, and the need to establish privacy rules for the use of commercially sourced data and for the machine-aid-ed reading of bulk data (i.e., use of algorithms). From the traveler's perspective, privacy statutes typically make exceptions for law-enforcement and intelligence information, putting actual redress out of reach in many circumstances. There is also agreement that privacy notices need to be improved, and that there needs to be a more uniform set of rules and a central privacy authority in the federal government.

Most importantly, as one pair of commentators has written, "the basic prem-ise of classifying data according to the status of the person (as a US person or a non-US person) or location of collection (within or without the United States) is problematic in today's interconnected, globalized environment. Updating these categorizations would benefit US interests as much as European ones."[185]

Criticisms within Europe of the European system of protecting privacy are no less sweeping. A recent study by Rand Europe has suggested that the entire EU Privacy Directive needs to be rethought.[186] A basic theme of the report is that the EU data-protection framework has to be restructured in order to provide *de facto* — as opposed to *de jure* — redress for individuals. This report is particu-larly critical about EU attitudes toward making privacy agreements with third countries, noting that "[d]e facto, the test being applied to third countries is not an adequacy test, but an equivalence (i.e. transposition) test."[187] The report also noted that processes for notifying the public about changes in the handling of personal information that affect them and the role of the data-protection authorities in accountability and enforcement are inconsistent and ineffective.

Canadian privacy practice and law is also a work in progress. Canada's legal privacy-protection regime more closely resembles that of the European Union than it does that of the United States. Canada has two federal privacy laws: the Privacy Act (1983) and the Personal Information Protection and Electronic Documents Act (2000). Each of its provinces and territories has its own privacy legislation on the collection, use, and disclosure of personal information held by government agencies. Like the European Union, Canada has an independent federal privacy authority in addition to provincial and territorial privacy commissioners.

Given the substantial challenges to privacy law and practice on both sides of the Atlantic, it is obvious that no party has a monopoly on best practices. An exchange of ideas about the different systems and a policy of mutual accommodation would help in upcoming negotiations on privacy issues.

Due to legal changes under the Lisbon treaty, which grants the European Union and its Parliament more authority over security-related matters, the European Union is in a state of constitutional flux. For this reason, the European Union is not in a position to insist on its current approaches being the last word. Whichever directions EU and US legislation and privacy governance take, any binding agreement must have built-in opportunities for adjustment that will make them responsive to new technologies.

The European Union also should take note that on the US side, there is an impetus for updating US privacy laws. As mentioned above, there is great concern about the fact that the 1974 Privacy Act does not adequately address the issues raised by the explosion of information practices and surveillance techniques that has occurred since the passage of the 1974 legislation.[188]

Meanwhile, all parties should remember that the OECD privacy principles, APEC principles, and the 1990 UN resolution on computer privacy do not require a specific structure for a privacy or accountability entity. A respectful mutual recognition of this fact would reflect the kind of comity that ought to characterize US-EU relations. The most important objective, on which both

North Americans and Europeans agree, is to have effective accountability, transparency, and appeals for information sharing among governments.

US Government Actions

The US government can take several steps that would help contribute to the success of negotiations on a set of transatlantic privacy principles.

First, DHS should focus with DOJ and DOS on working with their European counterparts to implement the US-EU MLAT agreement. The MLAT provides an important opportunity for deepening information sharing in critical areas of mobility security including counterterrorism and countering human trafficking and smuggling. Its privacy provisions will provide a testing ground and allow the practical experience to fuel negotiations for a binding international agreement that builds on the now-agreed-upon common principles for US-EU sharing of information for law-enforcement purposes. In addition, the US-EU MLAT will serve as a model for a comparable agreement within North America.

Second, DHS should provide Congress, EU bodies, and publics on both sides of the Atlantic with a well-explained account of the benefits of traveler personal information for crime control and counterterrorism. Annual reporting requirements on mobility security measures need to be developed to demonstrate that PNR and API programs are effective and can vindicate individual privacy interests.

Third, DHS should continue to improve TRIP and there should be an interagency process for ensuring that effective fixes are carried through the entire federal watchlist system, especially at TSC.

Fourth, the HLCG Common Principles group should include DOS participation at a senior level. Making a senior DOS official the department's focal point for international privacy policy could provide important support and cohesion to negotiations that potentially encompass a wide range of departments and agencies.

Fifth, US negotiators should enter negotiations armed with a far more detailed knowledge of the privacy laws and practices of the 27 EU Member States. The United States is currently in the position of defending its practices against criticisms based on what the European Union says, not on what countries actually do. Transatlantic negotiations should recognize that both sides' privacy laws are in their early stages of development.

Sixth, the United States should consider the EU model of having an independent privacy office, a version of which has also been suggested as a model for privacy governance by GAO.[189] An independent office could be especially useful in serving as a trusted third party to assess incidents in which sensitive or classified material is involved. The five-member Privacy and Civil Liberties Oversight Board mandated in the 2004 9/11 legislation may meet the level of independence and authority familiar to Europeans operating in a parliamentary system. This oversight board should be activated, and consideration should be given to its independence within an international context.

Seventh, US privacy advocacy and human rights groups across the spectrum, and law professors should apprise themselves of transatlantic privacy and data-security issues and factor them into ongoing discussions of proposals for updating US privacy laws. The United States needs to have its own debate on the applicability of privacy law to noncitizens. The United States has agreed to the principle that privacy is a human right in Article 12 of the Universal Declaration of Human Rights and Article 17 of the International Covenant on Civil and Political Rights. These should be a foundation for any review.

Eighth, US privacy laws should be updated, and a central point for privacy and data security policy coordination should be established.

Toward International Standards?

With the support of the European Union, ICAO, which develops international travel document standards, has proposed the adoption of international standards for PNR[190] (discussed in greater detail in chapter 11).[191] Especially from the perspectives of airlines and governments, an international information-sharing agreement for PNR information is worth considering. However, this is premature absent an EU-wide standard and a US-EU agreement. Only three EU Member States — the United Kingdom, France, and Denmark — use PNR data for passenger screening. Although the European Union has announced an intention to develop an EU-wide system, the European Commission has not announced plans to build such a system.[192] Indeed, national authorities can find themselves at odds with Brussels in incorporating PNR data into their layered civil-security defenses.[193] Nevertheless, as the PNR agreement continues to operate, DHS should seek to expand the parties to it and begin planning for an international standard.

DHS is well on its way to consideration of a long-term vision for international mobility-related information sharing. This can be accomplished through a single transatlantic agreement covering all mobility-related information sharing (allowing for national level variations as appropriate), sector-specific agreements, or the incorporation of comprehensive information-sharing provisions in broader mobility security agreements. In the interim, it should be a crucial policy priority to complete the US-EU privacy and data-security framework agreement.

Conclusion

Information sharing was invoked in the aftermath of 9/11 as a means to prevent future attacks and as an alternative to the tactics of US law-enforcement agencies. An important lesson of the first post-9/11 phase of transatlantic discussion is that although information-sharing policy is conceptually straightforward, it is challenging to develop and implement.

The United States needs to press forward on expanding information sharing to gain access to more passport and related civil-registry information in real time in order to strengthen visa-issuance and port-of-entry admission processes, as well as to complete more terrorist identity-sharing agreements. Expanded sharing of information about certain refugee and asylum applications among the 5CC may also prove beneficial and appropriate for extension to other countries.

However, information sharing must be accompanied by adequate legal redress for foreign citizens and US travelers who are subject to myriad errors in the normal course of the operation of bureaucratic systems. Otherwise, friction will arise with allies and the US public may be reluctant to support further significant investment in this process.

DHS and other US agencies working together must make a greater effort to explain privacy and data-security protections to the public. A good place to start would be the development of a periodic report setting forth the security and cost benefits of mobility-related information systems on which DHS and DOS currently rely to screen travelers and migrants.

It is important to complete a legal transatlantic privacy and data-security agreement. Implementation of the US-EU MLAT, including provisions for training, is also a critical next step. A transatlantic agreement, encompassing at least Canada, the United States, and the European Union would provide a solid foundation for broader multilateral information-sharing agreements to secure human movement. Before this effort begins in earnest, DHS and its partner agencies need to consider whether broad or sector-specific negotiations make more sense.

Information sharing concerning mobility security and the privacy and data-security foundations that support it have emerged as major dimensions of a transatlantic civil security alliance. It is not too soon to begin thinking about how the effort can be expanded to other VWP countries or other fora such as the G-20.

Notes

1. "Defense of the citizen" is a phrase from: Christopher Coker, *War in an Age of Risk* (Cambridge, UK: Polity, 2009), 132.

2. Jean-Louis Bruguiere in "Trail of a Terrorist," *Frontline* (a Public Broadcasting Service TV program), posted October 25, 2001, www.pbs.org/wgbh/pages/frontline,/shows/trail/etc/synopsis.html; National Commission on Terrorist Attacks upon the United States, *The 9/11 Commision Report: Final Report of the National Commission on Terrorist Attacks upon the United States* (New York: W.W. Norton & Company Ltd., 2004), 383.

3. Rey Koslowski, *Real Challenges for Virtual Borders: The Implementation of US-VISIT* (Washington, DC: Migration Policy Institute, MPI, 2005), www.migrationpolicy.org/pubs/Koslowski_Report.pdf.

4. The International Civil Aviation Organization (ICAO) is discussed in more detail in chapter 11.

5. National Commission on Terrorist Attacks upon the United States, *9/11 and Terrorist Travel*; *Intelligence Reform and Terrorism Prevention Act of 2004*, Public Law 108-458, 108th Cong., 2nd sess.; and pending Senate bill S. 1261 on PASS ID in the 111th Congress.

6. The report of the 9/11 Commission states that, "When people travel internationally, they usually move through defined channels, or portals. They may seek to acquire a passport. They may apply for a visa. They stop at ticket counters, gates, and exit controls at airports and seaports. Upon arrival, they pass through inspection points. They may transit to another gate to get on an airplane. Once inside the country, they may seek another form of identification and try to enter a government or private facility. They may seek to change immigration status in order to remain. Each of these checkpoints or portals is a screening — a chance to establish that people are who they say they are and are seeking access for their stated purpose, to intercept identifiable suspects, and to take effective action." See National Commission on Terrorist Attacks upon the United States, *The 9/11 Commission Report*, 385.

7. Statement for the record of David Heyman, Assistant Secretary, Policy, US Department of Homeland Security (DHS), "Five Years After the Intelligence Reform and Terrorism Prevention Act (IRTPA): Stopping Terrorist Travel," before the Senate Committee on Homeland Security and Government Affairs, 111th Cong., 1st sess., December 9, 2009, http://hsgac.senate.gov/public/index.cfm?FuseAction=Files.View&FileStore_id=fca64800-f21e-4772-8ec2-f39bab662ffe; Statement for the record of Janice L. Jacobs, Assistant Secretary, Consular Affairs, Bureau of Consular Affairs (CA), US Department of State (DOS), "Five Years After the Intelligence Reform and Terrorism Prevention Act (IRTPA): Stopping Terrorist Travel," before the Senate Committee on Homeland Security and Government Affairs, 111th Cong., 1st sess., December 9, 2009, http://hsgac.senate.gov/public/index.cfm?FuseAction=Files.View&FileStore_id=790a6ddb-6d50-49a5-8247-a7aaf6073fba; Statement for the record of Rand Beers, Under Secretary, National Protection and Programs Directorate, DHS, "Five Years After the Intelligence Reform and Terrorism Prevention Act (IRTPA): Stopping Terrorist Travel," before the Senate Committee on Homeland Security and Government Affairs, 111th Cong., 1st sess., December 9, 2009, http://hsgac.senate.gov/public/index.cfm?FuseAction=Files.View&FileStore_id=16e8ac24-2fb2-4672-bf28-4c1e6f72113b.

8. Political scientist Kamal Sadiq refers to these documents as "feeder" documents, defined as "any document, paper or plastic, real or fake, seemingly state authorized and posing as proof of identity such that it gives access to other identity documents authorized by the state." See Kamal Sadiq, *Paper Citizens: How Illegal Immigrants Acquire Citizenship in Developing Countries*, 79–80 (New York: Oxford Univ. Press-USA, 2008).

9. National Commission on Terrorist Attacks upon the United States, *9/11 and Terrorist Travel*.

10. The State Department developed a simple low-cost machine readable travel-document reader and border-control entry system that has been implemented in developing country airports with the assistance of the International Organization for Migration (IOM). See Rey Koslowski, "International Cooperation On Business Travel and Tourism," Paper Presented at the Global Mobility Regimes Workshop of the German Marshall Fund, Washington, DC, November 20–21, 2009.

11. Remarks by an Immigration and Customs Enforcement (ICE) Forensic Document Lab senior official on September 30, 2009, at the Migration Policy Institute (MPI) in Washington, DC.

12. The 9/11 Commission called for real-time verification of travel documents, stating in its report, "We should move toward real-time verification of passports with issuing authorities. The further away from our borders that screening occurs, the more security benefits we gain." See National Commission on Terrorist Attacks upon the United States, *The 9/11 Commission Report*, 389.

13. Koslowski, *Real Challenges for Virtual Borders*.

14. Matt Sundeen, "The REAL ID Rebellion," *State Legislatures*, March 2008.

15. HHS (US Department of Health and Human Services), Office of Inspector General, *Birth Certificate Fraud* (Washington, DC: HHS, 2000), www.oig.hhs.gov/oei/reports/oei-07-99-00570.pdf.

16. Oriana Zill, "Crossing Borders: How Terrorists Use Fake Passports, Visas, and Other Identity Documents," *Frontline*, October 25, 2001, www.pbs.org/wgbh/pages/frontline/shows/trail/etc/fake.html.

17. HHS, *Birth Certificate Fraud*.

18. National Commission on Terrorist Attacks upon the United States, The 9/11 Commission Report. The Markle Foundation also published a paper that called for standardization of paper breeder documents and digitization of birth and death records to be searchable in all states. See Amitai Etzioni, "Reliable Identification for Homeland Protection and Collateral Gains," in *Creating a Trusted Network for Homeland Security* (Washington, DC: Markle Foundation, 2003), Appendix A, 78.

19. *The Intelligence Reform and Terrorism Prevention Act of 2004* (IRTPA), Public Law 108-458, December 17, 2004, §7211 (b)(3)(A).

20. Ibid.

21. Today, in a handful of "open-access" states, many in New England, birth certificates may be purchased by anyone, without verifying that the requester is the person on the certificate.

22. Centers for Disease Control and Prevention and the National Center for Health Center Statistics, Intelligence Reform & Terrorism Act — The Act, the Process and Update (Washington, DC: Centers for Disease Control, 2005), www.cdc.gov/nchs/ppt/bsc/bsc_charlieintel_sep05.ppt.

23. Ibid.

24. Garland Land, Executive Director of the National Association for Public Health Statistics and Information Systems, personal email correspondence with the author.

25. Todd B. Tatelman, *Intelligence Reform and Terrorism Prevention Act of 2004: National Standards for Driver's Licenses, Social Security Cards, and Birth Certificates* (Washington, DC: Congressional Research Service, 2005), www.fas.org/irp/crs/RL32722.pdf.

26. National Association for Public Health Statistics and Information Systems, "EVVE Pilot," (Silver Spring, Md.: NAPHSIS, Web site accessed on February 17, 2010), www.naphsis.org/index.asp?bid=1035.

27. States with EVVE are: California, Montana, Utah, North Dakota, South Dakota, Kansas, Oklahoma, Minnesota, Iowa, Missouri, Arkansas, Kentucky, Mississippi, Alabama, New Jersey, Rhode Island, and Hawaii. Implementation is in progress in: Michigan, Ohio, New York, Pennsylvania, and Massachusetts. See the National Association for Public Health Statistics and Information Systems, "Jurisdiction Implementation Status (updated December 2009)," Powerpoint Presentation, December 2009, www.naphsis.org/NAPHSIS/files/ccLibraryFiles/Filename/000000001190/EVVE_Implementation_Dec_2009%20with%20territories.ppt.

28. GAO (US Government Accountability Office), *Department of State: Undercover Tests Reveal Significant Vulnerabilities in State's Passport Issuance Process*, GAO-09-447 (Washington, DC: GAO, 2009), www.gao.gov/new.items/d09447.pdf.

29. Statement for the record of the National Association for Public Health Statistics and Information Systems, "Reevaluating Real ID: Strengthening Birth Certificate Verification," before the Senate Committee on Homeland Security and Governmental Affairs on July 15, 2009, 111th Cong., 1st sess., www.naphsis.org/NAPHSIS/files/ccLibraryFiles/Filename/000000001077/NAPHSIS%20on%20REAL%20ID-July%202009.pdf.

30. Ibid.

31. Ibid.
32. Janice Kephart, "The Appearance of Security: REAL ID Final Regulations vs PASS ID Act of 2009," (Washington DC: Center for Immigration Studies, April 2009), 3, www.cis.org/articles/2009/back409.pdf.
33. Ibid.
34. GAO, *Undercover Tests Reveal Significant Vulnerabilities in State's Passport Issuance Process.*
35. Ibid.
36. "India's New Identity Card," *The Economist*, July 2, 2009.
37. Sadiq, *Paper Citizens.*
38. The Open Society Institute is calling attention and helping to address this problem. For example, it is working to help the stateless of Kenya to organize themselves to fight for their right to an identity card, known as the *kitambulisho*, without which a passport may not be acquired. See Open Society Institute, Justice Initiative, *Report on Developments 2005-2007* (New York: Open Society Institute, 2007), www.soros.org/initiatives/justice/articles_publications/publications/developments_20071221/developments_20071221.pdf.
39. "Worries About Iraq's Biometric Database," *Homeland Security Newswire*, August 26, 2009, http://homelandsecuritynewswire.com/worries-about-iraqs-biometric-database.
40. A variety of working groups work toward enhancing travel-document security and a number of documents such as Resolution 32-18 of the Assembly and the ICAO Blueprint for the implementation of biometric information also serve to promote this objective. For more details see ICAO, *MRTD Report: Optimizing Security and Efficiency Through Enhanced ID Technology* 1, no. 1 (2006), www.icao.int/cgi/goto_m_atb.pl?icao/en/atb/fal/mrtd/MRTD_Rpt_V1N1_2006.pdf.
41. Recommendation made by the National Commission on Terrorist Attacks upon the United States, *The 9/11 Commission Report*, 565 n. 40.
42. James A Lewis, *Authentication 2.0 — New Opportunities for Online Identification* (Washington, DC: Center for Strategic and International Studies, 2008), http://csis.org/files/media/csis/pubs/080115_authentication.pdf.
43. Statement for the record of Jess T. Ford, Director, International Affairs and Trade, GAO, "State Department: Improvements Needed to Strengthen US Passport Fraud Detection Efforts," before the Senate Committee on Homeland Security and Government Affairs, 109th Cong., 1st sess., June 29, 2005, www.google.com/url?sa=t&source=web&ct=res&cd=1&ved=0CAcQFjAA&url=http%3A%2F%2Fhsgac.senate.gov%2Fpublic%2Findex.cfm%3FFuseAction%3DFiles.View%26FileStore_id%3D882eb9a7-e54d-4214-a8e2-31450692fe28&ei=s9MuS4S-Joa7lAfVm82XBw&usg=AFQjCNFmeZDluQM5ttwkYzw_Oey5uxq_cQ&sig2=C4OZ4UeyG0XkrvLjs3yIqg .
44. GAO, *Undercover Tests Reveal Significant Vulnerabilities in State's Passport Issuance Process.*
45. Diplomatic Security officials, interviews with the author.
46. Some states will therefore choose not to issue EDLs.
47. DHS, "Fact Sheet: Enhanced Driver's Licenses (EDL)," Press Release, December 5, 2007, www.dhs.gov/xnews/releases/pr_1196872524298.shtm.
48. Ibid.
49. Statement for the record of Timothy J. Healy, Director, Terrorist Screening Center, Federal Bureau of Investigation (FBI), US Department of Justice (DOJ), "Five Years After the Intelligence Reform and Terrorism Prevention Act (IRTPA): Stopping Terrorist Travel," before the Senate Committee on Homeland Security and Government Affairs, 111th Cong., 1st sess., December 9, 2009, http://hsgac.senate.gov/public/index.cfm?FuseAction=Files.View&FileStore_id=50242372-f66d-401f-b3a8-1feb2b2de6fa.
50. A Markle Foundation task force subgroup made a similar suggestion, suggesting that OMB convene a group to deal with identification issues. See Etzioni, "Reliable Identification for Homeland Protection and Collateral Gains."
51. A report by the Identity Theft Prevention and Identity Management Standards Panel (IDSP) making such a proposal is available at ANSI (American National Standards Institute), *Identity Veri-*

fication (New York: ANSI's Identity Theft Prevention and Identity Management Standards Panel, 2009), http://webstore.ansi.org/identitytheft. A project plan was developed and a team formed to take this work forward under the leadership of the North American Security Products Organization (NASPO) and ANSI-accredited standards developer.

52. DOS (US Department of State), "Department Organization," www.state.gov/r/pa/ei/rls/dos/436.htm.

53. At least three overstays living in the United States were known to the 9/11 hijackers: Eyad Alrabaabah, Agus Budiman, and Mohammed Belfas. Alrabaabah's address was listed by five of the hijackers as their residence when applying for Virginia licenses or identity cards. Budiman and Belfas were associates of Mohammed Atta. Budiman's address in Germany had been used by one of the other hijackers on his visa application.

54. These include H2-A (temporary agricultural worker) and H2-B (temporary nonagricultural worker) visas. The Department of Labor (DOL) has a more limited role for H1B (specialty occupation) visas, where there is no labor market test, except in the H-1B "dependent" context where there is an attestation.

55. H (speciality occupation), L (intercompany transferees), O (extraordinary ability), P (artists, athletes), Q (cultural exchange), R (religious workers), and E (investors) and TN (NAFTA traders) if petitions are filed.

56. Certain visas, including E, Treaty Trader, and Treaty Investor, have no expiration date and are valid for as long as the holder conforms to the conditions for admission.

57. According to a memorandum of understanding signed by the Department of Homeland Security (DHS) and DOS in 2002, "the Secretary of Homeland Security will establish visa policy, review implementation of that policy, and provide additional direction as provided by this memorandum, while respecting the prerogatives of the Secretary of State to lead and manage the consular corps and its functions, to manage the visa process, and to execute the foreign policy of the United States. The Secretary of Homeland Security will rely upon the expertise of the Department of State with respect to foreign policy, and the Secretary of State will respect the expertise of the Department of Homeland Security concerning threats to American security." See US Government Printing Office, *Memorandum of Understanding between the Secretaries of State and Homeland Security Concerning the Implementation of Section 428 of the Homeland Security Act of 2002* (Washington, DC: US Government Printing Office, 2008), http://frwebgate.access.gpo.gov/cgi-bin/getdoc.cgi?dbname=108_cong_documents&docid=f:hd131.108.pdf.

58. The United States offers some reasonably long-term visas: L (intercompany transferee) visas may be up to seven years, H (temporary worker) visas up to six years, J (exchange visitors) visas often extend to seven or eight years, and E (investor visas) are of indefinite duration so long as the investment continues. US long-term visas, however, are connected to a specific purpose — work for a particular sponsoring employer or attendance at a particular school — with very limited flexibility.

59. Under a provisional visa, most employment-based immigrants would be sponsored by employers for three-year visas and could gain visa portability after one year. By meeting criteria to demonstrate suitability for long-term residence, provisional visa holders would be eligible for a second three-year visa, and many could then adjust to lawful permanent residence and obtain a green card. For more details, see Demetrios G. Papademetriou, Doris Meissner, Marc R. Rosenblum, and Madeleine Sumption, *Aligning Temporary Immigration Visas with US Labor Market Needs: The Case for Provisional Visas* (Washington, DC: Migration Policy Institute, MPI, 2009), www.migrationpolicy.org/pubs/Provisional_visas.pdf; Doris Meissner, Deborah W. Meyers, Demetrios G. Papademetriou, and Michael Fix, *Immigration and America's Future: A New Chapter* (Washington, DC: MPI, 2006).

60. Statement for the record of Janice L. Jacobs, assistant secretary, Consular Affairs, Bureau of Consular Affairs (CA), DOS, "Five Years after the Intelligence Reform and Terrorism Prevention Act (IRTPA): Stopping Terrorist Travel," before the Senate Committee on Homeland Security and Government Affairs, 111th Cong., 1st sess., December 9, 2009. The terrorist watchlist is made up of 400,000 people, of which approximately 3,400 are considered a threat to civil aviation or

national security. Of these, approximately 170 live in the United States. Statement for the record of Timothy J. Healy, director, Terrorist Screening Center, Federal Bureau of Investigation (FBI), US Department of Justice (DOJ), "Five Years after the Intelligence Reform and Terrorism Prevention Act (IRTPA): Stopping Terrorist Travel," before the Senate Committee on Homeland Security and Government Affairs, 111th Cong., 1st sess., December 9, 2009.

61. Edward Alden, *The Closing of the American Border: Terrorism, Immigration, and Security Since 9/11* (New York: HarperCollins, 2008).

62. *The Enhanced Border Security and Visa Reform Act of 2002* provides that visitors from state sponsors of terrorism are subject to additional security reviews. Cuba, Iran, Sudan, and Syria are currently designated state sponsors of terrorism.

63. These countries include: Afghanistan, Algeria, Bahrain, Bangladesh, Egypt, Eritrea, Indonesia, Iran, Iraq, Jordan, Kuwait, Libya, Lebanon, Morocco, North Korea, Oman, Pakistan, Qatar, Somalia, Saudi Arabia, Sudan, Syria, Tunisia, United Arab Emirates, and Yemen. See DHS, US Immigration and Customs Enforcement (ICE), "Fact Sheet: Changes to National Security Entry/Exit Registration System (NSEERS)," December 1, 2003, www.ice.gov/pi/news/factsheets/nseersFS120103.htm.

64. DOS, *US Department of State Foreign Affairs Manual, Volume 9 – Visas* (Washington, DC: DOS, 2009), www.state.gov/documents/organization/106193.pdf.

65. Statement for the record of Patrick F. Kennedy, Under Secretary of State for Management, DHS, "Securing America's Safety: Improving the Effectiveness of Anti-Terrorism Tools and Interagency Communication," before the Senate Committee on the Judiciary, 111th Cong., 1st sess., on January 20, 2010.

66. DOS, *US Department of State Foreign Affairs Manual, Volume 9 – Visas*, www.state.gov/documents/organization/87515.pdf.

67. Pew Hispanic Center, *Modes of Entry for the Unauthorized Migrant Population* (Washington, DC: Pew Hispanic Center, 2006), http://pewhispanic.org/files/factsheets/19.pdf.

68. Edward Alden, "US Should Drop the 'Exit' from Its Entry-Exit System," *Security Debrief,* October 12, 2009, http://securitydebrief.adfero.com/2009/10/12/u-s-should-drop-the-exit-from-its-entry-exit-system/.

69. DHS, "US-VISIT: Current Ports of Entry," January 31, 2008, www.dhs.gov/files/programs/editorial_0685.shtml.

70. Graeme Hugo, "In and Out of Australia: Rethinking Chinese and Indian Skilled Migration to Australia," *Asian Population Studies* 4, no. 3 (2008): 267–91.

71. Michael Clemens and Sami Bazzi, *Don't Close the Golden Door: Our Noisy Debate on Immigration and its Deathly Silence on Development* (Washington, DC: Center for Global Development, 2008), www.cgdev.org/content/publications/detail/16129.

72. GAO (US Government Accountability Office), *Overstay Tracking: A Key Component of Homeland Security and a Layered Defense*, GAO-04-82 (Washington, DC: GAO, 2004), www.gao.gov/new.items/d0482.pdf.

73. Algorithms for this purpose have been developed by Lawrence Livermore Laboratory.

74. Senior DHS officials, conversation with the author.

75. DHS, Office of Immigration Statistics, *Yearbook of Immigration Statistics 2008: Table 25, Nonimmigrant Admissions by Class of Admission: Fiscal Years 1999 to 2008* (Washington, DC: DHS, 2008), www.dhs.gov/xlibrary/assets/statistics/yearbook/2008/table25d.xls.

76. The Pew Hispanic Center estimated that 4 to 5.5 million individuals overstayed their nonimmigrant visas in 2006. See Pew Hispanic Center, *Modes of Entry for the Unauthorized Migrant Population*.

77. In recent testing of an exit system at airports, US Customs and Border Protection (CBP) identified 400 overstays in 30 days at two ports of entry. Senior DHS officials, conversations with the author.

78. Senior DHS officials, conversations with the author.

79. GAO, *Visa Waiver Program: Actions Are Needed to Improve Management of the Expansion Process, and to Assess and Mitigate Program Risks*, GAO-08-967 (Washington, DC: GAO, 2008),

www.gao.gov/new.items/d08967.pdf; GAO, *Overstay Tracking*; GAO, *Illegal Immigration: INS Overstay Estimation Methods Need Improvement*, GAO/PEMD-95-20 (Washington, DC: GAO, 1995), www.gao.gov/archive/1995/pe95020.pdf; GAO, *Illegal Aliens: Despite Data Limitations, Current Methods Provide Better Population Estimates*, GAO/PEMD-93-25 (Washington, DC: GAO, 1995), www.gao.gov/cgi-bin/getrpt?PEMD-93-25.

80. GAO, *Visa Waiver Program*.

81. Ibid.

82. Ibid.

83. In a November 2008 letter to the chairman, US Senate Committee on the Judiciary, then–Homeland Security secretary Michael Chertoff confirmed that DHS used departure data as the starting point for its estimates of overstays. "Letter dated November 13, 2008, to the Honorable Patrick Leahy, chairman, Senate Committee on the Judiciary from Michael Chertoff, secretary, Department of Homeland Security." Expressing concerns about the data, Senator Dianne Feinstein (D-CA) responded to Secretary Chertoff that this certification does not meet the security requirement to track visa-waiver-program travelers, as it only certifies that DHS has tracked 97 percent of individuals who exit through US airports, not whether 97 percent of individuals who *entered* at airports actually left. "Letter dated November 18, 2008, to Michael Chertoff, secretary, Department of Homeland Security, from Sen. Dianne Feinstein."

84. Statement for the record of Rand Beers, under secretary, National Protection and Programs Directorate, DHS, "Five Years after the Intelligence Reform and Terrorism Prevention Act (IRTPA): Stopping Terrorist Travel," before the Senate Committee on Homeland Security and Government Affairs, 111th Cong., 1st sess., December 9, 2009. The United States Visitor and Immigrant Status Indicator Technology Program (US-VISIT) Data Integrity Group (DIG) verifies and validates records of individuals whose status indicates that they may be in-country overstays, and it refers leads to ICE. DIG also reviews and validates records of out-of-country overstays and posts them to various databases used by officials who encounter foreign citizens.

85. US-VISIT senior official, personal communication with the author.

86. GAO recommended that the secretary of homeland security: (1) designate an office with responsibility for developing overstay rate information for the purposes of monitoring countries' compliance with the statutory requirements of the Visa Waiver Program (VWP); (2) direct established office and other appropriate DHS components to explore cost-effective actions necessary to further improve, validate, and test the reliability of overstay data; and (3) direct the VWP Office to request an updated, validated study of estimated overstay rates for current and aspiring VWP countries, and determine the extent to which additional research and validation of these data are required to help evaluate whether nationals of particular countries overstay at excessively high rates. See GAO, *Visa Waiver Program*.

87. DHS is statutorily obligated to provide a system of dissemination for immigration-related information that affects US economic interests. See *Immigration and Nationality Act* (INA) Sec 103(d), USC 1103(d).

88. Papademetriou, Meissner, Rosenblum, and Sumption, *Aligning Temporary Immigration Visas with US Labor Market Needs*; Meissner, Meyers, Papademetriou, and Fix, *Immigration and America's Future*; Victor C. Johnson, *A Visa and Immigration Policy for the Brain-Circulation Era: Adjusting To What Happened in the World While We Were Making Other Plans* (Washington, DC: Association of International Educators, 2009), www.nafsa.org/uploadedFiles/NAFSA_Home/Resource_Library_Assets/Public_Policy/visa_immigration_for_brain_circulation.pdf.

89. Johnson Lazaro, "The Law on Overstaying," *Asian Journal Publications*, February 15–21, 2008, www.asianjournal.com/pdf/PDF/2008_SF/2008_02_15/2008_02_15_SF_sec3p%203.pdf.

90. "Diet Cracks Down on Overstayers, Widens Door for Refugees," *The Japan Times*, May 28, 2004, http://search.japantimes.co.jp/member/member.html?nn20040528a1.htm.

91. The Embassy of India in Peru, "Fines," www.indembassy.org.pe/english/servicios/visa.htm.

92. GAO, *Overstay Tracking*.

93. Ibid.

94. Visa categories B (tourist and business), F (student), J (exchange visitor), and M (trade school) fall into this category.

95. Thierry Balzacq, Elspeth Guild, Anita Szymborska, and Agnieszka Weinar, *An Analysis of the Current Common Consular Instructions* (Brussels, Belgium: European Parliament, 2006), www.libertysecurity.org/IMG/doc_CCI-English.doc.

96. Ibid.

97. The visa categories are not technically called "immigrant" or "nonimmigrant" as they are in the United States. These terms are used here to designate what the equivalents would be in the United States.

98. Adrien Gouteyron, *Un rapport d'information fait au nom de la commission des finances, du contrôle budgétaire et des comptes économiques de la nation sur les services des visas* (Paris, France: Sénat, 2007), www.diplomatie.gouv.fr/fr/IMG/pdf/Rapport_d_information_no353_-_Visas.pdf (hereinafter Senate Report).

99. Home Office, UK Border Agency, "About Us," www.ukvisas.gov.uk/en/aboutus/.

100. Home Office, UK Border Agency, "Launch of Britain's New Unified Border Agency," News Release, April 3, 2008, www.ukba.homeoffice.gov.uk/sitecontent/newsarticles/2008/ukborderagencylaunch.

101. Home Office, UK Border Agency, *Entry Clearance Statistics 2008-09* (London, UK: Home Office, 2009), www.ukvisas.gov.uk/resources/en/docs/2958881/visastats2008-09.

102. Home Office, UK Border Agency, "Entry Clearance Guidance Documents," April 3, 2009, www.ukvisas.gov.uk/en/ecg/ecgdocuments.

103. Home Office, UK Border Agency, "Entry Clearance Guidance — Appeals (APL)," www.ukvisas.gov.uk/en/ecg/appeals/.

104. Current developments in categories of persons with the right to appeal have yet to be updated at Home Office, UK Border Agency, "Appeals (APL) — Categories Which Have the Full Right of Appeal," www.ukvisas.gov.uk/en/ecg/appeals/fullrightsappeals.

105. Ibid.

106. Tribunals Service, Asylum and Immigration Tribunal, "Appeals," www.ait.gov.uk/Appeals/appealTypes.htm.

107. The Independent Monitor for Entry Clearance Refusals with Limited Rights of Appeal, *Report to the Secretary of State, File sample: October 2006 to March 2007, Visits: April to September 2007* (London, UK: Home Office, 2007), 41, www.ukvisas.gov.uk/resources/en/docs/2258700/2258727/IMReport-Nov07 (hereinafter IM report).

108. Ibid., 42.

109. Ibid.

110. As amended by paragraph 27 of schedule 7 of the *Nationality, Immigration and Asylum Act of 2002.* The distinction between the independent monitor's title (which refer to "refusals without the right of appeal") and the language in the title of the report (which refers to "refusals with limited rights of appeal") reflects the fact that every applicant has a limited right to appeal on human rights and race grounds; Ibid., 3.

111. Ibid., 4.

112. Nonfamily visitors, as would be expected, are those applicants seeking entry for a purpose other than to visit a family member. Ibid., 3; Office of Public Sector Information, *Statutory Instrument 2003 No. 518, The Immigration Appeals (Family Visitor) Regulations 2003* (London, UK: Crown, 2003), www.opsi.gov.uk/si/si2003/20030518.htm.

113. IM Report, 4.

114. Office of Public Sector Information, *Immigration and Asylum Act 1999* (London, UK: Office of Public Sector Information, 1999), www.opsi.gov.uk/acts/acts1999/ukpga_19990033_en_1; Citizens Advice, "Inquiry into Asylum and Immigration Appeals," October 8, 2004, www.citizensadvice. org.uk/index/campaigns/policy_campaign_publications/consultation_responses/cr_immigra-tionassylum/cr_committee_lcd.

115. Home Office, Border and Immigration Agency, *Visitors Consultation Paper* (London, UK: Home Office, 2007), 24, http://ukba.homeoffice.gov.uk/sitecontent/documents/aboutus/consultations/closed-consultations/visitorsconsultationpaper/visitorvisaconsultation.pdf?view=Binary.

116. "Tourist Visa Time 'To Be Halved,'" *British Broadcasting Company News*, December 18, 2007, http://news.bbc.co.uk/2/hi/7146527.stm.

117. "Visa Changes Would Mean No Right of Appeal for Failed Applicants," *The Asian News*, February 4, 2008, www.theasiannews.co.uk/news/s/1035035_visa_changes_would_mean_no_right_of_ap-peal_for_failed_applicants. Byrne said, "This is a controversial idea. I am sure it will meet with resistance."

118. In fact, the options question the issue in the Visitors Consultation Paper.

119. The Migration Review Tribunal (MRT) is "a statutory body that provides a final independent merits review of visa and visa-related decisions made by the Minister for Immigration and Citizen-ship . . . or, in practice, by officers of the Department of Immigration and Citizenship . . . acting as delegates of the Minister." See Australian Government, MRT, Refugee Review Tribunal (RRT), *Factsheet M10: Tribunal Brochure* (Sydney, Australia: MRT, RRT, 2009), www.mrt-rrt.gov.au/docs/factsheets/mrt/M10Brochure.pdf. The Department of Immigration and Citizenship is known as DIAC. Former names for agencies now collectively included in DIAC are: Department of Immigra-tion and Ethnic Affairs (DIEA), Department of Immigration and Multicultural Affairs (DIMA), and Department of Immigration and Multicultural and Indigenous Affairs (DIMIA).

120. Ibid.

121. Australian Government, MRT, RRT, *Migration Review Tribunal & Refugee Review Tribunal Annual Report 2006–2007* (Sydney, Australia: MRT, RRT, 2007), 1, www.mrt-rrt.gov.au/annrpts/mrt-rrt/ar0607/MRTRRTAR0607.pdf.

122. Australian Government, MRT, RRT, *Migration Review Tribunal and Refugee Review Tribunal Annual Report 2005–2006* (Sydney, Australia: MRT, RRT, 2006), 2, www.mrt-rrt.gov.au/annrpts/mrt-rrt/ar0506/MRTRRTAR0506.pdf.

123. Ibid.

124. Australian Government, *Factsheet M10*.

125. Ibid.

126. Australian Government, *Migration Review Tribunal and Refugee Review Tribunal Annual Report 2005–2006*, 2.

127. Australian Government, *Factsheet M10*.

128. The term applicant is used throughout the MRT documents describing the review process. It is im-portant to note that this "applicant" may be a different individual from the original visa applicant pursuant to the regulations governing who has standing to seek review.

129. Australian Government, *Factsheet M10*; Australian Government, *Migration Review Tribunal and Refugee Review Tribunal Annual Report 2005–2006*.

130. Australian Government, *Factsheet M10*.

131. Ibid.

132. Australian Government, *Migration Review Tribunal and Refugee Review Tribunal Annual Report 2005–2006*, 4.

133. Cases of "particular interest" include those that: (1) are representative of the range of decisions across visa classes, claims, source countries, and outcomes; (2) involve detailed consideration of legal arguments or policy issues; (3) involve complex or unusual facts; (4) are likely to be of signifi-cant external interest; or (5) have clear precedential value. See Australian Government, MRT, RRT, *Publication of MRT and RRT decisions*, MR11 (Sydney, Australia: MRT, RRT, 2009),

www.mrt-rrt.gov.au/docs/factsheets/MR11PublicationDecisions.pdf.

134. Australian Government, MRT, RRT, *Migration Review Tribunal, Refugee Review Tribunal, Annual Report 2008–2009* (Sydney: Commonwealth of Australia, 2009), www.mrt-rrt.gov.au/annrpts/mrt-rrt/ar0809/MRTRRTAR0809.pdf.

135. Ibid.

136. Ministère de la Santé et des Sports, *Décret n° 2000-1093 du 10 novembre 2000 instituant une commission de recours contre les decisions de refus de visa d'entreé en France: Journal officiel du 11 novembre 2000* (Paris, France: Ministère de la Santé et des Sports, 2000), www.sante.gouv.fr/adm/dagpb/bo/2000/00-45/a0453118.htm. "Il est institué auprès du minister des affairs étrangères un commission chargée d'examiner les recours contre les decisions de refus de visa d'entrée en France prises par les autorités diplomatiques ou consulaires, dont la saisine est un préalable obligatoire à l'exercise d'un recours contentieux, à peine d'irrecevabilité de ce dermier."

137. Ibid.

138. Ibid.

139. Stefan Batory Foundation, *Changes in Visa Policies of the EU Member States* (Warsaw, Poland: Stefan Batory Foundation, 2009), www.batory.org.pl/doc/Visa_Report_2009.pdf.

140. Senate Report.

141. Ibid., "Les voies de recours ne sont pas indiquées aux demandeurs de visas. Ceci suffit pour expliquer que la comisión ne subisse pas un afflux de recours alors sa saisine est gratuite, et se fair par simple lettre, et sans ministère d'avocat."

142. Ibid., "Les erreurs commises dans le cadre de la procédure de déliverance de visas ont un impacte significatif: Les conséquences des refus erronés de visas sont les suivantes: des recours qui prennent un temps précieux et apparaissent couteux; une perte de croissance économique pour la France (moindre fréquentation touristique, réduction du volume d'affaires); une perte de bien-être familial pour les demandeurs de visas et leurs proches; un effet d'image négtif pour la France."

143. Senate Report.

144. DHS, "Remarks by Homeland Security Secretary Michael Chertoff at Harvard University," News Release, February 6, 2008, www.dhs.gov/xnews/speeches/sp_1203020606566.shtm.

145. See Appendix 1, Selected Recommendations, for a discussion of the objections raised to consular officers' power since 1952, with citations.

146. American Academy of Religion, American Association of University Professors, Pen American Center, and Tariq Ramadan v. Michael Chertoff, 06 CV 588 (PAC), US District (S.D.N.Y. December 20, 2007), 20, www.aaup.org/NR/rdonlyres/EA0965BB-1124-48E5-B06E-8FA50F2CF6B1/0/AARvChertoff.pdf.

147. Ibid., 24.

148. 8 C.F.R. §103.1(f)(3)(iii).

149. *Ramadan v. Napolitano*, previously cited as *Am Acad of Religion v. Napolitano*, Docket 08-0826-cv, US Court of Appeals of the Second Circuit, 2009 US App LEXIS 15786, March 24, 2009, heard, July 17, 2009, decided. See Am Acad of Religion v. Chertoff, 463 F. Supp. 2d 400, 58 (SDNY 2006), reversed.

150. GPO, "Department of State, Visas: Documentation of Nonimmigrants under the Immigration and Nationality Act, as Amended," *Federal Register* 71, no. 126 (June 30, 2006), http://edocket.access.gpo.gov/2006/pdf/E6-10270.pdf.

151. Ibid., para 2, obtained by author.

152. DOS, "Nonimmigrant Visa Workload Fiscal Year 2005," October 18, 2005, http://travel.state.gov/pdf/fy%202005%20niv%20workload%20by%20category.pdf.

153. See, for example: Statement for the record of Mark A. Mancini, esq. partner, Wasserman, Mancini & Chang, "Nonimmigrant Visa Fraud," before the House Committee of the Judiciary, Subcommittee on Immigration and Claims, 106th Cong., 1st sess., May 5, 1999, www.aila.org/content/default.aspx?docid=3714. In his testimony, Mancini states, "The most frustrating part of these investigations for applicants and petitioners is the inability to get any information from the INS or the

consular post as to the status of the investigation, the reasons for the investigation, or any idea of how long it will take to be resolved. Since the majority of cases usually turn out to be *bona fide*, communication with the applicant or petitioner, who may be able to provide additional documentation to clear up the matter, should be the norm. At the very least, investigators should let the applicants know of the reasons for the investigation, and keep them informed as to the progress."

154. Rep. Barney Frank (D-MA) has introduced legislation to establish a board of visa appeals to review consular decisions on visa matters numerous times. See, for example, Library of Congress, "H.R.1345: To Amend the Immigration and Nationality Act to Establish a Board of Visa Appeals within the Department of State to Review Decisions of Consular Officers Concerning Visa Applications, Revocations, and Cancellations," April 19, 2001, http://thomas.loc.gov/cgi-bin/bdquery/D?d107:16:./temp/~bdJ3Gd.

155. Peter Andreas and Timothy Snyder, eds., *The Wall around the West: State Borders and Immigration Controls in North America and Europe* (Oxford, UK: Rowman & Littlefield Publishers, Inc., 2000). Andreas describes the shift in border security activity and strategic options for shaping it among the United States, Mexico, and Canada.

156. The United States and United Kingdom have cooperated to jointly screen visa applications for persons in the United States seeking to travel to the United Kingdom. Statement for the record of David Heyman, assistant secretary, Policy, US Department of Homeland Security (DHS), "Five Years after the Intelligence Reform and Terrorism Prevention Act (IRTPA): Stopping Terrorist Travel," 111th Cong., 1st sess., December 9, 2009.

157. Pending formal entry by the United States and New Zealand, Home Office, UK Border Agency, *Report of a Privacy Impact Assessment Conducted by the UK Border Agency in Relation to the High Value Data Sharing Protocol amongst the Immigration Authorities of the Five Country Conference* (London, UK: Home Office, 2009), www.bia.homeoffice.gov.uk/sitecontent/documents/managingourborders/strengthening/pia-data-sharing-fcc.pdf; Australian Government, Department of Immigration and Citizenship, Annual Report 2007–08 (Belconnen, Australia: Department of Immigration and Citizenship, 2008), www.immi.gov.au/about/reports/annual/2007-08/pdf/annual-report-2007-08-complete.pdf.

158. DHS (US Department of Homeland Security), "Homeland Security Presidential Directive 6: Directive on Integration and Use of Screening Information to Protect against Terrorism," August 25, 2008, www.dhs.gov/xabout/laws/gc_1214594853475.shtm.

159. Statement for the record of David Heyman, DHS, "Five Years after the Intelligence Reform and Terrorism Prevention Act (IRTPA)."

160. Interpol (International Criminal Police Organization), "APEC Endorses INTERPOL's Stolen Travel Document Database," Media Release, November 21, 2005, www.interpol.int/public/ICPO/PressReleases/PR2005/PR200546.asp.

161. Statement for the record of Rand Beers, under secretary, National Protection and Programs Directorate, DHS, "Five Years after the Intelligence Reform and Terrorism Prevention Act (IRTPA): Stopping Terrorist Travel," before the Senate Committee on Homeland Security and Government Affairs, 111th Cong., 1st sess., December 9, 2009.

162. DHS, *DHS Exhibit 300 Public Release BY08 (Form) / CBP — Advance Passenger Information System (APIS) (2008) (Item)* (Washington, DC: DHS, 2006), www.dhs.gov/xlibrary/assets/mgmt/e300-cbp-apis2008.pdf.

163. DHS, Customs and Border Protection (CBP), *Customs and Border Protection Passenger Name Record Privacy Statement for PNR Data Received in Connection with Flights between the US and the European Union* (Washington, DC: DHS, 2004), www.dhs.gov/xlibrary/assets/privacy/privacy_stmt_pnr.pdf.

164. ICAO (International Civil Aviation Organization), *Airline Reservation System and Passenger Name Record (PNR) Access by States, Facilitation (FAL) Division — Twelfth Session* (Montreal, Canada: ICAO, 2004), www.icao.int/icao/en/atb/fal/fal12/documentation/fal12wp074_en.pdf.

165. Ibid.

166. UK House of Lords, *European Union Committee, European Union — Twenty-First Report* (Lon-

don, UK: House of Lords, 2007), www.publications.parliament.uk/pa/ld200607/ldselect/ldeu-com/108/10809.htm#a32.

167. Council of the European Union, *Final Report by EU-US High Level Contact Group on Information Sharing and Privacy and Personal Data Protection* (Brussels, Belgium: Council of the European Union, 2008), www.dhs.gov/xlibrary/assets/privacy/privacy_intl_hlcg_report_02_07_08_en.pdf.

168. DHS, *Agreement between the United States of America and the European Union on the Processing and Transfer of Passenger Name Record (PNR) Data by Air Carriers to the United States Department of Homeland Security (DHS) (2007 PNR Agreement)* (Washington, DC: DHS, 2007), www.dhs.gov/xlibrary/assets/pnr-2007agreement-usversion.pdf.

169. John Kropf, "Networked and Layered: Understanding the US Framework for Protecting Personally Identifiable Information," in *World Data Protection Report 2006–07* (Arlington, VA: The Bureau of National Affairs, Inc., 2007), 3–7.

170. For a comprehensive discussion of US privacy actors, see Ibid., and John Kropf, "Independence Day: How to Move the Global Privacy Dialogue Forward," *Privacy and Security Law Report* 8, no. 2 (2008): 1–4; John Kropf, "US/EU: Common Ground for Public Safety and Security," Data Protection Law and Policy 7, no. 7 (2007): 4–5; Mary Ellen Callahan, "US: Finding Relief for Privacy Infringement," Data Protection Law and Policy 6, no. 6 (2009).

171. "Feingold Wants Answers on No-Fly List Gaffes," *The Washington Times*, May 2, 2008, www.washingtontimes.com/apps/pbcs.dll/article?AID=/20080502/NATION/99960651/1001.

172. Customs and Border Protection officers, interviews with the author.

173. Anita Ramasastry, "The New DHS/TSA Traveler Redress Inquiry Program: Why the System, Though More Efficient, Still Does Not Accord Travelers Sufficient Due Process," *Findlaw*, February 15, 2007, http://writ.news.findlaw.com/ramasastry/20070215.html.

174. DHS, Office of Inspector General, *Effectiveness of the Department of Homeland Security Traveler Redress Inquiry Program (Redacted)* (Washington, DC: DHS, 2009), www.dhs.gov/xoig/assets/mgmt-rpts/OIG-09-103r_Sep09.pdf.

175. DHS and FBI officials, interviews with the author.

176. Mark Richard and Leslie S. Lebl, "Security and Data Sharing: Transferring Information without Compromising Privacy," *Policy Review*, no. 154, (April and May 2009): 79–92, www.hoover.org/publications/policyreview/41862277.html.

177. For a comprehensive discussion of the privacy and data-security issues raised by US-EU information sharing, see Hiroyuki Tanaka, Rocco Bellanova, Susan Ginsburg, and Paul De Hert, *Transatlantic Information Sharing: At a Crossroads* (Washington, DC: Migration Policy Institute, MPI, 2010), www.migrationpolicy.org/pubs/infosharing-Jan2010.pdf.

178. Official Journal of the European Union, *Agreement on Mutual Legal Assistance between the European Union and the United States of America.* (Brussels, Belgium: European Union, 2003), http://eur-lex.europa.eu/LexUriServ/LexUriServ.do?uri=OJ:L:2003:181:0034:0042:EN:PDF.

179. The United States and the European Union also exchanged instruments for the extradition treaty. DOJ (US Department of Justice), "Attorney General Holder Speaks at EU/US Justice and Home Affairs Ministerial Meeting," Speech, October 28, 2009, www.justice.gov/ag/speeches/2009/ag-speech-091028.html.

180. Official Journal of the European Union, *Agreement on Mutual Legal Assistance between the European Union and the United States of America.*

181. Kropf, "Independence Day," 1–5.

182. The United States should also consider the establishment of a central privacy office, which would help assure Europeans that it has an effective privacy watchdog. See Tanaka, Bellanova, Ginsburg, and De Hert, *Transatlantic Information Sharing.*

183. Nineteen EU Member States are in the Organization of Economic Cooperation and Development (OECD): Austria, Belgium, Czech Republic, Denmark, Finland, France, Germany, Greece, Hungary, Ireland, Italy, Luxembourg, the Netherlands, Norway, Poland, Portugal, Slovak Republic, Spain, and Sweden.

184. Recent authoritative critiques in the United States include those by the Technology and Privacy Advisory Committee to the Department of Defense (DOD) in 2004, the Committee on Technical and Privacy Dimensions of Information for Terrorism Prevention and other National Goals of the National Research Council in 2008, and the Information Security and Privacy Board reporting to the secretary of commerce, the Government Accountability Office (GAO) in 2008, the director of the Office of Management and Budget, and the director of the National Security Agency (NSA) in 2009. These advisory groups' critiques are extensive, deep, and significant.

185. Mark Richard and Leslie S. Lebl, "Security and Data Sharing: Transferring Information without Compromising Privacy," *Policy Review* 154 (April 21, 2009): 79–92.

186. Neil Robinson, Hans Graux, Maarten Botterman, and Lorenzo Valeri, *Review of the EU Data Protection Directive* (Santa Monica, CA: RAND Corporation, 2009), www.rand.org/pubs/technical_reports/2009/RAND_TR710.pdf.

187. After 13 years, the European Union has found only five non-EU countries to have adequate legal frameworks (Switzerland, Canada, Argentine, Guernsey, Jersey, and the Isle of Man). Robinson, Graux, Botterman, and Valeri, *Review of the European Data Protection*.

188. DOD (US Department of Defense), Technology and Privacy Advisory Committee, *Safeguarding Privacy in the Fight Against Terrorism* (Washington, DC: DOD, 2004), www.defense.gov/news/Jan2006/d20060208tapac.pdf; Committee on Technical and Privacy Dimensions of Information for Terrorism Prevention and Other National Goals and the National Research Council, *Protecting Individual Privacy in the Struggle against Terrorists: A Framework for Program Assessment* (Washington, DC: National Academies Press, 2008).

189. GAO, *Congress Should Consider Alternatives for Strengthening Protection of Personally Identifiable Information*, GAO-08-795T (Washington, DC: GAO, 2008), www.gao.gov/new.items/d08795t.pdf.

190. ICAO, *Airline Reservation System and Passenger Name Record (PNR) Access by States, Facilitation (FAL) Division — Twelfth Session*.

191. Ibid. In 2004, the ICAO Facilitation Division, in its twelfth session, stated, "With respect to PNR access regimes, we believe that it is absolutely critical that ICAO and its Contracting States seek to develop standards with respect to what States may, or perhaps even should require under such programs. Globally agreed standards are necessary in light of recent non-coordinated developments, and should be agreed to ensure harmonization of data exchange methodologies and in-line data filtering processes. We believe that this is ICAO's key role in this debate, and the air transport industry would support such a course of action."

192. Statewatch, "EU-PNR Scheme Being Rewritten by the Council," www.statewatch.org/news/2008/oct/04eu-pnr-rewrite.htm.

193. John Leydan, "UK e-Borders Scheme Thrown into Confusion by EU Rules," *The Register*, December 18, 2009, www.theregister.co.uk/2009/12/18/e_borders_confusion/.

SECTION IV: PREVENTING LIFE-THREATENING, ILLEGAL, AND UNCONTROLLED MOVEMENT

INTRODUCTION

The third goal in securing human mobility should be to prevent dangerous, illegal, and uncontrolled movement. As discussed earlier in this volume, the first goal is to preempt and counter terrorists and criminals, focusing on immediate threats and risks. The second goal is to ensure the integrity of mobility infrastructure by seeking to optimize protective measures that ensure resilience in "steady-state" activities. To achieve the third goal, governments must seek to build global norms of the rule of law in mobility channels and to institutionalize new protective measures against terrorist and criminal exploitation of mobility channels. There also must be a reorientation of the underlying and long-term conditions, or upstream factors, that accompany or cause corruption of the mobility system.

Despite its label, *homeland security* has an inextricable global dimension. As a result, the Department of Homeland Security (DHS) has a distinct, evolving international role. As many have explained, domestic law and international strategy have become merged in the age of risk. To counter terrorists and criminals, DHS must, among other things, field global investigative teams directed against human-trafficking organizations (HTOs) and human-smuggling organizations (HSOs). And, to ensure the integrity of mobility infrastructure, DHS and its federal peers must negotiate with foreign partners concerning mobility-related information-sharing and privacy agreements.

It is in meeting this third goal of preventing dangerous and exploitative movement of people that DHS's international responsibilities are most visible. *Border security* and *immigration enforcement* emphasize US borders and enforcement efforts inside the United States. But by definition, illegal flows of people — whether terrorists, members of organized criminal enterprises, or migrants — move from one place to another. They may transit through a number of countries, adopt diverse travel tactics, and present multiple identities. Prevention of illegal entry into the United States can best and sometimes only take place outside the United States, at points of departure, and along transit routes. Thus the strategic framework of *securing human movement* incorporates critical relationships with governments and other organizations outside the United States.

There is frequent reference in homeland security policy discourse to *pushing the US borders out* and setting up *layers of border defense*. These phrases do not, however, adequately capture US mobility security strategy. It is true that the US military in its foreign bases and maritime operations does in fact push out US border defenses throughout the world. But in the context of civilian movement of people, the United States cannot *actually push its borders out*; US boundaries are fixed and cannot be unilaterally breached. The metaphor of a *layered defense* is also of limited utility. The United States cannot simply establish a layer wherever it believes one is needed, because layers are invariably in other people's countries. The military and intelligence officials may override these limitations; homeland security officials may not. As a result, DHS has to construct mutually beneficial agreements and promote collective action in order for the United States to secure human movement.

As countries reconfigure relationships in the post–Cold War world, governments ally, in part, through rules that authorize access to different states and economies. For leading powers, greater access indicates wider, more productive friendships. Free markets depend on people's ability to travel affordably, efficiently, and safely. Increased travel efficiency and access to other countries stimulates global economic growth and provides nations with a competitive advantage. It also promotes the well-being of individuals. Movement is recognized as a right, albeit a limited one, in the international treaties to which the United States is committed, and travel sanctions are a means of expressing solidarity and opprobrium. Mobility diplomacy matters because it offers governments important opportunities to safeguard citizens, spur economic growth, enhance individual freedom of movement, contain travel and border infrastructure costs, constrain dangerous individuals, and pressure rogue states.

Although many reflexively think of borders and the right to travel as something over which sovereign states have full authority, the United States has long participated in international agreements that recognize that no one sovereign authority has absolute control over the regulation of cross-border movement, including its own. Agreements set international rules about the terms, conditions, and infrastructure of international air and sea mobility. Since the September 11, 2001, attacks, the United States has been assertive in asking other countries to adopt regulations and approaches that comport with its own. Many countries and international institutions have responded with new or renewed declarations, standards, actions, foreign assistance, and structured discussions on various aspects of mobility security.

Channels for Discussion and Cooperation

Mobility security diplomacy is conducted in bilateral, regional, and multilateral arenas. The modes are government to government, government to individual, government to private-sector organization, and sometimes even private-sector organization to private-sector organization.

Bilateral relations have historically provided the basis for the most detailed and effective agreements over access rules and they still shape most meaningful mobility security agreements. This is especially true for governments that share boundaries. But regional boundaries are becoming more important, including for travel and migration purposes. In addition to Canada and Mexico, the United States shares regional border interests with maritime neighboring states in the Caribbean and the seven Central American states. Within the European Union (EU), Member States have largely dismantled their national borders for travel purposes (although not yet for security purposes). The European Union shares maritime borders with the Maghreb countries across the Mediterranean. And regionally, the European Union, Organization of American States (OAS), Asia-Pacific Economic Cooperation (APEC) group, Association of Southeast Asian Nations (ASEAN), and other regional economic and political entities have formed new agreements relating to mobility security.

Because threats to exploit global mobility systems pose collective challenges, they must be addressed on a global scale. Terrorism, transnational crime, airline hijackings, piracy, and pandemics cannot be dealt with effectively without worldwide collaboration on travel and migration. For this reason, international cooperation on many mobility-related issues occurs through the United Nations (UN), its related institutions, and other multilateral institutions.

Mobility security provisions may be the primary focus of international agreements or an integral piece of broader agreements. Thus, in the past decade, agreements about visa, travel, and refugee arrangements all have included enhanced security provisions. In agreements concerning passports, air and maritime transportation, mobility crimes, and bans on terrorist and other malefactor travel, the regulation of mobility has been the primary focus. A key question going forward is whether mobility security agreements should be stand-alone, combined with migration stabilization and development provisions, or form part of a larger civil security alliance structure. A related organizational question is the extent to which DHS, the Department of State (DOS), and the Department of Justice (DOJ), as well as the intelligence community and the military, should direct and manage mobility security relations.

Section IV highlights three sets of international mobility security partnerships. Chapter 10 discusses visa-free travel and registered-traveler agreements. Chapter 11 describes US relations with developing countries and its leveraging of international institutions, and chapter 12 discusses managing boundaries with Canada and Mexico.

Chapter 10: Mobility Security Agreements

Policy Preview: Mobility security agreements should become a pillar of larger civil security alliances. The United States should continue to bolster its mobility security partnership with the European Union (EU) by seeking to resolve the US-EU dispute over visa-waiver travel. Although security experts have repeatedly warned about vulnerabilities posed by the US Visa Waiver Program (VWP), the United States should continue to grow the program within a strengthened security framework. The registered-traveler program needs a formal and transparent structure as it moves from the pilot stage to permanent program. With the United States, Canada, the European Union, and the Asia-Pacific Economic Cooperation (APEC) countries moving to secure travel in different ways, the Department of Homeland Security (DHS) could convene a group to develop a vision of an interoperable multilateral travel system. A broader vision of mobility security will be required to achieve agreements with developing countries marked by large-scale illegal migration to the United States and/ or vulnerable to large-scale displacement of people.

Mobility security agreements are international agreements that set the rules for mutual security in mobility channels. These agreements cover issues such as lost and stolen passports, illegal movement, visa-free travel, and an emerging registered-traveler network. Together with information-sharing agreements, mobility security partnerships are the basis for building multilateral civil security alliances against mobile terrorists, criminals, and other risks. As more countries enter mobility security arrangements, it will become more important to establish multilateral mechanisms to monitor them. This chapter assesses existing mobility security agreements and suggests how they should be expanded and developed.

The *border security–immigration enforcement* paradigm implies that the United States can protect mobility channels unilaterally. Yet preventing exploitation and unlawful use of entry channels must necessarily be a joint endeavor.[1] Nations that value the rule of law, human rights, and global markets should be natural partners to the United States in safeguarding global mobility channels.[2] Countries rely on each other to certify the identity of travelers, verify their travel documents, and set and enforce standards for safe and orderly arrival and departure.

DHS is already beginning to take both a bilateral and multilateral approach to mobility security, as reflected by recent progress in information-sharing agreements with the European Union and EU Member States, commitments to twice-yearly ministerial meetings with Canada, and an inaugural Quadrennial Homeland Security Review (QHSR).[3]

The United States is party to four kinds of bilateral agreements that secure mobility channels. First, it has signed agreements with wealthy countries whose citizens can enter the United States for temporary periods without a visa, pursuant to the VWP. Second, US Customs and Border Protection (CBP) has a new initiative to foster a global registered-traveler system. This program speeds the processing of known, repeat, low-risk international travelers. For US travelers, this is the Global Entry System. Where there is a reciprocal program with another country, the registered-travel program becomes part of CBP's pilot Fast Low Risk Universal Crossing (FLUX) Alliance. Third, under CBP's Immigration Advisory Program (IAP), CBP and foreign counterparts reciprocally permit immigration inspectors to check travel documents of departing passengers destined for their respective countries.[4] Fourth, the United States has negotiated agreements with Haiti and Cuba to mitigate the risk of uncontrolled mass movements.

Both the visa-waiver agreements and the registered-traveler agreements are mobility security agreements that establish significant security-related standards that partner governments must meet.[5] Both types of mobility security agreements primarily impact travelers and migrants at the high end of the income scale.

Visa-Free Travel

Since the end of the Cold War, governments have increasingly established programs that allow foreigners to travel without undergoing passport or visa checks before crossing borders. The United States has four basic categories of access:

- US citizens have a constitutional right to enter the United States at will
- Citizens of 35 countries[6] may enter the United States without a visitor visa, based on an inspection at a port of entry, but must obtain visas for work and other long-term purposes
- Canadians do not require a visa
- Citizens of all remaining countries require a visa for any purpose and length of stay

The degree to which governments use access as a diplomatic instrument varies. Visa-free access to the United States is first and foremost determined based on the bilateral relationship between the United States and the foreign government. Thus, nationality remains the threshold question for the availability for visa-free travel to the United States. This is not the case for all governments. Brazil, for example, has a universal visa, valid for two years, which must be used within 90 days of issuance; it does not vary by nationality in its applicability. Also, regional visa policies have led to the emergence of regional politics surrounding visa negotiations, notably between the European Union and states outside of it.

Visa-free travel policies have been formulated on a regional basis in the European Union, the Schengen Area in Europe, the Common Travel Area of the United Kingdom and Ireland,[7] the Caribbean Community, the Southern Common Market (MERCOSUR) in Latin America, the Trans-Tasmanian Travel Arrangement between Australia and New Zealand, and the Nordic Passport Union. US citizens can likewise travel visa free to any country that participates in the US VWP (based on reciprocity), such as Japan, France, and Brunei.

Once the threshold question of nationality is satisfied, the United States fills in the specifics of duration of the consular visa and the number of stays associated with it largely based on the statutorily imposed principle of reciprocity — that is, both countries agree to accord each other's citizens comparable access benefits. The principle of reciprocity can be convoluted in its application and not always to the advantage of the United States. Until recently, US negotiations with other governments about lowering visa barriers were handled in bilateral channels, often by consular service to consular service, and were usually workmanlike discussions. As public expectations of access to countries rose, visa terms became an increasingly important economic and political issue for nations. And as new security issues were raised, Congress recognized the subject as a key civil security concern.

Requirements to Enter the US Visa Waiver Program

The 9/11 attacks and the attempted 2004 attack by the so-called shoe bomber, Briton Richard Reid, demonstrated that the security assumptions underpinning the initial phase of the VWP (from 1986 to 2000) were outdated. During the first phase of visa-free travel expansion, the United States admitted countries to the program that:

- Extended reciprocal visa-free travel rights to citizens of countries that granted such rights to US citizens traveling abroad
- Had a refusal rate of less than 3 percent for its citizens who had applied for US business and tourism visas[8]
- Had a machine-readable passport
- Satisfied other law-enforcement and security requirements, such as sharing information on blank and issued lost and stolen passports

These criteria largely remain in place. However, the Secure Travel and Counterterrorism Partnership Act of 2007[9] changed the terms of these requirements and strengthened the program as follows.

Concerns related to unauthorized immigration. VWP candidates whose nationals are denied US tourist and business visas at rates of less than 3 percent are automatically considered for entry. Congress lowered the threshold for program participation by permitting nations with less than 10 percent visa-refusal rates to be considered eligible if: (1) DHS has an air exit system which shows that 97 percent of its nationals have exited the United States from a US airport, (2) DHS has a fully operational Electronic System of Travel Authorization (ESTA), and (3) the VWP candidate country has met other security requirements (see below). [10] The statute also stipulates that if DHS does not have a biometric air exit system in place by July 1, 2009, its authority to waive the 10 percent visa-refusal-rate requirement would be suspended until it implemented such a system. The US Government Accountability Office (GAO), however, has concluded that having an air exit system that can verify the departure from the United States of 97 percent of foreign nationals does not help mitigate the risk of overstays from current and potential VWP countries.

Under its current practice, DHS matches departure records, provided by airlines, of visitors leaving the United States to any prior arrivals to, status changes in, or prior departures from the United States. This methodology, unlike one that would match individuals' arrival records to their departure records, does not offer information on overall or country-specific visa-overstay rates, which are essential to determining illegal immigration risks relating to the VWP.[11] The 2007 law states that the secretaries of DHS and the Department of State (DOS) will jointly set a maximum visa overstay rate for countries participating in the program once an air exit system is in place.

Pretravel authorization for individuals. The most significant new requirement is that foreign travelers have to obtain pretravel authorization from CBP. As of January 12, 2009, individuals must submit traveler information through ESTA.[12] Under ESTA, citizens traveling without visas submit — via a secure online connection — almost the same information prior to their travels as would otherwise be required upon their arrival.[13] They may complete the ESTA form individually or through a third party such as a friend, relative, or travel agent. ESTA provides an instantaneous online response whether the individual is traveling without a visa or not.[14] If approved, an ESTA authorization is valid for multiple entries over a two-year period or until the applicant's passport expires, whichever comes first.[15] Such an extended approval is possible because it is subject to recurrent vetting rather than point-in-time checking. Travel or entry eligibility can be revoked as soon as any new information that establishes ineligibility is placed in the database. In its pilot phase, between August 1, 2008, and January 11, 2009, ESTA use resulted in examinations in less than 1 percent of cases (0.41 percent) and a smaller rate of actual denials. The statute also requires travelers with passports issued on or after October 26, 2006, to obtain electronic passports that contain biographic information and a digital photograph.[16] In its initial phase there has been no fee associated with ESTA.

Exit monitoring of individuals. Congress mandated an exit-monitoring system for foreign travelers in 1996. It further required that by June 30, 2009, DHS implement a biometric exit system able to track whether each individual entering the United States by air leaves within the permitted travel period. As an interim measure, before entering into any new visa-free travel agreements, DHS was required to verify the departure of 97 percent of foreign nationals who exited through an airport. Since DHS missed the June 30, 2009, deadline, no new countries were added to the VWP.

Government mobility security cooperation. In order to maintain visa-free travel and lower visa barriers for additional countries, the United States raised the baseline travel-security requirements for partner governments. To participate, a country must already be cooperating with the United States on information sharing and counterterrorism initiatives, including prevention of terrorist travel. The program agreement with the United States must include a commitment to share information about travelers who represent a threat; to report information about the theft or loss of passports directly or through Interpol; and to readmit citizens, former citizens, or nationals when the United States seeks to deport them. Candidate governments must be able to satisfy the homeland security secretary regarding their airport security standards, air marshal programs, travel-document security standards, information sharing regarding terrorist threats, and other counterterrorism collaboration. In addition, DHS must determine that the partnership will not compromise security or law-enforcement interests or compliance with US immigration laws. The Directorate of National Intelligence (DNI) must perform an independent intelligence assessment that evaluates whether the country's participation in the US VWP would pose a threat to the United States.

Regionalism as a Factor in Visa Diplomacy

While political conflicts could reverse a trend toward open mobility, there has nonetheless been a long-term drive to expand visa-free travel and to lower visa barriers in other ways. One challenge has been to identify the fora in which to conduct the negotiations.

The United States has feuded with the European Union over whether visa-free travel should be determined bilaterally with Member States or with the European Union itself. Regionalism is the most important factor driving freedom of mobility, and the European Union is the prime example of that. Its formation has complicated US diplomacy and policymaking regarding mobility security because the United States has historically made decisions about visa-free travel on a bilateral basis. The leaders of the Eastern Europe countries that joined the European Union in 2004 and 2007[17] argued that their citizens should be able to travel to the United States on equal terms with other US European allies. Their case for inclusion in the VWP was buttressed by their support for US military operations in Iraq and Afghanistan, the backing of US members of Congress with constituencies from these countries,[18] concurrent discussions concerning missile defense placement in certain countries, and a pledge by President George W. Bush in November 2006 to expand the VWP.[19]

Nevertheless, a diplomatic dispute between the United States and the European Union erupted a year later because the United States insisted on bilateral negotiations with the Eastern European nations — running headlong into EU governance and structural issues. In the years after 9/11, EU governance evolved to make the European Commission (EC) a prominent player.[20] Within the EU structure, movement of people is an EU arena of policy authority, but security remains under the purview of the Member State governments. The European Commission argued that because it handled

Passenger Name Record (PNR) negotiations with the United States, visa-free travel was also within its purview. From the US perspective, the European Commission was not a suitable negotiating partner because it exercised too little actual operational authority. The individual EU Member State governments retain authority to negotiate security matters; they possess the information that needs to be shared and can share it quickly. In the wake of accession to the European Union in 2004 by ten new countries and in 2007 by two more — and the negotiation of the PNR agreements in 2004, 2006, and 2007 — the European Commission made visa-free travel an issue of its political sovereignty and constitutional integrity.

The lack of an equivalent security concern in Europe about visa-free travelers from the United States also reduced EU interest in the US-proposed security provisions. Difficult negotiations led to a deterioration of the level of trust, even eliciting accusations that the criteria for admission were being cooked. A low point came when the United States suddenly dropped Greece from the short list of countries to be admitted to the VWP in October 2008, despite having actively promoted an agreement in 2007 with Greece (which was the last of the pre-2004 accession EU Member States not yet admitted to the VWP). This decision was based on Greece's rejection of the former Yugoslav Republic of Macedonia's bid to enter NATO as long as it kept the name Macedonia.[21] Notwithstanding the friction, the United States in 2008 signed preliminary memorandas of understanding (MOUs) permitting visa-free travel with 13 countries, finalizing agreements with eight of the 13.

The United States did not conclude mobility security agreements with five EU Member States: Greece, Cyprus, Poland, Bulgaria, and Romania.[22] The Polish application to the US VWP, for example, was undermined in part by high levels of illegal immigration by Poles to the United States.[23] Cyprus's divided status deprives the United States of a negotiating partner for the security provisions of the agreement. Bulgaria and Romania will likely not be able to satisfy the law-enforcement and security prerequisites for admission to the program.

The admission of so many new countries prompted the European Commission and the Council of the European Union to take a more nuanced diplomatic approach. At the same time, the European Union continues to emphasize the principle of reciprocity according to which all EU Member States must be treated equally in matters regarding visa-free travel. The European Union was sharply critical of Canada's 2009 decision to drop the Czech Republic from its visa-waiver program due to a surge in applications for asylum from members of the Czech Roma.

US Strategic Interests in Visa-Free Travel

The fact that the United States lowered visa barriers for citizens of eight additional countries in 2008 despite concerns about the potential for terrorist entry is a testament to the strategic importance of expanding human mobility. This statement by a senior DHS official captures the rising interest in national practices hitherto treated as entirely sovereign purviews: "Our goals are to ensure domestic practices in key partner nations are adequate to minimize risks posed to the United States and to jointly respond to the illicit movement of terrorists and criminals."[24] Visa-free travel agreements expand and protect the common global travel channels, providing new opportunities to law-abiding individuals. By forming mobility security agreements that expand travel opportunities, the United States and its civil security allies enlarge the global sphere of economic freedom, democracy, and individual rights. They also demonstrate the greater appeal of societies that are open, democratic, and based on upholding individual rights.

US competitiveness is also at stake. Visa-free travel brings significant economic benefits. The global travel, tourism, and business environment is competitive. In 2007 US residents spent $104.7 billion in travel abroad ($76.2 billion within foreign countries and $28.5 billion on airfares), up 5 percent from 2006.[25] US travelers spent the most money in Mexico ($11.1 billion), the United Kingdom ($10.5 billion), Canada ($7.6 billion), Germany ($5.9 billion), and Japan ($4.7 billion).[26] In 2008 international visitors spent over than $142 billion on US travel and tourism-related goods and services.[27] Not surprisingly, US business associations and all the major stakeholders in the aviation and tourism industries advocate for continued expansion of visa-free travel to the United States.[28]

Emerging market states are also attractive places for foreign investment and trade. This is leading to pressure to reduce travel restrictions imposed by these countries as well, including in some cases for the complete waiver of all visa requirements. Mexico, for example, eliminated visa requirements for 46 new countries and territories between mid-January and early August 2009.[29]

Comparing US Visa Restrictions Against Other Countries'

The competitiveness of the travel-dependent market makes it important to keep track of the scope of visa-free travel to other economies. As of January 2010, the VWP allows nationals of 35 countries to enter the United States without obtaining a B-1 or B-2 visa for purposes of short-term business or tourist travel. Many travelers are reaping the advantages of lowered barriers to travel. Of the approximately 5.6 million business-related temporary admissions in 2008, slightly under half, 45.4 percent, arrived without pretravel visas.[30] Of the 29.4 million tourists who came to the United States in fiscal year 2008, just over half, 51.3 percent, arrived from countries whose citizens did not require pretravel visas. But the United States has lowered its visa barriers for fewer countries than have nearly all its key partners. Among Western-style democracies, only Australia admits visa-free visitors from fewer countries (see table 10.1 for visa-free travel regimes by region). The difference mostly involves countries with high or potentially high illegal immigration rates to the United States.

Table 10.1 Visa-Free Travel Regimes by Region (as of August 1, 2009)

United States* (39)	Canada (67)	Mexico (93)	European Union (66)	United Kingdom** (88)	Ireland (88)	Japan (62)	Australia (34)
Oceania							
Australia, New Zealand, Marshall Islands*	Australia, New Zealand, Papua New Guinea, Pitcairn Islands, Solomon Islands, Western Samoa	American Samoa, Australia, Cook Islands, French Polynesia, Guam Islands, Marshall Islands, Micronesia, New Caledonia, New Zealand, Niue Islands, Norfolk Islands, Palau, Pitcairn Islands, Tokelau, Wallis and Futuna Islands	Australia, New Zealand	Australia, Federated States of Micronesia, Kiribati, Marshall Islands, Nauru, New Zealand, Palau, Papua New Guinea, Samoa, Solomon Islands, Tonga, Tuvalu, Vanuatu	Australia, Fiji, Kiribati, Nauru, New Zealand, Samoa, Solomon Islands, Tonga, Tuvalu, Vanuatu	Australia, New Zealand	New Zealand***
Europe							
Andorra, Austria, Belgium, Czech Republic, Denmark, Estonia, Finland, France, Germany, Hungary, Iceland, Ireland, Italy, Latvia, Liechtenstein, Lithuania, Luxembourg, Malta, Monaco, Netherlands, Norway, Portugal, San Marino, Slovakia, Slovenia, Spain, Sweden, Switzerland, United Kingdom	Andorra, Austria, Belgium, Bulgaria, Croatia, Cyprus, Czech Republic, Denmark, Estonia, Finland, France, Germany, Gibraltar, Greece, Holy See (Vatican), Hungary, Iceland, Ireland, Italy, Latvia, Liechtenstein, Lithuania, Luxembourg, Malta, Monaco, Netherlands, Norway, Poland, Portugal, Romania, San Marino, Slovakia, Slovenia, Spain, Sweden, Switzerland, United Kingdom	Andorra, Austria, Azores Islands, Belgium, Bulgaria, Cyprus, Czech Republic, Denmark, Estonia, Faroe Islands, Finland, France, Germany, Gibraltar, Greece, Hungary, Iceland, Ireland, Italy, Latvia, Liechtenstein, Lithuania, Luxembourg, Malta, Monaco, Netherlands, Norway, Poland, Portugal, Romania, San Marino, Slovakia, Slovenia, Spain, Sweden, Switzerland, United Kingdom	Andorra, Austria, Belgium, Bulgaria, Croatia, Cyprus, Czech Republic, Denmark, Estonia, Finland, France, Germany, Greece, Holy See (Vatican), Hungary, Ireland, Italy, Latvia, Liechtenstein, Lithuania, Luxembourg, Malta, Monaco, Netherlands, Norway, Poland, Portugal, Romania, San Marino, Slovakia, Slovenia, Spain, Sweden, Switzerland, United Kingdom	Andorra, Austria, Belgium, Bulgaria, Croatia, Cyprus, Czech Republic, Denmark, Estonia, Finland, Former Yugoslav Republic of Macedonia, France, Germany, Greece, Holy See (Vatican), Hungary, Iceland, Italy, Latvia, Liechtenstein, Lithuania, Luxembourg, Malta, Monaco, Montenegro, Netherlands, Norway, Poland, Portugal, Romania, San Marino, Serbia, Slovakia, Slovenia, Spain, Sweden, Switzerland	Andorra, Austria, Belgium, Bulgaria, Croatia, Cyprus, Czech Republic, Denmark, Estonia, Finland, France, Germany, Greece, Holy See (Vatican), Hungary, Iceland, Italy, Latvia, Liechtenstein, Lithuania, Luxembourg, Malta, Monaco, Netherlands, Norway, Poland, Portugal, Romania, San Marino, Slovakia, Slovenia, Spain, Sweden, Switzerland, United Kingdom & Colonies	Andorra, Austria, Belgium, Bulgaria, Croatia, Cyprus, Czech Republic, Denmark, Estonia, Finland, France, Germany, Greece, Hungary, Iceland, Ireland, Italy, Latvia, Liechtenstein, Lithuania, Luxembourg, Macedonia, Malta, Monaco, Netherlands, Norway, Poland, Portugal, San Marino, Slovakia, Slovenia, Spain, Sweden, Switzerland, United Kingdom	Andorra, Austria, Belgium, Denmark, Finland, France, Germany, Greece, Holy See (Vatican), Iceland, Ireland, Italy, Liechtenstein, Luxembourg, Malta, Monaco, Netherlands, Norway, Portugal, San Marino, Spain, Sweden, Switzerland, United Kingdom/BNO
United States* (39)	Canada (67)	Mexico (93)	European Union (66)	United Kingdom** (88)	Ireland (88)	Japan (62)	Australia (34)
Asia							
Brunei Darussalam, Federated States of Micronesia*, Japan, Republic of Korea, Singapore	Brunei Darussalam, Hong Kong SAR, Japan, Republic of Korea, Singapore	British Indian Ocean Territory, Christmas Island, Hong Kong SAR, Japan, Macao SAR, Marianas Islands, Republic of Korea, Singapore	Brunei Darussalam, Hong Kong SAR, Japan, Macau SAR, Malaysia, Republic of Korea, Singapore	Brunei Darussalam, Japan, Malaysia, Maldives, Republic of Korea, Singapore, Timor-Leste	Brunei Darussalam, Hong Kong SAR, Japan, Macau SAR, Malaysia, Maldives, Singapore, Republic of Korea	Brunei Darussalam, Hong Kong BNO/SAR, Macau SAR, Republic of Korea, Singapore, Taiwan	Brunei, Hong Kong SAR, Japan, Malaysia, Republic of Korea, Singapore, Taiwan

	United States	Canada	Mexico	European Union	Japan	United Kingdom	Australia
North America							
Canada*, Bermuda*	United States	Canada, Coconut Island, Greenland, United States of America	Canada, Mexico, United States	Canada, Mexico, United States	Canada, Mexico, United States	Canada, Mexico, United States	Canada, United States
Latin America and Caribbean							
	Anguilla, Antigua and Barbuda, Bahamas, Barbados, Bermuda, British Virgin Islands, Cayman Islands, Falkland Islands, Montserrat, St. Kitts and Nevis, St. Lucia, St. Vincent, Turks and Caicos Islands	Anguilla, Argentina, Aruba, Bahamas, Barbados, Belize, Bermuda, British Virgin Islands, Cayman Islands, Chile, Costa Rica, Falkland Islands, Guadalupe, Martinique, Montserrat, Netherlands Antilles, Panama, Paraguay, Puerto Rico, Trinidad and Tobago, Turks and Caicos Islands, Uruguay, Venezuela, Virgin Islands	Antigua and Barbuda, Argentina, Bahamas, Barbados, Belize, Brazil, Chile, Costa Rica, El Salvador, Guatemala, Honduras, Nicaragua, Panama, Paraguay, Saint Kitts and Nevis, Uruguay, Venezuela	Antigua and Barbuda, Argentina, Bahamas, Barbados, Belize, Bolivia, Brazil, Chile, Costa Rica, Dominica, El Salvador, Grenada, Guatemala, Honduras, Nicaragua, Panama, Paraguay, Saint Lucia, Saint Vincent and the Grenadines, Trinidad and Tobago, Uruguay, Venezuela	Antigua and Barbuda, Argentina, Bahamas, Barbados, Belize, Bolivia, Brazil, Chile, Costa Rica, Dominica, El Salvador, Grenada, Guatemala, Guyana, Honduras, Nicaragua, Panama, Paraguay, Saint Kitts & Nevis, Saint Vincent & the Grenadines, Trinidad & Tobago, Uruguay, Venezuela	Argentina, Bahamas, Barbados, Chile, Costa Rica, Dominican Republic, El Salvador, Guatemala, Honduras, Suriname, Uruguay	
Middle East							
Israel	Israel	Israel	Israel	Israel	Israel	Israel	Israel, Turkey
Africa							
Botswana, Namibia, Swaziland, St. Helena	French Guinea, Mahore, Reunion, Saint Helena	Mauritius, Seychelles	Botswana, Mauritius, Seychelles	Botswana, Mauritius, Namibia, Seychelles	Botswana, Lesotho, Malawi, Mauritius, Seychelles, South Africa, Swaziland	Lesotho, Mauritius, Tunisia	

Source: DOS, "Visa Waiver Program," http://travel.state.gov/visa/temp/without/without_1990.html#countries; Canada: Citizenship and Immigration Canada, "Countries and Territories Whose Citizens Require Visas in Order to Enter Canada as Visitors," www.cic.gc.ca/EnGLIsh/visit/visas.asp; Mexico: Secretaría de Gobernación, Instituto Nacional de Migración, "Countries That Do Not Need Visas," www.inm.gob.mx/EN/index.php?page/met_need_visa; European Union: Official Journal of the European Communities, Council Regulation (EC) No 539/2001 of 15 March 2001 Listing the Third Countries Whose Nationals Must Be in Possession of Visas When Crossing the External Borders and Those Whose Nationals Are Exempt from that Requirement (Brussels, Belgium: Official Journal of the European Communities, 2001). http://eur-lex.europa.eu/LexUriServ/LexUriServ.do?uri=OJ:L:2001:081:0001:0007:EN:PDF; Official Journal of the European Union, Council Regulation (EC) No 1932/2006 of 21 December 2006 Amending Regulation (EC) No 539/2001 Listing the Third Countries Whose Nationals Must Be in Possession of a Visas When Crossing the External Borders and Those Whose Nationals are Exempt from that Requirement (Brussels, Belgium: Official Journal of the European Union, 2006), http://eur-lex.europa.eu/LexUriServ/LexUriServ.do?uri=OJ:L:2007:029:0010:0013:EN:PDF; United Kingdom: Home Office, UK Border Agency, "Appendix 1 — Visa requirements for the United Kingdom," www.ukba.homeoffice.gov.uk/policyandlaw/immigrationlaw/immigrationrules/appendix1/; Ireland: Department of Justice, Equality, and Law Reform, Irish Naturalisation and Immigration Service, Statutory Instruments S.I. No.239 of 2009: Immigration Act 2004 (Visas) Order 2009, www.inis.gov.ie/en/INIS/s.i.239%20final.pdf/Files/s.i.239%20final.pdf; Japan: Ministry of Foreign Affairs of Japan, "A Guide to Japanese Visas," www.mofa.go.jp/j_info/visit/visa/02.html; Australia: Australia Government, Department of Immigration and Citizenship, "Visas, Immigration and Refugees," www.immi.gov.au/visitors/tourist/976/eligibility.htm.

Notes: *Canada, the Federated States of Micronesia, Bermuda and the Marshall Islands do not participate in the US VWP but their citizens enjoy the same benefits as citizens of countries that participate in the program. **The United Kingdom maintains a list of countries for which it requires visas. All countries that are not on the list can travel visa free. ***New Zealand does not participate in the Electronic Travel Authority (Visitor) subclass 976.

The Future of Visa-Free Travel Agreements

As is shown in table 10.1, many governments with which the United States is developing mobility security standards are members of the North Atlantic Treaty Organization (NATO) and the Organization for Security and Cooperation in Europe (OSCE). These nations have committed to working directly against terror networks and to confronting states that safeguard, sponsor, or facilitate terrorism. Building new protections into common travel channels is an important dimension of that joint security agenda, in addition to sustaining economic competitiveness. However, NATO and OSCE are not the multilateral organizations most suitable to building a civil security alliance that incorporates mobility security as one of its dimensions.

Going forward, it will become increasingly difficult and undesirable for the United States to exclude governments that are part of that counterterrorism alliance and that seek to collaborate more deeply to achieve visa-free travel protected by mobility security agreements. It will also be difficult to deny visa-free travel to the nationals of governments that have substantial economic relationships with the United States. Some countries will not be eligible for visa-free travel due to foreign policy considerations, even where mobility security standards could be met. Other countries will represent important markets for the United States, but their governments will not be able to meet mobility security standards. Taiwan, for example, is a close US ally and has a market economy, but in considering an agreement with Taiwan, the United States must take into account its relationship to China.[31] Israel would appear to be another good candidate for admission, but Israel's security environment could complicate negotiations toward an agreement.

An Interim Level of Access

Decisions to lower visa barriers will have to be made on a case-by-case basis, taking into account mobility security; economic interest; and a range of other security, human rights, and foreign policy criteria.

Some members of Congress want tougher program standards for the VWP. Senators Dianne Feinstein (D-CA) and Jon Kyl (R-AZ) introduced the Strengthening the Visa Waiver Program to Secure America Act on January 12, 2009, to tighten requirements for entering into visa-free travel agreements.[32] Under this bill, governments would have to report lost and stolen passport information directly to the United States and to maintain a visa overstay rate of under 2 percent.[33]

For countries that cannot meet US mobility security standards for visa-free travel, but whose markets are important and whose travelers do not pose a risk, the United States should consider an interim level of access. Some individuals, for example, could be permitted to travel as participants in CBP's Global Entry trusted-traveler program and to use ESTA rather than being required to undergo the full visa process.

How to Move Forward

DHS and DOS should renew the US commitment to this type of mobility security agreement and seek to conclude new agreements in due course. The following steps should be taken:

Downplay Politics
Policymakers should give priority to implementing the core mobility security provisions of visa-free travel agreements, namely the sharing of information on dangerous individuals and passports, and passport and airport security standards.

Continue DHS-DOS Joint Decision Making
Mobility security agreements reflect a wide range of criteria and considerations, as the Taiwan example illustrates. For this reason, DHS and DOS must continue to share decision making about mobility security partnerships.

Enter into an Agreement with the European Union
The European Union has been highly cooperative with the United States on mobility security matters. The European Union has been a close and important partner with the United States in advancing document securitization; for example, joining the United States in supporting Interpol's development of a clearinghouse for worldwide reports by countries of lost and stolen travel documents (discussed in chapter 11). Going forward, the transatlantic community has much to learn from collaborating in the migration and civil security arenas — from integration, asylum, and refugee issues to visa cooperation to facilitating intercompany transfers and cooperating on foreign assistance for border and mobility management. The United States should take a step toward the European Union to reduce unnecessary tensions and strengthen the civil security alliance. The United States could enter a bifurcated agreement with EU Member States and the European Commission reflecting the current allocation of authority between EU central authorities and Member States. Specifically:

- The United States should acknowledge that the European Union is the authority for repatriation and readmission. Since the European Union is a single borderless entity for purposes of residence and labor, treating it as such for purposes of repatriation and readmission would be appropriate and potentially afford the United States more options in the event of the need to repatriate an EU citizen.

- The European Union should not be treated as one entity for the purpose of meeting mobility security standards that only Member State governments have the authority or are able to address. For example, the United States would be able to enter into a mobility security agreement with Poland as long as the government of Poland could meet the requisite mobility security standards and as long as the overall visa overstay rate for the European Union is below the overstay rate determined by the homeland security secretary with congressional approval.

Arriving at an interim accommodation with the European Union as it restructures its sovereignty arrangements under the new Lisbon agreement would also contribute to the goodwill needed to achieve a binding agreement on privacy and data-security principles, which would provide a solid foundation for mobility-related information sharing (discussed in chapter 9).

In response to these steps, the United States should be able to expect that the European Union will cease looking at visa reciprocity with third countries until it has resolved internal issues that cause it to treat EU nationals unequally for purposes of moving and working freely within the European Union. EU policymakers are fully aware of the unevenness among Member States on mobility security, and indeed have ongoing programs to try to address these issues. The European Union, for instance, allows its Member States to limit the entry of workers from the 2004 and 2007 accession states for up to seven years.[34] Since the diplomatic tension between the United States and the European Commission arose from the US decision to not admit all EU Member States to the VWP, Jacques Barrot, vice president of the European Commission and head of Justice, Freedom, and Security, stated that despite his mandate to negotiate visa-free travel to the United States for all EU citizens, the task "will not be done at any cost."[35] A continuing and escalating dispute over visa-free travel would not be helpful in the long run, and, in reality, the European Union is not in a position to retaliate and impose a visa ban on US or Canadian citizens. Tourism and trade would be the only losers if the European Union's bark actually became a bite.

Strengthen Security

Mobility infrastructure needs to be supported so as to deliver a high level of security.

- *ESTA*. The ESTA program has to be sufficiently staffed with analysts to perform the background checks that are its immediate purpose and to develop the preventive intelligence that is its most important long-term benefit.

- *Continuous improvements*. There need to be benchmarks, monitoring, and improvements with respect to erroneous decisions to admit (false positives) and to exclude (false negatives). Analysis that enables DHS to continually improve the program should be built in.

- *Recertification*. Congress requires DHS to perform a biannual recertification of compliance with the terms of the mobility security agreements providing for visa-free travel. Recertification should bring all participating countries onto a level playing field. Standards for recertification should be clear, and permit workable but not identical processes to be maintained by countries that were VWP participants before 9/11. The United States dropped two countries from its VWP after 9/11. In 2002 it expelled Argentina from the program due to fears that the economic crisis and political instability in the country would lead to increased levels of unauthorized immigration to the United States, and in 2003 it dropped Uruguay.

Increase Transparency

DOS publishes visa-refusal rates by country on its Web site. The Bureau of Consular Affairs (CA) should also report results from its validation studies, and differences among refusal rate, validation study, and DHS air exit-entry matching data should be reconciled to achieve as reliable an estimate of overstays as possible absent a full exit system. On its Web site, DHS should regularly publish information on overstay rates by nationality, with an explanation of the DOS-DHS methodology. At present, depending on the method used, findings concerning overstays may be available based on less than 90 percent of incoming travelers. Publication of overstay rates — even if the data are not perfect — would allow the American public to know the level of risk of overstays associated with particular countries.

International Registered-Traveler Programs

Government-sponsored registered-traveler programs lower travel barriers based on advance collection of personal identifying information and promote information sharing among governments. A registered traveler uses an automated process to enter the country rather than presenting travel documents to an inspector in the regular primary lane. The system that CBP is developing requires more attention for two reasons. First, it should have formal, transparent standards. Second, DHS should consider the implications of the gap developing between the US and EU approaches to securing the flow of people at airports.[36]

CBP has two incentives for investing in registered-traveler systems. The first is cost savings. As the number of travelers and the number of watchlisted persons increases, border services will need to become more efficient. By increasing use of automation, fewer new border officials and less new space may be needed, and CBP will be able to focus on lesser-known travelers and to better analyze risk. The second is the market-driven demand for efficient travel. A country's ability to expedite lawful movement is a factor in business decision making about desirable locations and travel destinations. As more countries automate entry, their travel regimes become ever more competitive. As with the VWP, security is not the reason for registered-traveler programs. But these programs bring security benefits. The National Strategy to Combat Terrorist Travel proposes the establishment of "international registered-traveler programs, on a multilateral basis, with partner nations to increase advance information on a greater number of travelers and allow for increased scrutiny of higher-risk travelers attempting entry into the United States."[37]

New international standards for travel documents are providing the necessary technological foundation for an international registered-traveler regime. ICAO requires all countries to issue only machine-readable passports after April 1, 2010, and to ensure that non-machine-readable passports issued after November 24, 2005, expire before November 24, 2015. ICAO also issued optional specifications for incorporating biometrics into travel documents through an integrated chip that is globally interoperable. The ICAO-specified chip can store any biometric data that a country chooses, including fingerprints, facial photographs, and iris scans. The United States, Japan, and EU Member States have biometric passports that contain at least a digital photograph. The European Commission will store two fingerprints and digital photographs on EU passports beginning in 2010.

Over the past decade, a number of governments have instituted registered-traveler programs. Different programmatic approaches are emerging in the transatlantic region and in Asia. The US system relies on fingerprints to establish identity and a passport-swipe process to establish citizenship and travel authorization. Japan initiated a trusted-traveler program in November 2008 for Japanese citizens and reentry permit holders who have registered their faces in digital format. However, the US, EU, and APEC-member models differ in how they verify and screen passport holders from their own and other countries.

US and International Registered Travel

US experimentation with registered-traveler programs began when immigration and customs port directors instituted their own programs with foreign counterparts, beginning in the mid-1990s. CBP's NEXUS alternative inspection program on the Canada border and Secure Electronic Network for Travelers Rapid Inspection (SENTRI) program on the Mexico border are the two major examples. Table 10.2 provides a snapshot of how the United States regulates access.

Table 10.2 Levels of Lawful Port of Entry Access to the United States

Relative level of ease for entering the United States	Type of Access	Type of Traveler	Visa or No Visa Required	Program/Regulation	Type of Document Required	Biometrics	Other Required Processes
Easiest		Prevetted citizens of U.S. and Canada	No Visa	NEXUS	NEXUS Radio Frequency Information Card (RFID) Card	Digital facial picture and fingerprints; or iris scan for NEXUS-Air	Online registration via Global Online Enrollment System (GOES)
		Prevetted citizens of U.S. and Mexico	No Visa	SENTRI	SENTRI RFID Card	Digital facial picture and 10 fingerprints.	Online registration via GOES
	Registered Traveler	Prevetted truck drivers of U.S., Canada, and Mexico	No Visa	Free And Secure Trade (FAST)	FAST RFID Card	Digital facial picture and 10 fingerprints.	Online registration via GOES
		Prevetted citizens of U.S.	No Visa	Global Entry	Global Entry Card	10 fingerprints stored and 2 fingerprints confirmed	Online registration via GOES
		Prevetted citizens of U.S. and Netherlands	No Visa	Fast Low Risk Universal Crossing (FLUX) Alliance	FLUX Card	10 fingerprints stored and 2 fingerprints confirmed; digital facial picture; iris-scan for Privium	Must participate in Global Entry to participate in the FLUX Alliance; Online registration via GOES
		Prevetted citizens of APEC economies	Visa	APEC Business Travel Card (ABTC)	ABTC	Digital facial picture	
	Standard Entry for citizens from the U.S., Mexico, Canada, the Bahamas, and the Caribbean region.	Citizens of the United States	N/A	Western Hemisphere Travel Initiative (WHTI)	WHTI-compliant travel document (passport, trusted traveler card, state-issued enhanced driver's license, etc). Passport required for entry or reentry into the U.S.		
		Prevetted citizens of Visa Waiver Program (VWP) countries	No Visa	Electronic System of Travel Authorization (ESTA)	Machine-readable passport or electronic passport depending on country of citizenship.[3] Ultimately all passports are expected to be electronic.	Must submit 10 fingerprints to US-VISIT	
	Standard Entry for non-U.S. citizens	Non-US citizens (except for a few visa categories)[1]	Visa or No Visa	United States Visitor and Immigrant Status Indicator Technology (US-VISIT)	Individuals seeking to enter under the VWP must have a machine-readable passport. Passport, Permanent Resident Card, nonimmigrant visa, or visa waiver program national.[3]	10 fingerprints	
		Non-US citizens who are students	Visa	Student and Exchange Visitor Information System (SEVIS)	Passport, Permanent Resident Card, or other nonimmigrant visa	10 fingerprints	
Hardest		Select non-US citizens[2]	Visa or No Visa	National Security Entry-Exit Registration System (NSEERS)	Passport, Permanent Resident Card, or other nonimmigrant visa	10 fingerprints	Student activity reporting via SEVIS if a student, in addition to the NSEERS special secondary process

Source: Migration Policy Institute

1. Exceptions to US-VISIT are available at: www.dhs.gov/xtrvlsec/programs/gc_1231972592442.shtm and www.dhs.gov/xtrvlsec/programs/editorial_0527.shtm
2. Certain citizens or nationals of Iran, Iraq, Libya, Sudan and Syria, as designated by the DHS Secretary in the Federal Register; nonimmigrants who have been designated by the State Department; and any other nonimmigrant, male or female regardless of nationality, identified by immigration officers at airports, seaports and land ports of entry in accordance with 8 CFR 264.1(f)(2).
3. Nationals of the Czech Republic, Estonia, Hungary, Latvia, Lithuania, Malta, the Republic of Korea, and the Slovak Republic must have an e-passport to enter under the VWP.

DHS's Screening Coordination Office and CBP plan to consolidate existing registered-traveler systems into Global Entry at all US ports of entry, develop reciprocal registered-traveler partnerships, and use uniform standards for these partnerships as a foundation for a transatlantic and expanded multilateral registered-traveler system.

The Global Entry registered-traveler program was initiated in 2008. The program offers expedited immigration and customs control at certain ports of entry to returning US residents. Applicants must submit information to the Global On-Line Enrollment System (GOES) and pay a $100 application fee for a five-year membership. Private-sector travel agents may be able to assist with applications on behalf of clients who have already provided most of the required information. A CBP officer then reviews the application, conducts an applicant background check, takes a photo and fingerprints, and interviews the applicant at a Global Entry enrollment center.

To use the system at airports, individuals approach a Global Entry kiosk where they enter their machine-readable US passport or a permanent residency card, submit four fingerprints of the right or left hand for biometric verification,[38] and use the kiosk touch screen to make a customs declaration. The biometrics in the passport or the green card are checked against those contained in the enrollment record.[39] Once accepted at the kiosk, the passenger receives a receipt. Travelers still may be selected intentionally or randomly for secondary inspection. As of November 4, 2008, Global Entry operated at 20 airports in the United States.[40]

In May 2008 the United States and the Netherlands signed the first transatlantic "fast-lane" agreement of an international expedited-traveler program. A unified application process called FLUX will allow US citizens with valid machine-readable passports to apply to become FLUX members through the US Global Entry program, and then apply to become members of the Dutch Privium program. Both CBP and a Dutch law-enforcement agency, the Netherlands Royal Marechaussee, must conditionally approve the application separately before individuals may receive an interview at a US Trusted Traveler Enrollment Center or at the Joint Enrollment Center at Amsterdam's Schiphol Airport.

CBP aims to consolidate rules for the US legacy systems and for the new Dutch agreement within one programmatic framework that can be replicated with other countries, beginning with the United Kingdom and Germany. The United States also signed an agreement with the United Kingdom in June 2008 to begin a pilot program.[41] An agreement with Germany is under consideration, as is integration with the APEC Business Travel Card (discussed below).[42]

Through registered-traveler programs, border services are delegating security decision making in part to other countries' border services. Under FLUX, the Dutch government effectively decides which Dutch citizens may enter the United States in an expedited manner, and CBP decides which US citizens may enter the Netherlands. Each government does its own checks of the names provided.

Because registered-traveler agreements are a form of mobility security agreement, a comprehensive framework needs to be formalized so that the terms of registered-traveler agreements are clear to Congress and the public. Essential elements that need to be spelled out are: (1) security standards; (2) processes for refreshing information; (3) privacy standards; (4) data security standards; (5) a mechanism for redress; (6) audit and reporting practice; (7) the rules and processes for verifying and auditing other countries' standards and practices; (8) a timetable for improvements and upgrades; (9) a plan for ongoing analysis of and response to exploitation of any country's system, especially by someone involved in terrorism or crime; and (10) a cost-benefit analysis.

It is not clear how popular such a registered-traveler program will become in the United States or how well the technology will work. Global Entry is the second US attempt at such a system. An earlier version, INSPASS, proved unworkable. Global Entry receives about 600 applications a day and enrolled about 13,400 people in two years, bringing the total to about 60,000 people.[43] NEXUS covers less than 10 percent of the regular cross-border traffic with Canada. Relative to the number of travelers, these numbers are minute.[44] Lack of public awareness, cost, and concerns over data security and privacy may account for the relatively modest use of the program.

The EU Approach to Automated Entry

The European Union and EU Member States are moving on a three-track system for automated entry. One mode of entry will be for EU passport holders. Another will apply to non-EU passport holders. A third — in some countries only — will apply to domestic and potentially foreign-registered travelers. Like the Netherlands, at least six other European countries — Finland,

France, Germany, Portugal, Spain, and the United Kingdom — are initiating registered-traveler programs for their own passport holders. These programs may be entirely government run, as in the United Kingdom, or operated under a public-private partnership, as in the Netherlands. They apply different biometrics: Portugal and Finland require only a digital facial image, France mandates fingerprints, the Netherlands and the United Kingdom require an iris scan, and Spain is considering implementing an automated border system that employs both fingerprints and facial recognition by March 2010.[45] FLUX at least theoretically has the potential to integrate all of these systems.

The European Commission has not objected to the development of separate national registered-traveler systems. But it is has launched a pilot program in Germany that takes a different approach to security for rapid, routine entry. This system will enable all EU passport holders to enter the European Union by swiping their passport. Identity is verified by biometrics included in the EU passport, facial recognition, and eventually fingerprints. No additional security checks are performed.

The mix of EU and national systems is one part healthy experimentation — the equivalent of the "laboratory of the states" in the United States — and one part EU internal disarray. National mobility authorities can find it difficult to stay in accord with Brussels on border-screening methods. For example, the United Kingdom and European Union have been at odds over the UK Border Agency's plan to collect and analyze advanced passenger information. The European Commission has written to the UK Border Agency that such information can only be collected if passengers are informed in advance that providing the information is not compulsory nor a condition of purchase and sale of the ticket.[46] If the European Union follows up on its declared intention of instituting a PNR analysis system, perhaps the UK plan or something like it would become permissible. However, the European Union has had great difficulty in establishing EU-wide information systems to which Member States have already agreed (i.e., the EU Visa Information System, or EU VIS, and SIS-II, the second-generation Schengen Information System); another large-scale IT system is not in the offing in the foreseeable future.

US citizens and other foreigners will not have access to the EU passport-swipe entry system. Intended to be installed by 2020, the system will potentially make it significantly easier for EU citizens to enter the European Union than for US citizens to enter the United States. It is not clear, once the EU passport-swipe system is in place, if joining an EU Member State's registered-traveler program will provide any added benefit. If not, there would be no obvious basis for the type of reciprocal program with the United States on which CBP is basing its plans for multilateral Global Entry.

On its face, automated entry for citizens based solely on a passport swipe appears to be less secure. But it may not be, depending on how the system is structured. For example, security might be assured by roving security personnel who visually inspect people and make spot checks. CBP could begin to assess the security risks associated with the benefit of universal automated entry using passports by calculating the number of referrals of US passport holders to secondary inspection that prove to be positive, and examine the basis on which these individuals were sent to secondary inspection.

APEC's Business Travel Card

A similar movement to streamline entry processing is taking place in the Pacific region. In 2007 APEC (to which the United States, Canada, and Mexico belong)[47] implemented an APEC Business Travel Card (ABTC). The ABTC travel document facilitates the short-term movement of individuals traveling within APEC for business purposes. It serves as a substitute for a visa or entry permit and allows the cardholder to be admitted to APEC countries through APEC-dedicated lanes at major airports.

The impetus for ABTC is expanding free trade in Asia. APEC members have committed to implementing these measures to the extent possible. Border officials have also embraced the potential for joint information-sharing systems that provide for mutual real-time verification of visitor travel documents. Such integrated arrangements would provide a significantly higher level of public confidence in the screening program and alleviate traveler delays when advanced passenger information results in a hit.

Like FLUX, the security dimension of ABTC is collaborative. Governments accept applications from their own citizens and check individuals who apply for an ABTC against their own and other participating APEC watchlists. Card holders are categorized as low-risk, freeing immigration officials to focus their resources and energies on other travelers.

The governance by APEC is more developed than for FLUX. In 1997 APEC established a Business Mobility Group, a subfora working group of the

APEC Committee for Trade and Investment (CTI) made up of government representatives of the departments responsible for immigration and consular affairs. The group meets three times per year at the APEC Senior Officials' Meetings to discuss matters of travel facilitation and securing human mobility. The APEC Business Advisory Council (ABAC), founded in 1995, recommends policies to CTI on matters relating to business travel.[48] As of November 2008, 18 of the 21 APEC countries used the ABTC to expedite business travel among their citizens.[49] Mexico joined the program in 2008.[50]

Unlike FLUX, the ABTC program includes countries with which the United States (and Canada) does not have visa-free travel agreements. Consequently, the ABTC is not available to US citizens. As a compromise, the United States and Canada offer foreign ABTC holders with access to "fast-track" immigration lanes usually reserved for crew members, and to dedicated-ABTC lanes at certain major international airports. But ABTC travelers must present a valid passport and a visa if applicable. Unlike those applying for visa-free travel through ESTA, ABTC holders are not precleared. The United States recognizes the ABTC for purposes of allowing access to the crew lines at ports of entry and for expedited visa appointments, but it is unwilling to allow the card to function in lieu of a visa.

ASEAN has also taken steps to enhance cooperation on cross-border movement. Members signed the ASEAN Tourism Agreement in November 2002, which included a provision on facilitating travel within ASEAN nations. In 2004 members also signed the ASEAN Framework Agreement for Integration of Priority Sectors to commit themselves to offer visa-free travel within ASEAN to ASEAN nationals. Then in 2006, members signed the ASEAN Framework Agreement on Visa Exemption that committed members to exempt citizens of ASEAN countries with valid passports from visa requirements for stays of up to 14 days.[51] In addition to facilitated and visa-free travel arrangements, the ASEAN directors general of immigration departments and heads of consular divisions hold meetings to discuss matters of mutual interest such as imposter detection and profiling techniques,[52] counterterrorism, border management, document security, immigration intelligence, and information sharing.[53]

Conclusion

At present, the United States, European Union, APEC, and ASEAN are acting largely independently of one another and taking different approaches to securing border crossing and regional movement. A multilateral global travel infrastructure, called the Electronic International Travel System (EITS) and based on a distributed network that provides real-time access to national data sets, was conceptualized shortly after 9/11. It is time to think more about this type of model. Going forward, DHS and DOS should assess how to achieve the optimum level of standardization, interoperability, and inclusiveness in mobility infrastructure. As stated by one DHS senior official, "[C]onsistent international standards for biometrics and data sharing are essential to developing compatible systems, and compatible systems are essential to hindering criminal enterprises as well as terrorists' ability to travel."[54] The goal is to keep technology costs as low as possible, maximize efficiency and access for travelers, maintain high security standards, and uphold human rights principles.

As a step in that direction, different incremental improvements and best practices can be monitored and integrated, as DHS is seeking to do for US identity management through its Credentialing Framework Initiative (CFI), which began in July 2008. The CFI guides the selection and coordination of credentialing activities and investments throughout DHS.[55] For example, it may be possible for the United States and such close partners as the Five Country Conference, the European Union, and other VWP countries to simplify, clarify, consolidate, and extend to other countries the types of provisions in existing agreements (see box 10.1).

Box 10.1 Securing Human Movement: US Agreements with Foreign Governments

INFORMATION SHARING
1. Homeland Security Presidential Directive 6* (HSPD-6)
    a. Terrorist identities
    b. Terrorist biometrics
2. Traveler EU-US PNR Agreement (2004, 2006, and 2007)
3. Traveler Advance Passenger Information (API) Law (Unilateral US measure under Intelligence Reform and Terrorism Prevention Act [IRTPA] 2004)
4. Lost and stolen passports under agreements with Interpol and through APEC's Regional Mobility Alert System (RMAS)
5. Enhancing cooperation in preventing and combating serious crime (2009)
    a. Sharing serious criminal biometrics (fingerprints and DNA)
6. High Value Data Sharing Protocol amongst the immigration authorities of the Five Country Conference (2009)**
    a. Sharing biometric fingerprint information of foreign criminals and asylum seekers
7. Enhancing Cooperation in Preventing and Combating Serious Crime (2009)***
8. Financial EU-US SWIFT Agreement (2007 and 2009 TBD)
    a. Financial data transferred for counterterrorism purposes

*The United States currently shares information on terrorist identities with 17 countries.
**The Five Country Conference, which includes Australia, Canada, the United States, the United Kingdom, and New Zealand, is a forum for cooperation on strategic initiatives on immigration and border security. Pending final formal entry by the United States and New Zealand.
***The countries with whom the United States has signed agreements on enhancing cooperation in preventing and combating serious crime are: the Czech Republic, Estonia, Germany, Greece, Hungary, Italy, Latvia, Lithuania, Malta, Portugal, Slovakia, Spain, and South Korea. All of these, except for South Korea, are EU Member States.

MOBILITY SECURITY
1. US Visa Waiver Program (2008)****
    a. Visa overstay rates
    b. Visa refusal rates of under 10 percent
    c. Counterterrorism information sharing
    d. Passenger information sharing
    e. Adequate passport security standards
    f. Electronic passport
    g. Adequate passport and travel-document issuance standards
    h. Airport security standards
    i. Air marshals
    j. Repatriation
    k. ESTA
    l. Reporting lost and stolen passports through Interpol or other means
    m. Repatriation of aliens with removal orders
2. Immigration Advisory Program (2004) at nine airports.
    a. Travel document safety
    b. Lost and stolen passports
3. Immigration Preclearance with Canada, Bermuda, the Bahamas, Aruba, and Ireland.
4. FLUX, SENTRI, and NEXUS.
    a. Registered traveler programs

****The United States will evaluate periodically the effect a VWP country has on the security, law enforcement, and immigration interests of the United States to determine continuation of membership for that country in VWP.

MOBILITY-RELATED CRIME CONTROL
1. US-Europol Agreements (2001 and 2002)
2. US-Eurojust Agreement (2006)
3. US-EU Extradition***** Agreement (2003)
4. US-EU Mutual Legal Assistance Treaty (MLAT 2003)*****
5. Enhancing Cooperation in Preventing and Combating Serious Crime (2009)******

*****The European Union and the United States exchanged legal instruments for the MLAT and extradition treaties in October 2009, which awaited implementation on February 1, 2010.
******The countries with whom the United States has signed agreements on enhancing cooperation in preventing and combating serious crime are: the Czech Republic, Estonia, Germany, Greece, Hungary, Italy, Latvia, Lithuania, Malta, Portugal, Slovakia, Spain, and South Korea. All of these, except for South Korea, are EU Member States.

Source: Migration Policy Institute research of existing agreements.

Joint Action to Preclude Illegal Travel and High-Volume Uncontrolled Movement of People

Traveler demand, economic competitiveness, and public- and private-sector budgetary factors provide an impetus for the type of travel-risk management and mobility security collaboration in which national and regional authorities in the developed world and among emerging economies are or should be beginning to engage. Such agreements provide an operational structure for mobility-related information sharing. They also provide a framework for other joint action to secure human mobility. Cooperative efforts already include air marshal programs, airport security standards, and pretravel document inspections. Closer collaboration on travel-ban lists and integrated operations against HTOs and HSOs are a logical next step.

The process of lowering visa barriers with allies, building a fast lane for international travel, and collaborating proactively against crime and victimization in international mobility channels should continue. It is a challenging undertaking in which failure to make progress would contribute to catastrophic consequences. Even transatlantic agreement is not a foregone conclusion. Achieving agreement about legal standards and supporting it with interoperability technology presents unprecedentedly complex hurdles that civil security authorities and diplomats are only beginning to recognize and define. Issues like the right to maintain multiple citizenships and travel on multiple passports have profound ramifications apart from the practical difficulties they present. Where developing countries are involved, incentives outside travel and migration, such as foreign assistance, will be required.

But diplomacy and law securing and maintaining the integrity of global legal mobility channels represent only one dimension of mobility security. Precluding the mass displacement or large-scale unregulated movement of people presents a greater challenge. This is not only because of the unequal distribution of resources among countries or the environmental or political forces that can precipitate such movements; it is because there is no real consensus about the principles that should guide the search for solutions. It is increasingly accepted that a civil security alliance, with a mobility security dimension, is an essential response to the threat posed by nonstate actors and other transnational risks. It is less clear what the goal should be for mobility security agreements that aim to prevent large-scale, uncontrolled, or precipitous movement. How does the right of departure square with governments' responsibility to protect their population? How does the right to pursue economic opportunity square with states' obligation to build the capabilities of their citizenry? How is democratic choice reconciled with an individual's freedom of movement? These issues have barely begun to be articulated or debated.

US-Cuban discussions regarding a safe and orderly migration process between Cuba and the United States are a small instance of such conundrums. The negotiations continue a movement toward broader mobility stabilization and security agreements. The talks have roots in mid-1990s migration accords that aimed to prevent an exodus of Cuban refugees to the United States, such as the 1980 Mariel boatlift and the 1994 wave of boat people. The agreement established the repatriation by US authorities of Cuban migrants intercepted at sea. Cuba promised to curb illegal migration.[56] Negotiations that were suspended in 2004 resumed in July 2009 in New York City and were ongoing. US agreements with Mexico, the Caribbean states, and Canada must go beyond travelers who use legal mobility channels. A broader range of issues and interests must be addressed in order to provide security to migrants and sending, transit, and receiving states because unauthorized migration levels are so high.[57]

Agreements with wealthy countries and high-end travelers, and with countries where there are large numbers of poor people, form a continuum rather than two clearly distinct categories. If the United States permits relatively open access to the United States for citizens from one group of democracies with market economies, it becomes difficult to articulate a principled basis for denying citizens from other free-market democracies access on comparable terms, so long as there is a framework in place that effectively ensures compliance with mobility rules. The United States requires the United Kingdom, Germany, and Australia to meet certain security collaboration standards as a condition of visa-free travel and other mobility security arrangements. Equivalent arrangements must now be pursued with states from which significant numbers of people are traveling to the United States through illegal channels, sometimes coming to fatal harm in the process.

But to craft such arrangements will require a profound reexamination of assumptions about movement with which we have been living for decades. Finding answers will be easier if the goal of jointly upholding the rule of law in mobility channels is kept in the foreground.

Chapter 11: International Institutions to Secure Human Mobility

Policy Preview: Civil security relating to human movement has an international dimension because many terrorists and criminals are mobile and belong to transnational organizations. The core goal of US international mobility policy should be to take a leadership role in promoting the rule of law in global mobility channels and to work closely with partners to set the terms of an international mobility security agenda. The United States should increase and coordinate international assistance for mobility and border-security management. It should work bilaterally, through regional entities, and through the United Nations (UN) and other international institutions to reduce illegal migration. It should also help establish a new organization of border and immigration professionals to support cooperative mobility security policies and practices.

Preclusion and its close cousin, *prevention*, encompass several measures to prevent terrorist travel, human trafficking, human smuggling, other transnational criminal travel, and illegal migration. The goal is to prevent these threats from reaching the United States. (This form of prevention is referred to as *preemption* in section II.)

Both preclusion and prevention involve building new norms, institutions, and practices that establish the rule of law in mobility channels, with the goals of enforcing travel bans, targeting transnational criminals, managing flows of people in a safe and orderly manner, and protecting national borders. This new civil security arena must be supported by diplomacy, development assistance, and the military. It is the main subject of this chapter. Mobility-related infrastructure and institution building enable the United States to gain greater cooperation from other states in preemptive action against terrorist and criminal travel and migration.

Preclusion also entails promoting good governance, regional stability, environmental health, and economic development. These upstream or at-the-source approaches attempt to preclude terrorist mobility, migration-triggering events, and large-scale, uncontrolled migration. Such migration may be by individuals who pose risks to themselves or others, or by sudden mass movements precipitated by natural disasters, economic crises, or a regime's failure to fulfill its responsibility to protect the population.

Lawful mobility channels are a global public good. Although national laws limit the reasons that people can gain access to countries and economies, the complex of laws, operations, and technology that comprises legal mobility channels is in principle available to everyone who seeks to move. International action to protect people on the move, to prevent dangerous individuals from moving, and to regulate large-scale migration preceded September 11, 2001, but has gathered steam since then. Much of the content of a preclusion agenda — environmental, labor migration, development, and counterinsurgency initiatives — is outside the scope of this book. However, mobility security policy must play a significant role in meeting this challenge.

All forms of prevention assume that states want to preserve and control their sovereign boundaries, even as they may wish to cooperate in lowering travel barriers, engaging in cross-border boundary management, or opening labor and migration channels. Prevention in the form of cooperative international efforts to build the rule of law in mobility channels is emerging in five contexts:

1. International and regional agreements, standards, and declarations about counterterrorism and crime control
2. International and regional institutions and foreign-assistance programs for security-related mobility management
3. Bilateral foreign assistance relating to mobility security
4. Regional consultative dialogues relating to migration and its management
5. Bilateral mobility partnerships

International and Regional Agreements for Mobility Security Cooperation

The protection of people traveling as refugees has been a major focus for the United Nations since 1951. Terrorist mobility is a more recent area of focus. The UN Security Council (UNSC) has taken action against terrorist travel in a series of resolutions imposing travel bans, beginning with Security Council Resolution 1267 in 1999. It has also imposed travel sanctions on rogue states and human rights violators (discussed in chapter 6.) Wealthy countries have constructed mobility security agreements in order to lower entry barriers and expedite travel for short-term visitors, as discussed in chapter 10. Mobility-related information sharing has also been a critical arena for multilateral counterterrorism and broader mobility security, as discussed in chapter 9.

International Declarations Concerning Securing Human Mobility

The foundation for international action to secure human mobility is Security Council Resolution 1373 (September 28, 2001). In that resolution, the Security Council used its Chapter 7 authority to mandate that countries control their borders and deny terrorists safe havens. The resolution in effect prescribes the means to implement travel bans and suppress trafficking and other mobility crimes. Resolution 1373 establishes the mission of the UN Counter-Terrorism Committee Executive Directorate (CTED) and directs states to prevent the movement of terrorists or terrorist groups "by effective border controls and controls on the issuance of identity papers and travel documents, and through measures for preventing counterfeiting, forgery, or fraudulent use of identity papers and travel documents."[58] It calls upon states to:

- "Find ways of intensifying and accelerating the exchange of operational information, especially regarding actions or movements of terrorist persons or networks; forged or falsified travel documents; traffic in arms, explosives or sensitive materials; use of communications technologies by terrorist groups; and the threat posed by the possession of weapons of mass destruction by terrorist groups."

- "Exchange information in accordance with international and domestic law and cooperate on administrative and judicial matters to prevent the commission of terrorist acts."

- "Ensure, in conformity with international law, that refugee status is not abused by the perpetrators, organizers, or facilitators of terrorist acts, and that claims of political motivation are not recognized as grounds for refusing requests for the extradition of alleged terrorists."

Resolution 1373 builds on prior UN and regional organization commitments. In November 2000, the UN General Assembly markedly expanded the UN role in protecting people from transnational criminal organizations, by adopting, after seven years of discussion, the UN Convention against Transnational Organized Crime ("Crime Convention").

Shortly after the Security Council acted against terrorist travel through Resolution 1373, the General Assembly in November 2001 adopted two protocols to the Crime Convention — the Protocol to Prevent, Suppress, and Punish Trafficking in Persons, Especially Women and Children, and the Protocol against the Smuggling of Migrants by Land, Sea, and Air. The Crime Convention, approved by 146 parties;[59] and the Protocol to Prevent, Suppress, and Punish Trafficking in Persons, Especially Women and Children, endorsed by 118 parties,[60] both entered into force in 2003. The Protocol against the Smuggling of Migrants by Land, Sea, and Air, with 111 parties, came into force in 2004.

The two protocols, which are optional for countries, introduce some of the same concepts and measures that are essential to the implementation of UN travel-ban resolutions. They define human smuggling and trafficking as criminal offenses. They promote action and cooperation in prevention, information sharing, investigation, maritime interdiction, cross-border communication, sanctions, training and technical assistance, and prosecution. Both protocols promote secure and high-quality travel documents and prescribe state-to-state information sharing about the misuse of travel documents and about the methods organized criminal groups use to traffic individuals across borders. They address officials from immigration agencies, law enforcement, international organizations, nongovernmental organizations (NGOs), and civil-society organizations.

The relatively new Convention against Corruption (2003) is not yet in force. As the first legally binding treaty to address corruption-related problems on a global basis, it has significant potential for contributing to efforts to shrink the illicit market in movement, which depends on the complicity of officials.

International Standard Setting for Securing Human Mobility

There are as yet no global standards for ports of entry or border management in the way that the Financial Action Task Force's (FATF's) 40 recommendations guide countries in securing banking systems[61] (this task force is an intergovernmental policymaking body whose mission is to combat money laundering and terrorist financing at the national and international levels).[62] The exception is travel documents, for which there are global standards and recommendations.

The original concern of the International Civil Aviation Organization (ICAO), established in 1944 and located in Montreal, was, as the name suggests, civil aviation. A group of UN Member States formed ICAO, recognizing that civil air transportation would play an important role in international relations after World War II ended. ICAO has emerged as a critical player in the evolving mobility security agenda because of its role in promoting what one scholar calls a "global documentary regime."[63]

Founded by the Convention on International Civil Aviation, better known as the Chicago Convention, the 190-member organization is made up of an assembly,[64] a council,[65] and a secretariat.[66] Several articles of the Chicago Convention give ICAO the responsibility to set standards for clearing individuals at ports of entry. Article 13 requires individuals to comply with the immigration, customs, and passport regulations of Contracting States. Article 22 requires Contracting States to adopt measures to avoid unnecessary delays at ports of entry. Article 23 requires Contracting States to establish immigration and customs procedures. Article 37 requires Contracting States to develop and implement international standards for immigration and customs clearance.

ICAO requires all of its Contracting States to adopt International Standards and Recommended Practices (SARPs). The Chicago Convention has 18 annexes laying out SARPs for different domains in international air transport. Annex 9, entitled "Facilitation," prescribes standards for travel documents. Annex 9 was originally adopted to reduce paperwork; standardize travel documents used for international travel; and simplify procedures for allowing aircrafts, passengers, and cargo to enter a country. As air travel expanded, ICAO and its member states became concerned about ever-increasing passenger arrivals. ICAO revised Annex 9 to establish more efficient inspection techniques based on risk management, to reduce lines at airports, and to permit enhanced security through detection of the use of fraudulent travel documents.

In 1980 ICAO provided specifications for the first machine-readable passports issued by Australia, Canada, and the United States. Annex 9 obligates Contracting States to issue machine-readable travel documents by 2010. Two years after the 9/11 terrorist attacks, ICAO issued new specifications for the inclusion of interoperable biometrics and a chip in the next generation of machine-readable passports. Although the incorporation of biometric data is a recommended practice rather than a mandate, an ICAO blueprint[67] sets out the biometric indicators that countries should adopt as the standard, which systems are necessary to obtain global interoperability, how to program the contactless integrated circuit chip to store biometric information, and how to adopt the ICAO-sponsored public key infrastructure to secure data from unauthorized access.[68] E-passports containing biometric information in integrated chips had been issued by 62 states as of September 2009, with others making preparations.[69]

UN World Tourism Organization (UNWTO)

UNWTO does not have a primary security role, but it is becoming increasingly involved in setting guidelines for matters such as issuance of travel advisories and visas, two critical aspects of mobility security.

Regional Declaratory Agreements

The Group of Eight's (G-8's) Counterterrorism Action Group (CTAG) formed a subgroup, the Roma-Lyons group, which has put forward a series of mobility security measures beginning with a Secure and Facilitated International Travel Initiative. In that initiative, the G-8 members committed to:

- Develop mechanisms for real-time data exchange to validate travel documents, watchlist information, and Advance Passenger Information System (APIS) and Passenger Name Record (PNR) information
- Exchange timely information on terrorist identities
- Provide input to International Criminal Police Organization's (Interpol's) stolen and lost travel document (SLTD) database
- Share best practices on law-enforcement and intelligence cooperation
- Strengthen standardized practices for secure passport issuance

Similarly, the Inter-American Committee against Terrorism (CICTE) of the Organization for American States (OAS) in March 2009 adopted a declaration sponsored by the government of Mexico, the Declaration on Strengthening Border Controls and International Cooperation in the Fight against Terrorism. This agreement calls for border controls, port-of-entry improvements, travel-document measures, and information sharing, among other provisions. Other such agreements are listed in box 11.1.

Box 11.1 Regional Conclusions, Agreements, and Conventions with Mobility-Related Provisions

1. OAS Convention to Prevent and Punish Acts of Terrorism Taking the Form of Crimes against Persons and Related Extortion that are of International Significance, concluded at Washington, DC, on February 2, 1971.

2. European Convention on the Suppression of Terrorism, concluded at Strasbourg, France, on January 27, 1977.

3. South Asian Association for Regional Cooperation (SAARC) Regional Convention on Suppression of Terrorism, signed at Kathmandu on November 4, 1987.

4. Treaty on Cooperation among States Members of the Commonwealth of Independent States (CIS) in Combating Terrorism, signed at Minsk, Belarus, on June 4, 1999.

5. Convention of the Organization of the Islamic Conference on Combating International Terrorism, adopted at Ouagadougou, Burkina Faso, on July 1, 1999.

6. Organization of African Unity (OAU) Convention on the Prevention and Combating of Terrorism, adopted at Algiers on July 14, 1999.

7. Conclusions adopted by the Council (Justice and Home Affairs) on September 20, 2001, in Brussels.

8. Asia-Pacific Economic Cooperation (APEC) Leaders' Statement on Counter-Terrorism on October 21, 2001.

9. Inter-American Convention against Terrorism, adopted on June 3, 2002.

10. Asia-Europe Meeting (ASEM) IV Declaration on Cooperation against International Terrorism — Fourth Asia-Europe Summit Meeting in Copenhagen on September 23–24, 2002.

11. Convention between the Kingdom of Belgium, the Federal Republic of Germany, the Kingdom of Spain, the French Republic, the Grand Duchy of Luxembourg, the Kingdom of the Netherlands and the Republic of Austria on the Stepping Up of Cross-Border Cooperation, Particularly in Combating Terrorism, Cross-Border Crime and Illegal Migration (Prüm Convention), signed in Germany on May 27, 2005.

12. Council Declaration on the EU Response to the London Bombings, July 13, 2005, Justice and Home Affairs, Charles Clarke.

13. Association of Southeast Asian Nations (ASEAN) Convention on Counter Terrorism, adopted on January 13, 2007, in Cebu, Philippines.

Source: UN General Assembly, Report of the Secretary-General on Measures to Eliminate International Terrorism (Doc.A/64/161) (New York, NY: United Nations, 2009), www.unhcr.org/refworld/type,THEMREPORT,,,4a9e2c190,0.html; Justice and Home Affairs Council, "Conclusions Adopted by the Council (Justice and Home Affairs)," September 20, 2001, http://ec.europa.eu/justice_home/news/terrorism/documents/concl_council_20sep_en.pdf; APEC, "APEC Leaders Statement on Counter-Terrorism," October 21, 2001, www.apec.org/apec/leaders__declarations/2001/statement_on_counter-terrorism.html; ASEM, "Declaration on Cooperation against International Terrorism," September 22–24, 2002, www.aseminfoboard.org/content/documents/Declaration_on_Cooperation_against_International_Terrorism.pdf; Council of the European Union, Convention between the Kingdom of Belgium, the Federal Republic of Germany, the Kingdom of Spain, the French Republic, the Grand Duchy of Luxembourg, the Kingdom of the Netherlands and the Republic of Austria on the Stepping Up of Cross-Border Cooperation, Particularly in Combating Terrorism, Cross-Border Crime and Illegal Migration, July 7, 2005, www.statewatch.org/news/2005/aug/Prum-Convention.pdf; Council of the European Union, "Council Declaration on the EU Response to the London Bombings," Press Release, July 13, 2005, www.consilium.europa.eu/uedocs/cms_data/docs/pressdata/en/jha/85703.pdf; ASEAN, "ASEAN Convention on Counter Terrorism," January 13, 2007, www.aseansec.org/19250.htm.

Multilateral Institutions and Foreign Assistance Programs

Security Council travel ban Resolution 1373 and the two General Assembly protocols formulate a relatively coherent mobility security agenda targeting terrorists and criminals who exploit global mobility channels. The goals, however, are ambitious. Many poorer states lack the capacity, means, and know-how to implement the international standards that promote these objectives, even where they embrace them.

A number of international and regional organizations help promote international norms to secure human mobility and provide funding and technical assistance to support the establishment of these norms in developing countries. It is important to have a sense of what their missions and activities are to begin to assess how well the current mix of institutions serves new mobility security needs. These organizations include selected United Nations entities such as the Security Council, CTED, UN Office on Drugs and Crime (UNODC), and the UN Development Program (UNDP), etc.; ICAO; Interpol; the International Organization for Migration (IOM); and World Border Organization–BORDERPOL (WBO-BORDERPOL).

Regional organizations taking a prominent role in mobility-related security assistance include: ASEAN, OAS, Frontex (the EU border organization), the Organization for Security and Cooperation in Europe (OSCE), and the International Center for Migration and Development (ICMPD).

The United Nations has several specialized bodies that oversee, provide policy guidance, and support capacity building relating to aspects of the movement of people. The United Nations High Commission on Refugees (UNHCR), formed in 1950 with headquarters located in Geneva, is responsible for upholding the rights and well-being of refugees, a critical human security mission. The International Labor Organization (ILO) and the Population Division of the Department of Economic and Social Affairs are also instrumental in shaping approaches to and understandings of the movement of people.

As the demands of civil security compel a further development of international law and practice relating to the movement of people, these historically important institutions will have to be reinvigorated or they will be superseded. ILO, for example, will either become an integral part of the solution to precluding illegal labor migration or it will become increasingly irrelevant. UNHCR will either be reconceived in an era of multimotivated migrants — not strictly "refugees" in the official meaning of the term, but not entirely voluntary travelers, as most often found in developed countries — or its prominent role will be eroded, to be replaced by international organizations that promote development and investment in communities drained by emigration.

The UNSC Counter-Terrorism Committee (CTC) and Counter-Terrorism Committee Executive Directorate (CTED)

The United Nations' focus on bolstering sovereign borders is primarily driven by its counterterrorism goals. The Security Council established two organizations that have become critical to implementing travel bans and effective border controls. First, Resolution 1373 established CTC to monitor states' implementation of this resolution. Modeled on the country-specific sanctions committees, CTC's main responsibility is to ask countries to implement measures to counter terrorist activities.[70] It urges states to:

- Deny safe haven, sustenance, or support for terrorists
- Cooperate with other governments in the investigation, detection, arrest, extradition, and prosecution of those involved in terrorism
- Criminalize assistance for terrorism in domestic law
- Bring violators to justice
- Share information with other governments on groups practicing or planning terrorist acts[71]

It also asks states to prohibit incitement to commit terrorist acts, to prevent incitement from occurring, and to deny safe haven to those who engage in such activities (Security Council Resolution 1624).

Second, the Security Council in Resolution 1535 expanded CTC's responsibilities to include facilitating technical assistance to countries and developing technical-assistance programs with international, regional, and subregional organizations.[72] Resolution 1535 plunged the Security Council into the business of border-related capacity building.

Third, Resolution 1535 also created CTED, which has about 40 staff members,[73] two of whom are responsible for border-related activity, and an $8 million budget.[74] CTED works with international organizations, regional bodies, and other institutions to promote assistance in areas of border and customs controls, terrorist financing, police and law enforcement, and refugee and migration law. In March 2008, Resolution 1805 extended the mandate of the CTED to December 31, 2010. CTED operates by preparing preliminary implementation assessments (PIAs) for Member States; as of November 2008, 88 PIAs were in the works. CTED also makes site visits, concentrating on lessons learned, best practices, and particular vulnerabilities according to the circumstances of the country visited.[75] In 2007 CTED convened its first international conference exclusively on effective border security and the prevention of terrorist travel.[76]

In June 2008 CTED issued a Global Implementation Survey concerning Resolution 1373, which recommended that CTC: (1) promote the implementation of international standards for customs, aviation, and maritime security; (2) encourage the adoption of best practices in border control where such practices have proven their effectiveness, as in the fields of travel-document security, traveler screening, and cargo security; (3) enhance coordination among police and border-control agencies; and (4) encourage states to gain and provide better access to international counterterrorism and criminal databases in order to enhance abilities to detect and exclude persons involved in terrorism. Based on its experience and expertise, CTED is preparing to publish a technical guide that will provide standards and criteria for fulfilling the Resolution 1373 mandates, including border controls. This will be the first international statement about standards for the maintenance of borders to safeguard human mobility.

Challenges Facing CTED

CTED plainly lacks the resources to offer effective technical assistance to states that need it.[77] At present, CTED performs a very useful matching role, facilitating bilateral funding as the primary channel through which countries deliver technical assistance. This may be the best arrangement possible at the moment, but the process would benefit from finding ways to ensure that technical assistance and subsequent implementation are distributed in an efficient and sustained manner. There are practical considerations as to how international organizations, including the United Nations, and national governments can best coordinate the mobility security assistance they are providing to states. There is unquestionably a great deal of waste and redundancy at present.

Some countries have made progress adopting and enforcing travel bans. Southeast Asian countries have instituted a number of new border-control programs with the support of bilateral donors whose assistance CTED facilitated, notably Australia, the United States, the European Union, Germany, the United Kingdom, the Netherlands, and Denmark. The United States, Australia, certain EU countries, Japan, New Zealand, and Singapore have invested substantial sums in new border controls.

As with all counterterrorism measures, success in implementing travel bans cannot be judged against an absolute standard of perfection. All UNSC members, including the United States, have highly visible problems with border management. Mobility infrastructure is bound to remain a work in progress for the indefinite future. This is not necessarily a bad thing, since there are many issues to be resolved about the compatibility of tightened border controls and individual rights. The impact of tightened travel-document standards on vulnerable minorities and migrants must also be considered.

Still, countries' lack of capacity to carry out their legal obligations means that there will be slow progress in implementing travel bans and complying with Resolution 1373. The pace has political implications, including undermining states' respect for the travel-ban program and, more broadly, for the Security Council.

The United Nations Office on Drugs and Crime (UNODC) and the United Nations Development Program (UNDP)

UNODC, located in Vienna with 20 field offices, includes a Terrorism Prevention Branch (TPB). The UN General Assembly in 2002 expanded TPB's scope to include offering states legal and technical assistance to implement the requirements of Resolution 1373. The UN Global Counter-Terrorism Strategy, adopted in 2006, also encourages UNODC to enhance its technical assistance to states and encourages Member States to avail themselves of this support. TPB works closely with CTC and CTED, and with other UN entities working on mobility-related security issues.

ICAO's Implementation and Capacity Building Working Group (ICBWG)

A number of countries are having difficulty meeting the 2010 ICAO deadline for deploying machine-readable passports due to insufficient political will; poor governance; and lack of funding, expertise, and capacity.[78] In September 2008 ICAO established ICBWG. The working group offers assistance and expertise to countries that are having difficulty meeting the deadline and implementing new mobility technologies, policies, and standards for travel documents.[79] ICBWG has identified 22 countries that do not issue machine-readable passports and others that issue passports that do not comply with ICAO standards.[80]

Organization for Security and Cooperation (OSCE) in Europe

As its name indicates, the OSCE Travel Document Security Program seeks to improve travel-document security throughout the OSCE region.[81] The program grew out of the Bucharest Plan of Action for Combating Terrorism, which was adopted in December 2001. The plan recognizes the close connection between terrorism and transnational organized crime, and the importance of effective border controls in preventing terrorist movement.

International Criminal Police Organization (Interpol)

The International Criminal Police Organization, better known as Interpol, established in 1923, is the world's largest police organization, with 187 member governments.[82] It is headquartered in Lyon, France, with regional offices in Argentina, Cameroon, Côte d'Ivoire, El Salvador, Kenya, Thailand, and Zimbabwe.[83] National Central Bureaus (NCBs) link Interpol's central staff to their respective governments and counterparts in other Member States. Member States contributed to Interpol's budget of 47.6 million in 2008.

Interpol's mandate is to support police and law-enforcement agencies in its member countries in their efforts to prevent crime and conduct criminal investigations. In particular, Interpol facilitates cross-border police cooperation. Its crime-related databases include approximately 178,000 nominal records (names and photographs) on known international criminals, missing persons, and unidentified bodies; SLTDs and stolen administrative documents, motor vehicles, and works of art; and fingerprints. Interpol databases hold information on 16.7 million lost or stolen travel documents, 6.2 million lost or stolen vehicles, 34,000 pieces of stolen artwork, 83,000 DNA profiles from 48 countries, and 100,000 sets of fingerprints, among others.[84]

In 2002 Interpol established the international SLTD database, which contains limited but useful information on almost 17 million travel documents that 145 Member States have reported stolen or lost.[85] Switzerland, for example, conducts approximately 300,000 SLTD searches per month and finds more than 100 individuals traveling on stolen passports.[86] NCB officials and increasingly also Member State border officials have access to Interpol databases 24 hours a day, seven days a week.[87]

The US Congress has repeatedly emphasized the importance of the Interpol database, making participation in the program a criterion for visa-free travel status. The Department of State (DOS) downloads lost and stolen US passport information twice daily directly to Interpol. All EU Member States satisfy, to varying degrees, the EU mandate to submit their information on lost and stolen passports,[88] as do all G-8 countries.[89] UNSC Resolution 1617 (2005) "urges all Member States to . . . ensure that stolen and lost passports and other travel documents are invalidated as soon as possible and share information on those documents with other Member States through the Interpol database."[90]

International Organization for Migration (IOM)

Established in 1951, IOM has offices in more than 100 countries and 125 Member States. Its primary purpose as expressed in its constitution is to provide services to governments in connection with the organized transfer of migrants, refugees, and displaced persons and to respond to requests for assistance relating to other migration issues. IOM has added countering human trafficking as a practice area since 1994. Governments have supported approximately 500 IOM projects in 85 countries, and IOM projects have offered assistance to 15,000 trafficked persons since 2001.[91] It also publishes research on human-trafficking routes and trends.

About one-tenth of IOM's budget is supplied by contracts with governments to assist states to build capacity in systems for visa entry, border management, and countering human trafficking.[92] For example, IOM is assisting South Africa in addressing its problems of lax control of travel documents, corruption, unauthorized migration, and porous borders. Based on the Protocol on the Facilitation on Movement of People for the Southern African Region, IOM is seeking to foster a regional approach to capacity building in Member States of the Southern African Development Community (SADC) in the areas of countertrafficking, travel-document security, border-management procedures, and training of immigration officers. It is also providing assistance in the areas of border operations, border police training, and effective asylum procedures to countries in East Africa and the Horn of Africa, West Africa, North Africa, the Western Mediterranean, South America, Central America and Mexico, the Caribbean, South and Southwest Asia, East and Southeast Asia, and Central Asia. Since 2001 IOM has offered support on migration management to developing states, executing over 200 IOM-government projects in more than 85 countries.

International Centre for Migration Policy Development (ICMPD)

Founded in 1993, ICMPD is an international organization that serves as a forum for informal consultations. It provides services in migration governance to state agencies that are charged with designing and implementing migration policies; fosters intergovernmental dialogue on migration by serving as the secretariat to the Budapest Process involving 50 European and Eurasian States and 10 international organizations; offers capacity-building projects in areas of institution building and legal reform relating to asylum, visas, human trafficking, and integrated border management; and conducts comparative policy research on migration.

With 11 member states,[93] 60 staff members at its headquarters in Vienna, and other staff located around the world in its regional offices, the organization offers services including border-related capacity building, antitrafficking projects, and the development of readmission mechanisms. ICMPD, for example, has helped the European Union in drafting guidelines for Integrated Border Management (IBM) in the Western Balkans. IBM is the EU term for collaboration in border management among EU Member States, and by extension, any regional cooperation.

International Dialogue about Managing Migration

The international community has invested considerable effort in consultative processes and dialogues on preventive approaches to illegal immigration and associated criminality. These nonbinding fora bring together representatives of governments, civil-society organizations, and international organizations at the regional level for informal discussions on migration-related problems and opportunities for cooperation.

IOM, which provides support for these dialogues, lists them as follows: the Intergovernmental Consultations on Asylum, Refugee and Migration Policies in Europe, North America, and Australia (IGC) (1985); Budapest Process (1991); Commonwealth of Independent States Process (1995); Puebla Process (1996); Manila Process (1996); Intergovernmental Asia-Pacific Consultations on Refugees and Displaced Persons (1996); Bangkok Declaration (1999); South American Meeting on Migration, Integration, and Development (1999); Migration Dialogue for Southern Africa (2000); and the Dakar Declaration (2000).[94] The United States has participated in the IGC, Budapest Process, and Puebla Process initiated by Mexico. However useful they have been for building relationships and trust, the dialogues do not appear to have led to any concrete actions.

International dialogue has also taken place within the Global Commission on International Migration (GCIM), where illegal immigration, migrants' security, and the need to respect human rights were highlighted as integral aspects of international migration policy.[95]

European Mobility Partnerships

Europe has not developed a better preventive approach to uncontrolled migration than has the United States. However, the EU and its Member States have pursued several collaborative efforts to stymie large-scale illegal migration. The European Union and the Republic of Moldova, for example, signed a joint mobility partnership declaration in June 2008 to establish a more efficient framework for legal migration, the reintegration of returning migrants, and the fighting of illegal migration. The project got off the ground with 13 million and the support of 14 EU Member States and its border agency, Frontex.

The French immigration minister announced in August 2007 that France would seek to sign agreements on managing immigration with 20 African countries. As of May 2009, France had signed agreements on joint-management flows and codevelopment with Senegal, Gabon, the Democratic Republic of Congo, Benin, Tunisia, Mauritius, Cape Verde, Burkina Faso, and Cameroon. France has made it a goal to sign seven agreements per year until 2011. The agreements address opportunities for legal migration, readmission of unauthorized immigrants, development, police cooperation, and border surveillance.

Spain has ratified similar agreements with Gambia, Guinea, and Mali. Article 8 of each agreement provides for mutual assistance in:

- Exchanging information between authorities on human trafficking and organized criminals
- Providing technical assistance to fight illegal immigration
- Training consular and immigration personnel of both countries, including special training for detecting false documents
- Cooperation to strengthen border controls
- Guaranteeing the security of national identification documents
- Capacity building in fighting illegal immigration and human trafficking
- Campaigns to inform the public about the risks of illegal immigration and human trafficking

Spain has also signed cooperation agreements with Peru, Guinea Bissau, and Niger. The agreement with Peru focuses on:

- Exchange of statistical information on migratory flows, and breaking up networks that fuel illegal migration, human trafficking, and fraudulent and stolen documents
- Exchange of information to help in investigations related to illegal immigration, human trafficking, and fraudulent and stolen documents
- Collaboration and information sharing among border and immigration officials in order to prevent illegal migration, fight human trafficking, and identify organizations that promote illegal activities

European mobility partnerships offer an example — that should be analyzed by Congress and the Department of Homeland Security (DHS) — of how to achieve a mutually beneficial way of securing human mobility channels between countries. French, Spanish, and EU agreements may also prove useful for addressing the conditions that foster illegal migration. Thus far they are too new to have had more than limited impact.[96]

US Leadership in International Mobility Security Relations

In looking ahead to the next phase of international efforts to secure human mobility, two steps are especially important: the coordination of foreign assistance to secure mobility and the establishment of international institutions that promote and develop strong border policies.

US Foreign Assistance for Border Management

The 9/11 attacks prompted the United States and other governments to increase their funding for mobility, travel-document, and border management. These increases came in addition to US activities — as well as those of travel and other affected industries — in fostering international agreements and organizations aimed at securing the movement of people. Unlike Canada and the United Kingdom, however, the United States has no dedicated, visible fund for foreign assistance relating to border management. Having a transparent source of funding or at least open accounting for international mobility assistance would be useful.

DHS agencies deliver a wide range of training and technical assistance, which takes the form of:

- Resident training in the United States
- Resident training at its four International Law Enforcement Academies (ILEAs)
- Deployable training delivered in country
- In-country technical assessments
- Short-term and long-term (in-country) advisory assistance
- Equipment and infrastructure support

DHS training and technical-assistance programs cover the full range of its competencies. It offers more than 150 courses of instruction and has tailored its training and technical-assistance packages to meet specific international customer and interagency needs, including in:

- Border patrolling and enforcement
- Checkpoint management
- Weapons of mass destruction (WMDs) detection
- Critical infrastructure protection
- Targeting and risk management
- Short-term and long-term border advisory assistance
- Fraudulent document detection
- Biometrics
- Maritime law enforcement
- Small-boat operations and maintenance
- Maritime assessments
- Short-term and long-term aviation advisory assistance
- Airport assessments
- Foreign-air-carrier security compliance
- Legislative infrastructure development

DHS has limited legislative authority and funding to sponsor international training and technical assistance. Nearly all of its work in this area is delivered on a reimbursable basis with funding provided by other US agencies, foreign governments, or international organizations. As a result, DHS's priorities are heavily influenced by its funding sources and their legislative authority and budgets, especially DOS and the Department of Defense (DOD). These funding agencies, often working through an interagency process, determine the countries that receive DHS assistance, the scope of the assistance provided, and its duration. Consequently, DHS mostly supports interagency initiatives.

In a typical year, DHS trainers and subject matter experts travel to more than 70 countries, with funding provided by more than 22 different interagency sources, including:

- International Maritime Education and Training (DOD)
- Foreign Military Sales (DOD)
- Export Control and Related Border Security (DOS)
- International Narcotics Law Enforcement (DOS)
- Antiterrorism Assistance (DOS)
- Section 1206 Defense Authorization Act (DOD)
- Section 1207 Defense Authorization Act (DOD/DOS)

Interagency and international requests for DHS training and technical assistance come through multiple entry points, including bureau training offices, working-group representatives, and regional offices. These requests are seldom coordinated across agencies. Depending on volume, DHS bureaus have to prioritize across unrelated programs, as they attempt to balance training demand with the availability of personnel resources. DHS agencies typically try to meet all interagency requests without regard to the relative standing of a particular program or country in their hierarchy of priorities. In addition to direct bilateral assistance, DHS, DOD, and DOS work through regional organizations like OSCE, ASEAN, and OAS.

Tracking all its international training and technical-assistance activities would enable DHS to make better decisions and spot successes and problems. Establishing such a database would be a good foundation for seeking expanded legislative authorities to support specific training and capacity-building efforts tied to mobility security goals.

One of the most visible US efforts is a program to provide border authorities with the ability to use an electronic watchlist. However, because this program requires dedicated computers and software, border authorities can have difficulty integrating it with other border systems that support immigration management and customs revenue collection.

For example, when mobility management software is provided from different sources — different governments, international organizations, or units within governments and international organizations — the recipient authorities need to be able to apply extra expertise, effort, and funds to integrate the various technologies and business processes. When developing countries do not have such resources, the latest technology upgrade may not be used optimally or at all.

World Borders Organization (WBO-BORDERPOL)
One way the United States can promote security in global mobility channels while pursuing a foreign policy committed to building international cooperation is to help establish an international organization dedicated to advancing mobility security. There is already a group of border officials advocating for the establishment of such an organization. WBO-BORDERPOL was chartered in 2003 in Ottawa, Canada, by border policing and immigration professionals as a nonprofit international association. BORDERPOL has observer and member border agencies from 11 countries[97] that advocate the establishment of a permanent, international organization to address

global borders issues. Governed by a BORDERPOL Exploratory Committee (BEXCOM), it is intended to support governments in moving toward founding a full-fledged international organization. As of February 2010, BEXCOM includes full-fledged representation or observers from 11 member countries. The organization has supported and convened annual meetings, during which senior representatives of border control and policing agencies of about 50 countries engaged in multilateral discussions and exchanges of views and experiences. This forum has formed ad hoc working groups which have explored various border security issues and published nonbinding reports.

There are a number of ways in which an intergovernmental WBO-BORDERPOL-type organization could be useful in making borders smarter and safer, drawing on the experiences and contributions of several existing organizations. For example, analogously to FATF, which is concerned with security in the global financial system and has 35 member (33 jurisdictions and 2 regional organizations), a world borders organization could develop and promote national and international policies to secure human mobility, act as a policymaking body, and publish recommendations to meet this objective. Supporting CTED, a world borders organization could propose and establish polices, standards, and recommended practices that are related to the movement of people across international borders, which are global in scope and are designed to bring a level of harmonization to world practices in border protection. Another purpose of such an organization would be to forge synergies and interrelationships with relevant specialized international, regional, and other organizations, from Interpol to APEC, the Caribbean Community (CARICOM), and IOM. Table 11.1 lists select major international organizations and private associations with complementary mandates to a WBO-BORDERPOL-type entity.

Table 11.1 Mandates of Select International Organizations Addressing Operational Mobility Security

International Criminal Police Organization (Interpol)	Facilitates cross-border police cooperation and supports and assists all organizations, authorities, and services whose mission is to prevent or combat international crime by, among other things, granting them access to its SLTD and other databases.
International Organization for Migration (IOM)	Helps ensure the orderly and humane management of migration, promote international cooperation on migration issues, assist in the search for practical solutions to migration problems, and provide humanitarian assistance to migrants in need, including refugees.
World Customs Organization (WCO)	Helps members communicate and cooperate on customs issues, develop agreed rules on customs procedures, and provide advice and assistance to customs services.
International Civil Aviation Organization (ICAO)	Works to achieve its vision of safe, secure, and sustainable development of civil aviation through cooperation among its member states and adopts standards, such as travel-document regulations, and recommended practices concerning air navigation.
United Nations Office on Drugs and Crime (UNODC)	Assists the United Nations in better addressing a coordinated, comprehensive response to the interrelated issues of illicit trafficking, abuse of drugs, crime prevention, criminal justice, and international terrorism.
International Air Transport Association (IATA)	Ensures that people and goods can move around the global airline network as easily as if they were on a single airline in a single country, and provides essential professional support to all industry stakeholders with a wide range of products and expert service.
European Police Office (Europol)	Improves the effectiveness and cooperation of the relevant authorities in EU Member States in preventing and combating terrorism, drug trafficking, and other serious forms of international organized crime.
European Agency for the Management of Operational Cooperation at the External Borders of the Member States of the European Union (Frontex)	Coordinates operational cooperation between EU Member States in the field of management of external borders; assists Member States in the training of national border guards, including the establishment of common training standards; and carries out risk analyses.
United Nations World Tourism Organization (UNWTO)	Promotes the development of responsible, sustainable, and universally accessible tourism and travel with an eye toward reducing poverty and helping developing countries achieve sustainable development.

Source: Migration Policy Institute.

Conclusion

Initiatives to address the forces that foster illegal movement and that undermine the rule of law in mobility channels are not well developed. Most of the international *talk* on migration in international and regional fora concerns labor and family movements. In contrast, considerably more *action* than dialogue or lawmaking characterizes mobility security programs internationally. Yet the largest *budgets* in international migration fund refugee protection and repatriation. Development assistance relating to mobility security and border control predominantly comes from counterterrorism, conflict-related, human trafficking, and other crime-control budgets. Clearly, it would be better if there were a balance among talk, action, and budgets, reflecting mobility security alliance priorities.

International discussion on mobility security is usually separate from that on labor migration, but European mobility partnerships break the mold. These experimental agreements include a mix of labor migration and security-related provisions and demonstrate a potential direction for the United States in its long-term dialogue with Mexico and other countries in the Western Hemisphere with high, uncontrolled emigration to the United States.

The United States, regional organizations, the United Nations, and other multilateral organizations have put considerable effort since 9/11 into constituting the rule of law in global mobility channels and supporting its implementation with foreign and technical assistance. These efforts serve: (1) to enable governments to implement UN travel bans; (2) to control mobility crimes that violate human rights pursuant to UN protocols concerning human trafficking and human smuggling; (3) to promote their own interests in safe, secure, and well-managed borders and countering terrorist mobility; and (4) to advance the individual's interest in pursuing the opportunities arising from globalization.

Mobility security diplomacy offers opportunities for strengthening civil security alliances, including by addressing development imperatives. This field should continue to be resourced and to be developed in an organized manner. A useful next step for the United States would be to take the lead in the establishment of a new WBO-BORDERPOL-like international organization of border and immigration professionals who can help the international community: (1) develop standards for port-of-entry and border management,

(2) conduct mutual assessments that advance their implementation, (3) share best practices, and (4) reinforce ICAO's travel-document standards. The United States, Canada, the European Union, and other wealthy governments should provide more foreign and technical assistance to developing countries to develop border and mobility-management capabilities.

To do so effectively, better coordination and new funding vehicles among leading and donor countries is necessary. Since the United States and European Union have fundamentally similar concerns but sometimes distinctly different approaches to border control, there is a risk of redundancy and even conflicting approaches. The United States should also work with other countries to strengthen the ability of the United Nations to support efforts against terrorist travel and transnational criminal movement. Mobility- and border-related assistance for counterterrorism, crime control, migration management, good governance, and revenue collection have different emphases and require the involvement of different agencies and resources.

It may seem like a futile undertaking to tackle global border controls given the number of cross-border conflicts and the degree of corruption in mobility-related agencies. But in fact improvements have been made through concerted efforts. Dedicating additional and better-coordinated resources to develop the law and appropriate governance structures in global mobility channels will reinforce the bilateral and regional mobility security agreements discussed in chapter 10. It will build a more solid foundation for the necessary bilateral, regional, and multilateral discussions aimed at precluding high levels of illegal migration and catastrophic displacements of people. Strengthening the legal underpinning and the governance of mobility security are critical dimensions of civil security. Without progress in this area, labor mobility and freedom of movement cannot be expanded.

CHAPTER 12: MANAGING BORDERS WITH OUR NEIGHBORS

Policy Preview: *A more strategic approach needs to be taken to the US-Canada mobility security relationship. It should be seen as one element of a civil security (homeland security) alliance, parallel to the US-Canada Basic Defense Agreement and North American Aerospace Defense Command (NORAD). The purpose of a civil security alliance is to preclude catastrophic harm to people on both sides of the border. As an element of a civil security alliance, a strategic mobility security partnership should be formalized that would incorporate such elements as: (1) regular joint threat and risk assessments, (2) deeper mutual assistance, (3) a transatlantic privacy and data-protection framework, (4) a one-stop preclearance system, (5) aligned admission standards, and (6) integrated surveillance and security operations in the border zone. SBInet should be reexamined and aligned with these goals. In any event, SBInet should not be employed at the northern border until proven at the southern border.*

This final chapter addresses securing the movement of people across the United States' shared boundaries with Mexico and Canada, with detailed attention to the US-Canada mobility security relationship. Of the more than 40 million trips abroad made by US citizens by air in 2008, nearly 24 percent (9.5 million) were either to Canada (3.6 million) or to Mexico (5.9 million).[98] In total, 20.3 million US travelers went to Mexico in 2008, while 12.5 million US travelers visited Canada.[99] Every day, approximately 300,000 people cross the US-Canada border[100] and 1 million cross the US-Mexico border.[101] Roughly 25 million people or 75 percent of Canadians live within 100 miles of the US-Canada border.[102] Thirty million people, or 95 percent of the Canadian population, live in a province that borders the United States,[103] and 72 million people living in the United States (24 percent of the US population) live in states that border Canada.[104] More than 75 million border crossings take place across the US-Canada border each year at 86 US ports of entry.[105] Between 1999 and 2008, an average of 248 million border crossings occurred annually at 26 US ports of entry on the US-Mexico border.[106]

Mobility security relations with Canada and Mexico have a special importance because of both countries' proximity to the United States and the volume of movement across US borders. In addition, the US public's confidence and resilience depend on a belief that the security relationships with its closest neighbors are well managed. The same holds true for Canadian and Mexican citizens. That confidence would be sorely tested in the wake of a terrorist event linked to conspirators with a nexus in Canada, Mexico, or the United States. There would be little public tolerance for perceived errors associated with such events. The US, Canadian, and Mexican publics would ask why protective measures that could have prevented an attack had not been adopted years before. More than likely, the security gap would be the result of some failed reform that had been left on the table and that would seem quite easy to resolve in retrospect. While the problem of not pursuing certain measures is a perennial aspect of risk management — since threats, hazards, and failures are so unpredictable, and vulnerabilities to them so pervasive — the public assumes that security relations with Canada and Mexico are receiving priority attention as a matter of course.

This is especially true for Canada, with which the United States has a military and unique nuclear defense alliance, a common constitutional and cultural heritage, and a comparable tradition of immigration. Moreover, extensive media coverage in both countries regarding border management has raised public expectations. Yet, discussions with Canada on several key mobility security issues have stalled since 2002. This impasse is consistent with the relative lack of attention and resources dedicated to US relationships with Canada (and Mexico) in comparison to that given to wars aimed at defeating and constraining al Qaeda overseas. In addition, because of the war against drug-trafficking organizations (DTOs) and the volume of illegal movement over the southwest border, the US relationship with Canada has received less attention than that with Mexico. Both deserve significantly more attention.

Differences in security priorities relating to mobility are not a problem with respect to Canada. As discussed in the introduction to section II, terrorist movement with chemical, biological, radiological, nuclear, or high yield explosive (CBRNE) weapons is the top US mobility-related security concern. Canada's intelligence service, too, has identified terrorism as the nation's greatest security threat. Powerful and violent transnational criminal organizations, such as the Mexican DTOs, human-trafficking organizations (HTOs), and violent gangs, are the next highest concern for the United States. For Mexico (and Central America), such organizations pose the greatest security threat.

Because al Qaeda-related terrorism has had a closer connection with Canada than with Mexico (notwithstanding US concerns of potential terrorist entry from Mexico or through the Caribbean), this chapter primarily addresses securing the flow of people between Canada and the United States. The discussion seeks to place the US mobility-related relationship with Canada (and with Mexico) into a homeland security framework. Thus far, analysis of border security issues has tended to focus on the problems that enhanced US border security policies have created for the free flow of people and goods between the two countries. Analysts often propose measures to facilitate these flows, to integrate markets, or to respond to borderland needs. They do not usually address the specific reasons for lack of progress on particular security issues, their importance, and how to break logjams.

To focus primarily on homeland security is *not* to assert that managing security risks is *more* important than protecting market economies and borderland communities. The two frameworks complement each other, but security merits careful, independent attention. Progress in denying terrorist access through a bilateral homeland security alliance would enhance bilateral commerce. This latter point is frequently made by Canadian commentators. Canada's border security and counterterrorism strategies are intelligence based. For the Canada-US border, Canada has advocated an approach that combines low-risk identification and expedited clearance with high-risk identification and interdiction.

Binational Movement of Terrorists and Criminals

Between 1999 and 2008, Canada admitted an average of 235,215 new permanent immigrants every year, including 247,243 in 2008[107] (see figure 12.1), whereas the United States on average admitted 981,340, including over 1.1 million in FY2008.[108] The United States also recorded approximately 32.7 million temporary (nonimmigrant) admissions during the same period, including 39.4 million admissions in FY2008.[109]

Figure 12.1 Total Permanent and Temporary Migration to Canada, 1984–2008

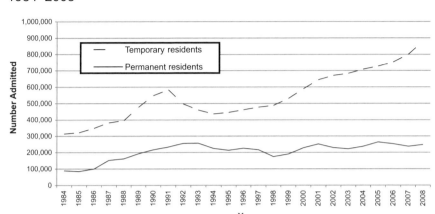

Source: Citizenship and Immigration Canada, "Facts and Figures 2008 — Immigration Overview: Permanent and Temporary Residents," August 25, 2009, www.cic.gc.ca/EnGLIsh/resources/statistics/facts2008/permanent/01.asp.

According to the 2006 census, Canada's permanent immigrant population numbered almost 6.2 million or 19.8 percent of the population.[110] As of 2006, the largest immigrant groups residing in Canada were from the United Kingdom (579,620), China (466,940), India (443,690), the Philippines (303,195), and Italy (296,850). The groups respectively made up 9.4 percent, 7.5 percent, 7.2 percent, 4.9 percent, and 4.8 percent of the total immigrant population.[111] Immigration from Pakistan comprised 6.2 percent of all permanent immigration flows to Canada in 2001, but its share declined to 3.3 percent in 2008.[112] The Canadian census lists an individual's last permanent or temporary residence as his place of origin, so, for example, the vast majority of the immigrants identified as being from the United Kingdom are migrants from South Asia.

Canada also faces significant illegal migration challenges. Smuggling organizations move roughly 10,000 people into Canada annually. Many are Chinese and Vietnamese who transit through Thailand, acquiring forged travel documents to use in entering Canada.[113] Recently, there has been an increase in migration of Indians using forged travel documents. Canadian officials have also noted increasing levels of unauthorized immigration from Mexico, especially since Mexican airlines began offering direct flights to Canada and the escalation of the drug wars in Mexico.[114] This situation has been exacerbated by a provision of the Canada-US Safe Third Country Agreement of 2002, which creates exceptions for certain asylum seekers from the requirement that they seek asylum in the first of the two countries that they reach. Canada in 2009 decided to impose a visa requirement on Mexican visitors to limit a spike in the number of Mexican asylum seekers entering Canada from the United States.

While the vast majority of immigrants and travelers to Canada (as to the United States) do not pose a security threat to people in Canada, the United States, or elsewhere, a small number do.

Canada is itself vulnerable to transnational terrorism. The Canadian Security Intelligence Service (CSIS) has reported that there are more representatives of international terrorist organizations operating in Canada than in any other country in the world, with the possible exception of the United States.[115] Canada's first major terrorist event, the 1985 bombing by Sikh militants of Air India flight 182 originating from Montreal's Mirabel airport, took the lives of 270 Canadians. Twenty-four Canadians were killed in the attacks on the World Trade Center (WTC) on 9/11. At least three al Qaeda propaganda releases since 2002 have explicitly threatened Canada and its oil industry. CSIS identifies the terrorist threat as "a real threat to the safety and security of Canadians" and as its operational priority for the foreseeable future.[116] In March 2009 an Islamist extremist, Momin Khawaja, was convicted of financing and facilitating terrorism and building explosive detonators for use in terrorist attacks targeting the United Kingdom.[117]

Counterterrorism raids in Toronto in 2006 led to the arrest of 18 members of an Islamist terrorist cell who were allegedly plotting to blow up several landmarks and to storm Parliament to kill the prime minister.[118]

Stating that "Canada has individuals who support the use of violence to achieve political goals," CSIS lists terrorist activities in Canada as including: "planning or helping to plan terrorist attacks in Canada or abroad; providing a Canadian base for terrorist supporters; fundraising; lobbying through front organizations; obtaining weapons and materials; and coercing and interfering with immigrant communities."[119] The Liberation Tigers of Tamil Eelam (LTTE) in Sri Lanka actively recruited and raised funds in Canadian immigrant communities until the end of the Sri Lankan civil war in 2009.[120] Canadian residents include persons who have attended terrorist training camps and are veterans of campaigns in Afghanistan, Bosnia, and Chechnya, as well as persons with insurgency combat experience in Iraq.

A much larger number of people seeking to enter the United States from Canada than from Mexico have been prevented from doing so as a result of hits on the US terrorist watchlist,[121] leading government officials to maintain that the threat from violent extremists in Canada outweighs the threat from Mexico.[122]

Terrorists have plotted in Canada against sites in the United States and US targets outside the country. In addition, several terrorists (albeit not the 9/11 terrorists, despite a popular misconception) have entered the United States from Canada. The leader of the 1993 WTC bombing, the blind cleric Omar Abdul Rahman, traveled to and from Canada for fundraising and recruitment. The Palestinian associated with the 1997 New York subway plot, Abu Mezer, entered the United States several times from Canada, before moving to the United States. The most well-known case is that of the would-be millennium bomber, Ahmed Ressam, who boarded a ferry from British Columbia with explosives hidden in his car to attack the Los Angeles International Airport.

In 2003 Canadian Abdel Rahman Jabarah bombed a residential area in Riyadh while his brother Mohammed Jabarah attempted to attack the US embassies in Singapore and Manila.[123] As a result of their alleged activity against US forces in Afghanistan, Omar Khadr is in US custody at Guantánamo Naval Base and his brother Abdullah is in Canadian custody pending extradition to the United States. One of the two men accused of planning an attack on a Danish newspaper that published cartoons offensive to many Muslims is a Canadian citizen who lived legally in Chicago, where he operated a travel agency and other businesses.[124]

Cross-border organized crime — human trafficking, firearms smuggling (in 2007, the Canada Border Services Agency [CBSA] seized 662 firearms at the border[125]), and transportation of illegal drugs and contraband — remains a significant problem. The Canadian government reports high levels of cigarette trafficking into its country from the United States. Illegal cigarette sales are funding the activities of organized criminal groups.[126] Such illicit activities fuel violence, undermine US and Canadian law, deplete federal and provincial tax revenues, and create unfair competition for legitimate Canadian businesses.

The Close US-Canada Strategic Security Relationship

Since the 1930s, the United States and Canada have cooperated with each other to facilitate and promote cross-border ties.[127] There are approximately 140 border-crossing points along the 5,525-mile US-Canada border, including 50 or so small country roads and paths through uncleared forests and hundreds of unmanned roads and paths.[128] In 2006 more than 30 million Americans and Canadians[129] — a total of 70 million travelers[130] and 35 million vehicles[131] — crossed the border.

The cross-border traffic of capital, goods, and people has brought major economic benefits to both countries. The Canada-US Free Trade Agreement (CUSFTA) of 1989[132] and the subsequent North American Free Trade Agreement (NAFTA) of 1994 have expanded cross-border commerce between the United States and Canada, which is the United States' largest trading partner. While most bilateral trade flows visibly across the border, more than 10 percent of it passes through pipelines and electrical transmission grids, which US and Canadian electric power companies have integrated.[133]

The trade agreements followed in the path of the deep security relationship that the United States and Canada have forged for over more than half a century. These bonds now encompass aspects of homeland defense and security, criminal investigations, and immigration policy. The International Boundary, as it is officially known, is the world's longest common border unprotected by military forces.

In 1958 the United States and Canada established what was then called the North American Air Defense Command in Colorado Springs in an effort to centralize operational control of continental air defense against military threats from the Soviet Union. Since then, the two countries have jointly strategized, monitored, coordinated, and conducted operations under what is now known as the North American Aerospace Defense Command (NORAD), a binational command formalized in the NORAD Agreement and the US-Canada Basic Defense Document. NORAD provides aerospace warning, aerospace control, and maritime warning for North America.[134]

Following the 9/11 attacks, the two nations, through NORAD, launched Operation Noble Eagle, which supplies airspace surveillance; a ready alert force; and an air defense system in the Washington, DC, area.[135] Noble Eagle includes air patrols of cities, military locations, and other critical-infrastructure locations by the National Guard and Reserve troops, as well as the Canadian Forces Air Force. By March 2009 Noble Eagle had flown more than 50,000 sorties, 70 percent of which were conducted by the Air National Guard.[136]

The NORAD agreement has been renewed ten times, mostly recently in May 2006, when a maritime component was added to its mandate. Armed fighters are on constant standby to patrol, identify, and intercept suspect aircrafts. In 2008 jet fighters responded to more than 200 incidents.[137]

The United States established the US Northern Command (NORTHCOM) in 2002 to provide command and control of the Department of Defense's (DOD's) homeland defense efforts and to coordinate defense support to civilian authorities.[138] NORTHCOM's Joint Task Force North (JTF-North) coordinates and manages military homeland security support to law-enforcement authorities "for the interdiction of suspected transnational threats within and along the approaches to the continental United States."[139] Operation Winter Freeze, for example, was a three-month operation in 2005 that brought the Army and Air Guard together with JTF-North to provide support to the Border Patrol in interdicting individuals seeking to enter the United States illegally along a 295-mile segment of the US-Canadian border.[140]

NORTHCOM and NORAD are two separate commands with an integrated headquarters under the command of a single general. NORTHCOM and Canada Command,[141] however, remain separate. JTF-North collaborates with a variety of US-Canada joint working structures, including Canadian law-enforcement and military agencies, their US counterparts, and the US-Canada Integrated Border Enforcement Teams (IBETs). IBETs, which consist of joint Border Patrol and Royal Canadian Mounted Police (RCMP) units, were instituted in the 1990s and have expanded dramatically since 9/11. The IBETs operate between designated ports of entry, identifying, investigating and interdicting persons, organizations, and goods that threaten the security of one or of both countries, or that are involved in organized criminal activity.[142] NORAD has undertaken a review of the requirements for northern (Arctic region) air operations and for Noble Eagle. US authorities continue to consider how NORTHCOM, NORAD, and Canada Command should interact, relate, and cooperate with one another. The three commands are jointly developing plans to provide a strategic framework for the bilateral defense and security of the United States and Canada. The evolution of the US-Canada strategic military relationship has been complicated by Canadian opposition to a US-proposed missile shield, as well as lack of an agreement about defense in the Arctic region as polar melting opens it up to traffic and resource exploitation.

The Canadian and US militaries also operate jointly through the North Atlantic Treaty Organization (NATO). The two governments' intelligence services share intelligence through a longstanding agreement among the United Kingdom, Canada, Australia, New Zealand, and the United States.

The Canada-US Civil Assistance Plan (CAP) of 2008 between NORTHCOM and Canada Command is a framework that allows both militaries to support each other during civil support operations, such as during floods, forest fires, hurricanes, earthquakes, and terrorist attacks. CAP was first used during the 2008 hurricane season when a Canadian airplane and medical crew assisted in the evacuation of medical patients from Louisiana.

CAP builds on an over-20-year history of formal cooperation by civil authorities during homeland security emergencies. In December 2008 the two countries renewed the Emergency Management Cooperation Agreement of 1986, continuing mutual assistance in providing supplies, equipment, emergency personnel, and professional and expert support through integrated response and relief efforts during cross-border emergency situations.[143] The 2003 electricity blackout in the northeastern and midwestern regions of the United States and the province of Ontario illustrates how interlinked cross-border homeland security emergencies can be.

The US-Canada Relationship with Regard to Securing the Movement of People

Since 9/11, Canada and the United States have not worked to secure mobility as productively and cooperatively as their long history of cooperation and their common interests would suggest that they should. The primary instinct of the United States after 9/11 was to tighten the common border. Canada's primary instinct was to take independent steps deemed sufficiently reassuring to the United States to preserve the open cross-border flow of people and commerce. Since 9/11 the two countries have issued a string of declarations, and agencies have individually entered into various memoranda of understanding, but no full-fledged mobility security or larger homeland security agreement has emerged that compares with the existing military alliance. More limited bilateral agreements such as the Smart Border Accord, Safe Third Country Agreement, Security Prosperity Partnership, and the Western Hemisphere Travel Initiative Document Compliance have been entered.

In May 2009 the two governments initiated what will be twice-yearly meetings by their respective cabinet officials responsible for civil security, the US homeland security secretary and the minister of public safety Canada. This bilateral dialogue takes place under the shadow cast by a persistent sense that the demands of security and economics conflict — in other words, that either security or the market must be paramount in border discussions, and that the United States and Canada have chosen opposite sides of the coin. For both countries to meet the full spectrum of their security needs, this idea must be replaced by one that more closely reflects the need for shared responsibility, institutional development, and respect for national frameworks.[144] This section explores how such a transformation might be accomplished, taking a realistic look at the current status of the relationship and the foundations on which progress can be made.

Unilateral Security Steps Taken by Canada and the United States

Most major post-9/11 assessments, decisions, programs, and expenditures involving securing the cross-border movement of people have been unilateral. Canada and the United States have each taken myriad independent actions to build stronger security measures into their immigration, border, and related intelligence and law-enforcement programs.

Canada has taken many steps to improve its counterterrorism and homeland security efforts as they relate to the cross-border movement of people. In particular, Canada:

- undertook a major reform to prevent the exploitation of its birth-certificate system by terrorists such as Ahmed Ressam
- fast-tracked fraud-resistant tamper-proof permanent residence cards
- established the Public Safety Canada ministry
- created the Canada Border Services Agency with armed personnel
- improved screening of immigrants, refugee claimants, and visitors
- imposed additional documentation requirements on applicants

- expanded government authority to use secret evidence to arrest and detain foreign nationals
- increased Customs, Immigration, and RCMP staffing; deployed more intelligence officers; and put undercover officers on aircrafts
- placed new explosive-detection systems at airports
- upgraded its border technology and enhanced infrastructure and emergency preparedness

The United States:
- significantly tightened its visa process and nonvisa travel program, adding the Electronic System of Travel Authorization (ESTA)
- established the Department of Homeland Security (DHS) and NORTHCOM
- instituted the United States Visitor and Immigrant Status Indicator Technology (US-VISIT) fingerprint program to check backgrounds of all foreign visa applicants, visitors, and lawful permanent residents (LPRs) against terrorist and criminal records
- instituted passenger targeting, using automated analysis of passenger information to detect risks through the US Customs and Border Protection (CBP) National Targeting Center
- increased CBP funding from $6 billion in FY2004 to $10.1 billion in FY2009,[145] mostly attributable to the Secure Borders Initiative (SBI), which seeks to double the size of the Border Patrol and to enhance both physical and virtual fencing (SBInet) at the border between ports of entry
- increased the number of Border Patrol agents along the US-Canada border from 340 before 9/11 to 1,798 in FY2009[146]
- required US and Canadian citizens to present identification establishing citizenship status when entering the United States, as per the Western Hemisphere Travel Initiative (WHTI)

US and Canadian unilateral efforts to further secure the lawful flow of people continue. Canada has announced a timeline to initiate its own fingerprint program to verify the identity of visa holders at ports of entry by 2013. It has also announced its commitment to reform its refugee program with the goal of making exploitation of the system more difficult. The United States is moving forward with the multi-billion-dollar SBInet program to build a virtual fence along its southern and northern borders. Millions of dollars of economic stimulus funding will be used to increase technology and improve infrastructure at ports of entry along the US-Canada border.[147]

The Status of a Joint Strategy to Secure the Cross-Border Flow of People

Although the major post-9/11 mobility-related security initiatives — birth certificate and refugee policy reform on the Canadian side, and US-VISIT, WHTI, SBInet, and ESTA on the US side — remain almost entirely unilateral, the two countries have made efforts to work together in the following areas:

- Terrorist-watchlist-related intelligence sharing
- Threat assessment
- Traveler-related biographic and biometric information sharing
- Risk assessment
- Security-related aspects of temporary visa policy
- Security-related aspects of refugee policy
- Traveler identity management
- Use of biometrics
- Standards for registered-traveler programs
- Border facilities, equipment, and technology
- Port-of-entry screening processes
- Preclearance for border crossers
- Land and maritime investigations and patrol
- The cross-border movement of people and goods during and after emergencies

The first of a series of joint declarations came on December 12, 2001, when the two nations signed the US-Canada Smart Border Declaration, building on previous agreements such as the 1995 Shared Accord on Our Border, the 1997 Border Vision, the 1997 Cross-Border Crime Forum, and the 1999 Canada-US Partnership Process.[148] The Smart Border Declaration included four thematic categories: securing the flow of people, securing infrastructure, securing the flow of goods, and coordinating and sharing information. The Smart Border Declaration's Action Plan for Creating a Secure and Smart Border identified the need to:

- Share lookout lists at visa-issuing offices
- Share information on refugees and asylum seekers, and Passenger Name Record (PNR) and Advance Passenger Information (API)
- Build compatible immigration databases in order to facilitate information sharing[149]

- Coordinate visa-free travel lists
- Negotiate a safe third-country agreement for refugees and asylum seekers
- Develop or improve biometric identifiers in permanent resident cards for NEXUS (a registered traveler system) and other travel documents
- Expand air preclearance programs
- Establish joint passenger analysis units at key US and Canadian international airports

The same month in which the two countries signed the Smart Border Declaration, the United States and Canada also issued a Joint Statement on Cooperation on Border Security and Regional Migration Issues. This agreement included commitments to review temporary visa policy, promote the development of common biometric document identifiers and standards, include Canadians in the FBI's Foreign Terrorist Tracking Task Force, expand the cross-border investigative IBETs, and increase the number of immigration officers overseas.[150]

These commitments have been echoed in subsequent joint statements by the United States, Mexico, and Canada. A report issued by the three governments acting through the Security and Prosperity Partnership (SPP) on March 23, 2005, reiterated the need to share watchlists and traveler information, establish risk-based screening standards, and facilitate cross-border travel by developing standards for secure travel documents.[151] In the North American Leader's Summit of August 2007, the leaders of the three countries named "smart and secure borders" one of the SPP's top priorities. In the North American Leaders' Summit in August 2009, the three governments stated that they were "investing in border infrastructure, including advanced technology, to create truly modern borders."[152] Their statement also called for reducing regulatory differences and for developing focused priorities and a specific timeline.

In May 2009 Homeland Security Secretary Janet Napolitano and Public Safety Canada Minister Peter Van Loan announced a Framework for the Movement of People and Goods across the border during and following an emergency.[153] This framework seeks to ensure that first responders will not be delayed at the border when emergency assistance is needed in either country, and that if the border closes for whatever reason, it will return to normal operations as quickly as possible.

Also in 2009 Canada, New Zealand, Australia, the United Kingdom, and the United States, which comprise the Five Country Conference (5CC), entered into a new agreement to share selected administrative information about travelers. Border and immigration services will be able to cross-check biographic and biometric records for refugee claimants and asylum seekers as a means of reducing risk and maintaining the integrity of their respective immigration systems.

Organizational Collaboration for Mobility Security

This hodge-podge of overlapping declarations is not without substance or ambition. Canada and the United States initiated three of the most important collaborative programs — airport preclearance, law-enforcement IBETs, and the joint registered-traveler program (NEXUS, at ports of entry) — before 9/11. In 2009 the two nations added to these initiatives two binational law-enforcement teams: the Integrated Maritime Security Operation (IMSO or Operation Shiprider) and the Border Enforcement Security Team (BEST).

Airport Preclearance
Under the US airport preclearance program, CBP officers at select overseas airports and ports conduct checks on travel documents, customs, and agricultural inspections for individuals seeking to enter the United States.[154] Precleared passengers arrive at a domestic terminal in the United States and exit the airport without further immigration checks.[155] The preclearance or preflight inspection program began in 1952 as a service for which the airlines paid the US government in order to relieve pressure from a growing number of passengers at certain US airports. Preclearance programs are now seen both as a way to increase efficiency in screening and to reduce risk by placing inspection outside national borders. Airport preclearance has not been extended to airports beyond Canada and a handful of other countries. Airport authorities in departing countries view preclearance as a hindrance to profits gained from passenger preflight shopping. Expansion of preclearance to land borders is a possibility, discussed below.

The Integrated Border Enforcement Teams (IBETs)
IBETs began as a pilot program in 1996, in northwest Washington and British Columbia, targeting cross-border organized crime between ports of entry.[156] Today IBETs investigate national-security risks, criminal smuggling of contraband and cash, human trafficking and smuggling, and immigration violations between ports of entry.[157] While part of an integrated program

involving joint investigations and shared intelligence, IBET agents remain attached to their own organizations. The program grew from two people to 20 prior to 9/11. As of January 2009, there were 15 IBET regions with IBET staff in 24 locations across the northern border.[158] As the first integrated US-Canada effort devoted to mobility security, IBETs merit more detailed attention.[159]

IBETs consist of five key agencies: RCMP, CBSA, CBP Office of Border Patrol, the US Immigration and Customs Enforcement (ICE), and the US Coast Guard (USCG). Canada does not have a border patrol but is considering establishing a mobile-border interdiction capability. An International Joint Management Team (IJMT) oversees a National Coordination Team (NCT), which supports the operational IBETs. Each IBET unit includes a Joint Management Team (JMT) responsible for operations. Joint Intelligence Groups (JIGs) fuse intelligence of member agencies. The IJMT initiates new activities and guides and promotes program policy. It meets four times a year with an annually rotating chair and representatives from each of the five member agencies. NCT has an office in Ottawa and a regular staff from the five participating agencies, and is responsible for the day-to-day administration of the 24 different IBET locations. The NCT fixes systemic problems, allocates budgets, and upholds common standards. Joint training sessions reinforce IBET's integration. The operational IBET agencies coordinate the involvement of local, state, and provincial authorities.

Registered Traveler Programs

The two governments have also worked to set security standards for participation in a program to expedite the movement of frequent border crossers. The NEXUS program allows registered travelers who have been prevetted to use dedicated, fast-track lanes at air, land, and marine ports of entry.[160] NEXUS cards with radio-frequency identification (RFID) tags have become an essential item for commuters and weekend visitors. NEXUS participants receive a biometric RFID card that facilitates smoother passage through ports of entry. A similar prescreening program has been implemented for cargo screening —the Free and Secure Trade for Commerce (FAST) program.

CBP has recently initiated the Global Entry program, which is intended to incorporate the different registered-traveler programs operating at different US ports of entry and to create a global standard that will permit reciprocal facilitated entry among numerous countries (see chapter 10).

NEXUS is an underused tool; like Global Entry, it is burdensome to join.[161] As of January 2009, NEXUS had 265,000 members, while Global Entry had 27,000 members who made 100,000 admissions through Global Entry as of November 2009.[162] The anticipated evolution from a standalone NEXUS program to standardization with Global Entry provides an opportunity for CBP and CBSA to determine and to address why more commuters and regular travelers are not joining these programs. Most importantly, it provides an impetus for Canada and the United States to design a roadmap for an interoperable registered-traveler system that also works with EU countries and other close partners. Ideally, such a system would ultimately become more global in scope.

Integrated Maritime Security Operation (IMSO)

In recent years, the United States and Canada have taken the IBETs concept a step further by incorporating joint operations in the maritime environment. A 2007 memorandum of understanding established the IMSO, more commonly known as Operation Shiprider. The US homeland security secretary and Public Safety Canada's minister formalized the agreement in May 2009. IMSO cross-designates USCG and Canadian officials to operate on each other's vessels under the supervision of the national authority for the boat. For example, USCG cross-designates RCMP officials as Coast Guard officers and RCMP cross-designates USCG officers as Supernumerary Special Constables. Twenty-five officers from each country have been trained at the USCG Maritime Law Enforcement Academy under a curriculum developed jointly by RCMP, USCG, and ICE. Upon graduation from the academy, officers are designated to serve as liaison officers with the other country. CBSA does not participate in the program for reasons that remain unclear. Legislation is pending in Canada to formalize Operation Shiprider.

The Shiprider mission is to patrol the shared maritime border in the Great Lakes and along the coextensive Pacific coastline. RCMP, CBP, and USCG are deploying automated, real-time communications marine radar surveillance technology to enhance interdiction capacity, including on a joint operational basis. Once designated, RCMP has the lead in Canadian waters with USCG providing support as directed, and vice versa in US waters. Thus, boaters of both countries may be stopped by officers from either country. The program's objective is to address cross-border crime in locations other than official ports of entry. Shiprider effectively removes the border as a jurisdictional obstacle for law enforcement that may be exploited by terrorists or criminals. Initial observations suggest that the joint patrols may have had a deterrent effect, pushing some criminal activity ashore.

Border Enforcement Security Team (BEST)

BEST is based on a strike-force concept to provide for law-enforcement collaboration at ports of entry. Already in effect on the Mexican border, BEST task forces as of fall 2009 had been established in two northern border locations, Blaine and Detroit. BEST task forces incorporate RCMP and CBSA personnel from Canada; ICE, CBP, and USCG personnel from the United States; and other federal, state, and local law-enforcement agencies. BEST operates similarly to Shiprider in that it cross-designates Canadian law enforcement to carry weapons and make arrest under ICE authorities in the United States at ports of entry.[163] By contrast, US law-enforcement officials may not carry firearms in Canada.

Western Hemisphere Travel Initiative

The US and Canadian governments have supported borderland states and provinces in developing mutually accepted Enhanced Driver's Licenses (EDLs) with RFID and citizenship information features for use at ports of entry.

Other Mobility Security Collaboration and Cooperation Efforts

In other arenas critical to mobility security, the United States and Canada are moving toward fully effective collaboration, but do not yet have an organizational partnership or close policy congruity. These arenas are intelligence sharing, threat and risk assessment, refugee programs, visa-free travel policy, and identity management.

Intelligence Sharing

Intelligence sharing is a bedrock element of the US-Canada security relationship. A memorandum of understanding between the two countries to share terrorist biographic information predates 9/11, but was reaffirmed and expanded after the terrorist attacks. Through their participation in the 5CC, Canada and the United States also share intelligence with the United Kingdom, Australia, and New Zealand. The case of Maher Arar, viewed as a possible terrorist by the United States but later exonerated by Canada, exposed obstacles to intelligence sharing arising from differences in how law-enforcement information is managed and how data security and privacy are maintained. The decision by US authorities to reject Arar's request to return to Canada, where he was a citizen, and instead to send him to Syria, where was tortured, has been a significant barrier to intelligence sharing for Canadian policymakers. This case speaks as much to the lack of an adequate framework for operational cooperation in counterterrorism investigations as it does to the need for more comprehensive information sharing.

Threat and Risk Assessment

At their summit in May 2009, DHS and Public Safety Canada leaders declared an intention to develop joint threat and risk assessments. A common understanding of threats and risks would provide a foundation for deeper strategic integration on security issues.[164]

Refugee Admissions

Canada and the United States have had moderate success in addressing standards for refugee admissions. The issue is twofold. First, lesser scrutiny or weaker precautionary procedures in refugee admissions by one country would subject the other to greater risk. Second, a more narrowly interpreted set of refugee rights by one country would potentially pressure the other to dilute its standards. While these standards are converging, differences in enforcement practice remain significant, especially with respect to older cases. The Canadian standards for refugee status are broader than those typically adopted by countries that base their decisions on a strict interpretation of a so-called "convention refugee." For example, while most countries offer temporary protection status to noncombatants involved in civil wars, Canada offers such individuals full refugee status, leading to permanent status. In addition, individuals who enter Canada as tourists or in other visa categories may make "inland claims" to refugee status, even when they are coming from Western democracies such as France, as Ahmed Ressam, the would-be millennium bomber, did. By contrast, in the United States, the Department of State (DOS) generally makes refugee determinations outside the United States, while DHS and the immigration courts consider political asylum claims in the United States.

In addition, persons denied refugee status in Canada have many subsequent opportunities to appeal their rejection. By contrast, persons without proper documents who request asylum or express a fear of return at a US border undergo an expedited review process involving an interview with an asylum officer. Unless the officer finds that the asylum seeker possesses a "credible fear" of persecution, the person is deported. This has led to criticisms that the United States is denying legitimate applicants, while in Canada backlogs of tens of thousands of cases have led to concerns over the exploitation of the system by applicants. Finally, Canada generally expects refugee applicants to appear at their hearings and to leave voluntarily if they are so ordered. Canada has lawful authority to detain refugee claimants and persons deemed inadmissible before a final determination, but this occurs only rarely. More commonly, claimants receive a temporary residence permit. By contrast, US immigration laws mandate detention in such cases.

As discussed, the US-Canada Safe Third Country Agreement of 2002 requires the two nations to cooperate in managing the flow of asylum seekers at common land-border crossings. In particular, migrants must apply for asylum in the country in which they first arrive unless they are exempt from this provision. Canada has four categories of exemptions: family members of Canadian citizens or permanent residents, unaccompanied minors, holders of certain Canadian documents, and public-interest cases. Exceptions include persons from countries from which travelers may enter Canada without a visa. Until 2009 the latter group of countries included Mexico. Public-interest exceptions include those who have been charged or convicted with a crime that could result in the death penalty, and people from Afghanistan, Burundi, the Democratic Republic of Congo, Haiti, Iraq, Liberia, Rwanda, or Zimbabwe.[165] The United States does not adhere to these exemption policies. It is as yet unclear to what degree Canadian reforms will further align the two national policies.

Visa-Free Travel Policy

Canada and the United States have waived visa requirements for citizens from different sets of countries (see chapter 9). In other words, they disagree over some of the countries whose nationals they believe can safely cross the perimeter of North America without a visa. Their lists of visa-waiver countries are not being harmonized. For example, Canada has recently cancelled nonvisa status from two countries — the Czech Republic, due to a spiking number of Roma refugee applicants, and Mexico, due to unexpectedly high numbers of refugee applicants. The United States requires visas from Mexico but not from the Czech Republic.

Travel Documents and Identity Management

The two countries have not agreed on a standard method for establishing personal identity in crossing the border. Pursuant to the Intelligence Reform and Terrorism Prevention Act, DHS instituted stricter standards for identification at the border through WHTI. The program requires all travelers (including US citizens) entering the United States from Mexico, Canada, Panama, Bermuda, and the Caribbean to present a passport or other secure document. Permissible documents include a passport, passport card, registered traveler card (NEXUS, FAST, or Secure Electronic Network for Rapid Inspection [SENTRI]), or an EDL. Children under the age of 16 are exempt from the WHTI requirements if they present a birth certificate or other proof of citizenship at the border. Canada and the United States have agreed to accept EDLs issued by the border states of New York, Vermont, Michigan, Washington, and the provinces of Ontario and British Columbia,[166] with additional Canadian provinces planning to issue them.[167]

Land Preclearance

Discussions between the United States and Canada on preclearance at land borders have been a disappointment. A preclearance program, as envisioned by the Smart Border Declaration, would accomplish three goals. First, it would increase security by screening passengers and cargo away from the border at the point of departure. Second, it would increase efficiency. When precleared travelers arrive at the border, immigration and customs officials need to conduct only minimal or no checks. The most efficient form of preclearance is when one country's exit is the other's entry, such as the juxtaposed controls performed between France and the United Kingdom at the Chunnel crossing. In theory, this form of preclearance should cut costs considerably by reducing the need for redundant infrastructure and staffing. Third, integrated staffing and procedures would lead to greater information sharing and additional collaboration. Preclearance programs recognize that resources freed from checking recognized low-risk individuals can be better deployed in checking unknown and higher-risk persons. This kind of intelligence-based approach to mobility security makes sense, particularly between allies.

In December 2004 the United States and Canada agreed to pilot a preclearance program at the Buffalo, New York–Fort Erie, Ontario Peace Bridge, and Thousand Islands Crossing in Ontario. The Buffalo port of entry was chosen because it does not have enough inspection lanes to process individuals and cargo while meeting security needs, even after adding two car lanes and three commercial lanes in 2005.[168] Under the pilot program, CBP officers were to be stationed at the Canadian side of the Peace Bridge in Fort Erie to inspect travelers and cargo before they entered the United States. Despite efforts between 2005 and 2007 to negotiate a workable program, the two governments were unable to come to an agreement. In April 2007 the nations agreed to provide Canada with a reciprocal preclearance area in the United States and to allow CBP officers to carry weapons at Fort Erie. However, DHS and its Canadian counterparts terminated negotiations over land preclearance and the concept of shared border management.[169] The two governments have not been able to agree on whether to allow:

- Individuals the right to withdraw their applications to enter the United States while at the land preclearance site in Canada ("turnarounds")
- CBP officers to question and fingerprint noncriminals in Canada
- CBP officers to search individuals and cargo without a warrant or probable cause, pursuant to US law in Canada[170]
- CBP officers to arrest suspected criminals or terrorists in the preclearance area in Canada rather than abiding by an agreement that the host country would have sole authority to make arrests at the preclearance site
- CBP officers to share information they collect at land preclearance sites with other US law-enforcement agencies

The Next Steps in Structuring a US-Canada Mobility Security Alliance

While the United States and Canada have taken significant steps to collaborate on securing the movement of people between the two countries, many issues still divide them. Paradoxically, the two governments have been able to integrate command and control of their common airspace — demonstrating mutual trust when it comes to nuclear weapons, for example — but have failed to integrate their regulation of cross-border movement. Agreements between the two countries have lacked the substantive commitments and dedicated follow-up needed to ensure their success.

On the ground, security is inadequate, as evidenced by the success of US Government Accountability Office (GAO) investigators in smuggling illegal goods between Canada and the United States without detection.[171] Finally, terrorism-related information sharing suffered a visible crisis in the handling of the Arar case.

Several factors make the time ripe for a reexamination of mobility security arrangements between the two countries. First, cabinet-level leaders in both countries have agreed to meet every six months, creating a high-level forum for these discussions. Second, DHS has completed work on its first Quadrennial Homeland Security Review (QHSR), which provides it with a firmer conceptual footing for international cooperation. Third, DHS is investing in border infrastructure on the northern border. It can either do so unilaterally or in cooperation with its closest ally. Fourth, the Canadian government has emphasized the importance of intelligence-led border security policies to enhance legitimate cross-border trade. Such policies would benefit significantly from closer coordination. Fifth, recent terrorism prosecutions in Canada and its agreement to a joint risk and threat assessment with DHS may create a significantly different environment for bilateral discussions.

The post-9/11 policy discussion about US-Canada mobility security relations began with the premise — especially prevalent among the Canadian public — that the United States has a terrorism problem and Canada does not. Security measures at the border and elsewhere have been viewed as a US need, and one that threatens Canada's vital economic interests. Numerous academic policy analyses have dwelt on differences in political values and preferences between the two nations. Bilateral discussions have highlighted Canadian efforts to soften Washington's hardening of the border. Under this view, security initiatives came from Washington, and mitigating initiatives came from Ottawa. Canadian officials have viewed many US measures as providing more but not better security, and as impairing trade.

Successful terrorism prosecutions have provided concrete evidence that the terrorism problem is a shared one, and have given Canadian leadership an opening to discuss terrorism with the public in a more open and persuasive manner. As an example, in a major speech delivered in October 2009, the director of CSIS, Richard Fadden, described attitudes toward terrorism in Canada as "a serious blind spot." Fadden argued that "security is a human right" with other rights forming "part of the genetic code of modern citizenship," and called for a "more nuanced debate worthy of a G-8 country." Noting that terrorists "are not couch potatoes," but rather are "part of this great global flux we all live in," he underlined the need to be "more mobile to defend Canada against threats."[172] Canadian public officials can also accurately state that border security measures assist in dealing with domestic criminality issues.

Such frank public discourse in Canada, combined with the renewed commitment to international cooperation in Washington, can pave the way for joint operational solutions within a larger framework of mutual commitment to civil security. With the Canadian public more cognizant of terrorism at home, US and Canadian officials have the opportunity to look at innovative ways to approach border management that reflect their longstanding and deep strategic alliance. The United States should not seek to replicate on the Canadian border its infrastructure and operations along the US-Mexico border, which include hundreds of miles of physical fencing. The Canada-US border also calls for a different approach.

Before leaping in to new rounds of discussions, it would be useful to think through their strategic aim. One starting point would be to establish a permanent binational high-level working group. This group would first consider the aims of what the United States is calling "homeland security" and what Canada has labeled "public safety." The phrase "homeland security" suggests that the focus of protection is the US or Canadian homeland territory as delimited by its borders, rather than the American or Canadian people wherever they are, including as they cross borders. The overall context should be *civil security or defense of the person*, not homeland security. The United States and Canada should explore the goals and substance of an alliance to protect civil security. For example, the two governments could agree to support each other and join in domain awareness, risk assessment, and building a resilient shared infrastructure, as well as the emergency response to which both have already agreed.

Such a homeland security framework would be complementary to the US-Canada Basic Defense Document. The White House National Security Council (NSC), on behalf of the president, should lead this effort for the United States, delegating its management to the homeland security secretary. This arrangement would bring all the relevant cabinet departments to the table, including the two defense departments and at some point the minister for international trade in Canada and the secretary of commerce in the United States.

Under a basic civil security framework agreement, there could be an array of specific treaties and informal agreements related to mobility security. Based on a mutual understanding of civil security and the strategic environment, Canada and the United States should renew their dialogue about the goals of securing the movement of people. It is likely that Canadian and US citizens do not so much want a hardened border as they want safe and lawful mobility channels. That mobility channels can be sites and vectors of attack, exploitation, and systemic collapse makes securing human mobility one of the major operational goals of civil security, comparable to securing cyberspace, financial flows, and the energy supply. However, the two countries should first articulate the common purpose of the civil security alliance in this area.

Specific security-related treaties and agreements will develop over time. Likely subjects include:

1.   *Threat and risk assessments.* The homeland security secretary and Canadian public safety minister have agreed to pursue joint threat and risk assessments.[173] After working through prototypes and pilots, such assessments should be built into existing intelligence-sharing agreements or otherwise formalized. The assessments have the potential to put the publics of the two countries on the same page concerning threats and risks, and could therefore provide a foundation for agreement about how to respond to them.

2.   *Mutual legal assistance and extradition.* Canada and the United States should review and update as necessary their mutual legal assistance and extradition treaties. Revised treaties should place all law-enforcement collaboration on the same footing, deepening and consolidating authority for the three separate border-related programs operating today (IBETs, Shiprider, BEST). These treaties should mirror the new treaties signed with the European Union.

CBSA is not included in IBETs. CBSA is not an exact counterpart to CBP in that it focuses exclusively on ports of entry and has no patrol function along the borders. Officials in Canada may want to reconsider fielding at least some Border Patrol counterparts through CBSA and including that agency in all joint law enforcement relating to the movement of people.

3.   *Data security/privacy.* An agreement on privacy and data security rules would provide a foundation for information sharing. Such an agreement should be developed within a transatlantic framework. For each type of information — intelligence, law enforcement, and traveler related — there needs to be agreement on: (1) with whom the information can be shared, (2) for what purposes, (3) how to safeguard the security of the information, (4) the consequences of a breach of security, and (5) scenario-specific processes to correct and secure redress for inaccurate information Canadian law provides

a legal framework for such information sharing, but more specific agreements may be required.

4. *Preclearance*. Although two preclearance programs are being piloted for traded goods, negotiations over preclearance for people at land borders have been terminated. To date, the two governments have not been able to agree on whether to allow:

- Individuals the right to withdraw their applications to enter the United States while at the land preclearance site in Canada
- CBP officers to question and fingerprint noncriminals
- CBP officers to search individuals and cargo without a warrant or probable cause, pursuant to US law[174]
- CBP officers to arrest suspected criminals or terrorists in the preclearance area as they would be able to do in the United States
- Sharing the information collected on the Canadian side of the border with other US law-enforcement agencies

Sufficient political will could overcome these obstacles. Two of these issues should be considered in the context of larger discussions. First, the issue of information-sharing terms belongs in an overall privacy/data-security framework agreement with the European Union. Second, arrest authority belongs in the overall mutual legal assistance and extradition discussion.

Beyond privacy/data security and arrest, the main obstacle boils down to whether US authorities have the right to fingerprint persons who, for whatever reason, decide not to seek entry into the United States. These persons, known as turnarounds, are few in number. Yet both Canadian and US officials acknowledge that they represent a potential security concern in that their actions may be part of border surveillance by persons or groups that pose criminal or security risks. Canadian officials have taken the position that detention and fingerprinting in such circumstances would not be permissible under the Canadian Identification of Criminals Act and would likely be contrary to Section 8 of Canada's Charter of Rights and Freedoms.

Fingerprints are routinely taken in Canada on a consensual basis, such as for employment. Persons who object to fingerprinting in Canada could be directed to alternative border crossings and be fingerprinted in the United States. As a legal matter, Canadian courts have held that searches that would be unreasonable in other circumstances may be reasonable when conducted at a border. Canada's Customs Act authorizes Canadian officials to search persons — a far more intrusive act than taking fingerprints — who enter areas designated for departure from Canada but who then fail to leave the country. In particular, it stipulates that:

SEARCH OF THE PERSON
98.(1) An officer may search. . .
(c)   any person who has had access to an area designated for use by persons about to leave Canada and who leaves the area but does not leave Canada . . . if the officer suspects on reasonable grounds that the person has secreted on or about his person anything in respect of which this Act has been or might be contravened, anything that would afford evidence with respect to a contravention of this Act.[175]

This law offers a rationale and a legal justification for permitting fingerprinting and temporarily detaining turnarounds subject to specific conditions, including visible notice. If deemed necessary, Canada could consider enacting an amendment to Section 98 of the Customs Act, which would specify that an officer may fingerprint a person who has chosen not to seek entry to the United States after entering the area designated for that purpose and that these fingerprints could be shared with designated US officials.

5.   *Entry standards.* Mutual commitments to manage risks associated with the movement of people should incorporate identity verification and security criteria relating to visa and nonvisa applicants. An initial area of focus should be visa-free travel. This program should be supported by a bilateral, and eventually transatlantic and international, watchlist of criminal and security risks, using facial recognition or other biometrics.

6.   *Border security* in between ports of entry. Canada and the United States should integrate management of the border between ports of entry in recognition of the fact that people who pose risks to one country — whether terrorists, smugglers of CBRNE weapons, human traffickers, human smugglers, or others — threaten the security of the other. At a minimum, the United States and Canada could create interlocking jurisdictional grids and staff them jointly, such that each section of the border would be overseen by one nation or the other. This work would be supported by a jointly deployed marine radar surveillance system operated by both countries as part of an integrated effort.

SBInet

There seem to be two practical obstacles to integrating security measures in the border zone. First, as discussed, Canada does not have an equivalent to the US Border Patrol. Thus, it does not have human resources *to* integrate with the Border Patrol. Canada is considering the structure of its border policing. Second, SBInet, the massive surveillance technology system which DHS is committed to installing on the southern and northern borders, is of questionable value from both a strategic and a technological viewpoint. SBInet fuses input from three sources of detection (radar, visual, and ground sensors), which are affixed to large towers, in an attempt to deliver a single communication to Border Patrol stations.

Beginning in 1994, the US Immigration and Naturalization Service (INS), the predecessor to DHS's immigration agencies, initiated a border blockade strategy. By lining up Border Patrol agents and vans along high-volume border-crossing routes, INS sought to deter migrants and potential smugglers from crossing illegally and to reduce the disorder and crime caused by large numbers of illegal crossings. The Border Patrol's goal of *prevention through deterrence*, underlying this strategy, survives today. While successful in some ways, *prevention through deterrence* has not stopped large-scale illegal entry by labor migrants and their family members. Nor does it adequately address the threat of terrorism or the scourge of human trafficking.

While US border apprehensions have fallen sharply in recent years, the degree to which this shift is attributable to stepped-up border enforcement or decreased US labor demand is uncertain. Figure 12.2, produced for the Migration Policy Institute (MPI), shows that illegal immigration is correlated with the business cycle; namely, fluctuations in migrant apprehensions along the southwest border have closely tracked changes in US labor demand since around the 2001 recession. Despite the frequent claims of law enforcement that the post- 9/11 increase in personnel at the border is responsible for fewer entries, it seems more likely that the combination of both ramped-up border security and decreasing labor-market demand is producing fewer border apprehensions and attempted crossings. Unlike for drug enforcement, data do not exist on what level of additional enforcement resources would be necessary to produce a lower rate of crossings and arrests.

Figure 12.2 Apprehensions as a Function of Labor Demand, Fiscal Years 1991 to 2008

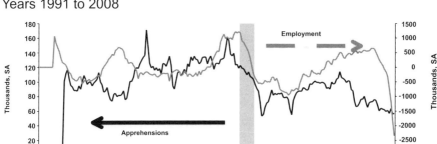

Source: Bureau of Labor Statistics and Department of Homeland Security data analyzed and provided to MPI by Pia Orrenius, senior economist, Federal Reserve Bank of Dallas.
Note: All data are monthly; data on employment represent deviations from long-run employment trends, plotted six months ahead.

In addition, the Border Patrol's reporting methods do not account for returns by deported migrants (recidivism). In other words, apprehensions do not speak to the percentage of migrants who are ultimately prevented from crossing illegally. The point is not that increased Border Patrol resources do *nothing,* but that they may not be doing *enough,* if the goal is to prevent illegal migration. Put differently, their cost-effectiveness has not been established. Meanwhile, the demand for additional border personnel continues without reference to the effectiveness of these resources or the need for them.

This analysis does not focus on the disconnect between short- or longer-term US labor-force needs and US admission policies. Nor does it speak to the Mexican government's desire to send unemployed labor north, or on some employers' noncompliance with US labor laws. If the goal is preventing large numbers of workers and their family members from crossing back and forth illegally, these issues need to be confronted.

Instead, this analysis focuses on the most important security problems identified by DHS and DOD: the potential for terrorism associated with large-scale use of CBRNE weapons, human smuggling with a terrorist or organized-crime linkage, and other high-impact crimes. *Prevention through deterrence* does not provide an adequate framework or sufficient tools to address our most pressing security-related challenges.

SBInet ultimately seeks to assess and classify threats, to coordinate responses among law-enforcement personnel, and to monitor the border. Yet it is not clear that SBInet can achieve these aims. According to DHS, SBInet "develops and deploys new integrated technology solutions to provide enhanced detection, tracking, response, and situational awareness capabilities."[176] In other words, this system seeks to apply what the military calls command, control, communication, and intelligence (C3I) systems at the border.

SBInet claims to provide a "common operating picture" for the Border Patrol. The quality of the real-time pictures of the border that it sends to Border Patrol field offices depends on data fusion from millimeter-wave radar and unmanned aerial vehicle (UAV) inputs to biometrics and remote cameras. Although the system is intended to fuse three types of signals into one message pinpointing an intrusion, the types of information being fused do not enable the system to distinguish between types of intrusions, whether those of a drug trafficker, a migrant, a terrorist, or even a wild animal. Thus, according to experts, the system runs the risk of information overload. In addition, significant technical and organizational issues stand in the way of fusing multiple streams of law-enforcement, sensor, and intelligence data from a variety of sources into a workable tool.[177]

In a series of scathing reports, GAO has pointed out that DHS did not specify planned activities and milestones, anticipated costs, staffing levels, and expected outcomes in its 2006 expenditure plan for SBInet.[178] In 2008 GAO criticized DHS for failing to specify its intended use of planned expenditures. It also cited the lack of an evaluation framework to assess program commitments and the lack of a schedule to guide the program's implementation. Since the program's inception, DHS has repeatedly delayed and modified deployment dates of SBInet technologies along the southwest border. In an independent review, DHS discovered that some SBInet technologies were unproven. In addition, SBInet pilot programs were poorly managed and lacked assessment structures. As a result, Border Patrol agents were forced to rely on previously available technologies, which had limited capabilities and performed poorly. While SBInet technology deployment was originally scheduled for the end of 2008, officials pushed this date back to 2011 and then again to 2016. Most recently, Homeland Security Secretary Janet Napolitano ordered a reassessment of the entire program following delays in the implementation of the first virtual fence along the southwest border.[179] DHS projects that SBInet will cost $6.5 billion over the life of the program.[180] As of September 2009,

DHS had spent $1 billion over three years on SBInet but had not yet produced an effective technological tool.[181]

These reports document the enormous resources being expended to erect a system that increases situational awareness, but that may not provide Border Patrol agents with actionable information. Even if this data can be fused, the question remains whether it will be of sufficiently high quality to justify the financial and environmental costs. In fact, the United States has been trying to build a system similar to this one for combat purposes for decades, but without success. Even if SBInet were ultimately able to function well, it may not be the right approach for US borders, where distinctions between types of intruders matter greatly, and where solutions need to be in place in the short term. At a minimum, the goals of the project need to be more precisely defined, and the project needs to be driven and tightly managed by a DHS senior-level team with IT experience rather than remain in the hands of contractor leadership.

SBInet should not be implemented immediately (if at all) on the US-Canada border. Canada is the closest US ally, and US-Canada cross-border communities are highly integrated. In addition, SBInet is far from a proven success or, as yet, a promising system. Under the circumstances, less costly, more community-friendly ways of managing risk should first be explored.

Technology alternatives should be explored from the perspective of the needs of an integrated border zone authority. The two countries should base their discussions on the premise that civil security must be driven by surveillance, interdiction, and joint solutions. Rather than a unilaterally administered virtual fence, simple cameras could be installed on both sides of the border that relay images to US-Canada fusion centers. In addition, radios and an internet connection could be provided, which links local landowners to US-Canada fusion centers and allows them to report anomalous incidents. Landowners could receive compensation for their participation in this program through slight modifications to the Department of Agriculture's or other existing federal programs. Such a program would be similar to the Sky Watch program in World War II, which had a Ground Observer Corps of more than 500,000 people providing round-the-clock surveillance of the US perimeters. It would engage citizens in protecting themselves and their communities, and would establish close, effective working relationships.

The United States and Canada should prioritize the development of a strong mobility security partnership, and should memorialize this partnership in substantial agreements that provide for (1) regular joint threat and risk assessments, (2) deeper mutual legal assistance, (3) a common transatlantic privacy and data-security framework, (4) a one-stop preclearance system, (5) alignment of entry standards, and (6) integrated protection in the border zone. If it cannot develop such agreements, then it may be necessary to turn towards a costly surveillance architecture. Even then, the SBInet system should not be instituted on the northern border until it has proven useful at the southern border.

Conclusion

Mobility security should be treated like other high-priority security arrangements between the United States and Canada. It should be approached as a common challenge, and resolved in a manner consistent with the two nations' long-standing alliance. Viewed from the perspective of the existing NORAD and Emergency Management Agreements, the failure to share the border security burden is difficult to understand.

A concerted effort should be made to place the civil security alliance with Canada on a firm strategic footing. As a first step, a series of agreements, some of which could have treaty status, should be adopted to secure human movement. Any outstanding areas of conflict can be solved with sufficient political will — and doing so would bring major benefits to both countries. In addition, the lessons learned could be applied to the more complex problems raised by the US-Mexico border.

NOTES

1. Carnegie Endowment for International Peace and Instituto Tecnológico Autónomo de México, *Mexico-US Migration: A Shared Responsibility* (Washington, DC: Carnegie Endowment for International Peace, 2001), www.carnegieendowment.org/pdf/files/M%20exicoReport2001.pdf.

2. The EU-US Joint Statement, "Enhancing Transatlantic Cooperation in the Area of Justice, Freedom and Security" of October 2009 is a milestone statement of the US-EU civil security partnership spanning mobility security to critical infrastructure protection. A section of the statement on "Facilitating Mobility in a Secure Environment" refers to completing visa-free travel between the United States and European Union; developing the working relationship on mobility and security matters, including border, readmission, and travel-document security policies; implementing a working arrangement between the Department of Homeland Security (DHS) and Frontex; improving our common understanding of migration and refugee issues, looking for joint responses in areas where both parties are affected; and expanding the US-EU dialogue toward these ends, http://. se2009.eu/polopoly_fs/1.21271!menu/standard/file/EU-US%20Joint%20Statement%2028%20October%202009.pdf.

3. Janet Napolitano, "Remarks by Secretary Napolitano at the Global Cyber Security Conference, August 2009," August 4, 2009, www.cfr.org/publication/20427/remarks_by_secretary_napolitano_ at_the_global_cyber_security_conference_august_2009.html.

4. CBP (Customs and Border Protection), "Immigration Advisory Program," Fact Sheet, www.customs.gov/xp/cgov/travel/inspections_carriers_facilities/immigration_advisory_prog.xml. Although the program preceded the establishment of the DHS, information about the Immigration Advisory Program is only available since 2004. As of August 2008 it included London-Heathrow, London-Gatwick, Manchester (UK), Tokyo, Seoul, Frankfurt, and Madrid, and IAP officers had produced 3,800 "no board" recommendations to air carriers and intercepted over 200 fraudulent documents. With the addition of Paris and Hong Kong, there are now nine participating countries.

5. Statement for the record of Susan Ginsburg, director, Mobility and Security Program, Migration Policy Institute (MPI), "Weaknesses in the Visa Waiver Program: Are the Needed Safeguards in Place to Protect America?" before the Senate Committee on the Judiciary, Subcommittee on Terrorism, Technology and Homeland Security, 110th Cong., 2nd sess., February 28, 2008, www. migrationpolicy.org/pubs/SGinsburgTestimony_02282008.pdf.

6. DOS (US Department of State), Visa Waiver Program (VWP) (Washington, DC: DOS, 2008), http://travel.state.gov/visa/temp/without/without_1990.html#countries.

7. From 2009, the Common Travel Area allowing for no passport checks may cease to function as it currently does. See David Sharrock, "New Border Control Will Abolish Free Movement between UK and Ireland," *Times Online*, October 25, 2007, www.timesonline.co.uk/tol/travel/news/article2733487.ece.

8. The refusal rate is the number of temporary business and tourism visas that US consular officers deny as a proportion of the total number filed by nationals of a given country. The statutory language is convoluted due to some politicking regarding Ireland. The refusal rate is used as a proxy for the number of visa holders that the State Department believes would overstay if permitted to enter the United States. Consular Affairs (CA) supports its estimates with "validation studies," statistically valid surveys that estimate of the level of overstays in a given geographic area based on return information.

9. *Secure Travel and Counterterrorism Partnership Act of 2007*, Senate and the House of Representatives, H.R.1, 110th Cong., 1st sess., H.R.1-73 (Washington, DC: Government Printing Office, 2007), http://frwebgate.access.gpo.gov/cgi-bin/getdoc.cgi?dbname=110_cong_bills&docid=f:h1enr.txt.pdf.

10. GAO (US Government Accountability Office), *Border Security: Stronger Actions Needed to Assess and Mitigate Risks of the Visa Waiver Program*, GAO-06-854 (Washington, DC: GAO, 2006), www. gao.gov/new.items/d06854.pdf.

11. GAO, *Visa Waiver Program: Actions Are Needed to Improve Management of the Expansion Process, and to Assess and Mitigate Program Risks*, GAO-08-967 (Washington, DC: GAO, 2008), www.gao.gov/new.items/d08967.pdf.

12. DOS, Visa Waiver Program (VWP).

13. DHS accepts applications for last-minute travel but recommends that travelers submit their application as soon as they make their travel plans.

14. DHS, *Visa Waiver Program: Passport Requirements Timeline* (Washington, DC: DHS, 2008), www.dhs.gov/xtrvlsec/programs/content_multi_image_0021.shtm.

15. DHS, "ESTA Web site Available in 13 Additional Languages for US-Bound Travelers from Visa Waiver Countries," News Release, October 15, 2008, www.dhs.gov/xnews/releases/pr_1224103683923.shtm.

16. Biometric information includes, at a minimum, a digital photograph of the individual. Additional options include fingerprints and iris scans. Those who obtained passports prior to October 26, 2006, must have either a machine-readable passport and/or a digital photograph.

17. The Czech Republic, Estonia, Hungary, Latvia, Lithuania, Poland, Slovakia, and Slovenia joined the European Union in 2004; Romania and Bulgaria joined in 2007.

18. Congressional interest continues. See Mike Quigley, "Quigley Gets Visa Waiver Extension for Poland into Immigration Reform Bill," Press Release, December 17, 2009, http://quigley.house.gov/index.php?option=com_content&task=view&id=205&Itemid=17. The press release states: "This is especially meaningful to the families of the thriving Polish community in the 5th district, and will make it much easier for their relatives to visit the United States. Poland has done so much for America, and it is our turn to repay this great nation." Quigley's provision would extend the VWP until June 30, 2011, overcoming its expiration due to the lack of the mandated air exit system.

19. The White House, "President Bush Participates in Joint Press Availability with President Ilves of Estonia," Press Release, November 28, 2006, http://georgewbush-whitehouse.archives.gov/news/releases/2006/11/images/20061128-4_p112806pm-0157-515h.html.

20. Mark Richard and Leslie S. Lebl, "Security and Data Sharing: Transferring Information without Compromising Privacy," *Policy Review*, no. 154, (April and May 2009): 79–81, www.hoover.org/publications/policyreview/41862277.html.

21. Commentaries : "US Excludes Greece from the Visa Waiver Program," *Greek-American News*, October 13, 2008, www.greeknewsonline.com/?p=9262.

22. The White House, "President Bush Discusses the Visa Waiver Program," Press Release, October 17, 2008, http://georgewbush-whitehouse.archives.gov/news/releases/2008/10/images/20081017-5_p101708jb-0301-515h.html.

23. DHS, "Remarks by Homeland Security Secretary Michael Chertoff at a Roundtable with Reporters from Select Visa Waiver Program Countries," Press Release, October 23, 2008, www.dhs.gov/xnews/releases/pr_1224850291152.shtm.

24. Statement for the record of David Heyman, Assistant Secretary, Policy, DHS, "Five Years After the Intelligence Reform and Terrorism Prevention Act (IRTPA): Stopping Terrorist Travel," before the Senate Committee on Homeland Security & Governmental Affairs, 111th Cong., 1st sess., on December 9, 2009, http://hsgac.senate.gov/public/index.cfm?FuseAction=Files.View&FileStore_id=fca64800-f21e-4772-8ec2-f39bab662ffe.

25. DOC (US Department of Commerce), International Trade Administration, Office of Travel and Tourism Industries, "Outbound Analysis 2007," Press Release, June 30, 2008, http://tinet.ita.doc.gov/outreachpages/download_data_table/2007_Outbound_Analysis.doc.

26. Ibid.

27. DOC, International Trade Administration, Office of Travel and Tourism Industries, *United States Travel and Tourism Exports, Imports, and the Balance of Trade: 2008* (Washington, DC: DOC, 2009), http://tinet.ita.doc.gov/outreachpages/download_data_table/2008_International_Visitor_Spending.pdf.

28. See also, Jena Baker McNeill, James Jay Carafano, James Dean, and Nathan Alexander Sales, *Visa Waiver Program: A Plan to Build on Success* (Washington, DC: The Heritage Foundation, 2009), www.heritage.org/Research/HomelandSecurity/bg2282.cfm.

29. The countries and territories that Mexico allowed to join its visa-free travel scheme between January 2009 and early August 2009 are: American Samoa, Anguilla, Aruba, Azores Islands, Bahamas, Barbados, Belize, Bermuda, British Indian Ocean Territory, British Virgin Islands, Cayman Islands, Christmas Island, Coconut Island, Cook Islands, Falkland Islands, Faroe Islands, French Guinea, French Polynesia, Gibraltar, Greenland, Guadalupe, Guam Islands, Macao SAR, Mahore, Marianas Islands, Marshall Islands, Martinique, Micronesia, Monteserrat, Netherlands Antilles, New Caledonia, Niue Islands, Norfolk Islands, Palau, Panama, Paraguay, Pitcairn Islands, Puerto Rico, Reunion, Romania, Saint Helena, Tokelau, Trinidad and Tobago, Turks and Caicos Islands, Virgin Islands, and Wallis and Furtuna Islands.

30. DHS, Office of Immigration Statistics, *Yearbook of Immigration Statistics 2008: Table 25, Nonimmigrant Admissions by Class of Admission: Fiscal Years 1999 to 2008* (Washington, DC: DHS, 2008), www.dhs.gov/xlibrary/assets/statistics/yearbook/2008/table25d.xls.

31. As of December 2009, the United States was reportedly organizing a working group to assess Taiwan's visa-security measures to determine whether or not to grant Taiwan membership to the VWP. "US Will Send Officials to Taiwan to Check Visa Security Measures," *Central News Agency*, December 2, 2009, www.etaiwannews.com/etn/news_content.php?id=1122878&lang=eng_news&cate_img=logo_taiwan&cate_rss=TAIWAN_eng.

32. 111th Congress, 1st session, S.203, "To Amend the Immigration and Nationality Act to Modify the Requirements for Participation in the Visa Waiver program and For Other Purposes," *Govit.com*, January 12, 2009, www.govit.com/vote/billtext.aspx?fname=s-s203is.html.

33. The nine databases to be used to determine visa overstay rates are: the Advanced Passenger Information System (APIS); the Automated Fingerprint Identification System (IDENT); the Central Index System (CIS); the Computer Linked Application Information Management Systems (CLAIMS); the Deportable Alien Control System (DACS); the Integrated Automated Fingerprint Identification System (IAFIS); the Nonimmigrant Information System (NIIS); the Reengineered Naturalization Applications Casework Systems (RNACS); and the Refugees, Asylum, and Parole System (RAPS).

34. Europa, "Free Movement of Workers: General Provisions," http://europa.eu/legislation_summaries/internal_market/living_and_working_in_the_internal_market/free_movement_of_workers/l23013a_en.htm.

35. European Parliament, "Round-up of Tajani and Barrot Hearings," Press Release, June 18, 2006, www.europarl.europa.eu/sides/getDoc.do?language=EN&type=IM-PRESS&reference=20080612FCS31557.

36. EU Member States are adopting different biometric standards and technologies for their e-border and trusted-traveler programs than those adopted by United States. For example, some EU Member States operate trusted-traveler programs based on iris scans.

37. NCTC (National Counterterrorism Center), *National Strategy to Combat Terrorist Travel* (Washington, DC: NCTC, 2006), www.nctc.gov/docs/u_terrorist_travel_book_may2_2006.pdf, 7. The NSCTT is discussed in chapter 4.

38. The four-fingerprint requirement began on June 9, 2009. Prior to this date, participants only needed to submit their right and left index fingerprints.

39. DHS, Customs and Border Protection (CBP), *Global Entry Program: Information Guide* (Washington, DC: DHS, 2009), www.cbp.gov/linkhandler/cgov/newsroom/publications/travel/global_brochure.ctt/global_brochure.pdf.

40. These 20 airports are: Boston-Logan International Airport (BOS); Chicago O'Hare International Airport (ORD); Dallas/Ft. Worth International Airport (DFW); Detroit Metropolitan Airport (DTW); Ft. Lauderdale Hollywood International Airport (FLL); George Bush Intercontinental Airport, Houston (IAH); Hartsfield-Jackson Atlanta International Airport (ATL); Honolulu

International Airport (HNL); John F. Kennedy International Airport (JFK); McCarran International Airport, Las Vegas (LAS); Los Angeles International Airport (LAX); Miami International Airport (MIA); Newark Liberty International Airport (EWR); Orlando International Airport (MCO); Philadelphia International Airport (PHL); San Francisco International Airport (SFO); San Juan-Luis Múñoz Marin International Airport (SJU); Orlando-Sanford International Airport (SFB); Seattle-Tacoma International Airport-SeaTac (SEA); and Washington-Dulles International Airport (IAD).

41. DHS, CBP, "US, United Kingdom Border Agencies Agree to Expedite Travel between Nations," Press Release, June 24, 2008, www.cbp.gov/xp/cgov/newsroom/news_releases/archives/2008_news_releases/june_2008/06242008_4.xml.

42. DHS, CBP, "Global Entry Program Description," Press Release, April 4, 2009, www.cbp.gov/xp/cgov/travel/trusted_traveler/global_entry/global_entry_discription.xml.

43. DHS, CBP, "CBP Debuts New Global Entry Area at Bush Intercontinental Airport," Press Release, May 18, 2009, www.cbp.gov/xp/cgov/newsroom/news_releases/may_2009/05182009_16.xml.

44. Christopher Sands, *Toward A New Frontier: Improving the US-Canadian Border* (Washington, DC: The Brookings Institution, 2009), www.brookings.edu/~/media/Files/rc/reports/2009/0713_canada_sands/0713_canada_report.pdf. The report points out that NEXUS is undersubscribed and that consolidation into Global Entry — a program open only for US citizens — could further undermine it. A solution is for the CBP to enter into an agreement with Canada for reciprocal participation as with the Netherlands. This essentially replicates the current arrangement but also expands traveler access, initially to the Netherlands.

45. José L. Lobo, "Interior implantará la 'frontera electrónica' en Barajas y El Prat para acabar con las colasInterior implantará la 'frontera electrónica' en Barajas y El Prat para acabar con las colas," *el confidencial*, August 5, 2009, www.elconfidencial.com/cache/2009/08/05/espana_74_colas_barajas_pasaporte_electronico.html.

46. John Leydan, "UK e-Borders Scheme Thrown into Confusion by EU Rules," *The Register*, December 18, 2009, www.theregister.co.uk/2009/12/18/e_borders_confusion/.

47. Asia-Pacific Economic Cooperation (APEC) is a multilateral economic forum, established in 1989, promoting economic growth, cooperation, trade, and investment in the Asia-Pacific region. It has 21 member economies including: Brunei, Darussalam, Canada, Chile, People's Republic of China, Hong Kong, China, Indonesia, Japan, Republic of Korea, Malaysia, Mexico, New Zealand, Papua New Guinea, Peru, the Republic of the Philippines, the Russian Federation, Singapore, Chinese Taipei, Thailand, the United States of America, and Vietnam.

48. ABAC (APEC Business Advisory Council), "Founding and Structure," www.abaconline.org/v4/index.php.

49. The 18 countries that fully administer the ABTC as a form of travel document are: Australia, Brunei Darussalam, Chile, China, Hong Kong (China), Indonesia, Japan, Korea, Malaysia, Mexico, New Zealand, Papua New Guinea, Peru, Philippines, Singapore, Chinese Taipei, Thailand, and Vietnam. See Singapore Immigration & Checkpoints Authority, *Application for APEC Business Travel Card System* (ABTC) (Singapore: Immigration & Checkpoints Authority), www.psi.gov.sg/NASApp/tmf/TMFServlet?app=ABTC-PUBLIC&Reload=true.

50. APEC, "Business Mobility Group," March 26, 2009, www.apec.org/apec/apec_groups/committee_on_trade/business_mobility.html.

51. ASEAN (Association of Southeast Asian Nations), *ASEAN Framework Agreement on Visa Exemption* (Kuala Lumpur, Malaysia: ASEAN, 2006), www.aseansec.org/18570.htm.

52. ASEAN, "Joint Statement of the ASEAN Directors-General of Immigration Departments and Heads of Consular Affairs Divisions of the Ministries of Foreign Affairs (DGICM) + Australia Consultation," Press Release, Kuala Lumpur, Malaysia, November 5, 2008, www.aseansec.org/22064.htm.

53. ASEAN, "Joint Press Statement of the Twelfth Meeting of the ASEAN Directors-General of Immigration Departments and Heads of Consular Affairs Divisions of Ministries of Foreign Affairs (DGICM)," Press Release, November 4–5, 2008, http://backup.immigration.gov.ph/asean-dgicm/index.php?option=com_content&view=article&id=113&Itemid=92; ASEAN, "Joint Press Statement of the ASEAN Directors-General of Immigration Departments and Heads of Consular Affairs Divisions of the Ministries of Foreign Affairs (DGICM)+Australia Consultation," Press Release, November 10, 2005, www.aseansec.org/17858.htm.

54. Statement for the record of Rand Beers, under secretary, National Protection and Programs Directorate, DHS, "Five Years After the Intelligence Reform and Terrorism Prevention Act (IRTPA): Stopping Terrorist Travel," before the Senate Committee on Homeland Security and Government Affairs,111th Cong., 1st sess., December 9, 2009.

55. For more information on the DHS Credentialing Framework Initiative see Statement for the Record of Kathleen Kraninger, Deputy Assistant Secretary for Policy, Screening Coordination, DHS, and Robert A. Mocny, Director, United States Visitor and Immigrant Status Indicator Technology Program (US-VISIT), National Protection and Programs Directorate, "Biometric Identification," before the House Appropriations Committee, Subcommittee on Homeland Security, 111st Cong., 1st sess., on March 19, 2009, www.dhs.gov/ynews/testimony/testimony_1237563811984.shtm; DHS, "DHS Screening and Credentialing," Powerpoint Presentation, January 2008, www.secure-idnews.com/audio/iab_0108/Cogswell.pdf.

56. The United States is seeking access to a deep-water Cuban port to return migrants safely and to ensure US diplomats can track their welfare upon repatriation. Cuba objects to US "wet foot, dry foot" policy, which facilitates immigration for Cubans who reach US shores as fueling human smuggling and undermining Cuban law. "Migration Talks with Cuba Put Off to February," *Reuters*, December 4, 2009, www.washingtonpost.com/wp-dyn/content/article/2009/12/03/AR2009120304738.html.

57. Robert Bach presents a vision of what such an agreement may encompass. See Robert Bach, "Missteps and Next Steps in US-Cuba Migration Policies," in *9 Ways for US to Talk to Cuba & for Cuba to Talk to US*, ed. Sarah Stephens and Alice Dunscomb (Washington, DC: The Center for Democracy in the Americas, 2009), www.box.net/index.php?rm=box_download_shared_file&file_id=f_238078916&shared_name=5r18tvkfm4.

58. UNSC (UN Security Council), "Resolution 1373 (2001) of 28 September 2001," http://daccess-dds-ny.un.org/doc/UNDOC/GEN/N01/557/43/PDF/N0155743.pdf?OpenElement.

59. United Nations Information Service, "Countries Invited to Sign, Ratify or Accede to Multilateral Treaties during the Treaty Event 23–25 and 29 September and 1 October 2008," Press Release, September 22, 2008, www.unis.unvienna.org/unis/pressrels/2008/unisinf281.html.

60. Anke Strauss, "Human Trafficking and Smuggling: OAS/IOM Introductory Course on the Human Rights of Migrants, Including Migrant Workers and Their Families," Powerpoint Presentation, International Organization for Migration (IOM), Washington, DC, March 6, 2008, www.google.com/url?sa=t&source=web&ct=res&cd=5&url=http%3A%2F%2Fwww.oas.org%2FDIL%2FESP%2Fmigrantes_curso_introductorio_2008_presentaciones_anke_strauss.ppt&ei=ZwTySfXDHIestgfit5WyDw&usg=AFQjCNHWsUplg6ZGyMD1taKdPAOSx7DhOQ&sig2=6DDDC9PxMSoEy9_a7pGVaA.

61. FATF (Financial Action Task Force), *FATF 40 Recommendations* (Paris, France: FATF, 2004), www.fatf-gafi.org/dataoecd/7/40/34849567.PDF.

62. For more information on FATF, see FATF, "About the FATF," www.fatf-gafi.org/pages/0,3417,en_32250379_32236836_1_1_1_1,00.html.

63. Kamal Sadiq, "A Global Documentary Regime? Building State Capacity in the Developing World," Presentation at conference on Global Mobility Regimes at the Levin Institute, New York (organized by the Rockefeller College of Public Affairs and Policy, Univ. at Albany, State Univ. of New York), April 27–28, 2009.

64. The assembly comprises all 190 Contracting States and meets every three years.

65. The council, comprising 36 members, is elected by the assembly for a three-year term and, as the governing body, provides direction to the International Civil Aviation Organization (ICAO). The council adopts and incorporates Standards and Recommended Practices (SARPS) as annexes to the Chicago Convention.

66. The council appoints a secretary general for a three-year term. The secretary general is head of the secretariat, chief executive officer of ICAO, and secretary of the council.

67. ICAO, "Biometric Identification to Provide Enhanced Security and Speedier Border Clearance for Travelling Public," Press Release, May 28, 2003, www.icao.int/icao/en/nr/2003/pio200309_e.pdf.

68. A variety of working groups are examining enhanced travel-document security and a number of documents such as Resolution 32-18 of the assembly and the ICAO blueprint for the implementation of biometric information also serve to promote this objective. For more details, see ICAO, "MRTD Report: Optimizing Security and Efficiency through Enhanced ID Technology," *ICAO MRTD Report* 1, no. 1 (2006), www.icao.int/cgi/goto_m_atb.pl?icao/en/atb/fal/mrtd/MRTD_Rpt_V1N1_2006.pdf.

69. ICAO representative, presentation by an ICAO representative at the "Border-Related Assistance to Developing Countries," Roundtable held under the Chatham House Rule at the Migration Policy Institute (MPI), Washington, DC, September 30, 2009.

70. Eric Rosand, Alistair Millar, and Jason Ipe, The UN Security Council's Counterterrorism Program: What Lies Ahead? (Washington, DC: Center on Global Counterterrorism Cooperation, October 2007).

71. UNSC, "Security Council Counter-Terrorism Committee," www.un.org/sc/ctc/aboutus.html. The Counter-Terrorism Committee (CTC) also asks governments to criminalize the financing of terrorism; freeze without delay any funds related to persons involved in acts of terrorism; and to deny all forms of financial support for terrorist groups.

72. Rosand, Millar, and Ipe, *The UN Security Council's Counterterrorism Program*.

73. UNSC, "Letter dated 7 February 2008 from the Chairman of the Security Council Committee Established Pursuant to Resolution 1373 (2001) Concerning Counter-Terrorism Addressed to the President of the Security Council," February 8, 2008, http://daccess-dds-ny.un.org/doc/UNDOC/GEN/N08/232/51/PDF/N0823251.pdf?OpenElement.

74. Advisory Committee on Administrative and Budgetary Questions, United Nations General Assembly, "Estimates in Respect of Special Political Missions, Good Offices and Other Political Initiatives Authorized by the General Assembly and/or the Security Council," October 27, 2008, http://daccess-dds-ny.un.org/doc/UNDOC/GEN/N08/568/00/PDF/N0856800.pdf?OpenElement.

75. Rosand, Millar, and Ipe, *The UN Security Council's Counterterrorism Program*.

76. Ibid.

77. S. Neil MacFarlane, "Charter Values and the Response to Terrorism," in *Terrorism and the UN: Before and After September 11*, ed. Jane Boulden and Thomas G. Weiss (Bloomington and Indianapolis, IN: Indiana Univ. Press, 2004).

78. Gary McDonald, "Overview of the ICAO MRTD Programme," Powerpoint Presentation presented at the Fourth Symposium and Exhibition on ICAO MRTDs, Biometrics and Security Standards, ICAO Headquarters, Montréal, Canada, October 6–8, 2008, www.icao.int/MRTDsymposium/2008/Presentations/3_McDonald.pdf.

79. Ibid.

80. Presentation by an ICAO representative at the "Border-Related Assistance to Developing Countries," Roundtable Held under the Chatham House Rule at MPI, Washington, DC, on September 30, 2009.

81. The Organization for Security and Cooperation in Europe (OSCE) has 56 participating states from Southeastern Europe, Eastern Europe, South Caucasus, Central Asia, Western Europe, and North America. Its 18 missions and field operations are in Southeastern Europe, the Caucasus, Eastern Europe, and Central Asia.

82. Peter Andreas and Ethan Nadelmann, *Policing the Globe: Criminalization and Crime Control in International Relations* (Oxford, UK: Oxford Univ. Press, 2006).

83. There is also a representative office at the United Nations in New York. About a third of Interpol staff are seconded or detached by their national bureaus. Interpol (International Criminal Police Organization), *Interpol: An Overview* (Lyon, France: Interpol, 2008), www.Interpol.int/Public/ICPO/FactSheets/GI01.pdf.

84. Interpol, "2009 — A Milestone Year for Interpol," Press Release, December 30, 2009, www.interpol.int/Public/ICPO/PressReleases/PR2009/flashPR2009118/PR2009118.asp; *Interpol*, Databases (Lyon, France: Interpol, February 2009), www.interpol.int/Public/ICPO/FactSheets/GI04.pdf.

85. Interpol, "Interpol Hosts European Troika Co-Operation Meeting to Boost Regional Security through Global Approach," Press Release, November 4, 2008, www.Interpol.int/public/icpo/pressreleases/pr2008/pr200860.asp.

86. Interpol, "19th Interpol Asian Regional Conference: Speech by Interpol Secretary General Ronald K. Noble," Speech, April 11, 2006, www.Interpol.int/Public/ICPO/speeches/AsianConfSG20060411.asp.

87. Interpol, *Databases*.

88. Commission of the European Communities, *Report from the Commission to the Council: Second Monitoring and Evaluation Report on the Operation Council Common Position 2005/69/JHA* (Brussels, Belgium: Commission of the European Communities, 2008), http://eur-lex.europa.eu/LexUriServ/LexUriServ.do?uri=COM:2008:0502:FIN:EN:PDF.

89. DOS (US Department of State), Bureau of International Information Programs, "G8 Countries Co-operate on Secure International Travel Initiative," Press Release, July 8, 2005, www.fas.org/asmp/campaigns/MANPADS/StateG8pressrelease_08July2005.html.

90. UNSC, *Resolution* 1617 (2005) Adopted by the Security Council at its 5244th Meeting (New York: UNSC, 2005), http://daccess-dds-ny.un.org/doc/UNDOC/GEN/N05/446/60/PDF/N0544660.pdf?OpenElement.

91. A list of 27 countertrafficking projects can be found at: IOM, "Project List," www.iom.int/1035/projectlist.htm.

92. IOM, *Migration Initiatives Appeal 2008* (Geneva, Switzerland: IOM, 2008), www.iom.int/jahia/webdav/shared/shared/mainsite/about_iom/docs/Migration_Initiatives_2008_Appeal.pdf.

93. The 11 member states are: Austria, Bulgaria, Croatia, Czech Republic, Hungary, Poland, Portugal, Slovakia, Slovenia, Sweden, and Switzerland.

94. IOM, *The Role of Regional Consultative Processes in Managing International Migration* (Geneva, Switzerland: IOM, 2001), www.iom.int/jahia/webdav/site/myjahiasite/shared/shared/mainsite/published_docs/serial_publications/mrs3.pdf.

95. Khalid Koser, "Irregular Migration, State Security and Human Security," Paper presented for the Policy Analysis and Research Programme of the Global Commission on International Migration, September 2005, www.gcim.org/attachements/TP5.pdf.

96. Jean-Pierre Cassarino, "EU Mobility Partnerships: Expression of a New Compromise," Migration *Information Source*, September 2009, www.migrationinformation.org/Feature/display.cfm?ID=741.

97. BORDERPOL members include: United Kingdom (UK Border Agency, Ports Police), New Zealand (Department of Labour, Immigration Service), Republic of South Africa (South African Police Service Border Division), Hungary (National Police Service), People's Republic of China (Public Security), Norway (National Police Service), Republic of Maldives (Department of Immigration and Emigration), and Burundi (Ministry of Public Security). Observer members include: Singapore (Immigration and Checkpoints Authority), United States of America (United States Border Patrol), and Azerbaijan (State Border Guard Service).

98. DOC (US Department of Commerce), International Trade Administration, Office of Travel & Tourism Industries, *US Citizen Air Traffic to Overseas Regions, Canada & Mexico 2008* (Washington, DC: DOC, 2009), www.tinet.ita.doc.gov/view/m-2008-O-001/index.html.

99. DOC, International Trade Administration, Office of Travel & Tourism Industries, "US Travel Abroad Declined in 2008. However, Fifth Straight Year of Record Spending," Press Release, June 29, 2008, http://tinet.ita.doc.gov/outreachpages/download_data_table/2008_Outbound_Analysis. doc.

100. DOS (US Department of State), "Background Note: Canada," November 2008, www.state.gov/r/pa/ei/bgn/2089.htm.

101. DOS, "Background Note: Mexico," May 2009, www.state.gov/r/pa/ei/bgn/35749.htm.

102. Embassy of the United States of America in Canada, "Did You Know? Why Canada is Important to the United States," 2007, http://ottawa.usembassy.gov/content/can_usa/pdfs/didyouknow.pdf.

103. The eight provinces that share a border with the United States are: British Columbia, Alberta, Saskatchewan, Manitoba, Ontario, Quebec, New Brunswick, and Yukon Territory. See Statistics Canada, *Population and Dwelling Counts, for Canada, Provinces and Territories, 2006 and 2001 Censuses — 100% Data*, December 19, 2008, www12.statcan.ca/census-recensement/2006/dp-pd/hlt/97-550/Index.cfm?TPL=P1C&Page=RETR&LANG=Eng&T=101.

104. The 13 US states that share a border with Canada are: Alaska, Washington, Idaho, Montana, North Dakota, Minnesota, Michigan, Ohio, Pennsylvania, New York, Vermont, New Hampshire, and Maine. See US Census Bureau, "B01003. TOTAL POPULATION — Universe: TOTAL POPULATION," 2008 American Community Survey, http://factfinder.census.gov/servlet/DTTable?_bm=y&-context=dt&-ds_name=ACS_2008_1YR_G00_&-CONTEXT=dt&-mt_name=ACS_2008_1YR_G2000_B01003&-tree_id=308&-geo_id=01000US&-geo_id=04000US02&-geo_id=04000US16&-geo_id=04000US23&-geo_id=04000US26&-geo_id=04000US27&-geo_id=04000US30&-geo_id=04000US33&-geo_id=04000US36&-geo_id=04000US38&-geo_id=04000US39&-geo_id=04000US42&-geo_id=04000US50&-geo_id=04000US53&-search_results=01000US&-format=&-_lang=en&-SubjectID=17631129.

105. This figure does not include all ports of entry but only those for which data are available. Data were taken from Research and Innovative Technology Administration, Bureau of Transportation Statistics, "Border Crossings: Border Crossing/Entry Data," July 2009, www.transtats.bts.gov/Fields. asp?Table_ID=1358.

106. This figure does not include all ports of entry but only those for which data are available. Ibid.

107. Citizenship and Immigration Canada, "Facts and Figures 2008 — Immigration Overview: Permanent and Temporary Residents," August 25, 2009, www.cic.gc.ca/EnGLIsh/resources/statistics/facts2008/permanent/01.asp.

108. DHS (US Department of Homeland Security), *Yearbook of Immigration Statistics 2008* (Washington, DC: DHS, 2009).

109. Ibid.

110. Statistics Canada, *Population by Immigrant Status and Period of Immigration, 2006 Counts, for Canada, Provinces and Territories — 20% Sample Data* (Ottawa, Canada: Statistics Canada, 2009), www12.statcan.ca/census-recensement/2006/dp-pd/hlt/97-557/T403-eng.cfm?Lang=E&T=403&GH=4&SC=1&S=99&O=A.

111. Statistics Canada, *Place of Birth for the Immigrant Population by Period of Immigration, 2006 Counts and Percentage Distribution, for Canada, Provinces and Territories — 20% Sample Data* (Ottawa, Canada: Statistics Canada, 2009), www12.statcan.ca/census-recensement/2006/dp-pd/hlt/97-557/T404-eng.cfm?Lang=E&T=404&GH=4&GF=1&SC=1&S=1&O=D.

112. Citizenship and Immigration Canada, "Facts and Figures 2008 — Immigration Overview: Permanent and Temporary Residents, Canada — Permanent Residents by Source Country," www.cic.gc.ca/English/resources/statistics/facts2008/permanent/10.asp.

113. Interpol (International Criminal Police Organization), *Trends in Illegal Immigration and Travel Document Fraud* (Lyons, France: Interpol, 2007), 20.

114. Jason Fekete, "Embrace 'Canadian values,' Urges Jason Kenney," *The Canwest News Service*, April 15, 2009.

115. The following DOS cable cites an August 2002 Canadian Security Intelligence Service (CSIS) report: DOS, "Canada: 2005 Country Report on Terrorism," Cable from US Embassy in Canada to the Secretary of State in Washington, DC, www.state.gov/documents/organization/133166.pdf.

116. CSIS (Canadian Security Intelligence Service), *Public Report 2007–2008* (Ottawa, Canada: CSIS, 2008), 8–14, www.csis-scrs.gc.ca/pblctns/nnlrprt/2007/PublicReport0708_Eng.pdf.

117. CSIS, "Remarks by Richard B, Fadden, Director, Canadian Security Intelligence Service, to the Canadian Association for Security and Intelligence Studies (CASIS) Annual International Conference," Remarks, October 29, 2009, www.csis-scrs.gc.ca/nwsrm/spchs/spch29102009-eng.asp.

118. "Another 'Toronto 18' Member Pleads Guilty," *CBC News*, January 20, 2010, www.cbc.ca/canada/toronto/story/2010/01/20/toronto-18-plea941.html. There had been two convictions and three guilty pleas as of this writing and prosecutions were ongoing.

119. CSIS, *Public Report 2007–2008* (Ottawa, Canada: CSIS, 2008), 10–11.

120. CSIS, *Public Report 2004–2005* (Ottawa, Canada: CSIS, 2005), www.csis-scrs.gc.ca/pblctns/nnlr-prt/2004/rprt2004-eng.pdf.

121. DHS officials, interviews with the author.

122. DHS officials, interviews with the author.

123. Ibid.

124. David Johnston and Eric Schmitt, "Ex-Military Officer in Pakistan is Linked to 2 Chicago Terrorism Suspects," *The New York Times*, November 18, 2009, www.nytimes.com/2009/11/19/world/asia/19mumbai.html.

125. RCMP (Royal Canadian Mounted Police), *Commissioner of Firearms 2007* Report (Ottawa, Canada: RCMP, 2008), www.rcmp-grc.gc.ca/cfp-pcaf/rep-rap/pdf/2007-comm-rpt-eng.pdf.

126. RCMP, "Vehicle Stop Leads to Seizure of Contraband Cigarettes," News Release, March 11, 2009, www.rcmp-grc.gc.ca/on/news-nouvelles/2009/09-03-11-cornwall3-eng.htm.

127. Michael Hart, "What About the Border?" *One Issue: Two Voices* (February 2008): 8–13, www.wilsoncenter.org/topics/pubs/Nontariff%20Barriers_1i2v8.pdf.

128. Embassy of the United States of America in Canada, "Border Facts," http://ottawa.usembassy.gov/content/textonly.asp?section=can_usa&subsection1=borderissues&document=borderissues_border-faq_0906.

129. Gary Hufbauer and Claire Brunel, "Economic Integration in North America," *One Issue: Two Voices* (February 2008): 2–7, www.wilsoncenter.org/events/docs/Nontariff%20Barriers_1i2v8.pdf.

130. GAO (US Government Accountability Office), *Various Issues Led to the Termination of the United States-Canada Shared Border Management Pilot Project*, GAO-08-1038R (Washington, DC: GAO, 2008), www.gao.gov/new.items/d081038r.pdf.

131. Ibid.

132. Hufbauer and Brunel, "Economic Integration in North America."

133. Hart, "What About the Border?"

134. NORAD (North American Aerospace Defense Command), "About Norad," www.norad.mil/about/agreement.html.

135. Lawrence Kapp, *Operations Noble Eagle, Enduring Freedom, and Iraqi Freedom: Questions and Answers about US Military Personnel, Compensation, and Force Structure* (Washington, DC: Congressional Research Service, 2005), www.fas.org/sgp/crs/natsec/RL31334.pdf.

136. Statement for the record of Victor E. Renuart, Jr., USAF Commander, United States Northern Command (USNORTHCOM) and NORAD, "United States Southern Command, United States Northern Command, United States Africa Command, and United States Transportation Command," before the US Senate Committee on Armed Services, 111th Cong., 1st sess., March 17, 2009, http://armed-services.senate.gov/statemnt/2009/March/Renuart%2003-17-09.pdf.

137. Thom Shanker and Eric Schmitt, "Air Defense Inspired by 9/11 Gets a Second Look," *The New York Times*, November 19, 2009, www.nytimes.com/2009/11/20/us/20terror.html.

138. USNORTHCOM assists the United States during natural and man-made disasters and pandemics by evacuating and transporting people and high-value cargo via military airlifts. Most responses are managed at the state or local level. USNORTHCOM also directs missile defense operations. Master Sgt. Bob Haskell, "Winter Freeze Wrap-Up," *USNORTHCOM News*, March 22, 2005, www.northcom.mil/news/2005/032205.html.

139. Statement for the record of Victor E. Renuart, Jr., "United States Southern Command, United States Northern Command, United States Africa Command, and United States Transportation Command."

140 "Putting the Freeze on the Bad Guys," *The On Guard* 32, no. 12 (2004), www.ng.mil/news/theonguard/2004/2004-12.pdf; Bernard F. Griffard and Bert B. Tussing, *Migration and Border Security: The Military's Role* (Carlisle, PA: US Army War College, 2009), www.csl.army.mil/usacsl/publications/IP_15_09_MigrationAndBorderSecurity.pdf.

141. Canada Command, established in 2006, is the operational military command responsible for all domestic and continental Canadian Forces operations (including the Navy, Army, and Air Force). It serves as the operational link with USNORTHCOM.

142. RCMP, "Integrated Border Enforcement Teams (IBETs)," March 3, 2009, www.rcmp-grc.gc.ca/ibet-eipf/index-eng.htm.

143. Canada News Center, "Canada and US Renew Emergency Management Cooperation Agreement," Press Release, December 12, 2008, http://news.gc.ca/web/article-eng.do?m=/index&nid=427669.

144. The White House, "Joint Statement by North American Leaders," Press Release, August 10, 2009, www.whitehouse.gov/the_press_office/Joint-statement-by-North-American-leaders/. The Summit is a modified continuation of the Security and Prosperity Partnership (SPP) launched by the Bush Administration.

145. Doris Meissner and Donald Kerwin, *DHS and Immigration: Taking Stock and Correcting Course* (Washington, DC: MPI, February 2009), www.migrationpolicy.org/pubs/DHS_Feb09.pdf.

146. Nadja Drost, "Heightened Security at U.S.-Canada Border Catching Few Terrorists," *Hearst Newspapers*, April 19, 2009, www.timesunion.com/AspStories/story.asp?storyID=791561; Terrence P. Jeffrey, "Administration Will Cut Border Patrol Deployed on U.S.-Mexico Border," *CNSNews.com*, September 24, 2009, www.cnsnews.com/news/article/54514.

147. Janet Napolitano, "Toward a Better Border: The United States and Canada," Speech made at the Brookings Institution, Washington, DC, March 25, 2009, www.brookings.edu/~/media/Files/events/2009/0325_us_canada/20090325_canada_transcript.pdf.

148. Deborah Waller Meyers, *Does "Smarter" Lead to Safer? An Assessment of US Border Accords with Canada and Mexico* (Washington, DC: Migration Policy Institute, MPI, 2003), www.migrationpolicy.org/pubs/6-13-0~1.PDF.

149. DHS, "Specifics of Secure and Smart Border Action Plan," Press Release, January 7, 2002, www.dhs.gov/xnews/releases/press_release_0036.shtm.

150. Meyers, *Does "Smarter" Lead to Safer?* Canada's Migration Integrity Officer Program (MIO) has reportedly had great success in preventing the arrival of persons who are inadmissible in Canada.

151. Government of Canada, Security and Prosperity Partnership of North America, *Report to Leaders*, June 2005, www.spp-psp.gc.ca/eic/site/spp-psp.nsf/eng/00098.html.

152. The White House, "Joint Statement by North American Leaders."

153. The agreement responds to two instances of disruption of first responders. In November 2007 an ambulance carrying an individual suffering from a heart attack in Detroit was stopped for secondary inspection on its way to a Windsor hospital by Customs and Border Protection (CBP). A few weeks earlier, a Quebec fire truck on its way to upstate New York to provide emergency support had likewise been stopped at the border.

154. DHS, CBP, "Preclearance Locations," July 28, 2009, www.cbp.gov/xp/cgov/toolbox/contacts/preclear_locations.xml. The United States also has preclearance agreements with Bermuda, the Bahamas, Aruba, and Ireland.

155. Preclearance port agreements with Canada include air and seaports. Preclearance locations in Canada include: Calgary International Airport, Edmonton International Airport, Halifax Robert L. Stanfield International Airport Level 2, Montreal Trudeau International Airport, Ottawa MacDonald-Cartier International Airport, Lester B. Pearson International Airport, Vancouver International Airport, Victoria and Port Angeles, and Winnipeg International Airport. See DHS, "Preclearance Locations."

156. RCMP, "Frequently Asked Questions," www.rcmp-grc.ca/secur/ibets-eipf-faq-eng. htm#contribution.

157. These regions include: Pacific (covers British Columbia and Washington); Okanagan (covers British Columbia, Idaho, and Washington); Rocky Mountain (covers Alberta and Montana); Red River (covers Manitoba, North Dakota, and Minnesota); Superior (covers Ontario, Michigan, and Minnesota); Sault St. Marie (covers Ontario and Michigan); Detroit/Windsor (covers Ontario and Michigan); Thousand Islands (covers Ontario and New York); Niagara Frontier (covers Ontario and New York); St. Lawrence Valley Central Region (covers Ontario and New York); Valleyfield (covers Quebec and New York); Champlain (covers Quebec, New York, and Vermont); Eastern (covers Quebec, Vermont, and Maine); and Atlantic (covers New Brunswick, Nova Scotia, and Maine).

158. RCMP, "IBETs across Canada," November 22, 2004, www.rcmp-grc.gc.ca/ibet-eipf/map-carte-eng. htm.

159. Jonathan Kent, "The IBETs and Integrated Border Management between Canada and the United States," *The Journal of the Royal Canadian Military Institute* 68, no. 2 (March–April 2008): 5–10, www.rcmi.org/archives/SITREP/08/08-2%20Sitrep.pdf.

160. DHS, CBP, "NEXUS Program Description," January 12, 2009, www.cbp.gov/xp/cgov/travel/trusted_traveler/nexus_prog/nexus.xml.

161. Christopher Sands, *Toward a New Frontier: Improving the US-Canadian Border* (Washington, DC: The Brookings Institution, 2009), www.brookings.edu/~/media/Files/rc/reports/2009/0713_canada_sands/0713_canada_report.pdf.

162. DHS, CBP, NEXUS (Washington, DC: DHS), www.cbp.gov/linkhandler/cgov/newsroom/fact_sheets/travel/nexus_fact.ctt/nexus_fact.pdf; DHS, "Secretary Napolitano Announces Rule Proposing Permanent Global Entry Program," Press Release, November 19, 2009, www.dhs.gov/ynews/releases/pr_1258657984894.shtm.

163. DHS, US Immigration and Customs Enforcement (ICE), *Border Enforcement Security Task Forces* (Washington, DC: DHS, 2009), www.ice.gov/pi/news/factsheets/080226best_fact_sheet.htm.

164. Public Safety Canada, "Joint Statement on the Canada-U.S. Border," Press Release, May 27, 2009, www.publicsafety.gc.ca/media/nr/2009/nr20090527-eng.aspx; Public Safety Canada, *Framework Agreement on Integrated Cross-Border Maritime Law Enforcement Operations between the Government of Canada and the Government of the United States of America* (Ottawa, Canada: Public Safety Canada, 2009), www.publicsafety.gc.ca/prg/le/_fl/int-cross-brdr-martime-eng.pdf.

165. CBSA (Canada Border Services Agency), *Canada-US Safe Third Country Agreement* (Ottawa, Canada: CBSA, 2009), www.cbsa-asfc.gc.ca/agency-agence/stca-etps-eng.html.

166. Nonborder states are unlikely to have an interest in issuing such cards as their costs will likely outweigh the revenues from them. .

167. "DHS and DOS Jointly Certify to Congress that Statutory Prerequisites for Implementation of WHTI Have Been Met," *Interpreter Releases* 86, no. 9 (March 2, 2009): 647–48.

168. GAO, *Various Issues Led to the Termination of the United States-Canada Shared Border Management Pilot Project.*

169. Ibid.

170. Ibid.

171. Statement for the record of Gregory D. Kutz, Managing Director, Forensic Audits and Special Investigations, GAO, and of John W. Cooney, Assistant Director, Forensic Audits and Special Investigations, GAO, *Border Security: Security Vulnerabilities at Unmanned and Unmonitored US Border Locations*, before the US Senate Committee on Finance, House Judiciary Committee Subcommittee on Immigration, Citizenship, Refugees, Border Security, and International Law, 110th Cong., 1st sess., September 27, 2007, www.gao.gov/new.items/d07884t.pdf.

172. CSIS, "Remarks by Richard B, Fadden, Director, Canadian Security Intelligence Service, to the Canadian Association for Security and Intelligence Studies (CASIS) Annual International Conference."

173. DHS, "Joint Statement by Secretary Napolitano and Canadian Public Safety Minister Peter Van Loan on the US-Canada Border," Press Release, May 27, 2009, www.dhs.gov/ynews/releases/pr_1243434829897.shtm; James Jay Carafano, Sharon Cardash, and Frank Cilluffo, *Canada and the United States: Time for a Joint Threat Assessment* (Washington, DC: The Heritage Foundation, 2009), www.heritage.org/Research/HomelandSecurity/upload/wm_2404.pdf.

174. GAO, *Various Issues Led to the Termination of the United States-Canada Shared Border Management Pilot Project*, GAO-08-1038R.

175. Department of Justice, Canada, *Customs Act (1985, c. 1 [2nd Supp.])* (Ottawa, Canada: Department of Justice Canada, 2009), www.canlii.org/en/ca/laws/stat/rsc-1985-c-1-2nd-supp/73617/rsc-1985-c-1-2nd-supp.html#history.

176. DHS, CBP, "More than 70 Percent of Tower Construction Completed for SBI's Northern Border Project in Detroit Sector," Press Release, December 1, 2009, www.cbp.gov/xp/cgov/newsroom/news_releases/archives/2009_news_releases/dec_2009/12012009_5.xml.

177. Christopher Bronk, *Managing the US-Mexico Border* (Houston, TX: James A. Baker III Institute for Public Policy of Rice Univ., 2007), www.bakerinstitute.org/publications/WWT_US-Mexico.pdf; Brady McCombs, "New 'Virtual Fence' on Verge of Going Up," *Arizona Daily Star*, February 8, 2009, www.azstarnet.com/sn/news/279334.

178. GAO, *Secure Border Initiative: Technology Deployment Delays Persist and the Impact of Border Fencing Has Not Been Assessed*, GAO-09-896 (Washington, DC: GAO, 2009), www.gao.gov/new.items/d09896.pdf; GAO, US Customs and Border Protection's Secure Border Initiative Fiscal Year 2009 Expenditure Plan, GAO-09-274R (Washington, DC: GAO, 2009), www.gao.gov/new.items/d09274r.pdf; GAO, Secure Border Initiative: DHS Needs to Address Significant Risks in Delivering Key Technology Investment, GAO-08-1086 (Washington, DC: GAO, 2008), www.gao.gov/new.items/d081086.pdf; GAO, Secure Border Initiative: Fiscal Year 2008 Expenditure Plan Shows Improvement, but Deficiencies Limit Congressional Oversight and DHS Accountability, GAO-08-739R (Washington, DC: GAO, 2008), www.gao.gov/new.items/d08739r.pdf; GAO, SBInet Expenditure Plan Needs to Better Support Oversight and Accountability, GAO-07-309 (Washington, DC: GAO, 2007), www.gao.gov/new.items/d07309.pdf; GAO, Border Security: Key Unresolved Issues Justify Reevaluation of Border Surveillance Technology Program, GAO-06-295 (Washington, DC: GAO, 2006), www.gao.gov/new.items/d06295.pdf.

179. Brady McCombs, "US to Revisit Glitch-Prone 'Virtual Fence' Set for Border," *Arizona Daily Star*, January 13, 2009.

180. GAO, "Briefing on U.S. Customs and Border Protection's Secure Border Initiative Fiscal Year 2009 Expenditure Plan, GAO-09-274R," Presentation prepared for the Subcommittees on Homeland Security, Senate and House Committees on Appropriations, www.gao.gov/new.items/d09274r.pdf; US House of Representatives, Homeland Security Committee, "Statement of Chairman Bennie G. Thompson: The Secure Border Initiative: SBInet Three Years Later," Press Release, September 17, 2009, http://homeland.house.gov/SiteDocuments/20090917103603-54387.pdf.

181. US House of Representatives, "Statement of Chairman Bennie G. Thompson: The Secure Border Initiative: SBInet Three Years Later."

Conclusion

Freedom of movement can only be expanded if the major problems associated with movement — terrorism, criminality, and large-scale illegal immigration — are addressed. A mobility framework that speaks primarily to curtailing illegal migration can neither meet the challenges posed by terror nor the needs of lawful travelers. *Securing human mobility* is a more useful way to further these dual goals. The primary strategic challenge should not be to restrict people's movement, but to advance the right to legal movement, even in the face of catastrophic risks.

The *securing human mobility* paradigm requires intensive collaboration related to civil security issues among allies, proactive strategies, compatible legal regimes, and long-term efforts to address the conditions that lead to large-scale, uncontrolled movements. In particular, this framework argues for redeployment of US security resources in order to:

- Preclude terrorism, human trafficking and smuggling, and transnational gang migration
- Reinforce the integrity and resilience of mobility infrastructure, safeguard mobility channels, and protect lawful travelers
- Preclude uncontrolled movements due to lack of opportunity, flight from terror, environmental collapse, pandemics, or for any other reason

The aim should be to provide security for the United States, its citizens, and its interests wherever they may be. The vision should be of a world where movement is as free as possible within the framework of sovereign laws and human rights.

Securing human mobility is an aspect of civil security. Civil security is, in turn, a strategic response to catastrophic risks. There are three types of risk that orient civil security strategy: terrorism; natural and environmental disasters and pandemics; and a collapse, for any reason, of a system on which our lives depend. Civil security defends the individual in the face of these risks, and thus preserves our democratic system and honors our fundamental values. It protects our mobility infrastructure in the same way it protects our cybersecurity and financial systems.

Promising Developments

This book has highlighted the major challenges, developments, and human rights issues associated with securing human mobility. A number of promising programs and ideas discussed in this book should be supported and strengthened. These include:

- The US-operated Human Smuggling and Trafficking Center (HSTC) and the Extra-Territorial Criminal Travel Strike Force (ECT), along with renewed efforts to combat official corruption
- A groundbreaking new mutual assistance treaty with the European Union, which could lead to joint human-smuggling investigations
- Focused deterrence programs to reduce gang violence and transnational gang migration
- Travel bans, which are among the new smart sanctions that the UN Security Council, the United States, and the European Union are using against rogue states and terrorists
- Mobility security agreements with allies
- Technology improvements, to expand freedom of movement in global travel channels
- Creative foreign assistance programs for mobility and border management, to help establish and solidify global standards for safeguarding human movement
- A US-EU agreement on privacy/data-security principles, which can serve as the foundation for further agreements

Major Challenges

The book has also identified several challenges that the United States confronts to security human mobility. These include:

- Expanding the investigative resources dedicated to cases with a terrorist nexus
- Building the analytical capacity of US law-enforcement and immigration agencies — within the Department of Homeland Security (DHS), US Immigration and Customs Enforcement (ICE), US Customs and Border Protection (CBP), and US Citizenship and Immigration Services (USCIS); and within the Department of State (DOS), the Bureaus of Consular Affairs (CA) and Diplomatic Security (DS) — to help them make the best use of

intelligence and investigative information

- Establishing and verifying identity for travel purposes, which requires better regulation of "breeder" documents, including US birth certificates
- The need for US mobility security and closer civil security alliances with both the European Union and Canada, which will require agreeing to a foundation of privacy and data-security rules
- The need for verifiable, mutually applicable standards for mobility security agreements, particularly those that rely on information-sharing protocols
- More cooperative and effective management of common borders with Mexico and Canada
- Establishment of a strategic foreign-assistance program for mobility security capacity building
- The need to make risk assessment, particularly comparing the costs and benefits of distinct mobility security strategies, central to policy-planning efforts
- Better public education on security measures, with the aim of securing greater cooperation and resilience in the response to terrorism
- Strengthening the legal foundations of the mobility security regime, including clarifying the scope of the right to privacy in the context of border- and travel-related surveillance, allowing appeals of visa denials, and understanding the limitations that international institutions and governments can impose on the right to movement

Without exception, every national security professional consulted during the research for this book supported broad immigration reform, as have presidents Bush and Obama. To be comprehensive, immigration reform would need to reduce the flow and the stock of unauthorized immigrants. Experts do not always agree on the design of reform legislation, of course. However, there is widespread agreement, including by this author, that civil security would be served by reducing the number of people — whose identities and immigration histories are not known to the government — who cross the border and circulate in the United States illegally. In addition, a broad and effective US-Mexico relationship dedicated to securing human mobility must be a part of any comprehensive solution to this dilemma.

Recommendations

Organizational and Institutional Issues

The *securing human mobility* framework leads to one principal recommendation related to the organization and responsibilities of DHS, and several that involve DHS and other entities. Mobility security is one of several "tier one" sectors over which DHS exercises homeland security authority. Others include public health, cyberspace, finance and banking infrastructure, and the energy supply. DHS exercises not only homeland security authority but also legacy authority in the immigration arena. It both implements immigration policy and exercises operational control (with DOS) over this function. DHS should be organized to take these different roles and authorities into account. As discussed in chapter 1, it should create two deputy secretary positions (as has been done at DOS and the Department of Justice, DOJ). One homeland security deputy secretary would have the portfolio for mobility (S2(M)), and the other would have the portfolio for all the other sectors of civil security (S2(C)).

Several other recommendations would buttress DHS's role in setting its legacy immigration, travel, and trade policy priorities within the parameters of the laws passed and resources appropriated by Congress. Immigration policymaking, even in this somewhat limited sense, may not be optimally served by its location within DHS. The purpose of homeland security is to protect and enhance US freedom of action in a world of catastrophic risk. This purpose encompasses precluding attacks, disruptions, and failures that prevent citizens from doing what they would otherwise lawfully do, that cause breakdowns of civil order, and that weaken the United States. In the same way that national security strategy does not set goals for the US economy, so civil security strategy should not set policy goals for immigration and for the financial and other systems that DHS is tasked with securing.

DHS must secure immigration flows and processes and effectively husband its resources, but it exercises a level of discretion in formulating immigration policy that goes beyond securing human mobility. Many of the policy considerations related to implementing immigration law — for example, whether to promote naturalization or to reform the US detention system (administratively) — do not clearly implicate DHS's US security responsibilities in the sense of reducing vulnerabilities. Of course, there is a security element to immigration policy, but security is not the main purpose of immigration policy any more than it is of energy policy.

To regulate immigration in the national interest, DHS must partner with experts who are not specifically concerned with homeland security. Since DHS manages the immigration system, some immigration policy expertise needs to be housed within it. This could be achieved, for example, by the establishment of a new assistant secretary for immigration policy who would be tasked with coordinating DHS's immigration-related functions.

Another promising idea is for Congress to establish a Standing Commission on Labor Migration, Competitiveness, and Immigration. This commission would not relieve DHS of any of its current responsibilities. Rather, it would provide analysis that would assist Congress and the executive branch in developing positive immigration policy goals.

The following additional changes would improve the ability of DHS and DOS to lead and to contribute to coordinated activity in support of mobility security:

- HSTC should be strengthened so that it can become the focal point (as was intended) for information sharing and integrated analysis on terrorist travel, human smuggling, human trafficking, and related issues.
- The DHS and DOS agencies involved in the movement of people should require cross-service and joint service as a condition of promotion to top leadership roles.
- ICE's ECT should become an interagency team under the direction of the National Security Council (NSC). (Alternatively, targeting could be delegated to HSTC.)
- DHS should create an office to contribute to the travel-ban policy, and HSTC could become a travel-ban clearinghouse for UN, foreign, and US travel sanctions.
- DHS should create an office of foreign and technical assistance for managing the movement of people; the office would coordinate DHS's intra- and interagency work in this area.
- DOS and DHS should support the establishment of an international organization for border and immigration authorities, which would be tasked with setting standards, conducting mutual assessments, and sharing best practices. Despite the entities that are already involved in some form of assistance related to facilitating and securing human mobility, there is no organization of professional border inspectors and guards with the international reach to develop policies and practices to improve global collaboration concerning the secure movement of people.

US prosperity depends on the nation's openness and attractiveness to the most talented and energetic people in the world. The legal framework for the movement of people must mature in the same way as the legal frameworks for other areas of global concern, such as the environment or trade. The mobility security framework must be consistent with US constitutional principles, and enable people to pursue economic opportunity, family reunification, and other lawful decisions in furtherance of US interests. The US commitment to its core principles will inspire greater international cooperation to address problems such as protection and recovery from chemical, biological, radiological, nuclear, or high yield explosive (CBRNE) attacks, global warming, and cyber disruptions. Such common efforts will ultimately reduce the pressures that lead to precipitous and dangerous mass migration. Securing human mobility is both an immediately pressing issue and one that will be of growing importance in building US security and essential civil security alliances for years to come.

ACKNOWLEDGEMENTS

I wish to thank Jonathan Ginsburg and Donald Kerwin for their essential support, inspiration, edits, and insights. David S. Aidekman's and Jim Chaparro's separate suggestions that I write such a book was its catalyst and ongoing inspiration. I am grateful to Alan Song and the Smith Richardson Foundation for their generous support. I wish to thank Demetrios Papademetriou, who gave me an institutional home and the extended support of the Migration Policy Institute which, due to his leadership, sets an always-rising bar for timely and intelligent migration policy analysis. Sophia Conroy and Nancy Chang of the Open Society Institute embraced my goal of focusing national security away from concepts tied to immigration policy; I am grateful for OSI's generous commitment to this undertaking.

Hiroyuki Tanaka played a fundamental role in bringing this project to fruition — from beginning to end, research to realization. Hiro is a superb researcher, keen policy observer, master of detail, able drafter, and incisive reader. I cannot thank him enough.

Kristi Severance provided substantial research and all-around support with commitment, writing élan, insight, and efficiency. I also thank a host of MPI interns for their able research assistance: Claire Bergeron, Christine Dehn, Uriah Ferruccio, Mary Lagdameo, Trudy Rebert, and Michael Roos. My thanks as well for their perspectives, background, referrals, and critiques to Deborah Meyers, Michelle Mittelstadt, Doris Meissner, Michael Fix, Kathleen Newland, Jeanne Batalova, Marc Rosenblum, Kirin Kalia, Aaron Terrazas, and April Siruno. Lisa Dixon was incomparably helpful. I am personally and professionally grateful for support from Gale Gearhart, Barbara Zinkant, Carolina Fritz, and Violet Lee.

My book seeks to move mobility security firmly into the framework of homeland, or "civil," security. The field of civil security as a core element of the doctrine of wars on terror is being conceptualized by legal and strategic thinkers, above all, by Philip Bobbitt, for whose friendship and comments I am grateful. Harvey Rishikof, Dave McIntyre, and Rick Noriega shared experience, insight, and perspective regarding this emerging field. Other especially valued interlocutors and critics include Bert B. Tussing, Theo Gemelas, Chris Bronk, Glenn Pierce, Russ Neuman, Monica del Carmen Serrano Carreto, Thomas

A. Tass, and Scott Newark. Among the helpful critics of draft chapters
were Anthony Braga, Scott Busby, Richard Friman, George Gavrilis, David
Kennedy, Mark Kleiman, Garland Land, Dan Martin, Barry Zellen, and
Jim Ziglar. Special thanks to John Brennan, Zbigniew Brzezinski, and Gil
Kerlikowske for their insights and interest.

Helping me through the maze of immigration law have been Jeanne Butterfield,
Robert Deasy, Deborah Drennan, David Martin, Elizabeth E. Stern, Margaret
Stock, Rose Mary Valencia, Stewart C. Verdery, Jr., Kathleen Campbell
Walker, Crystal Williams, and Palma Yanni.

I am also most grateful to Rey Koslowski, who generously introduced me
to many people who became important to this work. Others who were
instructive and thought-provoking were W. Russell Neuman, Jason Ackleson,
Francesca Bignami, David Cole, Felmon J. Davis, Susan Gzesh, Kamal Sadiq,
Kate Martin, John W. Donaldson, Chris Rudolph, Brent Backus, Bernard F.
Griffard, and Douglas V. Johnson.

The late Mark Richard and Steve Fischel were unfailingly helpful. I cherish the
memory of their warm encouragement and wise counsel, and of our humorous
sparring.

Additional thanks to Randel Johnson, Kelly Hunt, Angelo Amador, Laura
Reiff, Lynn Shotwell, and Rick Webster.

Thanks to Gregory Maniatis, Will Somerville, the Delegation of the European
Union to the United States, and to Sebastian Graefe and the Heinrich Boll
Foundation for the opportunity and support given to hold meetings with
European officials and counterparts.

Members of the transatlantic community, 5CC friends, and international
organization officials have been helpful throughout, forbearing from any facile
anti-Americanism without foregoing honesty, including Jonathan Faull,
Richard Barrett, Mike Smith, Brian Grant, Philippe Andrieux, Alec Attfield,
Jean-Eric Aubert, Haasan O. Baage, Telmo Baltazar, Mary Lynn Louise Becker,
Jack Bell, Arabelle Berneker, Tor Burman, Diane Burrows, Luis Cerdan Ortiz-
Quintana, Dennis Cole, George Costaris, Alan Craig, Taitu Deguefé, Tom
Dowdall, John Fothergill, Vincent Giuca, Ron Hendrix, Chris Hurrey, Katrin
Huber, Nigel Inkster, Rodney Irwin, Damon Jackman, Karsten Kloth, David

Knight, Anne Marie Lacoste, Richard Lewington, Peter MacDougall, Christian Mahr, Veronica Isabel Guillen Malagon, Jeremy Mell, Satko Mujagic, Scott Newark, Ronald K. Noble, John Oliver, Robert Orr, Richard Ots, Frank Paul, David Philp, Grzegorz Polak, David Quartemain, Serge Rinkel, Frank Schmiedel, Victor Shtoyunda, Rainer Stentzel, Brian D. Sullivan, Zoltan Szabo, Aleck Thomson, Michel Oude Veldhuis, Jim Versteegh, Juan Andres Villalgordo, Mike Vrolijk, Karl-Heinz Weidner, Ann Williams, Jim Williams, Bob Whalley, and Vladimirs Zaguzovs.

Especially helpful among European policy analysts and scholars have been Paul De Hert, Elizabeth Collett, Rocco Bellanova, Virginie Giraudon, Didier Bigo, Sergio Carrerra, Christina Boswell, Elizabeth Guild, and Mark Salter.

Numerous people helped with particular points and sources, especially Chris Kojm, Edward Alden, Parney Albright, Joseph Atick, David Biette, Alan Goodman, Michael Jacobson, Joanne Lin, Douglas Lovelace, Lisa Schirch, Tom Brenneman, Joseph Lapid, Edward Luttwack, Chris Sands, Tagi Sagafinejad, Steve Simon, Doug Smith, Winnie Reed, and Jill Wheeler. My colleagues on the Quadrennial Homeland Security Review advisory committee have been more helpful than they know, particularly Ruth David, Frank Ciluffo, Norm Augustine, and Dutch Leonard.

Civil security doctrine is being invented on the front lines, and this book was shaped by innumerable interviews and conversations with people in public service. Among the many currently or formerly in US government service whose experience and initiative provide the bedrock for this book are the following: Rowdy Adams, Jason Ahearn, Charles Allan, Stuart Baker, Lee Bargerhuff, Jack Barnhart, Ann Barrett, Charles Bartoldus, Ralph Basham, Diane R. Bean, Jane E. Becker, Jackie A. Bednarz, Joshua Black, Leonard Boyle, John B.Brennan, John L. Brummet, Donna Bucella, Mary Ellen Callahan, Edward Castillo, Jaime X. Castillo, Patricia Cogswell, Alan Cohen, John Cohen, Mary V.Connell, Don Crocetti, Henry Crumpton, Gregory M. Desbiens, Elaine Dezenski, Pamela E. Dieguez, Maureen B. Dugan, Lloyd M. Easterling, Tony Edson, Douglas Ellice, Paul M. Fitzgerald, Jess Ford, David Forsland, Bud Frank, Alcy Frelick, Mike Fullerton, Tina W. Gabbrielli, Harry Gallagher, Leslie Gerson, Ted K. Gong, David Gordner, Marc Gorelick, Jeffrey Gorsky, Roberta Griffith, Roy J. Hall, John Hamilton, Michael Hardin, Maura Harty, Scott L. Hatfield, Stephen R. Heifetz, Thomas F. Holley, John M. Hotchner, William H. Houston, John J. Ingham, Susan S. Jacobs, Robert

Jacksta, Janice L. Jacobs, Justin Jackson, Linda Kane, Barry Kefauver, Francine Kerner, David G. Kidd, Mark Koumans, Kevin Landy, Eric Larson, Leslie S. Lebl, Kent Lewis, John Kropf, Tim Longanacre, David M. Luna, Jeanne W. Maloney, Al Martinez-Fonts, Marianne K. Martz, Paul McHale, Miguel Mercado, Deborah W. Meyers, Patrick Minter, Larry Mitchell, Robert Mocny, Donna Montiel, Barry Moore, Paul M. Morris, John Morton, Michael C. Mullen, Eric Nordstrom, Bill Oliver, Jim Pritchett, Kenneth Propp, Michael Reilly, Sean W. Robinson, Paul Rosenzweig, Charles Rothwell, Nick Sabruno, Timothy B. Sampson, Christine Schellack, Jim Schnaible, Jonathan R. Scharfen, Andrew Simkin, Aileen (Lee) Smith, Laurel Smith, Ruth Smith, Derwood K. Staeben, Bruce Swartz, Jonathan Thompson, James F. Tomsheck, John Torres, Russell Travers, Joseph Uribe, Ken Wainstein, Jerry Walsh, and P. T. Wright.

My deep appreciation goes to MPI editors Donald Kerwin and Michelle Mittelstadt for their thorough, superlative editing, as well as to Fayre Makeig for her careful copy editing. I bear responsibility for any overstepping and errors in fact or judgment. I hope that our contributions prove useful and inspire others to add to them.

Finally, I am grateful to Francesca Jessup Arene, David E. Dreyer, Mark Ginsburg, and Emily Walker for always saying yes.

WORKS CITED

1997. "Once More Group of Tamils Landed." *De Telegraaf*, March 4. www.lankaweb.com/news/items00/0503-1.html.

2002. *Homeland Security Act of 2002*, Public Law 107-296, 107th Cong., 2nd sess., November 25. www.dhs.gov/xlibrary/assets/hr_5005_enr.pdf.

2002. *Immigration and Nationality Act* (INA), 8 USC §1182.

2003. 8 C.F.R. § 103.1(f)(3)(iii).

2004. "Al Qaida South of the Border: Rumsfeld — Human-Smuggling Rings Tied to Bin Laden's Terrorist Network." *WorldNetDaily*, February 16. www.wnd.com/news/article.asp?ARTICLE_ID=37133.

2004. "Diet Cracks Down on Overstayers, Widens Door for Refugees." *The Japan Times*, May 28. http://search.japantimes.co.jp/member/member.html?nn20040528a1.htm.

2004. "Putting the Freeze on the Bad Guys." *The On Guard* 32 (12). www.ng.mil/news/theonguard/2004/2004-12.pdf.

2004. "Report: Mexico is Al-Qaida Route to U.S.: Plans to Use Migrant Smuggling Paths to Set Up Operatives." *WorldNetDaily*, September 17. www.wnd.com/index.php?fa=PAGE.view&pageId=26596.

2004. "Terrorists obtain S. Africa Passports." *The Associated Press*, July 28. www.chinadaily.com.cn/english/doc/2004-07/28/content_352358.htm.

2004. *The Intelligence Reform and Terrorism Prevention Act of 2004 (IRTPA)*. Public Law 108-458, 108th Cong., 2nd sess., December 17. www.nctc.gov/docs/pl108_458.pdf.

2006. "Out of the Underworld — Criminal Gangs in the Americas." *The Economist*, January 6.

2007. "£1m Haul of Fake Passports as Police Smash Counterfeit Ring." *Daily Mail*, July 4. www.dailymail.co.uk/news/article-466192/1m-haul-fake-passports-police-smash-counterfeit-ring.html.

2007. *Department of State, Foreign Operations, and Related Programs Appropriations Act, 2008*. 110th Cong., 1st sess., January 4. http://frwebgate.access.gpo.gov/cgi-bin/getdoc.cgi?dbname=110_cong_bills&docid=f:h2764enr.txt.pdf.

2007. "Officers Seize 'Fake' Passports." *British Broadcasting Company News*, July 4. http://news.bbc.co.uk/1/hi/england/london/6269210.stm.

2007. "Passport Investigation Suggests Security Hole." *NBC News*, December 28.

2007. "Russian Federal Migration Service Offices Raided in Corruption Probe." *ITAR-TASS News Agency*, April 26.

2007. *Secure Travel and Counterterrorism Partnership Act of 2007*. Senate and the House of Representatives, H.R.1, 110th Cong., 1st sess., H.R.1-73. Washington, DC: Government Printing Office. http://frwebgate.access.gpo.gov/cgi-bin/getdoc.cgi?dbname=110_cong_bills&docid=f:h1enr.txt.pdf.

2007. "Tourist Visa Time 'To Be Halved.'" *British Broadcasting Company News*, December 18. http://news. bbc.co.uk/2/hi/7146527.stm.

2007. "US Attorney Reports Palestinian National and Former Colombian Detective Guilty of Conspiring to Support FARC and Alien Smuggling." *LawFuel.com*, November 15. www.lawfuel.com/ show-release.asp?ID=16112.

2008. "Commentaries: US Excludes Greece from the Visa Waiver Program." *Greek-American News*, October 13. www.greeknewsonline.com/?p=9262.

2008. "Feingold Wants Answers on No-Fly List Gaffes." *The Washington Times*, May 2. www. washingtontimes.com/apps/pbcs.dll/article?AID=/20080502/NATION/99960651/1001.

2008. "Visa Changes Would Mean No Right of Appeal for Failed Applicants." *The Asian News*, February 4. www.theasiannews.co.uk/news/s/1035035_visa_changes_would_mean_no_right_of_appeal_ for_failed_applicants.

2009. "111th Congress, 1st session, S.203, To amend the Immigration and Nationality Act to Modify the Requirements for Participation in the Visa Waiver Program and for Other Purposes." *Govit.com*, January 12. www.govit.com/vote/billtext.aspx?fname=s-s203is.html.

2009. "Arrests after Spain 'Forgery' Raids." *Aljazeera*, February 3, http://english.aljazeera.net/news/europ e/2009/02/200923105422941176.html.

2009. "DHS and DOS Jointly Certify to Congress that Statutory Prerequisites for Implementation of WHTI Have Been Met." *Interpreter Releases* 86 (9): 647–48.

2009. "DNA Test for UK Asylum Seekers Triggers Protests." *The Times of India*, November 6. http://timesofindia.indiatimes.com/world/uk/DNA-test-for-UK-asylum-seekers-triggers-protests/ articleshow/5201462.cms.

2009. "India's New Identity Card." *The Economist*, July 2.

2009. "Malaysia Unravels Indonesian Passport Forgery Syndicate." *Antara News*, March 3.

2009. "Migration Talks with Cuba Put Off to February." *Reuters*, December 4. www.washingtonpost.com/ wp-dyn/content/article/2009/12/03/AR2009120304738.html.

2009. "UK: Some Won't Need Visa Yet." *News 24*, February 9. www.news24.com/Content/SouthAfrica/ News/1059/c3c88c0980a04b16916f5eaa6d678f0a/09-02-2009-11-01/UK_Some_wont_need_visa_yet.

2009. US-VISIT senior official, personal communication with the author.

2009. "US Will Send Officials to Taiwan to Check Visa Security Measures." *Central News Agency*, December 2. www.etaiwannews.com/etn/news_content.php?id=1122878&lang=eng_news&cate_ img=logo_taiwan&cate_rss=TAIWAN_eng.

2009. "Worries about Iraq's Biometric Database." *Homeland Security Newswire*, August 26. http:// homelandsecuritynewswire.com/worries-about-iraqs-biometric-database.

2010. "Another 'Toronto 18' Member Pleads Guilty." *CBC News*, January 20. www.cbc.ca/canada/ toronto/story/2010/01/20/toronto-18-plea941.html.

AARO (Association of Americans Resident Overseas). "5.25 Million Americans Abroad Map." http://aaro.org/index.php?option=com_content&view=article&id=6&Itemid=6.

ABAC (APEC Business Advisory Council). "Founding and Structure." www.abaconline.org/v4/index.php.

ABS (Australian Bureau of Statistics). 2008. *Migration 2006–07*. Belconnen, Australia: ABS. www.ausstats.abs.gov.au/ausstats/subscriber.nsf/0/F15E154C9434F250CA2574170011B45B/$Fil e/34120_2006-07.pdf.

Abuza, Zachary. 2008. "Second Thai Counterfeit Passport Ring Broken Up This Month: Nearly 22,000 Passports Seized." *Counterterrorism Blog*, May 10. http://counterterrorismblog.org/2008/05/second_thai_counterfeit_passpo.php.

Adamson, Fiona B. 2006. "Crossing Borders: International Migration and National Security." *International Security 31* (1): 165–99.

Agunias, Dovelyn Ranneveig, ed. 2009. *Closing the Distance: How Governments Strengthen Ties with Their Diasporas*. Washington, DC: Migration Policy Institute (MPI).

Alden, Edward. 2008. *The Closing of the American Border: Terrorism, Immigration, and Security since 9/11*. New York: HarperCollins.

———. 2009. "US Should Drop The 'Exit' from Its Entry-Exit System." *Security Debrief*, October 12. http://securitydebrief.adfero.com/2009/10/12/u-s-should-drop-the-exit-from-its-entry-exit-system/.

American Academy of Religion, American Association of University Professors, Pen American Center, and Tariq Ramadan v. Michael Chertoff. 2007. 06 CV 588 (PAC), US District, (S.D.N.Y. December 20). www.aaup.org/NR/rdonlyres/EA0965BB-1124-48E5-B06E-8FA50F2CF6B1/0/AARvChertoff.pdf.

Andreas, Peter, and Ethan Nadelmann. 2006. *Policing the Globe: Criminalization and Crime Control in International Relations*. Oxford, UK: Oxford Univ. Press.

ANSI (American National Standards Institute). 2009. *Identity Verification*. New York: ANSI's Identity Theft Prevention and Identity Management Standards Panel. http://webstore.ansi.org/identitytheft.

APEC (Asia-Pacific Economic Cooperation). 2001. "APEC Leaders Statement on Counter-Terrorism." October 21. www.apec.org/apec/leaders__declarations/2001/statement_on_counter-terrorism.html.

———. 2009. "Business Mobility Group." March 26. www.apec.org/apec/apec_groups/committee_on_trade/business_mobility.html.

Archibold, Randal C. 2006. "US Blocks Men's Return to California from Pakistan." *The New York Times*, August 29. www.nytimes.com/2006/08/29/us/29hayat.html?ex=1314504000&en=dcda49ed0eeae90b&ei=5090&partner=rssuserland&emc=rss.

———. 2006. "Wait Ends for Father and Son Exiled by F.B.I. Terror Inquiry." *The New York Times*, October 2. http://query.nytimes.com/gst/fullpage.html?res=9505E7DE1430F931A35753C1A9609C8B63.

Archibold, Randal C., and Andrew Becker. 2008. "Border Agents, Lured by the Other Side." *The New York Times*, May 27. www.nytimes.com/2008/05/27/us/27border.html?pagewanted=print.

ASEAN (Association of Southeast Asian Nations). 2005. "Joint Press Statement of the ASEAN Directors-General of Immigration Departments and Heads of Consular Affairs Divisions of the Ministries of Foreign Affairs (DGICM) + Australia Consultation." Press Release, November 10. www.aseansec.org/17858.htm.

————. 2006. *ASEAN Framework Agreement on Visa Exemption*. Kuala Lumpur, Malaysia: ASEAN. www.aseansec.org/18570.htm.

————. 2007. "ASEAN Convention on Counter Terrorism." January 13. www.aseansec.org/19250.htm.

Advisory Committee on Administrative and Budgetary Questions, United Nations General Assembly.

————.2008. "Estimates in Respect of Special Political Missions, Good Offices and Other Political Initiatives Authorized by the General Assembly and/or the Security Council." October 27. http://daccess-dds-ny.un.org/doc/UNDOC/GEN/N08/568/00/PDF/N0856800.pdf?OpenElement.

————. 2008. "Joint Press Statement of the Twelfth Meeting of the ASEAN Directors-General of Immigration Departments and Heads Of Consular Affairs Divisions Of Ministries Of Foreign Affairs (DGICM)." Press Release, November 4–5. http://backup.immigration.gov.ph/asean-dgicm/index.php?option=com_content&view=article&id=113&Itemid=92.

————. 2008. "Joint Statement of the ASEAN Directors-General of Immigration Departments and Heads of Consular Affairs Divisions of the Ministries of Foreign Affairs (DGICM) + Australia Consultation." Kuala Lumpur, Malaysia, November 5. www.aseansec.org/22064.htm.

ASEM (Asia-Europe Meeting). 2002. "Declaration on Cooperation against International Terrorism." September 22–24. www.aseminfoboard.org/content/documents/Declaration_on_Cooperation_against_International_Terrorism.pdf.

Atick, Joseph. 2009. Personal exchange with the author.

Australian Government, Department of Immigration and Citizenship. 2008. *Annual Report 2007–08*. Belconnen, Australia: Department of Immigration and Citizenship. www.immi.gov.au/about/reports/annual/2007-08/pdf/annual-report-2007-08-complete.pdf.

————. "Visas, Immigration and Refugees." www.immi.gov.au/visitors/tourist/976/eligibility.htm.

Australian Government, Migration Review Tribunal (MRT), Refugee Review Tribunal (RRT). 2006. *Migration Review Tribunal and Refugee Review Tribunal Annual Report 2005–2006*. Sydney, Australia: MRT, RRT. www.mrt-rrt.gov.au/annrpts/mrt-rrt/ar0506/MRTRRTAR0506.pdf.

————. 2007. *Migration Review Tribunal and Refugee Review Tribunal Annual Report 2006–2007*. Sydney, Australia: MRT, RRT. www.mrt-rrt.gov.au/annrpts/mrt-rrt/ar0607/MRTRRTAR0607.pdf.

————. 2009. *Factsheet M10: Tribunal Brochure*. Sydney, Australia: MRT, RRT. www.mrt-rrt.gov.au/docs/factsheets/mrt/M10Brochure.pdf.

————. 2009. *Migration Review Tribunal, Refugee Review Tribunal, Annual Report 2008–2009*. Sydney: Commonwealth of Australia. www.mrt-rrt.gov.au/annrpts/mrt-rrt/ar0809/MRTRRTAR0809.pdf.

————. 2009. *Publication of MRT and RRT decisions, MR11*. Sydney, Australia: MRT, RRT. www.mrt-rrt.gov.au/docs/factsheets/MR11PublicationDecisions.pdf.

Bach, Robert. 2003. "Global Mobility, Inequality and Security." *Journal of Human Development and Capabilities* 4 (2): 227–45.

———. 2009. "Missteps and Next Steps in US-Cuba Migration Policies." *In 9 Ways for US to Talk to Cuba and for Cuba to Talk to US*, ed. Sarah Stephens and Alice Dunscomb. Washington, DC: The Center for Democracy in the Americas. www.box.net/index.php?rm=box_download_shared_file&file_id=f_238078916&shared_name=5r18tvkfm4.

Bachelet, Pablo. 2006. "US Uses Visas to Combat Corruption." *Miami Herald*, February 19.

Badger, T. A. 2003. "Probe Closes Visa Section of U.S. Consulate." *The Associated Press*, January 30.

Balzacq, Thierry, Elspeth Guild, Anita Szymborska, and Agnieszka Weinar. 2006. *An Analysis of the Current Common Consular Instructions*. Brussels, Belgium: European Parliament. www.libertysecurity.org/IMG/doc_CCI-English.doc.

Barry, Tom. 2009. "Mass Incarcerations of Immigrants." *Border Lines*, May 24. http://borderlinesblog.blogspot.com/2009/05/mass-incarceration-of-immigrants.html.

Beaverstock, Jonathan V., and James T. Boardwell. 2006. "Negotiating Globalization, Transnational Corporations and Global City Financial Centres in Transient Migration Studies." *In Competing for Global Talent*, ed. Christiane Kuptsch and Pang Eng Fong. Geneva, Switzerland: International Institute for Labour Studies, International Labor Office, and Singapore Management Univ..

Beers, Rand. 2009. "Five Years after the Intelligence Reform and Terrorism Prevention Act (IRTPA): Stopping Terrorist Travel." Statement for the record before the Senate Committee on Homeland Security and Government Affairs, 111th Cong., 1st sess., December 9. http://hsgac.senate.gov/public/index.cfm?FuseAction=Files.View&FileStore_id=16e8ac24-2fb2-4672-bf28-4c1e6f72113b.

Berti, Benedetta. 2002. "Reassessing the Transnational Terrorism-Criminal Link in South America's Tri-border Area." *Terrorism Monitor* 6 (18). www.jamestown.org/programs/gta/single/?tx_ttnews[tt_news]=611&tx_ttnews[backPid]=180&no_cache=1.

Black, Joshua. 2009. Interview with the author.

Blanke, Jennifer, and Thea Chiesa. 2007. *The Travel and Tourism Competitiveness Report 2007: Furthering the Process of Economic Development*. Geneva, Switzerland: World Economic Forum (WEF). www.weforum.org/pdf/tourism/Part1.pdf.

———. 2009. *The Travel & Tourism Competitiveness Report 2009*: Managing in a Time of Turbulence. Geneva, Switzerland: WEF. www.weforum.org/pdf/ttcr09/ttcr09_fullreport.pdf.

Bobbitt, Philip. 2008. *Terror and Consent: The Wars for the Twenty-First Century*. New York: Knopf.

Bossuyt, Marc. 2000. *The Adverse Consequences of Economic Sanctions on the Enjoyment of Human Rights: Review of Further in Fields with Which the Subcommission Has Been or May Be Concerned*. New York: United Nations, Economic and Social Council. www.unhchr.ch/Huridocda/Huridoca.nsf/e06a5300f90fa0238025668700518ca4/c56876817262a5b2c125695e0050656e/$FILE/G0014092.pdf.

Braga, Anthony A., *Problem-Oriented Policing and Crime Prevention* (Monsey: Criminal Justice Press, 2002): 78–81.

———. 2003. "Serious Youth Gun Offenders and the Epidemic of Youth Violence in Boston." *Journal of Quantitative Criminology* 19 (1): 33–54.

————. 2005. "Analyzing Homicide Problems: Practical Approaches to Developing a Policy-Relevant Description of Serious Urban Violence." *Security Journal* 18 (4): 17–32.

————. 2008. "Pulling Levers Focused Deterrence Strategies and the Prevention of Gun Homicide." *Journal of Criminal Justice* 36 (4): 332–43.

Braga, Anthony, David M. Kennedy, and George Tita. 2002. "New Approaches to the Strategic Prevention of Gang and Group-Involved Violence." In *Gangs in America*, third edition, ed. Ronald C. Huff. Thousand Oaks, CA: Sage Publications.

Braga, Anthony A., David M. Kennedy, Elin J. Waring, and Anne M. Piehl. 2001. "Problem-Oriented Policing, Deterrence, and Youth Violence: An Evaluation of Boston's Operation Ceasefire." *Journal of Research in Crime and Delinquency* 38 (3): 195–225.

Braga, Anthony A., Glenn L. Pierce, Jack McDevitt, Brenda J. Bond, and Shea Cronin. 2008. "The Strategic Prevention of Gun Violence among Gang-Involved Offenders." *Justice Quarterly* 25 (1): 132–62.

Brennan, John. 2009. "A New Approach to Safeguarding Americans." Remarks at the Center for Strategic and International Studies, Washington, DC, August 6.

Bronk, Christopher. 2007. *Managing the US-Mexico Border*. Houston, TX: James A. Baker III Institute for Public Policy of Rice Univ., www.bakerinstitute.org/publications/WWT_US-Mexico.pdf.

Brugiere, Jean-Louis. "Trail of a Terrorist." *Frontline*, October 25, 2001. www.pbs.org/wgbh/pages/frontline,/shows/trail/etc/synopsis.html.

Brzoska, Michael, ed. *Design and Implementation of Arms Embargoes and Travel and Aviation Related Sanctions: Results of the 'Bonn-Berlin Process.'* Bonn, Germany: Bonn International Center for Conversion. www.watsoninstitute.org/tfs/CD/booklet_sanctions.pdf.

Buddi, Mahesh. 2008. "'Immigration' Check Required." *The Times of India*, May 27. http://timesofindia.indiatimes.com/articleshow/msid-3075082,prtpage-1.cms.

Callahan, Mary Ellen. 2009. "US: Finding Relief for Privacy Infringement." *Data Protection Law and Policy* 6 (6).

Camarota, Steven A., and Jessica M. Vaughan. 2009. *Immigration and Crime, Assessing a Conflicted Issue*. Washington, DC: Center for Immigration Studies (CIS). www.cis.org/articles/2009/crime.pdf.

Canada News Center. 2008. "Canada and US Renew Emergency Management Cooperation Agreement." News Release, December 12, 2008. http://news.gc.ca/web/article-eng.do?m=/index&nid=427669.

Carafano, James Jay, Sharon Cardash, and Frank Cilluffo. 2009. *Canada and the United States: Time for a Joint Threat Assessment*. Washington, DC: The Heritage Foundation. www.heritage.org/Research/HomelandSecurity/upload/wm_2404.pdf.

Carnegie Endowment for International Peace and Instituto Tecnológico Autónomo de México. 2001. *Mexico-US Migration: A Shared Responsibility*. Washington, DC: Carnegie Endowment for International Peace. www.carnegieendowment.org/pdf/files/M%20exicoReport2001.pdf.

Carter, Sara A. 2009. "EXCLUSIVE: Hezbollah uses Mexican drug routes into US." *The Washington Times*, March 27. www.washingtontimes.com/news/2009/mar/27/hezbollah-uses-mexican-drug-routes-into-us/print/.

Cassarino, Jean-Pierre. 2009. "EU Mobility Partnerships: Expression of a New Compromise." *Migration Information Source*, September. www.migrationinformation.org/Feature/display.cfm?ID=741

Castaneda, Ruben. 2006. "Gang Members Describe Life Inside MS-13." *The Washington Post*, October 18.

Caulkins, Jonathan P., and Peter Reuter. 2009. "Towards a Harm-Reduction Approach to Enforcement." *Safer Communities* 8 (1): 9–23. www.ukdpc.org.uk/resources/Safer_Communities_Jan09_Special_Issue.pdf.

CBSA (Canada Border Services Agency). 2009. *Canada-US Safe Third Country Agreement*. Ottawa, Canada: CBSA. www.cbsa-asfc.gc.ca/agency-agence/stca-etps-eng.html.

CDC and NCHS (Centers for Disease Control and Prevention and the National Center for Health Statistics). 2005. *Intelligence Reform and Terrorism Act — The Act, the Process and Update*. Washington, DC: CDC. www.cdc.gov/nchs/ppt/bsc/bsc_charlieintel_sep05.ppt.

Chatelard, Geraldine. 2002. *Iraqi Forced Migrants in Jordan: Conditions, Religious Networks, and the Smuggling Process*. Florence, Italy: European Univ. Institute. www.aina.org/articles/chatelard.pdf.

Chin, Ko-Lin. 1996. *Chinatown Gangs: Extortion, Enterprise, and Ethnicity*. New York: Oxford Univ. Press.

CIA (Central Intelligence Agency). 2008. *The World Factbook: Rank Order — GDP (Purchasing Power Parity)*. Washington, DC: CIA. https://www.cia.gov/library/publications/the-world-factbook/rankorder/2001rank.html.

CIC (Citizenship and Immigration Canada). 2009. *Facts and Figures 2008*. Ottawa, Canada: CIC. www.cic.gc.ca/English/resources/statistics/facts2008/permanent/10.asp.

———. 2009. "Countries and Territories Whose Citizens Require Visas in Order to Enter Canada as Visitors." www.cic.gc.ca/EnGLIsh/visit/visas.asp.

Citizens Advice. 2004. "Inquiry into Asylum and Immigration Appeals." London, England: Citizens Advice.

Clarke, Richard A. 2008. *Your Government Failed You: Breaking the Cycle of National Security Disasters*. New York: Harper Collins, 119–41.

Clemens, Michael, and Sami Bazzi. 2008. *Don't Close the Golden Door: Out Noisy Debate on Immigration and its Deathly Silence on Development*. Washington, DC: Center for Global Development. www.cgdev.org/content/publications/detail/16129.

Coker, Christopher. 2009. *War in an Age of Risk*. Cambridge, UK: Polity.

Commission of the European Communities. 2008. *Report from the Commission to the Council: Second Monitoring and Evaluation Report on the Operation Council Common Position 2005/69/JHA*. Brussels, Belgium: Commission of the European Communities. http://eur-lex.europa.eu/LexUriServ/LexUriServ.do?uri=COM:2008:0502:FIN:EN:PDF.

Committee on Technical and Privacy Dimensions of Information for Terrorism Prevention and Other National Goals and the National Research Council. 2008. *Protecting Individual Privacy in the Struggle against Terrorists: A Framework for Program Assessment*. Washington, DC: National Academies Press.

Conference on Security and Co-operation in Europe. 1990. *Charter of Paris for a New Europe.* Paris, France: Conference on Security and Co-Operation in Europe. www.osce.org/documents/ mcs/1990/11/4045_en.pdf.

Cooney, John W. 2007. "Border Security: Security Vulnerabilities at Unmanned and Unmonitored US Border Locations." Stated for the record before the US Senate Committee on Finance, House Judiciary Committee Subcommittee on Immigration, Citizenship, Refugees, Border Security, and International Law, 110th Cong., 1st sess., September 27. www.gao.gov/new.items/d07884t.pdf.

Cornelius, Wayne. 2009. *Evaluating US Immigration Control Policy: What Mexican Migrants Can Tell Us.* San Diego, CA: Center for Comparative Immigration Studies.

Cornelius, Wayne A., and Idean Salehyan. 2007. "Does Border Enforcement Deter Unauthorized Immigration? The Case of Mexican Migration to the United States of America." *Regulation and Governance* 1: 139–53.

Cornelius, Wayne A., and Jessa M. Lewis. 2007. *Impacts of Border Enforcement on Mexican Migration: The View from Sending Communities.* Boulder: Lynne Rienner and UCSD Center for Comparative Immigration Studies.

Council of the European Union. 2005. "Convention between the Kingdom of Belgium, the Federal Republic of Germany, the Kingdom of Spain, the French Republic, the Grand Duchy of Luxembourg, the Kingdom of the Netherlands and the Republic of Austria on the Stepping Up of Cross-Border Cooperation, Particularly in Combating Terrorism, Cross-Border Crime and Illegal Migration." July 7. www.statewatch.org/news/2005/aug/Prum-Convention.pdf.

———. 2005. "Council Declaration on the EU Response to the London Bombings." Press Release, July 13. www.consilium.europa.eu/uedocs/cms_data/docs/pressdata/en/jha/85703.pdf.

———. 2008. *Final Report by EU-US High Level Contact Group on Information Sharing and Privacy and Personal Data Protection.* Brussels, Belgium: Council of the European Union. www.dhs.gov/xlibrary/ assets/privacy/privacy_intl_hlcg_report_02_07_08_en.pdf.

(CRS) Congressional Research Service. 2008. *Border Security: The Role of the U.S. Border Patrol.* Washington, DC: Congressional Research Service. www.fas.org/sgp/crs/homesec/RL32562.pdf.

Crush, Jonathan. 2008. "South Africa: Policy in the Face of Xenophobia." *Migration Information Source,* July. www.migrationinformation.org/Profiles/display.cfm?ID=689.

CSIS (Canadian Security Intelligence Service. 2005. *Public Report 2004–2005.* Ottawa, Canada: CSIS. www.csis-scrs.gc.ca/pblctns/nnlrprt/2004/rprt2004-eng.pdf.

———. 2008. *Public Report 2007–2008.* Ottawa, Canada: CSIS. www.csis-scrs.gc.ca/pblctns/ nnlrprt/2007/PublicReport0708_Eng.pdf.

———. 2009. "Remarks by Richard B, Fadden, Director, Canadian Security Intelligence Service, to the Canadian Association for Security and Intelligence Studies (CASIS) Annual International Conference." Remarks, October 29. www.csis-scrs.gc.ca/nwsrm/spchs/spch29102009-eng.asp.

Curry, G. David, Richard A. Ball, and Robert J. Fox. 1994. *Gang Crime and Law Enforcement Recordkeeping.* Washington, DC: US Department of Justice (DOJ). www.ncjrs.gov/txtfiles/gcrime.txt.

Dale, Maryclaire. 2008. "Feds: Russian Ring Made $3 Million on Asylum Fraud." *The Associated Press,* July 30. www.cis.org/node/707.

Dalleck, Matthew. 2008. "Civic Security." *Democracy* 7. www.democracyjournal.org/article.php?id=6567.

Davidson, Thomas. 2005. "Terrorism and Human Smuggling Rings in South and Central America." *Terrorism Monitor* 3 (22). www.jamestown.org/single/?no_cache=1&tx_ttnews%5Btt_news%5D=611.

Decker, Scott H. 2002. "A Decade of Gang Research: Findings of the National Institute of Justice Gang Portfolio." In *Responding to Gangs: Evaluation and Research*, ed. Winifred L. Reed and Scott H. Decker. Washington, DC: DOJ.

———. 2003. "Gangs, Youth Violence, and Policing: Where Do We Stand, Where Do We Go From Here?" In *Policing Gangs and Youth Violence*, ed. Scott H. Decker. Belmont, CA: Wadsworth.

Department of Justice, Canada. 2009. *Customs Act* (1985, c. 1 [2nd Supp.]). Ottawa, Canada: Department of Justice. www.canlii.org/en/ca/laws/stat/rsc-1985-c-1-2nd-supp/73617/rsc-1985-c-1-2nd-supp.html#history.

Department of Justice, Equality, and Law Reform, Irish Naturalisation and Immigration Service. 2009. *Statutory Instruments S.I. No.239 of 2009: Immigration Act 2004 (Visas) Order 2009*. www.inis.gov.ie/en/INIS/s.i.239%20final.pdf/Files/s.i.239%20final.pdf.

DHS (US Department of Homeland Security). 2002. "Specifics of Secure and Smart Border Action Plan." Press Release, January 7. www.dhs.gov/xnews/releases/press_release_0036.shtm.

———. 2005. "Homeland Security Secretary Michael Chertoff Announces Six-Point Agenda for Department of Homeland Security." Press Release, July 13. www.dhs.gov/xnews/releases/press_release_0703.shtm.

———. 2005. "Secretary Michael Chertoff, US Department of Homeland Security Second Stage Remarks." Press Release, July 13. www.dhs.gov/xnews/speeches/speech_0255.shtm.

———. 2006. *DHS Exhibit 300 Public Release BY08 (Form) / CBP — Advance Passenger Information System (APIS) (2008) (Item)*. Washington, DC: DHS. www.dhs.gov/xlibrary/assets/mgmt/e300-cbp-apis2008.pdf.

———. 2007. *Agreement Between the United States of America and the European Union on the Processing and Transfer of Passenger Name Record (PNR) Data by Air Carriers to the United States Department of Homeland Security (DHS) (2007 PNR Agreement)*. Washington, DC: DHS. www.dhs.gov/xlibrary/assets/pnr-2007agreement-usversion.pdf.

———. 2007. "Fact Sheet: Enhanced Driver's Licenses (EDL)." Press Release, December 5. www.dhs.gov/xnews/releases/pr_1196872524298.shtm.

———. 2007. *National Preparedness Guidelines*. Washington, DC: DHS. www.fema.gov/pdf/government/npg.pdf.

———. 2008. "DHS Screening and Credentialing." Powerpoint Presentation, January. www.secureidnews.com/audio/iab_0108/Cogswell.pdf.

———. 2008. "ESTA Web site Available in 13 Additional Languages for US-Bound Travelers from Visa Waiver Countries." News Release, October 15. www.dhs.gov/xnews/releases/pr_1224103683923.shtm.

———. 2008. *Homeland Security Presidential Directive 6: Directive on Integration and Use of Screening Information to Protect against Terrorism*. August 25. www.dhs.gov/xabout/laws/gc_1214594853475.shtm.

———. 2008. "Letter dated November 13, 2008, from Michael Chertoff, Secretary, Department of Homeland Security to the Honorable Patrick Leahy, Chairman, Senate Committee on the Judiciary." DHS, Washington, DC.

———. 2008. "Letter dated November 18, 2008, to Michael Chertoff, Secretary, Department of Homeland Security from Sen. Dianne Feinstein." DHS, Washington, DC.

———. 2008. "Remarks by Homeland Security Secretary Michael Chertoff at Harvard University." News Release, February 6. www.dhs.gov/xnews/speeches/sp_1203020606566.shtm.

———. 2008. "Remarks by Homeland Security Secretary Michael Chertoff at a Roundtable with Reporters from Select Visa Waiver Program Countries." Press Release, October 23. www.dhs.gov/xnews/releases/pr_1224850291152.shtm.

———. 2008. "U.S. Department of Homeland Security Announces 6.8 Percent Increase in Fiscal Year 2009 Budget Request." Press Release, February 4. www.dhs.gov/xnews/releases/pr_1202151112290.shtm.

———. 2008. "US-VISIT: Current Ports of Entry." January 31. www.dhs.gov/files/programs/editorial_0685.shtm.

———. 2008. *Visa Waiver Program: Passport Requirements Timeline*. Washington, DC: DHS. www.dhs.gov/xtrvlsec/programs/content_multi_image_0021.shtm.

———. 2009. "Joint Statement by Secretary Napolitano and Canadian Public Safety Minister Peter Van Loan on the US-Canada Border." Press Release, May 27. www.dhs.gov/ynews/releases/pr_1243434829897.shtm.

———. 2009. "Remarks by Secretary Napolitano at the Council on Foreign Relations." Press Release, July 29. www.dhs.gov/ynews/speeches/sp_1248891649195.shtm.

———. 2009. "Secretary Napolitano Announces Rule Proposing Permanent Global Entry Program." Press Release, November 19. www.dhs.gov/ynews/releases/pr_1258657984894.shtm.

———. 2010. *Quadrennial Homeland Security Review* (QHSR). Washington, DC: DHS, viii. www.dhs.gov/xabout/gc_1208534155450.shtm.

DHS, Customs and Border Protection (CBP). 2004. *Customs and Border Protection Passenger Name Record Privacy Statement for PNR Data Received in Connection with Flights between the US and the European Union*. Washington, DC: DHS. www.dhs.gov/xlibrary/assets/privacy/privacy_stmt_pnr.pdf.

———. 2008. *Performance and Accountability Report Fiscal Year 2008*. Washington, DC: DHS. www.cbp.gov/linkhandler/cgov/newsroom/publications/admin/par_fy08_pub.ctt/par_fy08.pdf.

———. 2008. "US, United Kingdom Border Agencies Agree to Expedite Travel between Nations." Press Release, June 24. www.cbp.gov/xp/cgov/newsroom/news_releases/archives/2008_news_releases/june_2008/06242008_4.xml.

———. 2009. "CBP Debuts New Global Entry Area at Bush Intercontinental Airport." Press Release, May 18. www.cbp.gov/xp/cgov/newsroom/news_releases/may_2009/05182009_16.xml.

———. 2009. *Global Entry Program: Information Guide*. Washington, DC: DHS. www.cbp.gov/linkhandler/cgov/newsroom/publications/travel/global_brochure.ctt/global_brochure.pdf.

———. 2009. "Global Entry Program Description." Press Release, April 4. www.cbp.gov/xp/cgov/travel/

trusted_traveler/global_entry/global_entry_discription.xml.

———. 2009. "More than 70 Percent of Tower Construction Completed for SBI's Northern Border Project in Detroit Sector." Press Release, December 1. www.cbp.gov/xp/cgov/newsroom/news_releases/archives/2009_news_releases/dec_2009/12012009_5.xml

———. 2009. "NEXUS Program Description." www.cbp.gov/xp/cgov/travel/trusted_traveler/nexus_prog/nexus.xml.

———. 2009. *Office of Internal Affairs: Assistant Commissioner*, James F. Tomsheck. Washington, DC: DHS. www.cbp.gov/xp/cgov/about/organization/assist_comm_off/internal_affairs.xml.

———. 2009. "Preclearance Locations." www.cbp.gov/xp/cgov/toolbox/contacts/preclear_locations.xml.

———. 2010. "Southwest Border Fence Construction Progress." Press Release, January 15. www.cbp.gov/xp/cgov/border_security/ti/ti_news/sbi_fence/.

———. *NEXUS*. Washington, DC: DHS. www.cbp.gov/linkhandler/cgov/newsroom/fact_sheets/travel/nexus_fact.ctt/nexus_fact.pdf.

DHS, Office of Immigration Statistics. 2006. *Yearbook of Immigration Statistics*. Washington, DC: DHS. www.dhs.gov/files/statistics/publications/yearbook.shtm.

———. 2008. *Yearbook of Immigration Statistics*. Washington, DC: DHS. www.dhs.gov/files/statistics/publications/yearbook.shtm.

DHS, Office of Inspector General. 2009. *Effectiveness of the Department of Homeland Security Traveler Redress Inquiry Program (Redacted)*. Washington, DC: DHS. www.dhs.gov/xoig/assets/mgmtrpts/OIG-09-103r_Sep09.pdf.

DHS, Risk Steering Committee. 2008. *DHS Risk Lexicon*. Washington, DC: DHS. www.dhs.gov/xlibrary/assets/dhs_risk_lexicon.pdf.

DHS, The Secure Borders and Open Doors Advisory Committee. 2008. *Preserving Our Welcome to the World in an Age of Terrorism*. Washington, DC: DHS. www.dhs.gov/xlibrary/assets/SBODAC_011608-Accessible.pdf.

DHS, US Immigration and Customs Enforcement (ICE). 2003. "Fact Sheet: Changes to National Security Entry/Exit Registration System (NSEERS)." December 1. www.ice.gov/pi/news/factsheets/nseersFS120103.htm.

———. 2007. *ICE Fiscal Year 2007 Annual Report: Protecting National Security and Upholding Public Safety*. Washington, DC: DHS. www.ice.gov/doclib/about/ice07ar_final.pdf.

———. 2008. "ICE Unveils Sweeping New Plan to Target Criminal Aliens in Jails Nationwide: Initiative Aims to Identify and Remove Criminal Aliens from All US Jails and Prisons." News Release, March 28. www.ice.gov/pi/news/newsreleases/articles/080414washington.htm.

———. 2008. "Los Angeles Man Arrested for Filing Nearly 1,000 Fraudulent Work Visa Petitions: Defendant Made Nearly $5 Million Charging Aliens for Fraudulent Filings." Press Release, July 31. www.ice.gov/pi/nr/0807/080731losangeles.htm.

———. 2008. *Operation Community Shield: Targeting Violent Transnational Street Gangs*. Washington, DC: DHS. www.ice.gov/pi/news/factsheets/opshieldfactsheet.htm.

———. 2009. *Border Enforcement Security Task Forces*. Washington, DC: DHS. www.ice.gov/pi/news/factsheets/080226best_fact_sheet.htm.

———. 2009. "ICE and DEA Strengthen Partnership to Fight Drug Trafficking." News Release, June 18. www.ice.gov/pi/nr/0906/090618washington.htm.

———. 2009. *ICE Fiscal Year 2008 Annual Report: Protecting National Security and Upholding Public Safety*. Washington, DC: DHS. www.ice.gov/doclib/pi/reports/ice_annual_report/pdf/ice08ar_final.pdf.

DOC (US Department of Commerce), International Trade Administration, Office of Travel & Tourism Industries. 2008. "2007 Sets All Time International Tourism Record for US." Press Release, March 10. www.commerce.gov/NewsRoom/PressReleases_FactSheets/PROD01_005355.

———. 2008. "Outbound Analysis 2007." Press Release, June 30. http://tinet.ita.doc.gov/outreachpages/download_data_table/2007_Outbound_Analysis.doc.

———. 2008. "US Sets New Records for Travel Abroad in 2007." Press Release, June 30. http://tinet.ita.doc.gov/outreachpages/download_data_table/2007_Outbound_Analysis.doc.

———. 2008. "US Travel Abroad Declined in 2008. However, Fifth Straight Year of Record Spending." Press Release, June 29. http://tinet.ita.doc.gov/outreachpages/download_data_table/2008_Outbound_Analysis.doc.
———. 2009. *United States Travel and Tourism Exports, Imports, and the Balance of Trade: 2008*. Washington, DC: DOC. http://tinet.ita.doc.gov/outreachpages/download_data_table/2008_International_Visitor_Spending.pdf.

———. 2009. *US Citizen Air Traffic to Overseas Regions, Canada and Mexico 2008*. Washington, DC: DOC. http://tinet.ita.doc.gov/view/m-2008-O-001/index.htm4l.

DOD (US Department of Defense), Technology and Privacy Advisory Committee. 2004. *Safeguarding Privacy in the Fight against Terrorism*. Washington, DC: DOD. www.defense.gov/news/Jan2006/d20060208tapac.pdf.

———. 2008. *National Defense Strategy*. Washington, DC: DOD. www.defense.gov/news/2008%20National%20Defense%20Strategy.pdf.

———. 2009. "2010 QDR Terms of Reference Fact Sheet." Press Release, April 27.

DOJ (US Department of Justice). 2008. "Foreign National Pleads Guilty to Conspiracy and Alien Smuggling Charges." Press Release, September 22. www.justice.gov/opa/pr/2008/September/08-crm-844.html.

———. 2009. "Attorney General Holder Speaks at EU/US Justice and Home Affairs Ministerial Meeting." Speech, October 28. www.justice.gov/ag/speeches/2009/ag-speech-091028.html.

———. 2009. "Project Safe Neighborhoods." www.psn.gov/.

DOJ, Federal Bureau of Prisons. 2009. "Quick Facts about the Bureau of Prisons." Press Release, December 25. www.bop.gov/news/quick.jsp#1.

DOJ, National Drug Intelligence Center. 2008. *Situation Report: Cities in Which Mexican DTOs Operate within the United States*. Washington, DC: DOJ. www.usdoj.gov/ndic/pubs27/27986/appendb.htm#start.

———. 2009. *National Drug Threat Assessment 2009*. Washington, DC: DOJ.

DOJ, Office of the Inspector General Audit Division. 2009. *The Federal Bureau of Investigation's Terrorist Watchlist Nomination Practices Audit Report 09-25*. Washington, DC: DOJ. www.usdoj.gov/oig/reports/FBI/a0925/final.pdf.

DOJ, Office of Justice Programs, National Institute of Justice. 2009. "Editor's Note: Evaluating the High Point Intervention." Press Release, March 24. www.ojp.usdoj.gov/nij/journals/262/evaluating-high-point-intervention.htm.

DOS (US Department of State). 2005. "Canada: 2005 Country Report on Terrorism." Cable from US Embassy in Canada to the Secretary of State in Washington, DC. www.state.gov/documents/organization/133166.pdf.

———. 2005. "Nonimmigrant Visa Workload Fiscal Year 2005*." http://travel.state.gov/pdf/fy%202005%20niv%20workload%20by%20category.pdf.

———. 2008. "Background Note: Canada." www.state.gov/r/pa/ei/bgn/2089.htm.

———. 2008. *Country Reports on Terrorism 2007*. Washington, DC: DOS. www.state.gov/documents/organization/105904.pdf.

———. 2008. *Report of the Visa Office 2008*. Washington, DC: DOS. www.travel.state.gov/visa/frvi/statistics/statistics_4391.html.

———. 2008. *Visa Waiver Program (VWP)*. Washington, DC: DOS. http://travel.state.gov/visa/temp/without/without_1990.html.

———. 2009. *Adjusted Refusal Rate — B Visas Only By Nationality Fiscal Year 2009*. Washington, DC: DOS. www.travel.state.gov/pdf/FY09.pdf.

———. 2009. "Background Note: Mexico." www.state.gov/r/pa/ei/bgn/35749.htm.

———. 2009. *Investigations*. Washington, DC: DOS. www.state.gov/m/ds/investigat/index.htm.

———. 2009. *Special Reports: Trafficking in Persons Report 2009*. Washington, DC: DOS. www.state.gov/documents/organization/123357.pdf.

———. 2009. *US Department of State Foreign Affairs Manual*, Volume 9 – Visas. Washington, DC: DOS. www.state.gov/documents/organization/106193.pdf.

———. "Department Organization." www.state.gov/r/pa/ei/rls/dos/436.htm.

DOS, Bureau of International Information Programs. 2005. "G8 Countries Cooperate on Secure International Travel Initiative." Press Release, July 8. www.fas.org/asmp/campaigns/MANPADS/StateG8pressrelease_08July2005.html.

DOS, Bureau of International Narcotics and Law Enforcement Affairs (INL). 2006. "US Strategy to Internationalize Efforts against Kleptocracy: Combating High-Level Public Corruption, Denying Safe Haven, and Recovering Assets." Fact Sheet, August 10, DOS, Washington, DC. http://armenia.usembassy.gov/root/pdfs/kleptocracy.pdf.

Drost, Nadja. 2009. "Heightened Security at U.S.-Canada Border Catching Few Terrorists." *Hearst Newspapers*, April 19. www.timesunion.com/AspStories/story.asp?storyID=791561.

DS (Diplomatic Security). 2009. Information obtained by author.

Dunn, Timothy J. 1996. *The Militarization of the U.S.-Mexico Border 1978-1992: Low-Intensity Conflict Comes Home*. Austin: CMAS Books.

EC (European Commission), External Relations. 2009. *Sanctions or Restrictive Measures*. Brussels, Belgium: EC. http://ec.europa.eu/external_relations/cfsp/sanctions/docs/index_en.pdf#4.

Embassy of the United States of America in Canada. 2007. "Did You Know? Why Canada is Important to the United States." http://ottawa.usembassy.gov/content/can_usa/pdfs/didyouknow.pdf.

———. 2009. "Border Facts." http://ottawa.usembassy.gov/content/textonly.asp?section=can_usa&subse ction1=borderissues&document=borderissues_borderfaq_0906.

Esquivel, J. Jesús. 2008. "Mexican Drug Cartels and Islamic Radicals Working Together." *Proceso*, July 14. http://einshalom.com/archives/1584.

———. 2008. "U.S. Government: Hamas, Hezbollah Collaborating with Mexican Drug Cartels." *Proceso*, July 16. www.blacklistednews.com/?news_id=550.

Etzioni, Amitai. 2003. "Reliable Identification for Homeland Protection and Collateral Gains." In *Creating a Trusted Network for Homeland Security*, Appendix A. Washington, DC: Markle Foundation.

EU-US Joint Statement. 2009. "Enhancing Transatlantic Cooperation in the Area of Justice, Freedom and Security." www.se2009.eu/polopoly_fs/1.21271!menu/standard/file/EU-US%20Joint%20 Statement%2028%20October%202009.pdf.

Europa. 2009. "Free Movement of Workers: General Provisions." http://europa.eu/legislation_ summaries/internal_market/living_and_working_in_the_internal_market/free_movement_of_workers/ l23013a_en.htm.

European Commission. *Security Budget*, 2007–2013. http://ec.europa.eu/research/fp7/index_ en.cfm?pg=security.

European Parliament. 2006. "Round-up of Tajani and Barrot Hearings." Press Release, June 18. www. europarl.europa.eu/sides/getDoc.do?language=EN&type=IM-PRESS&reference=20080612FCS31557.

Europol. 2007. *EU Organized Crime Threat Assessment 2007*. The Hague, the Netherlands: Europol. www.europol.europa.eu/publications/European_Organised_Crime_Threat_Assessment_%28OCTA%29/ OCTA2007.pdf.

———. 2008. *Facilitated Illegal Immigration into the European Union*. The Hague, the Netherlands: Europol. www.europol.europa.eu/publications/Serious_Crime_Overviews/Facilitated_illegal_ immigration_2008.pdf.

———. 2009. *Facilitated Illegal Immigration into the European Union*. The Hague, the Netherlands: Europol. www.europol.europa.eu/publications/Serious_Crime_Overviews/Illegal_Immigration_Fact_ Sheet_2009.PDF.

Fallows, James. 2009. "Civilize Homeland Security." *The Atlantic* (July/August). www.theatlantic.com/ doc/200907/ideas-homeland-security.

FATF (Financial Action Task Force). "About the FATF." www.fatf-gafi.org/pages/0,3417,en_32250379_3 2236836_1_1_1_1,00.html.

————. 2004. *FATF 40 Recommendations*. Paris, France: FATF. www.fatf-gafi.org/dataoecd/7/40/34849567.PDF.

FBI (Federal Bureau of Investigation), Human Smuggling and Trafficking Center (HSTC). 2004. *Front Companies: An Invaluable Source for Alien Smuggling Organizations*. Washington, DC: FBI.

Fekete, Jason. 2009. "Embrace 'Canadian Values,' Urges Jason Kenney." *The Canwest News Service*, April 15.

Flynn, Stephen E. 2004. *America the Vulnerable: How Our Government is Failing to Protect Us from Terrorism*. New York: HarperCollins.

————. 2007. *The Edge of Disaster*. New York: Random House.

Flynn, Stephen (project director), Gary Hart and Warren Rudman (cochairs). 2002. *America – Still Unprepared, Still In Danger*. New York: Council on Foreign Relations. www.cfr.org/publication/americastill_unprepared_ still_in_danger.html_.

Ford, Jess T. 2005. "State Department: Improvements Needed to Strengthen US Passport Fraud Detection Efforts." Statement for the record before the Senate Committee on Homeland Security and Government Affairs, 109th Cong., 1st sess., June 29. www.google.com/url?sa=t&source=web&ct=res&cd=1&ved=0CAcQFjAA&url=http%3A%2F%2Fhsgac.senate.gov%2Fpublic%2Findex.cfm%3FFuseAction%3DFiles.View%26FileStore_id%3D882eb9a7-e54d-4214-a8e2-31450692fe28&ei=s9MuS4S-Joa7lAfVm82XBw&usg=AFQjCNFmeZDluQM5ttwkYzw_Oey5uxq_cQ&sig2=C4OZ4UeyG0XkrvLjs3yIqg.

Franco, Celinda. 2008. *The MS-13 and 18th Street Gangs: Emerging Transnational Gang Threats?* Washington, DC: Congressional Research Service. www.fas.org/sgp/crs/row/RL34233.pdf.

Friman, H. Richard. 2008. "Migration and Security: Crime, Terror and the Politics of Order." In Immigration, Integration, and Security: America and Europe in Comparative Perspective, ed. Ariane Cebel d'Appollonia and Simon Reich. Pittsburgh: Univ. of Pittsburgh Press, 130–44.

————. 2009. "Drug Markets and the Selective Use of Violence." *Crime, Law and Social Change* 52 (3): 285–95.

Frontex. 2008. "Frontex and Fortress Europe." http://frontex.info.pl/content/frontex_and_fortress_europe.

Fuller, Thomas. 2002. "EU Passports: An Easy-to-Steal Tool for Terrorists." *The New York Times*, January 8. www.nytimes.com/2002/01/08/news/08iht-passport_ed3_.html?pagewanted=1.

Gardham, Duncan. 2009. "Hidden Threat from Al-Qaeda Sleeper Cells: Al Qaeda Terrorists are Exploiting Loose Visa and Immigration Rules to Enter Britain, the Security Services Fear." *The Telegraph*, November 27. www.telegraph.co.uk/news/6672806/Hidden-threat-from-al-Qaeda-sleeper-cells.html.

GAO (US Government Accountability Office). 1993. *Illegal Aliens: Despite Data Limitations, Current Methods Provide Better Population Estimates*, GAO/PEMD-93-25. Washington, DC: GAO. www.gao.gov/cgi-bin/getrpt?PEMD-93-25.

————. 1995. *Illegal Immigration: INS Overstay Estimation Methods Need Improvement*, GAO/PEMD-95-20. Washington, DC: GAO. www.gao.gov/archive/1995/pe95020.pdf.

———. 2004. *Overstay Tracking: A Key Component of Homeland Security and a Layered Defense*, GAO-04-82. Washington, DC: GAO. www.gao.gov/new.items/d0482.pdf.

———. 2005. *Combating Alien Smuggling: Opportunities Exist to Improve the Federal Response*, GAO-05-305. Washington, DC: GAO. www.gao.gov/new.items/d05305.pdf.

———. 2005. *Information on Criminal Aliens Incarcerated in Federal and State Prisons and Local Jails*, GAO-05-337R. Washington, DC: GAO. www.gao.gov/new.items/d05337r.pdf.

———. 2006. *Border Security: Key Unresolved Issues Justify Reevaluation of Border Surveillance Technology Program*, GAO-06-295. Washington, DC: GAO. www.gao.gov/new.items/d06295.pdf.

———. 2006. *Border Security: Stronger Actions Needed to Assess and Mitigate Risks of the Visa Waiver Program*, GAO-06-854. Washington, DC: GAO. www.gao.gov/new.items/d06854.pdf.

———. 2006. "Department of State, Visas: Documentation of Nonimmigrants under the Immigration and Nationality Act, as Amended." *Federal Register* 71, no. 126 (June 30): 37494–95. http://edocket.access.gpo.gov/2006/pdf/E6-10270.pdf.

———. 2006. *Illegal Immigration: Border-Crossing Deaths Have Doubled Since 1995: Border Patrol's Efforts to Prevent Deaths Have Not Been Fully Evaluated*, GAO-06-770. Washington, DC: GAO. www.gao.gov/new.items/d06770.pdf.

———. 2007. *SBInet Expenditure Plan Needs to Better Support Oversight and Accountability*, GAO-07-309. Washington, DC: GAO. www.gao.gov/new.items/d07309.pdf.

———. 2008. *Comprehensive Strategy Needed to Improve Passport Operations*, GAO-08-891. Washington, DC: GAO. www.gao.gov/new.items/d08891.pdf.

———. 2008. *Congress Should Consider Alternatives for Strengthening Protection of Personally Identifiable Information*, GAO-08-795T. Washington, DC: GAO. www.gao.gov/new.items/d08795t.pdf.

———. 2008. *Secure Border Initiative: DHS Needs to Address Significant Risks in Delivering Key Technology Investment*, GAO-08-1086. Washington, DC: GAO. www.gao.gov/new.items/d081086.pdf

———. 2008. *Secure Border Initiative Fiscal Year 2008 Expenditure Plan Shows Improvement, but Deficiencies Limit Congressional Oversight and DHS Accountability*, GAO-08-739R. Washington, DC: GAO. www.gao.gov/new.items/d08739r.pdf

———. 2008. *Various Issues Led to the Termination of the Untied States-Canada Shared Border Management Pilot Project*, GAO-08-1038R. Washington, DC: GAO. www.gao.gov/new.items/d081038r.pdf.

———. 2008. *Visa Waiver Program: Actions Are Needed to Improve Management of the Expansion Process, and to Assess and Mitigate Program Risks*, GAO-08-967. Washington, DC: GAO. www.gao.gov/new.items/d08967.pdf.

———. 2009. *Better Coordination with the Department of Homeland Security and an Updated Accountability Framework Can Further Enhance DEA's Efforts to Meet Post-9/11 Responsibilities*, GAO-09-63. Washington, DC: GAO. www.gao.gov/highlights/d0963high.pdf.

———. 2009. *Department of State: Undercover Tests Reveal Significant Vulnerabilities in State's Passport Issuance Process*. Washington, DC: GAO. www.gao.gov/new.items/d09447.pdf.

———. 2009. *Secure Border Initiative: Technology Deployment Delays Persist and the Impact of Border Fencing Has Not Been Assessed*, GAO-09-896. Washington, DC: GAO. www.gao.gov/new.items/d09896.pdf.

———. 2009. *US Customs and Border Protection's Secure Border Initiative Fiscal Year 2009 Expenditure Plan*, GAO-09-274R. Washington, DC: GAO. www.gao.gov/new.items/d09274r.pdf.

———. 2009. "Briefing on U.S. Customs and Border Protection's Secure Border Initiative Fiscal Year 2009 Expenditure Plan, GAO-09-274R." Presentation prepared for the Subcommittees on Homeland Security, Senate and House Committees on Appropriations. www.gao.gov/new.items/d09274r.pdf.

Gibson, Campbell, and Emily Lennon. 1999. "Historical Census Statistics on the Foreign-Born Population of the United States: 1850 to 1990." Working Paper No. 29, US Census Bureau, US Government Printing Office, Washington, DC.

Ginsburg, Susan. 2006. *Countering Terrorist Mobility: Shaping an Operational Strategy*. Washington, DC: MPI. www.migrationpolicy.org/pubs/MPI_TaskForce_Ginsburg.pdf.

———. 2008. "Weaknesses in the Visa Waiver Program: Are The Needed Safeguards in Place to Protect America?" Statement for the record before the Senate Committee on the Judiciary, Subcommittee on Terrorism, Technology and Homeland Security, 110th Cong., 2nd sess., February 28. www.migrationpolicy.org/pubs/SGinsburgTestimony_02282008.pdf.

Global Witness. 2008. "US Move to Ban Top Cambodian Officials Exposes Failure of Europe, Australia and Japan to Get Tough on Corruption." Press Release, January 22. www.globalwitness.org/media_library_get.php/569/US_move_to_ban_top_cambodian_officials_exposes_failure_of_europe_australia_and_japan_to_get_tough_on_corruption.doc.

Gouteyron, Adrien. 2007. *Un rapport d'information fait au nom de la commission des finances, du contrôle budgétaire et des comptes économiques de la nation sur les services des visas*. Paris, France: Sénat. www.diplomatie.gouv.fr/fr/IMG/pdf/Rapport_d_information_no353_-_Visas.pdf.

Government of Canada, Security and Prosperity Partnership of North America. 2005. *Report to Leaders*. June. www.spp-psp.gc.ca/eic/site/spp-psp.nsf/eng/00098.html.

Green, Eric. 2006. "US-Colombian Cooperation Nets Arrests of Alien Smugglers: Panama Also Helps in Solving Smuggling Case." *America.gov*, January 27. www.america.gov/st/washfile-english/2006/January/20060127170932AEneerG0.6159937.html.

Griffard, Bernard F., and Bert B. Tussing. 2009. *Migration and Border Security: The Military's Role*. Carlisle, PA: US Army War College. www.csl.army.mil/usacsl/publications/IP_15_09_MigrationAndBorderSecurity.pdf.

Halegua, Aaron. 2004. "The Targeting of United Nations Sanctions: Political, Economic and Ethical Explanations of Normative Change." Paper presented at the Annual Meeting of the International Studies Association, Le Centre Sheraton Hotel, Montreal, Quebec, Canada, March 17. www.allacademic.com//meta/p_mla_apa_research_citation/0/7/3/1/8/pages73180/p73180-1.php.

Harris, Kathleen. 2010. "Report: 14,000 Suspected Illegal Immigrants Detained Last Year." *Toronto Sun*, January 11. www.torontosun.com/news/canada/2010/01/11/12425881-qmi.html.

Hart, Michael. 2008. "What About the Border?" *One Issue: Two Voices* (February 2008): 8–13. www.wilsoncenter.org/topics/pubs/Nontariff%20Barriers_1i2v8.pdf.

Haskell, Master Sgt. Bob. 2005. "Winter Freeze Wrap-Up." *USNORTHCOM News*, March 22. www.northcom.mil/news/2005/032205.html.

Hayden, Michael V. 2008. "Transcript of Remarks." Landon Lecture Series, Kansas State University, April 30. www.cia.gov/news-information/speeches-testimony-archive-2008/landon-lecture-series.html.

Healy, Timothy J. 2009. "Five Years after the Intelligence Reform and Terrorism Prevention Act (IRTPA): Stopping Terrorist Travel." Statement for the record before the Senate Committee on Homeland Security and Government Affairs, 111th Cong., 1st sess., December 9. http://hsgac.senate.gov/public/index.cfm?FuseAction=Files.View&FileStore_id=50242372-f66d-401f-b3a8-1feb2b2de6fa.

Hegeman, Roxana. 2008. "Kan. Tribal 'Secretary of State' Gets Prison Term." *The Associated Press*, October 10. www3.signonsandiego.com/news/2008/oct/10/immigration-indian-tribe-10-10-08/.

Heyman, David, 2009. "Five Years after the Intelligence Reform and Terrorism Prevention Act (IRTPA): Stopping Terrorist Travel." Statement for the record before the Senate Committee on Homeland Security and Government Affairs, 111th Cong., 1st sess., December 9. http://hsgac.senate.gov/public/index.cfm?FuseAction=Files.View&FileStore_id=fca64800-f21e-4772-8ec2-f39bab662ffe.

Heyman, David, and James Jay Carafano. 2008. *Homeland Security 3.0: Building a National Enterprise to Keep America Free, Safe, and Prosperous*. Washington, DC: The Heritage Foundation and the Center for Strategic and International Studies. www.csis.org/files/media/csis/pubs/080918_homeland_sec_3dot0.pdf.

HHS (US Department of Health and Human Services), Office of Inspector General. 2000. *Birth Certificate Fraud*. Washington, DC: HHS. www.oig.hhs.gov/oei/reports/oei-07-99-00570.pdf.

Hiroyuki, Tanaka, Rocco Bellanova, Susan Ginsburg, and Paul De Hert. 2010. *Transatlantic Information Sharing: At a Crossroads*. Washington, DC: Migration Policy Institute, MPI. www.migrationpolicy.org/pubs/infosharing-Jan2010.pdf.

Ho-Gonzalez, William. 2008. "Combating International Criminal Travel Networks." *United States Attorneys' Bulletin* 56 (6): 20–24. www.justice.gov/usao/eousa/foia_reading_room/usab5606.pdf.

Home Office, Border and Immigration Agency. 2007. *Visitors Consultation Paper*. London, UK: Home Office. http://ukba.homeoffice.gov.uk/sitecontent/documents/aboutus/consultations/closedconsultations/visitorsconsultationpaper/visitorvisaconsultation.pdf?view=Binary.

Home Office, UK Border Agency. 2008. "Launch of Britain's New Unified Border Agency." News Release, April 3. www.ukba.homeoffice.gov.uk/sitecontent/newsarticles/2008/ukborderagencylaunch.

———. 2009. "About us." www.ukvisas.gov.uk/en/aboutus/.

———. 2009. "Appeals (APL) — Categories Which Have the Full Right of Appeal." www.ukvisas.gov.uk/en/ecg/appeals/fullrightsappeals.

———. 2009. "Entry Clearance Guidance — Appeals (APL)." www.ukvisas.gov.uk/en/ecg/appeals/.

———. 2009. "Entry Clearance Guidance Documents." www.ukvisas.gov.uk/en/ecg/ecgdocuments.

———. 2009. *Entry Clearance Statistics 2008-09*. London, UK: Home Office. www.ukvisas.gov.uk/resources/en/docs/2958881/visastats2008-09.

———. 2009. "New Countries Face Tough Visa Rules." Press Release, February 9. www.bia.homeoffice. gov.uk/sitecontent/newsarticles/newcountriesfacetoughvisarules. Homeland Security Council. 2007. *National Strategy for Homeland Security*. Washington, DC: The White House.

———. 2009. *Report of a Privacy Impact Assessment Conducted by the UK Border Agency in Relation to the High Value Data Sharing Protocol amongst the Immigration Authorities of the Five Country Conference*. London, UK: Home Office. www.bia.homeoffice.gov.uk/sitecontent/documents/managingourborders/ strengthening/pia-data-sharing-fcc.pdf.

———. "Appendix 1 — Visa requirements for the United Kingdom." www.ukba.homeoffice.gov.uk/ policyandlaw/immigrationlaw/immigrationrules/appendix1/.

Horowitz, Ruth. 1983. *Honor and the American Dream: Culture and Identity in a Chicano Community*. New Brunswick, NJ: Rutgers Univ. Press.

Howard, Russell D., and Colleen M. Traughber. 2007. "Summary of Conclusions: Combating Terrorism Working Group (CTWG)." *Connections* 6 (1): 104–05.

Hsu, Spencer S. 2009. "Border Deaths Are Increasing." *The Washington Post*, September 30. www. washingtonpost.com/wp-dyn/content/article/2009/09/29/AR2009092903212.html.

———. 2009. "US to Check Immigration Status of People in Local Jails." *The Washington Post*, May 19. www.washingtonpost.com/wp-dyn/content/article/2009/05/18/AR2009051803172.html.

Hufbauer, Gary, and Claire Brunel. 2008. "Economic Integration in North America." *One Issue: Two Voices* (February 2008): 2–7. www.wilsoncenter.org/events/docs/Nontariff%20Barriers_1i2v8.pdf.

Huff, Ronald C. 2002. "Gangs and Public Policy: Prevention, Intervention, and Suppression." In *Gangs in America*, Third Edition, ed. Ronald C. Huff. Thousand Oaks, CA: Sage Publications.

Hugo, Graeme. 2008. "In and Out of Australia: Rethinking Chinese and Indian Skilled Migration to Australia." *Asian Population Studies* 4 (3): 267–91.

ICAO (International Civil Aviation Organization). 2003. "Biometric Identification to Provide Enhanced Security and Speedier Border Clearance for Travelling Public." Press Release, May 28. www. icao.int/icao/en/nr/2003/pio200309_e.pdf.

———. 2004. *Airline Reservation System and Passenger Name Record (PNR) Access by States, Facilitation (FAL) Division — Twelfth Session*. Montreal, Canada: ICAO. www.icao.int/icao/en/atb/fal/fal12/ documentation/fal12wp074_en.pdf.

———. 2006. *MRTD Report: Optimizing Security and Efficiency through Enhanced ID Technology* 1, no. 1. www.icao.int/cgi/goto_m_atb.pl?icao/en/atb/fal/mrtd/MRTD_Rpt_V1N1_2006.pdf.

———. 2009. "Border-Related Assistance to Developing Countries." Presentation by an ICAO representative at the Roundtable held under the Chatham House Rule at the Migration Policy Institute (MPI), Washington, DC, September 30.

Interpol (International Criminal Police Organization). 2005. "APEC Endorses INTERPOL's Stolen Travel Document Database." Media Release, November 21. www.interpol.int/public/ICPO/ PressReleases/PR2005/PR200546.asp.

———. 2006. "19th Interpol Asian Regional Conference: Speech by Interpol Secretary General Ronald K. Noble." Speech, April 11. www.Interpol.int/Public/ICPO/speeches/AsianConfSG20060411.asp.

———. 2007. *Trends in Illegal Immigration and Travel Document Fraud.* The Hague, the Netherlands: Interpol.

———. 2008. *Interpol: An Overview.* Lyon, France: Interpol. www.Interpol.int/Public/ICPO/FactSheets/GI01.pdf.

———. 2008. "Interpol Hosts European Troika Co-operation Meeting to Boost Regional Security through Global Approach." Press Release, November 4. www.Interpol.int/public/icpo/pressreleases/pr2008/pr200860.asp.

———. 2009. "2009 — A Milestone Year for Interpol." Press Release, December 30. www.interpol.int/Public/ICPO/PressReleases/PR2009/flashPR2009118/PR2009118.asp.

———. 2009. *Databases.* Lyon, France: Interpol. www.interpol.int/Public/ICPO/FactSheets/GI04.pdf.

———. 2009. *People Smuggling.* The Hague, The Netherlands: Interpol. www.interpol.int/public/THB/PeopleSmuggling/Default.asp.

International Peace Institute. 2009. *Transnational Organized Crime: Task Forces on Strengthening Multilateral Security Capacity.* New York: International Peace Institute. www.ipacademy.org/media/pdf/publications/toc_final.pdf.

IOM (International Organization for Migration). 2001. *The Role of Regional Consultative Processes in Managing International Migration.* Geneva, Switzerland: IOM. www.iom.int/jahia/webdav/site/myjahiasite/shared/shared/mainsite/published_docs/serial_publications/mrs3.pdf.

———. 2003. *International Terrorism and Migration* (Geneva, Switzerland: IOM).

———. 2008. *Migration Initiatives Appeal 2008.* Geneva, Switzerland: IOM. www.iom.int/jahia/webdav/shared/shared/mainsite/about_iom/docs/Migration_Initiatives_2008_Appeal.pdf.

———. 2008. *World Migration Report 2008: Managing Labour Mobility in the Evolving Global Economy.* Geneva, Switzerland: IOM. www.iom.ch/jahia/webdav/site/myjahiasite/shared/shared/mainsite/published_docs/studies_and_reports/WMR2008/Ch1_WMR08.pdf.

———. 2009. "Project List." www.iom.int/1035/projectlist.htm.

Jacobs, Janice L. 2009. "Five Years after the Intelligence Reform and Terrorism Prevention Act (IRTPA): Stopping Terrorist Travel." Statement for the record before the Senate Committee on Homeland Security and Government Affairs, 111th Cong., 1st sess., December 9. http://hsgac.senate.gov/public/index.cfm?FuseAction=Files.View&FileStore_id=790a6ddb-6d50-49a5-8247-a7aaf6073fba.

Jasper, William F. 2005. "Communism's Resurgence." *The New American,* January 24.

Jeffrey, Terrence P. 2009. "Administration Will Cut Border Patrol Deployed on U.S.-Mexico Border." *CNSNews.com,* September 24. www.cnsnews.com/news/article/54514.

Johnson, Mary Helen. 2006. "National Policies and the Rise of Transnational Gangs." *Migration Information Source,* April 1. www.migrationinformation.org/Feature/print.cfm?ID=394.

Johnson, Victor C. 2009. *A Visa and Immigration Policy for the Brain-Circulation Era: Adjusting To What Happened in the World While We Were Making Other Plans.* Washington, DC: Association of International Educators. www.nafsa.org/uploadedFiles/NAFSA_Home/Resource_Library_Assets/Public_Policy/visa_immigration_for_brain_circulation.pdf.

Johnston, Rob. 2005. *Analytic Culture in the US Intelligence Community: An Ethnographic Study.* Washington, DC: Central Intelligence Agency (CIA).

Johnston, David, and Eric Schmitt. 2009. "Ex-Military Officer in Pakistan is Linked to 2 Chicago Terrorism Suspects." *The New York Times,* November 18. www.nytimes.com/2009/11/19/world/asia/19mumbai.html.

Jones, Susan. 2005. "US Denies Visa to Hindu Leader At Muslims' Urging." *Cybercast News Service,* March 18.

Justice and Home Affairs Council. 2001. "Conclusions Adopted by the Council (Justice and Home Affairs)." September 20. http://ec.europa.eu/justice_home/news/terrorism/documents/concl_council_20sep_en.pdf.

Kahn, Jeffrey. 2008. "International Travel and the Constitution." *UCLA Law Review* 56 (271): 271–350.

———. 2008. "International Travel and the Constitution." *American Bar Association National Security Committee Law Report* 30, no. 4 (November/December): 13–15.

Kapp, Lawrence. 2005. *Operations Noble Eagle, Enduring Freedom, and Iraqi Freedom: Questions and Answers about US Military Personnel, Compensation, and Force Structure.* Washington, DC: Congressional Research Service. www.fas.org/sgp/crs/natsec/RL31334.pdf.

Keefe, Patrick Radden. 2009. *The Snake Head: An Epic Tale of the Chinatown Underworld and the American Dream.* New York: Doubleday.

Kennedy, David M. 2002. "A Tale of One City." In *Securing Our Children's Future: New Approaches to Juvenile Justice and Youth Violence,* ed. Gary S. Katzman. Washington, DC: Brookings Institution Press.

———. 2007. "Making Communities Safer: Youth Violence and Gang Interventions that Work." Statement for the record before the House Committee on the Judiciary, Subcommittee on Crime, Terrorism, and Homeland Security, 110th Cong., 1st sess., February 15. http://judiciary.house.gov/hearings/February2007/021507kennedy.pdf?ID=736.

———. 2008. *Deterrence and Crime Prevention: Reconsidering the Prospect of Sanction.* London, UK: Routledge.

———. 2009. *Drugs, Race and Common Ground: Reflections on the High Point Intervention.* Washington, DC: DOJ. www.ojp.usdoj.gov/nij/journals/262/high-point-intervention.htm.

———. 2009. Personal communication with the author.

Kennedy, David M., and Anthony A. Braga. 1998. "Homicide in Minneapolis: Research for Problem Solving." *Homicide Studies* 2 (3): 263–90.

Kennedy, David M., Anthony A. Braga, Anne M. Phiel, and Elin J. Waring. 2001. Reducing Gun Violence: The Boston Gun Project's Operation Ceasefire. Washington, DC: DOJ. www.ncjrs.gov/pdffiles1/nij/188741.pdf.

Kennedy, Patrick F. 2010. "Securing America's Safety: Improving the Effectiveness of Anti-Terrorism Tools and Interagency Communication." Statement for the record before the Senate Committee on the Judiciary, 111th Cong., 1st sess., January 20. http://judiciary.senate.gov/pdf/1-20-09%20Kennedy%20Testimony.pdf.

Kent, Jonathan. 2008. "The IBETs and Integrated Border Management between Canada and the United States." *The Journal of the Royal Canadian Military Institute* 68 (2): 5–10. www.rcmi.org/archives/SITREP/08/08-2%20Sitrep.pdf.

Kephart, Janice. 2009. "The Appearance of Security: REAL ID Final Regulations vs PASS ID Act of 2009." Center for Immigration Studies, Washington DC, 3. www.cis.org/articles/2009/back409.pdf.

Khashu, Anita. 2009. *The Role of Local Police: Striking a Balance between Immigration Enforcement and Civil Liberties.* Washington, DC: Police Foundation. www.policefoundation.org/pdf/strikingabalance/Narrative.pdf.

Kleiman, Mark A. R. 2009. *When Brute Force Fails, How to Have Less Crime and Less Punishment.* Princeton, NJ: Princeton Univ. Press.

———. 2009. Personal communication with the author.

———. Personal communication with the author.

Kollwelter, Serge. 2007. "Immigration in Luxembourg: New Challenges for an Old Country." *Migration Information Source*, March 2007. www.migrationinformation.org/Profiles/display.cfm?id=587

Koring, Paul, and Campbell Clark. 2008. "Pressure Mounts to Repatriate Canadian Citizen." *The Globe and Mail*, May 3, 2008.

Koser, Khalid. 2005. "Irregular Migration, State Security and Human Security." Paper presented for the Policy Analysis and Research Programme of the Global Commission on International Migration (GCIM), September. www.gcim.org/attachements/TP5.pdf.

Koslowski, Rey. 2000. "The Mobility Money Can Buy: Human Smuggling and Border Control in the European Union." In *The Wall Around the West: State Borders and Immigration Controls in North America and Europe*, ed. Peter Andreas and Timothy Snyder. New York: Rowman & Littlefield.

———. 2005. *Real Challenges for Virtual Borders: The Implementation of US-VISIT.* Washington, DC: MPI. www.migrationpolicy.org/pubs/Koslowski_Report.pdf.

———. 2009. "International Cooperation on Business Travel and Tourism." Paper presented at the Global Mobility Regimes workshop of the German Marshall Fund, Washington, DC, November 20–21.

———. 2009. "International Migration and Human Mobility as a Security Issue." Paper presented for the International Studies Meeting, New York, February.

Kraninger, Kathleen. 2009. "Biometric Identification." Statement for the record before the House Appropriations Committee, Subcommittee on Homeland Security, 111st Cong., 1st sess., March 19. www.dhs.gov/ynews/testimony/testimony_1237563811984.shtm.

Kropf, John. 2007. "Networked and Layered: Understanding the US Framework for Protecting Personally Identifiable Information." In *World Data Protection Report 2006–07*. Arlington, VA: The Bureau of National Affairs, Inc., 3–7.

———. 2007. "US/EU: Common Ground for Public Safety and Security." *Data Protection Law and Policy* 7 (7): 4–5.

————. 2008. "Independence Day: How to Move the Global Privacy Dialogue Forward." *Privacy and Security Law Report* 8 (2): 1–5.

Kutz, Gregory D. 2007. "Border Security: Security Vulnerabilities at Unmanned and Unmonitored US Border Locations." Statement for the record before the US Senate Committee on Finance, House Judiciary Committee Subcommittee on Immigration, Citizenship, Refugees, Border Security, and International Law, 110th Cong., 1st sess., September 27. www.gao.gov/new.items/d07884t.pdf.

Lagdameo, Mary. 2008. "Human Smuggling from Fujian to New York." Master's Thesis, University of Southern California. http://digitallibrary.usc.edu/assetserver/controller/item/etd-Lagdameo-2050.pdf.

Land, Garland. 2009. Personal email correspondence with the author.

Laville, Sandra, Richard Norton-Taylor, and Vikram Dodd. 2009. "Student Visa Link to Terror Raids as Gordon Brown Points Finger at Pakistan." *The Guardian*, April 10. www.guardian.co.uk/uk/2009/apr/10/student-visa-terror-arrests-link.

Lazaro, Johnson. 2008. "The Law on Overstaying." *Asian Journal Publications*, February 15–21. www.asianjournal.com/pdf/PDF/2008_SF/2008_02_15/2008_02_15_SF_sec3p%203.pdf.

Laurence, Jonathan. 2007. *Integrating Islam: A New Chapter in Church-State Relations*. Washington, DC: MPI/Bertelsmann Stiftung.

Lebovic, James. 2006. "Deterrence and Homeland Security: A Defensive-Denial Strategy against Terrorists." John Hopkins Univ. National Center for the Study of Preparedness and Catastrophic Event Response (PACER), Baltimore, MD. www.pacercenter.org/pages/publications_briefs.aspx.

Levitt, Matthew, and Michael Jacobson. 2008. *The Money Trail: Finding, Following, and Freezing Terrorist Finances*. Washington, DC: The Washington Institute for Near East Policy. www.washingtoninstitute.org/templateC04.php?CID=302.

Lewis, James A. 2008. *Authentication 2.0 — New Opportunities for Online Identification*. Washington, DC: Center for Strategic and International Studies. http://csis.org/files/media/csis/pubs/080115_authentication.pdf.

Leydan, John. 2009. "UK e-Borders Scheme Thrown into Confusion by EU Rules." *The Register*, December 18. www.theregister.co.uk/2009/12/18/e_borders_confusion/.

Library of Congress. 2001. "H.R.1345: To Amend the Immigration and Nationality Act to Establish a Board of Visa Appeals within the Department of State to Review Decisions of Consular Officers Concerning Visa Applications, Revocations, and Cancellations." April 19, http://thomas.loc.gov/cgi-bin/bdquery/D?d107:16:./temp/~bdJ3Gd.

Lobo, José L. 2009. "Interior implantará la 'frontera electrónica' en Barajas y El Prat para acabar con las colasInterior implantará la 'frontera electrónica' en Barajas y El Prat para acabar con las colas." *el confidencial*, August 5. www.elconfidencial.com/cache/2009/08/05/espana_74_colas_barajas_pasaporte_electronico.html.

Loren, Brooke. 2009. "Mexican Border Vulnerable to Al Qaeda." *Associated Content*, February 19. www.associatedcontent.com/article/1470457/mexican_border_vulnerable_to_al_qaeda.html?cat=75.

Luna, David M. 2007. "Strategies to Fight Kleptocracy." Press Release, September 28. www.scoop.co.nz/stories/WO0709/S00763.htm.

MacFarlane, S. Neil. 2004. "Charter Values and the Response to Terrorism." In *Terrorism and the UN: Before and After September 11*, ed. Jane Boulden and Thomas G. Weiss. Bloomington and Indianapolis, IN: Indiana Univ. Press.

Mahnrood, Mazher. 2008. "Passport to Evil: We Smash Ring that Could Help Terrorists Slip Net." *News of the World*, August 24. www.newsoftheworld.co.uk/news/article16763.ece.

Majtenyi, Cathy. 2006. "Prominent Kenyans Banned from Entering US." *Voice of America*, May 24. www.tingroom.com/voastandard/2006/5/33040.html.

Mancini, Mark A. 1999. "Nonimmigrant Visa Fraud." Statement for the record before the House Committee of the Judiciary, Subcommittee on Immigration and Claims, 106th Cong., 1st sess., May 5. www.aila.org/content/default.aspx?docid=3714.

Manwaring, Max. 2007. *A Contemporary Challenge to State Sovereignty: Gangs and Other Illicit Transnational Criminal Organizations in Central America, El Salvador, Mexico, Jamaica, and Brazil*. Carlisle, PA: Strategic Studies Institute, US Army War College.

Martin, Stone. 2008. "The People Smuggling Gang Who 'Imported' Thousands to Britain." *Financial Times*, January 22.

Martin, Susan F., Patricia Weiss Fagen, and Andrew Schoenholtz. 2005. *The Uprooted: Improving Humanitarian Responses to Forced Migration*. Lanham, MD: Lexington Books.

Marshall, Steve. "PNG Immigration Officials Face Bribery Allegations." *ABC News*, October 8. www.abc.net.au/news/stories/2008/10/08/2384898.htm.

Mascini, Peter. 2006. "Can the Violent Jihad Do without Sympathizers." *Studies in Conflict and Terrorism* 29 (4): 343–57.

McCombs, Brady. 2009. "New 'Virtual Fence' on Verge of Going Up." *Arizona Daily Star*, February 8. www.azstarnet.com/sn/news/279334.

———. 2009. "US to Revisit Glitch-Prone 'Virtual Fence' Set for Border." *Arizona Daily Star*, January 13.

McDonald, Gary. 2008. "Overview of the ICAO MRTD Programme." Powerpoint presentation presented at the Fourth Symposium and Exhibition on ICAO MRTDs, Biometrics and Security Standards, ICAO Headquarters, Montréal, Canada, October 6–8. www.icao.int/MRTDsymposium/2008/Presentations/3_McDonald.pdf.

McGarrell, Edmund F., Steven Chermak, Jeremy M. Wilson, and Nicholas Corsaro. 2006. "Reducing Homicide through a Lever-Pulling Strategy." *Justice Quarterly* 23 (2): 214–31.

McIntyre, David. 2008. "Borders, Technology and Security: Strategic Responses to New Challenges." New Mexico State Univ.–U.S. Army Strategic Studies Institute Colloquium, Los Cruces, New Mexico, March 31.

McKenzie, David J. 2005. "Paper Walls Are Easier to Tear Down: Passport Costs and Legal Barriers to Emigration." Policy Research Working Paper 3783, World Bank, Washington, DC.

McNeill, Jena Baker, James Jay Carafano, James Dean, and Nathan Alexander Sales. 2009. *Visa Waiver Program: A Plan to Build on Success*. Washington, DC: The Heritage Foundation. www.heritage.org/Research/HomelandSecurity/bg2282.cfm.

Meissner, Doris, and Donald Kerwin. 2009. *DHS and Immigration: Taking Stock and Correcting Course.* Washington DC: MPI. www.migrationpolicy.org/pubs/DHS_Feb09.pdf.

Meissner, Doris, and Marc Rosenblum. 2009. *The Next Generation of E-Verify: Getting Employment Verification Right.* Washington, DC: MPI. www.migrationpolicy.org/pubs/Verification_paper-071709.pdf.

Meissner, Doris, Deborah W. Meyers, Demetrios G. Papademetriou, and Michael Fix. 2006. *Immigration and America's Future: A New Chapter.* Washington, DC: MPI.

Meyers, Deborah Waller. 2003. "Does "Smarter" Lead to Safer? An Assessment of US Border Accords with Canada and Mexico." *International Migration* 41 (4): 5–44. www.fina-nafi.org/triumvirat09/pdf/Meyers.pdf.

Millar, Alistair, Jason Ipe, David Cortright, George A. Lope, Anne Marbarger, and Kathryn Lawall. 2006. *Report on Standards and Best Practices for Improving States' Implementation of UN Security Council Counter-Terrorism Mandates.* Washington, DC: Center on Global Counter-Terrorism Cooperation.

Millar, Jane, and John Salt. 2007. "In Whose Interests? IT Migration in an Interconnected World Economy." *Population, Space and Place* 13: 41–58.

———. 2008. "Portfolios of Mobility: The Movement of Expertise in Transnational Corporations in Two Sectors — Aerospace and Extractive Industries." *Global Networks* 8 (1): 25–50.

Ministère de la Santé et des Sports. 2000. *Décret n° 2000-1093 du 10 novembre 2000 instituant une commission de recours contre les decisions de refus de visa d'entreé en France: Journal officiel du 11 novembre 2000.* Paris, France: Ministère de la Santé et des Sports. www.sante.gouv.fr/adm/dagpb/bo/2000/00-45/a0453118.htm.

Ministry of Foreign Affairs of Japan. 2009. "A Guide to Japanese Visas." www.mofa.go.jp/j_info/visit/visa/02.html.

Morgenthau, Robert. 2009. "The Link between Iran and Venezuela: A Crisis in the Making?" *The American Interest Online*, September 9. http://blogs.the-american-interest.com/contd/2009/09/09/the-link-between-iran-and-venezuela-a-crisis-in-the-making/.

Morton, Joe D. 2004. "Pushing the Border Out on Alien Smuggling: New Tools and Intelligence Initiatives." Statement for the record before the House Judiciary Committee, Subcommittee on Immigration, Border Security and Claims, 108th Cong., 2nd sess., May 18. http://commdocs.house.gov/committees/judiciary/hju93716.000/hju93716_0f.htm.

MPI (Migration Policy Institute). 2008. *Foreign-Born Population and Foreign Born as a Percentage of the Total US Population, 1850 to 2008.* Washington, DC: MPI. www.migrationinformation.org/DataHub/charts/final.fb.shtml.

Napolitano, Janet. 2009. "Oversight of the Department of Homeland Security." Statement for the record before the US Senate Committee on the Judiciary, 111th Cong., 1st sess., December 9. www.aila.org/content/default.aspx?bc=1019|6712|12178|30785.

———. 2009. "Remarks by Secretary Napolitano at the Global Cyber Security Conference, August 2009." Remarks, August 4. www.cfr.org/publication/20427/remarks_by_secretary_napolitano_at_the_global_cyber_security_conference_august_2009.html.

———. 2009. "Toward a Better Border: The United States and Canada." Speech made at the Brookings Institution, Washington, DC, March 25. www.brookings.edu/~/media/Files/events/2009/0325_us_canada/20090325_canada_transcript.pdf.

National Association for Public Health Statistics and Information Systems. 2008. "EVVE Pilot." www. naphsis.org/index.asp?bid=1035.

———. 2009. "Jurisdiction Implementation Status (updated December 2009)." Powerpoint Presentation, December. www.naphsis.org/NAPHSIS/files/ccLibraryFiles/Filename/000000001190/ EVVE_Implementation_Dec_2009%20with%20territories.ppt.

———. 2009. "Reevaluating Real ID: Strengthening Birth Certificate Verification." Statement for the record before the Senate Committee on Homeland Security and Governmental Affairs, 111th Cong., 1st sess., July 15. www.naphsis.org/NAPHSIS/files/ccLibraryFiles/Filename/000000001077/ NAPHSIS%20on%20REAL%20ID-July%202009.pdf.

National Commission on Terrorist Attacks upon the United States. 2004. *9/11 and Terrorist Travel.* Franklin, TN: Hillsboro Press.

———. 2004. *The 9/11 Commission Report: Final Report of the National Commission on Terrorist Attacks Upon the United States.* New York: W.W. Norton & Co.

———. 2004. "Entry of the 9/11 Hijackers into the United States: Staff Statement No.1." Washington, DC: National Commission on Terrorist Attacks upon the United States. http://news.findlaw.com/hdocs/ docs/terrorism/911comm-ss1.pdf.

National Network for Safe Communities. 2009. "Home." www.nnscommunities.org/.

National Research Council of the National Academies. 2002. *Making the Nation Safer: The Role of Science and Technology in Countering Terrorism.* Washington, DC: National Academies Press.

NCTC (National Counterterrorism Center). 2006. *National Strategy to Combat Terrorist Travel.* Washington, DC: NCTC. www.nctc.gov/docs/u_terrorist_travel_book_may2_2006.pdf.

Newland, Kathleen, Dovelyn Rannveig Agunias, and Aaron Terrazas. 2008. *Learning by Doing: Experiences of Circular Migration.* Washington, DC: MPI. www.migrationpolicy.org/pubs/Insight-IGC-Sept08.pdf.

NORAD (North American Aerospace Defense Command). "About Norad." www.norad.mil/about/ agreement.html.

Nuñez, Claudia. 2007. "Women Are The New Coyotes." *La Opinión,* December 23. http://news. ncmonline.com/news/view_article.html?article_id=170fbf6eecdd019ad7e93f66eda8d6b8.

Nuñez-Neto, Blas, Alison Siskin, and Stephen Viña. 2005. *Border Security: Apprehensions of "Other Than Mexicans" Aliens. Washington,* DC: Congressional Research Service. www.au.af.mil/au/awc/awcgate/crs/ rl33097.pdf.

Official Journal of the European Communities. 2001. *Council Regulation (EC) No 539/2001 of 15 March 2001 Listing the Third Countries Whose Nationals Must Be in Possession of Visas When Crossing the External Borders and Those Whose Nationals Are Exempt from that Requirement.* Brussels, Belgium: Official Journal of the European Communities. http://eur-lex.europa.eu/LexUriServ/LexUriServ.do?uri=OJ:L:2001:081: 0001:0007:EN:PDF.

Official Journal of the European Union. 2003. *Agreement on Mutual Legal Assistance between the European Union and the United States of America.* Brussels, Belgium: Official Journal of the European Union.

———. 2006. *Council Regulation (EC) No 1932/2006 of 21 December 2006 Amending Regulation (EC) No 539/2001 Listing the Third Countries Whose Nationals Must Be in Possession of a Visas When Crossing the External Borders and Those Whose Nationals are Exempt from that Requirement*. Brussels, Belgium: Official Journal of the European Union. http://eur-lex.europa.eu/LexUriServ/LexUriServ.do?uri=OJ:L:20 07:029:0010:0013:EN:PDF.

OECD (Organization for Economic Co-operation and Development). 2008. *International Migration Outlook Annual Report 2008* Edition. Paris, France: OECD.

OPSI (Office of Public Sector Information). 1999. *Immigration and Asylum Act 1999*. London, UK: OPSI. www.opsi.gov.uk/acts/acts1999/ukpga_19990033_en_1.

———. 2003. *Statutory Instrument 2003 No.518, The Immigration Appeals (Family Visitor) Regulations 2003*. London, UK: Crown. www.opsi.gov.uk/si/si2003/20030518.htm.

OSI (Open Society Institute), Justice Initiative. 2007. *Report on Developments 2005–2007*. New York: OSI. www.soros.org/initiatives/justice/articles_publications/publications/developments_20071221/developments_20071221.pdf.

Overseas Security Advisory Council. 2009. *El Salvador 2009 Crime & Safety Report*. Washington, DC: US Department of State (DOS). https://www.osac.gov/Reports/report.cfm?contentID=97810.

Papachristos, Andrew W. 2005. "Gang World." *Foreign Policy* (March/April): 53.

Papachristos, Andrew, Tracey Meares, and Jeffrey Fagan. 2006. "Attention Felons: Evaluating Project Safe Neighborhood in Chicago." Working Paper, Columbia Univ., Institute for Social and Economic Policy and Research, September. http://iserp.columbia.edu/files/iserp/2006_06.pdf.

Papademetriou, Demetrios G. 2007. *The Age of Mobility: How to Get More Out of Migration in the 21st Century*. Washington, DC: MPI. www.migrationinformation.org/transatlantic/age_mobility_032307.pdf.

Papademetriou, Demetrios, and Gregory Maniatis, lead writers. 2007. *Gaining from Migration: Towards a New Mobility System*. Washington, DC: MPI.

Papademetriou, Demetrios G., Will Somerville, and Hiroyuki Tanaka. 2009. "Talent in the 21st Century." In *Talent, Competitiveness and Migration*, ed. Bertelsmann Stiftung and MPI. Gütersloh, Germany: Bertelsmann Stiftung.

Papademetriou, Demetrios G., Doris Meissner, Marc R. Rosenblum, and Madeleine Sumption. 2009. *Aligning Temporary Immigration Visas with US Labor Market Needs: The Case for Provisional Visas*. Washington, DC: MPI. www.migrationpolicy.org/pubs/Provisional_visas.pdf.

———. 2009. *Harnessing the Advantages of Immigration for a 21st Century Economy: A Standing Commission on Labor Markets, Economic Competitiveness, and Immigration*. Washington, DC: MPI. www.migrationpolicy.org/pubs/StandingCommission_May09.pdf.

Passel, Jeffrey S., and D'Vera Cohen. 2008. *Trends in Unauthorized Immigration: Undocumented Inflow Now Trails Legal Inflow*. Washington, DC: Pew Hispanic Center. http://pewhispanic.org/files/reports/94.pdf.

———. 2009. *A Portrait of Unauthorized Immigrants in the United States*. Washington, DC: Pew Hispanic Center. http://pewhispanic.org/files/reports/107.pdf.

Pew Hispanic Center. 2006. *Modes of Entry for the Unauthorized Migrant Population*. Washington, DC: Pew Hispanic Center. http://pewhispanic.org/files/factsheets/19.pdf.

Pillar, Paul R. 2003. *Terrorism and US Foreign Policy*. Washington, DC: The Brookings Institution Press.

Presidential Proclamation. 2004. "To Suspend Entry as Immigrants or Nonimmigrants of Persons Engaged in or Benefiting From Corruption Proclamation 7750." *Federal Register* 69 (9): 2287–88. http://edocket.access.gpo.gov/2004/pdf/04-957.pdf.

Project on National Security Reform. 2008. *Forging a New Shield*. Arlington, VA: Project on National Security Reform and the Center for the Study of the Presidency.

Public Safety Canada. 2009. *Framework Agreement on Integrated Cross-Border Maritime Law Enforcement Operations between the Government of Canada and the Government of the United States of America*. Ottawa, Canada: Public Safety Canada. www.publicsafety.gc.ca/prg/le/_fl/int-cross-brdr-maritime-eng.pdf.

———. 2009. "Joint Statement on the Canada-U.S. Border." Press Release, May 27. www.publicsafety.gc.ca/media/nr/2009/nr20090527-eng.aspx.

Quigley, Mike. 2009. "Quigley Gets Visa Waiver Extension for Poland into Immigration Reform Bill." Press Release, December 17. http://quigley.house.gov/index.php?option=com_content&task=view&id=205&Itemid=17.

Quirk, Matthew. 2008. "How to Grow a Gang." *The Atlantic*, May, www.theatlantic.com/doc/print/200805/world-in-numbers.

Ramasastry, Anita. 2007. "The New DHS/TSA Traveler Redress Inquiry Program: Why the System, Though More Efficient, Still Does Not Accord Travelers Sufficient Due Process." *Findlaw*, February 15. writ.news.findlaw.com/ramasastry/20070215.html.

Ratha, Dilip. 2007. *Leveraging Remittances for Development*. Washington, DC: MPI. www.migrationpolicy.org/pubs/MigDevPB_062507.pdf.

RCMP (Royal Canadian Mounted Police). 2004. "IBETs across Canada." November 22. www.rcmp-grc.gc.ca/ibet-eipf/map-carte-eng.htm.

———. 2008. *Commissioner of Firearms 2007 Report*. Ottawa, Canada: RCMP. www.rcmp-grc.gc.ca/cfp-pcaf/rep-rap/pdf/2007-comm-rpt-eng.pdf.

———. 2008. "Frequently Asked Questions." www.rcmp-grc.ca/secur/ibets-eipf-faq-eng.htm#contribution.

———. 2009. "Integrated Border Enforcement Teams (IBETs)." March 3. www.rcmp-grc.gc.ca/ibet-eipf/index-eng.htm.

———. 2009. "Vehicle Stop Leads to Seizure of Contraband Cigarettes." News Release, March 11. www.rcmp-grc.gc.ca/on/news-nouvelles/2009/09-03-11-cornwall3-eng.htm.

Renuart Jr., and E. Victor. 2009. "United States Southern Command, United States Northern Command, United States Africa Command, and United States Transportation Command." Statement for the record before the US Senate Committee on Armed Services, 111th Cong., 1st sess., March 17. http://armed-services.senate.gov/statemnt/2009/March/Renuart%2003-17-09.pdf.

Research and Innovative Technology Administration, Bureau of Transportation Statistics. 2009. Border Crossings: Border Crossing/Entry Data. www.transtats.bts.gov/Fields.asp?Table_ID=1358.

Reyes, Alma Arámbula, and Gabriel Mario Santos Villarreal. 2007. *El flujo migratorio centroamericano hacia México*. Mexico City, Mexico: Servicios de investigación y análisis, Subdirección de Política Exterior. www.diputados.gob.mx/cedia/sia/spe/SPE-ISS-19-07.pdf.

Richard, Mark, and Leslie S. Lebl. 2009. "Security and Data Sharing: Transferring Information without Compromising Privacy." *Policy Review* 154 (April 21): 79–92. www.hoover.org/publications/policyreview/41862277.html.

Robinson, Neal, Hans Graux, Maarten Botterman, and Lorenzo Valeri. 2009. *Review of the European Data Protection*. Santa Monica, CA: The Rand Corporation. www.rand.org/pubs/technical_reports/2009/RAND_TR710.pdf.

Rollins, John, Liana Sun Wyler, and Seth Rosen. 2010. *International Terrorism and Transnational Crime: Security Threats, U.S. Policy, and Considerations for Congress*, R41004. Washington, DC: Congressional Research Service. http://assets.opencrs.com/rpts/R41004_20100105.pdf.

Rosand, Eric, Alistair Millar, and Jason Ipe. 2007. *The UN Security Council's Counterterrorism Program: What Lies Ahead?* Washington, DC: Center on Global Counterterrorism Cooperation.

Rudner, Martin. 2008. "Misuse of Passports: Identity Fraud, the Propensity to Travel, and International Terrorism." *Studies in Conflict and Terrorism* 31 (2): 95–110.

Rumbaut, Rubén G., Roberto G. Gonzales, Golnaz Komaie, and Charlie V. Morgan. 2006. "Debunking the Myth of Immigrant Criminality: Imprisonment among First- and Second-Generation Young Men." *Migration Information Source*, June 1. www.migrationinformation.org/Feature/print.cfm?ID=403.

Sadiq, Kamal. 2009. "A Global Documentary Regime? Building State Capacity in the Developing World." Presentation at Conference on Global Mobility Regimes, The Levin Institute, New York (Organized by the Rockefeller College of Public Affairs and Policy, Univ. at Albany, State Univ. of New York), April 27–28.

———. 2009. *Paper Citizens: How Illegal Immigrants Acquire Citizenship in Developing Countries*. Oxford, UK: Oxford Univ. Press.

Sageman, Marc. 2008. *Leaderless Jihad: Terror Networks in the Twenty-First Century*. Philadelphia: Univ. of Pennsylvania Press, 151.

Sands, Christopher. 2009. *Toward A New Frontier: Improving the US-Canadian Border*. Washington, DC: The Brookings Institution. www.brookings.edu/~/media/Files/rc/reports/2009/0713_canada_sands/0713_canada_report.pdf.

Saraswati, Muninggar Sri. 2005. "Government to Make Immigration Office More Independent." *The Jakarta Post*, December 31.

Schemo, Diana Jean. 2008. "Diploma Mill Concerns Extend Beyond Fraud." *The New York Times*, June 29.

Schweimler, Daniel. 2008. "Passport Scandal Hits Argentina." *British Broadcasting Company News*, July 13. http://news.bbc.co.uk/go/pr/fr-/2/hi/americas/7503844.stm.

Seabrooke, John. 2009. "Don't Shoot." *The New Yorker*, June 22. www.newyorker.com/reporting/2009/06/22/090622fa_fact_seabrook.

Secretaría de Gobernación, Instituto Nacional de Migración. 2009. "Countries That Do Not Need Visas." www.inm.gob.mx/EN/index.php?page=not_need_visa.

Security Council Report. 2008. "May 2008: Counter-Terrorism — Briefings to the Council." www.
securitycouncilreport.org/site/c.glKWLeMTIsG/b.4065781/k.C305/May_2008_brCounterTerrorism_
Briefings_to_the_Council.htm.

Shanker, Thom, and Eric Schmitt. 2009. "Air Defense Inspired by 9/11 Gets a Second Look." *The New
York Times*, November 19. www.nytimes.com/2009/11/20/us/20terror.html.

Sharrock, David. 2007. "New Border Control Will Abolish Free Movement between UK and Ireland."
The Times, October 25. http://travel.timesonline.co.uk/tol/life_and_style/travel/news/article2733487.ece.

Simpson, Cam. 2009. "Border Arrests Decline Again." *The Wall Street Journal*, November 11. http://
online.wsj.com/article/SB125781594948540097.html.

Singapore Immigration and Checkpoints Authority. 2009. "Application for APEC Business
Travel Card System (ABTC)." https://www.psi.gov.sg/NASApp/tmf/TMFServlet?app=ABTC-
PUBLIC&Reload=true.

Somerville, Will, Jamie Durana, and Aaron Mateo Terrazas. 2008. *Hometown Associations: An Untapped
Resource for Immigrant Integration?* Washington, DC: MPI. www.migrationpolicy.org/pubs/Insight-HTAs-
July08.pdf.

Spergel, Irving A., and David G. Curry. 1990. "Strategies and Perceived Agency Effectiveness in
Dealing with the Youth Gang Problem." In *Gangs in America*, ed. Ronald C. Huff. Newbury Park, CA:
Sage Publications.

Statewatch. 2008. "EU-PNR Scheme Being Rewritten by the Council." www.statewatch.org/news/2008/
oct/04eu-pnr-rewrite.htm.

Statistics Canada. 2008. *Population and Dwelling Counts, for Canada, Provinces and Territories, 2006 and
2001 Censuses — 100% Data.* www12.statcan.ca/census-recensement/2006/dp-pd/hlt/97-550/Index.cfm?
TPL=P1C&Page=RETR&LANG=Eng&T=101.

———. 2009. *Immigration in Canada: A Portrait of the Foreign-Born Population, 2006 Census:
Immigration: Driver of Population Growth.* Ottawa, Canada: Statistics Canada. www12.statcan.ca/census-
recensement/2006/as-sa/97-557/p2-eng.cfm.

———. 2009. *Place of Birth for the Immigrant Population by Period of Immigration, 2006 Counts and
Percentage Distribution, for Canada, Provinces and Territories — 20% Sample Data.* Ottawa, Canada:
Statistics Canada. www12.statcan.ca/census-recensement/2006/dp-pd/hlt/97-557/T404-eng.cfm?Lang=E
&T=404&GH=4&GF=1&SC=1&S=1&O=D.

———. 2009. *Population by Immigrant Status and Period of Immigration, 2006 Counts, for Canada,
Provinces and Territories — 20% Sample Data.* Ottawa, Canada: Statistics Canada. www12.statcan.ca/
census-recensement/2006/dp-pd/hlt/97-557/T403-eng.cfm?Lang=E&T=403&GH=4&SC=1&S=99&O
=A.

Stefan Batory Foundation. 2009. *Changes in Visa Policies of the EU Member States.* Warsaw, Poland:
Stefan Batory Foundation. www.batory.org.pl/doc/Visa_Report_2009.pdf.

Sterngold, James. 2001. "Bus Company is Accused of Traffic in Illegal Aliens." *The New York Times*,
December 11. www.nytimes.com/2001/12/11/us/bus-company-is-accused-of-traffic-in-illegal-aliens.html.

Strauss, Anke. 2008. "Human Trafficking and Smuggling: OAS/IOM Introductory Course on the Human Rights of Migrants, Including Migrant Workers and their Families." Powerpoint presentation, IOM, Washington, DC, March 6. www.google.com/url?sa=t&source=web&ct=res&cd=5&url=http%3A%2F%2Fwww.oas.org%2FDIL%2FESP%2Fmigrantes_curso_introductorio_2008_presentaciones_anke_strauss.ppt&ei=ZwTySfXDHIestgfit5WyDw&usg=AFQjCNHWsUplg6ZGyMD1taKdPAOSx7DhOQ&sig2=6DDDC9PxMSoEy9_a7pGVaA.

Stuijt, Adriana. 2009. "UK Cracks Down on South African Passport Holders from March." *Digital Journal*, February 10. www.digitaljournal.com/article/266934.

Sundeen, Matt. 2008. "The REAL ID Rebellion." *State Legislatures* (March).

Surgalla, Michael, and Arthur Norton. 2003. "International Aspects of Criminal Immigration Enforcement." *The United States Attorneys' Bulletin* 51 (5): 14–20. www.justice.gov/usao/eousa/foia_reading_room/usab5105.pdf.

Tang, Alisa. 2005. "Thailand Now Fake Passport Capital for Criminal Underworld, Terrorists." *The Associated Press*, September 8. www.irrawaddy.org/article.php?art_id=4963.

Task Force on Confronting the Ideology of Radical Extremism. 2009. *Rewriting the Narrative: An Integrated Strategy for Counterradicalization*. Washington, DC: The Washington Institute for Near East Policy. www.washingtoninstitute.org/pubPDFs/PTF2-Counterradicalization.pdf.

Tatelman, Todd B. 2005. *Intelligence Reform and Terrorism Prevention Act of 2004: National Standards for Drivers' Licenses, Social Security Cards, and Birth Certificates*. Washington, DC: Congressional Research Service. www.fas.org/irp/crs/RL32722.pdf.

The Embassy of India in Peru. 2010. "Fines." www.indembassy.org.pe/english/servicios/visa.htm

The Independent Monitor for Entry Clearance Refusals with Limited Rights of Appeal. 2007. *Report to the Secretary of State, File sample: October 2006 to March 2007, Visits: April to September 2007*. London, UK: Home Office. www.ukvisas.gov.uk/resources/en/docs/2258700/2258727/IMReportNov07.

The White House. 2006. "Fact Sheet: National Strategy to Internationalize Efforts against Kleptocracy." Press Release, August 10. http://georgewbush-whitehouse.archives.gov/news/releases/2006/08/20060810-1.html.

———. 2006. "President Bush Participates in Joint Press Availability with President Ilves of Estonia." Press Release, November 28. http://georgewbush-whitehouse.archives.gov/news/releases/2006/11/images/20061128-4_p112806pm-0157-515h.html.

———. 2008. "President Bush Discusses the Visa Waiver Program." Press Release, October 17. http://georgewbush-whitehouse.archives.gov/news/releases/2008/10/images/20081017-5_p101708jb-0301-515h.html.

———. 2009. "Joint Statement by North American Leaders." Press Release, August 10. www.whitehouse.gov/the_press_office/Joint-statement-by-North-American-leaders/.

The White House, Homeland Security Council. 2007. *National Strategy for Homeland Security*. Washington, DC: The White House. www.dhs.gov/xlibrary/assets/nat_strat_homelandsecurity_2007.pdf.

Tomsheck, James. 2009. Personal communication with the author.

Torpey, John. 1999. The Invention of the Passport: Surveillance, Citizenship, and the State. Cambridge, UK: Cambridge Univ. Press.

Transatlantic Satellite Debate. 2005. *What Lessons in the War against Terror can the EU and US Exchange?* Washington, DC: Friends of Europe. www.friendsofeurope.org/Portals/6/Documents/Reports/Atlantic%20Rendez-Vous%20-%2025%20April%202005.pdf.

Tribunals Service, Asylum and Immigration Tribunal. "Appeals." www.ait.gov.uk/Appeals/appealTypes.htm.

UK House of Lords, European Union Committee. 2007. *European Union — Twenty-First Report.* London, UK: House of Lords. www.publications.parliament.uk/pa/ld200607/ldselect/ldeucom/108/10809.htm#a32.

UN (United Nations). 1948. *The Universal Declaration of Human Rights.* New York: UN. www.un.org/Overview/rights.html.

———. 1966. *International Covenant on Civil and Political Rights* (ICCPR). New York: UN. www2.ohchr.org/english/law/ccpr.htm.

UN, Department of Economic and Social Affairs (DESA), Population Division. 2002. *International Migration from Countries with Economies in Transition: 1980–1999.* New York: DESA, Population Division. www.un.org/esa/population/publications/ewmigration/E-W_Migrationreport.pdf.

———. 2006. *International Migration 2006.* New York: DESA, Population Division.

———. 2009. *Statistics and Indicators on Women and Men.* New York: DESA, Population Division. http://unstats.un.org/unsd/demographic/products/indwm/tab1a.htm.

———. 2009. *Trends in International Migrant Stock: The 2008 Revision.* New York: DESA. http://esa.un.org/migration/index.asp?panel=1.

UN General Assembly. 2009. *Report of the Secretary-General on Measures to Eliminate International Terrorism* (Doc.A/64/161). New York: UN. www.unhcr.org/refworld/type,THEMREPORT,,,4a9e2c190,0.html.

UN Report of the Secretary General. 2009. *Implementing the Responsibility to Protect A/63/677.* New York: UN. www.documents-dds-ny.un.org/doc/UNDOC/GEN/NO9/206/10/pdf/NO920610.pdf?OpenElement.

Undocumented Worker Transitions. 2007. *Denmark Country Report: Work Package 2.* Roskilde, Denmark: Undocumented Worker Transitions. www.undocumentedmigrants.eu/londonmet/library/s15990_3.pdf.

UNHCR (United Nations High Commissioner for Refugees). 2009. *2008 Global Trends: Refugees, Asylum-Seekers, Returnees, Internally Displaced and Stateless Persons.* Geneva, Switzerland: UNHCR. www.unhcr.org/4a375c426.html.

———. 2009. *Implementing the Responsibility to Protect: Report of the Secretary-General.* New York: UN General Assembly. www.unhcr.org/refworld/category,REFERENCE,UNGA,,,4989924d2,0.html.

UNIS (United Nations Information Service). 2008. "Countries Invited to Sign, Ratify or Accede to Multilateral Treaties during the Treaty Event 23–25 and 29 September and 1 October 2008." Press Release, September 22. www.unis.unvienna.org/unis/pressrels/2008/unisinf281.html.

University of British Columbia. 2008. "UBC Legal Expert Releases Canada's First Stats on Foreign Human Trafficking Victims." Press Release, October 28. www.publicaffairs.ubc.ca/media/releases/2008/mr-08-143.html.

UNODC (United Nations Office on Drugs and Crime). 2009. *Global Report on Trafficking in Persons*. Vienna, Austria: UNODC. www.unodc.org/documents/human-trafficking/Global_Report_on_TIP.pdf.

———. 2009. *International Homicide Statistics (IHS): Intentional Homicide, Rate per 100,000 Population, 2004, Unless Otherwise Specified*. Vienna, Austria: UNODC. www.unodc.org/documents/data-and-analysis/IHS-rates-05012009.pdf.

UNSC (United Nations Security Council). 1999. *Resolution* 1267, S/RES/1267. New York: UNSC. http://daccess-dds-ny.un.org/doc/UNDOC/GEN/N99/300/44/PDF/N9930044.pdf?OpenElement.

———. 1999. *Security Council Committee Established Pursuant to Resolution 1267 (1999) Concerning Al-Qaida and the Taliban and Associated Individuals and Entities*. New York: UNSC. www.un.org/sc/committees/1267/index.shtml.

———. 2001. *Resolution 1373, S/RES/1373*. New York: UNSC. http://daccess-dds-ny.un.org/doc/UNDOC/GEN/N01/557/43/PDF/N0155743.pdf?OpenElement.

———. 2002. *Resolution 1390, S/RES/1390*. New York: UNSC. http://daccess-dds-ny.un.org/doc/UNDOC/GEN/N02/216/02/PDF/N0221602.pdf?OpenElement.

———. 2005. *Resolution 1617 (2005) Adopted by the Security Council at its 5244th Meeting*. New York: UNSC. http://daccess-dds-ny.un.org/doc/UNDOC/GEN/N05/446/60/PDF/N0544660.pdf?OpenElement.

———. 2006. *Focal Point for De-listing Established Pursuant to Security Council Resolution 1730 (2006)*. New York: UNSC. www.un.org/sc/committees/dfp.shtml.

———. 2007. "Letter Dated 29 March 2007 from the Secretary-General Addressed to the President of the Security Council." UNSC, New York. http://daccessdds.un.org/doc/UNDOC/GEN/N07/291/00/PDF/N0729100.pdf?OpenElement.

———. 2008. *Comparative Table Regarding the United Nations Security Council Committees Established Pursuant to Resolutions 1267* (1999), 1373 (2001) and 1540 (2004). New York: UNSC. www.un.org/sc/committees/1267/pdf/Revised%20comparative%20table_ENGLISH%20_7-11-2008_.pdf.

———. 2008. *Guidelines of the Committee for the Conduct of Work*. New York: UNSC. www.un.org/sc/committees/1267/pdf/1267_guidelines.pdf.

———. 2008. "Letter dated 7 February 2008 from the Chairman of the Security Council Committee Established Pursuant to Resolution 1373 (2001) Concerning Counter-Terrorism Addressed to the President of the Security Council." UNSC, New York. http://daccess-dds-ny.un.org/doc/UNDOC/GEN/N08/232/51/PDF/N0823251.pdf?OpenElement.

———. 2008. "Letter Dated 13 May 2008 from the Chairman of the Security Council Committee Established Pursuant to Resolution 1267 (1999) Concerning Al-Qaida and the Taliban and Associated Individuals and Entities Addressed to the President of the Security Council." UNSC, New York. http://daccessdds.un.org/doc/UNDOC/GEN/N08/341/88/PDF/N0834188.pdf?OpenElement.

———. 2008. "Letter Dated 10 June 2008 from the Chairman of the Security Council Committee Established Pursuant to Resolution 1373 (2001) Concerning Counter-Terrorism Addressed to the President of the Security Council." UNSC, New York. http://daccessdds.un.org/doc/UNDOC/GEN/N08/375/56/PDF/N0837556.pdf?OpenElement.

———. 2008. "Letter Dated 31 December 2008 from the Chairman of the Security Council Committee Established Pursuant to Resolution 1267 (1999) Concerning Al-Qaida and the Taliban and Associated Individuals and Entities Addressed to the President of the Security Council." UNSC, New York. http://daccessdds.un.org/doc/UNDOC/GEN/N09/206/16/PDF/N0920616.pdf?OpenElement.

———. 2008. *Report of the Analytical Support and Sanctions Monitoring Team Pursuant to Resolution 1735 (2006) Concerning Al-Qaida and the Taliban and Associated Individuals and Entities.* New York: UNSC. http://daccessdds.un.org/doc/UNDOC/GEN/N08/341/88/PDF/N0834188.pdf?OpenElement.

———. 2008. *Resolution 1822 (2008),* S/RES/1822. New York: UNSC. http://daccess-dds-ny.un.org/doc/UNDOC/GEN/N08/404/90/PDF/N0840490.pdf?OpenElement.

———. 2009. *Fact Sheet on Listing.* New York: UNSC. www.un.org/sc/committees/1267/fact_sheet_listing.shtml.

———. 2009. *Fact Sheet on the Travel Bans and its Exemptions.* New York: UNSC. www.un.org/sc/committees/1267/fact_sheet_travel_ban.shtml.

———. 2009. "Security Council Counter-Terrorism Committee." www.un.org/sc/ctc/aboutus.html.

UNWTO (United Nations World Tourism Organization). 2009. "Testing Times for International Tourism." News Release, June. www.unwto.org/media/news/en/press_det.php?id=4421&idioma=E.

US Census Bureau. 2007. *American Community Survey: Citizenship Status in the United States — Universe: Total Population in the United States.* Washington, DC: US Census Bureau. http://factfinder.census.gov/servlet/DTTable?_bm=y&-geo_id=01000US&-ds_name=ACS_2008_1YR_G00_&-SubjectID=17632063&-_lang=en&-mt_name=ACS_2008_1YR_G2000_B05001&-format=&-CONTEXT=dt.

———. 2008. *American Community Survey.* Washington, DC: US Census Bureau. www.census.gov/acs/www/.

———. 2008. "B01003. TOTAL POPULATION — Universe: TOTAL POPULATION." *American Community Survey.* http://factfinder.census.gov/servlet/DTTable?_bm=y&-context=dt&-ds_name=ACS_2008_1YR_G00_&-CONTEXT=dt&-mt_name=ACS_2008_1YR_G2000_B01003&-tree_id=308&-geo_id=01000US&-geo_id=04000US02&-geo_id=04000US16&-geo_id=04000US23&-geo_id=04000US26&-geo_id=04000US27&-geo_id=04000US30&-geo_id=04000US33&-geo_id=04000US36&-geo_id=04000US38&-geo_id=04000US39&-geo_id=04000US42&-geo_id=04000US50&-geo_id=04000US53&-search_results=01000US&-format=&-_lang=en&-SubjectID=17631129.

US Government Printing Office. 2008. *Memorandum of Understanding between the Secretaries of State and Homeland Security Concerning the Implementation of Section 428 of the Homeland Security Act of 2002.* Washington, DC: US Government Printing Office. http://frwebgate.access.gpo.gov/cgi-bin/getdoc.cgi?dbname=108_cong_documents&docid=f:hd131.108.pdf.

US House of Representatives, Homeland Security Committee. 2009. "Statement of Chairman Bennie G. Thompson: The Secure Border Initiative: SBInet Three Years Later." Press Release, September 17. http://homeland.house.gov/SiteDocuments/20090917103603-54387.pdf.

Van Fossen, Anthony. 2007. "Citizenship for Sale: Passports of Convenience from Pacific Island Tax Havens." *Commonwealth & Comparative Politics* 45 (2): 138–63.

Vaughan, Jessica M., and Jon D. Feere. 2008. *Taking Back the Streets: ICE and Local Law Enforcement Target Immigrant Gangs*. Washington, DC: Center for Immigration Studies (CIS). www.cis.org/ImmigrantGangsAnnounce.

Vick, Karl. 2009. "Iraq's Lessons, on the Home Front." *The Washington Post*, November 15. www.washingtonpost.com/wp-dyn/content/article/2009/11/14/AR2009111400915.html.

Vidino, Lorenzo. 2005. "Islamic Extremism in Europe." Statement for the record before the House Committee on International Relations Subcommittee on Europe and Emerging Threats, 109th Cong., 1st sess., April 27. www.investigativeproject.org/documents/testimony/303.pdf.

Vreja, Lucia Ovidia. 2007. "Trafficking Routes and Links to Terrorism in South Eastern Europe: The Case of Romania." *Connections* 6 (1): 27–45.

Wakeling, Stewart. 2003. *Ending Gang Homicide: Deterrence Can Work*. Sacramento, CA: California Attorney General's Office. www.popcenter.org/problems/drive_by_shooting/PDFs/Wakeling_2003.pdf.

Walsh, Delcan, Jason Burke, and Giles Tremlett. 2009. "Al-Qaida Connection: Foreign Passports Linked to Attacks on West Recovered." *The Guardian*, October 29. www.guardian.co.uk/world/2009/oct/29/al-qaida-pakistan-taliban-link.

Weaver, Jay. 2004. "Kendall Woman Sold Phony Visas, Feds Say." *Herald.com*, April 7. www.amren.com/news/news04/04/08/visafraud.html.

Webster, Michael. 2008. "Mexican Drug Cartels and Hezbollah Operating in Mexico and US." *Los Angeles Chronicle*, October 26. www.americanchronicle.com/articles/view/79021.

The White House. 1998. *International Crime Control Strategy*. Washington, DC: The White House.

Yale-Loehr, Stephen, Demetrios G. Papademetriou, and Betsy Cooper. 2005. *Secure Borders, Open Doors: Visa Procedures in the Post-September 11 Era*. Washington, DC: Migration Policy Institute MPI. www.migrationpolicy.org/pubs/Secure_Borders_Report0905.pdf.

Ziglar, James W. 2004. "Borders, Transportation, and Managing Risk." Before the National Commission on Terrorist Attacks Upon the United States, January 26. http://govinfo.library.unt.edu/911/hearings/hearing7/witness_ziglar.htm.

Zill, Oriana. 2001. "Crossing Borders: How Terrorists Use Fake Passports, Visas, and Other Identity Documents." *Frontline*, October 25, 2001. www.pbs.org/wgbh/pages/frontline/shows/trail/etc/fake.html.

Zimmer, Brian. 2007. "Interrupting Terrorist Travel: Strengthening the Security of International Travel Documents." Statement for the record before the US Senate Committee on the Judiciary, Subcommittee on Terrorism, Technology and Homeland Security, 110th Cong., 1st sess., May 2. http://judiciary.senate.gov/hearings/testimony.cfm?id=2733&wit_id=6437.

About the Author

Susan Ginsburg is a Migration Policy Institute nonresident fellow. She served on the Department of Homeland Security Quadrennial Homeland Security Review Advisory Committee and on the Secure Borders Open Doors Advisory Committee. As a senior counsel to the National Commission of Terrorist Attacks upon the United States (9/11 Commission), she was the team leader for its examination of how the 9/11 terrorists were able to enter the United States. Ms. Ginsburg served as chief of staff, senior adviser, and coordinator of firearms policy to the under secretary for enforcement at the Department of the Treasury from 1994 to 2001. She served as special assistant at the Department of State's Office of International Narcotics Matters from 1979 to 1981. A lawyer, Ms. Ginsburg has practiced civil litigation as a law firm associate and served as law clerk to Judge A. Leon Higginbotham of the Third Circuit US Court of Appeals. She also worked as a legislative assistant in the House of Representatives and for a public interest group. Ms. Ginsburg is the author of a number of publications, including Countering Terrorist Mobility: Shaping an Operational Strategy, published by the Migration Policy Institute in 2006.

About the Migration Policy Institute

The Migration Policy Institute (MPI) is an independent, nonpartisan, nonprofit think tank in Washington, DC, dedicated to analysis of the movement of people worldwide. MPI provides analysis, development, and evaluation of migration and refugee policies at the local, national, and international levels. It aims to meet the rising demand for pragmatic and thoughtful responses to the challenges and opportunities that large-scale migration, whether voluntary or forced, presents to communities and institutions in an increasingly integrated world.

Founded in 2001 by Demetrios G. Papademetriou and Kathleen Newland, MPI grew out of the International Migration Policy Program at the Carnegie Endowment for International Peace. MPI is guided by the philosophy that international migration needs active and intelligent management. When such policies are in place and are responsibly administered, they bring benefits to immigrants and their families, communities of origin and destination, and sending and receiving countries. **For more information visit www.migrationpolicy.org.**